Managing Financial Institutions

This book goes beyond traditional financial institutions textbooks, which tend to focus on mathematical models for risk management and the technical aspects of measuring and managing risk. It focuses on the role of financial institutions in promoting social and economic goals for the communities in which they operate for the greater good, while also meeting financial and competitive challenges, and managing risks.

Cooperman divides the text into eight easily teachable modules that examine the real issues and challenges that managers of financial institutions face. These include the transformative changes presented by social unrest, climate change and resource challenges, as well as the changes in how financial institutions operate in light of the opportunities that rapid innovations and disruptive technologies offer. The book features:

- Up-to-date coverage of new regulations affecting financial institutions, such as Dodd–Frank and new SEC and Basel III regulations.
- Material on project financing and new forms of financing, including crowdfunding and new methods of payment for financial institutions.
- New sustainable finance models and strategies that incorporate environmental, social, and corporate governance considerations.
- A new chapter on sustainable financial institutions, social activism, the greening of finance, and socially responsible investing.

Practical cases focusing on sustainability give readers insight into the socioeconomic risks associated with climate change. Streamlined and accessible, *Managing Financial Institutions* will appeal to students of financial institutions and markets, risk management, and banking. A companion website, featuring PowerPoint slides, an Instructor's Manual, and additional cases, is also available.

Elizabeth S. Cooperman is a Professor of Finance and Entrepreneurship and Co-Director of the Managing for Sustainability program at the University of Colorado Denver, USA. She serves as co-editor for the *International Review of Accounting, Banking and Finance*, and is a past president of the Midwest Finance Association.

Managing Financial Institutions

Markets and Sustainable Finance

Elizabeth S. Cooperman

Routledge
Taylor & Francis Group

NEW YORK AND LONDON

First published 2017
by Routledge
711 Third Avenue, New York, NY 10017

and by Routledge
2 Park Square, Milton Park, Abingdon, Oxon OX14 4RN

Routledge is an imprint of the Taylor & Francis Group, an informa business

Library of Congress Cataloging in Publication Data
Names: Cooperman, Elizabeth S. (Elizabeth Singleton), 1949- author.
Title: Managing financial institutions : markets & sustainable finance /
Elizabeth Singleton Cooperman.
Description: New York, NY : Routledge, 2016.
Identifiers: LCCN 2016031860| ISBN 9781138900035 (hbk) |
ISBN 9781138900028 (pbk) | ISBN 9781315707532 (ebk) |
ISBN 9781317480129 (mobi/kindle)
Subjects: LCSH: Financial institutions—Management. | Financial services
industry—Management. | Bank management.
Classification: LCC HG173 .C6756 2016 | DDC 332.1068—dc23
LC record available at https://lccn.loc.gov/2016031860

ISBN: 978-1-138-90003-5 (hbk)
ISBN: 978-1-138-90002-8 (pbk)
ISBN: 978-1-315-70753-2 (ebk)

Typeset in Times New Roman
by Book Now Ltd, London

To Mona Gardner and Dixie Mills, amazing professors and mentors, who began the journey of *Managing Financial Institutions* and without whom this book would never have existed; to dear family and friends, and especially to Bob, my precious muse, and to Gail and Mike, the best and *artistes extraordinaire*; and to students, the future, who are striving for a sustainable new world.

Contents

List of Figures

List of Tables

Preface

WE live in times with the world transforming around us, with rapid advances in technology, climate change risks, and accompanying social risks in the aftermath of the global financial crisis. These are challenging times, and the obligation of financial institutions to operate in a responsible way, including engagement in sustainable development, has never been more important, requiring socially and environmentally accountable financial institution management.

As Achim Steiner (2015, p. 1) in the foreword to the United Nations Environment Programme (UNEP) Inquiry Report for the Design of a Sustainable Financial System notes:

> The financial system underpins growth and development. In 2008 we witnessed some of the world's most sophisticated financial systems spawn the worst global financial crisis seen in decades. As markets in some developed countries collapsed, others in both developed and developing nations were inevitably dragged down… Aligning the financial system for sustainability is not some far-off notion, but is already happening. A "quiet revolution" is taking place as policy makers, and financial regulators address the need to forge robust and sustainable financial systems for 21st century needs.

Similarly, Luigi Zingales (2015, p. 1359) in his presidential address to the American Finance Association, "Does Finance Benefit Society" warns that:

> As a profession we financial economists have been too proud of the technical achievements and economic successes of our discipline and too complacent of its shortcomings. There is a large gap between our self perception and the outside perception of our role in society, a gap that can undermine the political viability of a well functioning financial system. A competitive and inclusive financial system can exist only if the rule of law is respected and expected to be respected in the future. Yet this expectation is unsustainable if there is major public resentment against the financial system at large.

Zingales points out that academics need to document "the contribution of finance to society," and at the same time realize that some criticisms are well founded, with the most important step being "an awareness of the problem," for solutions to work.

In the aftermath of the U.S. subprime crisis and the global great recession, there has been a great deal of public resentment towards the financial institutions, with a confidence poll by Gallop in 2015, showing only 28% of those polled in the U.S. having a great deal or quite a lot of confidence in banks as institutions compared to 40% on average historically (Jones, 2015). Similarly with the global recession, Europeans in a gallop poll of 124 countries in 2013 showed low confidence in financial institutions, with the lowest percentages for countries impacted most by the crisis, including only 11% having confidence in Cyprus and Spain, 17% in Greece, 16% in Italy, 15% in Ireland, and 26% or lower in Ukraine, Chile, Slovenia, Hungary, and Iceland (Loschky and Ray, 2014).

The great financial crisis is often depicted as a highly improbable event, i.e., as Taleb (2007) notes, a "black swan" event. Other notable books on the causes of the crisis point to corporate governance problems, as well as ethics and behavioral finance considerations. For instance, Morgenson and Rosner (2011) point out connections between hubris, "outsized ambition, greed, and corruption" leading to executives of government-sponsored mortgage agencies "to ignore warning signs of imminent disaster."

Similarly, Lewis's (2010) *The Big Short* (both the book and movie) focuses on human nature elements that brought about the crisis, including greed, unethical behavior, poor due diligence, the entrance of uneducated, untrained parties as underwriters, and gamesmanship, along with information avoidance. With subprime mortgage securitizations so complex that no one could understand them, and great laxity in underwriting standards with great demand for large volumes of loans to be generated for securitizations, subprime securities became speculative investments that were given high credit ratings by ratings agencies who received fee income for ratings. Complex, synthetic collateralized debt obligations (CDOs) and credit default swaps were also used for speculative purposes, adding fuel to the crisis.

Gary Gorton (2010) notes other changes in the banking system that contributed to the financial crisis, whereby with the advent of technology and huge amounts of securitizations the banking system includes a real securitized shadow banking system, where institutional investors, along with financial firms, engage in enormous short-term borrowings with repurchase agreement. With collateral tight, new forms of collateral such as commercial paper tied to mortgage securities contributed to collateral calls and liquidity runs on financial institutions.

Michael Lewis (2014) in *Flash Boys* similarly brings up other changes in financial markets, with technology that allows tremendous speed in trading a great competitive advantage. High-frequency trading using complex algorithms analyzing markets and making trades instantaneously, and trades hidden in dark pools, produced an uneven playing field for both large and small investors. New disruptive technology innovations from high-tech financial startups known as "FinTech" are also creating new competition, innovation and disruptive forces for traditional financial institutions, as well as new financial and technological risks.

Given the immense damage that arose from the global financial crisis, there has been a great backlash against many financial institutions, given their role in the financial system. Yet there is danger, since financial institutions are essential for an economy and for reducing inequality and alleviating poverty, with this backlash as well. Other notable authors point out benefits provided through financial innovations, including Sandor (2012) in *Good Derivatives:*

A Story of Financial and Environmental Innovation, and Shiller (2012) in *Finance and the Good Society*, where he points out the need for a democratization of finance that entails greater public participation, education and stewardship to allow greater public access and understanding of the workings of the financial system.

This text attempts to provide knowledge on the workings of financial institutions and markets and the changing environment in which they operate. The text is also unique in including coverage of environmental, social, and corporate governance (ESG) considerations for sustainable financial institution management.

A special tribute to Mona Gardner and Dixie Mills, the authors of *Managing Financial Institutions: An Asset and Liability Approach* for the first three editions, with whom I joined for the 4th and 5th editions. Much material in this text remains from the earlier editions, credited to the original authors.

Special thanks to Sharon Golan, Erin Arata and Maureen Allen for their support and encouragement, and to Michael Welply for excellent illustrations for the text.

REFERENCES

Gorton, Gary B. (2010). *Slapped by the Invisible Hand: The Panic of 2007*. Oxford: Oxford University Press.

Jones, Jeffrey M. (2015). "Confidence in U.S. institutions still below historical norms." Gallup, June 15, 2015. Accessed on March 31, 2016 at: http://www.gallup.com/poll/183593/confidence-institutions-below-historical-norms.aspx

Lewis, Michael (2010). *The Big Short: Inside the Doomsday Machine*. New York: W.W. Norton & Company, Inc.

Lewis, Michael (2014). *Flash Boys*. New York: W.W. Norton & Company, Inc.

Loschky, Jay and Julie Ray (2014). "Europeans give banks little credit." Gallup, August 14, 2014. Accessed on March 31, 2016 at: http://www.gallup.com/poll/174836/europeans-give-banks-little-credit.aspx

Morgenson, Gretchen and Joshua Rosner (2011). *Reckless Endangerment*. New York: Times Books/Henry Holt and Company.

Sandor, Richard L. (2012). *Good Derivatives: A Story of Financial and Economic Innovation*. Hoboken, NJ: John Wiley & Sons.

Shiller, Robert J. (2012). *Finance and the Good Society*. Princeton, NJ: Princeton University Press.

Steiner, Achim (2015). "Forward to the financial system we need: Aligning the financial system with sustainable development: Policy Summary." UNEP Inquiry Report, The Financial System We Need. October 2015.

Taleb, Nassim Nicholas (2007). *The Black Swan: The Impact of the Highly Improbable*. New York: Random House.

Zingales, Luigi (2015). "Presidential Address: Does finance benefit society." *Journal of Finance*, 70 (4), August, 1327–1363.

Overview

THIS text is designed to be used for undergraduate and graduate financial institutions and markets classes, as well as financial institution management classes. It provides both an overview of financial markets and central bank monetary policy and interest rates and hedging foreign exchange and interest rate risks, and the operations and managing considerations for financial institutions, including risk and financial performance analysis for financial institutions, capital management, and assets liability management for depository institutions along with coverage of insurance companies, mutual funds and pensions, securities firm and investment banks and diversified financial institutions, hedge fund and venture capital firms. Other topics include coverage of crowdfunding, shadow banking, and new FinTech types of financing. The text also includes coverage of social and environment and corporate social responsibility issues for financial institutions, which are crucial for the move for sustainable finance into the traditional finance arena.

The text is divided into eight modules that can be used as two-week modules for a full 15 to 16 week semester or as weekly modules for an 8 to 10 week quarter. Part 1 (Overview: Financial Services Industry and Its Environment) provides an overview of the financial services industry, including an outline of different financial institutions and how they operate, and their economic functions and objectives. Module I consists of one chapter, Chapter 1, on financial institutions as social creators and financial risk takers. Module II provides an overview of financial markets and their interest rate and regulatory environment in, respectively, Chapter 2, examining interest rate risk measurement and theories, and Chapter 3, presenting the regulatory environment, regulatory dialectic and new global regulations under Basel III.

Part 2 (Performance and Risk Analysis for FIs and ESG Considerations) examines the performance and risk analysis of financial institutions, focusing on depository institutions in Module III, with Chapter 4 presenting the analysis and Chapter 5 considering capital management. Module IV focuses on environmental and social responsibilities for financial institutions with a chapter, Chapter 6, on social and environmental risks and sustainable financial institutions and the greening of finance.

Part 3 (Managing Financial Institution Risks) focuses on defining and managing financial institution interest rate and foreign exchange risks, including an overview of foreign exchange rate determinants and risks and hedging foreign exchange risk in Chapter 7 and hedging interest rate risk with derivatives in Chapter 8 for Module V.

Part 4 (Asset and Liability Management) consists of Module VI covering asset and liability management and innovations, including Chapter 9 on loan analysis, credit risk, and environmental risk management, and Chapter 10 liquidity and liability management and securitization.

Part 5 (Overview: NonDepository Financial Institutions and New Forms of Financing) includes Module VII on contractual financial institutions and security firms, with Chapter 11 on insurance companies and Chapter 12 on mutual funds and pension management. Module VIII covers securities firms and venture capital and crowdfunding, with Chapter 13 presenting securities firms and investment banks and diversified financial institutions, and Chapter 14, hedge fund and venture capital, crowdfunding and shadow banking.

Part One

Overview

Financial Services Industry and Its Environment

Chapter 1

Financial Institutions as Social Value Creators and Financial Risk Takers

At its most basic definition, finance is the act of allocating capital to individuals and businesses that want to make productive use of it. In short finance creates social value.

(University of California, Haas School of Business Center for Responsible Business website)

Sustainable finance refers to any form of financial service integrating environmental, social and governance (ESG) criteria into the business or investment decisions for the lasting benefit of both clients and society at large.

(Swiss Sustainable Finance website)

WHEN financial markets and institutions are working well, they create social value by providing funds to businesses and individuals that these borrowers in turn can use for productive purposes. Financial institutions, for instance, often provide guidance and financing for small as well as medium-sized, and large businesses. Individuals can borrow from banks and savings associations to purchase homes they would otherwise never be able to afford. Consumers can also invest with mutual funds to save for dream retirements, their children's future college tuition, and other future goals. Without financial institutions, these dreams likely would not be possible. Similarly, businesses are able to engage in capital expenditures through financing by financial institutions, leading to greater hiring, that in turn increases employment in communities. Many banks are chartered to serve their communities and provide community outreach services as well. Venture capital and private equity firms provide financing for new innovations, such as the development of disruptive technologies to help solve environmental challenges. Hence, financial institutions stimulate growth and job creation and assist in financing technological innovations to help solve social and environmental problems in an economy.

However, if financial institution managers engage in practices only for their own benefit at the expense of their customers and stakeholders, or if they fail to understand the implications of risky business practices, great harm can be done that can lead to home foreclosures, business bankruptcies, job loss, and economic recessions, such as the U.S. subprime loan crisis and the great global recession.

Well-functioning financial institutions (FIs) are essential for economic growth, while poorly functioning FIs can contribute to economic losses, leading to poverty in developing countries. Central banks also depend on financial markets and institutions for their monetary policy operations to stimulate or cool down economies and to help control inflation or prevent deflation.

This chapter provides an overview of the different types of financial institutions, how they differ from nonfinancial firms, and the special types of risks they face. The chapter also discusses how FIs make profits, and the challenges of financial institutions to balance differing goals for different stakeholders including stockholders, customers, and regulators, as well as meeting environmental, social, and corporate governance (ESG) goals.

WHAT DO FINANCIAL INSTITUTIONS DO?

In the 21st century, we often take for granted the services provided by financial services firms, including checking accounts, online banking, debit and credit cards, home mortgages, car loans, business loans, life, health, auto, insurance, and investment and mutual funds. Financial institutions also provide financial planning, wealth management, and business working capital management and payment services. Likely you have relationships with at least three or more financial institutions or with a single large financial holding company that offers a variety of different types of financial services.

Financial institutions, as *financial intermediaries,* provide *indirect financing*, where they create *indirect securities* that have more desirable characteristics for borrowers and lenders (savers) than *direct securities* or loans exchanged directly between savers and borrowers. They also provide economic functions making an economy more efficient, such as liquidity, maturity, denomination, search, monitoring, and information financial intermediation benefits.

For example, banks, savings institutions, and credit unions (depository institutions) take in deposits from small savers (providing liquidity with checking, debit, credit card accounts) and pool deposits to make consumer, business, real estate, and agriculture loans to borrowers that desire longer maturities.

Such indirect financing provides advantages over *direct finance* (transactions directly between savers and borrowers) by reducing information, search, and monitoring costs, as well as providing lower costs and more efficient operations through *economies of scale* (cost advantages with a greater output and scale of operations) *and* a greater variety of financial services and products through *economies of scope* (with interrelationships and functional expertise allowing cross-selling of products). Financial institutions also provide *convenience benefits* with neighborhood branches, online banking services, branches, and debit and credit cards, mobile payments for transactions, and expertise, and working capital management and other special payment and certification and credit services.

Other types of financial institutions, such as *mutual funds* and wealth management firms allow savers advantages in terms of *diversification, portfolio selection, investment screening*, and *risk management services*. Mutual funds allow small savers to invest in *diversified*

5

*Financial
Institutions as
Social Value
Creators and
Financial Risk
Takers*

portfolios, managed by experienced portfolio managers at low costs. *Socially responsible investment (SRI) funds* in addition supply *screening services* for investors with portfolio selection on desired environmental or social or governance criteria. Investors can select different types of mutual funds based on their particular investment goals, maturity preference, and risk tolerance.

Investment and securities firms provide expertise and risk management as *portfolio and wealth managers*. By doing so, these firms reduce *risk management* costs. *Large banks and investment banks* also provide risk management services. This includes providing letters of credit that guarantee payment by other parties, facilitating trade transactions between different parties, such as importers and exporters, to reduce or eliminate the default risk between the parties. Other services include helping companies to hedge risks using derivatives (swaps, forward contracts, caps and floors based on future price movements of underlying instruments) against credit, interest rate, and foreign exchange risk, as well as assisting new businesses to raise capital, through initial public offerings, and later through secondary offerings and small business loans.

Contractual financial institutions (such as *insurance companies and pension funds* that involve long-term contracts) take on *specialized investment, maturity intermediation, and risk management services.* Insurance companies pool *premiums* from thousands of individuals and businesses as secondary securities (*policyholder reserves*) that they invest in intermediate-term and long-term securities providing income and capital gains to fund *contingent future payouts* to these policyholders in the event of property damage, theft, or loss of life. With the *pooling of premiums of a large number of customers*, insurance companies are able to provide risk management services at a much lower cost than if consumers or businesses had to save funds on their own to meet these contingencies.

Pension funds, as well as mutual funds and insurance companies carry out maturity intermediation services as well by allowing small investors to save for long-term goals, such as retirement by investing savings (pension fund contributions or insurance premiums) in diversified portfolios. They also provide retirement annuities, tax deferred investments, and other specialized investment products.

Many financial institutions are in the form of what is often called a universal bank or in the U.S. a financial institutions holding company (FHC) or *bank holding company* (BHC) that has subsidiaries that offer a variety of different financial services, such as an FHC that has commercial bank, mortgage bank, investment bank, mutual fund, and insurance company subsidiaries operating together under a diversified holding company umbrella.

SPECIAL GOVERNMENT POLICY-RELATED FINANCIAL SERVICES

Many financial institutions are government chartered or in some countries government owned. Such financial institutions are created to provide for economic needs for communities and specific sectors of the economy. Postal banks for instance in many countries provide banking services in post offices. Depository institutions also have an important role in sustaining the efficiency of the payments system and play a special role in the transmission of monetary policy. Banks and savings associations are often asked by governments to serve a policing role in apprehending criminals, intent on fraud or violation of a country's laws, as well as reporting suspicious behavior affecting the welfare of society. During financial crises, investment banks and commercial banks historically have often been called in to help stabilize the financial markets or banking systems.

Particular types of financial institutions are chartered for particular social purposes to provide a more effective home mortgage market, such as *savings institutions* and *government-sponsored enterprises (GSEs)*. GSEs purchase mortgage loans from financial institutions and securitize them, pooling mortgages and packaging them into securities, providing investors with a return based on the mortgage rates of the pool. If done properly with diversified mortgages packaged in pools to reduce a securitization's portfolio risk, this provides liquidity for depository institutions providing funds to make new loans, enabling greater liquidity in mortgage markets, which in turn allows greater amounts of mortgage loans to be made, promoting home ownership in an economy.

However, as revealed in the subprime loan crisis, when risky, complex, subprime loans were packaged together, with little due diligence and diversification and monitoring, such pools can create pools that are difficult to understand and lack transparency. Also, with inter-relationships among parties and pressures for creating a volume of securitizations to generate fee income, and inappropriately high ratings provided by credit agencies, this contributed to the global financial crisis. With U.S. home prices declining dramatically after peaking in mid-2006, subprime borrowers with adjustable rate mortgage loans were not able to make loan payments, leading to bankruptcies. With the mortgage loans underlying securitizations becoming worthless, this in turn made these collateralized debt obligations (CDOs) worthless and illiquid. This, along with fraudulent activities on the part of some FI managers, contributed to the collapse and U.S. government bailout. This also led to the take-over in 2008 of two huge GSEs, the *Federal Home Loan Mortgage Association* (FNMA, "Fannie Mae"), and the *Federal Home Loan Mortgage Corporation* (FHLMC, "Freddie Mac") (Morgenson and Rosner, 2011).

Hence, FIs, given the private nature of lending, are more likely to be prone to information asymmetries between managers and stakeholders, allowing managers to act in their own interests versus those of other stakeholders. When the financial system is working well, financial institutions can stimulate an economy and help individuals build wealth, and help to build a strong middle class, and reduce problems in a society.

OPPORTUNITIES AND RISKS FOR FINANCIAL INSTITUTIONS WITH TECHNOLOGY

With rapid changes in technology in the digital age, information has become more accessible to companies and individuals, reducing the role of FIs as monitors and information providers. For instance, technology allows large, creditworthy corporations to issue commercial paper, bonds, and engage in direct finance globally. Also, nonbank technology firms are able to enter the payments arena. Technology has increased the risks of technological failures, hacking, and dangers of illegal use, fraud, viruses, and embezzlement. Given the very technical nature of bank operations clearing millions of checks a day, technological advances have

7

*Financial
Institutions as
Social Value
Creators and
Financial Risk
Takers*

reduced the use of checks, lowering bank costs. However, with increased use of other types of payment mechanisms that are offered by nonfinancial institutions, technology also increases increasing competition for depository institutions, reducing their role in the payments mechanism. FinTech startups have been growing rapidly. These are firms that use technology to make payment or financial services more efficient or transparent, and that provide disruptive innovations, ranging from automated payment processors, to special payment apps, to person to person (P2P) and business to business (B2B) lending services to *robo* investment firms, among others. Apple, Google, Amazon, Facebook, and Samsung have also been entering the payments industry, including the development of digital payment apps, with investment in startups that are focused on retail banking markets rising from $2.2 billion in 2014 to $6.8 billion in 2015 (Henry, 2016; Lohr, 2016).

Technology has also brought opportunities to FIs. With technology, millions of loans have been pooled and packaged into securities, sold to investors, transforming financial institutions into more transaction-oriented institutions, reducing their monitoring (relationship-oriented) function. Other roles for FIs have gained importance, including retirement planning, wealth management, working capital management and risk management and other advisory services for companies, and automated clearinghouse (ACH) services, allowing direct disbursement from employers to employees within minutes. Client-based tools on websites of financial institutions, such as mutual funds, provide personalized information and financial planning advice, as well as the opportunity for live chats with representatives and help in opening accounts, and detailed real-time financial information and analysis for individual investors.

Many large banks have changed their delivery channels for payment services by making large technology investments to allow for online banking and the use of mobile phones and tablets for payments, among other mechanisms. Meara (2012) discusses a survey by Celent, a major technology strategy consulting firm, on emerging technologies. Survey results show that the majority of financial institutions surveyed viewed online channels, such as online account opening and loan originations, live online chats, person to person (P2P) payments, and remote check deposits through mobile phones, as more important strategically than branching systems, with large banks employing greater mobile banking advantages. Financial institutions are also engaging in branch transformations by making investments in technologies that improve sales and service effectiveness, including customer relationship management, customer analytics, and campaign management systems (Meara, 2012; The Financial Brand, 2012).

With greater use of technology, financial institutions also face new risks, including fraudulent transactions, hacking into customer accounts, and other disruptions. Financial institutions have been developing extremely secure security systems to keep criminals out, with banks generally liable for stolen funds as the result of cybercrimes (Landes, 2013). Financial institutions face greater competition, as well as assistance from and collaboration with technology companies. For example, *Apple Pay*, launched by Apple in October of 2014, allows payments with wallet-enabled devices, such as iPhones by using the Apple Pay app that allows up to eight different credit cards to be loaded up, as well as rewards-point cards. Over 500 companies, including major banks, credit card companies, and large merchants, participated in Apple Pay's introduction.[1] Security advances include the greater security of the payment app with a biometric fingerprint reader and encrypted details about transactions versus using credit card numbers (Quittner, 2014). Similarly, other easy to pay technologies developed by other technology firms offer mobile payments, including Google Wallet, and LoopPay acquired by Samsung, among many others. As noted by Popper (2016) a "Digital Disruption" report by Citigroup points out that nonbank firms, such as Tenpay and Alipay perform the majority of online payments in China, with Alipay having 3.3 times as large a payment volume in 2015 as America's most prominent player PayPal. Lohr (2016) points out that major banks have taken steps to address a shift led by millennials towards new digital financial services, including Citigroup's teaming up with Lending Club, an online lender, and its setting up of a special Citi FinTech unit, viewing FinTech as both an opportunity and a threat. FinTech companies also face challenges in terms of lacking legal and regulatory infrastructure, to allow greater financial services innovations (Lohr, 2016)

Entrepreneurs have also developed new disruptive technologies, such as *blockchain*, the technology underlying *Bitcoin***,** an electronic-only currency created on computers, not backed by any government or centralized authority. As noted by Irrera (2014), blockchain operates as an open, decentralized online ledger with each transaction record in a digital currency verified by a community of computer users. This allows digitization and codification and insertion of documents in the blockchain that creates an *indelible, untamperable* record. Blockchain, along with other new, disruptive technologies are revolutionizing the payments system by permitting safe transmissions over the internet as well for international payments, financial transactions, trading, and other settlements and clearings (Irrera, 2014).

Large banks, such as J.P. Morgan are also exploring the potential of blockchain, collaborating with nonbank firms, such as Digital Asset Holdings, to examine technological applications to cut costs and problems for trading and liquidity mismatches for loan funds. Similarly Goldman Sachs has been the leader in a consortium developing Symphony which is a communications tool using the blockchain technology (Mclannahan, 2016).

To understand how FIs operate and make profits and their special risks, the following sections discuss differences for FIs versus nonfinancial companies, including special differences in their assets and liabilities and income statements.

HOW DO FINANCIAL INSTITUTIONS DIFFER FROM NONFINANCIAL COMPANIES?

Financial versus Real Assets

To thrive, financial institutions must be profitable to create sustainable value. As noted by Deutsche Bank, in its discussion of its responsibility, "we want to create sustainable value: for our clients and employees, our shareholders and society. Our high-performance culture must go hand-in-hand with a culture of responsibility" (Deutsche Bank Responsibility, 2016).

Financial institutions have different management considerations from nonfinancial firms, with assets and liabilities predominantly financial contracts that promise cash flows to parties in contracts in the future. Differences for the balance sheets of a bank versus a manufacturing company with primarily real assets illustrate differences for financial institution operations and the special financial risks they take on.

9

*Financial
Institutions as
Social Value
Creators and
Financial Risk
Takers*

Benny's Manufacturing versus Benny's Bank

By way of comparison, Table 1.1 shows the assets for a manufacturing firm, *Benny's Manufacturing Firm* (*BMF*), versus a traditional bank, *Benny's Bank* **(BB).** Over 82% of BMF's assets are *real, physical assets* (inventory and equipment), while 96% of the assets for BB are *financial assets,* with a small percentage of real fixed assets. Benny's Bank's profits depend on *future cash flows* from financial contracts (loans and securities). Hence, BB has much more interest rate risk, credit risk, and liquidity risk than BMF. Financial assets, such as loans, entail *credit risk* of not being paid (defaulting). Financial institutions also have *interest rate risk*, since the market value of fixed-rate loans falls with a rise in interest rates. As shown in Table 1.2 for liabilities, BB is financed primarily with deposits, which entail *liquidity risk* since they are redeemable at any time (such as by writing a check or using a debit card), with these deposits invested in long-term loans.

As shown in Table 1.3, BB has *greater financial leverage with a 92% total debt to total asset ratio and a 12.5 equity multiplier (EM) (total assets to total equity).* This is compared to a 50% debt to assets ratio and an equity multiplier of 2 for BFM. Financial institutions hold a *much lower average equity to assets* than other firms (here 8% for BB versus 50% for BMF). BB has much greater capital risk, the risk of having an insufficient equity cushion to take losses against, with high financial leverage.

TABLE 1.1 | Comparison of assets

Benny's Manufacturing		Benny's Bank	
Assets ($ million)		Assets ($ million)	
Cash	10	Cash	20
Accounts receivable	350	Securities	724
Inventory	650	Loans	1,206
Plant and equipment	1,000	Building/equipment	60
Total assets	2,010	Total assets	2,010

TABLE 1.2 | Comparison of liabilities and equity

Benny's Manufacturing ($ million)		Benny's Bank ($ million)	
Accounts payable	10	Transaction deposits	1,000
Notes payable	500	Time deposits	649
Long-term bonds	500	Borrowings	200
Total debt	1,010	Total debt	1,849
Common stock	200	Common stock	61
Retained earnings	800	Retained earnings	100
Total equity	1,000	Total equity	161
Total liabilities and equity	2,010	Total liabilities and equity	2,010

TABLE 1.3 | Comparison of financial ratios for financial leverage

Benny's Manufacturing	Benny's Bank
Debt to assets = 50%	Debt to assets = 92%
Equity to assets = 50%	Equity to assets = 8%
Assets to equity = 1/0.50 = 2	Assets to equity = 1/0.08 = 12.5 (*Equity multiplier*)

With predominantly longer-term loans on its balance sheet financed by short-term deposits, BB has an asset/liability mismatch and greater interest rate risk than BFM, which has long-term fixed assets financed by long-term debt and equity. With *BB's greater interest rate risk*, if interest rates rise, the market value of BB's long-term assets will fall more than the market value of its short-term liabilities, resulting in a large fall in the market value of BB's equity (market value of assets less the market value of liabilities). With revenue from loans and expense for deposits, changes in interest rates will also affect BB's net interest income (interest revenue less interest expense).

Managing the Spread, Burden, and Loan Loss Provisions

Table 1.4 shows a comparison of income statements. BMF makes its revenues from the sale of inventory "real assets" to customers, with cost of goods sold (costs of inventory and labor to manufacture the firm's goods) as its largest expense, and a gross profit equal to sales revenues less cost of goods sold.

BB has a very different production function taking in deposits as inputs, and paying interest expense on these deposits used to produce loans to provide interest revenue to the bank. Hence, traditional profits for a bank include three primary components as shown on BB's income statement:

Net interest spread = Interest revenue − Interest expense

Burden = Noninterest expense − Noninterest revenue

Provision for loan losses (expense for expected loan losses).

Benny's Bank makes profits from its *net interest spread*, (interest revenue less interest expense). Benny's Bank also has a large *burden* expense (noninterest expense less noninterest revenue) for its operations. In addition, BB has a *provision for loan loss (PLL) expense*, estimated by its managers each year, based on expected future loan losses, an item that is added to its *accumulated loan loss reserves on the balance sheet* as protection against future losses, where net loans equals gross loans less *accumulated loan losses*.

A depository institution's *net interest margin (NIM)* is used as a measure of its traditional profitability, by taking the *interest spread as a percentage of total assets* (or if available more precisely as a percentage of total earning assets that pay interest). NIM is often divided into *[interest revenue / total assets] (IR%)* and *[interest expense / total assets] (IE%)* to see relative changes in each. Putting Benny's Bank income statement as

11

*Financial
Institutions as
Social Value
Creators and
Financial Risk
Takers*

TABLE 1.4 │ Comparison of income statements

Benny's Manufacturing ($ million)		Benny's Bank ($ million)	
Sales	400.00	Interest revenue	156.80
Cost of goods sold	100.00	Interest expense	45.96
Administrative expenses	10.86	Net interest spread	110.84
Earnings before interest and tax	289.14	Noninterest revenue	10.00
Interest expense	2.00	Noninterest expense	91.82
		Burden expense	81.82
Earnings before tax	287.14	Provision for loan losses	0.31
Taxes (30%)	86.14	Operating earnings before taxes	28.71
Net income	201.00	Taxes (30%)	8.61
		Net income	20.10

a percentage of total assets, its before-tax *operating return on assets* (operating earnings / total assets) *(OROA)* becomes:

$$\text{OROA before taxes} = (\text{NIM\%} - \text{Burden\%} - \text{PLL\%}).$$

Thus, to analyze a depository institution's performance, an analyst can focus on the NIM, Burden%, and PLL%, *along with any securities gains / losses to total assets (securities gain / loss%)* to see if its OROA has changed over time or to explain why it differs from its peer banks (similar size banks) or competitors.

Table 1.5 puts Benny Bank's income statement as a percentage of total assets to show these relationships, where each income statement item is divided by total assets to calculate interest revenue to assets (IR%), interest expense to assets (IE%), noninterest revenue to assets (NIR%), noninterest expense to assets (NIE%), and provision for loan losses to assets (PLL%).

TABLE 1.5 │ Common-size income statement for Benny's Bank

Benny's Bank %	Total assets
Interest revenue to assets (IR%)	7.80
Interest expense to assets (IE%)	2.29
Net interest margin (NIM)	5.51
Noninterest revenue to assets (NIR%)	0.51
Noninterest expense to assets (NIE%)	4.57
Burden to total assets (Burden%)	4.07
Provision loan losses to total assets (PLL%)	0.02
Operating income to total assets (OROA)	1.42
Net income to total assets (ROA)	1.00

TABLE 1.6 | Benny's Bank profitability ratio calculations

[Interest revenue / Total assets] (IR%) = [$156.80/$2,010] = 0.0780 or 7.80%
[Interest expense / Total assets] [IE%] = [$45.96/$2,010] = 0.0229 or 2.29%
Net interest margin (NIM) = [IR% − IE%] = [7.8% − 2.29%] = 5.51%
[Provision for loan losses / Total assets] [PLL%] = [$.31/$2,010] = 0.0002 or 0.02%
[Noninterest revenue / Total assets] (NIR%) = [$10/$2,010] = 0.0050 or 0.50%
[Noninterest expense / Total assets] (NIE%) = [$91.82/$2,010] = 0.0457 or 4.57%
Burden% = NIE% − NIR% = 4.57% − 0.50% = 4.07%
Operating ROA before taxes = [5.51% − 0.02% − 4.07%] = 1.42%
ROA = OROA (1 − t) = 1.42% (1 − 0.30) = 0.01 or 1%

As shown in Table 1.6 for Benny's Bank, dividing each item of the income statement by its total assets (TA) of $2,010 million: BB has a high Burden% of 4.07%, with a large NIE% and a small NIR%, and a low PLL% of 0.02%. However, BB's larger NIM% of 5.51%, allows the bank to make an OROA of 1.42%, and a return on assets (ROA) after taxes of about 1%, which is typical for banks (i.e. ROA after taxes of 1.42% [1 − 0.30 tax rate] equal to about 1%). An ROA of 1%, which is small, is typical for depository institutions, so even small changes in NIM%, Burden%, and PLL% need to be analyzed. This compares with BMC's ROA of 10%.

Depository Institution Return on Equity and Importance of the Equity Multiplier

The well-known Dupont system for ratio analysis analyzes how a firm is making its profits by multiplying a firm's net profit margin (NPM) (net income / revenues) times its asset utilization (AU) (revenues/assets) to get ROA (net income / assets):

ROA = NPM × AU.

For a bank, AU is equal to [(Interest revenue / Assets] (IR%) + [Noninterest revenues / Assets (NIR%). Thus, if you know a bank's ROA and AU, you can solve for its NPM as [ROA /AU].

A second equation shows the effect of financial leverage by multiplying a firm's ROA by the equity multiplier (assets/equity):

ROE = ROA × EM.

Hence, the Dupont ratios show that the return on equity (ROE) is a function of a bank's cost management relative to revenues (NPM), revenue generation to assets (AU), and financial leverage as represented by its equity multiplier (EM) as follows:

ROE = NPM × AU × EM.

These ratios for Benny's Manufacturing and Benny's Bank profitability ratios are shown for comparison in Table 1.7. BB has a NPM of about 12.05% and AU of 0.083 resulting in its

13

*Financial
Institutions as
Social Value
Creators and
Financial Risk
Takers*

TABLE 1.7 | Comparison of the two firms' profitability ratios

Benny's Manufacturing	Benny's Bank
Return on assets (ROA) = 10%	Return on assets (ROA) = 1%
Asset utilization (AU) = 0.199	Asset utilization (AU) = 0.083
Net profit margin (NPM) = 50.25%	Net profit margin (NPM) = 12.05%
Assets/equity = 1/0.50 = 2	Assets/equity = 1/0.08 = 12.5
	(Equity multiplier)
Return on equity (ROE) = 20%	Return on equity (ROE) = 12.5%

ROA of about 1%. With an equity multiplier of 12.5, its ROE is 12.5%. BMF has a high NPM of 50.25% and AU of 0.199, resulting in a ROA of about 10% and an EM of 2, and so a ROE of 20%. For BB if it had the same ROA, but if it was – 1% ROA, its ROE would be – 12.5%. Hence, higher financial leverage increases volatility on both the upside and downside.

Calculating Net Interest Spreads and Net Interest Margins

To see how interest expenses and interest revenues are calculated, suppose a different bank, *Bank Simple,* has the balance sheet (in $ million) shown in Table 1.8.

Bank Simple, as is the case for many banks, holds the majority of its assets in longer-term loans financed with predominantly short-term deposits as liabilities, (a maturity mismatch that creates greater interest rate risk).

Solving for Bank Simple's Interest Revenues and Interest Expenses

To solve for Bank Simple's net interest spread and net interest margin, interest revenue is the sum of each type of earning assets times its interest rate, and interest expense is the sum of each type of interest-paying liability times its interest rate. *So for Bank Simple:*

> *Interest revenues = ($50 × 0.06) + ($100 × 0.08) = $11 million*
>
> *Interest expenses = ($50 × 0) + ($50 × 0.05) = $2.5 million*
>
> *Interest spread = $11 million – $2.5 million = $8.5 million*
>
> *Net interest margin (NIM) = [$8.5/$150] = 0.0567 or 5.67%.*

Recall for a bank: OROA before taxes = (NIM – Burden% – PLL%). Suppose Bank Simple, with its NIM of 5.67%, has a Burden% of 3.67% and a PLL% of 1%, what is Bank Simple's operating ROA?

> OROA before taxes = NIM – Burden% – PLL%
> = 5.67% – 3.67% – 1% = *1%.*

Based on Bank Simple's equity multiplier of 3 × ($150 Assets / $50 Equity):

> Bank Simple's OROE = OROA × EM = 1% × 3 = 3%.

TABLE 1.8 | Balance sheet for Bank Simple

	Amount ($ million)	Rate (%)
Assets		
5-year loans	50	6
10-year loans	100	8
Total assets	150	
Liabilities		
Demand deposits	50	0
1-year time deposits	50	5
Total liabilities	100	
Equity	50	
Total liabilities and equity	150	

Bank Simple has very low financial leverage for a bank with 33.33% of its assets financed with equity, so its EM of 3 × is small. If Bank Simple instead had an EM of 10, assuming it had the same OROA, its OROE would go up to 1% × 10 = 10% (holding other factors constant, although likely interest expense would rise reducing the OROA a bit).

Different Risks Taken on by Financial Institutions

Financial institutions:

1 Often rely on their *interest spread* for profitability (**interest rate risk**).
2 Often rely on short-term financing (**liquidity risk**).
3 Often have *high financial leverage* (**capital risk**).
4 Often hold *financial assets* (**credit risk**).

Hence, FI managers need to manage *interest rate, liquidity, capital, and credit risks.*

How many of the different types of risks a particular type FI takes on varies for individual firms and different types of FIs, as does the risk tolerance of different FI managers. For instance, depository institutions have the greatest interest rate and liquidity risks. *Life insurance companies* have predominantly long-term assets (bonds, stock, mortgage, and real estate investments) and long-term policy reserves as liabilities, with matched maturities for assets and liabilities resulting in low interest rate risk. Property/casualty (P/C) insurance companies have more liquidity risk than life insurers, since their policies cover many unexpected events. Similarly *mutual funds* invest in stocks, bonds, and other investments as assets, and have shareholders investments as equity, both long-term, so have very low interest rate risk, but open-end mutual funds that redeem shares at any time have liquidity risk.

*Financial
Institutions as
Social Value
Creators and
Financial Risk
Takers*

Measuring Interest Rate Risk for Financial Institutions' NIM

Many FIs and particularly depository institutions take on the risk for their customers by making long-term fixed-rate loans financed by short-term liabilities. Since *fixed-rate loan rates will not change they are non-rate-sensitive assets*, while *deposits and short-term liabilities are rate-sensitive*, since their rates will go up if interest rates rise. *Rate-sensitive assets are maturing or price resetting assets, such as short-term securities that are maturing, or adjustable rate loans for a designated period, such as a 1-year period. Rate-sensitive liabilities are repricable or maturing short-term deposits and short-term liabilities.* Nonrepricable liabilities are liabilities such as long-term time deposits or bonds whose rates will remain the same for the 1-year or other designated time period.

The *repricing or funding gap* of an FI measures its interest rate risk for a fall in its NIM, which is the difference between its rate-sensitive assets (RSA) and rate-sensitive liabilities (RSL)

Funding gap = Rate-sensitive assets − Rate-sensitive liabilities.

Typically banks have a *negative funding gap*, with more rate-sensitive liabilities (deposits and short-term borrowings) than rate-sensitive assets (long-term loans and securities). *A negative funding gap implies a fall in a bank's NIM, if interest rates rise*, since its interest expense on rate-sensitive liabilities (RSL) will rise more than its interest revenue on its smaller amount of rate-sensitive assets (RSA). *Alternatively, if interest rates fall, a bank with a negative funding gap will have a rise in its NIM*, since the interest expense on its RSL will fall more than the interest revenue on its smaller amount of RSA.

If a depository institution has a *positive funding gap* (often the case if a bank sells or securitizes its long-term loans or sells these to another FI or has predominantly variable-rate loans), then the bank has a larger percentage of RSA than RSL. So *its NIM will go up when rates rise, with its IR% going up more than its IE%. But if rates fall, its IR% will go down more than its IE%, and its NIM will fall.*

A bank's funding gap has a direct link to a bank's net interest income (NII) spread. The expected change in a bank's NII with a change in interest rates is:

Change in NII = Funding gap × Expected change in rate.

For Bank Simple, for a 1-year funding gap (note funding gaps can be calculated for different periods), it has RSA of $0, since its loans have maturities $\geq$ 5 years. For RSL, its liabilities maturing in a year include $50 million demand deposits and $50 million time deposits of $100 million, so Bank Simple's funding gap is:

Funding gap = RSA − RSL = $0 − $100 million = − $100 million.

If rates rise by 1% (i.e., by 0.01), the expected change in Bank Simple's NII is:

Change in NII = − $100 million × 0.01 = − $1 million.

Even small changes in interest rates can have a big effect on a bank's net interest spread. If interest rates instead were expected to fall by 1% Bank Simple would expect a + $1 million rise in its NII.

If instead, the funding gap had been positive, or the bank had greater rate-sensitive assets than liabilities, if rates went up 1%, there would be an expected positive $ million rise in NII, and if rates fell 1%, an expected $1 million fall in NII.

Hence, a bank with a negative funding gap has the risk of a loss in its NII if interest rates rise (with its IE% rising more than its IR%), and a bank with a positive funding gap has the risk of a loss in its NII if interest rates fall (with its IR% falling more than its IE%).

The funding gap measures repricing or reinvestment risk, but does not measure price or market value risk, the risk of changes in the market value of assets and liabilities, and hence, changes in the value of equity (market value of assets – market value of liabilities). A better overall measure of interest rate risk is the duration gap, discussed later in Chapter 2, equal to the duration of a bank's assets less the duration of its liabilities. Often long-term assets less long-term liabilities for different periods, such as over 3, 5, 10, and 15 years are used as prox-ies to estimate overall interest rate risk as well, with greater interest rate risk when these two are mismatched. (Note funding gaps assume that rates for rate-sensitive assets and liabilities move together, which isn't always the case.)

Balance Sheet Indicators for Credit Risk

Taking on credit risk is an important intermediary role for FIs. Accordingly, more risky loans should pay higher rates for their greater credit risk. If a bank has a higher percentage of *nonpaying, noncurrent assets and other real estate owned (repossessed collateral to assets) (OREO)* on its balance sheet or a larger percentage of *net loan losses (actual loan losses less any recoveries),* these are indicators of greater credit risk. A bank's loan composition also reveals how risky its loan portfolio is. For instance, a larger percentage of construction and development real estate loans generally entail more risk, since their repayment depends on the successful completion and later purchase or rentals of constructed properties, such as shopping malls. Depository institution managers take a provision against expected future loan losses as an expense on their income statements, and this provision is accumulated in a total loan loss allowance account. Nonaccrual loans are loans with past due payments that are not currently accruing interest. Hence credit ratios reflect how well a bank is provisioning for loan losses, its earnings compared to net loan losses, and its percentage of net loan losses, among other indicators, including the types of loans it has on its balance sheet.

TABLE 1.9 | Some common credit risk ratios

Percentage net loans losses to total assets
Percentage net charge-offs to total loans and leases
Percentage noncurrent assets + other real estate owned (OREO) to total assets
Provision loan losses to total assets (PLL) to average total loans
Loan loss allowance to nonaccrual loans
Loan loss allowance to net loss
Earnings (net income) to net losses
Percentage growth rate in loans and leases
Composition of loan portfolio (types of loans and diversification)

17

*Financial
Institutions as
Social Value
Creators and
Financial Risk
Takers*

Banks with a larger percentage of net loan losses, a larger percentage of net charge-offs, a larger percentage of OREO and nonpaying loans, and lower earnings to net losses have greater credit risk (Table 1.9). Lower provisioning relative to net loan losses, and a lower loan loss allowance to nonaccrual loans or net losses have greater credit risk. How diversified a bank is in its lending is also key indicator for the credit risk of an institution's portfolio of loans, with a more diversified loan portfolio less vulnerable to an economic downturn for a particular industry sector. During the global financial crisis, undiversified real estate banks suffered much larger losses than diversified commercial banks.

Balance Sheet Indicators for Liquidity Risk

Balance sheet characteristics indicate liquidity risk in terms of both the asset side and the liability side of a bank's balance sheet. *On the asset side, if a bank is heavily loaned up, it has less liquidity* available to meet unexpected liquidity needs. If it has a larger percentage of short-term securities, it has stored liquidity to draw upon. *On the liability side, if a bank has more stable, insured core deposits* in contrast to short-term borrowings or large uninsured time deposits called purchased or volatile funds, it has less risk of deposits leaving the bank in the event of bad news, i.e., lower liquidity risk. Also, if a bank has a higher equity capital to total assets, it has lower liquidity risk, risk of depositors worrying about the solvency of the bank. On the off-balance sheet side, if a bank has a lower percentage of outstanding loan commitments, reflecting fewer liquidity needs for funds to make these loans, it has lower liquidity risk.

Indicators of Operating Risk

Depository institutions also have considerable operational risk, particularly for large complex organizations that are difficult to manage, making it difficult to monitor all operations. Technological innovations and the greater use of technology by FIs has increased this type of risk. Banks with higher burdens and higher noninterest expenses and a larger percentage of fixed assets tend to have greater operational risk. An often-used measure for bank operating inefficiency is a bank's *efficiency ratio* equal to noninterest expenses relative to net interest income and noninterest revenue, with a higher ratio indicating greater operating inefficiency, i.e., greater noninterest expenses relative to income sources.

Management culture and corporate governance factors also affect the financial performance and risk taking of financial institutions discussed in the final following sections for the chapter.

THE CHANGING MANAGERIAL OBJECTIVES FOR FINANCIAL INSTITUTIONS

Who Owns Financial Institutions?

Under traditional agency financial theory, the objective for financial managers is often assumed to be to maximize the wealth of the owners of the firm (i.e., stockholders), often operationalized as maximizing the firm's stock price based on expectations for future earnings per share (EPS) and the risk of the firm, whereby stock price is a function of expected EPS x price/earnings (P/E ratio).

From this perspective, other stakeholders are not explicitly considered, and short-term analyst expectations for future earnings are a paramount part of a firm's stock price valuation. Since stockholders have limited liability, with their maximum loss, their equity ownership stake and the opportunity for unlimited gains, stockholders often have incentives for greater risk taking. In contrast, debt-holders, uninsured depositors, regulators, and government insurance funds have preferences for managers to take on lower risk. Insured depositors may be less vigilant as monitors of bank managers, given their deposits are insured.

With reputational losses and unethical behavior by some financial institution managers and employees during the global financial crisis, there have been calls for a greater focus on ethics and reputation risk management, and on better *corporate governance* to prevent *agency problems*, where nonowner managers pursue their own interests at the expense of principals (owners) and other stakeholders, creating *agency costs*. Examples of this type of *managerial expense preference behavior* includes managers taking on lavish furnishings, large travel and expense accounts, or even fraud and embezzlement.

If compensation is tied to growth or number of transactions, managers may be encouraged to engage in risky types of behavior that benefit their personal bottom lines at the expense of their firm, such as an unprofitable merger that increases bank size and a manager's future compensation. During the U.S. subprime loan crisis, there were also numerous cases of conflicts of interest between managers and other stakeholders, with moral hazard problems created by perverse incentives for the compensation of managers, such as bonuses for making more loans versus judging the quality of loans and taking care in the underwriting. This was particularly the case with a huge demand for securitizations with no relationship between the loan underwriters or packagers of loan securitizations and the monitoring or follow-up on the loans that were made. Similarly, credit rating agents received fees paid by investment bankers for rating subprime securitizations, creating a conflict of interest. With the separation of owners and other stakeholders and managers, *corporate governance* is important for corporations, including the establishment of independent boards of directors as monitors of CEOs and other managers, and the development of policies to reduce potential moral hazard problems and agency costs.

Who are the Stakeholders for a Financial Institution?

In the post environment of the global financial crisis that began with the U.S. subprime loan crisis of 2008, institutional investors, central banks, governments, nongovernmental organizations (NGOs) and social activists have called for financial institutions to incorporate environmental, social, and governance (ESG) factors into their cultures and strategic management considerations. This includes assessing and managing climate change risks, as well as carrying out social, ethical, and governance responsibilities.[2]

Similarly, business schools have been asked to embrace ESG factors as a key curriculum component under the United Nations Principles for Responsible Management Education (PRME) (UNPRME, 2015), to train future business managers to consider that sustainability, corporate responsibility, and ethics as an integral part of management education (AACSB International, 2013).

In recent years, greater emphasis has been made for strategic decisions to include effects on other stakeholders, including the consideration of environmental, social, governance

19

*Financial
Institutions as
Social Value
Creators and
Financial Risk
Takers*

(ESG) factors in the decision-making framework. Research has also shown additional benefits with empirical findings that if firms include ESG factors in decisions, firms will maximize shareholders' wealth by attracting better and more loyal employees and customers, improving the bottom line and a firm's reputation and branding, avoiding the risk of reputation loss, and reducing exorbitant legal and high costs associated with environmental and social damages. Depository institutions in particular are also given charters to operate and receive deposit insurance based on serving their communities, with communities as important stakeholders.

In this vein, recently, there have been challenges to the concept of stockholders as the owners of a firm, and the fiduciary duty of directors to manage firms solely in shareholders' interests. From this perspective, a company should be managed in the interests of a "broad range of stakeholders," who benefit from the long-run success of the corporation (e.g., employees, creditors, managers, local governments, and others contributing to the firm's ability to succeed). In turn, all stakeholders delegate authority to an independent board of directors to monitor efforts and make determinations as to how each stakeholder can be rewarded and incentivized.

Samuelson and Padro (2015) at the Aspen Institute,[3] point out that the short-term demands of "quick-hit investors" are often at odds with the long-term interests of companies. They observe misconceptions about the commonly held view of shareholders as the sole owners of corporations including:

1 *Corporations own themselves versus being the property of shareholders,* since they are created as separate entities acting in the corporation's own name in terms of the ownership of assets with the design shielding shareholders from having to pay corporate debts or be responsible for obligations, with shareholders having limited liability.
2 *There is no legal mandate for a corporation "to maximize shareholder value" or to put the interests of stockholders ahead of the long-run interests of the corporation.* Consequently, many CEOs becoming engaged in sustainability and employee wellness visions have increased the long-run sustainability of their firms, despite some objections by stockholders or Wall Street analysts.
3 *Corporate law under the business judgment rule permits boards of directors and management to use their judgments to act "for the health of the enterprise"* and to determine the purpose of the firm and to "harness its potential," with more executives exhibiting the courage to examine the incentives and metrics that focus on short-term maximization of a corporation's stock price as a primary goal.

Chandler (2015), in a collection of articles on UN PRME principals, similarly points out, with respect to "Principle 2: Shareholders do not own the firm," that with rapid trading today on numerous exchanges, including high-frequency trading, stockholders are often not long-term stakeholders in a firm. Hence, firms need to be run using a more sustainable business model with long-term, close relationships to a broad range of stakeholders central to its mission focusing on long-term value over short-term profits. He also notes recent legal rulings supporting this view, including the UK Companies Act of 2006, that requires directors to act for the long-run success of a company to benefit all stakeholders (Bainbridge, 2002a,b,c; Blair and Stout, 2001a,b; Kaufman and Englander, 2005; Lan and Heracleous, 2010; Millon, 2000).

The Balancing Act of Financial Institutions Managers to Manage for Multiple Stakeholders in the Long-run Interests of the Financial Institution

Managerial objectives in financial institutions need to consider customers' needs, and to meet the needs of the community they serve. Customers of FIs are also suppliers of inputs for banks (deposits) that are used to provide outputs (loans) to other customers, as well as providing interest revenue for banks. In turn FIs provide liquidity for depositors. If a financial institution's reputation is damaged, this in turn can lead to depositors, as well as loan customers, leaving the bank, and even to deposit runs, that can affect a bank's solvency.

Financial institutions also have regulators as stakeholders, being subject to government regulations and often acting as agents for the government, such as depository institutions assisting in carrying out a government's fiscal and monetary policies or other public policies such as the distribution of credit to disadvantaged borrowers. Because governments often provide insurance for many financial institutions, they regularly employ examiners to monitor activities and ensure that managerial decisions don't strain or endanger insurance funds or violate regulations for the safety and soundness and integrity of financial institutions.

Thus, FI managers have a balancing act setting objectives and strategies that address multiple stakeholders: stockholders, debt-holders, customers, employees, and regulators. The concept of a single objective of maximizing shareholder wealth is considered to be too one-dimensional, as demonstrated by the U.S. subprime loan crisis of 2007 to 2008, and subsequent global financial crisis. The impact of strategic decisions on all stakeholders (depositors, borrowers, and other customers) should be considered in terms of environmental and social factors. Financial institutions also face climate change related risks that have to be managed, such as greater catastrophic risk for insurance companies, and stranded asset risks (with fossil fuel reserves affecting fossil fuel company valuations with unburnable reserves to avoid irreversible temperature changes globally). Given these risks, for instance for coal companies, some banks including JPMorgan Chase and BankAmerica decided not to make loans to coal companies in March 2016, and many major insurers have hired climate scientists to estimate the extent of climate change risk and future potential losses.

SUMMARY

Financial institutions are a unique set of business firms with primarily financial assets and financial liabilities, special regulatory restrictions, and special economic functions that have a significant effect on the efficiency and payments systems of a country's economy. Financial institutions are designed to offer intermediary or brokerage services to assist savers in allocating their funds. The services they provide reduce transactions and information costs, including search, portfolio selection, monitoring, risk management, and liquidity and maturity and intermediation costs to investors. With dramatic changes in information technology, financial institutions face greater competition from nonfinancial companies, including technology (FinTech) companies. Other risk management and financial services roles have increased with demand from customers for retirement and financial planning and other wealth management services. Corporate governance, reputation building, and managing credit and operational risk have become more important in the aftermath of the U.S. subprime loan crisis and the following great global recession, along with incorporating environmental, social, and corporate governance factors considerations into strategic decision making.

NOTES

1 These include Bank of America, Citibank, JPMorgan Chase and Wells Fargo, along with big credit card networks including MasterCard, Visa, and American Express.
2 See Blackburne (2013); CFA Institute (2015); First for Sustainability (2015); Global Alliance for Banking Values (2015); IISD (2015); McKinsey & Company (2013); Natural Capital Declaration (2015); Niven (2012); Rhodes (2015); Silverman (2013); Sustainable Banking @ Stanford (2015); Tomorrow's Company (2015); UNEP FI (2015); and Yeates (2014) among many others.
3 The Aspen Institute is an international nonprofit organization for educational and policy studies in Washington, DC, with a mission to foster leadership based on enduring value and to provide a nonpartisan venue for dealing with critical issues.

BIBLIOGRAPHY

AACSB International (2013). "Standard 9," AACSB International website. Accessed on January 29, 2015 at: http://www.aacsb.edu/en/accreditation/standards/2013-business/learning-and-teach/standard9/

Bainbridge, S. (2000a). "Why a board? Group decision-making in corporate governance." *Vanderbilt Law Review*, 55, 1–55.

Bainbridge, S. (2000b). "Director v. shareholder primacy in the convergence debate." *Transnational Lawyer*, 16, 45–62.

Bainbridge, S. (2000c). *Corporation Law and Economics*. New York: Foundation Press.

Blackburne, Alex (Ed.) (2013). *The Guide to Sustainable Banking, Blue & Green Tomorrow*. Accessed on January 29, 2015 at: blueandgreentomorrow.com

Blair, M. and L. Stout (2001a). "Corporate accountability: Director accountability and the mediating role of the corporate board." *Washington Law Review*, 79, 403–447.

Blair, M. and L. Stout (2001b). "Trust, trustworthiness, and the behavioral foundations of corporate law." *University of Pennsylvania Law Review*, 149, 1735–1810.

CFA Institute. (2015). *Environmental, Social, and Governance (ESG) Resources*. Accessed on January 24, 2015 at: http://www.cfainstitute.org/ethics/topics/Pages/esg_resources.aspx

Chandler, David (2015). "Principle 2: Shareholders do not own the firm." In *Corporate Social Responsibility: A Strategic Perspective*, New York: BEP Business Expert Press.

Deutsche Bank Responsibility (2016). "Our understanding of responsibility." Deutsche Bank's website. Accessed on August 22, 2016 at: https://www.db.com/cr/index_en.htm

First for Sustainability: Financial Institution, Resources, Solutions, and Tools (2015). Sustainable Banking website (An Innovation of International Finance Corporate (IFC) in Partnership with Ministry for Foreign Affairs of Finland and SIDA). Accessed on January 25, 2015 at: http://firstforsustainability.org/sustainability/sustainability-and-finance/

Gardner, Mona, Dixie Mills, and Elizabeth S. Cooperman (2005). *Managing Financial Institutions*, 5th ed., Mason, OH: Thomson/Southwestern Publishing.

Global Alliance for Banking Values (2015). Accessed on January 26, 2015 at: http://www.gabv.org

Henry, Zoe (2016). "8 emerging FinTech startups to watch in 2016." Inc., Brand View, January 16. Accessed on April 17, 2016 at: http://www.inc.com/zoe-henry/8-emerging-fintech-startups-2016.html

IISD (2015). "Sustainable banking," on the International Institute for Sustainable Development (IISD) website. Accessed on January 29, 2015 at: https://www.iisd.org/business/banking/sus_banking.aspx

Irrera, Anna (2014). "UBS CIO: "Blockchain technology can massively simplify banking." *Wall Street Journal*, WDJ.D Tech: Digits: Tech News & Analysis from the WSJ, October 27, 2014. Accessed on February 1, 2015, at: https://blogs.wsj.com/digits/2014/10/27/ubs-cio-blockchain-technology-can-massively-simplify-banking/ KEYWORDS=massively+simplify+banking

Kaufman, A. and E. Englander (2005). "A team production model of corporate governance." *Academy of Management Executive*, 19(3), 9–22.

Landes, Luke (2013). "What happens if your bank account is hacked?" *Forbes*. Accessed on February 1, 2015, at: http://www.forbes.com/sites/moneybuilder/2013/01/15/what-happens-if-your-bank-account-is-hacked/

Lan, Luh Luh and Loizos Heracleous (2010). "Rethinking agency theory, the view from law." *Academy of Management Review*, 35(2), 294–314.

Lohr, Steve (2016). "As more pay by smartphone, banks scramble to keep up." *New York Times*, January 18, 2016. Accessed on April 17, 2016 at: http://www.nytimes.com/2016/01/19/technology/upstarts-are-leading-the-fintech-movement-and-banks-take-heed.html?_r=0

McKinsey & Company (2013). "The search for a sustainable banking model," McKinsey & Company website. Accessed on January 29, 2015 at: http://www.mckinsey.com/insights/financial_services/the_search_for_a_sustainable_banking.model

Mclannahan, Ben (2016). "JPMorgan in blockchain trial project." *Financial Times*, February 1, 2016, p. 15.

Meara, Bob (2012). "Emerging technologies in retail banking: The long road to customer centricity." CELENT website, August 17. Accessed on February 1, 2015 at: http://www.celent.com/reports/emerging-technologies-retail-banking-long-road-customer-centricity

Millon, D. (2000). "New game plan or business as usual? A critique of the team production model of corporate law." *Virginia Law Review*, 86, 1001–1044.

Morgenson, Gretchen and Joshua Rosner (2011). *Reckless Endangerment: How Outsized Ambition, Greed, and Corruption Led to Economic Armageddon*. New York: Times Books, Henry Holt and Company.

Natural Capital Declaration (2015). website. Accessed on January 25, 2015 at: http://www.naturalcapitaldeclaration.org/financial-institutions/

Niven, James (2012). "Sustainable banking: The business case." Guardian sustainable business: Values-led business, *The Guardian*, April 3, 2012. Accessed on January 29, 2015 at: http://www.theguardian.com/sustainable-business/sustainable-banking-ethical-investment-business-case

Popper, Nathaniel (2016). "'Fintech' start-up boom said to threaten bank jobs." *The New York Times*, March 30, 2016. Accessed on March 31, 2016 at: http://www.nytimes.com/2016/03/31/business/dealbook/fintech-start...

Quittner, Jeremy (2014). "How apple pay may change the world of payments." *INC. Technology*, October 17, 2014. Accessed on February 1, 2015 at: http://www.inc.com/jeremy-quittner/apple-pay-launch-moves-needle-on-digital-payments.html

Rhodes, William (2015). "Banks need to lead on cultural change." The Bretton Woods Committee, January 6, 2015. Accessed on January 24, 2015 at: http://www.brettonwoods.org/in_the_news/banks-need-to-lead-on-cultural-change

Samuelson, Judith and Miguel Padro (2015). "What business leaders & shareholders get wrong." *The Aspen Journal of Ideas*, Winter 2014/2015, 82–84.

Silverman, Ross (2013). "Bank of England Governor calls for change in banks' culture." *The Telegraph*, August 8, 2013. Accessed on January 24, 2015 at: http://www.telegraph.co.uk/finance/bank-of-england/10230186/Bank-of-England-governor-calls-for-change-in-banks-culture.html

Sustainable Banking @ Stanford (2015). SB@S website. Accessed on January 24, 2015 at: https://www.sustainablebanking.stanford.edu

Swiss Sustainable Finance. "What is sustainable finance." Swiss Sustainable Finance website. Accessed on September 9, 2016 at: http://www.sustainablefinance.ch/en/what-is-sustainable-finance-_content---1--1055.html

The Financial Brand (2012). "Emerging technologies in retail banking: The long road ahead," The Financial Brand website, October 25. Accessed on February 1, 2015 at: http://thefinancialbrand.com/25875/bank-and-credit-union-technology-trends/

Tomorrow's Company (2015). "Tomorrow's value: Achieving long-term financial returns: A guide for pension fund trustees." Accessed on January 29, 2015 at: http://www.law.harvard.edu/programs/corp_gov/long-term-value-creation-roundtable-2014-materials/tomorrows-value-achieving-long-term-financial-returns_EX.pdf

UNEP FI Guide to Banking and Sustainability (2011). United Nations Environment Programme (UNEP) Finance Initiative: Innovative financing for sustainability. Accessed on January 24, 2015 at: http://www.unepfi.org/fileadmin/documents/guide_banking_statements.pdf

*Financial
Institutions as
Social Value
Creators and
Financial Risk
Takers*

UNEP FI (2015). United Nations Environment Programme Finance Initiative. Accessed on January 26, 2015 at: http://www.unepfi.org

UN Principles for Responsible Management Education (UNPRME) (2015). Accessed on January 24, 2015 at: http://www.unprme.org

University of California, Haas School of Business Center for Responsible Business website. Accessed on April 17, 2016 at: http://responsiblebusiness.haas.berkeley.edu/programs/sustainablefinance.html

Yeates, Clancy (2014). "Australian Super calls on banks to access climate change risk." *The Sydney Morning Herald*, December 26, 2014. Accessed on January, 24, 2015 at: http://www.smh.com.au/business/banking-and-finance/australian-super-calls-on-banks-to-assess-climate-change-risk-20141224-12d16q.html

QUESTIONS AND PROBLEMS

Questions

1   What are some of the important economic functions for financial institutions? What is the difference between indirect and direct finance, and how does indirect finance facilitate and transform financial transactions between savers and borrowers?

2   How do the assets and liabilities differ for a financial institution versus a nonfinancial firm? Why do financial firms have so much financial leverage?

3   What is a favorite financial institution that you have a relationship with? What factors led you to choose that particular firm? How much did the financial institution's reputation and trustworthiness have in your decision?

4   Do you agree with the common financial concept that financial institution managers should maximize stockholders wealth? Why or why not. What other stakeholders influence the management objectives of financial institutions? Give an example of a situation where the objectives of regulators and stockholders might be in conflict.

5   Briefly discuss differences between depository, contractual, and investment types of financial intermediaries. Give examples for banks, mutual funds, insurance companies, and pension funds of what their roles are in terms of financial services and the benefits they provide to consumers and businesses.

6   Define a depository institution's NIM, Burden%, and PLL%. If a firm has a NIM of 5%, a NIR% of 1%, NIE% of 3%, PLL% of 1%, and equity to assets ratio of 10%, what are the firm's operating ROA and ROE before taxes?

7   Why should financial institution managers be concerned with environmental, social, and governance (ESG) issues as well as profitability in their strategic decisions?

8   Pick a large financial institution's website, and find its sustainability or corporate social responsibility report or summary of environmental, social, and governance activities. What are some activities that the financial institution is engaging for environmental, social, or governance areas?

9   What are different risks that depository institutions (banks, credit unions, savings institutions) face? Why do depository institutions have greater liquidity, interest rate, and credit risk than contractual and investment institutions? Financial institutions are often cited as being in the risk business; how do financial institutions reduce risk for consumers and borrowers?

10 How does the separation of ownership and management complicate the theory of the firm? Give an example of expense preference behavior on the part of a manager.

11 In the aftermath of the U.S. subprime loan crisis and the great global recession, regulatory proposals have been made to limit bank executive salaries and bonus structures. Find an article on recent regulations in this area. Do you think this is a good idea? Why or why not?

Problems

1 The Felicity Bank has the following balance sheet:

Assets		
Fixed-rate loans (30 years)	$50 million	(Rate 8%)
Total assets	$50 million	
Liabilities and equity		
Deposits (less than 1 year)	$42 million	(Rate 5%)
Equity	$8 million	
Total liabilities and equity	$50 million	

a   What is the bank's 1-year funding gap (RSA – RSL)? What risk does the bank have for interest rate movements with this funding gap?

b   Calculate the bank's expected net interest income (interest revenue less interest expense) for the coming year? What is the bank's expected net interest margin (net interest income / total assets)?

c   If rates go up for deposits by 5% to 6%, what is the bank's new net interest income and net interest margin?

d   What is the bank's equity to total assets ratio? What is the bank's equity multiplier? If the bank has a PLL% of 0.50%, and a Burden% of 1%, what is the bank's operating ROA based on its current expected NIM you calculated in #b? What is its expected operating ROE?

2   Alby Singleton at Bank Sussman in San Francisco is examining the bank's ROE under the following conditions: NIM is 4.2%, EM is 11, the marginal tax rate is 35%, total assets are $1,750 million, the burden is $40 million, and the provision for loan losses $0. What is the bank's operating ROE? If the bank decides to increase the equity multiplier to 12, holding other factors constant, what will be the new expected operating ROE?

3   The board of directors of the First National Bank of Lizzie has approved a target ROE of 16%, target EM of 12. The bank has a marginal tax rate of 35%, total assets of $850 million, interest expense of $80 million, burden of $11.5 million, PLL of $1 million. What does the bank's target NIM need to be? What target interest revenues must the bank have to meet its financial goals? If interest expenses rise to 10% above target, what ROE will the bank actually earn?

25

*Financial
Institutions as
Social Value
Creators and
Financial Risk
Takers*

4 The First Caroline Bank and Trust Company has a ROA of 1%, ROE of 12.57%, and net income of $11,798,000. What is the bank's equity multiplier and equity to total assets ratio. What is the bank's total assets and total equity? If the bank increases total liabilities by $10 million and reduces equity by the same amount, and with the higher interest expense, net incomes falls to $11.5 million, what will the new ROE be? What do these changes reveal about the impact of financial leverage?

5 Terrell Savings Bank is preparing a financial plan based on the following data: target ROE of 15%, tax rate of 35%, total assets of $700 million, total liabilities of $640 million, and provision for loan losses of $1 million. What is the bank's current equity multiplier? Given this EM, what before tax income must the bank earn to reach its target ROE? What is the bank's NIM, assuming a Burden% of 1.1% of total assets?

Chapter 2

Interest Rates: Theories and Duration as an Overall Risk Measure

Central banks across Asia are racing to cut interest rates, but they may not be doing it fast enough to stave off economic malaise. The problem is weak inflation. Policy makers appear to have been surprised by how slowly prices are rising, and the slowdown is starting to weigh on economic growth across the region. If prices drop for too long, companies invest less and people's pay shrinks. Asia is not experiencing such outright deflation yet, but the risks are rising.

(Gough, 2015)

Interest rates reflect the underlying fundamentals of the economy. The severe recession triggered by the financial crisis and the subsequent slow recovery have led to lower expected real returns from investments. More broadly, the level of equilibrium real interest rates (which equate the supply of saving with the demand for investment) is quite low. Coupled with low inflation, low equilibrium real interest rates have translated into low nominal interest rates.

(Genay and Podjasek, 2014)

As noted in Chapter 1 discussing the effect of interest rates on the profitability and risk of depository institutions, an understanding of interest rate theories is of key importance to financial institution managers. During the U.S. subprime loan crisis in 2007 to 2008, and the following great recession, central banks engaged in monetary policies, including quantitative easing policies, to increase the money supply and keep interest rates low in order to stimulate their countries' economies. As shown in Figure 2.1, in the United States the Fed Funds rate, the rate reflecting borrowing and lending for excess reserves between banks, fell dramatically. By 2010, this rate was close to 0%. Later in 2015 it rose to 0.25% and in 2016 to 0.50%. Figure 2.1 shows shadowed areas for recessions. Note, during recessions, interest rates typically fall with lower demand for funds.

Historically, interest rates can be quite volatile, often with short-term interest rate changes leading long-term rate changes. Rates generally rise (but not always) during expansions, with a greater demand for funds, and fall during recessions, when there is lower business demand

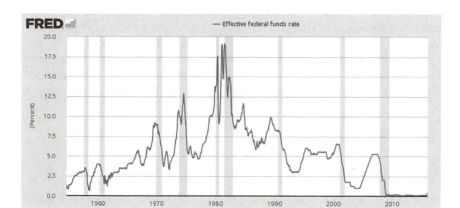

FIGURE 2.1 | Fred Graph: Trends in U.S. Fed Funds rate over time (percentage).

Source: Board of Governors of the Federal Reserve System (US) Federal Reserve Economic Data (FRED).

and demand for funds in an economy. Short-term rates typically lead long-term rates in terms of rising and falling, with long-term rates often taking longer to change.

Central banks are also concerned about expectations for interest rates, particularly how the level of interest rates will affect the health of the economy, as well as a country's foreign exchange rate. As noted in the quotes at the beginning of the chapter, central banks face a difficulty in deciding when to act in their open market operations to stimulate or contract the money supply to prevent inflation or deflation, using interest rates as a target that is watched carefully.

Investors and households are also concerned about different types of investments, such as fixed-rate bonds and variable-interest rates for home mortgages and mortgage securities, among other financial instruments. The subprime loan crisis is a case in point when interest rates rose and subprime borrowers with adjustable rate mortgages were not able to make higher loan payments, contributing to nonpayments and abandonment of homes by borrowers that in turn contributed to over 2.2 million of loan foreclosures in 2007 alone. These loan losses, along with large losses on subprime mortgage loan securities, put many financial institutions on the brink of failure. Similarly, portfolio managers of fixed-rate bond portfolios need to be aware of likely trends in interest rates for hedging against interest rate risk.

Hence, it is important to have an understanding of interest rates, types of interest rate risk, duration as an overall measure of interest rate risk for bonds and for financial institutions, and an understanding of interest rate theories used to try to anticipate future changes in interest rates discussed in this chapter.

INTEREST RATE RISK DEFINED

Risk is part of life and risk for financial assets such as securities is the potential variation of returns on an investment. Expected risks are incorporated into investment decisions by investors; risks arise from changes investors don't anticipate. Part of decision making includes trying to forecast changes, but even the most astute forecaster will make errors, so no investor can be completely protected from interest rate risk. For investors there are two types of interest rate risk, the risk of capital losses if fixed-rate securities have to be sold prior to maturity when interest rates rise (price risk), and the risk of lower reinvestment income if interest rates fall and maturing cash flows have to be reinvested at lower rates. These two risks and an overall measure of both risks, duration, are discussed in the following sections.

REINVESTMENT AND PRICE RISK

For fixed-rate securities, there are two types of interest rate risk:

1 *Price risk:* the risk of a capital loss if interest rates go up and the price of the security going down if it has to be sold prior to maturity.
2 *Reinvestment risk:* the risk of lower reinvestment income for coupons for a coupon bond or other maturing cash flows, that can result in a lower than expected annual return.

To understand these risks, it is good to look at the relationship between bond yields and prices, as an example of the inverse relationship between fixed-income security prices and market interest rates on similar bonds.

THE PRICE YIELD RELATIONSHIP

There is an inverse relationship between interest rates and fixed-rate bond prices. Fixed-rate bonds typically come in two types:

1 *Zero coupon bonds*, with no coupons and a single payment at maturity, that are priced at a discount from their maturity values, with only a single maturity payment.
2 *Coupon bonds* that pay coupons over a specified period, such as annually or semi-annually, and a maturity value the final year of payment for the bond.

For each bond type, the price or market value of the bond is the present value of its cash flows as discussed below for zero coupon and coupon bonds respectively.

ZERO COUPON BOND VALUATION

A zero coupon bond's price is the present value of its maturity value t years in the future discounted at the market rate y^* for similar bonds where:

Zero coupon price $(P_0) = $ (Cash flow in year t)$/(1 + y^*)^t$

where y^* is the market interest rate on similar bonds (discount rate) and t, the number of years later when the cash flow will be received. If the market interest rate for similar bonds rises, the price (value) of the security will fall.

Example If you buy a 10-year maturity zero coupon bond *that has no coupons, just a single payment at maturity* of $1,000, and the market rate for similar bonds is 5%:

$$P_0 = \$1,000/[(1.05)^{10}] = \$613.91.$$

PRICE RISK FOR THE ZERO COUPON BOND

Since zero coupon bonds only have a single cash flow, they only have price risk. If interest rates rise to 6%, for instance, the price of the zero coupon will fall to:

$$P_0 = \$1,000/[(1.06)^{10} \text{ to } \$558.40.$$

The bond has a loss in its market value of ($558.40 – $613.91) = $55.51. Holding default risk constant, if the bond is held to its 10-year maturity, however, investors will lock in the expected yield to maturity (y^*) of 5%.

VALUATION FOR A COUPON BOND

For a coupon bond, the price is equal to the present value of the coupon payments and the single maturity payment, each discounted at market rate, y^*:

Coupon bond (P_0) = PMT (PVIFA y^*, t) + Maturity value (PVIF y^*, n)

where PVIFA is the present value of the annuity factor $\{[1 - (1/(1 + y^*)^n]/y^*\}$ used to find the present value of the coupon payments (PMT) each occurring at their respective time, t, and PVIF is the present value factor $[1/(1 + y^*)^n]$ to find the present value of the single payment maturity value in year n.

Example If you buy a 10-year maturity coupon bond that has an annual coupon payment of $50, and a maturity value of $1,000, and the market rate for similar bonds is 5%:

$$P_0 = \$50 \text{ (PVIFA 5\%, 10)} + \$1,000 \text{ (PVIF 5\%, 10)}$$
$$= \$50 (7.7217) + \$1,000 (0.6139) = \text{about } \$1,000.$$

Note since the coupon rate is 5% and y^* is 5%, the bond sells at its maturity value of $1,000, so no calculation was really needed. If the coupon rate is greater than y^*, the bond will sell at a premium above its maturity value, and if the coupon rate is less than y^*, the bond will sell at a discount.

Coupon paying bonds have both price risk (if sold prior to maturity) and reinvestment risk for coupon payments if market rates change over the life of the coupon bond.

REINVESTMENT AND PRICE RISK FOR THE COUPON BOND

If interest rates rise to 6% over the life of the coupon bond right after it is issued, the value of the bond will fall, since it will be offering a coupon rate (CR) < new y^*. The new price of the coupon bond if rates rise to 6% will be:

$$P_0 = \$50 \ (\text{PVIFA } 6\%, 10) + \$1,000 \ (\text{PVIF } 6\%, 10)$$
$$= \$50 \ (7.3601) + \$1,000 \ (0.5584) = \$944.49.$$

A loss in value of ($944.49 – $1,000) = ($55.51).

Hence, the coupon bond if it has to be sold prior to maturity will have to be sold at a price lower than its purchase price at a capital loss. Note, although for this particular example, the price changes are similar for the two bonds, price swings for zero coupon bonds, since they don't have coupon payments, are generally larger than for coupon bonds.

Reinvestment Risk

The zero coupon bond has no reinvestment risk over its life, if the bond is held to maturity, since there are no coupon payments to reinvest. For the coupon bond, there will be reinvestment risk if rates fall, since its expected yield to maturity of 5% depends on the coupon payments being reinvested at the 5% expected annual compound rate. If the coupons have to be reinvested at a lower interest rate, this reduces the future value of the coupons and the bond's annual compound yield.

Hence, given price and reinvestment risk, the yield an investor expects to get when purchasing a bond (ex ante effective annual yield) can differ from the ex post (actual) effective annual yield the investor receives.

Calculating Ex Post (Actual) Effective Annual Yields

The actual (ex post) effective annual yield (EAY) that investors receive is calculated as:

$$\text{EAY} = \{[\text{FV/PV}]^{1/n}\} - 1$$

where PV is the price you paid for the bond (present value of cash flows at that time), and FV is the future value, what you actually receive in year n, the number of years of your investment holding period. Note you are basically taking a geometric mean by taking the ratio of the future value to the present value to the $1/n$ power. You can think of this equation as what you have at the end of your investment period (FV) divided by what you paid for that investment when you bought it (PV), and putting this on an annual compound basis to get your annual compound rate of return by taking this to the $1/n$ power. This will give you $(1 + y^*)$, so you subtract 1, to get the average annual compound return you received over your holding period of n years.

EXAMPLES: EFFECTIVE ANNUAL YIELDS FOR DIFFERENT RATE SCENARIOS

Here are some example cases for finding the EAYs under different interest rate scenarios. For Case 1, the 10-year coupon bond is held to maturity. For Case 2 rates fall to 4% over the life of the bond, and it is held to maturity. For Case 3, rates rise in year 8 to 6%, and the bond is sold at the end of year 8 for the market price at that time, based on the present value of the remaining two coupons and maturity value that the buyer of the bond will receive.

Case 1: A Bond is Held to Maturity and $y*$ Is Constant over the Bond's Life

Example Given a 10-year coupon bond, with a 5% coupon rate, and $1,000 maturity value, with a price of $1,000, with $y* = 5\%$ held to maturity:

FV if held to maturity = Coupon PMT (FVIFA $y*$, n) + Maturity value

where FVIFA is the future value of the annuity factor, $\{[(1 + y*)^n - 1]/y* \}$.
So, if $y*$ remained at 5% over the life of the bond and is held for 10 years:

FV = $50 (FVIFA 5%, 10) + $1,000 = $50 (12.5779) + $1,000
  = $628.90 + $1,000 = $1,628.90

EAY = $\{[\text{FV/PV}]^{1/10}\} - 1 = [\{1,628.90/1,000\}^{0.10}] - 1 = 0.05$ or 5%.

In this case since the bond was held to maturity and the coupons could be invested over the entire period at the 5% annual compound rate, the ex ante expected annual yield is equal to the ex post annual yield of 5%.

Case 2: Reinvestment Risk

The same bond is held to maturity, but right after purchase rates go down to 4% and stay at that rate for 10 years. The future value of the bond's coupons are calculated plus the $1,000 maturity value that you'll have earned at the end of the 10 years, so:

FV = $50 (FVIFA 4%, 10) + $1,000 = $50 (12.006) + $1,000 = $1,600.30

EAY = $\{[\text{FV/PV}]^{1/10}\} - 1 = [\{1600.30/1000\}^{0.10}] - 1 = 0.0481$ or 4.81%.

Because of the drop in interest rates (reinvestment risk), since the coupon payments had to be reinvested at a much lower rate, the investor received an effective annual ex post yield of 4.81% less than the expected ex ante yield of 5%.

Case 3: Price Risk

Where for the same coupon bond, rates stay at 5% for 8 years, but y^* rises to 6% when the bond is sold at the end of year 8 (two coupons and maturity payment remain).

In this case, since the bond is sold prior to maturity, the investor will receive the FV of eight coupon payments invested at 5% plus the price the bond sells for at the end of year 8, equal to the present value of its remaining 2 years of cash flows.

FV of coupons for 8 years = Coupon PMT (FVIFA 5%, 8)

P_0 Bond sales price = PMT (PVIFA 6%, 2) +

Maturity value (PVIF 6%, 2),

so:

FV of coupons = $50 (FVIFA 5%, 8) = $50 (9.5491) = $477.46

Price sell bond for = $50 (PVIFA 6%,2) + $1,000 (PVIF 6%, 2)
$$= \$50 (1.8334) + \$1,000 (0.8900) = \$981.67$$

$$\text{EAY} = [\text{FV/PV}]^{1/8} - 1 = \{[(477.46 + 981.67)]/1,000\}^{1/8} - 1$$
$$= \{[1.4591]^{0.125}\} - 1 = 0.0484 \text{ or } 4.84\%.$$

Because the bond was sold prior to maturity and with y^* rising to 6%, the bond had to be sold at a capital loss, so the investor received an EAY of 4.84% less than the expected ex ante yield of 5%, illustrating price risk.

DURATION AS AN OVERALL MEASURE OF INTEREST RATE RISK

Duration is a measure of overall interest rate risk first developed by Frank Macaulay over 50 years ago, and is widely used as an overall measure of interest rate risk that encompasses both price and reinvestment risk.

Duration in simple terms can be thought of as the weighted average time over which cash flows from an investment are expected, where the weights are the relative time-adjusted present values of the cash flows. Duration is superior to maturity as a measure of interest rate risk, since maturity ignores the fact that, for most securities, such as coupon bonds with high coupon payments, substantial cash benefits are received before the maturity date. Duration is also a measure of the overall interest rate risk or responsiveness of a bond's market price to a change in market rates.

The formula for duration is in simple terms:

DUR = Sum (PV of weighted cash flows x t) / Sum (PV of cash flows) where t is the time when the cash flow comes in. Since the sum of (PV of cash flows) is the price of a bond, the formula can also be expressed as the sum (PV of cash flows x t) divided by the bond's price. Duration goes down as coupon rates go up, the reinvestment rate y^* goes up, and as maturity (n) goes down.

EXAMPLE CALCULATING BOND DURATION

Suppose an insurance company issues a $1 million guaranteed investment contract that guarantees an annual effective yield (y^*) of 8% for 5 years. In other words, the investor is promised that he/she will receive $1 million $(1.08)^5 = \$1.469$ million in 5 years, that is, an 8% annual realized return on the investment.

The firm has two investment alternatives, both with a $1,000 maturity value:

1 *Bond 1:* 5-year bonds with an 8% coupon rate and $1,000 par value, which sells for $1,000 per bond, with $y^* = 8\%$.
2 *Bond 2:* 6-year bonds with an 8% coupon rate and $1,000 par value, which sells for $1,000 per bond, $y^* = 8\%$.

Bond 1 The duration of Bond 1 is:

Year t	Cash flow ($)	PVIF 8%	PV cash flow ($)	t x PV cash flow ($)
1	80	0.9259	74.07	74.07
2	80	0.8573	68.58	137.16
3	80	0.7938	63.50	190.50
4	80	0.7350	58.80	235.20
5	1080	0.6806	735.05	3,675.25
		Sum	1,000.00	4,312.18

Duration = Sum (Weighted PV cash flow / PV cash flow (bond's price)
= [$4,312.18/$1,000] = 4.312.

Note: For a coupon bond, its duration will always be less than its maturity years, while a zero coupon bond has a duration equal to its maturity, so no calculation is needed.

Bond 2 For finding the duration of Bond 2, we'll use a shorter formula:

$$DUR = N - \{[Coupon\ PMT / (P_0 \times y^*)]\ [N - (1 + y^*)(PVIFA\ y^*, N)]\}$$

where N = years to maturity, P_0 = price, y^* = market yield to maturity rate, and PVIFA is the present value of the annuity factor for a rate of y^* and N maturity years).

$$DUR = 6 - \{[80/(1,000 \times 0.08)]\ [6 - (1.08)(4.6229)]\} = 4.993.$$

The 6-year maturity Bond 2 actually has a duration of just about 5 years, which would be closest to the holding period for the insurance firm of 5 years.

Immunizing a Bond or Bond Portfolio against Interest Rate Risk by Duration Matching to the Number of Years in an Investment Horizon

By duration matching a bond or bond portfolio to its number of holding period years (i.e., the investment horizon desired), the bond can be protected (*immunized*) against interest rate risk, helping to lock in the desired EAY, subject to some limitations discussed a little later.

Example Duration matching for a 5-year investment horizon with Bond 2 that had a 5-year duration to get at least the annual return desired of 8%.

Scenario 1: Suppose rates rise to 9% after Bond 2 is purchased, and Bond 2 is held for 5 years, and sold at the end of year 5.

FV of coupons = 80 (FVIFA 9%, 5) = 80 (5.9847) = $478.78.

Price sell bond for in year 5 with 1 year of cash flows remaining:

= $1,080 (PVIF 9%, 1) = $1,080 (0.9174) = $990.83

Total FV at the end of year 5 = $478.78 + $990.83 = $1,469.61.

Note: The coupon reinvestment income is larger than expected.
Offsetting the capital loss when the bond is sold at the end of year 5.

EAY = (FV/PV) $^{1/n}$ − 1 = (1,469.61/1,000)$^{0.20}$ − 1 = 0.08 or 8%.

[The higher coupon reinvestment income offset the capital loss, so the desired effective annual rate of 8% or the amount desired at the end of the 5 years of $1,469 for each bond purchased is achieved.]

Scenario 2: Suppose rates go down to 7% after the bond is purchased, and Bond 2 again is held for 5 years, the desired holding period, and sold at the end of year 5:

FV of coupons = 80 (FVIFA 7%, 5) = 80 (5.7507) = $460.06.

Price sell bond for in year 5:

= $1,080 (PVIF 7%, 1) = $1,080 (.9346) = $1,009.37

(since the bond has 1 year remaining to maturity).

Total FV at the end of year 5 = \$460.06 + \$1,009.37 = \$1,469.43

$$\text{EAY} = (\text{FV/PV})^{1/n} - 1 = (1,469.43/1000)^{0.20} - 1 = 0.08 \text{ or } 8\%.$$

[The lower coupon reinvestment income was offset by the capital gain, so the desired annual return or \$1,469 in 5 years is achieved.]

By matching the desired holding period with a bond with the same duration, the bond is immunized against interest rate risk, helping to assure the desired 8% effective annual compound return.

Similarly, the investor could have purchased a 5-year zero coupon bond that offered an 8% annual yield to maturity, and held the bond to its 5-year maturity period, again matching the duration of the bond to the duration of the investor's holding period to immunize against interest rate risk.

Immunization Assumptions and Limitations

Under certain assumptions, immunization by duration matching as shown in the example above immunizes a bond portfolio for interest rate risk. With a flat yield curve and only one unexpected parallel shift in the curve, the realized annual return over the holding period in the example resulted in the ex post and ex ante annual yield being the same. However, if market changes occur in the middle of an investment period, an investor may be less than perfectly immunized. Another problem is finding a bond with the expected duration for the desired holding period, particularly for longer periods of time. Zero coupon bonds and stripped securities, bonds stripped of their coupon payments, held to maturity are useful for duration matching, since all cash flows come in at maturity.

Financial institutions that promise to make cash payments to others at specified dates in the future, such as pension funds and life insurance companies, can use duration matching to enhance the probability that cash will be available to meet these payments by investing in assets with a weighted average duration equal to that of their future cash obligations, called dedicated portfolios. Immunized portfolios, however, are not protected from default risk, and there may be changes in anticipated yields as the result of unanticipated changes in tax laws, and immunization can reduce unexpected gains when interest rates change in a favorable direction.

MODIFIED DURATION

The approximate change in the value of an asset or liability using a bond's duration can be calculated as:

$$\text{Approximate change in value} = -\text{Duration} \times ((\text{Change } y^*)/(1 + y^*))]$$

where y^* is the yield to maturity at a point in time, and change y^* is the expected change in rate expressed as a fraction, such as a 1% rise in rates would be expressed as 0.01. Investors often calculate modified duration (MD) to make it easier to quickly calculate the approximate change in a security's value, where:

$MD = [DUR/(1 + y*)]$.

For Bond 1, for instance, with a duration of 4.312, and $y*$ of 8%,

MD Bond 1 $= [(4.312/(1.08)] = 3.99$.

The approximate change in price for Bond 1 with a 1% change in $y*$

$= - MD \times$ Change rate $= - 3.99 (0.01) = - 0.0399$ or $- 3.99\%$.

Given a price of $1,000, the price will change by about:

Approximate change price $= - 0.0399 \times \$1,000 = - \$39.90$.

Because duration assumes a linear relationship between $y*$ and a bond's price, and this relationship is actually convex (i.e., capital gains are larger than capital losses for a given change in rate), the change in price is approximate and will be slightly off as an approximation. For large portfolios convexity adjustments can be made.

ESTIMATING INTEREST RATE ELASTICITY

It is also a short step, once you have a bond's modified duration, to estimate a measure of interest rate elasticity (E) for a financial asset, which may be a more reasonable proxy for the interest rate risk of holding that asset, without regard to any given expected change in $y*$. Interest rate elasticity is defined as the percentage price change expected for a 1% change in $y*$:

$E = - $ (Modified duration)($y*$).

For Bond 1 for instance,

$E = - 3.99 (0.08) = - 0.3192$.

For Bond 1, for every 1% change in the bond's yield of 8% (for instance, a change in 8% $\times$ 0.01 of 0.08%) the bondholder could expect a price change of 0.3192% in the opposite direction of the yield change. Interest rate elasticity is useful in comparing the interest rate risk of bonds with different yields and without having to estimate expected yield changes.

DURATION GAPS AS A MEASURE OF AN FI'S OVERALL INTEREST RATE RISK

In Chapter 1, a funding gap was introduced to measure a bank's risk for a change in its net interest spread, measuring reinvestment and refinancing risk. The risk of a change in the market value of a bank's assets and liabilities, and, hence the value of its equity (value of assets – value of liabilities) is measured by its duration gap (D-gap) where Dur-assets is the weighted average duration of a bank's assets, and Dur-liabilities is the weighted average duration of a bank's liabilities, and the leverage ratio (total liabilities / total assets) represents the percentage of financing with liabilities that is multiplied by the duration of liabilities to get the D-ap as:

D-gap = Dur-assets – (Total liabilities / Total assets)(Dur-liabilities).

Just like for bonds, where the approximate change in the value of a bond can be calculated using duration, the approximate change in the value of equity to assets can be calculated using a financial institution's duration gap, as follows:

% Change in value of equity / Total assets =

– D-gap [Change y^* / $(1 + y^*)$]

where y^* is proxied by the average rate in assets

Approximate change in value of equity = % Change $\times$ Total assets

The approximate change in the value of equity with a change in interest rates can be calculated as above by multiplying by its total assets, since the earlier formula is the percentage change in equity relative to total assets.

A bank with a positive duration gap has more long-term assets than liabilities, so the value of equity will fall if interest rates rise (i.e., negative funding gap), with the value of its assets falling more than the value of its liabilities. A bank with a negative duration gap has more long-term liabilities than assets, so the value of equity will fall if interest rates fall (i.e., a positive funding gap), with a larger rise in the value of its liabilities with the fall in interest rates than the rise in the value of its assets.

Often on depository institution reports, proxies are used for duration, such as the value of long-term assets less the value of long-term liabilities to get a net position for a particular time period, such as 1, 3, 5, and 10 or more years.

EXAMPLE: CALCULATING THE DURATION OF ASSETS AND DURATION OF LIABILITIES AND D-GAP FOR FLATBUSH AVENUE BANK

Dur-assets = Sum [Each asset type / Total assets) $\times$ its Duration]

Dur-liabilities = Sum [Each liability type / Total liabilities) $\times$ its Duration]

Dur-gap = Dur-Assets – [(Total Liabilities / Total Assets) $\times$ Dur-Liabilities].

Calculating the duration gap for Flatbush Avenue Bank

		Duration
Assets ($ million)		
Cash	10,000	0
T-bills (6-month, 6% rate)	40,000	0.50
Loans 10-year, 10% fixed rate	50,000	4.73
Total assets	100,000	
Liabilities ($ million)		
Transaction deposits	40,000	0
Certificates of deposits (1 year)	50,000	1
Total liabilities	90,000	
Equity	10,000	
Total liabilities and equity	100,000	

$$Dur\text{-}assets = [(10,000/100,000) \times 0] + [(40,000/100,000) \times 0.50]$$
$$+ (50,000/100,000) \times 4.73] = 0 + 0.20 + 2.365 = 2.565$$

$$Dur\text{-}liabilities = [(40,000/90,000) \times 0] + [(50,000/90,000) \times 1]$$
$$= 0 + 0.556 = 0.556$$

$$D\text{-}gap = Dur\text{-}assets - [(Liabilities\ /\ Total\ assets) \times Dur\text{-}liabilities]$$
$$= \{2.565 - (90,000/100,000)(0.556)\} = 2.565 - 0.500 = 2.065.$$

If rates rise 1%, what will be the approximate change in the value of equity? *Note:* For the average asset rate use 7.4% as the weighted average asset rate [i.e., $(0.40 \times 6\%) + (0.50 \times 10\%) = 7.4\%)$].

$$Approximate\ \%\ change\ in\ value\ of\ equity = -D\text{-}gap\ (Change\ y^*/(1 + y^*)$$
$$= -2.065\ (0.01)/(1.074) = -0.0192\ \text{or about}$$
$$-1.92\%$$

$$Approximate\ change\ in\ the\ value\ of\ equity = (-0.0192 \times \$100,000\ \text{million})$$
$$= -\$1,920\ \text{million.}$$

Since the bank had a positive duration gap, with a rise in rates the duration of its assets fell more than the duration of its liabilities, resulting in a drop in the market value of the bank's equity.

Financial institutions can reduce duration gaps by having a better duration match of assets and liabilities, or changing the liability to asset ratio that affects the duration of liabilities. However, there is a cost of immunization:

1 If the bank switches to more long-term liabilities, these are more expensive, so would reduce the bank's not interest spread and NIM.
2 If the bank switches to more variable-rate assets, these will have lower rates, since this passes the interest rate risk on to the borrower, so would also lower the bank's net interest spread and net interest margin.

Thus, by reducing its duration gap, the bank passes on interest rate risk to its customers. For instance, by having more adjustable rate mortgages, borrowers have greater interest rate risk. Consequently, these borrowers will demand a lower initial base interest rate for this risk. Similarly, customers who invest in longer-term time deposits have greater interest rate and liquidity risk with longer-term fixed-rate deposits, and they demand a higher interest rate for taking on this risk.

Hence, by hedging this way, a depository institution will lower its net interest income and NIM. Financial institutions can also hedge their funding or duration gaps using derivatives instead, such as interest rate futures, options, and swaps discussed later in Chapter 8.

LIMITATIONS TO DURATION AS A MEASURE OF A FINANCIAL INSTITUTION'S INTEREST RATE RISK

Duration gaps have some limitations as a measure for interest rate risk, including:

1   Duration assumes a flat yield curve with the same discount rate used for each cash flow every year.
2   Duration assumes a parallel shift in the yield curve with both short-term and long-term rates rising by the same amount when rates change, which often isn't the case.
3   A D-gap measure does not adjust for changes in asset and liability mix with a change in interest rates. For instance, when rates fall by 2% or more, mortgage holders may refinance mortgages or depositors may withdraw deposits and invest in other higher yielding investments.
4   For very large portfolios using duration, it is important to adjust duration calculations for convexity, to provide a more exact estimate for the change in value with a change in y^*. The adjustment is the second derivative of the bond price equation with respect to a change in y^* with a change in price called convexity. PVCF below is the present value of each cash flow. The formula for an expected change in value including convexity is:

$$\% \text{ Change in value} = - \text{DUR} \times [\text{Change } y^*/(1 + y^*)] + 0.50 \times \text{Convexity} \times (\text{Change } y^*)^2$$

where:

$$\text{Convexity} = \text{Sum } \{\text{PV of each CF} \times (t)(t + 1)\}/\{\text{Sum (PVCFs)}(1 + y^*)^2\}.$$

This adjustment results in a smaller rise in the percentage change in value versus duration. Thus convexity helps to get a closer estimate to the actual change in price with a rise of rates, which adds to the accuracy of this calculation. For small amounts of bonds, the added accuracy will be small, but for large million dollar bond portfolios, the addition of convexity can make for a much more accurate forecast of the approximate expected change in value of the bond portfolio.

For instance for a 5-year 8% annual coupon bond selling at its maturity value with $y^* = 8\%$, its duration will be 4.312 and its convexity will be 21.05. Calculating the expected percentage change in value for the bond with a 1% rise in rates = [−4.312 (0.01/1.08)] + Convexity Adjustment of [(0.5)(21.05)(0.01)^2], which equals − 0.0399 + 0.00105 = − 3.89%. This compares with a larger expected change including only duration of − 3.99%,

SIMULATION AND SCENARIO ANALYSIS

One weakness of both funding gaps and duration gaps is the assumption that assets and liabilities remain the same after an interest rate rises or fall. In reality with a fall in rates (generally of about 2% or more), for instance, loan customers tend to prepay their fixed-rate loans and refinance at lower rates with their bank or another financial institution. Thus the bank's asset mix may change considerably if rates fall significantly. Similarly, depositor customers may withdraw funds from long-term certificates of deposit (CDs) and be willing to take withdrawal penalties to be able to reinvest funds in higher yielding assets when rates rise. However, with static duration and funding gap measures, mix and volume changes in assets and liabilities are not considered.

To estimate mix and volume changes in financial assets and liabilities with interest rate changes, depository institution managers use simulation or scenario analysis packages that consider mix and volume changes in assets and liabilities and changes in the institution's net interest margin under different scenarios. Regulators also ask depository institutions to perform such an analysis with the interest rate sensitivity (S) component of their regulatory CAMELS rating (Capital, Assets, Management quality, Earnings, Liquidity, and Sensitivity).

Given FI interest rate risk, it is important to understand theories of interest rates that help FI managers recognize expectations for future changes in interest rates discussed in the following sections.

LOANABLE FUNDS THEORY OF INTEREST RATES

It is important to understand theories in order to explain interest rate movements. One prominent theory is the Loanable Funds Theory of Interest Rates, which is widely used by analysts and focuses on the amount of funds available for investment (the supply of loanable funds) and the amount of funds that borrowers want (the demand for loanable funds). *The intersection of the demand curve for loanable funds and supply curve for loanable funds determines the equilibrium "real" interest rate in an economy.*

The demand curve for loanable funds consists of demand for funds primarily in net with demands by businesses and the government for funds to borrow. Greater amounts of funds are demanded at lower interest rates (i.e., lower borrowing costs), so the demand for funds curve is downward sloping as shown in Figure 2.2. The supply curve for loanable funds consists of the supply for loanable funds provided primarily by net savers (investors) plus increases in the money supply (and velocity of money). More funds are supplied at higher interest rates, so the supply curve for loanable funds is upward sloping as depicted in Figure 2.2. The real rate of interest in an economy is determined by the intersection of the demand and supply curves.

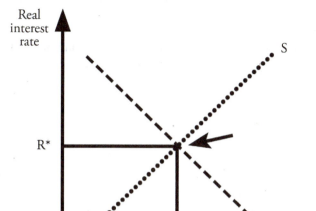

FIGURE 2.2 | Determinants for the supply of loanable funds by investors. Note: S is the supply curve for loanable funds; D is the demand curve for loanable funds; R* is the equilibrium interest rate at the point where the supply and demand curves for loanable funds intersect; and Q* is the quantity of loanable funds at this intersection point.

Factors that affect the supply of loanable funds include:

1   Wealth in an economy (increasing loanable funds available).
2   Expected returns (higher, greater loanable funds will be supplied).
3   Risk (greater risk, fewer loanable funds supplied).
4   Liquidity (increases in liquidity in an economy, greater funds supplied).
5   Changes in the money supply (affected by central bank open market operations).

Factors that affect the demand curve for loanable funds include:

1   Expected profitability of investment opportunities (greater profitable investment opportunities, such as new technologies, the greater the demand for loanable funds) (supply of bonds).
2   Expected inflation (lowers the real cost of borrowing increasing the opportunity for financing and the demand for loanable funds).
3   Government deficits (with deficits, governments need to borrow more increasing the demand for loanable funds).

The loanable funds theory can be used to make predictions for expected future rates (i.e., the equilibrium real rate) with changes in factors affecting respectively the supply of loanable funds (such as risk aversion, liquidity needs, expected returns) and changes in factors affecting the demand for loanable funds (such as expected inflation, government budget deficits, new investment opportunities and technologies).

For example suppose a central bank is engaging in an expansionary policy increasing the money supply and, hence, the supply of loanable funds. This would result in a shift outward for the supply curve, so it will interact with the demand for funds at a lower equilibrium interest rate as shown in Figure 2.3:

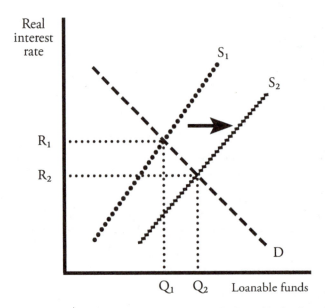

FIGURE 2.3 | Shift out in the supply curve for loanable funds with an increase in the money supply intersecting with the demand curve at a lower equilibrium interest rate. Note: S is the supply curve for loanable funds; D is the demand curve for loanable funds; R is the equilibrium interest rate at the point where the supply and demand curves for loanable funds intersect; and Q is the quantity of loanable funds at this intersection point.

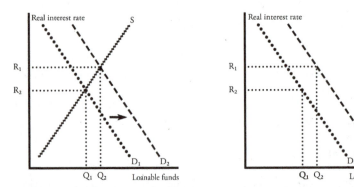

FIGURE 2.4 | Shift out for the demand curve for loanable funds. Note: S is the supply curve for loanable funds; D is the demand curve for loanable funds; R is the equilibrium interest rate at the point where the supply and demand curves for loanable funds intersect; and Q is the quantity of loanable funds at this intersection point.

As another example, suppose new business opportunities come up, increasing the demand by businesses for loanable funds. As shown in Figure 2.4, this would result in a shift outward in the demand for loanable funds curve intersecting at a higher equilibrium real interest rate with the supply curve for loanable funds, resulting in a higher equilibrium real interest rate.

Under the loanable funds theory, holding other factors constant, factors increasing or decreasing the supply and demand for loanable funds can shift these curves and have an effect on the real equilibrium interest rate.

THE FISHER EFFECT: NOMINAL VERSUS REAL INTEREST RATES

The loanable funds theory provides an explanation for the determination of real interest rates in an economy. A 20th-century economist, Irving Fisher, is widely credited with laying the foundation for the study of the relationship between interest rates and expected inflation. The Fisher effect distinguishes between nominal rates (i_n) the stated rate on a bond that includes the real rate (r), and an inflation premium (IP) for any expected loss in purchasing power over the life of the bond. Under the Fisher effect:

$$(1 + i_n) = [(1 + r)(1 + IP)]$$

where i_n is the nominal interest rate that investors demand, r is the real interest rate that investors want to earn, and IP is the inflation premium for expected inflation.

Solving for i_n, the nominal rate investors will demand for loss of expected purchasing power:

$$i_n = [(1 + r)(1 + IP)] - 1.$$

For example, if an investor desires a real interest rate of 2% (ex ante) and the expected inflation rate next year is 2%, the nominal rate demanded will be:

$$i_n = [(1.02)(1.02)] - 1 = 0.0404 \text{ or } 4.04\%.$$

Similarly, an investor can solve for the ex post real rate earned by solving for r^* where:

$$r^* = [(1 + i_n) / (1 + IP)] - 1.$$

For example, if an investor had a nominal rate on a bond of 8%, and the actual inflation rate over the year was 3%, the ex post real rate, r^*, earned would be:

$$r^* = [(1.08)/(1.03)] - 1 = 0.0485 \text{ or } 4.85\%.$$

Sometimes if compounding effects are small, simpler formulas are sometimes used, where:

$$i_n = [r + IP]$$

and

$$r^* = [i_n - IP].$$

INCORPORATING TAX EFFECTS INTO THE FISHER EQUATION

Since investors are taxed on the inflation premium as well as the real interest rate, they should demand a before tax inflation premium that includes the tax on the inflation premium that they will have to pay. Including tax effects, the Fisher relationship can be adjusted by adding a before tax inflation premium, where:

Before tax inflation premium = Expected inflation rate / $(1 - t)$.

So, the nominal rate (i_n) investors will require will include this adjusted IP.

For example if investors desire a real rate of return of 4% before taxes (2.9% after taxes) and expect inflation to be 4%, and they have a marginal tax rate of 28%, the before tax inflation premium = 4% / $(1 - 0.28)$ = 5.56%.

The nominal rate investors will require for the expected rise in inflation including tax effects will be:

$$i_n = (1.04)(1.0556) - 1 = 0.09782 \text{ or } 9.782\%.$$

So if investors will make an after tax return of 9.782% $(1 - 0.28)$ = 7.043%, and if inflation is actually 4%, their ex post after tax return will be $[(1.07043)/(1.04)] - 1$ = about 2.9%, their desired real after tax return.

THEORIES FOR THE RISK PREMIUMS AND TERM STRUCTURE OF INTEREST RATES

Different factors affect interest rates for particular bonds, including risk premiums, the premium demanded for greater *default risk* (i.e., investors demand a lower price for bonds with higher risk, with a higher yield for more risky bonds). The default risk premium on a bond is often defined as the risk spread equal to: the risky bond rate with default risk, R_d, less the risk free rate, R_f, on default-free bonds, such as a U.S. Treasury bond with the same maturity, i.e.,

Risk spread = $R_d - R_f$.

Bond rating agencies, such as Moody's and Standard and Poor's, rate bonds according to their credit risk, categorizing bonds into different risk categories (Aaa or AAA; Aa or AA; Baa or BBB, Ba or BB; B, Caa, Ca, or CCC, CC, and D grades). Bonds with greater risk tend to have larger risk premiums, with greater risk premiums for lower grade securities that have greater default risk. Often financial institutions, such as depository institutions and insurance companies, are required by regulators to only hold investment grade securities (BBB, Ba) or higher that have lower default risk. Depository institution managers also have similar risk classifications for loans that they make. Bond risk premiums tend to go up during recessions, since companies face more financial difficulties and tend to go down during expansions.

Bonds also have *liquidity risk* premiums, with shorter-term, more liquid money market securities (with less than 1 year to maturity) and securities that are more marketable (with a large secondary market and dealers/brokers facilitating sales) having more liquidity (ease of being sold with little or no loss of value).

Income tax considerations also affect yields on bonds. Bonds that are tax-deductible, such as municipal bonds that are exempt from state taxes, because of their low tax status can offer lower yields (sell at higher prices). To compare bond rates that are tax-deductible, the *tax equivalent yield* is often calculated to treat municipal bonds as if they would be taxed as tax-deductible bond rates, by dividing by $(1 - t)$, where t is the marginal tax rate of the investor. For instance, if an investor is comparing a taxable bond to a nontaxable bond with similar default risk and the same maturity, and the taxable bond has a 10% rate and the nontaxable bond has an 8% rate, the tax equivalent yield for the nontaxable bond if the investor's marginal tax rate was 25% would be equal to 8% / (1 − 0.25) = 10.67% for comparison on a taxable basis.

Maturity considerations also affect yields with longer-term securities for homogeneous bonds (having all other characteristics the same) typically having a higher yield (but not always), i.e., a *maturity risk premium*. Explanations for differences in long-term and short-term rates are discussed in the next section.

THE TERM STRUCTURE OF INTEREST RATES

The term structure of interest rates is the relationship between y^* and time to maturity for a homogeneous group of bonds, with the same characteristics otherwise including default risk and marketability. Typically, yield curves are constructed for government securities, such as U.S. Treasury securities that have the same default risk, but often also for other types of corporate bonds with the same credit ratings.

Yield curves for bonds typically are upward sloping with higher rates for longer-term than shorter-term securities, but often have other shapes as shown in Figure 2.5.

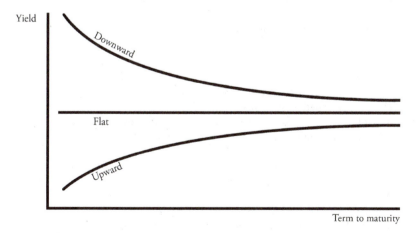

FIGURE 2.5 | Yield curve shapes. A: Upward sloping, B: Flat, and C: Downward sloping.

Upward sloping yield curves typically appear during expansions, flat yield curves in transition periods, and downward sloping yield curves at times during recessions. At times when there is a liquidity problem for short-term securities, such as banks refusing to lend after a financial crisis, a humped yield curve will appear, with medium-term short-term securities having the highest rates and a downward sloping yield curve that flattens out for longer-term rates.

Theoretical explanations for the typical yield curve shape include:

1   *Expectations theory.* If investors think yields will rise in the future, they will demand a higher rate for longer-term bonds that will be equal to the average of current and expected yields for similar short-term bonds over the life of the longer-term bond.

2   *Liquidity premium theory.* Under the liquidity premium theory, like the expectations theory, longer-term rates are a function of current and expected short-term rates, but also a function of a liquidity premium demanded by investors for greater liquidity risk for longer-term bonds, explaining the typical upward slope of the yield curve.

3   *Market segmentation theory.* Under the market segmentation theory, investors have preferences of different maturities, such as pension funds or life insurance companies wanting longer-term securities for a longer-term investment horizon.

4   The *preferred habitat theory* is a modification of the market segmentation theory that allows some substitutions among security market segments, if a premium exists to induce them to switch.

These theories are used as well to predict expectations by investors for future short-term rates known as forward rates in between current long-term and short-term rates.

Mathematics and Predictions for the Pure Expectations Theory

PURE EXPECTATIONS THEORY

Mathematically, including compounding, we can set the theory up as a formula:

$$(1 + {_1}r_n) = [(1 + {_1}r_1)(1 + {_2}f_1) \dots (1 + {_n}f_1)]^{1/n}$$

where: ${_1}r_n$ = a security with *n* years to maturity issued today in year 1;

${_1}r_1$ = a one-year security issued today in year 1;

${_2}f_1$ = the expected (forward) rate for a 1-year security issued next year in year 2;

${_n}f_1$ = the expected (forward) rate for a 1-year security issued in year *n*.

(Note the first subscript is the year in which a bond is issued, and the second subscript is the maturity for the bond. For instance the long-term bond ${_1}r_n$ is a bond issued today in year 1, with *n* years to maturity.)

The formula basically states that the long-term bond with n years to maturity will be equal to the geometric average of the current 1-year bond today and all the expected 1-year rates (known as forward rates) for the life of the bond.

Example. Under the expectations theory, what should the rate on a long-term 5-year fixed-rate bond be if the current 1-year rate is 5%, and rates are expected to be 6% in year 2, 7% in year 3, 8% in year 4, and 9% in year 5?

The 5-year rate should be just about the average rate of the expected short-term rates over the life of the long-term bond, i.e., for the above 5-year bond, the expected rate:

$$= [5\% + 6\% + 7\% + 8\% + 9\%]/5 = 7\%.$$

Or more precisely considering compounding effects:

$$(1 + {}_1r_5) = [(1.05)(1.06)(1.07)(1.08)(1.09)]^{0.20} = 1.06991; \text{ so } {}_1r_5 = 6.991\%.$$

Predictions for future rates under the pure expectations theory are:

1   If the yield curve is upward sloping, future rates are expected to rise.
2   If the yield curve is flat, future rates are expected to stay the same.
3   If the yield curve is downward sloping, future rates are expected to fall.

USING THE TERM STRUCTURE TO FORECAST EXPECTED INTEREST RATES

Expectations theory

Long-term rates = geometric average of the current and expected rates over the life of the long-term bond:

$$1 + {}_1r_n = [(1 + {}_1r_1)(1 + {}_2f_1) \cdots (1 + {}_nf_1)]^{1/n}$$

where: ${}_1r_n$ = a current bond with n years to maturity, issued today in year 1;
   ${}_1r_1$ = current bond with 1 year to maturity, issued today in year 1;
   ${}_2f_1$ = expected (forward) rate for a 1-year bond issued next year, year 2;
   ${}_nf_1$ = expected (forward) rate for an *n*-year bond issued in year *n*.

(Note the first subscript is the year of issue for the bond and the second subscript is the maturity.)

A long-term bond should have the same annual average rate as any combination of maturity bonds over its life, such as a 10-year bond being the average of the current 5-year bond rate and expected 5-year bond rate issued 5 years from today as follows:

$$1 + {}_1r_{10} = [(1 + {}_1r_5)^5(1 + {}_5f_5)^5]^{1/10}.$$

We can also solve for the expected 5-year (forward) rate for 5 years from now ${}_5f_5$ if we know the current 5-year and 10-year bond rates. We can solve for ${}_5f_5$ by first taking each side of the equation above to the 10th power, so:

$$(1 + {}_1r_{10})^{10} = [(1 + {}_1r_5)^5(1 + {}_5f_5)^5].$$

Then solve for

$$(1 + {}_5f_5)^5 = (1 + {}_1r_{10})^{10}/[(1 + {}_1r_5)^5].$$

Then solve for

$$(1 + {}_5f_5) = [(1 + {}_1r_{10})^{10}/[(1 + {}_1r_5)^5]^{1/5}.$$

So in general, solving for a forward rate where j is its maturity:

$$1 + {}_if_j = [(1 + {}_1r_n)^n/[(1 + {}_1r_m)^m]^{1/j}$$

where the subscript *i* is year of issue for the forward (expected) rate and the subscript *J* is the maturity for that forward rate, and *n* is the maturity of the current longer-term bond, and *m* is the maturity of the current shorter-term bond.

Example Solving for an Expected (Forward) Rate

Suppose for homogeneous bonds (same type and risk), an 8-year bond today has a 5% rate, and a 4-year bond today has a 4% rate. Under the expectations theory, what rate do investors expect for a 4-year bond issued 4 years from today?

Answer:

$$1 + {}_if_J = [(1 + {}_1r_n)^n/[(1 + {}_1r_m)^m]^{1/J}.$$

So:

$$1 + {}_4f_4 = [(1 + {}_1r_n)^8/[(1 + {}_1r_m)^4]^{1/4}.$$

So:

$$1 + {}_4f_4 = [(1.05)^8/(1.04)^4]^{1/4}$$
$$= \{[1.4775/1.1699]^{0.25}\} - 1 = [1.2629]^{0.25} = 1.0601.$$

So the expected 4-year bond rate 4-years from now is:

$${}_4f_4 = 0.0601 \text{ or } 6.01\%.$$

Check: 8-year rate $= [(1.04)^4(1.0601)^4]^{1/8} - 1 = [1.16986 \times 1.26295]^{0.125} - 1 = 0.05$ or 5%.

Note: To take any number to a power, such as $[1.2629]^{0.25}$, just enter the number, such as here 1.2629, in a simple mathematical calculator, and then press your "y^x" key and enter the power, here 0.25, and then press your "=" key, and you'll have the answer, here 1.0601.

Since the expected 4-year rate > the current 4-year rate, rates are expected to rise in the future. Note intuitively since the 8-year bond has an annual compound rate of 5% compared to the 4% for the 4-year bond, even without calculations, because the annual rate for the 8-year bond rate is so much higher than the 4-year bond rate, that this suggests investors expect a rise in the 4-year bond rate in the future under the expectations theory.

Mathematics and Predictions for the Liquidity Premium Theory

Mathematically the liquidity premium theory is similar to the expectations theory, but includes a liquidity premium for longer-term rates given their greater liquidity risk.

LIQUIDITY PREMIUM THEORY

Long-term rates = geometric average of the current and expected rates over the life of the long-term bond plus a liquidity premium:

$$1 + {}_1r_n = [(1 + {}_1r_1)(1 + {}_2f_1) \cdots (1 + {}_nf_1) + L_n]^{1/n}$$

where; ${}_1r_n$ = a current bond with n years to maturity, issued today in year 1;

$\quad {}_1r_1$ = a current bond with 1 year to maturity, issued today in year 1;

$\quad {}_2f_1$ = the expected (forward) rate for a bond with 1 year to maturity, issued next year, year 2;

$\quad {}_nf_1$ = the expected (forward) rate for a bond with n years to maturity, issued in year n;

$\quad L_n$ = the liquidity premium for a bond with n years to maturity.

(Note the first subscript is the year of issue for the bond and the second subscript is the maturity.)

This theory explains why the yield curve is generally upward sloping, since a liquidity premium is demand for longer-term bonds.

Solving for expected forward rates using the liquidity premium theory, the liquidity premiums (L_n and L_m) for respective long-term and intermediate-term bonds need to be subtracted before doing the calculations.

$$1 + f_J = \{[(1 + ({}_1r_n - L_n)]^n / [(1 + ({}_1r_m - L_m)]^m\}^{1/J}.$$

Then the expected rate under the liquidity premium theory is $f_J + L_J$, adding back the liquidity premium for the maturity J of the bond you're solving for.

The forward rate you're solving for excludes the liquidity premiums that were incorporated in the long-term bonds. Then, add back in a liquidity premium to the forward rate you solved for with maturity J.

Forecast Example Using the Liquidity Theory

$$1 + {}_i f_J = \{[(1 + ({}_1 r_n - L_n)]^n / [(1 + ({}_1 r_m - L_m)]^m\}^{1/J}.$$

Suppose for the same example we used before we're solving for the forward rate for a bond issued in year 4 (i) with a 4-year maturity (J), and looking at a current 8 (n) year bond with a 5% rate and a current 4 (m) year bond with a 4% rate. However, we estimate that investors require a 0.50% liquidity premium (L_8) for the 8-year bond, and a 0.20% liquidity premium (L_4) for the 4 year bond.

So:

$$1 + {}_4 f_4 = \{[(1 + ({}_1 r_8 - L_8)]^8 / [(1 + ({}_1 r_4 - L_4)]^4\}^{1/4}.$$

Step 1 Deduct the liquidity premiums for the current 8-year bond and current 4-year bond. So the adjusted current 8-year bond rate is 5% – 0.50% = 4.5%, and the adjusted current 4-year bond rate is 4% – 0.20% = 3.8%.

Step 2 Then solve for the forward rate as above using the adjusted rates without liquidity premiums. Plugging these numbers into the equation:

$$1 + {}_4 f_4 = [(1.045)^8 / (1.038)^4]^{1/4} - 1 = [1.4221/1.16089]^{0.25} = 1.0521.$$

Subtracting 1 to get ${}_4 f_4 = 0.0521$ or 5.21%.

Step 3 The 5.21% rate is the expected forward rate without a liquidity premium, so we need to add back the liquidity premium for a 4-year bond of 0.20%, so the expected 4-year bond rate 4 years from now is equal to:

$$({}_4 f_4 + L_4) = 5.21\% + 0.20\% \ L = 5.41\%.$$

Since the expected 4-year rate of 5.41% > the current 4-year rate of 5%, rates are expected to rise under the liquidity premium theory, but not by as much as expected under the expectations theory, where the expected 4-year rate was 6.01%.

Predictions of Expected Rates under the Segmented Market Theory

Under the segmented market theory for each short or intermediate term or long-term segment, different investors will have different preferences for short- or long-term securities, so interest rates would be forecast using the loanable funds theory for each different market, based on supply and demand factors for different securities. Under the segmented market theory discontinuities in the yield curve would be expected.[1] The segmented theory is unrealistic, since despite preferences, traders would arbitrage across markets if rates in one or the other market were out of line. However, supply and demand factors, such as lower amounts of short-term securities available could have an effect on rates in the short-term market, for instance. The preferred habitat theory is similar, but assumes that short- and long-term investors have preferences, but are willing to switch to other markets if yields are higher. Institutional investors do have preferences, such as money market mutual funds seeking out short-term money market securities, and long-term bond portfolio managers seeking out long-term bonds, and depository institutions for liquidity purposes may have preferences for short-term securities. By looking at supply and demand factors rates for short- and long-term bonds can be predicted under this theory.

SUMMARY

All financial institutions are affected by interest rates since financial institutions hold primarily financial assets and financial liabilities, so it's important to understand different aspects of interest rate risk, and interest rate risks and theories. Since interest rates and prices are inversely related, valuations for fixed-rate assets and liabilities are affected by changes in interest rates. Interest rates have both price risk, the risk of a fall in value for a fixed-rate security if rates rise, and reinvestment risk, the risk of a fall in the future value of coupon payments if rates fall and the coupons have to be reinvested at a lower rate. Duration is a measure of overall interest rate risk encompassing both types of risk.

By duration matching the duration of a bond with the number of years in an investor's investment horizon, the risk of not getting a desired yield to maturity can be reduced. Financial institutions have duration gaps equal to the duration of assets less [the fraction of liabilities to total assets] times the duration of liabilities.

Theories of interest rates are useful in understanding factors that affect interest rates, including the loanable funds theory where there is demand for loanable funds in net by businesses and government and suppliers of loanable funds are net savers (investors), along with changes in the money supply. The intersection of the demand and supply curves in an economy determine the real equilibrium interest rate. The Fisher effect is another theory that separates out nominal and real interest rates with nominal rates, including an inflation premium above the real interest rate expected to compensate for expected lost purchasing power with inflation. Other factors affecting interest rates are default risk, liquidity risk, and maturity risk, with risk premiums required by investors for different types of risk. Theories on the term structure of interest rates help to explain the relationship between the time to maturity and yield to maturity for homogeneous groups of bonds and provide valuable insights for expectations by investors for future interest rates and a better understanding of the relationships between rates and maturity.

NOTE

1   Other theoretical models have been and are on-going in their development including work by Cox, Ingersoll, and Ross that recognize in addition to the expectations theory, other factors that are important in determining expectations including inflation, uncertainty, and productivity.

BIBLIOGRAPHY

Abken, Peter (1990). "Innovations in modeling the term structure of interest rates." *Economic Review* (Federal Reserve Bank of Atlanta), 65 (July/August), 2–27.

Cox, John C., Jonathan E. Ingersoll, Jr., and Stephen A. Ross (1981). "A re-examination of traditional hypotheses about the term structure of interest rates." *Journal of Finance*, 36 (September), 769–799.

Cox, John C., Jonathan E. Ingersoll, Jr., and Stephen A. Ross (1985). "A theory of the term structure of interest rates." *Econometrica*, 53 (March), 385–408.

Fisher, Irving (1930). *The Theory of Interest*. New York: Macmillan.

Genay, Hesna and Rich Podjasek (2014). "What is the impact of a low interest rate environment on bank profitability?" *Chicago Fed Letter: Essays on Issues* (Federal Reserve Bank of Chicago), 324 (July), 1–4.

Gough, Neil (2015). "Asia rushes to lower rates, but maybe not fast enough." *The New York Times*: International Business, March 12, 2015. Accessed on March 25, 2015 at: http://www.nytimes.com/2015/03/13/business/international/asia-central-bank-rate-cuts-too-slow.html?ref=topics&_r=0

Ho, Thomas and Sang-Bin Lee (1986). "Term structure movements and pricing interest rate contingent claims." *Journal of Finance*, 41 (December), 1011–1029.

Malkiel, Burton (1966). *The Term Structure of Interest Rates: Theory, Empirical Evidence, and Applications*. Princeton, NJ: Princeton University Press.

McCulloch, Huston J. (1975). "An estimation of the liquidity premium hypothesis." *Journal of Political Economy*, 83 (January/February), 95–119.

Meiselman, David (1962). *The Term Structure of Interest Rates*. Englewood Cliffs, NJ: Prentice Hall.

Polakoff, Murray E. (1981). "Loanable funds theory and interest rate determination." In *Financial Institutions and Markets*, 2nd ed., Eds. Murray E. Polakoff, and Thomas A. Durkin. Boston: Houghton Mifflin, pp. 483–510.

Roley, V. Vance (1981). "The determinants of the treasury yield curve." *Journal of Finance*, 36 (December), 1103–1126.

Roll, Richard (1970). *The Behavior of Interest Rates*. New York: Basic Books.

Schiller, Robert J., John Y. Campbell, and Kermit L. Schoenholtz (1983). "Forward rates and future policy: Interpreting the term structure of interest rates." In *Brookings Paper on Economic Activity*. Washington DC: Brookings Institution, pp. 173–223.

Van Horne, James (1965). "Interest rate risk and the term structure of interest rates." *Journal of Political Economy*, 73 (August), 344–351.

QUESTIONS AND PROBLEMS

Part 1: Review for Duration, Modified Duration, and Expected Annual Return

1 What is the market price, duration, and modified duration for a 4-year coupon bond with a 10% annual coupon rate, maturity value of $1,000, with yield to maturity (YTM) of 10%?

2 What is the market price, duration, and modified duration for a 4-year zero coupon bond with a maturity value of $1,000, and a market rate for similar bonds, i.e. YTM of 10%. Which of the two bonds in #1 and #2 has greater overall interest rate risk? Explain why.

3 Explain the difference between reinvestment risk and price risk. For the two bonds in #1 and #2 above, which has the greater reinvestment risk? Price risk? If you have a 4-year investment horizon, which bond would be best to invest in to immunize against overall interest rate risk? Explain why.

4 If you buy a 5-year bond with a 10% annual coupon rate and $1,000 maturity value and YTM of 10%, what is the bond's duration and modified duration?

5 Suppose you invest in the 5-year bond in #4 with an annual 10% coupon rate and $1,000 maturity value and YTM of 10% for a 4-year investment horizon, and, for a price of $1,000. Right after you buy the bond, rates go up to 12%, and you sell the bond at the end of year 4.

   a What price will the bond sell for at the end of year 4?
   b What is the future value of the coupon payments you receive at the end of year 4?
   c What will your effective annual yield be at the end of year 4?

6 For the bond in #5, suppose instead, right after you purchase the bond, rates fall and stay at 8% over the life of the bond.

   a What will be the price you sell the bond for at the end of year 4?
   b What will be the future value of your coupon payments at the end of year 4?
   c What will be your annual compound yield at the end of year 4?

7 The Cool Bank of Alaska has the following questions it would like to ask you about its bank. The bank's balance sheet is as follows:

		Duration
Assets		
Cash	$50 million	0
Long-term loans 6% rate	$550 million	8 years
Total assets	$600 million	
Liabilities and equity		
Short-term deposits 1% rate	$540 million	1 year
Equity	$60 million	
Total liabilities and equity	$600 million	

   a What is the Cool Bank's NIM?
   b What is the Cool Bank's 1-year funding gap?
   c What is the Cool Bank's duration gap?
   d What is the expected change in NII based on the funding gap if rates rise 1%? Based on the bank's duration gap, what is the expected change in the value of bank equity if rates rise 1%?

Part 2: Review for Real and Nominal Interest Rates

8 Explain the difference between real and nominal interest rates.
9 If you desire a 2% real rate of return and inflation is expected to be 2%, what nominal rate of return would you demand on a security to be compensated for loss of purchasing power?
10 If you purchased a bond that has an 8% annual compound rate, and the actual inflation rate over the year was 3%, what was your real rate of return on the bond?
11 If you have a marginal tax rate of 25%, and desired a 2% real rate of return after taxes and inflation is expected to be 2%, what nominal rate of return would you demand?

Part 3: Review Loanable Funds Theory

12 Describe in your own words the loanable funds theory and how interest rates are determined, including a graph for the loanable funds theory with the demand and supply curve and discussing who the net demanders and suppliers of funds are.

13 Using the loanable funds theory, explain what would happen to the real equilibrium interest rate under the following scenarios: (a) The Fed has an expansionary policy increasing the money supply. (b) A new technology is developed that offers new ideas to businesses for new products. (c) Wealth in the economy decreases with a recession. (d) Governments have a large deficit to finance.

Part 4: Review Yield Curve Theories and Expected Interest Rates

14 If the current 10-year bond rate is 5% and a 5-year bond rate has a 4% rate, what is the expected rate for a 5-year bond issued 5 years from today? What are future rates expected to do? Explain why?

15 For # 14, if the 10-year liquidity premium is 0.50% and the 5-year liquidity premium is 0.25%, what is the expected rate for a 5-year bond issued 5 years today under the liquidity premium theory? What are future rates expected to do? Explain why?

16 Briefly explain what the segmented market theory would expect if the government plans on selling short-term T-bills to finance a deficit, in terms of the effect on short-term and long-term interest rates and the yield curve. What are the weaknesses of the segmented market theory for the term structure of interest rates?

Chapter 3

The New Regulatory Environment and the Regulatory Dialectic

Banking is a very treacherous business because you don't realize it is risky until it is too late. It is like calm waters that deliver huge storms.

(Taleb, 2007)

The origin of the U.S. Financial crisis is that commercial banks and investment banks lent vast sums—trillions of dollars—for housing purchases and consumer loans to borrowers ill-equipped to repay. The easy lending pushed up housing prices around the U.S., which then ratcheted still higher when speculators bought houses on the expectation of yet further price increases. When the easy lending slowed and then stopped during 2006 to 2007, the housing prices peaked and began to fall. The housing boom began to unravel and now threatens an economy-wide bust.

(Sachs, 2008, p. 1)

The Dodd–Frank Wall Street Reform and Consumer Protection Act or Dodd–Frank Act, represents the most comprehensive financial regulatory reform measures taken since the great depression.

(Morrison & Foerster, 2010, p. 1)

IN the aftermath of the global financial crisis, regulatory bodies globally instituted new regulations for financial institutions and derivative markets, including the new Basel III regulations and in the U.S. new regulations under the Dodd–Frank Act, along with regulations across countries across the globe. The Dodd–Frank Act, for example, includes new regulations affecting the oversight and supervision of financial institutions, new consumer financial laws and a new agency, the Bureau of Consumer Financial Protection for greater consumer finance protection oversight. On the financial market side, Dodd–Frank also includes more stringent oversight and regulation and capital requirements for over-the-counter derivatives, credit rating agency reform, and regulations for the securitization market. Other regulations apply to corporate governance and executive compensation for financial institutions, and the registration of advisers of private funds, among others.

Similarly under Basel III major new regulatory changes for major international banks include:

1. *Under Pillar 1: Capital*: New capital requirements and types of capital for banks to hold, with greater emphasis on the quality of capital, and new capital conservation and countercyclical capital buffers.

2. *Under Pillar 1: Risk coverage*: A strengthening of the capital treatment for certain complex securitizations and more rigorous credit analysis for securitization exposures that are externally rated, higher capital for trading and derivatives activities, a strengthening of the counterparty credit risk framework and risk-weightings for banks to hold more capital for exposure to central counterparties.

3. *Under Pillar 1: Containing leverage*: A stronger nonrisk-based leverage capital ratio.

4. *Under Pillar 2: Risk management and supervision*: Supplemental capital requirements for off-balance sheet risk exposure and securitization activities, along with better incentives in place for better risk management over the long-term, including sound compensation practices, valuation practices, and stress testing and accounting standards for financial instruments and improved corporate governance.

5. *Under Pillar 3: Market discipline*: Revised disclosure requirements for securitization exposure and the sponsorship of off-balance sheet vehicles and on the details of regulatory capital components and their reconciliation and a comprehensive explanation for how regulatory capital ratios are calculated.

6. *Under Pillar 3: Liquidity coverage ratio disclosure*: A new liquidity coverage ratio (LCR) requires banks to have sufficient liquid assets of high quality to withstand a 30-day period of stressed funding. In addition a net stable funding ratio (NSFR) addresses liquidity mismatches in the longer term encompassing the entire balance sheet. This ratio provides an incentive for banks to utilize stable sources of funding, along with regulatory supervisory monitoring of banks for sound liquidity principles. In addition to meeting the Basel III requirements, global systematically important financial institutions (SIFIs) designated by a country's regulators must have greater loss absorbency capital reflecting the much greater risks that they present to the financial system, that are met with a progressive common equity tier (CET 1) capital requirement ranging from 1 to 2.5% based on a financial institution's systematic importance (Basel III, 2016).

Financial institution managers need to understand all regulations affecting their institutions and the rationale for regulations. Financial institutions also need to understand central bank operations, which became particularly important during the aftermath of the financial crisis, with new monetary policy techniques used including quantitative easing (QE) policies to stimulate economic activity by increasing the money supply in an economy and lowering interest rates. This chapter looks at the regulatory environment of financial institutions and provides an overview of the effect of central bank actions on interest rates and the economy.

WHY ARE FINANCIAL INSTITUTIONS REGULATED?

Since financial institutions are crucial to the efficient operating of the payment system, and their assets and liabilities are financial contracts, and deposits are often at least partially guaranteed by governments to build confidence in the financial system, they are heavily regulated to protect the financial system and the economy.

Governments regulate financial markets and institutions and the rationale provided for doing so includes the following aims, among others:

1   *Ensure the stability in economies* by maintaining safety and soundness of the financial system, ensuring that the economy is not disrupted, and avoiding contagion effects across financial institutions.
2   *Protect consumers* (prevent fraud and misrepresentation), given information asymmetries between consumers and financial institutions and the private nature and confidentiality of financial transactions.
3   *Promote market and institution efficiency and liquidity* to ensure that payment systems are efficiently operated for speedy, transparent, efficient operations, and to assure liquidity in an economy.
4   *Promote social policies*, such as assuring that banks are providing funds to the community in which they are lending, providing services for the unbanked, and acting as agents of a government to prevent fraud and assure security in the payments system.

Depending on the economic development of a country, financial markets and financial institutions operate in tandem, allowing economies to develop and thrive. In some countries with weaker financial markets, greater dependence is placed on financial institutions. Often there is a trade-off between efficiency and safety and soundness. Financial institutions and regulations also help solve problems common to financial contracts to ensure fairness and instill trust. In addition financial institution managers perform information and monitoring services to prevent fraud and misrepresentation. Given the nature of operations for financial institutions with financial contracts between parties, common problems include:

1   *Asymmetric information:* The inequality of information between savers and borrowers and financial institutions, given the private nature of financial contracts and at times incomplete information about future prospects of borrowers.
2   *Adverse selection:* A higher likelihood that potential customers who are more uncreditworthy or that take on greater risks are more likely to seek out financial products, such as loans and insurance.
3   *Moral hazard:* The risk or hazard that a borrower once having received a loan or insurance policy, for instance, might be tempted to engage in undesirable and risk-taking activities that increase the risk that a loan might not be paid back or that an insurance company will have to pay out more than expected for future losses.
4   *Conflicts of interest:* When a party in a financial contract has incentives to act in his/her own interests versus the interests of other parties.

Financial institutions help to reduce these drawbacks by providing information, analysis, and monitoring services, and designing contracts that reduce the problems. To help to avoid adverse selection and moral hazard problems for instance, insurance policies may include a large deductible, whereby an insurance policyholder has a stake in taking precautions and reducing potential risks. Similarly, requiring a significant down payment or setting the loan up with a higher loan-to-value ratio for a borrower taking on a home mortgage loan, gives the borrower an incentive not to walk away from the loan.

WHO ARE THE REGULATORS?

Within an economy, there are a number of different regulators to monitor financial institutions and markets. Often the structure of the regulatory system is based on a historic process, so at times the structure may seem complex. In the United States, for example, there are many regulatory bodies that were often created in response to crises that occurred at different times:

1   *The Securities and Exchange Commission (SEC)*, established in 1934 under the Securities Exchange Act. The SEC regulates organized exchanges and financial markets, including requirements for disclosure and restricting insider trading. The SEC is also responsible for regulating investment companies and investment advisers and mutual funds.
2   *The Federal Reserve System (FED)*, established in 1913, serves as a lender of last resort, promotes an elastic money supply, maintains a nationwide payment system, and tightens bank supervisions. The Fed operates as a central bank for the transmission of monetary policy and is a regulator for all depository institutions, including reserve requirements and chief regulator of bank holding companies and financial holding companies, as well as the Bureau of Consumer Financial Protection established under the Dodd–Frank Act of 2010 to protect consumers.
3   *Office of the Comptroller of the Currency (OCC)*, established in 1863, to create a uniform national currency under the National Currency Act. The OCC charters and examines federally insured commercial banks; it was created during the U.S. civil war by the Union to create a stable currency and avoid inflation. In 1864 under the National Banking Act, the OCC was authorized to grant federal bank charters that originated the dual system of federal and state chartered banks.
4   *State banking and insurance commissions* regulating state chartered banking and insurance companies, respectively; and the Federal Insurance Office, created under the Dodd–Frank Act of 2010 under the Treasury to compile information on the insurance industry, including affordable insurance products for minorities and underserved communities, and to monitor the insurance industry for systemic risks.
5   *National Credit Union Administration (NCUA)*, which charters, regulates and examines federally chartered credit unions and administers the National Credit Union Share Insurance Fund (NCUIF) that provides deposit insurance to protect deposits of credit union (CU) members at insured CUs.
6   *National Association of Insurance Commissioners (NAIC)* that has no legal power, but significant political clout for the regulation of insurance companies, given the federal government has the potential right to regulate insurance companies under the *McCarran–Ferguson Act of 1945*, but does not exercise that right if individual states adequately establish and enforce standards for the industry.
7   *Federal and state pension fund regulators*, including the *Pension Benefit Guaranty Corporation (PBGC)* that guarantees the benefits of defined benefit pension funds for public corporations regulated by the *Employee Retirement Income Security Act* of 1974.

As in many countries both federal (national) and regional (local) regulators operate together, with dual bank examinations often required. Similar types of government pension funds operate in other countries, and similar other types of regulators.

TYPES OF REGULATIONS FOR FINANCIAL INSTITUTIONS

Regulations fall into many different types including but not exclusive to:

1 *Balance sheet regulations* on the type of assets and liabilities financial institutions hold to protect against financial institutions taking on excessive risk.
2 *Capital regulations* on the types and amounts of capital financial institutions must hold as protection against future losses.
3 *Consumer protection regulations* that protect consumers from fraud and misrepresentation, given information asymmetries.
4 *Safety/soundness regulations and examinations* to ensure the safety and soundness of financial institutions.
5 *Social policy related regulations*, since many financial institutions, such as banks, are chartered to serve the needs of their community.
6 *Central bank related regulations and requirements* to ensure the efficiency of the payment system and to assist in central bank operations.
7 *Restrictions on mergers and acquisitions and entry and exit* to maintain competition and prevent monopoly powers, and to assure the safety of the banking system.

Regulations are subject to change by governments as they become obsolete or new regulations are needed. Regulations often trend from regulatory leniency during periods of economic growth to regulatory stringency in periods following financial crises. In the post global financial crisis environment, for example, new regulations were passed to provide better capitalization and liquidity for international banks under Basel III, and to protect consumers and prevent banks from engaging in risky activities under the U.S. Dodd–Frank Act of 2010.

Often during periods of reregulation following financial crises, there may be a *period of regulatory stringency*, which may hurt an economy, if banks are afraid to make new loans, reducing liquidity in the banking system, and having a contraction effect on the economy. Similarly, during periods of deregulation, there may be a *period of regulatory laxity*, leading to a regulatory dialectic over time, with adjustments made to regulations as needed.

WHY DO REGULATIONS CHANGE: KANE'S REGULATORY DIALECTIC

Edward Kane, a renowned professor of finance introduced the concept of a *regulatory dialectic*[1] to capture the impact of regulations on managerial decisions. The word *dialectic* refers to changes occurring through a process of action and reaction by opposing forces;

in his classic presentation, the philosopher Hegel described the process as: (1) *thesis*, an initial set of arguments or rules; (2) *antithesis*, a conflicting set of arguments or responses; (3) *synthesis*, a change or modification resulting from an exchange or interaction among opposing forces.

The regulatory dialectic includes different stages including the following:

1   **Thesis**: *Regulations* are passed for safety and soundness, consumer protection, and market efficiency and liquidity purposes, often in response to a crisis.
2   **Antithesis**: *Ways to get around regulations* are developed by financial institution managers in order to compete and follow customers globally, given technological, globalization, competition, and market forces changing the environment they operate in, with some regulations becoming obsolete. In other cases, managers attempt to circumvent regulations to take on greater risks or take advantage of profitable opportunities that may increase risk taking.
3   **Antithesis reaction:** Regulators pass amendments to previous regulations activities to remove the methods used by financial institutions to avoid regulations.
4   **Synthesis: Deregulation**: In response to intense lobbying by financial institutions for the removal of regulations, such as regulations that may be obsolete, making it difficult for financial institutions to compete;
5   **New antithesis**: *A financial crisis* occurring as the result of some financial institution managers engaging in aggressive risk-taking activities that threaten the safety and soundness of the financial system.
6   **New thesis: Reregulation**: In the aftermath of a financial crisis threatening the safety and soundness of the financial system, new comprehensive regulations are passed to ensure the safety of the financial system, and provide periods of greater financial stringency, and the regulatory cycle begins again.

The regulatory dialectic has been used to analyze regulatory changes that occur over time for the USA and other countries. Historically, there are lots of examples for the regulatory dialectic for diverse countries. An illustration follows for the United States following each stage in the regulatory dialectic over time.

Illustration of the Regulatory Dialectic in the USA, 1930s to the Present

1. Thesis New Regulations were created in the aftermath of the banking crisis of the 1930s, with nearly 10,000 bank failures. New regulations focused on the safety and soundness of the banking system, and to prevent the risk-taking activities leading to the banking crisis. Earlier the *McFadden Act of 1927* placed geographic restrictions on bank branching. *The Banking Act of 1933 (Glass–Steagall)* limited commercial banking to pure banking activities (no investment or insurance activities allowed), and put ceilings on deposit rates under *Regulation Q*, to prevent "rate wars" that could threaten solvency. Glass–Steagall also established the *Federal Deposit Insurance Corporation* (FDIC) to insure bank deposits, giving the government a stake in the event of a bank failure, involving greater regulation and examination of banks by the FDIC.

2. Antithesis Bank managers found ways to get around each of these regulations. With environmental changes including security firms developing new cash management and money market checking accounts, banks suffered disintermediation, with customers leaving banks that offered low rates. Initially to avoid rate ceilings, banks offered depositors *"implicit" interest* through gifts to depositors, such as toasters or other products and services that did not violate the "explicit" interest rate ceilings. Large banks also began a strategy of *liability management* by issuing short-term, uninsured securities for financing, such as negotiable certificates of deposit (CDs), Eurodollar CDs, bankers' acceptances and commercial paper that could be traded in financial markets to replace lost deposits, and as nondeposit funding were not included under Regulation Q.

To avoid the separation of banking, investment, and insurance activities within commercial banks, *one bank holding companies (OBHCs)* were created with nonbank activities carried on by different subsidiaries that technically were not part of the bank subsidiary. Similarly, to avoid geographical branching restrictions, banks developed *multi-bank holding companies (MBHCs)* with subsidiaries in different counties or states that were not technically a branch. These loopholes allowed banks to follow their customers into different parts of the country, facilitating working capital management and lending and consolidation of deposits for their customers. Bank holding companies (BHCs) facilitated bank growth and acquisition activities, allowing them to be larger financial institutions and to have different product lines, other than commercial banking.

3. Antithesis reaction Patching up regulations by regulators was done to curb these activities. For OBHCs and MBHCs new bank holding company acts and amendments were passed to restrict de facto branching and to reduce other abuses, including a new requirement that nonbank subsidiary activities be bank related and requiring Federal Reserve approval.

4. Synthesis: Deregulation In response to lobbying and the financial distress of savings institutions and the savings and loan crisis of the late 1980s, Regulation Q's rate ceilings under Glass–Steagall were gradually phased out in the 1980s, and savings institutions were given greater powers to make some nonmortgage loans and variable-rate loans to reduce their interest rate risk.

Later in the 1990s, with demographic and technological changes, branching restrictions for banks became obsolete, reducing the efficiency of the banking system, with business customers operating nationally having to use several banks in different regions to handle their banking needs. States began negotiating interstate agreements allowing branching among certain states in different regions. After considerable lobbying, national branching restrictions were removed under the *Riegle–Neal Interstate Banking and Branching Efficiency Act (IBBEA) of 1994*, which allowed bank holding companies to consolidate their subsidiaries across state lines, with full interstate branching phased in by 1997.

In the 1990s financial institutions in the United States faced intense competition from international banks that could engage in investment banking and insurance activities as universal banks. New technology also made separation of activities and customers inefficient, and business customers often wanted to be able to take all their financial services to one BHC. Extensive lobbying efforts were made by the financial services industry with investment banks, insurance companies, and other financial services companies urging Congress to allow commercial banks, investment banks, and insurance companies to merge with each other (at this time, prohibited under the Glass–Steagall Act of 1933).

In 1998, confronting Congress with this issue Citibank merged with Travelers Group, a large diversified financial services firm. Citibank was given two-years' forbearance by regulators for the merger in violation of Glass–Steagall, in anticipation of expected changes in regulations to allow the merger.

In November of 1999, the *Financial Services Modernization Act*, known as the *Gramm–Leach–Bliley Act (GLB)*, was passed, removing 60 years later the restrictions of the Glass–Steagall Act of 1933. Under GLB, banks, securities firm, and insurance companies could be owned by each other, and a new *financial holding company (FHC)* organization was set up with the Fed, as the chief regulator for FHCs that could be chartered to engage in a list of different financial activities approved by the Fed. To be approved as a FHC by the Fed a financial institution must be both well-capitalized and well-managed, with a satisfactory rating on its most recent Community Reinvestment Act exam (an act to ensure that BHCs were serving their communities' lending needs).

5. New antithesis In the mid-1990s to early 2000s, in the United States, the Fed followed a monetary policy of keeping interest rates low, which fueled a housing market boom. With interest rates low, some financial institution managers, particularly at large mortgage banks, looked for higher returns by underwriting more risky subprime loans that could be packaged and sold to investors as *collateralized debt obligations (CDOs)*, and *synthetic CDOs*, that were highly levered. With a change in culture with investment banking part of large bank holding companies, on the investment banking side there was a strong pull, along with strong market demand for mortgage-backed securitizations, which offered higher rates for investors and generated significant fee income. Large mortgage banks, like Countrywide Financial, also became chartered as thrift holding companies, allowing them to engage in banking type activities and less regulated mortgage securitizations. With greater demand for mortgage-backed securities (MBS), new loan underwriters were hired with bonuses based on loan volume versus loan quality, and new low documentation (low doc) standards were used for loans that failed to verify salaries and information on borrowers.

As noted in the beginning quote by Jeffrey Sachs (2008), a feeding frenzy to make huge volumes of new loans and securitize these has occurred. Loans were poorly underwritten based on rising home price collateral considerations versus the ability of borrowers to repay the loans, and loans were poorly written as adjustable rate mortgages, that with rising rates and loan payments later, subprime loan customers were unable to afford. With large financial holding companies becoming too large to monitor and trillions of dollars of complex securitizations occurring, regulators had difficulties monitoring large financial institutions. There was also interconnectedness between large banks underwriting loans and investment banks and credit agencies that rated risky, complex securitizations as investment grade.

Consequently, when the real estate market bubble collapsed in 2007, the United States faced a huge, somewhat unexpected financial crisis. Large amounts of credit default swaps (CDS) were issued by large financial institutions, with large payoffs to financial institutions as buyers in the event of what seemed like an improbable loan default or credit event. With the crisis, these CDS had to be paid off by the issuers, putting AIG, Lehman Brothers, and other issuers on the brink of bankruptcy as well. Many CDS were used for speculative purposes as well. In addition, nonregulated shadow banks (hedge funds, private equity firms) invested in complex CDOs that offered higher yields for accredited investors used also as collateral for overnight loans. When the market for CDOs collapsed, the short-term lending market collapsed with insufficient collateral available for these repurchase agreements, creating an additional liquidity crisis.

6. Synthesis: Reregulation In response to the U.S. subprime loan crisis, new regulations were passed to reduce the risk-taking activities of financial institutions, and to provide greater protection to consumers, along with higher capital requirements and other regulations under the *Dodd–Frank Act of 2010* as mentioned at the beginning of the chapter. A new *Bureau of Consumer Protection* was established to protect consumers, the *Financial Stability Oversight Council (FSOC)* to oversee financial institutions whose failure could affect the U.S. economy, and new capital and liquidity requirements were mandated.

Under the new Basel Committee on Bank Supervision, *Basel III* regulations were approved by 27 member jurisdictions and 44 central banks and supervisory authorities and endorsed by G20 leaders at the end of 2010, with recommendations that banks satisfy enhanced capital requirements by 2019. Individual countries are charged with making modifications for their own needs and priorities for the implementation of Basel III in a timely fashion.

A NEW REGULATORY DIALECTIC?

Following the passage of new regulations, some critics have argued that some aspects of the Dodd–Frank Act were too stringent as a new antithesis following the synthesis of reregulation in the aftermath of the financial crisis. Complaints have set off legal proceedings and lobbying by some financial institutions. The new FSOC in the United States designated several nonbank financial institutions as systematically important financial institutions (Sifi), required to hold additional capital and have additional oversight. MetLife, a giant insurance firm, challenged its identification as a Sifi by the council, based on use of a flawed and inadequate analysis in making this designation. In March of 2016, the U.S. District Court, ruled in favor of MetLife challenging this aspect of Dodd–Frank. MetLife's challenge could also lead to other legal challenges from major insurance firms, such as Prudential. General Electric, designated as a Sifi, also requested removal of its Sifi status, by divesting tens of billions of assets for its GE Capital division (Gray and Jopson, 2016; Jopson and Gray, 2016; Mclannahan, 2016a).

Public debate also continues over whether new regulations following the global financial crisis are too stringent and might have unintended consequences in the desire for greater trading transparency. An example is more stringent margin requirements or insurance and extra capital requirements mandated for banks using less standardized, over-the-counter, more tailored and illiquid swaps with global banks. These regulations have resulted in the majority of swap deals being transacted via clearing houses, leading to problems for a large number of over-the-counter trades being unable to be cleared (Stafford, 2016). Hence, the regulatory dialectic continues. Community banks have also complained of excessive regulations that increase costs for their operations, when their banks were not involved in the excesses of the subprime loan crisis.

THE EXAMINATION PROCESS

A major function of depository institution regulators is to examine the financial condition and operations of firms they supervise. With a number of different regulators for depository institutions, in the United States the *Federal Financial Institutions Examination Council (FFIEC)*, established in 1979, coordinates procedures for assuring compliance with a variety of regulations. The FFIEC includes representatives from the Board of Governors of the Fed, the FDIC, the OCC, and the NCUA. The FFIEC controls requirements for financial reporting and the disclosures that must be made to regulators, and also negotiates sharing of information across agencies and training programs for examiners of member agencies. The FFIEC also provides public performance and risk information for depository institutions that are downloadable as uniform bank performance reports (UBPR) (at: http://www.ffiec.gov).

Since 1993, regulators in the United States have used a set of so-called *tripwires* to identify unsafe or unsound banking practices, establishing minimum standards for almost every area under management's influence or control. The Fed, FDIC, OCC, and the NCUA use a uniform rating system with the acronym *CAMELS,* which assigns ratings of 1 to 5 (best to worst) to an depository institution's *Capital, Assets, Management, Earnings, Liquidity, and Sensitivity to market and interest rate risk* (added in 1997). CAMELS are viewed together to determine whether a depository institution's capital is adequate. The quality of assets and liabilities and off-balance sheet items are classified as good, substandard, doubtful, or losses. To evaluate management ability, examiners consider not only the quality of the bank's management, but also the quality of its board of directors.

Other countries have similar evaluation and examination processes to attempt to identify problems right away for depository institutions in order to avoid potential problems for financial institutions in these different areas of risk for banks. These risks in turn are also affected by economic conditions, with a country's central bank influential in monitoring, as well as doing research on economic conditions for the purpose of carrying out a country's monetary policies.

Major world banks are also required to undergo stress tests. In the United States, for instance, in early April 2016, 33 of the world's largest banks carried out a Comprehensive Capital Analysis and Review (CCAR), submitting documents to the Fed for the qualitative part of this review. Stress tests determine if banks have the resources and "wherewithal" to be able to withstand a major shock like the failure of Lehman Brothers. Banks that pass the stress tests are cleared to pay out a certain amount of cash as dividends or buybacks to shareholders. If an institution fails the stress test, this puts a stigma on the bank, affecting its share price, and puts pressure on executives. Part of the stress test is quantitative examination of whether a large bank has sufficient capital to be able to get through a major "slump." For instance, in 2016, the framework included a scenario of a larger recession in Europe and negative short-term interest rates for a nine-quarter planning period. The Fed is also allowed to reject capital plans if flaws are found in a bank's controls and risk management for the qualitative part of the stress test (Mclannahan, 2016b).

WHY HAVE A CENTRAL BANK?
OPERATIONS AND REGULATIONS

Historically, nations that do not have a central bank and a regulated currency have been plagued with problems when major banking panics occur; for instance, in the USA during the "Wildcat Banking" and "Free Banking" eras. Problems include having:

1   *An unsatisfactory currency*, such as multiple currencies across regions or states, so that the value of a currency received is undeterminable, leading to fraud and unredeemable currency.

2   *A deficient payment system*, with difficulty verifying and using currency for purchases or transferring currency to other parties, resulting in a lack of liquidity in the payments system.

3   *Periodic panics* associated with currency crises and lack of regulation for banks with no curbs in risk-taking activities and fraud that results in widespread bank failures, contagion, and a widespread recession or depression.

4   *Lack of control over the money supply*, leading to inflation and economic problems for a country.

5   *No lender of last resort* in the event of bank panics and contagion across healthy banks.

ROLES OF CENTRAL BANKS

Central banks have diverse roles that differ in different countries but generally include *issuing new currency* and withdrawing and destroying old damaged currency, *making discount loans* for banks suffering severe liquidity needs backed by risk-free collateral, *setting reserve requirements* for banks, *bank examinations, evaluating proposals for bank mergers and activities*, as well as *collecting data on business and economic conditions*, serving as a *liaison with the business community*, and doing *economic and other research* related to monetary policy. Central banks also engage in open market operations and *international coordination* with other countries for monetary policy, and act as lender of last resort during financial crises, a tool widely utilized during the U.S. subprime loan crisis of 2007 to 2008.

Central banks are organized differently in different countries. The Federal Reserve Bank (Fed) in the United States was initially founded to maintain some control over the private banking system under the Federal Reserve Act of 1913, in response to major financial panics in the United States in the 1800s and early 1900s.

The Fed was created as an independent government entity, to avoid problems of political pressures put on its operations (often associated with inflation). The Fed has 12 regional district banks spread across the USA, with directors of district banks including three professional bankers, three prominent business leaders from industry, labor, agriculture, or the consumer sector, and three directors appointed by the Board of Governors to represent the public interest. The Board of Governors of the Fed includes seven members including the chairman who are nominated by the President of the United States and confirmed by the Senate for full terms of 14 years, with the Chairman and Vice Chairman similarly named by the President and confirmed by the Senate for four-year terms (Board of Governors, 2015a).

The Fed's monetary policy tools include setting reserve requirements for banks (percentage reserves that must be held for transaction deposits), setting the discount rate for collateralized borrowing from the Fed, and open market operations. Of these, open market operations are the most effective, since reserve requirements and discount rate changes depend on actions by banks, such as banks lending more with lower reserve requirements or borrowing more from the Fed if the discount rate for borrowing from the Fed is lower. Open market operations by increasing and decreasing the money supply have a more direct effect on interest rates to stimulate or contract financial markets and stimulate or slow down economic activity in an economy.

It was not until the 1920s that the Fed began using *open market operations*, when Benjamin Strong, head of the New York Fed, avoided a recession in 1932 by purchasing large amounts of government securities from the nonbank public (investors) that in turn put funds in investors' bank deposit accounts enabling banks to make more loans and stimulating the economy (Board of Governors, 2015a).

In the aftermath of the global depression of the 1930s, the *Federal Open Market Committee (FOMC)* was established as a separate legal entity to engage in open market operation decisions (buying and selling government securities from the nonbank public). *These sales are implemented at the New York Fed.* To implement open market operations by a central bank, an economy must have a well-developed market for government securities, so many emerging markets rely more on other monetary policy tools, including reserve requirements and discount loans.

OVERVIEW OF A CENTRAL BANK'S OPEN MARKET OPERATIONS

Central banks have a key implementing monetary policy to control the money supply and to ensure the efficiency of the payments system, keeping price levels stable (avoiding inflation), and ensuring the liquidity of financial markets. In the United States, the Fed has the primary objective of keeping price levels stable (avoiding inflation), but also during recessions and financial crises the Fed has an additional objective of stimulating the economy and at times reducing the unemployment rate by doing so. When the economy appears to be overheating with an unacceptably high rate of inflation, the Fed usually adopts a constrictive policy and the Central Bank conducts open market operations, entailing selling government securities to the nonbank public, reducing deposits and reserves in the financial system. Reducing bank lending when the economy appears to be dragging instead and needs pepping up, the Fed will generally adopt an expansionary policy and increase the money supply using open market operations. This entails buying government securities from the nonbank public and putting deposits and reserves into the economy, whereby banks can lend more.

The target that the Fed uses to judge the effect of its operations is the *Fed Funds rate*, the interest rate that depository institutions charge on the excess reserves that they lend to one another. Under the loanable funds theory, with the Fed increasing the supply of loanable funds under an expansionary policy, the supply curve for loanable funds shifts outward, intersecting at a lower real equilibrium interest rate (Fed Funds rate). Similarly, if the Fed decreases the supply of loanable funds under a constrictive policy, the supply curve for loanable funds shifts inward, intersecting at a higher equilibrium interest rate.

Open Market Operations for an Expansionary Policy

To see the effect of open market operations, it's helpful to look at balance sheet accounts for the Fed, the banking system, and the nonbank public. For example, if the Fed conducts an open market purchase, buying $5 billion of bonds from the nonbank public, the nonbank public's asset account will decrease in security holdings by $5 billion, and its checkable deposits will increase by $5 billion. As shown in Figure 3.1, the supply curve of loanable funds shifts out.

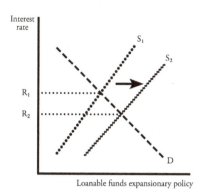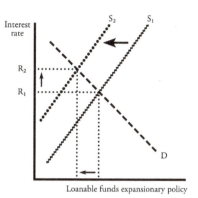

FIGURE 3.1 | Shift out for the supply curve for loanable funds. Note: S is the supply curve for loanable funds; D is the demand curve for loanable funds; and R is the equilibrium interest rate at the point where the supply and demand curves for loanable funds intersect.

Nonbank public

Assets:	Securities	− $5 billion
	Checkable deposits	+ $5 billion

In turn, the banking system will have an increase in checkable deposits as liabilities of $5 billion, and an increase in reserves as an asset of $5 billion.

Banking system

Assets:	Reserves	+ $5 billion
Liabilities:	Checkable deposits	+ $5 billion

For the Federal Reserve System's accounts, securities will go up by $5 billion as assets and reserves will go up as liabilities by $5 billion.

Fed Reserve system

Assets:	Securities	+ $5 billion
Liabilities:	Reserves	+ $5 billion

The net effect of the Fed's open market purchases is an expansion of reserves and deposits in the banking system, allowing banks to make more loans, and with an expansion of the money supply, a lower equilibrium interest rate.

Open Market Operations for a Contraction Policy

Similarly, for a contraction policy, the Fed instead sells securities to the nonbank public, reducing checkable deposits and reserves in the banking system. For a $5 billion purchase of securities from the nonbank public under a contraction policy, the balance sheet accounts for the nonbank public would be a $5 billion increase in securities and $5 billion decrease in checkable deposits as assets. Figure 3.1 shows a shift back in the loanable funds supply curve.

Nonbank public

Assets:	Securities	+ $5 billion
	Checkable deposits	− $5 billion

In turn, the banking system will have a decrease in checkable deposits as liabilities of $5 billion, and decrease in reserves as an asset of $5 billion.

Banking system

Assets:	Reserves	− $5 billion
Liabilities:	Checkable deposits	− $5 billion

For the Federal Reserve system, securities will go up down by $5 billion as assets and reserves will go down as liabilities by $5 billion.

Fed Reserve system

Assets:	Securities	− $5 billion
Liabilities:	Reserves	− $5 billion

Hence, there is a contraction of reserves and deposits and less lending by banks in the economy, slowing the economy down and reducing the money supply, resulting in a higher real interest rate, which discourages businesses from borrowing.

WHAT IS QUANTITATIVE EASING?

With the subprime loan crisis of 2007 to 2008 threatening the economy, the Fed engaged in a unique, new massive expansionary monetary policy to stimulate the economy and prevent deflation, known as *quantitative easing,* along with an additional new policy, known as *Operation Twist*.

Under quantitative easing (QE), the Fed purchased huge amounts of U.S. Treasury notes and mortgage securities from its member banks including longer-term securities, instead of short-term Treasury securities as in typical Fed open market operations. This had the effect of lowering yields, including in the long-term sector. Since purchases were made from member banks, the Fed in essence created loanable funds by paying for its purchases by crediting the bank for its bond purchases.

The intent of QE is to lower borrowing costs, stimulating banks to lend more and companies to borrow more with low rates. The Fed tied its bond-purchase program also to a target of significant improvement in the labor market (i.e., expansion of jobs). Most studies show that QE helped to reduce borrowing costs in the United States, with a positive effect on employment. Critics of QE worry about risks, including the large size of the Fed's giant balance sheet and the potential for inflation (Saphir, 2012).

The Fed engaged in three rounds of bond purchases known as QE1, QE2, and QE3 over 2008 to 2014, with a gradual tapering off from June 2013 on, and purchases halted by October 29, 2014, with the Fed's balance sheet having accumulated about $4.5 trillion in assets. Hence, QE differs from open market operations by the enormity of its operations. The Bank of England, the European Central Bank (ECB), the Swiss National Bank, the Swedish National Bank, and the Bank of Japan also have engaged in quantitative easing activities, including bond purchases for the European Central Bank in 2015 and 2016 to stimulate the economy (Jolly and Ewing, 2015).

Under *Operation Twist,* also known as the maturity extension program, instead of purchasing short-term Treasury securities from the nonbank public (investors), the Fed sold or redeemed $667 billion of short-term Treasury securities by the end of 2012 and used the proceeds of this sale to buy long-term Treasury securities. By reducing the supply of longer-term Treasury securities, this increased prices for these securities (i.e., reducing the interest rate), with the effect of lowering long-term corporate bond rates to encourage businesses investing in new projects with low rates for financing stimulating the economy (for greater details, see Board of Governors, 2012). The net effect of Operation Twist was successful in lowering the slope of the yield curve with lower rates for longer-term securities after the policy was implemented. With the huge amount of FOMC purchases of securities during 2009 to 2013 under QE, the Federal Reserve's balance sheet grew tremendously from less than $1 trillion in assets in 2007 to over $3.5 trillion in assets in 2013, with about $2 trillion of these assets long-term Treasury security purchases.

THE FED'S RESCUE: MORAL HAZARD VERSUS SAFETY AND SOUNDNESS TRADE-OFF

With financial institutions with large subprime holdings facing deposit runs, and stock sell-offs by investors, regulators had difficult choices of whether or not to rescue huge financial institutions to avoid systemic risk in the financial system. Regulators were concerned that if failures were not allowed to take place, this would be a bad signal to other financial institutions engaging in great risk taking. At the same time, the Fed needed to protect the safety and soundness of the financial system. At the beginning of the crisis in April 2008, regulators decided to rescue Bear Stearns, a huge investment bank that had large losses from its two hedge funds that had liquidity problems and could not meet their obligations. Since a failure of Bear Stearns would have significant repercussions for other financial institutions and investors globally, the Fed negotiated and subsidized a merger with another large financial institution, JPMorgan Chase, to protect the financial system.

As the crisis worsened, more mega financial institutions with huge losses endured a liquidity crisis. With credit agencies downgrading MBS and their prices tumbling, the value of MBS held for future sales under mark-to-market accounting had to be reduced on balance sheets, reducing the value of a firm's equity (market value of assets – market value of liabilities), resulting in insolvency with a zero or lower market value for equity. In contrast to the decision for Bear Stearns, Lehman Brothers, a large global investment bank, was allowed to fail.

Investors and regulators were shocked by the market reactions to this failure, including a huge downturn in stock markets, given the worldwide links of Lehman Brothers with other financial institutions. Other major Wall Street firms including Merrill Lynch, Morgan Stanley, and Goldman Sachs, that had lent money to hedge funds with large subprime loan holdings, faced severe liquidity problems, and were unable to borrow in financial markets.

Given the systematic effects and distress for other financial institutions and markets, the Fed switched back to a safety and soundness rationale. This included a government infusion for an arranged takeover of Merrill Lynch by Bank of America to prevent its failure, and a conversion of Goldman Sachs and Morgan Stanley to bank holding companies to allow them access to liquidity by borrowing from the Fed. The Fed engaged in rescues and arranged take-overs to prevent other large BHCs from failing, including a merger for Wachovia with Wells Fargo and for Washington Mutual to be acquired by JPMorgan Chase. With a large number of bank failures, there was considerable contagion in the financial markets, with investors unsure about the quality of assets or involvement of other financial institutions in subprime lending. This resulted in widespread selling of bank stocks, regardless of the quality of the bank, and a further huge downturn in the stock market.

In September/October 2008, AIG, a giant insurance company, was forced to pay out enormous sums on credit default swaps, and was taken over in the form of a conservatorship by the government. The huge government-related mortgage agencies, Fannie Mae and Freddie Mac also had to be rescued and put under government conservatorship. At this point, stronger governmental measures to reinstate confidence in the financial system had to be taken.

On October 3, 2008, Congress signed the Emergency Economic Stabilization Act creating a $700 billion Troubled Assets Relief Program (TARP) to purchase subprime assets from banks. "Mark-to-market" accounting rules were also eased to stop widespread MBS sales, and the Fed announced it would provide $900 billion in short-term loans to banks. On October 7, the Fed also announced it would lend as emergency funds $1.3 trillion directly to companies outside of the financial sector. Other central banks joined in (in the United Kingdom, China, Canada, Sweden, Switzerland, and the EU) to engage in expansionary monetary policies to reduce rates to stimulate the world economy.

By October 14, 2008, a new program whereby the U.S. government took on an equity position in banks to inject $250 billion of public funds was initiated under TARP, and on October 21 the Fed announced it would purchase $540 billion in short-term debt from money market mutual funds to ease liquidity problems. For the remainder of the year additional capital was infused into markets. This included a government rescue of Citigroup by infusing $20 billion of capital. The Fed also pledged additional funds of $800 billion, including $600 billion to purchase mortgage bonds issued or guaranteed by Fannie Mae, Freddie Mac, Ginnie Mae, and the Federal Home Loan Banks.

For the rescue efforts, safety and soundness and instilling confidence in financial markets and institutions dominated as the rationale for regulatory actions.

NEW REGULATIONS IN THE GLB ENVIRONMENT

Overview: Dodd–Frank Act of 2010

The objectives of legislation in the United States following the subprime loan crisis included restoring confidence and accountability in the banking system and creating a solid foundation for the economy to grow and for job creation. Highlights of the legislation presented by the

U.S. Committee on Financial Services (2010) include greater regulatory oversight, regulatory warning systems, transparency, consumer and investor protections, proposals for changes in compensation system incentives that encourage risk taking, and restrictions on some non-banking activities. Provision includes:

1   *Consumer protection*: The Bureau of Consumer Financial Protection was established as an "independent watchdog" under the Fed to protect U.S. consumers, including transparent, accurate information on mortgages, credit cards, and other financial products, with protection from fees that are hidden, along with any abusive terms or deceptive practices.
2   *Ending too big to fail bailouts*: Charged to develop safe ways to liquidate large failed financial institutions and ways to discourage FIs from becoming too large, and giving the Fed greater authority for system-wide support but no longer allowing the Fed to prop up individual financial institutions to prevent future taxpayer funded bailouts. Under the *Volcker Rule*, the Dodd–Frank Act prohibits proprietary trading and sponsorship of hedge funds and private equity firms, including restrictions on these types of activities for non-bank financial institutions supervised by the Fed. Large, complex financial companies are required to periodically submit plans for their quick and orderly liquidations, and a liquidity mechanism created for the FDIC to wind down significant financial companies that pose systematic risks.
3   *Advance warning systems*: The Financial Stability Oversight Council (FSOC) was created to identify and respond to risks emerging in the financial system, including the Treasury Secretary, Fed, SEC, OCC, FDIC, NCUA, the Commodity Futures Trading Commission (CFTC), the Federal Housing Finance Agency (FHFA), and the Consumer Financial Protection Bureau. The FSOC makes recommendations to the Fed for rules for capital, leverage, liquidity, and risk management, among others, including special rules for large, complex financial institutions that pose risks to the financial system, and has the potential to regulate nonbank financial companies and the divestment of assets for large, complex firms by a 2/3 vote if a firm's activities or failure poses a significant risk to the stability of the financial system. The FSOC is charged with making information on risks transparent in reports and testimony to Congress, and to establish a floor for capital requirements.
4   *Transparency and accountability for exotic instruments* is included with a charge to eliminate loopholes associated with risky and abusive practices, including those for over-the-counter derivatives, asset-backed securities, hedge funds, mortgage brokers, and payday lenders. Special provisions were also included for greater transparency for the extraction industry, among others.
5   *Executive compensation and corporate governance provisions* for financial institutions that receive government assistance under the Emergency Economic Stabilization Act of 2008 were instituted with guidelines to ensure that top executive compensation is aligned not just with the interests of shareholders and financial institutions, but also with taxpayers providing assistance. The Dodd–Frank Act also included provisions for proposals to be created to give stockholders a stronger position on pay and corporate affairs, including a nonbinding vote on executive compensation and other matters.

In response to this provision, the SEC in 2013 adopted a proposed rule on the CEO pay ratio disclosure for financial institution compensation for financial institutions with total assets of $1 billion or more, including CEO pay ratio (CEO pay to the median pay), along with:

1   *Disclosures about incentive-based compensation arrangements* and prohibitions for encouraging inappropriate risk taking.

2   *Special prohibitions and requirements for larger financial institutions* with $50 billion or more in total consolidated assets, requiring that executive officers defer for three years at least 50% of any incentive-based compensation and incentive-based compensation payments adjusted for losses incurred by the covered financial institution after the compensation was awarded initially. Additional requirements include directors charged with identifying employees that expose an institution to large losses (such as traders with huge position limits), and overseeing the incentive-based compensation arrangement for that person.

3   *Establishing policies and procedures*: A covered financial institution would be barred from establishing an incentive-based compensation arrangement unless the arrangement was adopted under policies and procedures developed and maintained by the institution and approved by its board of directors (see SEC 2011-57). The rule also provides guidance on determining the CEO pay ratio including the determination of the median employee and calculation of total compensation, required disclosure and the timing of disclosure (Meridian, 2013).

4   *Protection for investors*: Provisions are included for new tougher rules on transparency and accountability for credit rating agencies. Provisions also include greater funding and resources for the SEC, reducing risks posed by securities, and better oversight of the municipal securities industry, among others. The Deposit Insurance Corporation for depository institutions was also increased to $250,000, which was retroactive to January 1, 2008.

5   *Greater regulatory powers for enforcement and oversight* are provided to allow regulators to aggressively pursue financial fraud conflicts of interest, and system manipulation benefitting special interests at the expense of consumers and businesses.

Dodd–Frank also requires that financial and bank holding companies and nonbank financial companies having consolidated assets greater than $10 billion to conduct and report on self-imposed stress tests semi-annually. The 19 largest complex banking organizations with assets greater than $100 billion also have a stress test conducted by the Fed that includes estimating the effect on their revenues, losses, and reserve requirements of two adverse economic scenarios for future years. The Federal Reserve also introduced in 2011 a Comprehensive Capital Assessment Review (CCAR) program evaluating the capital planning process of institutions with greater than $500 billion in assets.

Community banks (categorized as banks with $10 billion in assets) are required to determine their ability to withstand adverse economic conditions, and to submit to regulators a plan for their risk management practices. Supervisory guidelines increased for banks that have a significant concentration of commercial real estate lending.

Living Will Requirement for Eight Largest U.S. Banks

Large international banks are also subject to Basel III's regulatory framework. The Dodd–Frank Act requires the eight largest banks deemed "too big to fail" that are systemically important financial institutions (SIFIs) to develop "living wills," which are bankruptcy action plans, with the FSOC given the implicit right to break up huge banks if living wills are not viable. These "living wills" are detailed plans explaining how they would dismantle their operations and financial contracts in an orderly fashion to avoid contagion effects during a financial crisis. In April of 2016, the FDIC and Federal Reserve received plans for Bank of America, Bank of New York, Mellon, JPMorgan Chase, State Street and Wells Fargo. Under the Dodd–Frank rules, banks that have had plans rejected are given 90 days to revise plans, unless given a longer time for revisions by regulators. Five of the largest banks submitted plans that were rejected as not being credible plans by regulators who gave these banks 6 months until October 1, 2016 to fix their plans (Popper and Eavis, 2016). Citigroup, whose wind-down plan was passed in response to new regulations (regulations pushing banks to become "simpler and safer"), sold 60 businesses, shrunk retail branches around the world, reduced its bank's holdings by $700 billion, and oversaw a decline in 40,000 jobs, by means of layoffs (Popper and Corkery, 2016). In recent years many politicians have pushed for the breaking up of mega banks following the subprime crisis.

Overview: New Basel III Regulatory Framework

The Basel Committee on Banking Supervision[2] at the Bank for International Settlements developed a new regulatory framework for banks (Basel III) with new capital standards that began to be implemented beginning January 1, 2013. Member countries are required to translate the new Basel III rules into national laws and regulations, with different core components of Basel III having different implementation dates.

Basel I of 1988 (phased in by 1993 in the United States) provided minimum risk-based capital requirements for large international banks along with a higher minimum core equity to total assets ratio. Basel 1 had some problems with risk-based capital ratios calculated by categorizing assets into different risk categories based on their general risk: that is, government securities a 0% weight, 50% for mortgage loans, and 100% capital to be held on other types of loans, such as commercial loans. Off-balance sheet items were also converted to risk-based assets. With the subprime loan crisis, mortgage loans and mortgage-backed securities had much greater risk, but had less capital held as protection against losses.

Basel II initiated in 2004 contained three pillars including: (1) *capital charges against market, operational, and credit risk* that allowed large banks to use their own advanced internal risk-based measures or a standardized advanced measurement approach to calculate their risks and capital charges; (2) an *effective supervisory review process* of the banks' internal assessments of their individual capital allocations to determine if they were sufficient; and (3) *market discipline and transparency* with risk and capital positions of banks made more transparent to allow market discipline to reinforce pillars 1 and 2. Basel II encompassed a great effort to evaluate risk sensitivity, but for some large international banks their capital requirements were lower based on internal risk-based measures versus community banks that continued to operate under Basel I. Gaps still remained that large international banks could exploit, and with new technological innovations and sophisticated products, regulators had difficulty understanding and evaluating these and how they affected bank risks. There was also perhaps too much reliance on market discipline.

The new international regulatory framework for banks under Basel III includes a comprehensive set of reform measures that were developed by the Basel Committee on Banking

Supervision "to strengthen the regulation, supervision and risk management of the banking sector" including: (1) improvement in the banking sector's ability for shock absorption that comes about from financial and economic stress, regardless of the source; (2) improvement in risk management and governance; and (3) strengthening the transparency and disclosure of banks. Two approaches to supervision that are complements include: (1) bank-level, microprudential regulation at the microlevel to help increase the resilience during periods of stress for individual banking institutions; and (2) system-level, macroprudential regulations to reduce system-wide risks that can arise in the banking sector, in addition to "procyclical amplification" of these risks over time. The two approaches to regulation are noted to be complementary, since greater individual bank resilience reduces the risk of system-wide risk with shocks (Basel Committee, 2016).

Components of Basel III include: (1) *capital adequacy reforms* beginning implementation on January 1, 2013; (2) *new frameworks to measure credit risk and hence risk-based assets* to be implemented beginning January 1, 2016; (3) a *liquidity coverage ratio* to be implemented from January 1, 2015; (4) a *leverage ratio* with disclosure starting in 2015; and (5) a *net stable funding ratio* under review to have a minimum standard introduced in 2018. As of 2010, the Committee began to periodically monitor the progress of a sample of internationally active banks in their adjustment to new Basel III standards for capital and liquidity, including 101 Group 1 banks with Tier capital in excess of 3 billion euros that are internationally active, and 109 Group 2 other banks (Basel Committee, 2013).

Highlights of Basel III include: (1) a *higher overall capital requirement*; (2) a *narrower definition of qualifying regulatory capital*; (3) *high capital charges for banking book and trading book exposure*; (4) a *new capital leverage ratio*; and (5) *two new liquidity ratios* (a liquidity coverage ratio phased in starting in 2015 and a stable funding ratio phased in starting in 2018). Under Basel III the quality and quantity of capital will increase; a new capital conservation buffer will be instituted and a new countercyclical capital buffer will be phased in with higher capital taken on in good times to protect against needs for capital for losses in bad times; and banks that do not have capital ratios meeting targets will have restrictions placed on their capital distributions and other discretionary payments.

Within different countries, many other regulations to prevent abuses and to reduce risk taking have been introduced. In the United Kingdom, for instance, the Chancellor of the Exchequer created in 2010 a new Independent Commission on Banking, chaired by Sir John Vickers, to consider structural and other nonstructural reforms to the UK banking sector for the promotion of financial stability and completion. The Vickers Report to be enacted in Parliament by 2015 and completed by 2019 has three main recommendations that include: (1) putting European retail banking assets, liabilities and services as separate subsidiaries to separate retail operations from investment banking; (2) protecting retail deposits (savings) above unsecured loans if a bank goes under, providing greater incentives for monitoring by unsecured lenders; and (3) requiring the retail components of larger UK banks with an international presence to maintain capital at 17–20% of their UK balance sheet versus 7% under Basel III and 10% suggested by the UK Treasurer. Critics point out that UK banks will have to raise significant capital, which could make them uncompetitive with other international banks, and could also reduce lending by UK banks (The Money Principle, 2015).

THE REGULATORY DIALECTIC AND NEW REGULATORY CONCERNS

Dermine (2013) points out the more stringent regulations for bank capital, liquidity, and corporate structure intended to protect the global banking system could have unintended consequences in terms of reducing lending, and increasing more securitization of assets, and moving more financial intermediation to shadow banking. With greater capital required for the 19 largest U.S. banks and financial holding companies, bank executives have also questioned whether it would be better to break-up the bank to avoid this penalty (Eavis, 2015). Critics have also been concerned that new rules are too complex, and by hurting financial institution profitability may be weakening the financial system. Whether this is the case is yet to be seen as the regulatory dialectic continues.

SUMMARY

Regulators oversee financial institutions, to help facilitate an efficient payment system and the safety and soundness of an economy. Financial institution managers also need to be continuously aware of central bank monetary policies, since they have a significant effect on interest rates. It is also important to understand factors that contribute to financial crises to avoid repeating mistakes that have been made in the past, and to recognize the reaction of regulators in stemming crises, such as the recent global financial crisis.

Financial regulations have often followed a regulatory dialectic, as suggested by Ed Kane, whereby there is a thesis in terms of regulations passed for safety and soundness or to promote efficiency of the banking system. With changes in economic conditions and technology, regulations become less useful, and financial institutions find ways to avoid regulations with new innovations, as an antithesis, followed by regulatory actions to amend or patch up regulations to prevent this regulatory avoidance. Eventually with lobbying and pressures for change, as a synthesis, deregulation comes about. This in turn can lead to greater risk taking by financial institutions, leading to more stringent regulations, leading to a new regulatory dialectic cycle. The recent global financial crisis and U.S. subprime loan crisis have resulted in a new regulatory cycle to protect the banking system with new capital and liquidity requirements, consumer protection, and corporate governance regulations and financial oversight including greater regulation for derivative activities and greater oversight for large financial institutions that are important to the economy, whose failure could lead to a more widespread economic crisis in the future.

NOTES

1 Kane (1977) introduced the regulatory dialectic, which was further developed in articles (1981), (1989), and (1996), among others.
2 The Basel Committee includes representatives from organizations with senior banking supervisory authority and central banks from Argentina, Australia, Belgium, Brazil, Canada, China, France, Germany, Hong Kong SAR, India, Indonesia, Italy, Japan, Korea, Luxembourg, Mexico, the Netherlands, Russia, Saudi Arabia,

Singapore, South Africa, Spain, Sweden, Switzerland, Turkey, the United Kingdom, and the USA, with the governing body the central bank governors and noncentral bank heads of supervision of the member countries. Meetings are usually held at the Bank for International Settlements (BIS) in Basel, Switzerland, the location of the committee's permanent Secretariat (Basel Committee, 2013).

BIBLIOGRAPHY

Basel Committee on Banking Supervision (2013). "Report to G20 Finance Ministers and Central Bank Governors on Monitoring Implementation of Basel III regulatory reform." Bank for International Settlements, August 2013. Accessed on February 24, 2015 at: http://www.bis.org/publ/bcbs260.pdf

Basel III (2014). "International Regulatory Framework for Banks (Basel III)." Bank for International Settlements. Accessed on April 5, 2016 at: http://www.bis.org/bcbs/basel3.htm

Basel III (2016). "Basel Committee on Banking Supervision Reforms—Basel III Summary Table." Bank for International Settlements. Accessed on April 5, 2016 at: http://www.bis.org/bcbs/basel3/b3summarytable.pdf

Bloomberg (2009). U.S. European Bank Writedowns and Losses, November 5, 2009. Accessed on February 23, 2015 at: http://www.reuters.com/article/2009/11/05/banks-writedowns-losses-idCNL554155620091105

Board of Governors of the Federal Reserve System (2012). Federal Reserve website. Accessed March 12, 2012 at: http://www.federalreserve.gov/faqs/money_15070.htm

Board of Governors of the Federal Reserve System (2015a). Federal Reserve website. Accessed on February 26, 2015 at: http://www.federalreserve.gov/aboutthefed/bios/board/default.htm

Board of Governors of the Federal Reserve System (2015b). About-the-Fed-History. Accessed on February 19, 2015 at: https://federalreserveeducation.org/about-the-fed/history

Committee on Financial Services (2010). Overview: Dodd–Frank Wall Street Reform and Consumer Protection Act, June 29, 2010, 1–15.

Dermine, Jean (2013). "Banking regulations after the global financial crisis: Good intentions and unintended evil," Working Paper, INSEAD.

Eavis, Peter (2015). "The break-up question over JPMorgan Chase." *The New York Times*, January 14, 2015. Accessed on January 26, 2015 at: http://dealbook.nytimes.com/2015/01/14/the-break-up-question...

Getter, Darryl E. (2012). U.S. Implementation of the Basel Capital Regulatory Framework, November 14, 2012, Congressional Research Service. Accessed on February 28, 2013 at: www.crs.gov,7-5700/R42744.

Gorton, Gary B. (2010). *Slapped by the Invisible Hand: The Panic of 2007.* Oxford: Oxford University Press.

Grant Thornton (2011). "Beyond banks: New incentive compensation rules reach entire industry." Accessed on February 26, 2015 at: http://www.grantthornton.com/staticfiles/GTCom/Financial%20services/FSandFI%20 files/Incentive%20compensation%20rules%20reach%20entire%20industry-Grant%20Thornton-May%20 2011.pdf

Gray, Alistair and Barney Jopson (2016). "MetLife escapes 'too big to fail' label." *Financial Times*, March 31, 2016, p. 1.

Home Foreclosure Statistics (2014). July 8, 2014. Accessed on February 24, 2015 at: http://www.statisticbrain. com/home-foreclosure-statistics/

Joint Economic Committee (2007). "The subprime lending crisis: The economic impact on wealth, property values and tax revenues and how we got here." Report and Recommendations by the Majority Staff of the Joint Economic Committee, Senator Charles E. Schumer, Chairman and Rep. Carolyn B. Maloney, Vice Chair, October 2007. Accessed on February 19, 2015 at: http://www.jec.senate.gov/archive/Documents/Reports/10 .25.07OctoberSubprimeReport.pdf

Jolly, David and Jack Ewing (2015). "E.C.B. stimulus calls for 60 billion euros in monthly bond-buying," *New York Times*, January 22, 2015, pp. 1–5. Accessed on March 1, 2015 at: http://www.nytimes.com/2015/01/23/business/ european-central-bank-bond-buying.html?_r=1

Jopson, Barney and Alistair Gray (2016). "Financial. Dodd–Frank challenge: MetLife ruling shakes US post-crisis laws." *Financial Times*, April 1, 2016, p. 15.

Kane, Edward J. (1977). "Good intentions and unintended evil: The case against selective credit allocation." *Journal of Money, Credit and Banking*, 9 (February), 55–69.

Kane, Edward J (1981). "Accelerating inflation, Technological innovation, and the decreasing effectiveness of banking regulation." *Journal of Finance*, 36 (May), 355–367.

Kane, Edward J. (1989). "Changing incentives facing financial-services regulators." *Journal of Financial Services Research*, 2, 265–274.

Kane, Edward J. (1996). "De jure interstate banking: Why only now?" *Journal of Money, Credit, and Banking*, 28 (1996), 141–161.

Latham & Watkins (2015). "Regulatory capital reform under Basel III." Powerpoint presentation, March 2011, Global Association of Risk Professionals (GARP). Accessed on February 26, 2015 at: http://www.garp.org/media/583507/regulatorycapitalreformbaseliii_nicolaides032311.pdf (also available at: www.lw.com/presentations/understanding-**basel-III**-2014).

Lewis, Michael (2010). *The Big Short: Inside the Doomsday Machine*. New York: W.W. Norton & Company.

Lewis, Michael (2011). *Boomerang: Travels in the New Third World*. New York: W.W. Norton & Company.

Mayer Brown (2012). Basel Committee releases final text of Basel III framework. Accessed on February 4, 2012 at: http://www.mayerbrown.com/publications/article.asp?id=10235

Mclannahan, Ben (2016a). "GE Capital in move to be stripped of US 'Sifi' label." *Financial Times*, April 1, 2016, p. 11.

Mclannahan, Ben (2016b). "US stress-test puts finance industry on edge." *Financial Times*, April 4, 2016, p. 16.

Meridian (2013). "SEC posts proposed rule on CEO pay ratio." Meridian client update. Accessed on February 26, 2015 at: http://www.meridiancp.com/wp-content/uploads/sec-posts-proposed-rule-on-ceo-pay-ratio.pdf

Mishkin, Frederic S. and Stanley G. Eakins (2015). *Financial Markets and Institutions*, 8th ed. New York: Pearson.

Morgenson, Gretchen and Joshua Rosner (2011). *Reckless endangerment: How Outsized Ambition, Greed, and Corruption Led to Economic Armageddon*. New York: Times Books: Henry Holt & Company.

Morrison & Foerster (2010). "The Dodd–Frank Act: A cheat sheet." Morrison & Foerster. Accessed on April 5, 2016 at http://media.mofo.com/files/uploads/images/summarydoddfrankact.pdf

Popper, Nathaniel and Michael Corkery (2016). "Regulations enforce a diet for Citigroup: A trend of megabanks becoming just big." *New York Times*, April 16, 2016, A1, B6.

Popper, Nathaniel and Peter Eavis (2016). "5 Banks are still too big to fail, regulators say." *New York Times*, April 14, 2016, A1, B3.

Raman, Ravi (2016). "Basel III: An easy to understand summary." White Paper, iCreate Software Banking Intelligence. Accessed on April 5, 2016 at http://www.icreate.in/pdf/Basel%20III%20-%20An%20easy%20to%20understand%20summary.pdf

Sachs, Jeffrey D. (2008). "How to fix the U.S. financial crisis." *Scientific American*, December 1, 2008, pp. 1–10. Accessed on April 5, 2016 at: http://www.scientificamerican.com/article/fixing-financial-crisis/

Saphir, Ann (2012). "The Fed's Q3: How does it work and what are the risks." Reuters.com, September 13, 2012. Accessed on September 13, 2012 at: http://www.reuters.com/article/2012/09/13/us-usa-fed-easing-idUSBRE88C1CT20120913

SEC (2011). "SEC proposes rules on disclosure of incentive-based compensation arrangements at financial institutions," U.S. Securities and Exchange Commission, Washington DC., March 2, 2011. Accessed on February 26, 2015 at: http://www.sec.gov/news/press/2011/2011-57.htm

Subprime Mortgage Crisis (2015). *Business Today*, Case Study, February 18, 2015, 1–2. Accessed on this date at: http://www.businesstoday-eg.com/case-studies/case-studies/subprime-mortgage-crisis.html

Stafford, Philip (2016). "Risky derivatives trades face higher costs." *Financial Times*, February 5, 2016, p. 24.

Taleb, Nassim Nicholas (2007). *The Black Swan: The Impact of the Highly Improbable*. New York: Random House.

The Money Principle (2015) "New UK banking regulation." Accessed on February 26, 2015 at: http://www.themoneyprinciple.co.uk/new-uk-banking-regulation/

Additional Resources

To see Frontline's "Inside the Meltdown" just click on the link on the PBS Website (if available in your area; no need to sign in) or go to: http://video.pbs.org/video/1082087546/ This video lasts about an hour (great overview for the U.S. subprime loan crisis).

QUESTIONS AND PROBLEMS

1   Find an article for a different country and its central banking activities. How are that country's central bank activities and organization similar and different from that of the U.S. Federal Reserve? Explain why a strong government security market is necessary for a central bank's open market operations. How is monetary policy implemented in the country you examine?

2   During the recent global financial crisis, regulators faced the trade-off between conflicting goals of dealing with moral hazard problems of avoiding "too big to fail" financial institutions who engaged in excessive risk taking to fail and rescuing these institutions to prevent contagion in the financial system from a safety and soundness rationale.

3   Explain in your own words the concept of the regulatory dialectic and give an example. Using current articles in the financial news or on the Web, identify a recent regulatory decision and explain the reaction of financial institution managers to it and what objection financial institution managers may have.

4   What were the primary causes of the global financial crisis? Were all financial institution managers to blame? What ideas do you have to help prevent this from happening in the future?

5   Explain in your own words how central banks engage in monetary policies to expand the money supply and to contract the money supply, respectively. Show asset and liability accounts for each for the nonbanking public, banking system, and the Federal Reserve for each type of policy using respectively purchases and sales of $500 billion.

6   Summarize the Dodd–Frank Act major provisions of 2010. What do you think of the provisions in terms of reducing the likelihood of a future financial crisis? Do you agree with some critiques that the regulations are too stringent or too lenient? Explain why.

7   Summarize the Basel I, II, and III frameworks. What problems did Basel I and II have? How will the Basel III framework attempt to remedy these? Do you agree or disagree that there might be unintended consequences with the new framework.

Part Two

Performance and Risk Analysis for FIs and ESG Considerations

Chapter 4

Financial Performance and Risk Analysis

Risk comes from not knowing what you're doing.

(Warren Buffett, cited in Berman, 2014)

UNDERSTANDING how financial institutions operate and how to analyze their financial statements and performance and risk ratios is of key importance for financial institution managers and financial analysts. During the global financial crisis, many investors were shocked by the problems experienced by both large and small banks that seemed to come out of nowhere, when a careful financial analysis would have revealed the brewing of significant problems for many banks, particularly real estate lenders.

In the United States, in the first quarter of 2016, only one federally insured bank failed, and there were zero bank failures in 2006, just prior to the U.S. subprime loan crisis that began in 2007. From 2007 to 2015, 514 federally insured banks and savings associations failed. A number of weaker depository institutions also engaged in federally assisted and unassisted mergers. The number of FDIC-insured commercial banks fell by almost 24% from 2006 to 2014, falling from 7,408 to 5,646. For FDIC-insured savings institutions the number of institutions fell by about 32% from 2006 to 2014 from 1,279 to 867 in 2014.

Having a good understanding of financial statements and being able to analyze financial statements for depository institutions is very important to determine both an institution's strengths and its weaknesses. Since financial firms purchase and sell and invest in money, they are subject to greater fraud and accounting complexities than nonfinancial firms. Financial assets and liabilities are promises of future payments, so are subject to greater market risk for changes in the values of assets and liabilities, and hence the value of equity (market value of assets less the market value of liabilities). Financial statements may not reveal all an investor needs to know about a financial institution, but they do provide clues about how well the institution has been doing, as well as signaling risks and trends.

Because financial reports are affected by accounting rules and regulatory rules and with financial institutions having many very untypical items, financial analysts and FI managers need to understand the subtleties of bank financial statements. Also, elements of a bank's strategy can be revealed along with strengths and weaknesses for strategic planning purposes. This chapter examines the financial statements of depository institutions, and their performance and risk analysis.

SOURCES OF INDUSTRY PERFORMANCE INFORMATION

Although often for insured banks, credit unions, and saving institutions, regulatory information or ratings may be protected for the safety and soundness of the financial system, such as to avoid contagion or bank runs, regulators also provide detailed financial information, available to the public, as well as other private sources. For publicly traded financial and bank holding companies and banks, there are detailed annual reports with financial statements. Depository institutions are required to report data to regulators routinely, so a number of sources for data are available.

In the United States, the *Federal Financial Institutions Examination Council (FFIEC)* website (http://www.ffiec.gov) has links where you can click on UBPR, which allows you to search for and download a *bank's uniform bank performance report (UBPR)* that gives in addition to financial statements, details on the composition of assets, liabilities, yields and cost of funds, operating cost information and efficiency ratios, and risk characteristics, and trend and peer comparisons for similar size banks. On the website, you'll see: FFIEC Financial Institution Information, UBPR, Users Guide, and FDIC Directory, where if you click on UBPR, you can search for a U.S. FDIC-insured bank's UBPR; or first look up the bank in the FDIC Institutions Director, with a User's Guide as well that can be downloaded.

Other reports and information are also on the FFIEC website, including links to the *National Information Center (NIC)* that provides data for financial and bank holding companies, links to bank holding company reports, and other links and information, including details of bank consumer compliance ratings. The NIC home page (http://www.ffiec.gov/nicpubweb/nicweb/nichome.aspx) also provides an institution search for bank and financial holding companies in the United States. Holding companies with greater than $10 billion in assets, and bank holding company peer group reports and other reports also can be found there.

The Federal Deposit and Insurance Corporation (FDIC) website (www.fdic.gov) also provides industry analysis data including bank data and statistics; information on failed banks; information on international deposit insurance and how the FDIC fosters communication and coordination among the deposit insurance systems of other countries; and research and analysis for regional and national bank trends in the United States (http://www.fdic.gov/bank/).

Different countries often have similar national sources for information. Private groups such as Bauer Financial (www.bauerfinancial.com) and SNL Financial (www.snl.com) provide detailed financial data and bank rating information that can be purchased. Since many large banks are publicly traded, annual reports can be found online or if publicly traded in the United States can be downloaded on the Securities and Exchange Commission (SEC) website at http://www.sec.gov; if you click on filings, you'll see a link to the Edgar database, which provides online filings (http://www.sec.gov/edgar/searchedgar/companysearch.html).

The Yahoo finance website (http://www.yahoo.com/finance) also has summary financial statements for publicly traded bank and financial holding companies. The U.S. National Credit Union Administration website (http://www.ncua.gov) provides information for credit unions. Annual reports for large banks and financial institutions are also posted online, including financial statements, such as the annual report for Deutsche Bank (https://annualreport.deutsche-ank.com), with links to click on for financial statements. Many different countries also publish public data on commercial banks and savings institutions.

OVERVIEW OF COMMERCIAL BANK FINANCIAL STATEMENTS

Sources of funds for banks include (liabilities) checkable deposits; nontransaction deposits; and borrowings, including federal funds purchased and repurchase agreements, trading liabilities, other borrowed funds, subordinated debt, and other liabilities.

Uses of funds (assets) include cash and due (that includes reserves, cash items in the process of collection, and vault cash), interest-bearing balances, securities, federal funds sold and reverse repurchase agreements, securities (held as secondary reserves), and a bank's primary use for funds, loans.

Commercial banks facilitate the flow of funds in an economy by accepting funds from depositors and providing them to borrowers. In effect, banks buy funds from deposits at low, insured rates and sell funds at higher rates to borrowers.

TRADITIONAL OPERATING PROFITS FOR DEPOSITORY INSTITUTIONS

As discussed in Chapter 1, a bank's net interest margin (NIM) is a measure of the profitability of its traditional lending activities. Accordingly, traditional operating profits for banks are generally calculated as the *net interest income (NII)*, (interest revenue less interest expense) *less the provision for loan losses (PLL)* (expense deducted for expected loan losses) *less the net operating expenses (burden)* (noninterest expense less noninterest revenue).

Operating profit before taxes and security gain/loss = NII – PLL – Burden.

If this is put as a percentage of average total assets, the operating return on assets (OROA) becomes:

OROA before taxes and security gain/loss = NIM – PLL% – Burden%.

A bank's interest spread is its interest revenue from its earning assets less its interest expense from its interest paid on deposits and other liabilities. Thus, it's important to be familiar with the different types of assets and liabilities that a depository institution holds.

OVERVIEW OF TYPES OF ASSETS (SOURCES OF INTEREST REVENUES)

On a bank's balance sheet, items are listed from the most liquid to the least liquid as shown in Table 4.1, which gives the typical balance sheets for all FDIC-insured banks in the United States in 2014, and their percentages of total assets (i.e., a common size balance sheet). Each of these items are discussed below:

Cash and Due

Commercial banks hold short-term assets for liquidity and transactions, since deposits can be withdrawn at any time. Typical short-term assets for banks include:

1 *Vault cash* that covers deposit withdrawals.
2 *Deposits held at Federal Reserve Banks and other financial institutions* to meet the largest portion of a bank's reserve requirements; these are not really liquid assets. Smaller banks often hold deposits at other financial institutions (compensating balances) as payments for check clearing, advisory services, and other services provided by their correspondent banks.
3 *Cash in the process of collection (CIPC).* CIPC includes checks written against other financial institutions but not yet cleared. Since cash type holdings earn low or no interests, banks try to minimize these holdings within safe limits for the liquidity needed.

TABLE 4.1 | FDIC statistics on depository institutions: Balance sheet*

Assets and liabilities	Percentage total average assets
Assets	
Cash and due from depository institutions	12.80%
Interest-bearing balances	11.34%
Securities	20.27%
Federal funds sold and reverse repurchase agreements	2.46%
Net loans and leases	51.95%
Loan loss allowance	0.78%
Trading account assets	4.52%
Bank premises and fixed assets	0.77%
Other real estate owned	0.14%
Goodwill and other intangibles	2.39%
All other assets	4.69%
Liabilities and capital	
Total liabilities	88.84%
Total deposits	75.57%
Interest-bearing deposits	55.67%
Deposits held in domestic offices	63.93%
Fed Funds purchases and repurchase agreements	2.03%
Trading liabilities	2.04%
Other borrowed funds	6.23%
Subordinated debt	0.67%
All other liabilities	2.30%
Total equity capital	11.16%

*As of December 31, 2014; all U.S. national FDIC-insured commercial banks; percentage of average assets; 5,642 commercial banks reporting.

Source: www2.fdic.gov

As shown in Table 4.1, in 2014, for U.S. national banks insured by the FDIC, *cash and due was about 12.80%* of total average assets and *interest-bearing balances about 11.34%*, a total of about *24.14%* of total average assets held on average for the 5,642 commercial banks reporting.

Securities

Commercial banks hold securities for both liquidity and as a source of profit, with short-term securities held primarily for liquidity purposes and longer-term securities as a source of profitability, particularly for countercyclical profitability when loan demand is low. In 2014, the average FDIC-insured banks held about *20.27%* of average total assets in securities. Regulators *require banks to hold securities with low default risk*. Banks can generally hold unlimited amounts of U.S. Treasury and federal agency securities, including mortgage-backed securities issued by government agencies and general obligation municipal securities (those guaranteed by the general funds of the issuers), as well as limited amounts of investment grade (BBB/Baa ratings or better) securities. Banks must classify investment securities as *"held to maturity"* (held at book value) or *"available for sale"* (held at market value).

Short-term Securities (Less Than 1 Year to Maturity)

Banks hold short-term securities for liquidity purposes as a primary form of stored liquidity:

1   *Fed Funds sold (FFS)* are excess reserves at the Fed that are traded among banks. If a bank has excess reserves (i.e., excess cash and deposits held at the Federal Reserve for the Fed's reserve requirements), it can lend this to another bank that has deficit reserves and make interest on this money. Fed Funds sold are assets, while Fed Funds purchased are liabilities. The Fed Funds rate is an indicator of liquidity in bank markets and, as noted, is used by the Fed in the United States as a target for its FOMC operations. Maturities are tailor-made, ranging from overnight to a year.
2   *Repurchase agreements (repos).* Repos represent the short-term sale of Treasury bills or other liquid securities by a bank to another, agreed to be repurchased at a higher price by the borrowing bank (i.e., an exceptionally short-term, collateralized loan). *To the lending bank, this repurchase agreement is a short-term asset, called a reverse repurchase agreement.* Repos can be tailor-made for any maturity, but generally are overnight or very short-term. In 2014, in the United States FDIC-insured banks held *on average about 2.46%* of average total assets as FFS and repos.
3   *Trading account assets* are securities, primarily Treasury or municipal securities traded by large banks (with > $1 billion in assets) to make a short-term profit. Large banks often serve as government security dealers and/or municipal security underwriters, bearing any market risk for these issues. They make profits by selling securities for prices greater than their purchase price. These trading account securities must appear on the balance sheet at market value, with any market value losses or gains reflected in income. In 2014, on average *4.52%* of bank assets were held as trading account assets, *with 4.91% on average* held by large banks with > $1 billion in assets.

Other short-term securities (held for liquidity by large banks) include other types of short-term securities as well, such as commercial paper and bankers' acceptances or negotiable CDs, and Treasury bills and agency bills, discussed in more detail later in Module VI Asset and Liability Management and Innovations.

Longer-term Investment Securities

To reduce their interest rate risk, banks generally prefer to avoid securities with maturities greater than ten years. National banks cannot own stock except shares they acquire as loan collateral or stock they hold in Federal Reserve banks. So longer-term securities are kept for secondary liquidity and to generate countercyclical income. When loan demand goes down, a bank's investment security generally gets larger. Often a portion of securities are not available for sale and cannot be held for liquidity if they are secured for *pledged deposits*: Tax, state, city government deposits that are uninsured government deposits are often pledged deposits whereby an equivalent portion of the security portfolio is pledged for these (so cannot be sold for liquidity).

Loans and Leases

Loans are the primary asset class for commercial banks, with net loans and leases about *51.95% of average total assets* for FDIC-insured banks in 2014. On a bank's balance sheet loans appear as *gross loans* held at book value. On the balance sheet a contra account, a*llowance for loan losses (about 0.77% in 2014 for FDIC-insured commercial banks)*, follows gross loans and is *a cumulative account whereby loan loss provisions are added each year less net loan loss charge-off (net loan losses less recoveries).*

Net loans = Gross loans – Loan loss allowance.

Major Different Types of Loan Held by Insured Banks

Table 4.2 shows the different types of loans held by FDIC-insured commercial banks in 2014 as a percentage of average total assets. Commercial banks are diversified with different types of banks specializing in different areas, but on average in 2014, 25.59% of total assets were real estate loans, 11.40% commercial and industrial loans, and 8.96% consumer loans (loans to individuals), and 0.52% farm loans.

1 **Real estate loans.** Real estate loans are secured by real property and generally have longer-term maturities, and hence greater interest rate risk, market value, and prepayment risk. Banks often sell or securitize loans (package loans into portfolios that are sold as pass-through securities to investors) to reduce this risk.

   Different types of real estate loans include: (1) construction and land development loans (about 1.54% of FDIC-insured bank assets in 2014) that are more risky than other types of loans since their repayment depends on successful completion of the development and high occupancy rates once the development is completed; (2) commercial real estate loans (about 7.29% of total average assets) that also depend on successful occupancy rates; (3) 1–4 family residential which tend to be less risky loans (14.14%), and farmland (0.56%) and real estate in foreign offices (0.46%).

2 **Commercial loans.** Commercial loans generally are intermediate term (a few months to five or more years to maturity). Banks generally are not allowed by regulators to lend

TABLE 4.2 | FDIC statistics on depository institutions: Loans as percentage average assets*

Net loans and leases	Percentage total average assets
Gross loans and leases	52.73%
Loan loss allowance	0.78%
Net loans and leases	51.95%
All real estate loans	25.59%
Construction and land development	1.54%
Commercial real estate (CRE)	7.29%
CRE owner occupied	3.11%
Other nonfarm residential	4.17%
Multifamily residential real estate	1.61%
1–4 family residential	14.14%
Farmland	0.56%
Real estate loans to foreign offices	0.46%
Farm loans	0.52%
Commercial and industrial loans	11.40%
Loans to individuals (consumer loans) (includes credit cards, other revolving credit plans, automobile loans, and other loans to individuals)	8.96%
Other loans and leases Includes loans to foreign governments and official institutions, obligations of states and political subdivisions in the U.S., other loans, and lease financing receivables and loans to depository institutions and acceptances of other banks.	6.27%

*As of December 31, 2014 includes all U.S. national FDIC-insured commercial banks; percentage of average assets; 5,642 commercial banks reporting.

Source: www2.fdic.gov

more than 15% of equity capital or 25% if a loan is collateralized by risk-free securities to one borrower. Thus, often syndicates with other banks are used for large loans.

3   **Loans to individuals (consumer loans).** These include credit card loans and related plans, automobile loans, and other loans to individuals for car, education, and home improvement expenses, among others. Consumer loans are generally short-term (few months to three years), so have less interest rate risk.

4   **Other loans and leases.** These include other types of loans and leases not previously listed including those to foreign governments and official institutions, such as obligations of states and political subdivisions in the United States, lease financing receivables, and loans to depository institutions and acceptances of other banks. These loans include loans of non-Fed Funds to other financial institutions, loans to brokers, dealers, and individuals for securities purchases; loans to nonprofit organizations, agricultural loans, and loans to governments, among others.

Other Assets

Other assets listed include bank premises and fixed assets, other real estate owned, intangible assets, and other items that are not significant enough to merit their own categories. Other assets in 2014 for U.S. FDIC-insured banks were about 4.69% of average total assets.

Bank Premises and Fixed Assets, and Other Real Estate Owned and Goodwill and Intangibles

Bank premises and fixed assets encompass both the depreciated value of bank buildings and equipment. Banks have low operating leverage compared to other businesses, with just 0.77% of total average assets bank premises and fixed assets in 2014. Other real estate owned (OREO) includes property taken as collateral for unpaid loans, listed at market value. Problem banks carry large OREO accounts. Intangible assets include goodwill often associated with bank mergers and acquisitions.

BANK LIABILITIES AND EQUITY CAPITAL

Bank Deposits

As shown in Table 4.1, the majority of the *average bank's liabilities are deposits, 75.57% of average total assets* for banks in 2014. Also, banks are highly financially levered, with liabilities for FDCI-insured commercial banks about 88.84% of total average assets, and total equity capital 11.16%, that is, an equity multiplier of (1/ 0.1116) or 8.96 x. Given an average ROA of 1% for FDIC-insured commercial banks in 2014, this implies an 8.96% average ROE (ROA × EM).

Bank deposits are generally divided into two general categories:

1 *Transaction deposits* that have check-writing privileges (reserve requirements are required for most of these deposits).
2 *Nontransaction deposits*, that is, savings and time deposits.

They are also often categorized into:

1 *Core (insured deposits)* which are stable insured deposits that tend to stay with the banks, so have less liquidity risk.
2 *Purchased funds or volatile (large time) deposits* that are large time deposits and include jumbo CDs and brokered deposits—interest-sensitive, so may leave the bank with bad news or more competitive rates elsewhere (pay higher rates, so more expensive).

Banks desire greater numbers of core deposits that are cheaper and have less liquidity risk on the liability side.

Transaction accounts (checking accounts) include many different types of accounts, generally with higher rates and lower service charges for higher minimum amounts deposited, such as negotiable order of withdrawal (NOW) accounts or Super NOW accounts that require larger minimums and pay slightly higher interest. *Demand deposits* are primarily for check writing for business demand deposits. Previously, under Regulation Q, banks in the U.S. Federal Reserve System were prohibited from paying interest on demand deposits. In July 2011, the Federal Reserve Board approved a final rule to repeal this restriction under Section 627 of the Dodd–Frank Wall Street Reform and Consumer Protection Act (Fed, 2011).

Nontransaction deposits include *money market deposit accounts (MMDAs)*, where banks often limit the number of checks that can be written each month. *Other savings deposits* include different types of savings deposits that let savers withdraw funds, but not write checks. *Time deposits* are often called certificates of deposit (CDs) and set fixed maturity dates. Banks often impose *prepayment penalties* equal to stated numbers of interest payments, for early withdrawals. Relatively small CDs (those for less than $100,000) are often called *retail CDs*, while larger time deposits are called jumbo CDs. FDIC deposit insurance covers the balances of NOW accounts, MMDAs, savings, and retail CDs up to $250,000 per depositor, per insured bank, for each account ownership category. These *core (insured) deposits*, are coveted, since they tend to be stable and have low interest rates, so are less costly and entail less interest rate risk.

Purchased funds, often called "volatile liabilities" include: Negotiated "jumbo CDs" of large, well-known banks typically having denominations of $1 million and trading in a well-established secondary market. Securities firms often broker jumbo CDs that are up to the insured deposit limit for large banks, allowing customers to buy securities with high rates, called brokered CDs. Other types of uninsured borrowed funds are also included. Since these types of funds are very sensitive to interest rate changes and can leave the bank at any time if there is bad news or other banks offer higher rates, they increase a bank's liquidity risk, as well as being more expensive than core deposits. Regulators have imposed restrictions on the use of brokered deposits to well-capitalized banks, since they have been associated with bank crises in the past.

Nondeposit Liabilities

Nondeposit liabilities representing about 13.27% of FDIC-insured commercial bank liabilities in 2014 include: Fed Funds purchased and repurchase agreements, FHLB advances, trading account liabilities, other borrowed money, subordinated debt, and other liabilities:

1   *Fed Funds purchased and repos* (borrowed funds, often overnight) are excess reserves borrowed from other financial institutions, and repurchase agreements (repos) are short-term collateralized borrowing, selling low-risk securities, such as Treasury bills with the agreement to purchase them back at a higher price in the very near future (often the next day), *often engaged in by large banks as liability managers.*
2   *Other borrowed funds* (short-term commercial paper, Eurodollar CDs, bankers' acceptances) are short-term securities that can be traded prior to maturity discussed in Module VI under liability management. Other types of borrowed money, including *FHLB advances* (short-term borrowings from the Federal Home Loan Bank System), are often used, among other short-term borrowings.
3   *Subordinated debt* (with maturities of 1 year or greater); claims subordinate to depositors, so included at times as secondary capital for regulatory capital requirement purposes.
4   *Other liabilities* includes taxes and dividends payable, acceptances and trade credit outstanding, among other miscellaneous items that do not fit in other categories.

Bank Equity Capital

Bank equity capital includes common stock (both the par legal value and surplus amount paid over a legal par value), and retained earnings (often reported in bank financial statements as undivided profits). Equity accounts also often include other equity or contingency reserves. The amount reflects reserves against losses on securities or other contingencies. Smaller banks tend to have higher equity ratios on average, since they are less diversified and have less external sources of financing, so need a larger equity capital cushion.

BANK INCOME STATEMENTS

Table 4.3 shows a typical bank income statement for the average FDIC–insured commercial bank in the United States. Since each of the items shown are a percentage of total average assets, the net interest income % is the average NIM of 2.77%, the difference between the IR% (total interest income %) of 3.06% and the IE% (total interest expense %) of 0.29. The noninterest income % (NIR%) is 1.61% on average and the noninterest expense (NIE%) is 2.77%, or a burden expense % of 1.16% (NIE% – NIR%).

This gives a pre-tax net operating income % (OROA before taxes) of 1.42%. On average the security gain % was 0.02% and the average tax rate was 0.44%, resulting in an average net income % (ROA) of 1%. This very small ROA of 1% is very typical for banks, emphasizing the importance of the equity multiplier (EM) for generating a good ROE, in this case with the EM of 8.96, an average of 8.96%.

Using Income Relationships to Forecast Target NIMs

Forecasting NIM Based on a Target OROA (Before Taxes and Security Gains)

Given: NIM – PLL% – Burden%, a target NIM can be solved for as:

Target NIM = Target OROA + PLL% + Burden %.

Example Suppose a bank manager has a marginal tax rate of 30%, and a target OROA of 1.25% after taxes, so the required before tax OROA is solved for as 1.25% / (1.30) which equals a desired 1.786% before tax OROA. Also, suppose the bank expects to have a PLL% of 0.30%, and a Burden% of 1.5%.

What is the target NIM that the bank needs to make to achieve its desired 1.786% target OROA before taxes?

Solving for Target NIM = Target OROA + PLL% + Burden%

Target NIM = 1.786% + 0.30% + 1.50% = 3.586%.

The bank would have to earn a 3.586% target NIM to get its desired 1.786% target OROA before taxes.

TABLE 4.3 | FDIC statistics on depository institutions: Income statement*

Income and expense	Percentage total average assets
Total interest income	3.06%
Total interest expense	0.29%
Net interest income	2.77%
Provision for loan and lease losses	0.18%
Total noninterest income	1.61%
Fiduciary activities	0.22%
Service charges on deposit accounts	0.23%
Trading account gains and fees	0.16%
Additional noninterest income	1.00%
Total noninterest expense	2.77%
Salaries and employee benefits	1.26%
Premises and equipment expense	0.30%
Additional noninterest expense	1.21%
Pre-tax net operating income	1.42%
Securities gains (losses)	0.02%
Applicable income taxes	0.44%
Net income	1.00%
Net charge-offs	0.26%
Cash dividends	0.59%
Sale, conversion, retirement of capital stock	0.02%

*As of December 31, 2014; includes all U.S. national FDIC-insured commercial banks; percentage of average assets; 5,642 commercial banks reporting.

Source: www2.fdic.gov/SDI

Forecasting a Target ROA and NPM Based on a Target ROE

Given the Dupont relationships discussed in Chapter 1, where:

$$ROE = ROA \times EM$$
$$ROA = NPM \times AU$$

and putting these together:

$$ROE = NPM \times AU \times EM,$$

where:

ROA = [Net income / Assets] or your net income % of total assets;

EM = [Total assets / Equity] or {1 / [Equity/Assets]};

NPM = [Net income / Revenues];

AU = [Revenues /Assets].

Suppose a bank manager has a desired target ROE of 16%, and the bank has an EM of 10 x, and its IR% (interest revenue to assets) is 5% and its NIR% is 3%, what is the bank's target ROA? What is the bank's AU? What is the bank's target NPM?

Solving for *Target ROA* = Target ROE / EM = [16% / 10] = 1.6%:

AU = [Revenues/Assets] = IR% + NIR% = 5% + 3% = 8% or 0.08 as a fraction.

Solving for *Target NPM* = [Target ROA / AU as a fraction] = [1.6% / 0.08] = 20%

Proof:

ROE = NPM × AU × EM = 20% × 0.08 × 10 = desired 16%.

Overview of a Bank's Performance Analysis Using a Uniform Bank Performance Report

To analyze a depository institution, it's helpful to use a common size income statement, where each income statement item is put as a percentage of average total assets. Uniform bank performance reports (UBPRs) published for U.S. federally insured depository institutions provide such an analysis

Typical performance ratios on the first page of a uniform bank performance report are shown on the sample UBPR format for a fictional Bank Star (Table 4.4) for the years 2007, 2006, and 2005, before the U.S. subprime loan crisis. On page 01 of a UBPR report, the top half is a bank's earning and profitability analysis, with the bank's income statement put as a percentage of average total assets (i.e., a common size income statement). Hence, with each item as a percentage of average total assets, the interest income is the IR%, the interest expense, the IE%, the net interest income, the NIM% for the bank, the noninterest income, the NIR%, the noninterest expense, the NIE%, the provision for loan and lease losses, the PLL%, the pre-tax net operating income, the OROA, and the net income, the ROA. Note the "TE" after interest income stands for tax equivalent, with any nontaxable interest revenue put on a before tax basis by dividing by $(1 - t)$, so it is before tax, tax-equivalent income.

Using the earnings and profitability analysis at the top of the first page of each UBPR, an analyst can examine the trends in ROA and why they changed over time and also compare these to the PG2 (similar size peer banks) each year, to examine the strengths and weaknesses of the bank. For this example for Bank Star, which is a bank with $1,636,242,000 or about $1.636 billion in average total assets, it is compared to similar size banks, categorized as Peer Group 2 (PG2).

Analysis of Why ROA Changed Over Time for Bank Star from 2005 to 2007

Looking at the trends on the sample UBPR earnings and profitability analysis, you can see that the ROA (net income %) went down from 1.15% in 2005, and then up to 1.42% in 2006,

TABLE 4.4 | UBPR for Bank Star, p. 01: Earnings and profitability and risk analysis

	12/31/2007		12/31/2006		12/31/2005	
Average assets ($000)	1,636,242		1,024,807		657,369	
Net income ($000)	11,842		14,549		7,571	
Number of banks in peer group	297		286		1,075	
Earnings and profitability	Bank	PG2	Bank	PG2	Bank	PG2
% Average assets						
Interest income (TE)	8.25	6.73	8.31	6.52	7.07	5.84
− Interest expense	4.51	3.07	4.03	2.73	3.07	1.89
Net interest income (TE)	3.74	3.66	4.28	3.82	4.00	3.96
+ Noninterest income	0.24	0.95	0.30	0.97	0.33	0.88
− Noninterest expense	1.48	2.79	1.68	2.74	2.03	2.86
− Provision: loan and lease losses	1.34	0.28	0.64	0.16	0.49	0.17
= Pretax operating income (TE)	1.16	1.58	2.27	1.96	1.82	1.84
+ Realized gains/losses securities	0.00	0.00	0.00	0.00	0.00	0.00
= Pretax net operating income (TE)	1.16	1.57	2.28	1.95	1.82	1.85
Net operating income (OROA)	0.72	1.08	1.42	1.30	1.15	1.27
Margin analysis						
Average earning assets %	95.8	93.5	95.9	93.4	96.2	93.7
Average interest-bearing funds to average assets	86.4	81.3	85.4	80.8	85.6	78.8
Interest income (TE) to average earning assets	8.61	7.22	8.67	7.02	7.34	6.24
Interest expense to average earning assets	4.71	3.29	4.20	2.92	3.18	2.01
Net interest income (TE) to average earning assets	3.90	3.95	4.47	4.12	4.16	4.24
Loan and lease analysis						
Net loss to average total loans and leases	0.25	0.24	0.20	0.14	0.32	0.13
Earnings coverage of net loss (X)	11.9	22.7	17.9	47.9	9.09	47.2
Loans and leases allowance to net losses (X)	8.95	11.2	6.53	19.2	3.50	21.0
Loans and leases allowance to loans and leases not held for sale	1.83	1.24	1.02	1.18	0.94	1.23
Loans and leases allowance to total loans and leases	1.83	1.22	1.02	1.16	0.94	1.22
Noncurrent loans and leases to gross loans and leases	1.38	1.08	1.06	0.59	0.74	0.49

(Continued)

TABLE 4.4 | (Continued)

Earnings and profitability	Bank	PG2	Bank	PG2	Bank	PG2
Liquidity						
Net noncore funding dependence	69.3	29.3	57.9	27.3	45.3	22.3
Net loans and leases to assets	79.8	72.1	78.4	71.3	76.5	69.4
Capitalization						
Tier 1 leverage capital	8.67	8.73	9.97	8.70	8.61	8.88
Cash dividends to net income	0.00	46.7	0.00	44.1	0.00	36.2
Retained earnings to average total equity	8.03	4.56	15.5	6.93	13.4	8.00
Growth rates						
Assets	49.3	10.5	66.2	13.0	52.9	11.9
Tier 1 capital	29.2	9.94	89.5	14.2	42.6	13.0
Net loans and leases	51.9	11.9	70.4	15.1	45.0	13.4
Short-term investments	-24.	13.3	-47.	69.	151.	104.
Short-term noncore funding	94.9	17.9	122.	31.2	35.3	29.9

Note: TE, tax equivalent; X, times covered

but then declined to 0.72% in 2007. Using OROA = NIM − PLL% − Burden%, we can see why the ROA changed each year. Since the Burden% (Noninterest Expense % − Noninterest Revenue %) has not been calculated we can calculate this for each year as (NIE% − NIR%). Note on the UBPRs, since each figure is calculated separately, subtracted amounts may be slightly off for NIM or other figures (so these are recalculated here, so NIMs, and OROAs are slightly different, but the same trends).

	12/31/2007		12/31/2006		12/31/2005	
	Bank	PG2	Bank	PG2	Bank	PG2
IR%	8.25	6.73	8.31	6.52	7.07	5.84
IE%	4.51	3.07	4.03	2.73	3.07	1.89
NIM	3.74	3.66	4.28	3.79	4.00	3.95
NIE%	1.48	2.79	1.68	2.74	2.03	2.86
NIR%	0.24	0.95	0.30	0.97	0.33	0.88
Burden%	1.24	1.84	1.38	1.77	1.70	1.98
PLL%	1.34	0.28	0.64	0.16	0.49	0.17
OROA	1.16	1.54	2.26	1.86	1.81	1.80

Reason for Bank Star's OROA Going Up in 2006 and PG2 Comparison

As shown above for Bank Star (BK), the reason its OROA rose in 2006 from 2005 was the result of a rise in its NIM by 0.28% (28 basis points) from 4% to 4.28%, and a fall in its Burden% by 0.32% from 1.70% to 1.38%, despite a rise in its PLL% by 0.15%.

The rise in the NIM by 0.28% was the result of a larger rise in its IR% by 1.24% than the rise in its IE% by 0.96% with a rise in rates in 2006, suggesting a positive funding gap.

The 0.32% fall in the Burden% was the result of large fall in the NIE% by 0.35% relative to a small 0.03% fall in the NIR%. Hence, the burden improvement was due to improved cost efficiency.

Compared to the PG2 in 2005 and 2006, Bank Star has a much higher IR%, but also a higher IE%. With the much higher IR%, Bank Star has higher NIM each year than its peers. Bank Star also has a lower NIE% each year, but a lower NIR%, and a lower Burden% each year than the PG. However, Bank Star has a higher PLL% than the PG2 each year. Hence, Bank Star has strengths in terms of a higher IR% and lower NIE% than the PG, but weaknesses in terms of a lower NIR%, a higher IE%, and higher PLL% than its peers.

The PG2 in contrast to Bank Star has a fall in NIM in 2006 by 0.16% with the rise in rates, with a larger rise in IE% by 0.84% compared to a rise in IR% by 0.68%, suggesting a negative funding gap. However, despite the fall in NIM, the PG2 OROA went up slightly in 2006 by 0.06% (6 basis points), because of a decline in the Burden% by 0.21% (with a drop in NIE% by 0.12% and rise in NIR% by 0.09%) and a slight 0.01% fall in PLL%.

Reason for Bank Star's OROA Going Down in 2007 and PG2 Comparison

In 2007, Bank Star had a large drop in its OROA by 1.10% (48.67% drop from 2006) as the result of a 0.54% lower NIM%, and a 0.70% higher PLL% (a 109% rise over 2006), despite a drop in the Burden% by 0.14%. The drop in the NIM% was the result of a very small rise of 0.06% in the IR%, offset by a large 0.48% rise in IE%. The Burden% fell as the result of a 0.20% fall in NIE%, despite a small 0.06% fall in NIR%. Hence, Bank Star has a problem with a rising IE% and a rising PLL%. In this case with the rise in rates and larger rise in the IE%, this suggests that Bank Star has a negative funding gap.

Compared to the PG2 in 2007, Bank Star still has a higher IR%, but a much higher IE% than the PG2, resulting in less of a difference in the NIM from the PG2 in 2006, only 0.08% (8 basis points) higher. Bank Star continues to have a much lower NIR%, but a lower NIE%, resulting in a lower Burden% than the PG2 as a strength. Bank Star's PLL%, however, is much higher than the PG2, having more than doubled in 2007.

The PG2 also had a drop in OROA in 2007 but not as large, just by 0.32%, as the result of a fall in NIM by 0.13%, and a rise in Burden% by 0.07%, and rise in PLL% by 0.12%. The fall in the NIM was the result of a rise in rates, with a larger rise in IE% by 0.34% compared to a rise in IR% by 0.21%, suggesting a smaller negative funding gap. The slight rise in burden was the result of a slight rise in NIE% by 0.05% and a slight fall in NIR% by 0.02.

Dupont Analysis for Bank Star and the PG2

At the bottom of page 01 of a UBPR, you'll see risk ratios for different bank risks. If you look under Capitalization towards the bottom you'll see the Tier 1 leverage capital ratio for the bank and PG2 as follows:

Capitalization	12/31/2007		12/31/2006		12/31/2005	
	Bank	PG2	Bank	PG2	Bank	PG2
Tier 1						
Leverage capital	8.67	8.73	9.97	8.70	8.61	8.88

The Tier 1 leverage capital for banks is essentially the equity to total average assets ratio. So you can solve for the EM for each year as:

EM = [1 / (Tier 1 leverage capital ratio as a fraction)].

To solve for the NPM and AU, given the ROA, you first need to find the AU. The AU% each year is just the sum of interest revenue to average assets + noninterest revenue to average assets, which gives you total revenue to average assets. Hence:

AU = IR% + NIR%.

Then you can solve for

NPM = [ROA / (AU as a fraction)],

since NPM × AU equals ROA, so solving for NPM = ROA / AU.

For example for Bank Star in 2007, AU = IR% 8.25% + NIR% 0.24% = 8.49%, so NPM = ROA/AU = [0.72% / 0.0849] = 8.48%.

Having AU and NPM, you can analyze their trends to see why the ROA changes based on revenue generation and cost efficiency. You can also solve for the ROE = ROA × EM.

Since the Tier 1 leverage capital ratio is 8.67%, then the EM = (1 /.0867) = 11.53. So the ROE for Bank Star = ROA × EM = (0.72% × 11.53) = 8.30%. As a check for the NPM calculation, ROE = NPM × AU × EM = 8.48% NPM × AU .0849 = ROA of 0.72% × EM of 11.53 = ROE of 8.30%.

ROE analysis%	2007		2006		2005	
	Bank	PG2	Bank	PG2	Bank	PG3
ROE	8.30	12.38	14.24	14.94	13.35	14.30
ROA	0.72	1.08	1.42	1.30	1.15	1.27
EM	11.53	11.46	10.03	11.49	11.61	11.26
AU	8.49	7.68	8.61	7.49	7.40	6.72
NPM	8.48	14.06	16.49	17.36	15.54	18.90

Performing a Dupont Analysis for Bank Star, its ROE rose in 2006 as the result of a higher ROA, despite a lower EM. The ROA rose as the result of high AU and a higher NPM, indicating improvements in both revenue generation and cost management.

In 2007, the ROE fell as the result of a much lower ROA, despite a higher EM. The ROA fell as the result of a lower NPM, as well as a slight decline in AU. Hence, Bank Star in 2007 is having problems with managing costs with the lower NPM, resulting in its lower ROA, and a lower ROE, despite a higher EM in 2007.

Doing a peer comparison, Bank Star had a lower ROE in 2005 as the result of a lower NPM, despite a higher AU and a slightly higher EM. In 2006, Bank Star's ROE was closer but lower than the PG ROE, despite a higher ROA, because of a lower EM. The higher ROA was the result of higher AU, despite a lower NPM. In 2007, Bank Star's ROE was much lower as the result of a lower ROA, despite a slightly higher EM. The lower ROA was the result of a much lower NPM, despite a higher AU. Both Star Bank and the PG2 had declines in NPM over the three years, resulting in lower ROAs.

Analyzing the Risk Profile for Bank Star

The lower half of page 01 of the Bank Star's UBPR, provides a snapshot of the bank's margin analysis and risk profile by presenting different risk ratios.

Margin Analysis and Interest Rate Risk Analysis

Margin analysis provides more details on a bank's NIM based on average earning assets, including a summary of volume effects in terms of the percentage of average earning assets. Bank Star has a slightly larger percentage of earning assets each year, helping to explain its higher IR%. The percentage of average interest-bearing funds also helps to explain a bank's IE%. Bank Star has a higher percentage of interest-bearing funds, helping to explain its higher IE%. Looking at the trends, you can also see that with rates rising in 2006, the NIM based on earning assets rose, suggesting a positive funding gap for Bank Star. However, the PG2 has a fall in NIM, suggesting a negative funding gap. In 2007, the NIM fell for both Bank Star and the PG2 with what appears to be a rise in rates at this time with the IR% and IE% rising for the PG2, and just the IE% rising for Bank Star. For both Bank Star and the PG2, with the large rise in IE%, the NIM fell, consistent with a negative funding gap for each.

LOAN AND LEASE ANALYSIS AND CREDIT RISK ANALYSIS

The loan and lease analysis provides a snapshot of the credit risk for the bank. The net loss to average total loans and leases provides trends and peer comparison for the percentage of actual loan losses. The net loss percentage for Bank Star is slightly higher each year than the PG2. The noncurrent loans and leases (non-CUR LN&LS) to gross loans and leases (Gross LN&LS) is the percentage of loans that are nonpaying relative to gross loans, a ratio that is higher for Bank Star each year than the PG2. This suggests greater future credit risk for Bank Star, and explains the reason for managers to have taken a larger PLL% over time, with the percentage of noncurrent loans and leases also rising each year. Since Bank Star appears to have greater credit risk, it should be holding a higher loan and lease allowance to loans and to net losses than its peers. In 2005 and 2006, Bank Star's loan allowance to total loans and leases was lower than its peers, but higher in 2007. The bank's loan loss allowance to net losses was much lower each year than its peers, but rose in 2007. The earnings coverage to net losses indicates the bank's ability to withstand losses from earnings each year. Bank Star has a much lower ratio than its peers each year. This suggests greater credit risk for Bank Star than the PG2.

LIQUIDITY

The liquidity ratio net noncore fund dependence gives the trends for a bank's liquidity risk on the liability side with large noncore fund dependence making a bank more vulnerable to liquidity risk, if noncore fund depositors or liability holders withdraw their funds from the bank with bad news or higher rates offered by other banks or for other investments. The net loans and leases to assets ratio indicates how loaned up a bank is on the liability side, with a higher ratio indicating less liquidity on the asset side. Bank Star clearly has greater liquidity risk in both areas with a higher percentage of net loans that has risen over time and a much higher percentage of net noncore fund dependence that has also been rising each year. As shown under growth rates, Bank Star has had a negative growth rate in short-term investments in 2007 and 2006, also suggesting lower liquidity on the asset side, and has a much higher short-term noncore funding ratio than the PG2 each year, suggesting greater liquidity risk on the liability side as well.

CAPITALIZATION AND GROWTH RATES

Bank Star in 2007 and 2005 has a lower Tier 1 leverage capital ratio than the PG2, but this was slightly higher than the PG2 in 2006. Bank Star's Tier 1 capital ratio fell by 13% from 9.97% in 2006 to 8.67% in 2007. Tier 1 capital grew at a lower rate than assets in 2007 and 2005, but at a higher rate in 2006. Bank Star has been retaining earnings at a higher rate than the PG2 each year, but its retained earnings to average total equity fell in 2007. The PG2 paid larger dividends to net income each year, with a 0% dividend payout for Bank Star. Bank Star has greater interest rate, credit, liquidity, and capital risk than the PG2, which should be of concern to the bank's managers. The higher IE% for Bank Star could reflect a risk premium for this greater risk profile.

Analyzing the Burden for Bank Star More Closely

To analyze more closely the trends in Bank Star's Burden%, we can look at page 3 of its UBPR that provides ratios for different types of noninterest expenses as shown in Table 4.5 for 2007 and 2006. The reasons for Bank Star's lower NIE% include lower personnel, occupancy, and other operating expenses each year, resulting in much lower total overhead expense to average assets each year. Since Bank Star had a lower NIR%, but lower NIE%, its overhead less noninterest income (NIR%) is still lower than the PG2. Bank Star's efficiency ratio (noninterest expense divided by the sum of net interest income and noninterest revenue) is lower (better) than the PG2 in 2006, but similar in 2007, due to Bank Star's lower net interest income that year. In terms of personnel expense to assets, Bank Star has a lower ratio each year, and higher assets to employee ratio, suggesting efficiency on the personnel side.

Analyzing Bank Star's NIM: Asset and Liability Rates and Mix

Looking at the lower half of page 03 of Bank Star's UBPR, the yields on different assets are shown, including the yield on total loans, followed by the cost (interest rate) for all interest-bearing liabilities, followed by information on different types of deposits and other liabilities. To explain Bank Star's higher IR%, its average yield is higher than the PG2 each year as are rates on each type of loan. To explain its higher IE%, similarly its cost of interest-bearing deposits is much higher each year than the PG2, as are its rates for each type of deposit and other borrowed money. The only liability rate that is lower for Bank Star relative to the PG is for Fed Funds purchased in 2007. The much higher average loan rate and much higher cost of interest-bearing funds each year suggests a risk premium for more risky loans, given Bank Star's higher net loan losses, and accordingly higher rates on uninsured time deposits and other borrowed money. Bank Star's interest rate fell on each type of loan and investment securities over time, with the exception of consumer loans explaining the larger fall in its IR% while the rate on each type of liability fell, but by a lesser amount.

TABLE 4.5 | UBPR for Bank Star, p. 03: Noninterest expenses and yields and cost of funds

	2007		2006	
	Bank	PG2	Bank	PG2
% Average assets				
Personnel expenses	0.60	1.41	0.60	1.48
Occupancy expenses	0.17	0.40	0.02	0.39
Other operating expenses	0.86	1.05	0.68	0.88
Total overhead expenses	1.63	2.92	1.48	2.79
Overhead less noninterest revenue	1.64	1.94	1.24	1.77
Efficiency ratio	66.6	66.92	37.2	59.55
Personnel expenses/assets	51.51	65	46.41	64.1
Assets/employee	8.48	5.1	9.31	4.83
Yields on total loan	7.37	6.52	9.15	7.83
Real estate	7.12	6.42	8.99	7.71
Commercial	8.29	6.58	10.01	8.45
Consumer	10.57	7.84	10.54	8.35
Investment securities	4.61	5.01	5.69	5.11
Fed Funds sold	2.53	2.06	5.15	5.11
Cost of interest bearing deposits	4.65	2.75	5.26	3.7
Transaction deposits	1.15	1.13	1.61	1.77
Savings deposits	2.08	1.51	3.23	2.58
Uninsured time	5.23	3.92	5.70	4.86
Fed Funds purchased	1.51	2.39	4.27	4.39

(Continued)

TABLE 4.5 | (Continued)

	2007		2006	
	Bank	PG2	Bank	PG2
Other borrowed money	4.58	3.58	4.95	4.86
All interest bearing funds	4.63	2.81	5.22	3.83

Analyzing Bank Star's Trends in Asset and Liability Mix

Analyzing Bank Star's loan mix, it's clear why Bank Star's IR% and its average rate on loans are so much higher than the PG2. Bank Star has a lower percentage of real estate loans than its peers, but the types of real estate loans it has are much riskier, with a larger percentage of construction and development loans and only a small percentage of less risky 1–4 family residential loans. Rates on more risky construction on development loans should be higher with the inclusion of a risk premium. Bank Star also has a larger percentage of agricultural loans, and lower percentages for consumer and commercial loans. Hence, Bank Star's higher IR% reflects higher loan rates for taking on additional risk with a larger percentage of more risky types of real estate loans, as shown in Table 4.6, including a large percentage of construction and development loans.

In terms of liabilities, Bank Star has a bit larger percentage of deposit financing, but a much lower percentage of cheaper core deposits than the PG2, helping to explain Bank Star's higher IE%. Bank Star also has a larger percentage of brokered deposits and uninsured deposits in its liability mix that demand higher rates, contributing to its higher IE%.

In terms of trends for asset mix, Bank Star increased its percentage of construction and development loans and agricultural loans slightly, and had a decline in its percentage of consumer and commercial loans. For liabilities, the percentage of core deposits went up, but was still much lower than the PG2 in 2007, and insured time deposits and brokered deposits went up and uninsured deposits went down. Bank Star appears to be undiversified and has greater credit risk in terms of holding more risky types of real estate loans. On the liability side, with a large percentage of brokered deposits and uninsured deposits, and a lower percentage of core deposits that are more stable deposits, Bank Star has great liquidity risk. Its higher rates on liabilities may also reflect a risk premium for Bank Star's more risky loan profile, with uninsured deposits and borrowings having a much higher rate than the PG2.

Detailed Risk Analysis Using Credit, Liquidity, Interest Rate, and Capital Ratios from Bank Star's UBPR Report

UBPRs provide detailed risk ratios for each of the different areas of a bank's risk. Selected ratios from each of these pages are included in Table 4.7 for 2007. UBPRs show concentration ratios as the total average amounts of different types of loans to total bank capital. As can be shown for Bank Star, the bank has considerable credit concentration risk with very large and much higher percentages for construction and development and agricultural loans than the peer averages. If these loans have problems, such as during the subprime loan crisis, the bank would have very serious problems covering losses.

Interest rate risk ratios taking long-term loans less long-term liabilities for greater than 1-year and greater than 3-year periods to get a net position show lower risk for rising rates

TABLE 4.6 | UBPR for Bank Star, p. 06: Balance sheet percentage composition and p. 07A: Loan mix (selected ratios taken from pages)

	2007		2006	
	Bank	*PG2*	*Bank*	*PG2*
% Average assets				
Net loans and leases	79.54	71.73	77.94	70.87
% Total loans				
Real estate loans	66.05	74.93	65.04	74.79
Construction and development	32.09	18.81	30.11	16.86
1–4 family residential	5.31	19.44	6.45	20.62
Other real estate loans	27.66	32.92	28.48	33.14
Agricultural loans	23.29	0.73	20.45	0.72
Commercial loans	10.03	15.36	12.28	14.90
Consumer loans	1.54	4.34	2.15	4.86
Liabilities				
Total deposits	80.72	78.13	81.18	78.30
Core deposits	23.77	56.29	14.68	56.85
Demand deposits	1.31	5.58	2.60	6.97
NOW accounts	0.33	2.37	1.16	2.77
Money market deposits	4.19	21.18	3.98	21.04
Other savings	3.70	10.37	3.49	10.00
Insured time deposits	45.03	18.46	24.85	16.51
(Brokered insurance deposits)	30.80	3.79	21.41	3.21
Uninsured time deposits	26.15	15.28	45.09	16.01
Fed Funds purchased	0.64	3.46	0.47	3.41
FHLB borrowings	8.77	5.01	8.57	4.98
Equity				
Bank capital	9.02	9.99	9.13	9.76

Note: NOW accounts, negotiable order of withdrawal accounts.

than the PG2 with lower net positions in 2007. Bank Star also has a lower percentage of off-balance sheet items.

For liquidity risk, however, there are indicators of significant problems for Bank Star. The bank appears to have significant problems with its high dependence on brokered deposits, including a larger percentage that will mature in a year, and a large noncore fund dependence, with the ratio of short-term investments to noncore funds very small. Given the larger credit and liquidity risk that Bank Star has, it should be holding a larger percentage of equity capital to average total assets, but its Tier 1 capital ratio is slightly smaller than the PG2 average.

TABLE 4.7 | UBPR for Bank Star, Selected risk ratios: credit, liquidity, interest rate risk, off balance sheet, and capital risk

	2007	
	Bank	PG2
Credit risk concentration		
% Bank capital		
Construction and development loans	275.28	147.33
Agricultural loans	203.90	5.47
Commercial loans	71.92	114.91
Consumer loans	11.49	31.48
Total retained earnings loans	583.74	581.62
Interest-rate risk		
Loans/securities > 3 years	18.64	31.11
Liabilities > 3 years	2.05	2.57
Net 3 year position	16.59	28.12
Loans/securities > 1 year	32.64	47.20
Liabilities > 1 year	21.08	8.70
Net 1 year position	11.56	37.72
% Off-balance sheet items	11.95	21.85
Liquidity risk		
% Loan commitments	11.41	19.46
Net noncore funding deposit	69.29	32.11
Brokered deposits < 1 year	74.05	57.02
Brokered deposits to deposits	45.50	5.74
Short-term investments to short-term noncore deposit	5.13	19.71
Tier 1 capital%	*8.67*	*8.73*

What Happened to Bank Star?

The real bank of a different name on which Bank Star was modeled was closed by the Federal Deposit Insurance Corporation (FDIC) in April 2009, after being under a cease and desist enforcement action in December 2008. The FDIC observed in December 2008 that the bank was following unsafe or unsound banking practices and violations of law and/or regulations including: (1) operating with an inadequate level of capital protection for the kind and quality of assets it held; (2) failing to provide adequate allowance for loan and leases losses; and (3) operating without adequate liquidity or regard for its funds management with a risky bank asset and liability mix—this included a heavy reliance on short-term, volatile deposits as a source of funds for longer-term investments; (4) creating high levels of concentration of credit; (5) operating the bank with inadequate earnings to fund growth, dividend payments, and the augmentation of capital; and (6) operating with uncontrolled growth without regard to protecting capital. Hints of these problems were shown earlier when doing the analysis that we did for Bank Star.

IMPORTANCE OF COMPARISONS FOR PEER BANKS

Large banks have considerable differences when compared with community banks with less than $1 billion in assets, so it's important to do peer comparisons for similar banks.

There has been a great deal of consolidation in the banking industry in the United States and globally. To illustrate this, at the end of 2013 there were 5,880 FDIC-insured banks. This compares to 12,351 in 1990 and 8,317 in 2000, and 7,527 in 2005. Following the subprime loan crisis from 2007 to 2013, the number of FDIC-insured financial institutions in the United States fell by 1,414 (from 7,294 in 2007 to 5,880 in 2013) with a large number of mergers, including 408 mergers for failing banks and other unassisted FDIC mergers (source: www2. fdic.gov).

It's important for peer comparisons to compare banks with similar size peer banks, since very large and smaller banks have very different income and balance sheet statements, with smaller banks often having larger net interest spreads and NIMs, but lower percentages of noninterest revenue. For instance, compare income statements for FDIC-insured commercial banks with assets of $100 million to $1 billion to commercial banks with assets greater than $1 billion (all shown as a percentage of total average assets in 2014):

2014 Comparison for profitability measures for small and large banks

Percentage average assets	Banks $100 million to $1 billion	Banks more than $1 billion
Net interest margin	3.47%	2.71%
Provision for loan losses	0.13%	0.19%
Noninterest revenue	0.97%	1.67%
Noninterest expense	3.09%	2.74%
Burden%	2.12%	1.07%
Pre-tax operating income	1.22%	1.45%

Before securities gains and losses and extraordinary items (source www.fdic.gov).

Similarly balance sheets can be quite different for community banks versus large banks with greater than $1 billion in assets, with greater trading account assets and larger bank premises and fixed assets for very large banks on the asset side, and larger percentages of more volatile, noncore deposit funds and other liabilities and subordinated debt, with greater liability management, for larger banks. Very large banks also tend to be more diversified in terms of their loan portfolios on average and to have larger percentages of credit card loans and consumer loans, and a lower percentage of real estate loans and a lower percentage of net loans to average total assets. Very large banks also have much more off-balance sheet activities.

TYPES OF OFF-BALANCE SHEET ACTIVITIES

Very large banks particularly engage in off-balance sheet (OBS) activities that are often activities that create potential or contingent liabilities in the future. These items include contingent loan commitments, such as unused loan commitments, letters of credit, securities borrowed and lent, participations in acceptances, securities committed to be purchased or sold, nonrecourse mortgage sales, futures contracts (financial, foreign exchange and others), interest rate swaps and option contracts. Smaller banks generally have the majority of their off-balance sheet activities in loan commitments. Banks gain fee income, a source of noninterest income for many off-balance sheet activities, such as loan commitments and letters of credit, that as contingent liabilities may expire unused. Since these items require no advance commitment of funds, they are considered to be contingent "off-balance sheet" liabilities.

Different Types of Off-Balance Sheet Items

Loan commitments Include bank commitments for revolving lines of credit, credit lines backing the commercial paper of large corporations, and note issuance facilities where banks agree to purchase short-term notes if a borrower is unable to sell them elsewhere. Unused loan commitments often serve as one measure of a bank's liquidity risk, with a high percentage indicating high potential liquidity needs if borrowers call on these commitments.

Letters of credit Often used in international trade when lenders agree to provide financing for customers to purchase specific goods. Upon documentation of the completion of a transaction between the customer and a third party, the bank fully expects to advance funds. A standby letter of credit is a similar instrument with an important difference. Rather than making a definite commitment to finance a transaction, the bank states its obligation to pay a third party only if the bank's customer defaults. Standby letters are used in commercial transactions and also to enhance the marketability of municipal bonds or to guarantee the performance on construction contracts, acting as insurance for risk-averse third parties.

Securities lent or borrowed (often associated with when-issued securities) Associated with large banks' security dealer and underwriting activities reflecting commitments to buy or sell securities in the future, often associated with issuing securities prior to issue, exposing banks to the risk of a fall in market value with changes in interest rates or market conditions. Banks that are U.S. government dealers engage in these activities with weekly auctions.

Other OBS liabilities Include loans sold with recourse whereby banks have some liability remaining that's associated with a loan sale, among other items that leave the bank with the potential for some future commitment, that are not large enough to merit a separate category.

Interest rate contracts Used predominantly to hedge activities associated with interest rate risk, with the exception of very large (greater than $1 billion in average total assets) banks that earn fees acting as brokers/dealers for interest contracts for other parties. In addition, banks engage in hedging credit risk with credit derivatives and very large banks also often act as brokers/dealers for these contracts.

Foreign exchange contracts These set terms for future exchanges of foreign currency. Many very large banks deal in forward contracts for foreign currencies, agreeing with customers to buy or sell foreign currencies in the future at currently agreed upon rates. Contracts on other commodities and equity are similarly futures or forward contracts dealing with purchases or sales of commodities or stock in the future at current agreed upon prices.

Differences among Banks, Credit Unions and Savings Institutions

Different countries have different types of depository institutions in addition to commercial banks. In the United States two other major types of depository institutions are savings institutions and credit unions. Many large bank holding and financial holding companies also have savings institutions as subsidiaries.

Savings Institutions

Savings institutions are often called thrifts, because they traditionally promote thriftiness and cater to individual small savers and make primarily home mortgage loans. Many thrifts were established in the United States as mutual organizations owned by their customers (i.e., depositors). Over time, in order to compete and raise capital, the majority of thrifts converted to stock charters, particularly after the thrift crisis of the late 1980s. Thrifts unlike banks have predominantly real estate loans, with regulations placing limits on the percentage of small business loans and consumer loans that they can make. In 2014, for example, 867 FDIC-insured savings institutions in the United States had about 62% of assets in net loans and leases and 43% of these were in real estate loans, 11% in loans to individuals, 6% in commercial and industrial loans, and 2% in other loans and leases. Because real estate loans tend to be long-term, often fixed-rate loans, thrifts have greater interest rate risk than banks, and often have negative funding gaps. On the liability side, thrifts tend to have greater deposit financing, averaging 88%, with 65.88% core (retail) deposits for FDIC-insured thrifts in 2014.

Thrifts, like smaller commercial banks, generally depend on traditional bank earnings, the NIM for their profitability, with an average NIM of 3.26% in 2014, and a 0.38% provision for loan losses percentage. The average thrift in 2014 had a NIR% of 1.94% and NIE% of 3.11%, resulting in an average burden expense % of 1.17%, and an average OROA before security gains and extraordinary items and taxes of 1.71%.

Credit Unions (CUs)

Credit unions are similar to mutual savings institutions by being owned by their customers (depositors) and developed to promote thrift among their members. Credit unions originated in the mid 19th century in Germany, and the concept was brought to the United States in the early 1900s. During the 1920s and the Great Depression of the 1930s, CUs grew quickly, reflecting the rapid development of consumer activism and labor organizations under a "common bond" concept. In the United States in 1934, Congress passed the Federal Credit Union Act to charter federal credit unions. Because CU profits go to individual members in the form of dividends, cheaper loans, and higher interest rates, CUs are not taxed. To join a CU, a person must be within its field of membership, such as employee groups, associations, religious or fraternal affiliations, and residential areas. Many CUs depend heavily on volunteer labor and donated facilities. In recent years credit unions have loosened common bond require-ments for credit union membership.

Credit unions can be state or federally chartered. Federally chartered CUs are regulated by the National Credit Union Administration (NCUA) and insured by the National Credit Union Share Insurance Fund (NCUSIF), as are state-chartered CUs. Deposits of CUs are referred to as shares. The NCUA also provides a Central Liquidity Facility (CLF) as a lender of last resort. As a quasi-public organization, the CLF has the authority to borrow from public sources and has a credit line with the U.S. Treasury department. Congress also charges the NCUA with enforcing a broad range of federal consumer laws and regulations for federally chartered CUs and also in certain instances to state-chartered CUs. Community Development Credit Unions (CDCUs) are a special type of credit union intended to serve specific communities in lower income or under-served areas. Community credit unions serve an entire community and have a wide market in which to seek members in return for extending services to all regardless of economic status or financial sophistication. Credit unions have predominantly members with consumer loans and home mortgage loans, with limited powers to make a smaller percentage of small business loans.

SUMMARY

Financial performance analysis for a depository institution encompasses performance and an institution's risk profile, including credit risk, interest rate risk, liquidity risk, capital risk, and operating risks, as well as for very large institutions off-balance sheet risks. Since depository institutions make profits from taking on different risks, there will always be risks, but financial institution managers need to manage these risks, reduce risks where possible, and hold sufficient capital against these risks. It's important to carefully compare banks to peer banks of similar size and focus to avoid bias in comparison. Managing the net interest margin, burden, and provision for loan losses as key profitability measures is important, with trends in profitability and risk measures providing indicators of strengths and weaknesses for depository institutions.

BIBLIOGRAPHY

Berman, J. (2014). "The three essential Warren Buffett quotes to live by." *Forbes*, April 22, 2014. Accessed on August 25, 2016 at: http://www.forbes.com/sites/jamesberman/2014/04/20/the-three-essential-warren-buffett-quotes-to-live-by/#6b4418b132f5

Fed (2011). Press Release Board of Governors of the Federal Reserve System, July 14, 2011. Accessed on February 6, 2016 at: http://www.federalreserve.gov/newsevents/press/bcreg/20110714a.htm

FDIC (2016). Federal Deposit Insurance Corporation, Reports & Analysis. Accessed on April 6, 2016 at: www.fdic.gov

FFIEC (2016). Uniform Bank Performance Reports. Accessed on April 6, 2016 at: www.ffiec.gov

Gardner, Mona J., Dixie L. Mills, and Elizabeth S. Cooperman (2005). *Managing Financial Institutions*, 5th ed. Mason, OH: Thomson/Southwestern.

CASE/WEB EXERCISE

Look up the financial statements or the UBPR for a bank you are interested in. For UBPRs go to www.ffiec.gov and do a financial and risk analysis for the bank for a trend analysis and compare to its peers for the last two years.

QUESTIONS AND PROBLEMS

1   Roscoe–Yuko Savings Bank in New York has total assets of $500 million and an EM of 10. A competitor of equal size has an equity to assets ratio of 8%. Both managers forecast interest revenues to assets (IR%) from 7% to 13%, and interest costs to assets as 6%. Both have a Burden% of 1.5% and a PLL% of 0.50%, and a marginal tax rate of 30%.

   a   What is the potential ROE range for each bank?
   b   Which bank would be better off during an upturn? During a downturn?
   c   If there was a high probability on the IR% being 13%, which bank would you prefer to invest in?

2   The board of directors of the Oakleigh–Elizabeth Regional Bank has requested a presentation on the relationship between financial leverage and return on equity. The bank has assets of $2 billion and a leverage ratio (total equity to total assets) of 10%. Net income in the coming year is expected to be between 1.2% and 2% of total assets (i.e. ROA).

   a   At the bank's current capital level, what is the expected ROE for the low and high low range for ROA, respectively?
   b   The new chief financial officers hoped to persuade the directors to operate aggressively by increasing the equity multiplier to 12. If they do, interest expense will rise because of the increased reliance on borrowed funds. The estimated range of ROA changes runs from a low of 0.5% to a high of 1.9%. What will be the resulting range for ROE?
   c   Based on these estimates, what recommendation should the directors follow?

3   Do a financial performance and risk analysis for Community Banks of Colorado in Greenwood Village, Colorado for 12/30/2008 to 12/31/2009 (source: public data provided by the FFIEC uniform bank performance report at: www.ffiec.gov).

TABLE P4.1 | Problem 3: Community Banks of Colorado, Greenwood Village, CO., 2008 to 2009: Uniform bank performance report, for 9/30/2011, Summary ratios, p. 01

Earnings and profitability	12/31/2009		12/31/2008	
	PG2	Bank	PG2	Bank
% Average assets				
Interest income	4.35	4.87	5.87	5.74
Interest expense	2.44	1.57	2.61	2.31
Net interest income	*1.91*	*3.30*	*3.26*	*3.43*
Noninterest income	0.63	0.93	0.59	0.86
Noninterest expense	2.59	3.12	2.37	2.92
Provision loan losses	3.01	1.50	1.18	0.94
Pre-tax operating income	*− 3.06*	*− 0.39*	*0.30*	*0.43*
Realized gain/losses securities	0.04	0.03	0.00	− 0.04

(Continued)

(Continued)

Earnings and profitability	12/31/2009		12/31/2008	
	PG2	Bank	PG2	Bank
Pre-tax net operating income	− 3.02	− 0.36	0.30	0.39
Margin analysis				
As % total average assets				
% Earnings assets	94.21	93.37	93.04	93.47
% Interest-bearing funds	82.95	82.90	79.59	82.61
As % average earning assets				
Interest income	4.62	5.23	6.31	6.16
Interest expense	2.59	1.69	2.81	2.47
Net interest income	2.03	3.54	3.50	3.69
Loan and lease analysis (%)				
Net loss to average loans	2.89	1.54	0.48	0.81
Earnings coverage net losses	− 0.02	3.15	3.44	6.51
Loan loss allowance to net losses	0.94	2.31	3.55	4.14
Loan loss allowance to total loans	2.97	2.07	1.71	1.59
% Loans past due	8.26	3.74	3.72	2.52
Liquidity (%)				
Net noncore fund dependence	33.00	27.70	49.61	36.39
Net loans to assets	73.05	67.51	86.54	72.57
Capitalization				
% Tier 1 leverage capital	6.15	8.31	8.51	8.40
% Dividends to net income	0.00	25.08	319.40	36.00
% Retained earnings to equity	− 32.55	− 8.06	− 4.78	− 2.51
Growth rates				
Total assets	1.25	5.39	7.23	9.82
Tier 1 capital	− 24.34	5.13	− 4.06	7.54
Net loans and leases	− 14.53	− 0.69	3.08	10.38

Source: FDIC (http://www.ffiec.gov/UBPR.htm), accessed on April 23, 2016.

a   Using page 01 of Community Bank of Colorado's UBPR (Table P4.1) that includes an earnings and profitability analysis (common size income statement, explain why the bank's OROA (operating net income before security gains and taxes as a percentage of average assets) changed using the relationship:

$$OROA = NIM - Burden\% - PLL\%.$$

(Note NIM is the net interest income provided since it's a percentage of average assets, the Burden% is the noninterest expense % given – noninterest revenue%, and the provision for loan losses is the PLL%.)

b Also, using the Tier 1 leverage ratio under Capitalization at the bottom of the page, find the bank's EM in 12/30/2008 and 12/31/2009. Using the ROA (net income given as a percentage of average assets at the top of the UBPR), find the ROE for each of the 2 years. How did changes in the EM affect changes in the ROE?

c Do the same process and explain why the OROA and ROE differ for its peers compared to the Community Bank of Colorado. What strengths and weaknesses are revealed for the Community Bank of Colorado?

d Find the asset utilization (total revenues to average assets) for 12/30/2008 and 12/31/2009 for the bank and its peers by adding the interest income (interest income to average assets provided) and noninterest income (noninterest income to average assets provided). Using the OROAs each year, find the NPM equal to OROA divided by asset utilization expressed as a fraction. Evaluate the trends in NPM and AU for the bank and compared to its peers each year.

e Looking at the risk ratios at the bottom of the page, what trends occurred in 2008 to 2009 for the bank's liquidity, capitalization, and credit risks and how do these compare to the PG2 peer banks? Based on the changes in the bank's and the peer's NIM, what type of funding gap do they likely have? (To see what rates did for these years, look at the interest income [interest income as a percentage of average assets] and [interest expense as a percentage of average assets] as proxies for the average loan and liability rate each year.)

f Summarize the strengths and weaknesses for Community Banks of Colorado from your analysis in terms of profitability and risk.

4 Do the same analysis for the questions above but for 9/30/2011 and 9/30/2010 (Table P4.2).

TABLE P4.2 | Problem 4: Community Banks of Colorado, Greenwood Village, CO., 2010 to 2011: Uniform bank performance report, for 9/30/2011, Summary ratios, p. 01

Earnings and profitability	9/30/2011		9/30/2010	
	Bank	PG2	Bank	PG2
% Average assets				
Interest income	3.60	4.35	3.92	4.56
Interest expense	1.22	0.80	1.72	1.13
Net interest income	2.38	3.55	2.20	3.43
Noninterest income	− 0.50	0.93	0.13	0.93
Noninterest expense	3.10	2.97	2.37	2.90
Provision loan losses	1.41	0.55	2.93	0.96
Pre-tax operating income	− 2.63	0.96	− 2.97	0.50

(Continued)

(Continued)

Earnings and profitability	9/30/2011		9/30/2010	
	Bank	PG2	Bank	PG2
Realized gain/losses securities	0.05	0.05	0.07	0.07
Pre-tax net operating income	− 2.58	1.01	− 2.90	0.57
Margin analysis				
As % total average assets				
% Earnings assets	92.37	92.93	92.39	92.98
% Interest-bearing funds	83.43	81.19	84.08	85.57
As % average earning assets				
Interest income	3.89	4.69	4.24	4.92
Interest expense	1.32	0.86	1.86	1.22
Net interest income	2.57	3.83	2.38	3.70
Loan and lease analysis (%)				
Net loss to average loans	4.22	0.90	2.02	1.25
Earnings coverage net losses	− 0.38	5.58	− 0.02	4.33
Loan loss allowance to net losses	1.01	3.66	2.33	2.98
Loan loss allowance to total loans	4.74	2.08	4.89	2.16
% Loans past due	12.88	3.14	12.23	3.95
Liquidity (%)				
Net noncore fund dependence	− 7.91	7.99	− 5.46	11.95
Net loans to assets	72.76	61.90	72.89	64.52
Capitalization				
% Tier 1 Leverage Capital	1.64	9.50	4.88	8.80
% Dividends to net income	0.00	21.78	0.00	19.46
% Retained earnings to equity	− 127.30	4.17	− 49.96	0.25
Growth rates				
Total assets	− 22.57	4.21	− 9.01	3.45
Tier 1 capital	− 73.15	8.55	− 28.37	5.24
Net loans and leases	− 22.71	0.04	− 8.44	− 2.32

Source: FDIC (http://www.ffiec.gov/UBPR.htm), accessed on April 23, 2016.

5 Do a performance and risk analysis for Meridian Bank with the first page of its Uniform Bank Performance report listed in Table P4.3. Meridian is a small community bank operating in Illinois with $46,849,000 in total assets. Its peer group (PG) is for 274 similar

size insured banks operating in the United States at this time. Figures are given for 9/30/2008 and 9/30/2007. Note for the earnings and profitability analysis (common size income statement) each item is as a percentage of average assets.

TABLE P4.3 | Problem 5: Meridian Bank, Eldred, IL, 2007 to 2008: Earnings and risk analysis, Summary ratios, p. 01

Earning and profitability	2008		2007	
	Bank	PG	Bank	PG
% Average assets				
Interest income (TE)	5.29	6.10	5.51	6.64
− Interest expense	2.67	2.21	3.31	2.60
Net interest income (TE)	2.62	3.89	2.19	4.05
+ Noninterest income	0.77	0.60	1.45	0.63
− Noninterest expense	5.16	3.34	5.11	3.35
− Provision: loan and lease losses	4.58	0.13	0.33	0.10
Pretax operating income (TE)	− 6.35	1.05	− 1.79	1.22
+ Realized gains/losses securities	0.01	0.00	0.00	0.00
Pretax net operating income (TE)	− 6.34	1.01	− 1.79	1.22
Net Operating Income	− 6.34	0.82	− 1.79	0.98
Margin analysis				
Average earning assets to average assets	84.29	92.93	83.63	93.16
Average interest-bearing funds to average assets	78.00	74.27	77.65	74.54
Interest income (TE) to average earn assets	6.28	6.58	6.59	7.15
Interest expense to average earning assets	3.17	2.38	3.96	2.79
Net interest income (TE) to average earning assets	3.11	4.20	2.62	4.36
Loan analysis				
Net loss to average total loans and leases	3.76	0.14	0.74	0.13
Earnings coverage of net losses (X)	− 0.80	24.72	− 3.90	29.84
Loans and leases allowance to net losses	0.99	17.47	0.86	20.37
Loans and leases allowance to total loans and leases	3.95	1.42	0.57	1.41
Total loans and leases − 90+ days past due	0.71	0.29	0.50	0.25
− Nonaccrual	4.56	0.83	4.48	0.59
− Total	5.27	1.26	4.98	0.93
Liquidity				
Net noncore funding dependence new $250M	8.09	9.91	6.80	9.79
Net loans and leases to assets	65.46	63.66	54.67	64.02

(Continued)

(Continued)

Earning and profitability	2008		2007	
	Bank	PG	Bank	PG
Capitalization				
Tier 1 leverage capital	0.84	10.34	6.89	10.41
Cash dividends to net income	0.00	38.66	0.00	36.87
Retained earnings to average total equity	− 94.07	2.90	− 21.12	4.22
Growth rates				
Total assets	− 21.20	5.64	76.83	5.15
Tier 1 capital	− 89.08	3.75	− 20.99	4.47
Net loans and leases	− 5.65	4.87	22.71	5.72
Short-term investments	− 72.25	8.22	323.13	51.35
Short-term noncore funding	− 55.27	6.76	− 28.03	14.96

a Explain why Meridian's OROA (net operating income% given) changed from 2007 to 2008 from the perspective of its NIM, Burden%, and PLL%. Explain additionally, why the NIM changed in terms of changes in the interest income (IR%) and interest expense (IE%) provided, and why the Burden% changed in terms of the change in the noninterest income (NIR%) and noninterest expense (NIE%) percentages of average assets provided.

b Looking at the margin analysis, given the changes in the IR% and IE%, did rates go up or down over the period? Given the change in the bank's NIM%, what funding gap does this imply?

c Do a peer comparison for Meridian versus the PG's OROA, examining NIM, Burden%, and PLL% and their components. What weaknesses are revealed for Meridian in this analysis?

d How do the percentages of earnings assets and average interest-bearing assets and IR%, IE% and NIM% compare for Meridian to its peers. Explain why Meridian's NIM% differs from its peers?

6 Meridian analysis: Do a more detailed analysis including a risk, burden, and detailed NIM analysis for rate, mix, and volume trends and differences between Meridian and its peer (PG) banks.

a For the loan and lease analysis, liquidity, and capital analysis listed from page 01 above analyze those of Meridian Bank compared to its peers.

b Analyze Meridian Bank's burden by comparing the different expense ratios that the bank has compared to its peers (PG13) as shown in Table P4.4, along with the overall efficiency ratio and overhead less noninterest income ratio.

c For a more detailed analysis of NIM, look at the yield for assets and rates for liabilities, shown below the burden analysis. How do Meridian's loan and liability rates compare to its peers and how can this help explain Meridian's trends in its NIM? Also look at the loan mix table in Table P4.4; how does the loan composition for Meridian differ from its peers? How does this affect differences in the IR% of

Meridian for trends and compared to its peers. Look at the liability mix in the table as well; how does the composition of liabilities differ from its peers, and how does this affect differences and trends in its IE%?

d   Summarize strengths and weaknesses for Meridian compared to its peers and any recommendations you might have.

TABLE P4.4 | Problem 6: Meridian Bank, Eldred, IL, 2007 to 2008: Earnings and risk analysis, Summary ratios, p. 01

Burden and rate and mix analysis	2008		2007	
	Bank	PG	Bank	PG
Burden analysis				
Personnel expense	2.77	1.86	3.07	1.89
Occupancy expense	1.01	0.46	0.93	0.46
Other operating expenses (incl. intangibles)	1.38	1.00	1.12	0.98
Total overhead expense	5.16	3.34	5.11	3.35
Overhead less noninterest income	4.39	2.69	3.66	2.68
Efficiency ratio	152.19	73.63	140.17	71.26
Average personnel expense per employee ($000)	41.63	48.29	35.06	46.84
Analysis of asset rates				
Yield on:				
Total loan and leases (TE)	7.01	7.70	7.42	8.21
Loans in domestic offices	7.01	7.68	7.42	8.19
Real estate	7.00	7.41	7.07	7.75
Secured by 1–4 family residential property	7.18	7.61	N/A	0.00
All other loans secured by real estate	6.92	7.28	N/A	0.00
Commercial and industrial	6.34	7.74	7.54	8.38
Individual	8.43	9.06	9.40	9.12
Total investment securities	4.92	4.80	5.20	4.77
US Treasury	4.50	4.57	5.01	4.51
Mortgage-backed securities	5.09	4.39	5.39	4.27
Interest-bearing bank balances	8.42	2.98	4.21	4.05
Fed Funds sold and repos	2.85	2.53	5.42	5.28
Analysis of liability rates				
Total interest-bearing deposits	3.46	2.93	4.22	3.42
Transaction accounts	1.88	0.80	1.87	1.05

(Continued)

(Continued)

Burden and rate and mix analysis	2008		2007	
	Bank	*PG*	*Bank*	*PG*
Other savings deposits	2.11	1.42	2.61	1.84
Time deposits over $100M	4.14	3.98	4.66	4.68
All other time deposits	4.18	4.06	4.86	4.53
Federal Funds purchased and repos	2.77	2.09	10.45	4.45
Other borrowed money	0.00	3.49	5.86	4.30
Subordinated notes and debentures	N/A	6.73	N/A	5.91
All interest-bearing funds	3.43	2.96	4.27	3.47

% Average gross loans and leases	2008		2007	
	Bank	*PG 13*	*Bank*	*PG 13*
Loan mix				
Real estate loans	70.68	53.09	65.19	52.56
Construction and development	11.61	2.78	8.88	2.38
1–4 family construction	0.83	1.11	N/A	3.40
Other construction and land development	11.12	1.42	N/A	4.04
Secured by farmland	3.22	12.94	2.87	13.13
1–4 family residential	23.48	21.99	20.16	22.44
1–4 family first lien loans	23.37	20.63	19.97	21.18
Multifamily	1.79	0.33	2.28	0.29
Nonfarm nonresidential	30.58	11.21	31.00	10.32
Owner occupied nonfarm nonresidential	24.26	4.44	N/A	7.99
Other nonfarm nonresidential	6.61	5.40	N/A	10.36
Agricultural loans	0.55	18.39	0.56	19.36
Commercial and industrial loans	18.28	15.05	24.34	14.34
Loans to individuals	10.45	10.01	9.85	10.43

% Average assets	2008		2007	
	Bank	*PG 13*	*Bank*	*PG 13*
Liability mix analysis				
Demand deposits	13.34	14.06	11.38	13.85
All NOW and ATS accounts	9.26	12.07	6.50	12.07

Money market deposit accounts	6.62	6.14	7.52	5.76
Other savings deposits	7.76	8.95	7.45	8.88
Time deposits at or below insurance limit	40.53	29.21	43.50	29.74
– Fully insured brokered deposits	0.00	0.43	0.00	0.43
Core deposits	77.50	71.52	76.35	71.45
Time deposits above insurance limit	10.88	13.29	14.07	12.97
Total deposits	88.39	86.05	90.42	85.74
Federal Funds purchased and repos	4.10	0.35	0.42	0.39
Total other borrowings	0.02	0.01	0.05	0.01
Memo: short-term noncore funding	13.72	12.64	13.50	12.39

Note: NOW: negotiable order of withdrawal accounts; ATS: automatic transfer service accounts.

Capital Management

The impact of the recent financial crisis has significantly changed the supervision and regulation of financial organizations. Countries such as the U.K., Switzerland and Sweden are not only planning on implementing the tougher Basel III capital standards, but are also considering whether they should require institutions to hold capital significantly above Basel III capital levels.

(Rosengren, 2013)

Given the score and speed with which the recent and previous crises have been transmitted around the globe as well as the unpredictable nature of future crises, it is critical that all countries raise the resilience of their banking sectors to both internal and external shocks.

(Basel III, 2010a)

DURING the U.S. subprime loan crisis of 2007 and 2008 and global financial crisis, many financial institutions had inadequate capital to cover the unexpected losses that they experienced. This was particularly the case for several large financial institutions that were systemically important, whose failures had significant contagion effects, contributing to the potential collapse of other financial institutions to which they were tied.

Lehman Brothers, for instance, as an internationally active financial institution, did business in 40 countries and 650 legal entities outside the United States and was also counterparty to many other financial institutions, resulting in contagion effects globally. As noted by Wiggins and Metrick (2015), the clients and counterparties of Lehman entailed millions of dollars of potential losses, based on their exposure with Lehman Brothers failure. In addition, Lehman Brothers had a huge derivative book, large involvement with collateralized debt obligations associated with subprime mortgages. Lehman Brothers also used wholesale, short-term funding, and when confidence was lost for Lehman in the financial markets, sources of short-term funding refused to renew that financing. In addition, Lehman Brothers' capital ratio (Tier 1 and Tier 2 relative to risk-weighted assets) in 2007 was only about 7.27% (compared to a 9.87% ratio earlier in 2003), which was insufficient to cover its losses, contributing to its bankruptcy (Christopoulos, Mylonakis, and Diktapanidis, 2011; Rosengren, 2009).

Following the global financial crisis, to prevent this from happening again, new capital regulations have been enacted globally for depository institutions, including a new framework under Basel III developed by the Basel Committee on Banking Supervision at the Bank for International Settlements (BIS). The revised Basel III Framework was approved in 2010, including phase-in schedules by 27 member jurisdictions and 44 central banks and supervisory authorities, endorsed by leaders for the governments of G20 nations. Different countries are allowed to make modifications for their particular priorities and needs, with full implementation recommended by 2019 (Basel III, 2010a; Getter, 2012).

This chapter discussed how capital is defined including the market versus book value of equity, the role of capital as a cushion against losses, preferences by different agents for capital, regulatory definitions of capital and capital adequacy, and the evolution of regulations by the Basel Committee for Basel I, Basel II, and Basel III, and how banks use capital charges in setting loan rates under a risk-adjusted return on capital framework.

DIFFERENT DEFINITIONS OF CAPITAL

Capital is the equity cushion protecting against potential losses on a financial institution's assets, as well as other operating losses. Since equity capital is equal to total assets less total liabilities, for a firm to be solvent its total assets must be greater than its total liabilities (i.e., positive equity capital). Generally, for banks, equity capital includes common stock and retained earnings (undivided profits).

Regulatory capital is different. For depository institutions, regulators have often allowed some long-term debt and other items that have claims below insured deposit funds as secondary capital for regulatory purposes. Since capital also provides a role in protecting a federal insurer (and hence taxpayers) from having to pay out for insured deposits, long-term claims by debt-holders are subordinated to depositors in case of insolvency.

Typically, balance sheet measures for equity capital are based on accounting versus market value of equity. Book value accounting measures for equity have often been criticized as not revealing the true value from a market perspective for the value of a financial institution's equity capital. The following section discusses the difference between the market value of equity versus the book value.

MARKET VERSUS BOOK VALUE OF CAPITAL

For depository institutions, the use of book value accounting can cause particular distortion, since the economic value of a financial institution depends on financial assets and liabilities, whose market value changes significantly with interest rates. For accounting purposes, most depository institution assets, with the exception of securities available for sale and trading securities, are held at their historical (book) value. Since any changes in the market value of assets or liabilities are not considered, the historical book value of assets can create distortions for investors trying to analyze depository institutions. However, with market value accounting the value of financial assets and liabilities would have to be updated constantly in volatile markets.

For example, looking at the Market King Bank, based on book value accounting, its balance sheet looks as follows:

Assets ($ thousand)		Liabilities and equity ($ thousand)	
Cash	1,000	Deposits	65,800
90-day T-bills	19,000	Total liabilities	65,800
4-year loans (10%rate)	50,000	Equity	4,200
Total assets	70,000	Total liabilities and equity	70,000

Under book value accounting, the equity to total asset ratio is $4,200 / $70,000 which equals 0.06 or 6%. Regardless of how interest rates change, the equity to asset ratio based on the book value of assets and liabilities will remain the same. If the bank has to sell its loans, however, they could be sold at a capital loss if interest rates on similar loans rise above the 10% fixed rate on these loans. Market King Bank has loans that at the time they were made had a market value and book value of $50,000 thousand, with an annual loan payment of $15,773.52 thousand at the end of each of the four years, so the present value of the loan payments is equal to $15,773.52 thousand times the PVIFA 4, 10% (present value of annuity factor for 4, 10% of 3.16987), which equals $50,000 thousand, the market value of the loans.

Under market value accounting, the market value of the financial assets and liabilities will change with changes in interest rates. For instance, suppose the market rate on other similar 4-year loans rises to 11% right after the loans are made. On the bank's balance sheet the loans book value will remain at $50,000 thousand and total assets at $70,000. However, the market value of the loans if they are sold will now equal $15,773.52 loan payment x (3.10245, PVIFA, 11%, 4), which equals $48,936.56 thousand. Hence, holding other factors constant, the new market value of equity will be lower by $1,063.44 thousand (total assets of $68,936.56 thousand less $70,000 thousand). Hence, the bank in market value terms has lower equity capital of ($4,200 – $1,063.44) equal to $3,136.56 and an equity to total asset ratio of ($3,136.56 / $68,936.56) equal to 0.0455 or 4.55%.

The Financial Accounting Standards Board (FASB) requires banks, other financial institutions and nonfinancial firms with assets of $150 million or greater to disclose in footnotes in their financial statements the fair market value of all financial instruments on their balance sheets, as well as liabilities. In 1993, FASB issued a rule requirement requiring market value accounting for investments held for sale by banks. Securities not held for sale (held to maturity) could still be reported at book value. A majority of total bank securities are held for sale, thus requiring that the majority of investments be held at market value. With the subprime mortgage crisis of 2007 to 2008, many banks that held mortgage securities had market value losses that had to be reported. Depository institutions are also required to report their market sensitivity under the "S" in CAMELS ratings, with reports on the expected loss in the market value of equity with unfavorable interest rates.

WHY IS CAPITAL IMPORTANT?

Capital is important as a cushion against future losses. It protects deposit insurance funds in the event of losses, ensuring the integrity of the payments system and provides long-term funds for long-term investment and growth. Capital also provides confidence for uninsured depositors and uninsured debt-holders. Having adequate capital also provides protection against regulatory interference, contributes to higher credit ratings, provides extra borrowing capacity, and provides an optimal capital structure that offers a lower weighted average cost of capital.

An example for capital as a cushion against losses is the Euphoria Savings Association below:

Assets ($ millions)		Liabilities and equity ($ millions)	
T-bills	30	Deposits	92 (80 insured)
Loans	70	Equity	8
Total assets	100	Total liabilities and equity	100

The current equity to assets ratio is 8%. Given this equity cushion, the market value of Euphoria's loans would have to fall by $8 million or by 11.43% ($8/$70) before depositors' interests would be threatened after equity capital is wiped out. If the bank instead had only $2 million in capital, it would only take a $2 million fall in the value of loans or a 2.86% fall in the value of loans ($2 /$70) for depositors' interests to be threatened. With a higher equity to assets ratio, the bank will have a lower cost of borrowing, and have an easier time attracting investors and have less regulatory interference, and have higher credit ratings on any debt it issues.

THEORETICAL VIEWS ON OPTIMAL CAPITAL RATIOS

Preferences of Stockholders for Financial Leverage

With higher financial leverage, stockholders can put in a smaller investment, using funds provided by debt-holders to finance assets to produce a higher return for stockholders. Stockholders have limited liability, so the maximum they can lose is their relatively small equity investment, providing an incentive for stockholders to prefer higher financial leverage and risk taking. Debt-holders in contrast prefer a higher equity cushion to protect their interests, and have incentives to monitor managers for excessive risk taking and demand higher risk premiums on their debt if the bank takes on greater risk. However, insured depositors, since they know they will be bailed out by regulators, may have little incentive to monitor the bank where they deposit their funds. Hence, there is a moral hazard problem, with little monitoring by depositors of their interests. In contrast, regulators prefer higher capital ratios to protect deposit insurance funds. Managers may prefer lower risk to protect their employment, but if managers are also stockholders at some point in ownership, they may prefer greater risk taking and lower capital ratios.

Buser, Chen, and Kane (1981) point out in a theoretical model that without deposit insurance, banks would have lower optimal debt to assets ratios, since uninsured debt-holders would demand higher risk premiums (a higher interest rate) if banks took on great financial leverage. This view goes along with research showing much higher equity to asset ratios for many banks of 30% or higher prior to deposit insurance in the United States. Regulators try to offset incentives for stockholders to take on unlimited debt by having regulatory minimum capital ratios, with regulators willing to accept a compromise to convince banks to be members of deposit insurance funds.

An example of this moral hazard problem is if an investor owns a bank with all equity financing of $5 million that is invested in $5 million in loans, with a 50% probability of not defaulting and having a $5 million profit, and a 50% chance of defaulting with a loss to the investor of $5 million. No rational investor would accept this arrangement, since the expected return would be equal to:

$$[0.50 \times \$5 \text{ million}] + [0.50 \times -\$5 \text{ million}] = \$0.$$

However, if the investor only invests $1 million and raises $4 million in insured deposits with a 10% interest rate resulting in a $400,000 annual interest expense, then the expected return becomes:

$$[0.50 \times (\$5 \text{ million} - \$0.40 \text{ million})] + [0.50 \times -\$1 \text{ million}] = \$1.8 \text{ million}.$$

Hence, using other people's money for financing makes the investment look like a good deal, even if there is a 50% chance of a $1 million loss, given the upside potential of a $1 million gain. However, if an investor is risk adverse and wants to grow without raising expensive external equity, maintain good credit ratings, have a comfortable equity margin over regulatory minimums, and wants to avoid regulatory interference, the investor may still have incentives to hold additional capital.

Pricing Loans for Risk-Adjusted Return on Capital

Practical considerations in managing capital include protection for economic risk, the risk of significant losses, and the amount of capital held should include a bank's credit, market, and business risks. Banks also consider the capital held by peer banks with similar risks, and capital associated with equivalent bond ratings.

Large money center banks often use a risk-adjusted return on capital (RAROC) approach to give a particular asset a capital charge based on the amount of capital that needs to be held on an asset according to its risk, with a higher equity to asset percentage allocated to more risky assets. Hence, more risky assets require a higher return (higher loan rate, for instance) to cover the cost of the extra capital that has to be held for them.

As an example, suppose the Good Capital Bank decided that based on the risk of its commercial loans, the bank will allocate equity capital equal to 12% of the loans value as a cushion against losses (i.e., equity to assets of 12%) in addition to their required loan loss provision of 1.25%.

RAROC = before tax charge for additional risk.

The bank's estimated cost of equity capital (average ROE) is 15% after taxes, so the additional capital cost of the loans will be:

Capital charge after taxes = 15% (ROE) × 0.12 capital allocated = 1.80%.

So the before tax charge is equal to 1.80% / (1 − *t*), and if the marginal tax rate for the bank is 40%:

Before tax RAROC capital charge = 1.80% / (1 − 0.40) = 3%.

So a 3% capital charge will be added to the loan rate for commercial loans to cover the additional cost of holding extra capital for greater risk.

Because of the higher capital requirement, the bank will add the 3% capital charge (RAROC) to the costs of the loan that include its cost of liability funds to fund the loan, hypothetically 5%, the required loan loss provision of 1.25% plus other direct expense of 0.80% plus an indirect expense of 0.40% plus an overhead expense of 0.50%, that will give a total required loan rate of 10.95%.

With the RAROC charge, the bank must earn a higher return on its traditional commercial lending activities than for other assets that have a lower regulatory and risk-based equity to asset requirement. This could make commercial loans less attractive than other types of investments that offer higher spreads.

Kimball (1998) points out that banks use different models to determine the appropriate equity to asset ratio to hold for different asset classes based on their risk, that vary from simple methods to very sophisticated ones. Examples are: (1) just using the equity to asset ratios that other financial institutions hold for a particular one-line type of business, such as capital held by credit card banks, etc. (2) using a bank's probability of insolvency ratio $(Z) = (ROA^* + K)$ divided by the standard deviation of ROA, where for a target Z^* ratio that the bank desires for each of its operations, the optimal K^* (equity to asset) ratio for each of the bank's operations is solved for as $K^* = \{[Z \times STD\ (ROA)] - ROA^*\}$. The Z-ratio gives the number of standard deviations by which ROA would have to fall before the bank's book value of equity would be exhausted, with a lower Z-ratio showing greater insolvency risk. (3) Using a similar approach but adjusting this allocation downward based on the diversification of the bank into other products, whereby for a diversified bank, the desired K^* would be lowered.

REGULATORY CAPITAL REQUIREMENTS

The U.S. regulatory capital minimum ratios effective on January 1, 2015 for all banks include the following under the interim final rules for the phase in of Basel III that will occur gradually through 2019. The U.S. regulatory minimum ratios and PCA (prompt corrective action) ratios are listed in Tables 5.1 and 5.2 (FDIC Reg. Cap., 2015). The tables show required minimum capital ratios based on different types of regulatory capital including:

1 *Tier 1 leverage capital to total assets (leverage ratio)*, which is similar to a total equity to total assets ratio;
2 *Common equity to risk-based capital ratios*, where the denominator is risk-weighted assets where weights are given for different types of assets based on their risk for the percentage of capital that needs to be held on each category.

The numerators for each capital ratio use different types of regulatory capital.

Tier 1 includes equity capital to total assets. While CET 1 is a new definition of equity capital that includes predominantly common stock and retained earnings with some adjustments. Tier 1 is equity capital with some additions, and total capital includes both Tier 1 and

TABLE 5.1 | U.S. banks and saving associations' new regulatory minimums

Tier 1 leverage capital	4.0%
Common equity Tier 1 risk-based capital ratios:	
Capital (CET 1)	4.5%
Tier 1 risk-based capital	6.0%
Total risk-based capital	8.0%

TABLE 5.2 | U.S. banks and savings associations' capital classifications prompt corrective action (PCA) ratios by categories of capitalization

	Tier 1 leverage %	*CET1 to RBC%*	*Tier 1 RBC*	*Total RBC%*
Well capitalized	$\geq 5\%$	$\geq 6.5\%$	$\geq 8\%$	$\geq 10\%$
Adequate capital	$\geq 4\%$	$\geq 4.5\%$	$\geq 6\%$	$\geq 8\%$
Undercapitalized	$< 4\%$	$< 4.5\%$	$< 6\%$	$< 8\%$
Significantly undercapitalized	$< 3\%$	$< 3\%$	$< 4\%$	$< 6\%$
Critically undercapitalized	Tangible equity / Total assets $\leq 2\%$			
	where Tangible equity = CET1 + outstanding non-Tier 1 perpetual preferred stock.			

CET1: common equity Tier 1; RBC: risk-based capital.

Resources can be found at www.fdic.gov/regulations/capital

Tier 2 capital, where Tier 2 capital allows additional noncommon equity types of capital to be included.

In the following section the definitions for each of these types of capital are discussed in more detail for new U.S. capital regulations.

TYPES OF CAPITAL ALLOWED FOR U.S. DEPOSITORY INSTITUTIONS

Regulators have different definitions of capital, and traditionally have allowed depository institutions to hold two types of capital: Tier 1, core or tangible equity capital and Tier 2, supplemental capital.

Under Basel III, a new capital ratio: common equity Tier 1 (CET 1) is set as:

Core equity Tier 1 (CET 1) capital includes primarily:

Common stock (par and surplus).

Retained earnings (undivided profits).

For U.S. capital regulations, adjustments are also made, including adding back in accumulated other comprehensive income and other disclosed reserves and common shares issued by consolidated subsidiaries held by minority interest that meet CET 1 criteria, less regulatory deductions and dividends removed according to accounting standards.

As shown below for the third quarter of 2015, the typical CET 1 based on average equity capital as a percentage reported by the FDIC was as follows:

Core equity Tier 1 capital (known as CET 1 capital)

Components on average for equity capital as percentage average total assets for all insured banks and savings institutions as of September 9, 2015

Perpetual preferred stock	0.05*
Common stock	7.86 (par and surplus)
Undivided profits	3.42 (retained earnings)
Average bank equity capital	11.33 for U.S. insured banks

*Note a small amount of perpetual preferred stock is included. Under Basel III requirements that are being phased in gradually by January 1, 2018, cumulative preferred stock and all hybrid instruments (such as convertible preferred stock, along with trust-preferred stock) is *now excluded* from Tier 1 equity capital. These are being phased out under the rationale that troubled institutions would be unwilling to defer dividends.

Source FDIC: As of September 30, 2015 for U.S. federally insured institutions, reported by FDIC at: www.fdic.gov

Hence, the average equity capital to total average assets ratio (leverage ratio) was 11.33%, in the well-capitalized category for the leverage ratio. U.S. federally insured banks had an average CET 1 to risk-based capital ratio at this time of about 9.25%, also on average in the well-capitalized category.

Basel III also redefines additional Tier 1 capital (AT 1 capital) AT 1 capital under Basel III includes noncommon equity Tier 1 instruments that qualify as more loss absorbing, that have no obligation for payment in the event of default with no circumstances under which distributions are obligatory and with no credit-sensitive dividend feature (i.e., dividend/coupon reset periodically, based in whole or in part on a bank's current credit standing).

Basel III also redefines the type of nonequity capital allowed as Tier 2 capital Tier 2 Capital under Basel III includes nonequity capital that is allowed as secondary capital, where the investor has no rights to accelerate payment in the future. The instrument may not have a credit-sensitive dividend/coupon reset periodically based on a bank's current credit standing and must be subordinated to depositors and general creditors of the bank.

In the United States under Basel III, Tier 2 capital is defined as:

1 Limited allowance for loan and lease losses (up to 1.25% risk-weighted assets).
2 Qualifying preferred stock and subordinated debt including bank-issued SBLF (Small Business Lending Fund) and TARP (Troubled Asset Relief Program) instruments currently qualifying as Tier 1 capital in the United States (with previous limits under Basel II eliminated on subordinated debt; limited preferred stock and the amount of Tier 2 capital included in total capital).

For U.S. FDIC-insured banks and savings associations as of September 30, 2015, the average Tier 2 capital to risk-based assets ratio was 1.10% (as reported by the FDIC, www.fdic.gov). Taking the total Tier 1 and Tier 2 capital to risk-based assets, the average is 10.35%, in the well-capitalized category. Under Basel III, a capital conservation buffer is also required as discussed in the following section.

Capital Conservation Buffer

A capital conservation buffer is added under Basel III to ensure that large international banks build up a capital buffer in favorable periods that can be drawn upon later in unfavorable periods when losses occur. When banks draw down on this buffer, they are required to rebuild them by reducing distributions of earnings that are discretionary, such as reducing dividend payments, or bonus payments to managers and staff. Banks can also raise external equity capital to rebuild depleted capital. Thus, the Basel III capital conservation buffer of 2.5% phased in by January 1, 2019, comprised common equity Tier 1 capital providing an amount above the regulatory minimum capital requirement as a buffer against losses, with regulatory restrictions on capital distributions, if the buffer becomes depleted.

Starting in January 2016, the capital buffer requires an additional 0.625% with rises over the years to the final level of 2.5% of risk-weighted assets by January 1, 2019 for U.S. banks (i.e. 1.25% in 2017, 1.875% in 2018) (Lekatis, 2011).

BRIEF OVERVIEW HISTORY OF REGULATORY CAPITAL REQUIREMENTS

Basel I in a Nutshell

With hundreds of failures for savings and loans associations and commercial banks in the1980s and the 1990s, including the failures of large international banks and savings associations (i.e., this includes the failures of: Bank of Credit and Commerce International (BCCI) in 1991, with $20 billion in assets, as the result of widespread fraud; Long-Term Credit Bank of Japan in 1989, with more than $19.2 billion in bad debt; Bright Banc Savings Association, in Texas in 1989, with $5 billion in assets; Bank of New England in 1991, with assets of $21.8 billion; Continental Illinois National Bank and Trust in 1984, with almost $40 billion in assets, among hundreds of savings and loan failures (Knufken, 2009).

These failures and differences in capital requirements for international banks led to capital reforms. In addition to higher capital requirements in the United States under the Federal Deposit Insurance Corporation Improvement Act (FDICIA), phased in by 1993, Basel I of 1988 was phased in by 1993, as proposed by the Bank for International Settlements (BIS). Key elements include: (a) a minimum leverage: core equity to total assets ratio; (b) Minimum Tier 1 to total risk-based asset ratio; and (c) Minimum (Tier 1 + Tier 2) to total risk-based asset ratio.

Risk-based assets Risk-based assets weigh how much capital must be held on particular types of assets, such as 0% for Federal Reserve balances, U.S. government securities, and other securities with low default risk, 20% for cash items in the process of collection, general obligation municipal bonds, Fed Funds sold, and other types of low default risk securities, 50% for secured mortgage loans on 1 to 4 family mortgages fully secured by first liens and other municipal revenue bonds, and 100% for commercial and consumer loans, corporate bonds, commercial paper, and other assets not included in other categories as more risky assets. Off-balance sheet items with more risk are also converted to risk-based assets that are also given weights and included as part of total risk-based assets. After Basel I was passed the average U.S. commercial bank equity to asset ratio rose from about 7.83% in 1993 to about 9.10% in 2003.

Problems with Basel I Overly simple rules allowed for "regulatory arbitrage" and poor risk management under Basel I. For instance, subprime mortgage loans were put in a 50% risk category, with less capital held on these as mortgage loans. Hence, within risk-weighted buckets the quality of loans could vary; yet the capital that had to be held for less risky and more risky loans within buckets could differ widely.

With large bank trading losses, in 1998, the BIS Market Risk Amendment was put in place requiring banks with significant trading activity to hold additional capital for market risk, using either their own internal risk measurement model or a standardized process developed by the BIS committee. Many banks use a value at risk (VAR) approach.

Overview of Basel II

Basel II of 2004 tried to alter bad behavior by having a more market-based approach for large international banks, which for the United States entailed ten very large international banks, who could opt in to Basel II.

Basel II contains three pillars:

1 *Pillar 1: Capital charges against market, operational, and credit risk.* Banks could use their advanced internal risk-based measures or a standardized advanced measurement approach to calculate their risks and accordingly capital charges.
2 *Pillar 2: An effective supervisory review process.* Supervisors were mandated to review banks' internal assessments of their individual capital allocation and adequacy to determine if they were sufficient.
3 *Pillar 3: Market discipline and transparency.* Risk and capital positions of banks were to be made more transparent to allow market discipline to reinforce the efforts of the other pillars.

Basel II included a great effort to evaluate risk sensitivity, but treated risk exposures and banks very unequally, with community banks subject to previous Basel I ratios and large international banks often having lower capital requirements based on internal risk-based measures. Basel II also placed more reliance on the discipline of the market.

Problems for Basel II These include a number of gaps that still existed that large international banks could exploit, with advanced internal risk-based measures often resulting in banks holding lower capital than community banks using the Basel I approach. Also, with new innovations and sophisticated products developed with new technologies, supervisors had difficulty evaluating these new products and their effect on bank risk.

Overview of Basel III

Basel III addressed the shortcoming of Basel II, including the impact on trading books, bank liquidity, and bank leverage. Basel III has three pillars including:

1 *Pillar I:* Enhanced minimum capital and liquidity requirements.
2 *Pillar II:* Enhanced supervisory review process for firms with risk management and capital planning.
3 *Pillar III:* Enhanced risk disclosure and market discipline.

Basel III redefines common equity Tier 1 (CET 1) capital, and additional Tier 1 capital as mentioned earlier. It also implements a new capital conservation buffer, and for the FDIC in the United States revises prompt corrective action (PCA) thresholds and adds the new ratio to the PCA framework, and changes the risk weights for certain assets and off-balance sheet exposures (FDIC Reg. Cap., 2015).

Basel III increases capital requirements for banks and makes certain bank activities more capital intensive than in the past. Banks still have a choice for measuring credit risk for risk-weighted assets including:

1 *A standardized approach* with fixed weights as in Basel 1, with little differentiation between safer and more risky assets, so generally with the highest capital requirement.
2 *Foundation internal risk-based (IRB) measures* for credit risk using more sophisticated formulas that use internally developed inputs for the probability of default (PD) and inputs for the loss of default (LGD), exposure at default (EAD) and maturity (M). This method provides a better differentiation for calculating required capital needed for safer versus more risky assets.
3 *An advanced IRB measure for credit risk* that uses more sophisticated formulas and inputs that are internally determined for PD, LGD, EAD, and M. With an internal risk management system and data, a transition to advanced IRB can be implemented.

Under Basel II, banks had strong incentives to move to an IRB status to reduce their total required regulatory capital. Banks must hold capital for their trading book exposures and exposures not held in their trading books to cover credit losses that are unexpected that may happen over a one-year holding period (Latham & Watkins, 2011; Mayer Brown, 2012). Generally, a risk-weighted capital charge is equal to the amount of exposure (EA) × risk weight for exposure (RW) × capital requirement (under Basel II about 8%).

Basel III includes:

1 A higher overall capital requirement.
2 A narrower definition of qualifying regulatory capital.
3 Higher capital charges for banking book and trading book exposures.
4 A new leverage ratio.
5 Two new liquidity ratios (a liquidity coverage ratio phased starting in 2015 and a stable funding ratio phased in starting 2018; discussed in Chapter 10 on liquidity management for depository institutions).

Under Basel III, the quality and quantity of capital increases:

1 *Will rise substantially including the minimum requirement for common equity* (doubling from 2% before deductions to 4.5% after deductions from 2013 to 2015).
2 *A new 2.5% capital conservation buffer will begin in 2016 to 2019* that must be met by Tier 1 (CET 1) capital after deductions. This results in an increase in the total equity to asset requirement, with banks in practice likely to hold more to avoid regulatory penalties, by, for example, not paying dividends to retain more earnings if this falls below a given buffer zone;
3 *A new 0% to 2.5% countercyclical capital buffer will be phased in during January 2016 to 2019.* This countercyclical capital buffer is required to be met with Tier 1 capital and serves as an extension to the capital conservation buffer. The percentage required to be held for this buffer depends on a bank's geographical and credit exposures.

At Basel III's completed phase-in as of January 1, 2019, banks must meet regulatory target ratio minimum requirements to avoid restrictions on capital distributions and discretionary payouts. Basel III Pillar I minimum capital requirements phased in by 2019 include a minimum common equity capital ratio of 4.5%, a minimum Tier 1 capital ratio of 6%, a minimum total (Tier 1+ Tier 2) capital ratio of 8%, and a minimum conservation buffer of 2.5%. This results in a minimum total capital plus conservation buffer of 10.5%. There is also an optional minimum countercyclical buffer of 2.5%. So the minimum total capital including the conservation buffer and optional countercyclical buffer ratio will be 13%. Additional capital requirements for additional loss absorbency are required for globally systemically important banks (G-SIBs). (FDIC Reg. Cap., 2015; Getter, 2012, 2014; Latham & Watkins, 2011; Mayer Brown, 2012).

In the United States, Basel III was adopted in 2013 to be phased in by 2018 and fully implemented by 2023. The United States also imposed new rules under the Dodd–Frank Act of 2010 in response to the U.S. subprime loan crisis of 2007 to 2008.

The status of Basel III adoption varies by country with some countries moving faster than others for its implementation. The Bank for International Settlements website has links (http://www.bis.org/publ/bcbs/b3prog_dom_impl.htm) that include stages of implementation and links and documents for implementation alphabetically by country. An example for the United States for its stages of implementation for Basel III is discussed below.

Revised Regulatory Capital Rules (as of January 1, 2015) for all U.S. FDIC-Insured Banks

Tier 1 leverage capital is as a percentage of total assets, while other ratios are as a percentage of risk-weighted assets. Other interim final rule changes include:

1 Creating a new capital ratio: common equity Tier 1 risk-based capital ratio.
2 Implementing a capital conservation buffer.
3 Revising prompt corrective action (PCA) thresholds and adding a new ratio to the PCA framework.
4 Changing risk weights for certain assets and off-balance sheet exposures.

All capital ratios will use the new definitions of *common equity Tier 1 capital*, additional Tier 1 capital, and Tier 2 capital.

Additional Tier 1 capital includes noncumulative perpetual preferred stock, including surplus and qualifying Tier 1 minority interest less certain investments in financial institutions. *Tier 2 capital* includes limited allowance for loan and lease losses plus preferred stock and subordinated debt plus qualifying Tier 2 minority interest with FDIC minus Tier 2 investments in financial institutions. For institutions with $250 billion or greater in assets or $10 billion or more in foreign exposures they may elect to use accumulated other comprehensive income (AOCI) and advanced approaches, where CET 1 capital includes common stock and retained earnings plus or minus limited AOCI items, plus or minus deductions and adjustments plus qualifying CET 1 minority interest. For banks that do not make this election, limits are less for accumulated other comprehensive income (AOCI) (FDIC Reg. Cap., 2015).

Deductions for common equity Tier 1 capital include goodwill, deferred tax assets, other intangibles, gain on sale of securitization exposures, and certain investments for other financial institutions' capital instruments (with ownership of over 10% of another financial institution's shares considered to be significant). Other adjustments include the deduction of unrealized gains and adding unrealized losses on cash flow hedges.[1] For Tier 2 previous limits on subordinated debt, limited life preferred stock, and the amount of Tier 2 capital included in total capital were eliminated (FDIC Reg. Cap., 2015).

TYPICAL RISK WEIGHT BUCKETS FOR RISK-WEIGHTED ASSETS

Category 1: 0% weight for assets that have low risk including Federal Reserve balances, Organization for Economic Cooperation and Development (OECD) government securities, U.S. government securities, and some U.S. agency securities, among other very low risk assets.

Category 2: 20% weight for other low risk assets including cash in the process of collection, OECD interbank deposits and guaranteed claims, some non-OECD bank and government deposits and securities, general obligation municipal bonds, Fed funds sold, some mortgage-backed securities, claims collateralized (backed) by the U.S. Treasury, and some other government securities, among other low risk assets.

Category 3: 50% weight for other municipal revenue bonds, secured mortgage loans on 1–4 family residential mortgage properties, fully-secured by first liens.

Category 4: 100% weight: All other on-balance sheet assets including commercial and consumer loans, corporate bonds, commercial paper, and other assets not included in other categories.

With Basel III, some changes in risk weightings for more risky assets were made, and these are discussed in a later section.

To calculate risk based on balance sheet assets, the dollar amounts of total assets in each category are multiplied by their respective fraction weights, and the sum is taken. Risk-based off-balance sheet assets must also be converted to credit equivalent assets, and then put in risk categories and multiplied by risk weights to get total risk-based capital required for risk-based capital ratios.

The risk-based categories for credit equivalent off-balance sheet items are generally as follows:

Category 1 (0% risk weight): For very low risk items, such as unused commitments with an original maturity 1 year or less or conditionally cancellable commitments.

Category 2 (20% risk weight): For lower risk items, such as commercial letters of credit, bankers' acceptances conveyed, and other short-term self-liquidating trade-related items.

Category 3 (50% risk weight): For standby letters of credit, other performance warranties and unused portions of loan commitments with original maturities exceeding 1 year, and revolving underwriting facilities.

Category 4 (100% risk weight): For direct credit substitutes including general guarantees, sale and repurchase agreements with recourse, and forward agreements to purchase assets.

Because risk weight buckets do not always reflect the credit risk of individual assets in each bucket (for instance, for off-balance sheet items that are used for hedging and liquidity purposes), there have been some criticisms that broad risk weight buckets may penalize some banks taking lower risks.

Example: Risk-based capital ratios for Winter Green Bank

Tier 1 (CET 1 capital):	Common equity	$1,880,937
	Less adjustments	$291,335
	CET 1 capital	$1,589,602
Tier 2 capital:		$161,113
Total Tier 1 and Tier 2 capital		$1,750,715

Balance sheet risk categories to calculate risk-based assets

Asset type × weight	
Category 1: 0% weight	$2,879,180 × 0 = $0 capital needed to be held
Category 2: 20% weight	$6,126,605 × 0.20 = $1,225,321
Category 3: 50% weight	$860,398 × 0.50 = $403,199
Category 4: 100% weight	$9,539,748 × 1 = $9,539,784
Total on-balance sheet risk-based assets	= $11,168,304

Off-balance sheet risk categories to calculate OBS risk-based assets (credit equivalent amounts of off-balance sheet items are calculated and placed in similar risk-weighted categories):

Off-balance sheet risk categories for OBS assets

Asset type × weight	
Category 1: 0% weight:	$12,139 × 0 = $0
Category 2: 20% weight	$73,180 × 0.20 = $14,636
Category 3: 50% weight	$22,252 × 0.50 = $11,126
Category 4: 100% weight	$1,983,830 × 1 = $1,983,830
Total off-balance sheet risk-based assets	= $2,009,592

Calculating total risk-based assets (RBAs) less adjustments

Total RBA = RBA + OBS RBA = $11,168,304 + $2,009,592 = $13,177,896
Total RBA after technical adjustments = $12,465,170
Total assets after adjustments = $18,765,337

Calculating the capital ratios for the bank based on these figures:

Tier 1 to Risk-based assets = [$1,589,602 million / $12,465,170 million] = 0.1275 or *12.75%*.

Tier 1 to Total assets = [$1,589,602 million / $18,756,337 million] = *8.48%* (Tier 1 leverage%).

Tier 1 and Tier 2 to Risk-based assets = $1,750,715 million / $12,465,170 million = *14.04%*.

Hence, Winter Green Bank is well capitalized by the standards:

Tier 1 leverage%	CET 1 to RBC%	Tier 1 RBC	Total RBC%
≥ 5%	≥ 6.5%	≥ 8%	≥ 10%

Changes in Risk-Weighted Buckets under Basel III

In the United States banks continue to use 50% and 100% risk weights, with 1–4 family residential mortgages still in the 50% weight category. Changes that have been made include weights for *high volatility commercial real estate (HVCRE)*, past-due asset exposures, securitizations (structured investments), equity exposures, equity exposures to investment funds for on balance sheet assets, and certain credit conversion factors for off-balance sheet items, and a risk-weighting substitution for collateralized and guaranteed exposures.

For HVCRE loans, there is a *150% risk weight*. HVCRE loans are categorized as total acquisition, development, and construction (ADC) loans less: (1) ADC loans meeting certain criteria, including if the borrower has contributed in cash or unencumbered "readily marketable assets" at least 15% of the "as completed" value, the loan-to-value (LTV) ratio is at or below the maximum supervisory LTV, and the borrowed contributed capital is by contract required to maintain throughout a project's life; (2) 1–4 family residential projects; (3) ADC loans secured by properties for agricultural purposes; and (4) community development loans.

Past-due assets of 90 days or more past-due or nonaccrual also have higher risk weights for revenue bonds, multi-family loans, consumer loans, commercial and industrial loans, non-farm nonresidential loans, and agricultural loans.

Structured securities and securitizations, such as private label collateralized mortgage obligations (CMOs), trust preferred collateralized debt obligations (TruPS, CDOs) and asset-backed securities have risk weights based on one of three approaches (eliminating a ratings-based approach): a gross up approach, a simplified supervisory formula approach, or a 1,250% risk weight. The chosen approach must be applied consistently with due diligence, and the 1,250% option can be used regardless of which approach was selected to any of a bank's securitization exposures. The simplified supervisory formula approach assigns a risk weight based on the weighted average risk weight of underlying collateral, the relative size and seniority of a particular security in a structure, and the delinquency level of underlying collateral. The gross up methods involves capital required for subordinated tranches based on the amount of the tranche held by a bank and the pro-rata support provided to senior tranches. A securitization cannot be assigned a weight less than 20% (FDIC Reg. Cap., 2015).

GSIB FRAMEWORK UNDER BASEL III

Globally systematically important bank holding companies (GSIB) in the United States are subject to the Federal Reserve Board's risk-based capital surcharge framework, as determined by: (1) their *size* (total exposure), (2) *interconnectedness* (intra-financial system assets, intra-financial system liabilities, and securities outstanding); (3) *substitutability* (payments activity, assets under custody, and underwritten transactions in debt and equity markets); (4) *complexity* (notational amount of over-the-counter (OTC) derivatives); and (5) *cross-jurisdictional activity* (cross-jurisdictional claims and cross-jurisdictional liabilities) (Board of Governors, 2016).

Eight systematically important banks (SIFIs) will be required by the Federal Reserve Board to hold a minimum Basel III leverage ratio of 6%, and 5% for their insured bank holding companies as of July 2013. The Federal Reserve Board of Governors also incorporated a liquidity coverage ratio (LCR) introduced under Basel II for U.S. banking organizations with assets greater than $10 billion, and systematically important financial institutions. The Basel III LCR is based on (high-quality liquidity assets) / (total net liquidity outflows) over 30 days being greater or equal to 100%. The U.S. version is more stringent by having a denominator that considers total net cash outflows over a particular period.

Systematically important financial institutions under the Dodd–Frank 2010 Wall Street Reform Act include Bank of America, JPMorgan Chase, Citigroup, and Wells Fargo, and an estimated 100 large BHCs were estimated to need to raise a total of $4.5 billion in capital by the end of the phase-in of new capital requirements in 2019 to meet new capital requirements (Puzzanghera, 2013).

CRITICISMS OF BASEL III

Although Basel III is only now beginning its evaluation, it has faced some criticism, including the challenge of providing individual financial institutions with buffers that are sufficient to protect them from extreme events and, hence, protect against systemic risk for the banking system. Critics argue that Basel III overly relies on complex analytic methods that previously did not protect banks, and that it puts a large burden on institutions and regulators to closely monitor these models. In particular, specific loan types in risk buckets are not adjusted for their individual credit risk, which may lead to misallocations of capital across different sectors. Some proponents argue that overreliance on models for operational risk and value at risk models does not consider breakdowns caused by people, process and technology that have become increasingly important in recent years. From this perspective, critics note that using simple leverage ratios may be a better and less costly solution (Rossl, 2013).

Other critics point out that the new regulatory scheme doesn't really address the problem of calculation of risk weights under Basel II that led to the accumulation of what seemed like risk-free assets, such as mortgages that were actually risky pools of subprime mortgages given triple A ratings by regulators. Currently lending to AA-rated sovereigns, for instance, has a zero risk weight, which could increase this lending and could result in a future crisis. These critics suggest that regulators need to be more responsive to marketplace changes and products that generate a higher return with low risk (Basel III, 2010b).

SUMMARY

During the U.S. subprime loan crisis and subsequent global financial crisis, financial institutions were severely undercapitalized and, with intricate global connections, there were significant systemic effects across other financial institutions when major global financial institutions were on the brink of bankruptcy. To try to prevent this from occurring in the future, new higher capital regulations were passed under Basel III, including a new additional capital conservation buffer to be phased in by 2019. By requiring higher capital ratios, the hope is that banks will be able to withstand larger losses in the event of a crisis.

Capital management for banks also entails a risk-adjusted return on capital (RAROC) for pricing loans and other risky assets, with a risk premium for the additional capital that needs to be held for more risky assets. Banks also need to consider capital needed for future growth, for maintaining excellent credit ratings. Capital also provides confidence for uninsured depositors and uninsured debt-holders, protection against regulatory interference, contributes to higher credit ratings, provides extra borrowing capacity, and provides an optimal capital structure that offers a lower weighted average cost of capital.

NOTE

1 Other threshold deductions are also included for significant investments in other unconsolidated financial institutions' common stock, for mortgage servicing assets (MSAs) and for deferred taxes that are related to temporary timing differences, with threshold deduction amounts greater than 10% individually or greater than 15% for the aggregate CET 1 capital, with amounts not deducted generally subject to a 250% risk weight.

BIBLIOGRAPHY

Basel III (2010a). "A global regulatory framework for more resilient banks and banking systems." Bank for International Settlements, December 2010 (rev, June 2012, p. 2).

Basel III (2010b). "Basel III: Third time's the charm?" *The Economist*, September 13, 2010. Accessed on February 12, 2016 at: http://www.economist.com/blogs/freeexchange/2010/09/basel_iii

Board of Governors (2016). "GSIB framework denominators." Basel Regulatory Framework, Board of Governors of the Federal Reserve System, January 13, 2016. Accessed on February 14, 2016 at: http://www.federalreserve.gov/bankinforeg/basel/denominators.htm

Buser, Stephen A., Andrew H. Chen, and Edward J. Kane (1981). "Federal deposit insurance, regulatory policy, and optimal bank capital." *Journal of Finance*, 36 (March), 51–60.

Christopoulos, Apostolos G., John Mylonakis, and Pavios Diktapanidis (2011). "Could Lehman Brothers' collapse be anticipated? An examination using CAMELS rating system." *International Business Research,* 4(2). Accessed on February 11, 2016 at: http://www.ccsenet.org/journal/index.php/ibr/article/viewFile/10009/7111

FDIC Reg. Cap. (2015). "FDIC regulatory capital interim final rule." Accessed on February 12, 2016 at: https://www.fdic.gov/regulations/resources/director/rulemaking/RegCapIntFinalRule.pdf

Getter, Darryl E. (2012). "U.S. implementation of the Basel capital regulatory framework," November 14, 2012, Congressional Research Service, www.crs.gov,7-5700/R42744

Getter, Darryl E. (2014). "U.S. implementation of the Basel capital regulatory framework." Congressional Research Service. Accessed on August 27, 2016 at: https://www.fas.org/sgp/crs/misc/R42744.pdf

Kimball, Ralph C. (1998). "Economic profit and performance measurement in banking." *New England Economic Review* (Federal Reserve Bank of Boston), (July/August), 35–53.

Knufken, Drea (2009). "25 Biggest bank failures in history." Business Pundit, May 7, 2009. Accessed on February 12, 2016 at: http://www.businesspundit.com/25-biggest-bank-failures-in-history/

Latham & Watkins (2011). "Regulatory capital reform under Basel III." January 2011. Accessed on February 12, 2015 at: https://www.lw.com/upload/pubContent/_pdf/pub3946_1.pdf

Lekatis, George (2011). "Basel III: Understanding the capital conservation buffer." Treasury NL, May 5, 2011. Accessed on February 14, 2015 at: http://www.treasury.nl/blog/basel-iii-understanding-the-capital-conservation-buffer/

Mayer Brown (2012) "Basel Committee releases final text of Basel III Framework." Accessed on February 4, 2012 at: http://www.mayerbrown.com/publications/article.asp?id=10235.

Puzzanghera, Jim (2013). "Federal reserve adopts tougher capital requirements for banks." *Los Angeles Times*, July 2, 2013. Accessed on February 14, 2016, at http://www.latimes.com/business/la-fi-mo-federal-reserve-basel-banks-20130702-story.html

Rosengren, Eric S. (2009). "Challenges in resolving systemically important financial institutions." Federal Reserve Bank of Boston, Keynote Speech, The Institute of Regulation and Risk North Asia, Hong Kong, May 5, 2009. Accessed on February 11, 2016 at: https://www.bostonfed.org/news/speeches/rosengren/2009/050509.pdf

Rosengren, Eric S. (2013). "Bank capital lessons from the U.S. financial crisis." Federal Reserve Bank of Boston, Bank for International Settlements Forum on Key Regulatory and Supervisory Issues in a Basel III World Keynote Address, February 24, 2013. Accessed on February 11, 2016 at: http://www.basel-iii-accord.com/

Rossl, Clifford (2013). "Banks' model risk worse than ever, thanks to Basel III." *American Banker*, July 11, 2013. Accessed on February 13, 2015 at: http://www.americanbanker.com/bankthink/model-risk-worse-than-ever-thanks-to-basel-iii-1060517-1.html

Wiggins, Rosalind Z. and Andrew Metrick (2015). "The Lehman Brothers Bankruptcy H: The global contagion." Yale Program on Financial Stability Case Study 2014: 3H-V1, October 1, 2014, Revised April 8, 2015. Accessed on February 11, 2016 at: http://som.yale.edu/sites/default/files/files/001-2014-3H-V1-LehmanBrothers-H-REVA.pdf

QUESTIONS AND PROBLEMS

Problems

1   The Precipice Bank has the following balance sheet (in $ million)

Assets		Liabilities and equity	
Cash	20	Deposits	850
Treasury securities	75	Subordinated debt	15
Mortgages	740	Common stock	10
Fixed assets	70	Retained earnings	30
Total	905		905
Off-balance sheet items (credit equivalent in 50% risk-based category)			
Long-term loan commitments:		$ 500 million	
Interest rate swap agreement:		$ 100 million	

Because of severe economic difficulties in the savings and loans region, $50 million of the mortgages are in default, requiring a 200% risk weight by regulators.

a   Calculate the firm's risk-based assets, Tier 1 capital and Tier 2 capital, and its regulatory capital ratios (Tier 1 capital to risk-based assets, Tier 2 capital to total assets, and Tier 1 + Tier 2 capital to risk-based assets.

b   What regulatory category of capitalization would Precipice fall under for U.S. banks under Basel III?

2 Euphoria Savings Bank has the following balance sheet (book values in $ thousand):

Assets ($ thousand)		Liabilities and equity ($ thousand)	
Cash	300	Deposits	40,500
T-bills	7,000	Equity	1,800
Consumer loans	35,000		
Total assets	42,300	Total liabilities and equity	42,300

Note the consumer loans are 3-year fixed-rate loans with a 12% annual rate (1% monthly rate). Assume that with an interest rate change, the market values of the T-bills and deposits will not change (having very short-term maturities).

    a   Calculate the market value change in the consumer loans if the interest rate on similar consumer loans has risen to 15%.

    b   What is the difference between the book value of equity and the market value of equity (given this rate change)? Compare capital ratios for the book value of equity and the market value of equity with this change?

    c   Do the same problem, but assume instead that the interest rate on similar consumer loans has fallen to 8%.

Hint: The monthly loan payment for the consumer loans = loan amount / (present value interest factor of an annuity 36 payments, 1%)

$$= \$35{,}000{,}000 / [1 - (1 / (1.01)^{36}] / 0.01 = \$35{,}000{,}000 / 30.1075$$
$$= \$1{,}162{,}501 \text{ a month}$$

Questions

1 Why is the market value of equity so different from the book value of equity for depository institutions? What happens to the market value of equity if interest rates rise and a bank has long-term assets financed by short-term deposits? Explain why.

2 What is the purpose of capital? Why is capital particularly important for depository institutions? Give an example from the U.S. subprime crisis or the global financial crisis that followed.

3 What are the different preferences of stockholders, managers, regulators, and insured and uninsured depositors for how much capital banks should have? Why does deposit insurance create a moral hazard?

4 What is Basel III and what are its primary capital ratios? How has Basel III improved upon Basel II? What are the weaknesses and strengths of Basel III?

5 What is RAROC? How does RAROC help in allocating capital for a bank's economic risks? How is it used to price loans?

6 What are practical considerations that a bank needs to bear in mind when selecting the best capital structure?

7 What is a globally systematically important bank holding company (GSIB)? How are GSIBs determined?

Chapter 6

Social and Environmental Risks and Sustainable Financial Institutions

Concepts such as natural wealth and the circular, green economy have moved from the margins to become the substance of economic strategies and policies for businesses and nations. Clean energy will underpin tomorrow's global energy system and there is little doubt that the challenge, although considerable, is essentially one of transition.

(Steiner, 2015)

For too many years, we failed to rein in the excesses building up in the nation's financial markets. When the credit bubble burst in 2008, the damage was devastating. Millions suffered. Many still do. We're making the same mistake with climate change. We're staring down a climate bubble that poses enormous risks to both our environment and economy. The warning signs are clear and growing more urgent at the risks go unchecked.

(Paulson, 2014)

As expressed by Achim Steiner (2015), the United Nations Under-Secretary General and Executive Director of the United Nations Environment Programme (UNEP), there has been a growing recognition and a *quiet revolution taking place* in the aftermath of the global financial crisis for sustainable finance whereby:

[T]he financial system must be not only sound and stable, but also sustainable in the way it enables the transition to a low-carbon, green economy. Therefore to achieve the sustainable development we want will require a realignment of the financial system with the goals of sustainable development.

Harry Paulson, former U.S. Secretary of the Treasury (2014) observes as well that there are major concerns about the potential for a "climate bubble" that could occur in the future, with the need to transition to a less fossil fuel dependent economy to avoid a temperature rise of 2°C, which climate scientists agree would result in catastrophic climate change (McGlade and Elkins, 2015; Meinhausen, et al., 2009). The U.S. National Oceanic and Atmospheric Administration (NOAA) (2015) reported that based on a maximum carbon budget of less than 1,000 billion tons of CO_2 released in the atmosphere to avoid such a temperature rise, only about 565 gigatons of CO_2 ($GtCO_2$) can be emitted.

In December of 2015, COP21, the conference of parties for the 21st Climate Change Conference of the United Nations resulted in the submission of *intended nationally determined contributions* (INDCs) to the UN Framework Convention on Climate Change, as climate action plans for lowering global emissions for 155 countries to the UN, representing almost 90% of global carbon emissions. The INDCs are noted to be a floor versus a ceiling for action, with additional negotiations and commitments needed to keep temperatures from rising above 2°C, but an improvement over a *business as usual* path that would result in a rise of greater than 4°C, with the agreement ratified in October 2016 (United Nations, 2016).

As pointed out on the COP21 website (United Nations, 2015), globally businesses have "been at the forefront of efforts to persuade government leaders to reach a meaningful global climate agreement." Many businesses including financial institutions have taken actions to report their carbon emissions to the CDP (formerly the Carbon Disclosure Project) and/or the Global Reporting Initiative (GRI), creating and working to meet targets to reduce future carbon emissions. By doing so, they have also increased their operating efficiencies and substantially reduced their operating costs with lower energy usage, increasing overall profitability.

In the United States 75 large corporations joined the original signatories for a total of 154 companies signing up for the American Business Act on Climate Pledge to take aggressive action against climate change, including ambitious company-specific goals, with signatory companies having a combined market capitalization of greater than US$7 trillion.

Financial institutions have significant roles to play in mitigating climate change risks, including accompanying socioeconomic risks. These roles include:

1   providing financing for sustainable development, including funding for new emerging technologies for alternative energy sources and funds to reduce socioeconomic problems for poor communities;
2   evaluating and monitoring companies they make loans to for environmental and social risks, as an important fiduciary duty;
3   acting as shareholder activists through both negotiation with companies and using shareholder proxy resolutions for annual meetings to put pressure on companies to reduce negative environmental and social impacts;
4   providing insurance and risk management services and new insurance products to protect against catastrophic climate change related future events;
5   managing sustainably and reducing their own carbon footprints;
6   taking advantage of opportunities to develop innovative new products and services and sustainable financing techniques for the mitigation of environmental and social welfare problems and educating its stakeholders; and
7   participating in thought leadership and development with governments, industry, peers, and nongovernment organizations to promote policy changes to mitigate climate change risks.

This chapter provides an overview of FI risks associated with climate change, sustainable management strategies that financial institutions have undertaken, and sustainability frameworks that have evolved to assist financial institutions in these endeavors, along with an overview of socially responsible investment funds, and new green bonds and social bonds, and project type financing.

CLIMATE CHANGE RISKS

The Intergovernmental Panel on Climate Change (IPCC, 2014) in its "Climate Change 2014: Impacts, Adaptation, and Vulnerability" assessment report warned of increased risk of flooding and threats to food and water security with the effects of climate change already happening across continents and oceans. Key risks associated with climate change listed include storm surges, flooding on coasts, sea-level rises for communities on coasts, and disruption and flood risks associated with inland flooding for some regions, and extreme weather events that can result in breakdowns of infrastructure networks and critical electricity, water supply, emergency and health services (Lloyds, 2014).

The World Economic Forum (WEF, 2015) similarly points out extreme weather events, natural catastrophes, and failure of climate change adaptation as three of the top ten global risks, with the lack of proper adaptation leading to the spread of infectious diseases, energy price shock, and biodiversity loss and ecosystem collapse.

Similarly, large financial institutions have taken positions on climate change risk, such as Citi's (2007) position taken on its website:

> In February 2007 Citi issued a Position Statement on Climate Change that calls on Congress to immediately create a market-based national policy to reduce GHG [greenhouse gas] emissions, with the ultimate goal of contributing to the development of an integrated global framework. We believe in this national policy to reduce GHG emissions, with the ultimate goal of contributing to the development of an integrated global framework. We believe this national policy should bring clarity and certainty to markets, emphasize that a transition to environmentally sustainable energy will foster economic activity and opportunity, generate jobs, and protect the environment, and recognize emissions-reduction efforts undertaken prior to the enactment of a national legislative framework to encourage early action.

Citi also lists its roles in mitigating climate change, including: promoting cost-effective energy efficiency, renewable energy, and other low-carbon alternatives to conventional power generation; applying enhanced diligence in evaluating the financing of fossil fuel power plants in the United States; educating stakeholders including governments on changes to mitigate climate change risks; and pursuing business opportunities by developing products and services to help clients transition to and be successful in a carbon-constrained economy, with strategic advice on climate-related opportunities, financing and investing in renewable energy and clean technology, carbon trading in markets allowing trading, and partnering with energy service companies and utilities to finance client energy-efficiency retrofits, among others (Citi, 2007).

For financial institutions, there are a number of different financial risks associated with risks of climate change including:

1   *Carbon asset risk*, the risk of fossil fuel companies losing value with the transition towards a low fossil fuel economy, including having large reserves of fossil fuel become unburnable "stranded assets," with future regulatory restrictions likely to be imposed by governments to avoid serious effects of climate change.

2   *Catastrophic weather-related events* that can affect businesses that financial institutions lend to, increasing the default risk for loans and loss on investments for banks and security firms, and resulting in large payouts for severe climate change weather event damages for property/liability insurance companies.

3   *Environmental health and socioeconomic risks* associated with greater prevalence of infectious diseases and poor air quality and lung diseases, associated with climate change, affecting health insurers, among other financial institutions. Socioeconomic risks include social unrest resulting from unfavorable climate change for poorer, emerging economies, including droughts, flooding, and food scarcity.

A discussion of financial institution engagement to mitigate different climate change risks follows. A more detailed discussion and leadership by the financial services industry can be found in a report published by UNEP (2015) on "Financial institutions taking action on climate change."

CARBON ASSET RISK AND INSTITUTIONAL INVESTOR ENGAGEMENT

In 2011 and 2013 the Carbon Tracker Initiative (2011, 2013), as well as later research reports by HSBC in 2012, 2013 and 2015, Citi, and Goldman Sachs (Randall, 2014), expressed urgent concerns about stranded assets, large fossil fuel reserves that will likely be unburnable in the future (i.e., becoming stranded assets), to avoid a rise in global temperatures associated with catastrophic climate change. This suggests much lower valuations for fossil fuel companies and the potential for a carbon bubble, with today's valuations not reflecting potential unburnable reserves for fossil fuel companies. Institutional investors with large portfolios that include fossil fuel company stocks have been particularly concerned about stranded asset risk, which has the potential for huge price drops in portfolios. Central banks and other government organizations and sovereign funds have also issued concerns, including the Bank of England warning of "huge financial risk" from fossil fuel investments (Carrington, 2015; HSBC, 2015).

In response to the climate change risk associated with the burning and continued exploration for reserves by major fossil fuel companies, and the potential for valuation losses for stranded assets, a divestment movement began in 2011 that included Go Fossil Free and Divest-Invest, encouraging divestment and reinvestment in alternative energy sources globally. By the end of 2014, 181 institutions and local governments and 656 individuals managing over $50 billion in assets made a pledge to divest from fossil fuels, focusing on coal, as the largest emitter of carbon emissions. This group includes socially responsible mutual funds, pension funds for sovereign funds, municipalities, and universities around the world, with 17 of the world's largest philanthropic foundations divesting from fossil fuels over 2011 to 2015.

139

*Social and
Environmental
Risks and
Sustainable
Financial
Institutions*

Often large pension funds and other institutional investors have engaged in letters, negotiation, and carbon risk shareholder resolutions targeting major fossil fuel companies that are the largest carbon emitters. In 2013, a group of 70 major institutional investors, including major pension funds, private equity investors, and socially responsible investment firms managing over $3 trillion in assets, delivered letters to the 45 major fossil fuel companies as globally the top CO2 emitters requesting that the companies address new business models for a less carbon dependent world in the future. These letters were followed by formal shareholder resolutions at annual meetings of major fossil fuel companies, requesting that stranded asset risks be addressed in annual reports. In 2015, for the first time, shareholder proxy resolutions were presented to major fossil fuel companies that uniquely demanded a return of capital to investors for stranded asset risks, if companies continue to make large capital expenditures for the acquisition of new, large fossil fuel reserves. Many of the stock resolutions are facilitated by nonprofit organizations including As You Sow (www.asyousow.org) and Ceres (www.ceres.org) that promote environmental and social corporate responsibility by means of shareholder advocacy and coalition-building strategies, along with sustainability leadership with investor and company networks (Byrd and Cooperman, 2015, 2016).

In other activist activities by institutional investors, legal actions have been used. Under the U.S. Securities and Exchange Commission (SEC) ruling in 2010, publicly traded companies are mandated to address the risks posed by climate change in their regular security filings. In April of 2015, 62 institutional investors mandated that the SEC hold firms more accountable for not disclosing their climate change risks in a letter to the SEC. Later in October 2015, the New York City and New York State comptrollers, administrations with large public pension funds, sent letters to the SEC with a similar request for greater climate change risk disclosure. In other actions, in November 2015, the New York attorney general began an investigation of Exxon Mobil as a major fossil fuel company for not revealing the seriousness of climate change risk to investors. Investor concerns were related to falling prices for fossil fuel companies over 2011 to 2015, with coal company stock prices in particular falling dramatically, such as for Peabody Energy, a major U.S. coal company, whose share price fell from $1,000 per share in 2011 to $4 in 2015 (Gilles, 2016; Gillis and Krauss, 2015).

CARBON RISK IN THE BANKING SECTOR FOR LOANS

Boston Common Asset Management (2014) points out that the financial institution industry's assets that are in portfolios that are distributed across sectors makes them particularly vulnerable to economic and political uncertainty created by climate change, including a transformed environment with new regulations and adaptations and lending and underwriting activities, leading to both direct and indirect ownership in companies with high-carbon assets. Environmental risks for banks include the risk of inadequate credit risk assessment and loan pricing, changing regulatory environments, legal and reputational risks, uncertain demand in the future for high-carbon fuels, and misalignment of incentives of bankers. The report states that, for risk management, stress tests need to be performed to examine the effects of adverse climate events, that portfolios need to be rebalanced for climate change risks, and loan pricing and investment analysis needs to consider risk premiums for the legal and reputation aspects of investments and potential shifts in consumer behavior that can affect the demand for fuels that are carbon based (Boston Common, 2014).

In December of 2015, U.S. banks with $50 billion or more in assets required to have stress tests by the Federal Reserve expected tougher stress tests in the future, given their exposure to oil and dramatically falling prices for crude oil to below $36 per barrel, an 11-year low changing the outlook for energy companies and the financial sector, with rising default risk for many oil and gas loans to exploration and oil producers who could have more difficulty paying their loans with low oil prices (Noonan, 2015). In December of 2014, similar warnings were provided in an analysis by Goldman Sachs that estimated that $930 billion of investments in future oil projects were at risk as they were no longer profitable with a 49% drop in crude prices at that time over the previous six months (Randall, 2014).

HOW SUSTAINABILITY BENEFITS FINANCIAL INSTITUTIONS

From a financial perspective, sustainable management practices increase a firm's operating efficiency, reducing costs and increasing profitability. Sustainability encompasses managing for profitability to remain viable and maximize shareholder wealth, but extending this objective to create social and environmental value for all stakeholders as well. Many large banks, such as Bank of America, Westminster Bank, and Tridos, became leaders in sustainability early on with energy reduction projects, use of renewable energy and energy reductions, use of solar power, and recycling, and other sustainability ventures generating large cost savings (Bouma, Jeucken, and Klinkers, 2002; Jeucken 2002; Kalla 2011).

As noted on the First for Sustainability (2015) website, there are two components of sustainability that benefit financial institutions, by:

1 *Providing an evaluation of both environmental and social risks* to strengthen lending and investment portfolios, reducing financial, liability, and reputational risks arising from ESG issues.
2 *Identifying and taking advantage of environmental business opportunities* to develop innovative products that are both profitable and provide environmental and social benefits (e.g., the evolution of renewable energy, energy efficiency, cleaner production processes and technologies, carbon finance, and sustainable supply chains, among others).

By incorporating environmental, social, and governance (ESG) goals in business models, financial institutions differentiate themselves from competitors and increase profitability by being able to attract a more talented, committed workforce. This also results in greater access to capital by increasing goodwill, with better public perceptions and branding as a result. In addition, FIs become more efficient by reducing energy and resource costs, as well as future potential legal costs and payments for environmental and social damages (First for Sustainability, 2015).

Many FIs provide lending support to companies in sustainable industries seeking solutions to environmental and social problems. Financial institutions also have been innovative in developing financial products that support environmental and social goals, including green bonds and social impact bonds, as well as developing financial instruments to protect against catastrophic events associated with climate change. Over 720 socially responsible

141

*Social and
Environmental
Risks and
Sustainable
Financial
Institutions*

investment (SRI) firms and mutual funds use ESG criteria for their portfolios. The Forum for Sustainable and Responsible Investment (US SIF, 2014) reported that by the end of 2014, SRI was $4.85 trillion in the United States, along with $1.35 trillion both invested and used for shareholder resolution strategies, and $0.37 trillion for shareholder resolutions alone, totaling $6.57 trillion in SRI. The Global Sustainable Investment Alliance (GSIA, 2014) reported global sustainable investment assets to have expanded from $13.3 trillion at the beginning of 2012 to reach a total of $21.4 trillion at the beginning of 2014, representing a 61% growth rate that outpaced the growth of total professionally managed assets. Many private equity and venture capital funds use ESG criteria, including venture capital funds that provide substantial funding to the Clean Tech sector. FIs also often provide education and support to help customers be more environmentally conscious, such as charging lower rates for loans for energy efficient cars and products (Cooperman, 2011, 2013; Global Clean Technology Venture Investment, 2013; Goossens, 2012; GSIA, 2014; Hull, 2013; KKR, 2015; US SIF, 2014).

On the social side, financial institutions have engaged in employee volunteering and other social programs, and some countries have passed regulations that require large financial institutions do so. In Canada, legislation was initiated that requires public accountability statements (PAS), including an outline of economic and social contributions to their communities, from all financial institutions with over $1 billion in equity. Some institutions have engaged in meeting these obligations through employer-supported volunteer programs for employees. In the United States, the Community Reinvestment Act (CRA) encourages depository institutions to meet the credit needs of the communities in which they operate.

Many large international banks such as Deutsche Bank have developed employee engagement programs that support employee engagement activities with over 25% participation by 19,562 volunteers for 2,948 volunteer projects and support for 2,479 partner organizations, and 25,030 volunteer days globally (Deutsche Bank Responsibility, 2014). Citigroup and other large banks have also posted Environmental Commitment on their websites along with strategies to reduce their environmental footprint, and manage their environmental and social risks. Targets for reductions in carbon emissions are also provided, as are contributions towards climate initiatives. Many large financial institutions have joined the Equator Principles, the Global Reporting Initiative (GRI), CDP (formerly the Carbon Disclosure Project) and the United Nations Principles for Responsible Investment (UNPRI), among other organizations discussed below, promoting responsible lending practices and greenhouse gas (GHG) emission reductions (Cooperman, 2013).

EQUATOR PRINCIPLES

The Equator Principles (EP) originally was started in 2002 with 10 global banks which agreed upon guidelines on social and environmental issues on loans to developing countries. Today the Equator Principles encompasses all project loans of $10 million or more across different industry sectors and a credit risk management framework for assessing and managing environmental and social risk for project transactions. As of January 2016, 83 EP Financial Institutions (EPFIs) operating in 36 countries have officially signed on, encompassing 70% of international project finance debt in emerging markets. Members commit to incorporate and implement the Equator Principles in their internal environmental and social policies, and procedures and standards for the financing of projects. EPFIs do not provide loans to projects with clients that will not or are unable to comply with the Equator Principles. EPFIs report at different times in the calendar year based on their reporting periods. The Equator Principles website contains publicly available EP best practice and documents for download, including guidance for EPFIs in incorporating environment and social considerations into loan documentation (Cooperman, 2011, 2013; Epstein 2008; Equator Principles, 2016).

The Carbon Principles (CP)

In February 2008, three major banks, Citi, JPMorgan Chase, and Morgan Stanley proclaimed common coal power financing policies, known as the Carbon Principles, to address environmental and regulatory risks associated with carbon emissions. The principles came out of public concerns for plans for more than 100 new coal-fired power plants, which would move the United States further into a utility carbon-intensive sector resulting in additional hundreds of millions of tons of new CO_2 emissions each year. The Carbon Principles presents due diligence conditions on banks for financing the construction of new U.S. coal-fired power plants. Signatories to CP commit to:

1. *Encouraging clients to engage in cost-effective energy efficiency*, renewable energy, and other low-cost carbon alternatives, taking into account the potential value added of avoiding CO_2 emissions.
2. *Applying an enhanced diligence process in evaluating the financial and operational risk of fossil fuel generation financing*, posing the prospect of domestic CO_2 emissions controls and using the result for the determination of whether a transaction is eligible for financing and under what terms.
3. *Educating clients, regulators, and other industry participants regarding the additional diligence that is required for "fossil fuel generation financings,"* and encouraging regulatory and legislative changes that are consistent with the Carbon Principles. In 2009 the scope of CP also included the financing for public power and electric companies. Other major bank signatories by 2010 included Wells Fargo & Co. and Credit Suisse (Morgan Stanley, 2008).

There have been some critics that say banks need to do more, including a report by the Rainforest Action Network (RAN) in 2010 that found little difference in the financing of coal plants for the five major CP banks versus five other major banks. The report urges a more aggressive and urgent focus and actions for the CP signatories, including greater public debate for governments to make policy changes to mitigate climate risk, better assessment of loans for GHG emission risk and not granting funding to coal extraction projects, providing more financing for renewable energy production and emission reduction technologies, and developing more services to assist clients in addressing climate change (RAN, 2010).

The Climate Principles

The Climate Principles provide a framework similar to the Carbon Principles for European banks for best practices for the financial sector regarding climate change. This includes a comprehensive industry framework in response to climate change adopted by Credit Agricole, Munich Re, Standard Chartered, Swiss Re, and HSBC. The Climate Principles are

143

*Social and
Environmental
Risks and
Sustainable
Financial
Institutions*

proactive in engaging with a network of stakeholders to raise awareness about climate change and reducing GHG emissions; engaging with suppliers on climate change issues; and supporting the adoption of effective and efficient regulation and policy to reduce GHG emissions, including engaging policymakers and key stakeholders individually or through industry and multi-stakeholder initiatives.

Specific commitments are included for:

1 *Asset management:* including carbon and climate risks and opportunities into research and investment decisions.
2 *Retail banking:* making customers aware of their impacts and developing products and services for customers to address these impacts and reduce carbon footprints.
3 *Insurance and reinsurance:* developing skills and tools to assess carbon and climate risks for clients and providing advice, products and services to help customers reduce both carbon and climate risks.
4 *Corporate banking:* developing and implementing a process to assess the financial implications of carbon and climate risks for loans and investing activities, and educating clients on measuring and reducing these risks.
5 *Investment banking and markets:* advising clients on financial implications of carbon and climate risk, *for structured lending and venture capital*; generating viable financing solutions for investment in low-carbon technologies and greenhouse gas reduction products; *for trading*, developing expertise in emissions trading, weather derivatives, renewable energy credits, and other, climate-related commodities and promoting these.
6 *Project finance:* seeking opportunities to reduce project-related GHG emissions, quantifying, monitoring, disclosing, and reporting direct and indirect GHG emissions, and the evaluation of options to reduce or offset GHG emissions for the design and operation of a project (The Climate Principles, 2016).

UN Principles for Responsible Investment (UNPRI)

The UNPRI initiative includes an international network of investors that work together to put in practice six Principles for Responsible Investing, with the goal for investors to understand and include these in their ownership practices and investment decisions to contribute to a more sustainable global financial system. As of February 2016, there are 1,380 signatories, including asset owners, investment managers, and service providers with $59 trillion assets under management.

The six principles include: (1) incorporating ESG issues into investment analysis and decision making; (2) being active owners and incorporating ESG issues into ownership policies and practices; (3) seeking appropriate disclosure on ESG issues for the companies which are invested in; (4) promoting the acceptance and use of the Principles within the investment industry; (5) working together to enhance effectiveness in implementing the Principles; and (6) reporting on activities and progress towards implementing the Principles (UNPRI, 2016).

CDP (Formerly the Carbon Disclosure Project)

The Carbon Disclosure Project, renamed to the CDP to include all greenhouse gases, is an organization that is based in the United Kingdom. The CDP works with 822 institutional investors holding $95 trillion in assets to help assess the environmental risk in their investment portfolios, and with thousands of companies and governments to reduce their GHG emissions, along with other business and government actions. The CDP is the largest collector globally of self-reported climate change, water and forest risk data for companies and other organizations. Many large financial companies are signatories and members including Aegon, Allianz Global Investors, Aviva Investors, Axa Group, Bank of America, Blackrock, Boston Common Asset Management, BP Investment Management, California Public Employees Retirement System (CALPERS), California State Teachers Retirement Fund (CalSTRS), Calvert Asset Management Company, Goldman Sachs Asset Management, HSBC Holdings, Key Bank, Legg Mason, London Pension Fund Authority, Norges Bank Investment Management, and TIAA-CREF, among many others financial institutions.

Wolfsberg's AML Principles

The Wolfsberg Group, an association of 13 global banks that came together in 2000 at the Chateau Wolfsberg in north-eastern Switzerland, along with representatives from Transparency International. The group drafted and later published "The Wolfsberg anti-money laundering principles for private banking." It also published research on the financing of terrorism and measures FIs can consider to prevent money laundering and corruption in their own operations. The Wolfsberg Group includes Banco Santander, Bank of America, Bank of Tokyo–Mitsubishi UFJ, Barclays, Citigroup, Credit Suisse, Deutsche Bank, Goldman Sachs, HSBC, JPMorgan Chase, Societe Generale, Standard Chartered Bank, and UBS (Wolfsberg Group, 2015).

Natural Capital Declaration

The Natural Capital Declaration is a global statement that demonstrates the financial sector's commitment to work towards the integration of natural capital criteria into financial products and services. Signatories include international financial institutions, such as Althella Ecosphere, ASN Bank, Banco Pichincha, Banorte-Ixe, Caisse des Depots, Caixa Economica Federal, Calvert Investment, China Merchants Bank, Financiera Rural, FIRA–Banco de Mexico, First Green Bank, FMO, Infraprev, International Finance Corporation, Kenya Commercial Bank, MN (a large Dutch asset management firm), Mongeral Aegon, MS&AD Insurance Group Holdings, National Australia Bank, Nedbank, PaxWorld Management, Ping An Bank, Rabobank Group, Robeco, Sovereign, Standard Chartered, Sumitomo Mitsui Trust Holding, UniCredit, VicSuper, and Yes Bank, as working group members with 12 other large banks and wealth and asset management firms as observers.

The Natural Capital Declaration is supported by both the UNEP Finance Initiative and the Global Canopy Program (GCP). Signatories acknowledge and reaffirm the importance of "natural capital" in the maintenance of a sustainable global economy, and the importance of leadership from the financial sector in reducing the ecological footprints of customers, whose impacts have significant financial risks. The declaration includes a call to action for governments to develop long-term frameworks for disclosure of environmental risks and to incentivize financial institutions and other organizations to take natural capital into account as a cost used for financial decision making and valuations. The declaration recognizes the significant role financial institutions have to play for reforms to include natural capital in decisions made within the financial system (Natural Capital Declaration, 2016).

The Social Capital Protocol

The Social Capital Protocol is similar to the Natural Capital Protocol, but envisions decision making by businesses to be in harmony with, and measure and value interactions with people and society, with a call for collaboration with business to create such a platform including tools, frameworks, and standards. A position paper calling for collaboration by the World Business Council for Sustainable Development (WBCSD) points out that, although there are many tools and approaches for measuring social impacts, businesses are calling for a more widely accepted approach that includes: (1) clarification for businesses to develop best practices approaches for social performance, tools, and standards; (2) increasing positive social impacts of business throughout a firm's operations and supply chain; and (3) increasing business credibility with a solid foundation and framework for external reporting and disclosure of social impacts and dependencies.

SOCIALLY RESPONSIBLE INVESTMENT (SRI) MANAGERS AND MUTUAL FUNDS

Socially responsible investing has become more mainstream in recent years with a number of sustainability indexes reflecting the performance of ESG funds, including the Dow Jones Sustainability Indexes (DJSI), the FTSE4Good Index series, the Goldman Sachs GS SUSTAIN ESG index, the Domini 400 Social Index, MSCI World, and the KLD Broad Market Social Index (BMSI) among many more. Mutual funds provide different types of ESG funds and index funds, and socially responsible investment (SRI) funds have grown dramatically. Social Funds (www.socialfunds.com) lists numerous SRI mutual funds. Some funds are offered by SRI companies such as Calvert, Green Century, Domini, and Pax World, while others are offered by large mutual fund companies, including TIAA-CREF, Vanguard, and others, and others firms that are more regionally focused, such as First Affirmative Financial Network, LLC, a professional SRI firm in Colorado that allows individually tailored portfolios to be created for individual investor customers (Cooperman, 2013). There are also many ESG asset managers. For example, Green Alpha Advisors is an asset management firm that addresses core economic concerns and risks associated with "resource scarcity and the worst effect of climate change, examining innovations that address these risks and that improve economic productivity," as well as managing a specialty portfolio for the Sierra Club (SCGA) (Green Alpha, 2016).

Fung, Law, and Yau (2010) point out different strategies used by SRI companies to create SRI portfolios, including: (1) investment screens that can be either positive or negative types of screening; (2) best-in-class screenings with comparisons and rankings of firms in specific industry sectors or other selected groups or benchmark indexes; (3) active engagement with companies that are considered, with a certain amount of capital invested in the company, such as through bank lenders or private equity investors; (4) shareholder advocacy and activism to support specific causes; and (5) approaches that include a combination of these strategies or use additional ESG metrics for portfolio creation.

Investment managers of funds often use their own funds to engage in shareholder proxy resolution campaigns for social environmental health issues, assisted by nonprofit advocate groups, such as the As You Sow Foundation and Ceres, with groups of investors often joining together to submit a joint environmental health shareholder resolution.

According to the Forum for Sustainable and Responsible Investment in its 2014 Report on Sustainable and Responsible Investing Trends in the United States, socially responsible investments in the United States were $6.57 trillion in 2014, growing from $3.74 trillion in 2011. Top environmental shareholder resolutions filed in 2014 included those on climate change, pollution/toxics, and sustainability reporting. Top social shareholder resolutions were predominantly related to political contributions, and top governance issues were executive compensation and independence of the chair of the board. Also, from 2012 to 2014, institutional investor policies to restrict investments in weapons manufacturers grew to affect $355 billion in assets, which was a four-fold increase (US SIF 2016).

SUSTAINABILITY REPORTING

Sustainability reporting has also been an important way for an institution to both commit to sustainability practices and to report to and engage stakeholders, and to attract investments from socially responsible investors (SRIs). It also is a way to showcase what an institution has accomplished, and its awareness of the environmental and social risks and hazards it faces. As pointed out by Kalla (2011), sustainability reporting can also help institutions obtain global rankings in such as the Dow Jones Sustainability Index (DJSI) that tracks the financial performance for companies that are sustainability driven.

Although sustainability reporting is not mandated by regulations, stakeholders of companies including consumers have preferences for sustainable companies, which provides branding advantages for companies, as well as benefitting companies with reductions in their carbon footprints and also improving company efficiency by reducing energy costs. Globally as of 2011 there were close to 300 financial institutions reporting on sustainability performance (Kalla 2011).

GLOBAL REPORTING INITIATIVE'S (GRI) G3 GUIDELINES

Approximately 7,500 reports with reporters in 90 different countries use the GRI framework including the G3 guidelines, which include a special supplement on the financial services sector. The GRI is an independent, international organization that assists businesses, government, and other organizations to both understand and communicate the impact of business on climate change, human rights, corruption, and other crucial sustainability issues. GRI sustainability reporting standards are the most widely used standards for sustainability reporting and disclosure. The key vision for GRI is "to empower decision makers everywhere" with the GRI's sustainability standards and multi-stakeholder network to be able to move towards a more sustainable economy and world. Key values are a multi-stakeholder process and network that is inclusive, transparency as a catalyst for change, informed decision making through the GRI standards, the need for a global perspective to change the world, and that public interest should be driving each decision that an organization makes. The GRI has special GRI guidance for different industries, including what stakeholders want to know, and this includes guidance for banks, diverse financials and insurance (GRI 2016; GRI Topics 2016).

SUSTAINABILITY ACCOUNTING STANDARDS BOARD (SASB)

Climate change sustainability disclosure is becoming increasingly valued by investors and stakeholders. Recognizing this importance, the Sustainability Accounting Standards Board (SASB) was established in the United States as an independent nonprofit organization, accredited by the American National Standards Institute (ANSI) to provide sustainability accounting standards for use by publicly listed corporations in their financial statements to disclose material sustainability issues. In early 2016, the Institute of Management Accountants (IMA), a global accounting association, became aligned proactively with SASB to advance the disclose of such valuable nonfinancial information in corporate reports (UN PRI, 2016). SASB has developed standards for 80 industries in 10 sectors based on the work of multi-stakeholder industry working groups, including over 2,800 individuals with combined $23.4 trillion in assets under management and $11 trillion in market capital (SASB, 2016). Standards have been developed in the financial field, for instance for the commercial banking, investment banking and brokerage, asset management and custody activities, consumer finance, mortgage finance, security and commodity exchanges and insurance areas. The standards include the integration of environmental, social, and governance factors in practices and disclosures, and inclusion of the underserved, and management of systematic and climate change risks, among others (SASB, 2016).

SOCIAL BANKS AND ENVIRONMENTAL OR ECO BANKS

A group of banks, social banks and environmental or eco banks and credit unions, have been formed with environmental and social goals in addition to economic goals, providing a culture where environmental and social goals are prominent, as well as sustaining profitability to allow their institutions to thrive. Similarly, a number of large banks have inaugurated programs for microlending (Drake and Rhyne, 2002; Institute for Social Banking, 2015).

Weber and Remer (2011) point out that there are many different definitions of social banks, but one of the best definitions for a social bank is a bank that aims for a positive impact through banking on "people, the environment and culture." They also point out that banks that consider themselves to be "core social banks" include 28 banks that are often members of the Global Alliance for Banking on Values (GABV, 2015) or the Institute for Social Banking (ISB, 2015), which was founded by a group of European social banks and financial service providers to offer training and education in social banking. In addition, they point out different classifications for social banks, including social banks that provide poverty alleviation and other ethical banks, for which ethical principles take precedence over the maximization of profits. Also, there are social banks that focus more on microcredit lending, and those that focus on sustainable or environmentally related, sustainable loans and mortgages and socially responsible investments.

The GABV (2016) is an international banking network that has a commitment to the advancement of positive changes in banking values, including transparency of banking business models, sustainability with indicators to report the social and ecological impact of banking within a regulatory framework, and diversity having an important part for "reframing regulations for the financial sector." GABV member banks include independent licensed financial institutions that have combined assets of over $100 billion operating in countries across Asia, Africa, Australia, Latin America, North America, and Europe. The ISB (2015) offers a Massive Open Online Course (MOOC) on social banking and other academic programs and certificate courses and research in partnership with the GABV as well.

Banks, savings institutions, and credit unions have also taken a more environmentally responsible focus. Boulder Valley Credit Union (BVCU) in Boulder, Colorado is an example of an eco-conscious credit union, which embodies a culture of environmental responsibility, providing sustainability education for its customers and offering discounts on financing of solar power for homes, and working as well with other eco-friendly business partners to promote an environmentally conscious community. BVCU began as a pioneer for eco-friendly credit union. It uses a SunPower solar electric system producing emission-free clean solar electricity, and has on its website the life-time energy generation, with the power generated offsetting 14 tons of CO_2 pollution each year for the 30 to 40 years of life for the system. Permaculture Credit Union in New Mexico is another environmentally oriented credit union that adopted an ethical code where no loans it made would go to businesses that are exploitative and investments are made into sustainable projects and its community. Alpine Bank, an independent community bank in Colorado, obtained an ISO 14001 certification for its environmental management, including its use of clean energy, water conservation, and recycling and use of recycled paper and green cleaners (Cooperman, 2011, 2013).

Alternative new community-focused banks provide loans that are environmentally focused, such as green buildings and green energy based projects including New Resource Bank in San Francisco, First Green Bank of Florida, Green Bank in Houston, Common Good Bank in western Massachusetts, e3bank in Philadelphia, and One Earth Bank into Austin, Texas (Cooperman, 2013). NY Green Bank, a division of NYSERDA, is a bank that advances New York clean energy investments. It is a state-sponsored, specialized financial entity that partners with the private sector to create a sustainable energy system that is more efficient and reliable for a more extensive deployment of clean energy assets that can encourage economic development, reduce environmental impacts, and allow the advantages of more green energy for each public dollar that is spent (NY Green Bank, 2016).

ESG INVESTING BY SPECIALIZED AND CONVENTIONAL VENTURE CAPITAL FIRMS

Venture capital firms are also heavily involved in ESG investing, especially for the Cleantech sector. Some VC firms are subsidiaries of other firms, such as for Google, which made agreements to fund almost $2.5 billion in clean energy wind and solar projects. In 2014, Clean Tech Investment rose 16% to $310 billion, a five-fold increase from a decade ago, with solar the largest single contributor with huge cost-competitiveness improvements (Murray, 2015). Government and corporate spending is estimated to be an additional $300 billion in 2014, and, according to Dow Jones Venture Source, the biggest venture funding events for sustainable companies include funds from Franklin Square Capital Partners, Triangle Peak Partners, Accel Partners, Foundation Capital, Madrone Capital Partners, Sequoia Capital, Collaborative Fund, Far East Organization, Founders Fund, Khosla Ventures, Google Ventures, Brightpath

149

*Social and
Environmental
Risks and
Sustainable
Financial
Institutions*

Capital Partners, E.ON Venture Partners, GE Ventures, DAG Ventures, GAF Corp., GSV Capital Corp., GSV Ventures, Kleiner Perkins Caufield & Byers, Element Partners, T. Rowe Price Group, Inc., British Petroleum, DSM Venturing, Monitor Venture Associates, Eastwood Capital Corp., and Oak Investment Partners, among many others.

Money managers with over $4.9 trillion in assets under management have also been involved in shareholder proxy resolutions to get corporations to change particular practices that cause environmental, health, or other social dangers. Pension funds, such as the California Public Employees' Retirement System (CalPERs) have put pressure on firms in their portfolios to change policies that are detrimental to the environment or society, and many pension funds will not invest in companies that do not meet ESG standards.

Private equity firms, such as KKR & Co. L.P., provide financial assistance and expertise to their portfolio companies to help them become more energy efficient and sustainable under a *Green Portfolio program*, given the rationale that better environmental performance also results in better business performance.

GREEN BOND ISSUANCE AND PUBLIC/PRIVATE PARTNERSHIPS FOR GREEN ENERGY PROJECTS

Financial institutions are also instrumental in the issuance of climate-aligned bonds. Climate-aligned bonds are bonds whose assets are invested in low-carbon or clean energy projects, such as low-carbon transport and clean energy. As the Climate Green Bonds Initiative (2015) notes, *green bonds* are created for financing projects with positive environment and/or climate benefits. In 2014, the green bond market had $36.6 billion issued, which was triple the $1.1 billion issued in 2013 (Climate Bonds, 2016b). Bloomberg New Energy Finance (2015) points out that green bond issuance included a large amount of issues by supranational, sovereign and agency bonds, issued by international financial institutions, agencies and provinces to finance green projects; corporate bonds explicitly labeled as green; U.S. municipal bonds to finance green projects; and smaller amounts for project bonds that are backed by renewable energy projects; and asset backed securities associated with green projects (Bloomberg New Energy Finance, 2015).

Climate bonds are generally fixed-income bonds that have a link in some way to climate change solutions, and issued for this purpose, such as for mitigation (i.e., GHG emission reduction projects, adaptation-related projects, clean energy, energy efficiency or climate adaptation projects, such as, flood defenses, adaptation to warming waters, natural resource management and conservation, capacity building, infrastructure planning and development, among others). Governments, multinational banks and corporations issue these. Most are "use of proceeds" bonds, and include project bonds where a special purpose vehicle (SPV) is used for a particular project; or asset-backed securities, where the cash flows are securitized in one bond, such as a loan portfolio for renewable energy projects; or covered bonds where an investor has recourse to the issuer balance sheet, typically for a bank as well as a pool of high-quality assets, often mortgages as well. The European Investment Bank began the use of "climate awareness bonds" that permit companies to issue bonds with themes verifying that funds are invested for these purposes, such as activities related to climate change. As theme bonds, institutional investors and sovereign wealth funds can invest in areas that are important to stakeholders with the same credit risk and return profile as standard bonds. They also transmit political signals to other stakeholders and allow governments to provide direct funding for climate change mitigation, which might qualify for preferential tax treatment (Climate Bonds, 2016a).

Most green bonds are issued as green based on the "use of the proceeds" and/or as asset-linked bonds, where proceeds are "earmarked" for green projects, but are backed by an issuer's "entire balance sheet." There are also green project bonds and green securitized bonds. An example of a *green use of proceeds bond* that is *issuer linked* is a bond earmarked for green projects, with full recourse to the issuer, so the bond will have the same credit rating as an issuer's other bonds. A *green "use of proceeds" revenue bond* is also earmarked for green projects, but revenue streams from the issuers through fees, taxes, etc., are used for the collateral for the debt. A *green project bond* is for the specific underlying green projects with recourse only for the project's assets on the balance sheet; and a green securitized bond is either earmarked for a green project or funds go directly into the underlying green projects with recourse for the group of projects, such as in a covered bond or another structure (Climate Bonds, 2016a,b).

Across different countries, government/private partnerships are often used to finance energy projects. Renewable finance sources of project capital tend to be complex, since with a high cost, government subsidies are often needed to attract private investors. Often this subsidy is in the shape of tax credits that can be in the form of accelerated depreciation or production or investment tax credits. Project sponsors often also borrow against future energy savings. Partnership groups, such as the U.S. Partnership for Renewable Energy Finance (US PREF), facilitate investments in the energy industry, including renewable energy. Members of PREF, for instance, meet, as an educational program group, with policymakers about renewable energy finance policies and the effect proposed policies would have on the market (Cooperman, 2013; US PREF, 2016).

SOCIAL IMPACT BONDS

Social impact bonds (SIBs) have become popular recently as a way to finance social change and have been issued in California, Colorado, New York, Ohio, and elsewhere. For a social impact bond donors and other investors supply money to a nonprofit organization that has an innovative way to solve a social problem. SIBs are unique by entailing a contract that is performance-based where private and/or philanthropic lenders loan funds to accomplish a specific objective. Investors are then repaid based on whether a program achieves its goals. Examples include reducing the number of offenders returning to prison. In Denver, a recent SIB program for this purpose received funds from investors that included philanthropic foundations and a major bank, The Northern Trust Company, along with other government funds and grants. Program partners included the Colorado Coalition for the Homeless as a service provider, the Corporation for Supportive Housing, providing project management, and other service providers and managers. Funds will be used to provide housing and supportive care management services for about 250 homeless individuals, who otherwise would use emergency services, such as the police, jail, courts, and emergency rooms. Instead, preventive services will be used to provide stable housing and supportive services, with savings and benefits reducing costs to the criminal justice system that in turn are captured by the City to use to repay lenders for their upfront investments to cover the costs to finance the program. Repayment to investors in turn is contingent on the program achieving its outcome targets including, based on previous studies, an expected 35–40% reduction in jail bed days, and an 83% housing stability rate, with repayment less if such outcomes are not achieved (Denver Foundation, 2016).

PUBLIC AND PRIVATE PARTNERSHIPS TO FINANCE ALTERNATIVE ENERGY PROJECTS

Public/private partnerships have also been used to provide renewable energy, with project-level financing more accessible to firms for clean technology schemes. Under this type of partnership, a bond similar to a social impact bond is often issued, whereby cost savings generated are returned to investors or to an energy company providing guarantees of future energy savings for bank loans based on repayment with cash flows generated by future energy savings. An example in Cooperman (2013) is the upgrading of the Colorado State Capital Building to geothermal energy in July 2013. The upgrading replaced existing pumps and equipment, allowing geothermal energy for the air conditioning/heating system, with Chevron Energy Solutions performing the upgrade, as a private guarantor of future savings for the bank loan. The U.S. Department of Energy (DOE) also provided a $4.1 million grant towards the overall $5.5 million project, and the state paid $1.5 million to finance the project's completion. As a result, the public/private funding mechanism resulted in zero cost to taxpayers and more than $8 million in utility savings, and more than 91.2 million pounds of carbon emissions were offset. Careful auditing by an accounting firm of future energy savings was used to attract bank loan financing, with savings of $100,000 in heating and cooling costs expected for the first year and higher savings for subsequent years (Casey, 2013; Cooperman 2013).

SUMMARY

Financial institutions have made great strides in managing sustainably, reducing GHG emissions by operating more efficiently and using renewable energy sources, and encouraging customers to do so as well, and providing funds for alternative energy sources, and for some financial institutions refusing to lend to companies with poor environmental or exploitative practices. Yet, much remains to be achieved, including better financial decision-making models integrating ESG criteria into financial institution management strategies, as well as the incorporation of ethical frameworks across company cultures. Many financial institutions have engaged in sustainability management and are responding to multiple stakeholders. Challenges have arisen with climate change for mitigation efforts, and risk management for FIs as well. New innovations in financial markets, including green bonds, social impact bonds, and private/public project financing, have facilitated clean technology and social financing efforts.

BIBLIOGRAPHY

Bloomberg New Energy Finance (2015). "Annual clean energy investment overview." Luke Mills, Bloomberg New Energy Finance, January 8, 2015. Accessed on February 6, 2016 at: http://about.bnef.com/presentations/clean-energy-investment-q4-2014-fact-pack/content/uploads/sites/4/2015/01/Q4-investment-fact-pack.pdf

Boston Common (2014). "Financing climate change: Carbon risk in the banking sector." Boston Common Asset Management, July 2014. Accessed on January 28, 2015 at: http://www.bostoncommonasset.com/documents/ThoughtPiece-2014-07-FinancingClimateChange.pdfl wealth at the expense of customers and society.

Bouma, Jan Jaap, Marcel Jeucken, and Leon Klinkers (Eds.) (2002). *Sustainable Banking: The Greening of Finance.* Sheffield, UK: Greenleaf Publishing.

Byrd, John and Elizabeth S. Cooperman (2015). "Carbon bubble & divestment trouble: Investors reactions: An analysis." *Journal of Environmental Investing,* 6(1), 75–88.

Byrd, John and Elizabeth S. Cooperman (2016). "Shareholder Activism for Stranded Asset Risk: An Analysis of Investor Reactions for Fossil Fuel Companies." Working Paper, University of Colorado Denver, 2016.

Carbon Tracker Initiative (2011, 2013). "Unburnable carbon: Are the world's financial markets carrying a carbon bubble?" Accessed on August 26, 2016. Available at: http://www.carbontracker.org/wp-content/uploads/2014/09/Unburnable-Carbon-Full-rev2-1.pdf

Carrington, Damian (2015). "Bank of England warns of huge financial risk from fossil fuel investments." *The Guardian,* March 3, 2015. Accessed on April 8, 2016 at: http://www.theguardian.com/environment/2015/mar/03/bank-of-england-warns-of-financial-risk-from-fossil-fuel-investments

Casey, Chris (2013). "Gold-domed loan transforms into gold standard of efficiency." Newsroom, University of Colorado Denver. Accessed in May 2013, at: http://www.ucdenver.edu/about/newsroom/newsreleases

Citi (2007). "Citi's response to climate change." Citi website. Accessed on April 8, 2016 at: http://www.citibank.com/citi/citizen/data/cr07_ch11.pdf

Climate Bonds (2015). "Explaining green bonds." Climate Bonds Initiative. Accessed on February 7, 2015 at: https://www.climatebonds.net/market/explaining-green-bonds

Climate Bonds (2016a). "Understanding climate bonds." Climate Bonds Initiative. Accessed on February 7, 2016 at: https://www.climatebonds.net/market/explaining-green-bonds

Climate Bonds (2016b). "Understanding green bonds." Climate Bonds Initiative. Accessed on February 8, 2015 at: https://www.climatebonds.net/market/explaining-green-bonds

Cooperman, Elizabeth S. (2011). "Sustainable banking: Boulder Valley Credit Union," Chapter 8. In Fred Andreas, E.S. Cooperman, B. Gifford, & G. Russell (Eds.), *A Simple Path to Sustainability: Green Business Strategies for Small and Medium-Sized Businesses,* Santa Barbara, CA: ABC-CLIO (Pager Publications), pp. 118–136.

Cooperman, Elizabeth S. (2013). "The greening of finance: A brief overview." *International Review of Accounting, Banking and Finance,* 5(1) (Spring), 42–59.

CDP (2016). CDP: Driving Sustainable Economies. CDP website. Accessed on February 6, 2016 at: https://www.cdp.net/en-US/Pages/About-Us.aspx

Denver Foundation (2016). "Fact sheet: Denver social impact bond program to address homelessness." The Denver Foundation. Accessed on August 28, 2016 at: http://pfs.urban.org/pfs-project-fact-sheets/content/denver-social-impact-bond-program

Deutsche Bank Responsibility (2014). "Employee engagement: Pass on your passion." Deutsche Bank website. Accessed on February 9, 2015, at: https://www.db.com/cr/en/our-people/employee-engagement.htm

Drake, Deborah and Elisabeth Rhyne (Eds.) (2002). *The Commercialization of Microfinance: Balancing Business and Development.* Bloomfield, CT: Kumara Press Inc.

Epstein, Marc J. (2008). *Making Sustainability Work: Best Practices in Managing and Measuring Corporate Social, Environmental, and Economic Impacts.* Sheffield, UK: Greenleaf Publishing.

Equator Principles (2016). Equator Principles website. Accessed on January 25, 2016, at: http://www.equator-principles.com

First for Sustainability (2015). "Sustainability and finance." First for Sustainability website. Accessed on January 25, 2015 at: http://firstforsustainability.org/sustainability/sustainability-and-finance/

Fung, Hung-Gay, Sheryl A. Law, and Jot Yau (2010). *Socially Responsible Investment in a Global Environment.* Northampton, MA: Edward Elgar.

153

*Social and
Environmental
Risks and
Sustainable
Financial
Institutions*

GABV (2015). Global Alliance for Banking on Values website. Accessed on January 26, 2015 at: http://www.gabv.org

GABV (2016). Global Alliance for Banking on Values website. Accessed on April 9, 2016 at: http://www.gabv.org/our-banks

Gilles, David (2016). "When investors aren't told about climate change." *The New York Times*, January 24, 2016, p. 7.

Gillis, Justin and Clifford Krauss (2015). "Exxon Mobil investigated for possible climate change lies by New York Attorney General." *The New York Times*, November 5, 2015. Accessed on January 27, 2015 at: http://www.nytimes.com/2015/11/06/science/exxon-mobil-under-investigation-in-new-york-over-climate-statements.html?_r=0

Global Clean Technology Venture Investment (2013). Cleantech Group website, accessed on January 3, 2013 at: http://www.cleantech.com

Goossens, Ehren (2012). "U.S. sustainable investments rise to record \$3.7T: US SIF." *Bloomberg News*, November 15, 2012. Accessed on July 29, 2013 at: http://www.bloomberg.com/news/print/2012-11-15/u-s-sustainable-investments-rise-to-record-3-7t-us-sif.html

Green Alpha (2016). "Green Alpha: About us." Green Alpha website. Accessed on April 8, 2016 at: reenalphaadvisors.com/about-us/

GRI (2016). "About GRI." Global Reporting Initiative website. Accessed on February 8, 2016 at: https://www.globalreporting.org/information/about-gri/Pages/default.aspx

GRI Topics (2016). "Sustainability topics for sectors: What do stakeholders want to know? Banks, diverse financials insurance." Global Reporting Initiative. Accessed on February 8, 2016 at: https://www.globalreporting.org/resourcelibrary/34-Banks.pdf

GSIA (2014). "Global sustainable investment review 2014." Global Sustainable Investment Alliance. Accessed on August 28, 2016 at: http://www.gsi-alliance.org/wp-content/uploads/2015/02/GSIA_Review_download.pdf

HSBC (2015). "Keeping it cool: Oil, CO2 and the carbon budget." HSBC Global Research: Climate Change, March 2015. Accessed on April 8, 2016 at: https://www.research.hsbc.com/midas/Res/RDV?p=pdf&key=I6wwvBhH8M&n=448964.PDF

Hull, Dana (2013). "Cleantech as VC interest shrinks, corporate investors swoop in." *San Jose Mercury News*, May 26, 2013, 1–6.

IISD (2015). "Sustainable banking." International Institute for Sustainable Development (IISD) website. Accessed on January 29, 2015 at: https://www.iisd.org/business/banking/sus_banking.aspx

Institute for Social Banking (2015). Institute for Social Banking: Education and Research website. Accessed on January 24, 2015 at: http://www.social-banking.org/the-institute/what-is-social-banking/

IPCC (2011). "Renewable energy sources and climate change mitigation." Intergovernmental Panel on Climate Change. Accessed on April 9, 2016 at: http://srren.ipcc-wg3.de/report

IPCC (2014). "Climate change 2014: Impacts, adaptation, and vulnerability." Accessed on August 28, 2016, at: http://www.ipcc.ch/report/ar5/wg2/

Jeucken, Marcel (2002). *Sustainable Finance and Banking: The Financial Sector and the Future of the Planet*. London: Earthscan Publications.

Kalla, Chaltanya (2011). "Sustainability—the way ahead for banking and financial institutions." *Finesse*, November 2010 – February 2011, EY. Accessed on January 25, 2016 at: http://www.ey.com/IN/en/Industries/Financial-Services/Banking---Capital-Markets/Finesse-2---Sustainability

KKR (2015). Green Portfolio, KKR website. Accessed on January 24, 2015, at: http.www.green.KKR.com/why-go-green).

Lloyds (2014). "IPCC warns of severe and pervasive impacts from climate change." Accessed on February 4, 2016 at: https://www.lloyds.com/news-and-insight/news-and-features/emerging-risk/emerging-risk-2014/ipcc-warns-of-severe-and-pervasive-impacts-from-climate-change

McGlade, Christophe, and Paul Elkins (2015). "The geographical distribution of fossil fuels unused when limiting global warming to 2°C." *Nature*, 517 (January 8), 187–190.

McKinsey & Company (2013). "The search for a sustainable banking model." McKinsey & Company website. Accessed on January 29, 2015 at: http://www.mckinsey.com/insights/financial_services/the_search_for_a_sustainable_banking.model

Meinshausen, M., N. Meinshausen, W. Hare, C.B. Raper, K. Frieler, R. Knutti, D.J. Frame, and M.R. Allen (2009). "Greenhouse-gas emission targets for limiting global warming to 2°C." *Nature* 458 (April 30), 1158–1163.

Morgan Stanley (2008). "The Carbon Principles." Morgan Stanley website. Accessed on January 28, 2016 at: http://www.morganstanley.com/globalcitizen/environment/CarbonPrinciplesFinal.pdf

Murray, James (2015). "Clean Tech investment surges back in 2014." Renewable Energy: Guardian Environment Network. Accessed on February 6, 2016 at: http://www.theguardian.com/environment/2015/jan/09/solar-power-led-clean-energy-investment-surge-in-2014

Natural Capital Declaration (2016). Natural Capital Declaration website. Accessed on February 6, 2016 at: http://www.naturalcapitaldeclaration.org/financial-institutions/

NOAA (2015). "Weekly Manua Loa CO2 records." U.S. National Oceanic and Atmospheric Administration website. Accessed on March 1, 2015 at: http://www.esrl.noaa.gov/gmd/ccgg/trends/weekly.html

NY Green Bank (2016). "Welcome to NY Green Bank." Accessed on February 6, 2016 at http://greenbank.ny.gov/About/Overview

Noonan, Laura (2015). "US banks hit by cheap oil as OPEC warns of long-term low." *Financial Times*, December 23, 2015. Accessed on February 7, 2015 at: http://www.ft.com/cms/s/0/23d9c0ca-a95a-11e5-955c-1e1d6de94879.html#axzz3zWT4OsjT

Paulson, Henry M. (2014). "The coming climate crash: Lessons for climate change in the 2008 recession." Sunday Review, Opinion, *The New York Times*, June 21, 2014. Accessed on January 26, 2016 at: http://www.nytimes.com/2014/06/22/opinion/sunday/lessons-for-climate-change-in-the-2008-recession.html?smid=tw-share&_r=1

PR Newswire (2016). "SASB and IMA announce memorandum of understanding." PR Newswire, February 2, 2016. Accessed on February 5, 2016 at: http://www.prnewswire.com/news-releases/sasb-and-ima-announce-memorandum-of-understanding-300212790.html

Quittner, Jeremy (2015). "Top 10 venture capital-backed green companies." Inc.com. Accessed on February 6, 2016 at: http://www.inc.com/jeremy-quittner/venture-capital-flows-to-sustainability-companies-and-earth-day.html

RAN (2010). "The principle matter: Banks, climate & the Carbon Principles." Rainforest Action Network. Accessed on February 5, 2016 at: http://d3n8a8pro7vhmx.cloudfront.net/rainforestactionnetwork/legacy_url/1424/ran_the_principle_matter_carbonprinciplereport.pdf?1402698593

Randall, Tom (2014). "Bankers see $1 trillion of zombie investments stranded in the oil fields." Bloomberg, December 17, 2014. Accessed on April 8, 2016 at: http://www.bloomberg.com/news/articles/2014-12-18/bankers-see-1-trillion-of-investments-stranded-in-the-oil-fields

SASB (2016). "Accounting for a sustainable future." Sustainability Accounting Standards Board. www.sasb.org. Accessed on February 5, 2016 at: http://www.sasb.org/standards/download/

SASB Commercial Banks (2014). "Commercial banks: Research brief." Sustainability Accounting Standards Board. www.sasb.org. Accessed on February 5, 2016 at: http://www.sasb.org/wp-content/uploads/2014/05/SASB_Commercial_Banks_Brief.pdf

SASB Financial Services (2014). "Disclosure guidance integrated banking & financial services: Technical bulletin." Sustainability Accounting Standards Board. www.sasb.org. Accessed on February 5, 2016 at: http://www.sasb.org/wp-content/uploads/2014/02/Financials_Sector_Technical_Bulletin_022514.pdf

SASB Investment Banking (2014). "Investment banking & brokerage: Research brief." Sustainability Accounting Standards Board. www.sasb.org. Accessed on February 5, 2016 at: http://www.sasb.org/wp-content/uploads/2014/05/SASB_Investment_Banking_Brief.pdf

Social Capital (2016). "The Social Capital Protocol." World Business Council for Sustainable Development (WBCSD). Accessed on February 8, 2016 at: http://www.wbcsd.org/SocialCapital.aspx

Steiner, Achim (2015). "Forward to the financial system we need: Aligning the financial system with sustainable development: Policy Summary." UNEP Inquiry Report, The Financial System We Need. October 2015.

The Climate Principles (2016). "The Climate Principles: A framework for the finance sector." Accessed on February 6, 2015 at: http://www.theclimategroup.org/_assets/files/The-Climate-Principles-English.pdf

Tridos Bank (2015). "01 sustainable banking." Tridos Bank website. Accessed on January 29, 2015 at: www.tridos.com

UNEP (2015). "Financial institutions taking action on climate change." United Nations Environment Programme, Accessed on April 8, 2016 at: http://investorsonclimatechange.org/wp-content/uploads/2014/09/FinancialInstitutionsTakingActionOnClimateChange_Final.pdf

United Nations (2015). "What is COP21?" United Nations Conference on Climate Change. Accessed on January 26, 2015 at: http://www.cop21.gouv.fr/en/learn/what-is-cop21/

United Nations (2016). "Sustainable development goals: About COP21." United Nations website, Accessed on April 8, 2016 at: http://www.un.org/sustainabledevelopment/cop21/

UN PRI (2016). "UN PRI: Principles for Responsible Investment: About the PRI initiative." Accessed on February 6, 2016 at: http://www.unpri.org/about-pri/about-pri/

US PREF (2016). "U.S. partnership for renewable energy finance." Accessed on February 8, 2016 at: http://uspref.org

US SIF (2014). "Report on US sustainable, responsible and impact investing trends." Accessed on August 28, 2016 at: http://www.ussif.org/trends

US SIF (2016). The Forum for Sustainable and Responsible Investment, 2014 Trends Report. Accessed on February 6, 2016 at: http://www.ussif.org/content.asp?contentid=40

Weber, Olaf and Sven Remer (2011). *Social Banks and the Future of Sustainable Finance.* London: Routledge.

WEF (2015). "Global risks 2015, 10th ed." World Economic Forum Insight Report. Accessed on February 4, 2016 at: http://www3.weforum.org/docs/WEF_Global_Risks_2015_Report15.pdf

Wolfsberg Group (2015). "The Wolfsberg Group: Global bank: Global standards." September 7, 2015. Accessed on January 5, 2015 at: http://www.wolfsberg-principles.com

QUESTIONS AND PROBLEMS

1   What roles do financial institutions have to play in helping to mitigate climate change and socioeconomic risks? How do these roles help financial institutions to engage in risk management and also help to improve profitability as well as providing benefits to stakeholders. Provide an example for a particular type of financial institution.

2   Discuss some of the different risks associated with climate change and give examples. What is stranded asset risk, and why is the banking sector affected by carbon risk?

3   In the United States what mandate does the Securities and Exchange Commission demand for publicly traded companies? What criticisms have institutional investors made in association with a potential carbon bubble?

4   Give examples of how financial institutions have engaged in sustainability management. What savings have been made? Give examples of how large financial institutions have incorporated sustainability within their organizations.

5   What are social banks and eco banks? Find an example of each on the web.

6   What are the Equator Principles, and what do signatories pledge?

7   What respectively are: (1) the Carbon Principles; (2) the Climate Principles; (3) the UN Principles of Responsible Investment; (4) the Carbon Disclosure Project; (5) Wolfsberg's AML Principles; (6) the Natural Capital Declaration and what do signatories commit to?

8   What is a socially responsible investment (SRI)? How have SRI financial institutions engaged companies as social activists? What are the different ways SRI firms screen companies to create a SRI portfolio?

9   Discuss the purpose of sustainability reporting and the GRI Initiative. What is SASB, and what is its mission?

10 How did the U.S. subprime loan crisis create reputational damage for FIs? What are ways that FIs can redeem their reputations? How might compensation policies have led to greater risk taking?

11 How can ESG considerations be integrated into lending and capital budgeting decisions? How would such an integration help financial institutions to make better decisions and reduce risks?

12 What is a climate-related bond? What is a green bond? A social impact bond? What are different ways these bonds are structured? Why are public/private partnerships important for financing renewable alternative energy projects?

Part Three | # Managing FI Risks

Chapter 7

International Markets, FX Risks, and Hedging FX Risk

The first step in the risk management process is to acknowledge the reality of risk.

(Tremper, 2015)

More countries are adopting a managed floating exchange rate system, especially as a number of emerging countries try to safeguard their currencies from increased volatility in foreign exchange markets triggered by monetary easing measures from advanced countries.

(*Nikkei Asian Review*, 2014)

WITH greater globalization, international financial institutions face considerable foreign exchange (FX) risk, so it is important to understand the different types of foreign exchange regimes that countries operate under and different factors that affect foreign currency rate. The International Monetary Fund (IMF) in its 2014 *Annual Report on Exchange Arrangements and Exchange Restrictions (AREAER)* notes a trend for additional foreign exchange liberalization by many countries with a slow global recovery from the Great Recession as well as increased capital flow volatility. Globally, with market conditions improving, most countries returned to more stable FX rate regimes and a relaxing of controls on current and capital transactions (IMF, 2014).

With globalization of markets, countries around the world are affected by monetary policies and crises in other countries that affect investment flows across countries, with international investors looking for higher interest rates and stronger currencies for investments. This was clear in 2015 to 2016 with financial crises in Greece, China, and Brazil having significant global affects, resulting in greater volatility in FX rates, and more recently when the results for the BREXIT vote for United Kingdom to leave the European Union were reported on June 24, 2016. This led to a fall in the value of the U.K. pound sterling, which fell 12% after the referendum, its lowest point in 30 years (Martin and Blitz, 2016). This chapter examines foreign exchange rate regimes, theories for determinants of FX rates, and central bank interventions to manage FX rates, and FX markets and foreign currency risk hedging techniques using derivatives.

TYPES OF FOREIGN EXCHANGE RATE REGIMES IN DIFFERENT COUNTRIES

Different countries are diverse in their types of exchange rate regimes chosen by their government and maintained by their central banks. These include *fixed* or *pegged* exchange rate regimes and *floating* or *manage*d float regimes. Categories can also be subdivided for fixed-rate regimes into: (1) *hard pegs* where an exchange arrangement is made with no separate legal tender, or a currency board arrangement where another country's currency is used; (2) *soft pegs* where a country has a fixed pegged exchange rate but with a horizontal band within which it can float, and a *crawling peg* allows depreciation or appreciation of a currency to happen gradually, such as adjusting for factors such as inflation. There are also other arrangements, such as *currency boards, dollarization, and stabilized arrangements*, crawl-like arrangements, and pegged exchange rates with horizontal bands, among others. Under a currency board arrangement, a country has a tie for its currency with another larger country, and under dollarization, a country adopts the currency of another larger country, such as the U.S. dollar. Floating rate regimes based on market determined FX rates can be: (1) *free floating*; or (2) *managed float* where intervention can be engaged by central banks if rates get seriously out of line (IMF, 2014; Stone, Anderson, and Veyrune, 2008).

It is interesting to note that Ecuador, which previously in 2000 changed its currency to the U.S. dollar, in 2015 is changing its monetary system to use digital currencies, a process that began in December 2014 by permitting qualifying users to set up accounts to become a means for real transactions to support its dollar-based monetary system. As of February 2015, real transactions are allowed under this first state-run electronic payment system. Although other countries, such as Sweden, have widely used digital currencies, this is the first state-sponsored system (Rosenfeld, 2015).

The IMF (2014) *AREAER* report notes a rise in the number of member countries (includes 188 IMF member countries) with a soft peg, which likely reflects pressure on currencies of emerging market economies as the result of capital flow volatility necessitating greater exchange rate management. About 36 countries that are members of the IMF had managed float arrangements and 29 free-floating arrangements, representing about 35% of IMF member countries. Thirteen countries had no legal tender using the U.S. dollar or the euro or other exchange rate anchors, and about 25 countries and regions use a fixed exchange rate system, where currencies are pegged to the U.S. dollar (IMF, 2014; *Nikkei Asian Review*, 2014; Stone, et al., 2008).

In evaluating and understanding FX rate risk, it is important to understand why economies as members of the International Monetary Fund (IMF) began using a gold standard after World War II in 1945, and why IMF country members went off of a gold standard for the value of their currencies, beginning in 1972, and the pros and cons of using fixed FX currency rates versus floating FX rates, discussed in the following sections.

PREVIOUS GOLD STANDARD AND FIXED-RATE REGIMES

Countries that use *fixed or pegged exchange rate regimes* keep the value of their currencies pegged relative to another currency known as the anchor currency, so that exchange rates remain fixed. For decades prior to the creation of the Federal Reserve, the United States and several other countries agreed upon a fixed-rate gold standard as an anchor, with gold as a defined standard of value used to maintain a fixed exchange rate between currencies based on the price of gold.

Under a gold standard, economic problems often arose with little control over the money supply, with rises in gold production or circulation increasing the supply of a currency leading to inflation, and contractions in gold production or circulation leading to deflation and recession, leading to bank panics. For instance, the United States suffered great inflation in the later 1800s following the California Gold Rush of 1848 to 1855, when great amounts of gold were available. Historically, data show dramatic swings in prices under gold standard periods. Also with a fixed exchange rate for gold when countries paid for imports, these countries experience a reduction in the money supply of their countries, leading to deflation. Net exporter countries receiving greater gold have an increase in their money supply and increased inflation. A scarcity of gold can also limit the ability of an economy to grow. With the money supply determined by the rate of gold production, this also limits the ability of central banks to respond to crises. Friedman and Schwartz (1963), for instance, suggest that the gold standard limited the U.S. central bank's response during the Great Depression of 1929 to 1941 (Bordo, Choudri, and Schwartz, 2002; Friedman and Schwartz, 1963; Mayer, 2010; Timberlake, 1993, 2005).

While hard pegged fixed exchange rate regimes do not allow a currency to fluctuate, a pegged float regime (or soft peg) allows a country's currency to float within a band of values that can be either fixed or adjusted at times, such as the Danish krone that is pegged to the euro and allowed to float within +/− 15% against the euro or at a smaller range if necessary. China also has recently moved more towards a soft peg system.

At the end of World War II in 1945, under the Bretton Woods Agreement (named after Bretton Woods, New Hampshire, where the agreement was negotiated), the U.S. dollar was established as a global currency, with the United States holding significant gold reserves and emerging as a post-war economic power. The conversion of U.S. dollars into gold was established initially as one U.S. dollar convertible into gold at $35 per ounce. This fixed FX rate was maintained by central bank interventions (selling and buying of dollar assets) held as international reserves to keep currencies in line. The World Bank and the International Monetary Fund (IMF) were also created to assist in monitoring the new system. Countries agreed not to attempt to lower a country's currency value simply to increase trade, but could intervene to regulate their currencies to avoid economic destabilization and to allow for adjustments to currency values for rebuilding of countries following World War II (Amadeo, 2014).

Later in the early 1970s, a high inflation rate in the United States and a large U.S. trade deficit occurred, along with a recession (i.e., a condition of stagflation with a recession with inflation). With a fixed rate, the value of the U.S. dollar remained high, while in market value terms it should have fallen. Pressure was placed on central banks in other countries in the Bretton Woods system, including Japan and Germany that had a higher balance of payments, to do FX market interventions to increase the value of their currencies relative to the U.S. dollar. Countries preferred not to do this, since an increase in their FX rates would increase prices for their countries' goods, and hence reduce exports. The United States made the decision to reprice its dollar to $1/$42 of an ounce of gold. This policy had unfortunate results by contributing to a run on U.S. gold reserves, with individuals rushing to redeem U.S. dollars for gold (Amadeo, 2014).

By 1971, the United States decided to abandon the gold standard, and to change to a floating rate system that allows the U.S. dollar to change relative to the value of other currencies, beginning in 1972. By 1973, the value of gold was also allowed to go up and down with the market, rather than having a fixed price. The fixed rate used under the Bretton Woods system also ended, with IMF member countries allowed to choose any FX arrangement they wanted, except for pegging their currency to gold. Countries could choose to allow their currencies to float freely, be pegged to another currency or a basket of currencies or adopting another country's currency, or participating in a currency block or being a part of a monetary union (IMF, 2015a).

The U.S. dollar still remains as a popular reserve currency, although other currencies are used as reserve currencies, such as the euro, British pound, and Japanese yen. The IMF has special drawing rights (SDR) that can be used as an international reserve asset, allowing countries the ability to exchange SDRs for usable currencies to supplement their international reserve holdings. The SDR was as of 2015 in denominations as a basket of primarily four currencies (the U.S. dollar (41.9%), the euro (37.4%), pound (11.3%), and yen (9.4%). This compares with the use of 16 currencies in the 1970s in an attempt to be more inclusive. Some analysts argue that greater diversification is needed to provide a more orderly balance of payment adjustment and to reduce dependence on dollar liquidity, which can create global concerns if there is a sudden U.S. monetary policy tightening. In this spirit, the IMF approved China's yuan as a reserve currency in November 2015 to take effect on October 1, 2016, with the yuan having a 10.92% weight in the basket of currencies, 41.73% for the U.S. dollar, 30.93% for the euro, 8.33% for the yen, and 8.09% for the British pound (IMF, 2014; Mayeda, 2015).

From the mid-1970s, onward, the IMF helped to respond to balance of payment problems for poorer countries through a concessional loan program, the Structural Adjustment Facility, which was succeeded by the Enhanced Structural Adjustment Facility in 1987. This change was in response to a number of international crises, including a crisis in Mexico in 1982, where the IMF had to coordinate a global response including commercial banks as well to avoid country failures by calming the panic, with painful reforms for debtor countries and additional cooperative global measures needed. Other central roles of the IMF include helping the transition of countries in the former Soviet bloc to transition from central planning to market driven economies in the 1990s after the fall of the Berlin wall in 1989, providing funds to help reduce panics during the Asian Financial Crisis in 1997, and during the Great Recession following the U.S. subprime loan crisis. Significant reforms took place in the 1990s including the IMF working closely with the World Bank to alleviate debt burdens of poor countries. The Heavily Indebted Poor Countries (HIPC) Initiative was launched in 1996, with the aim to ensure that no poor country faces a debt burden that it cannot manage. To help accelerate progress for the United National Millennium Development Goals in 2005, the HIPC Initiative was supplemented with the Multilateral Debt Relief Initiative (IMF, 2015a,b,c; Mandeng, 2015).

Under managed float, central banks continue to intervene when currencies become too out of line, with limits in their ability to do so for countries that have large trade deficits, since they may deplete international reserves. Under a fixed exchange rate system and a gold standard system, this can pose an even greater potential for international reserve depletion discussed in the following sections.

INTERVENTIONS TO MAKE ADJUSTMENTS TO AN EXCHANGE RATE

To maintain a fixed-rate FX rate, a country's central bank must intervene to keep the rate fixed with another country's currency. For instance, in the case of an undervalued currency, a central bank intervenes by a sale in the foreign exchange market of some of its international reserves (holdings of assets denominated in a foreign currency). The problem with doing this is that such an *unsterilized intervention* results in a decline in currency in circulation. As follows, the central bank would sell international reserves in return for currency, increasing the circulation of international reserves versus the country's currency. The net effect, however, would be a reduction in the country's currency in circulation, which with this contraction in the money supply could lead to a recession.

Central bank	
Assets	Liabilities
International reserves: − $50 billion	Currency in circulation: − $50 billion

To avoid a contraction of the monetary base, a central bank can do a sterilized intervention by engaging in an off-setting expansionary policy by buying government securities at the same time to offset the fall in currency in circulation, as shown below, known as a *sterilized intervention*, with the central bank's balance sheet looking as follows:

Central bank	
Assets	Liabilities
International reserves: − $50 billion	Currency in circulation: − $50 billion
Government securities: + $50 billion	Currency in circulation: + $50 billion
	Net change in currency $0

As shown for the above example, with the offsetting purchase of government securities by the central bank from the nonbank public in return for currency, this results in a net change in the monetary base of $0.

Similarly, if a country had an overvalued currency that it wished to lower, it would engage in the opposite policy of buying international reserves in return for currency from the nonbank public, increasing the currency in circulation under an unsterilized interventions resulting in a central bank balance sheet of:

Central bank	
Assets	Liabilities
International reserves: + $50 billion	Currency in circulation: + $50 billion

This open market operation would reduce the supply of international reserves in circulation, reducing the supply of the foreign currency relative to the country's currency, but also increasing the amount of currency in circulation, which could lead to inflation. To offset this action, the country would engage in a sterilized intervention by selling government securities in the same amount to the nonbank public in return for currency (nonbank public deposits), reducing the money supply in circulation, resulting in a "0" net change in the monetary base as shown below:

Central bank	
Assets	Liabilities
International reserves: + $50 billion	Currency in circulation: + $50 billion
Government securities: − $50 billion	Currency in circulation: − $50 billion
	Net change in currency: $0

Under agreements between industrialized nations that are trading partners for managed float regimes, joint interventions are used when FX rates are significantly out of line as well. In 1987, the Group of Five (G5) agreed to coordinate efforts to keep the U.S. dollar within a specified trading range relative to the currencies of other countries. In 1987, the Group of Five was expanded to the Group of Seven (G7) including Canada, France, Germany, Italy, Japan, the United Kingdom, and the United States that also meet to discuss global issues, discussed in more detail in a following section on the G7 (CFR, 2015).

FIXED-RATE FOREIGN EXCHANGE REGIMES

Advantages of fixed exchange rates include having a known exchange rate between trading partners, such as importers and exporters, and allowing estimation of costs and prices that can be beneficial for encouraging trade and capital investments. A country on a fixed-rate regime may also benefit from a more disciplined monetary policy to reduce inflation, or for larger countries, a peg that allows a lower FX rate that's attractive for exports to a trading partner (i.e., making goods cheaper).

However, there are many disadvantages for fixed FX regimes, including no automatic mechanism for balance of payment adjustments, and a fixed rate may not reflect market factors for supply and demand between trading partners. If a fixed rate for a country becomes out of line, such as a currency becoming overvalued, a government's central bank will have to intervene to maintain the fixed rate with the pegged currency, and may run out of international reserves, which could lead to an eventual currency devaluation to reset the par exchange rate at a lower level. A smaller country also faces a loss of control over its monetary policy, having to react to monetary policy actions of a larger country. Trading partners on managed float or floating rate regimes may also become disgruntled if a fixed currency rate is kept too low, resulting in a lower cost of goods than its trading partners that leads to greater exports for the country with a low fixed rate relative to its trading partners.

There are speculative dangers with fixed FX rate systems, since international speculators can sell or short sell a currency, which can result in a sharp drop in the real value of its exchange rate.

FLOATING OR MANAGED FLOAT REGIMES

In contrast to fixed-rate regimes, a floating exchange rate regime allows exchange rates to change daily in response to market forces allowing supply and demand forces to apply in determining the FX rate for different currencies. Under managed float regimes the option remains for trading partner central banks to intervene to prevent large changes in exchange rates or to reduce exchange rate volatility. This in turn makes it easier for firms and consumers to purchase or sell goods and services abroad and plan for the future.

Floating exchange rates serve to help adjust a country's monetary surpluses and deficits, which also affect the exchange rate for its currency. If a country has a large international deficit, it tends to import more from other countries and export less, resulting in more demand for the currency of other countries and less for its own currency. Economic forces for trading partners of countries with floating exchange rates help to make adjustments. If a country's FX rate falls, its goods become relatively cheaper, increasing demand for that country's goods and increasing exports.

When a trading partner, however, has a pegged versus floating exchange rate, such an economic adjustment cannot happen, which can cause frictions between trading partners with managed float, since their goods will remain expensive relative to their fixed-rate trading partner. Managed float is the most frequently employed FX regime, including for the British pound, the U.S. dollar, the Japanese yen, and the euro, for example. Under a floating rate system, however, small economies may be subject to large FX swings caused by recent quantitative easing policies of larger countries (*Nikkei Asian Review*, 2014).

INTERNATIONAL POLICY COORDINATION

One potential goal of monetary policy is to promote a satisfactory trade balance between trading partners. Under a managed float system, the U.S. dollar has had a role as the world's primary reserve currency, with foreign countries purchasing U.S. Treasury debt as dollar-denominated assets to hold foreign exchange reserves. Reserves that countries hold include money market instruments and bonds in a reserve currency, as well as gold and International Monetary Fund special drawing rights. These reserves are then used for FX exchange rate interventions.

Conerly (2013) points out that to be a reserve currency, the country whose currency is used needs to have government securities with a liquid (can be sold quickly) and deep (having an ample amount of securities that can be purchased and sold that will not have a big effect on the securities' prices) market. Hence, the U.S. dollar has been a popular reserve currency for these reasons, as well as having a large economy and having assets that are likely not to default or lose value (i.e., not likely to have credit downgrades. Because central banks want diversification, countries use other types of reserves, with the U.S. dollar, about 60% of currency reserves that are identifiable, with other currencies used as reserves including the euro, the pound sterling, and the yen, among others.[1]

G5, G7, AND G20 AGREEMENTS

In 1985, the United States and four other major industrialized nations—the Group of Five (G5) made an agreement to coordinate efforts to keep the U.S. dollar within a specified trading range relative to the currencies of other countries. In 1987, the Group of Five was expanded to the Group of Seven (G7), including Canada, France, Germany, Italy, Japan, the United Kingdom and the USA; for meetings there are also representatives from the European Central Bank, the IMF, the World Bank, the Financial Stability Board, and the European Union. The actual range that currencies will be kept to before an intervention is needed is a closely guarded secret by the G7 governments, representing perceptions of the best collective interests of the nations. Experts believe that policymakers set a very flexible target rather than a narrow one. To carry out the agreement, central banks in the G7 nations buy or sell dollar reserves in the exchange markets whenever its value threatens to break outside the range. If open market purchases and sales of dollars fail to reverse what the group considers an undesirable trend, the non-U.S. G7 central banks sometimes attempt to increase or decrease interest rates in their own countries to counteract differentials.

Following the U.S. subprime loan crisis, of 2007 to 2008, when the Fed in the United States engaged in quantitative easing to stimulate the U.S. economy that lowered interest rates in the U.S., other emerging economies faced problems, with their currency values rising as foreign capital left the United States for higher yields in other countries. With globalization and the removal of restrictions, emerging economies have also seen a free flow of capital, with about 40% of emerging economies officially floating their currencies.[2]

All the members of the G7 are also part of the G20, a forum for international economic cooperation, including Argentina, Australia, Brazil, Canada, China, France, Germany, India, Indonesia, Italy, Japan, Mexico, Russia, Saudi Arabia, South Africa, South Korea, Turkey, the United Kingdom, the United States, and the European Union. The Group of 20 finance ministers and central bank governors was established in 1999 for industrialized and developing economies in a global economy to discuss key issues. The G20 has also been involved in global economic coordination, with many analysts noting that the G20 was most effective during the financial crisis, with G20 leaders meeting in Washington, DC after the fall of Lehman Brothers, cooperating to provide liquidity and limit the contagion of the banking crisis (CFR, 2015; G20, 2014).

TYPES OF FOREIGN EXCHANGE RISK

Operating in a global environment, large international financial institutions face considerable foreign exchange risks. There are four major types of foreign exchange risk associated with unfavorable FX changes or economic risks including:

1. Transaction FX risk exposure is when a party is paid in one currency and must pay for the transaction in another currency.

For example: Suppose a U.S. international bank agrees to finance a short-term seasonal working capital loan to a French exporter for €50 million. At the time of the loan, suppose the direct spot rate is €1 equals US$1.057, or in other words, the indirect spot exchange rate is US$1 is (1/1.057) or €0.9461. The U.S. bank expects a repayment of the loan in 3 months in euros. The U.S. bank is worried about fall in the value of the euro in 3 months when the loan amount is repaid. Suppose the euro 3 months later falls to €1 = 0.9513 U.S. dollars.

The bank had been expected to receive $52.85 million, but three months later only receives $47.565 million as the result of the fall in the value of the euro as follows:

Expected receipt = €50 million × $1.057 = $52.85 million

Actual receipt = €50 million × 0.9513 = $47.565 million

Opportunity loss spot positions = *($5.285 million).*

Hence the bank has considerable transaction FX risk.

2. Translation FX exposure risk is when assets and liabilities for a financial institution are in different currencies, whereby the market value of a firm's equity is:

Value of equity = Value of assets − Value of liabilities.

For example: Suppose a multinational bank has assets in U.S. dollars financed with British pounds as liabilities. If the British pound rises relative to the U.S. dollar, the market value of its liabilities will be greater than the market value of its assets, resulting in a decline in the value of equity.

Translation FX exposure can be particularly severe for banks in countries during a currency crisis. Examples include the foreign exchange crises in 1997 for Indonesia and Thailand, when financial institutions in these countries borrowed in U.S. dollars to finance loans that would be paid back in Indonesian and Thai currencies. During the crisis, when the Indonesian rupiah and Thailand baht fell in value to the U.S. dollar, the value liabilities of these banks was greater than the value of assets, resulting in a severe fall in the value of equity, putting these banks on the brink of bankruptcy. Similarly, on a country level, in 1999 Brazil's debt service was 25% dollar linked, so when the value of the Brazilian real fell relative to the U.S. dollar, the cost of the loan repayments became very expensive and were difficult to repay.

3. Country risk exposure is the risk of a nationwide default by a government on its debt regardless of the condition of a particular borrower; for instance if a government announces that all dollar debts will not be repaid. This can be a default on bonds, loans, or other financial commitments. An example is Argentina's debt crisis in December 2014, with Argentina in negotiation with a group of U.S. hedge funds over unpaid debt, insisting that the hedge funds accept reduced payments, despite a U.S. court order for a full repayment of $1.3 billion debt plus interest. In July 2014, Argentinian President, Cristina Fernandez, announced that the face value of bonds to the funds would not be repaid, and the funds declined an offer under terms of bond swaps similar to Argentina's default in 2002 (Misculin and Raszewski, 2014).

4. International economic risk is the risk of a change in the net present value of expected future after-tax cash flows as the result of the three above types of exposure. For instance, if a country has an economic crisis, a plunge in the value of its currency, or other catastrophic event, this can create economic exposure to international companies and FIs with projects and investments in these countries. A good example is the effect of the subprime loan crisis in the U.S. in 2007 and 2008, which affected investors globally holding U.S. subprime collateralized debt obligations (CDOs) as well as having an economic impact with lower sales for exporters of goods to the United States from other countries.

THEORIES OF FOREIGN EXCHANGE RATE DETERMINATION

Modern Asset Theory: Supply and Demand Factors for Goods and Services Affecting FX Rates

Similar to the Loanable Funds Theory of Interest Rates, supply and demand for a country's currency, just like the supply and demand for bonds or any other asset, have significant effects on a country's FX rate. Different factors that affect the demand and supply for a foreign currency include:

1 *The relative supply and demand for goods and services in different countries.* Trade imbalances that lead to trade or balance of payment deficits affect currency and exchange rates. More specifically if a country has goods and services that are very attractive, this can increase the demand for its goods and products (i.e., shift out in the demand curve for its currency resulting in a rise in its FX relative to other countries).
2 *The relative inflation rates among countries.* Relatively high inflation in one country leads to a depreciation in its currency relative to currencies in other countries that have lower inflation rates. If one country has greater inflation than another country, its products will be very expensive, and there will be less demand for its currency, causing the value of its currency relative to other currencies to fall.
3 *The relative real interest rates in different countries.* Relatively high real interest rates in one country will be accompanied by appreciation of its currency relative to currencies with lower real interest rates, since demand for that currency by international investors will increase.

These supply and demand economic factors can be used to help forecast expected movements in FX rates in the short run. Governments also often attempt to intervene to keep the stability of their currencies with trading partners as discussed earlier for the G7.

Similar to the loanable funds theory, modern asset theory, as shown in Figure 7.1, shows supply and demand factors as determining FX rates. In this case for instance, the supply curve for euros and demand curve for euros intersection determines the US dollar (USD) FX price per euro. The demand for curve for euros is similarly downward sloping and the supply curve is upward sloping. If for instance, with quantitative easing policies the supply curve for euros shifts outward, this would result in a lower intersection with the demand curve for euros, resulting in a lower dollar price per euro (i.e., a decline in the FX rate for the euro in U.S. dollars). Such a decline over time would make European goods cheaper for U.S. importers to import, increasing exports for European countries.

Recent Examples of FX Rate Volatility Demonstrating Supply and Demand Factors

Examples of FX risks and factors affecting interest rates include the case of the Brazilian real (R$), which was introduced in 1994 as the "new real," with the exchange rate fixed, so that R$1 = US$1, with the Central Bank of Brazil controlling the exchange rate. In 1999, with

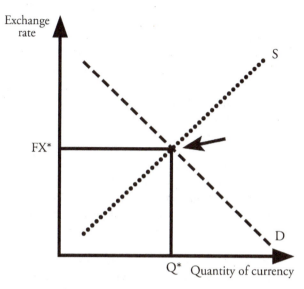

FIGURE 7.1 | Supply and demand as determinants for foreign exchange rates: Example for euro/US$. Note: S is the supply curve for the foreign currency for a country; D is the demand curve for that currency, FX* is the equilibrium foreign exchange rate at the point where the supply and demand curves for the currency intersect, and Q* is the quantity of that currency at this intersection point.

disruption in international markets with a Russian Bond Default, the Central Bank of Brazil released control over the exchange rate, and the real suffered a devaluation to R$2 = US$1. By 2002, the real had fallen to R$4 = US$1. In 2007, however, with the U.S. subprime loan crisis, the value of the real to the U.S. dollar, rose to R$0.5 = US$1 (Oanda, 2015). In 2010 when the Brazilian real was moving sharply higher, in contrast its neighbor countries engaged in devaluations to make their goods cheaper and more attractive for world trade (Buttonwood, 2015).

In September 2015, the Brazilian real dropped the most among the world's 16 major currencies, with concerns about Brazil, as Latin America's largest economy faltering increased, with Brazil's bonds downgraded by Standard & Poor's (S&P) to junk status. Further economic problems for Brazil included the downgrade of a major oil producer, Petroleo Brasileiro SA, to junk bond status as well by S&P. Reasons for the downgrade included: (1) increasing foreign debt; (2) falling prices of export commodities that represent a large portion of Brazil's revenue (including sugar, coffee, and soybeans), rising inflation and interest rates, and a depreciation in the real; (3) domestic political instability rising; (4) difficulties by the government in its handling of Brazil's rising debt; and (5) an outlook that was negative based on corruption and scandals, including the Petrobas scandal (Blakely, 2015). In October 2015, amid severe economic problems and a court ruling attempt to delay a resolution to impeach the president of Brazil at this time, stock prices on Brazil's Sao Paul Stock, Mercantile and Futures Exchange (Bovespa) based on an index of about 50 stocks traded on the exchange, fell, as did those on the Ibovespa, along with a drop in emerging markets, with a plunge in China's imports providing bad news for the Brazilian economy. As of October 14, 2015, the Brazilian real traded at 3.81 relative to the U.S. dollar (Sambo and Godoy, 2015).

Hence, similar to interest rate determination by supply and demand factors, supply and demand factors affect FX rates. These factors include relative inflation, demand for a country's goods and services, relative interest rates, and also risk perceptions for a country's investments, along with how FX rates are managed by a country. Factors that increase the demand for a country's currency will have a positive effect on the value of that country's currency, while factors such as inflation, high relative prices for goods and services, less attractive types of goods or services, or low interest rates for investors that reduce the demand for products and goods have a negative effect on FX rates. Similarly, the supply of a currency affects FX rates, with an increase in the supply of a currency having a dampening effect on a country's FX rate. An example is when a country's central bank engages in quantitative easing policies that dramatically increase the supply of that country's currency. With a greater supply of currency, the supply curve for loanable funds shifts outward, intersecting with the demand curve at a lower equilibrium interest rate in that country. The lower interest rate makes investments in bank deposits or bonds in that country less attractive, reducing the demand for that country's currency and putting downward pressure on the country's FX rate.

Finance experts also recognize that forecasts for FX rates are incomplete without acknowledging the role of expectations, such as revealed in forward and futures contracts foreign currency rates. Balance of payments also are important in understanding market adjustments for FX rates.

BALANCE OF PAYMENTS AND FX RATES

Balance of payments is a bookkeeping account for international receipts and payments that directly affect the movement of funds among nations from private and government transactions. The current account reflects international transactions that involve currently produced goods and services, with the trade balance in the account the net receipts from trade (i.e. the difference between exports and imports). When merchandise imports are greater (fewer) than exports, there is a trade deficit (surplus) for a country. There is also a capital account equal to the net receipts from capital transactions, with flows of capital into (out of) a country registered as receipts (payments). A country has a positive capital account when net capital flows into a country are positive.

The balance of payments provides an array of factors that affect the supply of a currency (exports of merchandise and services from another country, transfers of private and official funds to another country, and long-term and short-term investments in another country) and demand for a currency (imports of merchandise and services from the country, transfers of funds private and official to the country from another country, and long-term and short-term investments from another country). Holding other factors affecting supply of a country's currency constant, if factors affecting the demand for a country's currency increase, this results in a rise in the value of that currency, and similarly, if any of the factors affecting the supply for the country's currency increase, this results in a fall in the value of that currency. Hence, holding other factors constant, countries with greater net exports to other countries and fewer net imports would be expected to have a higher relative FX rate. However, in the long run, the higher FX rate under a floating exchange rate system makes that country's goods more expensive, which would lead to lower demand for that country's goods for exports, reducing trade imbalances.

THEORY OF INTEREST RATE PARITY FOR FOREIGN EXCHANGE RATES IN THE LONG RUN

Brief Overview Theory of Purchasing Power Parity (PPP)

A well-known theory for how FX prices should act in the long run is the theory of purchasing power parity (PPP) that has been found to hold at times for long-term FX relationships, but not so much for short-term. PPP is based on the law of one price, that is, if two countries are producing identical goods, the price of a good should be the same globally regardless of the country producing it. If costs are different, the FX rate should adjust to make the price identical. Hence, exchange rates for any two currencies will adjust to reflect changes in the price levels of the two countries, implying that if one country's price level rises relative to another's, such as with inflation, its currency should depreciate (i.e., the other country's currency should appreciate). PPP cannot fully explain exchange rates, since it assumes that all goods are identical in both countries, which may be unreasonable for different products, and PPP does not take into account that there may be trade barriers or FX or capital flow restrictions, so prices might not be allowed to rise or fall relatively for different currencies.

Interest Rate Parity and FX Rates

Under PPP, expected returns in a country including FX appreciation or depreciation should be equal across countries, where returns on domestic deposits adjusted for FX changes should equal the return on foreign deposits adjusted for FX changes. Thus, interest rate parity conditions include: (1) expected returns in the long run equal to the return plus appreciation or less depreciation in a foreign currency should be the same on deposits and perfect substitutes; (2) the expected return on a country's deposits should equal the expected return on foreign deposits including expected FX rate changes; and (3) only when interest parity holds will both outstanding deposits of two countries be held willingly by large investors.

From this perspective if one country has a higher deposit rate than another country, the relative FX rates will adjust until the deposit rate in each country plus the appreciation (less the depreciation) will be equal in the long run. So, for instance, if the U.S. rate on deposits was 1% and the European Union rate on deposits was 2%, you would expect in the long run that there would be an appreciation in the FX rate for the U.S. dollar (i.e., a depreciation in the euro), so their rates plus rate of change in the value of each currency would be equal.

Different Types of Foreign Exchange Rates

In the foreign exchange market there are several different markets:

Spot market rates, which is the market for current exchange rates for currency, reported generally on an immediate (two-day) basis.

Forward transaction rates that are agreed upon exchanges for a future date (carried out with a broker/dealer over-the-counter) that can be tailor-made for any amount or delivery date.

Futures transaction rates that are contracts on a formal exchange, guaranteed by the exchange, to buy or sell a currency, security or commodity for a future date, with liquidity, since contracts can be reversed at any time to get out of a position, taking your gain or loss at that time (reversed prior to the future date) and with very standardized contracts for a specific date, contract amount, and type of currency.

Spot Market Rates

Spot market rates for foreign exchange are available in the financial section of newspapers and on financial sites on the web (such as www.x-rates.com or www.exchange-rates.org, among others) and these include graphs and tables for current and historical rates for different currencies. On April 19, 2015, spot rates for the U.S. dollar relative to other different currencies listed on www.x-rates.com were:

	Direct rate	Inverse (indirect) rate
Euro	0.924658	1.081481
British pound	0.668309	1.496314
Indian rupee	62.549466	0.015987
Australian dollar	1.281206	0.780515
Canadian dollar	1.222452	0.818028
Singapore dollar	1.344543	0.743747
Swiss franc	0.950742	1.051810
Japanese yen	118.968431	0.008406
Chinese yuan renminbi	6.195849	0.161398

The indirect rate is the value of each currency in U.S. dollars, and the direct rate, the value of a U.S. dollar in the other currency. For instance, on this date, if you exchanged euros for dollars, €1 would be worth US$1.081481. If you had dollars to exchange for euros, US$1 would be worth (1/1.081481) or €0.924658.

FX rates can be quite volatile. An example is the euro in the spring of 2015. On April 14, 2015, the euro closed at 1.053712, but by April 19, 2015 the euro rose to 1.081481, a rise of +2.69% in just a few days. If a U.S. importer expected to pay €100 million for goods, and planned on exchanging dollars to make this payment on April 19, this would represent a rise in his expected cost from the week before, that is:

Expected cost in $ = €100 million × 1.053712 = $105.3712 million

New cost in $ = €100 million × 1.081481 = $108.1481 million

Rise in cost in $ = ($2.7769 million).

Alternatively, if instead a U.S. exporter expected to receive €100 million over this time period, this would be a rise of $2.7769 million in revenues expected to be received when converting the euros to U.S. dollars on April 19 versus April 14, since the value of the euro went up.

Expected revenue in $ = €100 million × 1.053712 = $105.3712 million

New revenue in $ = €100 million × 1.081481 = $108.1481 million

Rise in revenue in $ = $2.7769 million.

As in the example above, even for a short period, with volatile FX rates, there can be considerable FX rate risk. These risks can be hedged in financial markets using forward or futures contracts or options on futures contracts.

HEDGING FOREIGN EXCHANGE RISK

The Forward Currency Market

Given significant foreign exchange rate volatility and risks, investors, corporations, and financial institutions use the forward currency market to reduce their risks. The forward currency market is an over-the-counter market with brokers and dealers, where arrangements are made between two parties to exchange a specified amount of one currency for another at a specified future date and a specified rate of exchange. The forward rate that is agreed upon may differ from the spot rate at the time of the negotiation, since it is based on future expected FX rates along with transaction costs. Forward rates are quoted daily along with spot rates often for 1-month (30 days), 3-months (90 days), and 6-months (180 days) forward. The FX over-the-counter market involves several hundreds of dealers that are primarily banks ready to buy and sell deposits in foreign currencies with most of the trades for buying and selling deposits denominated in a foreign currency. Most FX trades are transactions greater than $1 million, while small trades are generally made through dealers, with higher rates charged for smaller trades.

Advantages of forward contracts are that they are not standardized, and can be locked in a given FX rate for the future. *They can be customized for the needs of each trader with negotiations for any denomination, type of currency, and for any given delivery date.* Forward contracts are arranged electronically by means of a foreign currency dealer or through large, international financial institutions. Also, forward contracts do not have margin requirements or daily resettlement required for futures contacts, so do not have to be monitored daily and do not need sources of liquidity to meet margin calls.

Disadvantages of forward rates include higher brokerage fees, and forward contracts are not guaranteed, so depend on the reputation of the broker/dealer, and there is no secondary market for forward contracts, so traders face default risk and a lack of liquidity compared to futures contracts.

Foreign Currency Futures

Futures contracts are sold on futures exchanges with contracts to buy or sell currency, commodities, and securities in the future for given specified types, amounts, and delivery dates under standardized contracts that are guaranteed by the exchange. Contracts can be traded and reversed prior to the future date, where a trader offsets the contract with a reverse trade (for instance if the contract is to buy offset by a contract to sell) and can take the gain or loss and get out any time before the delivery date. Thus, futures contracts have the advantage of liquidity and low default risk, since they are guaranteed to go through by the exchange.

With futures, if foreign exchange rates move the opposite way than expected (i.e., so there is a spot gain), the futures contract will have futures loss that must be taken. Options on futures contracts are also often available at a premium cost, giving the option if rates moved the opposite way to that expected, not to have to exercise the contract. Futures contracts require *margin requirements*, that is, a small percentage of the value of the contract as a deposit in the form of cash, a bank letter of credit, or short-term government securities.

Futures contracts also involve *daily resettlement* at the end of each day's trading, where daily losses are taken against the margin and daily gains added to the margin. If the amount of the margin goes below a somewhat lower *maintenance margin*, there will be a *margin call*, and additional funds must be put in to bring the account back up to the initial margin. Hence trading in futures involves liquidity being available for potential margin calls with daily resettlement. To control the exposure to risk of traders, the exchanges set a maximum amount by which the price of a contract is allowed to change. When that limit is reached on a given day, the price cannot move farther, and subsequent trades will take place only if they are within the limits.

For example for the CME Group (www.cmegroup.com), euro/USD FX futures have a contract size of €125,000, have contracts for March, June, September, and December, have a minimum price increment of $6.25/contract, and have options on futures contracts for €125,000, and a maintenance margin requirement of $3,550 at the time of this writing (April 2016).

For hedging with futures contracts, the net hedging result will be the futures gain less the spot loss if rates move as expected. A perfect hedge would result in a net hedging position of zero (less the margin holding opportunity cost and any brokerage fees). However, since futures prices don't always move exactly the same as spot prices, you may have a larger or smaller gain on the futures position than your hedged position, known as *basis risk*. This can occur also with rounding up or down for the number of contracts, since contracts are not sold in fractional units. It can also occur if you're using *cross-hedging*, that is, hedging with a foreign currency other than your spot position if a futures contract for a particular currency is not available. If futures prices move more than spot prices for the instrument you are hedging, for instance, this can result in a larger future gain than your spot loss if FX rates go the way you expected, but a larger future loss than your spot gain if FX rates go the other way. To reduce this risk you can estimate a hedge ratio using historic prices for your futures and spot positions to adjust for the number of contracts you need; this is discussed in a later section.

Short versus Long Hedges

For hedging with futures contracts against foreign exchange risk, a hedger wants to take a futures position that will result in a futures contract gain to offset a spot position loss if a foreign exchange rate moves in an unfavorable way for the spot position hedge. *If a hedger wants to hedge against a spot loss with a rise in a FX rate, a long futures position should be taken (position to buy the foreign currency).* Then if the FX rate rises, the hedger has a contract to buy the foreign currency at the lower rate on the contract, and a gain can be made by offsetting the position by reversing the trade with a contract to sell the currency at a higher rate, making a futures contract gain.

If a hedger wants to hedge against a spot loss with a fall in a FX rate, a short futures position should be taken (position to sell the foreign currency). Then if the FX rate falls, the hedger has a contract to sell the foreign currency at the higher rate on the contract, and a gain can be made by reversing the trade with a contract to buy the currency at a lower rate, making a futures contract gain. Of course if rates go the opposite way than expected, there will be a futures loss that will be offset by a spot gain, in either case locking in a net zero change position, subject to basis risk.

Calculating the Correct Number of Contracts for a FX Hedge with Futures

To find the correct number of contracts to use for a hedge, you divide the amount you want to hedge in your spot position in a foreign currency by the amount of foreign currency per futures contract:

No. contracts = [FX position to hedge / FX futures contract amount] × HR

where HR stands for hedge ratio, if cross-hedging with a different currency for the futures contract, representing the ratio of how much historically the FX spot position's change in price moves relative to the FX futures contract position change in price.

For example, if the exporter mentioned earlier in April is going to receive €100 million in June, and a euro futures contract on the CME is for €125,000, the number of contracts (assuming a hedge ratio of 1) needed for the hedge will be:

No. contracts = [€100,000,000 / €125,000 per contract]
            = 800 futures contracts for the hedge.

Since the exporter is concerned about the value of the euro going down in the future, this should be a short hedge (hedge to sell euros), so if the euro goes down and there is a spot opportunity loss, there will be a gain on the futures hedge to offset the spot loss.

Alternatively, if an importer has to pay €100 million in June, and wants to hedge against a higher expense in U.S. dollars if the euro rises, this should be a long hedge (hedge to buy euros), so if the euro goes up and there is a higher spot position expense, there will be a gain on the futures hedge to offset this higher expense.

In either case, the hedger can just reverse the trade (take on the opposite contract) and take the futures gain to offset the spot loss if rates go the way expected.

OVERVIEW FX FUTURE CONTRACT PRICES

An example of FX future contract prices for a euro/USD FX futures contract can be found on the CME Group website (www.cmegroup.com website traded on Globex, an electronic trading platform that is used for derivative, futures, and commodity contracts that has continuous trading) accessed on April 13, 2016 as:

Product	Contract	Last	Change	Open	High	Low	Globex volume
Euro FX futures	June 2016	1.1295	− 0.01225	1.1405	1.14115	1.1288	197,579

The last quote for the June 2016 euro/USD FX futures contract is given and the change from the previous day, and the opening price, high and low price for that day's trading, and the volume of contracts. The prices are the euro in U.S. dollars, so the last price for the contract on this day is $1.1295 per euro. The contract size is €125,000 per contract. So for instance, if you were expecting to receive €100 million in June, and wanted to hedge against a fall in the value of the euro, you would take a short position (position to sell euros at the given price), where you would make a gain if the value of the euro falls if you reverse your trade, making the difference between the euro sales price and buy price. Options are also offered for this contract in terms of puts (right to sell) and calls (right to buy) this FX futures contract that do not have to be exercised, but have a premium cost.

FX FUTURE HEDGING EXAMPLE

Suppose on April 19, 2015, a U.S. importer wants to hedge against a higher cost the company will have to pay for the €100,000,000 owed in June to an exporter. So the firm is afraid that the value of the euro will rise. At this time in April for this example, the value of the euro in U.S. dollars was $1.081481. The future price for a June euro contract on that date was $1.1295, with the expectation implied that the value of the euro would rise. The U.S. importer wants to hedge against a potential rise in the euro, so takes on a *long futures contract (contract to buy euros) that will result in a futures gain if the euro futures price rises.*

Calculating the number of contracts for the hedge, as before:

No. contracts = [€100,000,000/€125,000 per contract]
= 800 futures contracts for the hedge.

June hedging results Suppose in June when the payment is due, the spot value of the euro rises to US$1.11948, and the futures price rises to $1.1595, what are the spot and futures gains or loss, and the net hedging position?

Since the euro rose the importer will have a higher price to pay in U.S. dollars, so a spot loss = [€100,000,000] × [change in price of euro]:

Spot loss = [€100,000,000] × [$1.11948 new price − $1.081481 previous price],

which equals

[€100,000,000] × [$0.03800], *a spot loss of $3,800,000*

Since the importer took a long position and the euro futures price rose, there will be a futures gain equal to 800 contracts × €125,000 per contract × [change in price of euro]:

Futures gain = 800 contracts × €125,000 [$1.1595 − $1.1295]
= €100,000,000 [$0.0300] = *Gain of $3,000,000*

So

Net hedging result = Spot loss – Futures gain
= Net hedging loss of $3,800,000 – $3,000,000 = ($800,000).

The importer did not have a perfect hedge but reduced his spot loss by the futures gain. This provides an example of basis risk, with futures prices for the euro changing less than spot prices. Additional futures contracts would have helped reduce the net hedging loss.

To adjust for greater volatility in the spot prices than futures prices in this example, a hedge ratio could be estimated using historic prices for futures prices and spot prices, these could be regressed against each other, and a hedge ratio calculated to make an adjustment for the number of future contracts to take on for the hedge. In this case, the hedger did not have a perfect hedge, with spot prices moving more than futures prices; however, the net hedging loss was much less than if the spot position had not been hedged, which would have resulted in a spot position opportunity loss of $3,800,000.

Note, if this had been the exporter expecting to receive euros in the future, a short position would have been taken, and the net hedging result would have been a spot gain less a futures loss, which would have resulted in a net hedging position of a gain of $800,000 instead.

THE HEDGE RATIO

Although there are other ways of defining a hedge ratio, the relative variability of prices in cash and future instruments is often used to minimize the variability in price changes to which the hedger is exposed, where:

$$HR = \frac{\text{Covariance for changes in spot and future prices}}{\text{Variance change in future prices}}$$

The covariance is a statistic that measures the extent to which two variables move together and the variance in futures prices is a measure of future price volatility. Students of regression analysis may realize that the covariance between the two variables divided by the variance of one of the variables is the beta coefficient in a simple regression between the two variables. Thus, the hedge ratio can be estimated by regressing past price changes in the cash instrument to be hedged against past price changes in a futures instrument. The beta of the regressions is the hedge ratio for the proposed hedge.

Suppose for the previous example, the hedge ratio for euro spot and future prices was 1.27, then the number of futures contracts to get would be:

No. contracts = [100,000,000/125,000] × 1.27 HR = 1,016 contracts

For the previous example, then

Futures gain = 1,016 contracts × 125,000 [1.1595 – 1.1295] = 3,810, 000

So,

Net hedging result = Futures gain − Spot loss
= Net hedging gain of $3,810,000 − $3,800,000 = $10,000.

HEDGING WITH OPTIONS AND SWAPS VERSUS FUTURES

Options and Options on Futures Contracts

Options can also be used for hedging FX risk. Options on futures contracts can be purchased for a premium that allow the hedger the right but not the obligation to not exercise the option in the event that FX rates go the opposite way to that expected, so a futures loss will not have to be taken against a spot gain. Call options on futures contracts are options to purchase futures contracts in the future or for buying/selling particular currencies, and put options on futures contracts are options to sell future contracts in the future. The cost of the options is a premium cost that can be large, so it's often better to get an options contract for a position where there is more likely to be volatility or a high likelihood that rates will move in an unexpected direction where price changes will cover the premium cost. An example would be the case of a U.S. exporter who expects to receive €100,000,000 in June for sales made in Europe in April, and wants to hedge against a fall in the value of the euro in June. The exporter would want to get a short position in futures or alternatively a put option on a futures contract. At this time, the value of the euro in U.S. dollars was $1.081481. As noted above, the future price for a June euro contract on that date was $1.1295, with the expectation implied that the value of the euro would rise. The number of contracts desired would be [€100,000,000 divided by €125,000 per contract] or 800 contracts.

June hedging results Suppose in June when the payment is due, the spot value of the euro rose to US$1.11948, and the futures price rose to $1.1595, what are the spot and futures gains or loss, and the net hedging position? Since the euro rose, the exporter will receive a higher dollar value for euros than expected, a spot gain of €100,000,000 × [$1.11948 new price − $1.081481 previous price] = a spot gain of $3,800,000. The exporter will receive a futures contract short position loss equal to 800 contracts × €125,000 [1.1295 − 1.1595] equal to $3,000,000. So the net hedging result will be the difference between the spot gain and loss, that is, spot gain equal to a $800,000 net hedging gain. If an option on a futures contract had been used instead, the put option on the futures contract would not have to be taken, and there would be just a spot gain of $3,800,000 less the premium cost for the option as the net hedging result. As long as the premium cost for the options on futures contracts was less than the futures loss, the hedger would have been better off getting the options on the futures contracts.

Currency Swaps

A currency swap involves an agreement for the exchange of different currencies by two parties at a future date at the same exchange rate. Periodic interest payments are made during the term of the swap. Currency swaps can be tailor-made for longer-term, custom-made arrangements over several years to reduce foreign exchange risk. For instance, a Japanese bank doing business in the United States may be receiving interest revenues in dollars from loans in U.S. dollars, but be financing this loan with debt in Japan denominated in yen. To reduce the foreign exchange risk, the Japanese bank could arrange a currency swap of payments through an intermediary broker with another institution that has the opposite problem, receiving interest revenues, for example in Japanese yen and paying expenses for financing in U.S. dollars. Advantages of swaps are that they can be tailor-made for long periods of time and flexibility. Disadvantages include legal and brokerage fees, and that they are less liquid and more difficult to get out of if a situation changes. Some swaptions (an option giving the right but not the obligation to engage in a swap) are available as well.

SUMMARY

With globalization, exchange rates have been very volatile in recent years, particularly following the great recession. With quantitative easing used in the USA and Europe and other countries as an economic stimulus, there have been significant foreign exchange rate effects across countries. Understanding factors that affect FX rates and ways to hedge against foreign exchange risks are of key importance for financial institution managers. FX rates are expressed in terms of how much one unit of currency is worth relative to another currency. Different types of FX rate risks include transaction, balance sheet, and economic risks.

Similar to the loanable funds theory, a supply and demand theory for foreign exchange rates helps to examine potential effects of changes on future FX rates, with factors increasing the demand and supply for a currency, such as: higher interest rates, lower inflation, and new technologies putting upward pressures on foreign exchange rates; and central bank interventions that decrease or increase the supply of a currency also having a significant effect, with increases in supply reducing FX rates and decreases increasing FX rates, holding other factors constant.

In the long run purchase price parity predicts an equilibrium between FX rates between country trading partners with FX rates adjusting. Hence, under the law of one price, if two countries produce an identical good, the price of the goods in the two different countries should be equal with exchange rates adjusting to make prices identical in the long run across countries.

To hedge FX rate risk, forward, futures, options, and currency swaps can be used. Forward contracts can be tailor-made for any amount or delivery date, so are better for smaller positions, but entail greater counterparty risk and generally must be carried through, so lack liquidity. Futures contracts are for large standardized amounts, for particular delivery dates, and particular currencies, and are sold and guaranteed by an exchange; and trades can be reversed at any time, so they have low counterparty default risk and are very liquid. Margin requirements and daily resettlement entail the need for a hedger to have sufficient liquidity to meet margin calls, and futures have basis and cross-hedging risks and can be used generally to hedge for a year or less. Options on futures contracts allow the option of not exercising the contract if rates go the opposite way to that expected, and have a premium cost. Currency swaps are tailor-made and allow hedging for longer time periods, allowing longer-term exchanges of currency between parties to hedge ongoing foreign exchange risks.

NOTES

1 See Conerly (2013) for a detailed discussion of the future of the dollar as a world reserve currency versus other potential currencies.
2 See *The Economist* (2010) for a more detailed discussion.

BIBLIOGRAPHY

Amadeo, Kimberly (2014). "Bretton Woods System and 1944 Agreement: How Bretton Woods introduced a New World Order." Accessed on June 22, 2015 at: http://useconomy.about.com/od/monetarypolicy/p/Bretton-Woods-International-Monetary-System-And-1944-Agreement.htm

Blakely, Renee (2015). "Standard & Poor's downgrades Brazil's credit rating to junk." Market Realist, September 11, 2015. Accessed on October 14, 2015 at: http://marketrealist.com/2015/09/standard-poors-downgrades-brazils-credit-rating-junk/

Bordo, M., Ehsan Choudri, and Anna Schwartz (2002). "Was expansionary monetary policy feasible during the Great Contraction? An examination of the gold standard constraint." *Explorations in Economic History*, 39(1), 1–28.

Buttonwood (2015). Buttonwood's Notebook: Financial Markets: Exchange rates and the economy. "Devaluations didn't work." *The Economist*, September 30, 2015. Accessed on October 14, 2015 at: http://www.economist.com/blogs/buttonwood/2015/09/exchange-rates-and-economy?zid=305&ah=417bd5664dc76da5d98af4f7a6 40fd8a

CFR (2015). CFR Backgrounders "The Group of Seven (G7)." Council on Foreign Relations. Accessed on April 13, 2016 at: http://www.cfr.org/international-organizations-and-alliances/group-seven-g7/p32957

Conerly, Bill (2013). "Future of the dollar as world reserve currency." *Forbes*, October 25, 2013. Accessed on April 17, 2015 at: http://www.forbes.com/sites/billconerly/2013/10/25/future-of-the-dollar-as-world-reserve-currency/

Friedman, M. and A.J. Schwartz (1963). *A Monetary History of the United States, 1867–1960*. Princeton, NJ: Princeton University Press and National Bureau of Economic Research.

"G20: What is it and how does it work?" (2014). *The Telegraph*, November 12, 2015. Accessed on April 13, 2015 at: http://www.telegraph.co.uk/finance/g20-summit/5075115/G20-what-is-it-and-how-does-it-work.html

IMF (2014). *Annual Report on Exchange Arrangements and Exchange Restrictions 2014*. International Monetary Fund, October 2014. Accessed June 22, 2015 at: http://www.imf.org/external/pubs/nft/2014/areaers/ar2014.pdf

IMF (2015a). "The end of the Bretton Woods system, 1972–81." International Monetary Fund. Accessed on April 12, 2016 at: https://www.imf.org/external/about/histend.htm

IMF (2015b). "Debt and painful reforms (1982–89)." International Monetary Fund. Accessed on April 12, 2016 at: https://www.imf.org/external/about/histdebt.htm

IMF (2015c). "Societal change for Eastern Europe and Asian upheaval (1990–2004)." International Monetary Fund. Accessed on April 12, 2016 at: https://www.imf.org/external/about/histcomm.htm

IMF (2015d). "Globalization and the crisis (2005–present)." International Monetary Fund. Accessed on April 12, 2015 at: https://www.imf.org/external/about/histglob.htm

Mandeng, Ousmene (2015). "IMF must grab this chance to shake up the currency system." Markets & Investing, *Financial Times*, June 23, 2015, p. 24.

Martin, Katie and Roger Blitz (2016). "Banks staff up for fierce currency movements," *Financial Times*, June 27, 2016, p. 19.

Mayeda, Andrew (2015). "IMF approves reserve currency status for China's yuan." *Bloomberg*, November 30, 2015. Accessed on April 12, 2016 at: http://www.bloomberg.com/news/articles/2015-11-30/imf-backs-yuan-in-reserve-currency-club-after-rejection-in-2010

Mayer, David A. (2010). *The Everything Economics Book: From Theory to Practice, Your Complete Guide to Understanding Economics Today*. Avon, MA: Adams Media.

Misculin, Nicolas and Eliana Raszewski (2014). "Argentina's debt crisis seen rumbling on until 2015 election." *Reuters*, December 30, 2014. Accessed on April 15, 2015 at: http://www.reuters.com/article/2014/12/30/us-argentina-debt-analysis-idUSKBN0K81DL20141230

Mishkin, Frederic S. and Stanley G. Eakins (2012). *Financial Markets and Institutions*, 7th ed. New York: Prentice Hall.

Nikkei Asian Review (2014). "IMF finds more countries adopting managed floating exchange rate system." *Nikkei Asian Review*, August 19, 2014. Accessed on April 13, 2016 at: http://asia.nikkei.com/Markets/Currencies/IMF-finds-more-countries-adopting-managed-floating-exchange-rate-system

Oanda (2015). "Brazilian real." Accessed on October 14, 2015 at: http://www.oanda.com/currency/iso-currency-codes/BRL

Rose, Andrew K. (2015). "Exchange rate regimes in the modern era: Fixed, floating, and flaky." Working Paper, University of California Berkeley. Accessed on April 16, 2015 at: http://faculty.haas.berkeley.edu/arose/FFF.pdf

Rosenfield, Everett (2015). "Ecuador becomes the first country to roll out its own digital cash." Currencies, CNBC, February 9, 2015. Accessed on April 13, 2016 at: http://www.cnbc.com/2015/02/06/ecuador-becomes-the-first-country-to-roll-out-its-own-digital-durrency.html

Sambo, Paula and Denyse Godoy (2015). "Brazil's real, Ibovespa lead world losses amid political crisis." Bloomberg Business, October 13, 2015. Accessed on October 15, 2015 at: http://www.bloomberg.com/news/articles/2015-10-13/brazil-real-drops-as-china-imports-slump-adds-to-pessimism

Stone, Mark, Harald Anderson, and Romain Veyrune (2008). "Exchange rate regimes: Fix or float?" *Finance and Development*, 45(1). Accessed on June 22, 2015 at: http://www.imf.org/external/pubs/ft/fandd/2008/03/basics.htm

The Economist (2010). "Beyond Bretton Woods 2: Is there a better way to organize the world's currencies?" *The Economist*, November 4, 2010. Accessed on April 17, 2015, at: http://www.economist.com/node/17414511

Timberlake, R. (1993). *Monetary Policy in the United States, an Intellectual and Institutional History*. Chicago: University of Chicago Press.

Timberlake, R. (2005). "Gold standards and the real bills doctrine in U.S. monetary policy." *Econ Journal Watch*, 2(2), 196–233.

Tremper, Charles (2015). "Charles Tremper quotes." Accessed on April 13, 2016 at: http://www.quotehd.com/quotes/charles-tremper-quote-the-first-step-in-the-risk-management-process-is-to-acknowledge-the

QUESTIONS AND PROBLEMS

1   Discuss the different types of foreign exchange risk for a financial institution including: (a) transaction exposure; (2) translation exposure; and (3) economic exposure, as three types of foreign exchange risk.

2   Suppose a Denver bank in the United States gives a loan to a bank in London of one million British pounds with a spot rate of £1 = \$1.424 with the loan to be paid back in pounds with a 10% rate, financed at a 8% rate paid in U.S. dollars.

   a   What type of FX rate exposure does the Denver bank have?
   b   What would be the change in the market value of the loan if the value of the British pound fell to \$1.255?
   c   What would be the effect on the market value of the bank's equity? How would the spread on the loan change with the change in the value of the British pound?
   d   What would be the change in the interest spread?

3   Discuss using a supply and demand for currency framework the different factors that affect foreign exchange rates. Describe how relative interest rates, the supply and demand for goods and services in different countries, and relative interest rates affect foreign exchange rates for a country.

4   Using a supply and demand framework, discuss what would happen to the value of a country's currency if: (a) the central bank uses a contraction policy to raise interest rates; (b) the inflation rate rises in a country; (c) a new technology is developed in a country that increases the demand for that country's goods globally.

5   In April a U.S. Export Company is expecting to receive in June from its European customer €500 million, and wants to hedge against a fall in the value of the euro relative to the U.S. dollar in June. In April the spot exchange rate euro is US$1.08909. The CME currency future settle rate for June euro FX futures contracts is €1 = US$1.0902, with each contract for €125,000 per contract.

   a   What position and how many contracts should the financial manager take to hedge against a rise in the euro? Explain why. (Hint: No. contracts = amount of euros hedging / €125,000 per contract. Always take a position that will give you a futures gain to offset your spot loss in the event of what you want to hedge.)

   b   Suppose in June the spot rate for the euro rises to $1.0950 and the futures settle rate has risen to $1.0961. Calculate the spot opportunity loss or gain for the company and the futures gain or loss. What is the net hedging result?

   c   Would the U.S. Company have done better getting options on a futures contract for this hedge? Explain why or why not. What is the maximum loss for an options contract if it isn't exercised?

6   In April, the Mountain King Company, a U.S. company is expecting to pay in June its European customer €900 million, and wants to hedge against a rise in the value of the euro relative to the U.S. dollar in June.

   In April the spot exchange rate euro is US$1.136. The CME Group future settle rate for June euro FX futures contracts is €1 = US$1.1418, with each futures contract for €125,000 per contract.

   a   What position and how many contracts should the financial manager take for the hedge? Explain why. (Hint: No. contracts = amount of euros hedging / €125,000 per contract.)

   b   Suppose in June the spot rate for the euro falls to US$1.095 and the futures settle rate falls to US$1.1019. Calculate the spot opportunity loss or gain for the company and the futures gain or loss. What is the net hedging result?

   c   Would the Mountain King Company have done better getting options on the euro futures contract for this hedge? Explain why or why not.

7   Find an article on a country such as Brazil, Venezuela, Japan, or China, or the European Union, and the trends in their currency values, and how central banks have attempted to intervene. Discuss the success or failure of these interventions.

Chapter 8

Hedging Interest Rate Risk with Derivatives

[B]y hedging now, in advance of a prospective change in sentiment, companies would be assured of protection if rates spike sooner than widely expected.

(Kawaller, 2014)

It is shown that the known risks of derivatives portfolios can generally be measured and managed well at the firm level. However, derivatives can create systemic risks when a market participant becomes excessively large relative to particular derivatives markets. Overall, the benefits of derivatives outweigh the potential threats.

(Stulz, 2004)

FINANCIAL institutions by their nature, as well as corporations with large amounts of financial assets and liabilities, are subject to great interest rate risk. Interest rate risk management includes the use of financial derivatives, contracts that derive their value based on the performance of an underlying security or portfolio. Derivatives are also used to hedge credit risk. Hedging techniques for interest rate risk include a variety of different types of derivatives to choose from, including using forward contracts, futures contracts, options on futures contracts, interest rate swaps, caps, and options on futures contracts, and swaps. As pointed out in the first quote above, by taking derivative positions, companies can hedge against expected and unexpected interest rate risks. However, as noted in the second quote, which later came to pass with credit default swaps during the U.S. subprime loan crisis, there is systemic risk when market participants become excessively large relative to particular derivatives markets.

Major U.S. bank holding companies are the greatest users of derivatives for both hedging and trading purposes and often serve as dealers/brokers for derivatives. This chapter provides an overview of different types of derivatives and uses for hedging focusing on interest rate risk.

USE OF DERIVATIVES BY U.S. INSURED COMMERCIAL BANKS AND SAVINGS INSTITUTIONS

For the third quarter of 2015, the U.S. Office of the Comptroller of the Currency (OCC, 2015) reported net credit exposure for insured U.S. commercial banks and savings associations for derivatives as $444.6 billion. The notional value of derivatives (total value of the underlying asset at its spot price) was $192.2 trillion. About 76.9% of total derivative notional amounts were interest rate derivatives, and about 4.3%, credit derivatives. A total of 1,411 insured U.S. commercial banks and savings associations reported derivatives activities.

Four large major U.S. commercial banks had 90.8% of the total U.S. banking industry notional amounts, and 80.5% of net current credit exposure (NCCE) from derivatives. Large commercial banks use derivatives for trading revenue as well as hedging, and as acting as dealers/brokers for other financial institutions. Trading risk for U.S. commercial banks and savings institutions, measured by value at risk (VAR), rose for the top five dealer banking companies by 2.9% to $357 million. The top four commercial banks with the majority of derivatives (JPMorgan Chase, Citibank, Goldman Sachs Bank, and Bank of America) held derivatives that are about 34.7 times larger than their total assets, as shown in Table 8.1. Other commercial banks, savings associations, and trust companies held much lower amounts, with derivatives about 1.92 times larger than their total assets (OCC, 2015).

TABLE 8.1 | Notional amounts of derivative contracts for U.S. banks and savings institutions, September 30, 2015

	Total assets ($ million)	Total derivatives ($ million)	Interest rate derivatives ($ million)
Top four commercial banks	5,035,977	174,541,078	143,250,636
Other commercial banks, savings associations and trust companies with derivatives	9,187,420	17,659,771	10,711,292
Total amount	14,223,397	192,200,849	153,961,928
Top four commercial banks with derivatives by rank			
1 JPMorgan Chase Bank	1,954,125	51,907,395	47,515,937
2 Citibank	1,337,821	51,201,146	35,361,239
3 Goldman Sachs Bank	127,605	43,621,441	40,129,410
4 Bank of America	1,616,426	27,811,096	20,244,050

Figures only include contracts subject to risk-based capital requirements. Numbers may not add due to rounding.

Source: Office of the Comptroller of the Currency, OCC Bank Derivatives Report, Quarter 3, 2015 (OCC, 2015).

FUTURES EXCHANGES

Futures contracts and other derivatives are traded on organized exchanges globally. Five of the largest exchanges by number of contracts traded ranked by *Futures Industry Magazine* in March 2015, based on 2014 volume in terms of the number of contracts traded and/or cleared include: (1) CME Group, which includes the Chicago Mercantile Exchange, Chicago Board of Trade (after merger of the two in 2007), and the New York Mercantile Exchange; (2) Intercontinental Exchange, which includes ICE Futures Europe, NYSE Amex, NYSE Arca, ICE Futures U.S., ICE Futures Canada, and Singapore Mercantile Exchange; (3) Eurex, which includes International Securities Exchange and International Securities Exchange Gemini; (4) the National Stock Exchange of India; and (5) BM&F Bovespa (FIA, 2015b).

The Futures Industry Association (FIA) reports on data for 75 futures and options exchanges globally. The CME Group alone had a volume of over 3.5 billion. The total number of futures and options traded on exchanges globally rose to 24.78 billion, a rise of 13.5% from 2014. For the 28 Asia-Pacific exchanges, 2015 volume was 9.7 billion, a 33.7% growth rate, with 25 North America exchanges having a volume of 8.2 billion, a – 0.2% growth rate, and 14 European exchanges having a volume of 4.8 billion, a 8.2% growth rate. Latin America, the fourth largest region fell 4.4% to 1.45 billion in volume (Acworth, 2016; FIA, 2016). The advantage of trades on futures exchanges are that they are guaranteed by the exchange as the clearing house for contracts, and markets are efficient and transparent with high volumes of trades for standardized contracts. Also, clearing house exchange allows for reversing of trades to get out of contracts, allowing great liquidity. The clearing house takes care of clearing and settlement. The FIA reported in March 2015 a total of 21,867,438,547 futures and options traded and/or cleared at 75 exchanges worldwide, including 37.8% in North America, 32.2% in the Asia Pacific, 20.4% in Europe, 6.9% in Latin America, and 2% for exchanges in other regions (FIA, 2015a).

FUTURES CONTRACTS

Overview of Futures Contracts

Futures contracts are standardized contracts backed up by the exchange that are traded on an exchange for future delivery/sale of a commodity or security. In practice delivery is generally not taken. Instead, an investor simply reverses his/her contract and makes a gain or loss on the contract. There is great liquidity on futures exchanges, with investors allowed by reversing a trade to get out of contract at any time.

While futures contracts on agricultural products have been available for over a century, the Chicago Board of Trade (CBOT) was the first organized exchange to introduce an interest rate futures contract in October 1975. Earlier in 1972, the International Monetary Market (IMM) of the Chicago Mercantile Exchange (CME) introduced the first futures contracts on foreign currency.

The CME and the CBOT completed a merger on July 12, 2007, transforming into the CME Group Inc. which also includes the New York Mercantile Exchange, serving the risk management needs of customers globally and bringing buyers and sellers together using the CME Globex electronic trading platform in addition to trading floors. Products include futures and options based on interest rates, equity indexes, commodities, foreign exchange, energy, among others including alternative investment products, including weather and real estate (CME Group, 2007).

A futures contract is a commitment to buy or sell a specific commodity or security of designated quality at a specified price and date in the future (the delivery date). The specified price is an estimate of the price that is expected to prevail at a future time. *A distinguishing feature of trading is that the two sides of a futures contract do not trade directly with another, but rather trade with a clearing house.* The clearing house acts as a buyer to each seller and seller to each buyer, which eliminates the need for direct contact between traders. The *clearing house guarantees the performance of the contract* and assumes responsibility for the creditworthiness of buyers. At the end of each trading date, the clearing house settles all accounts, pays profits earned by some traders, and collects payment due from others.

Contracts are *standardized* and the clearing house assumes the default risk for contracts, so a seller or buyer of a futures contract can easily offset (*reverse the trade* by purchasing the opposite contract) or cancel (get out of a contract by reversing a trade taking gains or losses) before the delivery date. Standardization of futures contracts allows the market to function efficiently. For instance, for interest rate futures, the contract size, maturity and coupon rate for coupon bonds are predetermined to facilitate efficient trading.

Hence, futures contracts sold on an exchange are very liquid. *About 98% of contracts involve reverse trades and close out of positions, whereby the gain or loss is taken versus taking actual delivery.* Futures are traded globally on different futures exchanges around the world, with a total volume of 21.87 billion contracts traded on exchanges worldwide in 2014, and in November 2015, trading in interest rate, credit, and foreign exchange products on swap execution facilities averaged $370.2 billion per day (FIA, 2015a).

FUTURES CONTRACTS VERSUS FORWARD CONTRACTS

Futures contracts differ from forward contracts that are over-the-counter (made through brokers and dealers) and nonstandardized, with trades not guaranteed by a clearing house and trades having to be carried through (not liquid like futures or allowed to be reversed prior to their maturity date). Futures contracts are standardized contracts with specific underlying commodities or securities, specific amounts per contract, and specific delivery dates. Thus, they are not tailor-made for particular customers. Forward contracts can be tailor-made for amounts, delivery date, and types of securities, so work better for hedging smaller amounts and for commodities or types of currency or securities that are unusual or have unusual delivery dates, since minimum amounts per contract can be large for futures contracts and only particular types of securities and currency and commodities are traded for particular dates. Futures contracts in contrast to forward contracts are rarely settled by actual delivery and are usually closed out prior to maturity. Futures contracts also have margin requirements and daily resettlement, with margin calls to replenish margins if daily losses erode the initial margin below a maintenance margin amount. Hence, hedgers have to have sources of liquidity available to cover margin calls to provide funds to get back to the margin required for the contract. About 98% of futures contracts simply reverse trades and close out their positions—taking the gain or loss versus actual delivery, while forward contracts entail actual delivery at a specified date in the future. Hence, forward contracts are less liquid and difficult to reverse, if a situation changes, and a hedger wants to get out of a contract.

Characteristics of Financial Futures Transactions

The margin Future traders are required to post an initial margin (often no more than 5% of the contract's face value), set by the exchange depending on the price volatility of a contract. Daily losses are taken against the margin, and a minimum *maintenance margin* is set, whereby the contract holder has to add an additional amount to get back to the margin amount. *Daily resettlement (mark to market)* is made at the end of each day, whereby the clearing house requires a trader to settle the account, with any losses charged against the trader's margin account. An example would be a $2,000 margin and a $1,500 maintenance margin for a contract. The margin account can go down to $1,500, but if it gets below $1,500, funds must be added to get back to the $2,000 original margin.

Limits on price changes To control traders' exposure to risk, the exchanges set a maximum amount by which the price of a contract is allowed to change. When the limit is reached on a given day, the price cannot move farther, and subsequent trades will take place only if they are within the limits, although risk of losses still exists, with several days of limit moves in a row, for instance, adding up to substantial losses.

Basis and cross-hedging risk Since futures contracts are standardized and only for certain underlying securities or commodities, they have basis risk (the risk of futures prices not moving the same as the spot position that is being hedged), particularly since standardized contracts are only for particular commodities and securities, so a cross-hedge with a different but similar security/commodity must be used.

INTEREST RATE FUTURES CONTRACTS

Interest rate futures contracts are standardized to buy and sell securities that pay interest, such as money market securities or bonds with gains or losses based on movements in interest rates. The type of underlying instrument, the face value of the contract, the daily price limits, and the delivery months for interest rate futures contracts are very standardized and set by the clearing house, such as the CME Group as a major futures exchange.

Long positions in interest rate futures are positions to buy money market securities or bonds at a given time in the future, and *short positions* are positions to sell securities in the future. Note that a gain will be made on a long position on a bond futures contract if bond prices rise (i.e., interest rates fall). A gain will be made a short position on a futures contract if bond prices fall (i.e., interest rates rise).

With a long position you have a contract to buy bonds at a given contract price for a given time in the future. If interest rates fall (i.e., bond prices rise), you can reverse your trade and take an offsetting short position contract, and take your gain. In this case, your gain will be equal to the new higher futures bond price—(the lower contract price on the long contract) x (amount per contract x no. contracts you purchased). This futures gain can offset a spot position loss, such as a plan to purchase bonds in the future and having to pay a higher price than currently for the bonds, because bond prices rose**.** *Hence, to hedge against a fall in interest rates (rise in bond prices), a long position should be taken for interest rate futures.*

With a *short position you have a contract to sell bonds* at a given contract price for a given time in the future. If interest rates rise (i.e., bond prices fall), you can reverse your trade and take an offsetting short position contract, and take your gain. In this case, your gain will be equal to (the higher price on the short contract – the new lower futures contract buy price) x (amount per contract x no. contracts you purchased). This futures gain can offset a spot position loss, such as a loss on a bond portfolio if rates rise and the value of the bond portfolio falls. *Thus, to hedge against a rise in interest rates (fall in bond prices), a short position should be taken for interest rate futures.*

Of course with any futures hedge, if rates (bond prices) go the opposite way expected for the hedge, there will be a futures loss that will offset a spot opportunity gain, as a disadvantage. However, the hedger is willing to forgo this spot opportunity loss for the peace of mind of reducing the risk of an unfavorable interest rate change that entails a large spot loss by having a futures gain to offset this loss.

DIFFERENT TYPES OF INTEREST RATE FUTURES OFFERED BY EXCHANGES

The CME Group, a major futures exchange, as an example of different types of futures contracts that are offered, provides a variety of interest rate products including futures and options on widely followed U.S. Interest Rate benchmarks that include Eurodollars, U.S. Treasury securities, 30-Day Fed Funds, and interest rate swaps. Short-term interest rate (STIR) futures contracts on the CME include Eurodollar futures and options and Fed Fund futures. Advantages of STIR futures contracts and options are that they reflect expectations for interest rates in the marketplace and are actively traded (CME Group, 2016a,b).

Other STIR contracts that are traded on European and Asian exchanges include the Euribor, the Euroyen, and the Euroswiss. The CME Group posts information and educational articles on different interest rate products on its website (www.cmegroup.com) for specific information on each product. Longer-term interest rate futures products by the CME Group include longer-term securities across the yield curve including U.S. Treasuries for different maturities, such as the 2-year, 5-year, and 10-year T-note futures, and 10-year U.S. Treasury bond futures, among others, and interest rate swap futures for 2, 5, 7, 10, 20, and 30 years in U.S. dollars and 2-year euro deliverable interest rate swap futures (CME Group, 2016a,b).

EURODOLLAR FUTURES CONTRACTS

Eurodollar futures are one of the most popular short-term interest rate (STIR) futures contracts for hedging interest rate risk that were introduced by the CME Group in December 1981. They are one of the most widely traded STIR futures, with the CME group no longer offering T-bill futures, given that T-bills were very thinly traded in the past decade, making them illiquid.

Eurodollars are U.S. deposits in banks outside the United States. The CME Eurodollar time deposit futures reflect the offered interest rate for a 3-month $1 million deposit that is offered on U.S. denominated deposits that banks hold outside the U.S. Since Eurodollars are outside the United States, they are outside the Fed's jurisdiction, so subject to lower levels of regulation and banking regulations, and offer a higher interest rate than T-bills of the same maturity. Eurodollars generally are held in different financial centers globally as offshore time deposits.

The pricing for Eurodollar futures reflects the interest rate offered on U.S. dollar denominated deposits held by banks outside the United States, reflecting the 3-month U.S. Dollar LIBOR (London Interbank Offered Rate) interest rate expected on the settlement date of the contract. The TED (T-bill and Eurodollar) spread (difference between the rates on 3-month futures contracts for U.S. Treasuries and 3-month contracts for Eurodollars with the same expiration month) is often used as an indicator of credit risk, with a higher spread providing investor sentiment of greater default risk for interbank loans (Blystone, 2014; CME, 2006).

Eurodollar futures contracts are backed by 90-day Eurodollars, with a contract amount of $1 million per contract. Contracts mature during the months of March, June, September, or December, and extend outward up to 10 years in the future. Eurodollar futures are also used for trading to take advantage of changing expectations about the shape of the yield curve and to price and hedge interest rate swaps (Blystone, 2014; CME, 2006; Labuszewski & Co., 2004).

Information on LIBOR used to set Eurodollar Rates

LIBOR (the London Interbank Offered Rate) is the rate major international banks offer for short-term Eurodollars to each other, with a secondary market that actively allows the sale of Eurodollar certificates of deposit (CDs) by investors before these deposits mature, similar to negotiable CDs. Eurodollars are frequently also used by large U.S. banks as an alternate source of short-term borrowing to Fed Funds, so the two rates are strongly correlated, along with other money market security rates (FRBSF, 2006).

The LIBOR rate is a key global benchmark rate used for setting adjustable rates, swaps, and an estimated $450 trillion of deals for 2012. Each day a group of leading banks submit the interest rates they are willing to lend at to each other, providing rates for 10 currencies that cover 15 different loan lengths, ranging from overnight to one year, with the 90-day LIBOR as the most important rate. After the top and bottom quartiles are removed, an average is calculated for the remaining rates, as LIBOR. In recent years, several major banks were accused of manipulation for the LIBOR rate with traders at several major international banks colluding to affect the results for LIBOR by submitting rates higher or lower than actual estimates. Regulators punished several large banks with huge fines for market manipulation. Following the LIBOR scandal a government commission made a major review of LIBOR and its rate setting, with oversight moved from the British Bankers' Association to the Intercontinental Exchange (ICE). Currently, rates are set based on actual transactions, with detailed records kept. Also, specific criminal sanctions were imposed for the manipulation of any benchmark interest rates (BBC, 2015).

Eurodollar Futures Prices

Table 8.2 shows prices for Eurodollar futures on the CME Group website (www.cmegroup.com) at the end of the day for trading on January 11, 2016 for different STIR contracts, the majority of which are Eurodollar futures. The information includes the type of contract, future date for

TABLE 8.2 | Eurodollar futures prices for STIR contract on the CME Group website, January 11, 2016

Product	Contract	Last	Change	Open	High	Low	Globex volume
Eurodollar futures	Mar. 2016	99.310	+0.005	99.305	99.315	99.305	7,679
Eurodollar futures	Jun. 2016	99.200	0.00	99.190	99.200	99.190	15,604
Eurodollar futures	Sep. 2016	99.090	0.00	99.075	99.090	99.070	10,955
Eurodollar futures	Dec. 2016	98.965	− 0.005	98.955	98.965	98.950	18,534
Eurodollar futures	Mar. 2017	98.885	− 0.01	98.845	98.855	98.840	7,977
Eurodollar futures	Jun. 2017	98.740	− 0.015	98.730	98.740	98.725	7,114
Eurodollar futures	Sep. 2017	98.635	− 0.015	98.620	98.635	98.620	5,996
Eurodollar futures	Dec. 2017	98.530	− 0.01	98.520	98.530	98.510	4,213

Source: CME Group website at: www.CMEGroup.com (accessed on January 11, 2016, at 9 pm MST).

the contract, the last (latest) price for the contract, the percentage change from the previous day, the open price, high and low prices, and Globex trading volume. The change column shows the change in price between the most recent "last" and the previous day's settlement price. The "high" column gives the highest trade, and the "low" column the lowest trade. The "open" column gives the first trade price of the session for the contract. The "volume" column provides the total number of contracts traded during the trading day as noted on the CME group website.

Understanding the Quoted Prices for Eurodollar Futures

Eurodollar futures are priced similar to T-bills, using discount yields that are used by convention in trading. Recall that T-bills and Eurodollars are sold at a discount from their maturity value, as noncoupon securities, similar to zero coupon bonds. Prices are quoted in terms of the IMM (International Monetary Market) index where the IMM index is equal to 100 less the yield on the security (previously the IMM was a division of the CME, with references continuing today), where:

IMM index = 100% − Yield %.

Here for example, for the March 2016 Eurodollar future (based on a 90-day Eurodollar) contract *with a $1 million par value, the last (similar to a closing price) is listed as 99.310, implying a yield of 0.69%, i.e.*

Yield = 100% − IMM index = 100% − 99.310% = 0.69%.

The pricing is set, so if the value of the futures contract changes by one basis point (0.01%), this is a $25 change in the contract value. This can be shown by using the formula for the basis point value (BPV) of an n = 90-day, $1 million face value money market instrument using the formula below:

Basis point value = Face value × (n/360) × 0.01% (as a fraction 0.0001).

So,

Basis point value = $1,000,000 × (90/360) × 0.0001 = $25.00.

The tick size (minimum allowable price fluctuation) that is usually established is one-half of a basis point (0.005%), equal to $12.50; this minimum is usually set to one-quarter basis point (0.0025%) for the nearby expiring contract month equal to $6.25 per contract (CME, 2016c). For the March 2016 contract, the change in price was + 0 .005% or half a basis point on Jan 11, 2016, equal to $12.50 per contract for the day.

Calculating the Gain or Loss on a Eurodollar Futures or T-bill Futures Contract

Since one-half basis point in the discount rate is worth $12.50, a change in one basis point (0.01%) is worth $25, making it easy to calculate the gain or loss on a Eurodollar or T-bill futures contract.

For example, suppose you took a short position in the March 2016 Eurodollar futures contract for 5,000 contracts with the quoted price of 99.31% (discount yield of 0.69%). In March you reverse your trade by taking a long position in the contract, and suppose the new quoted price is 99.11% (discount yield of 0.89%). Since the discount rate went up (price went down), you'll make a gain on the futures contract. The amount of the gain will be equal to 99.31% – 99.11% which equals 0.20% or (20 basis points) × ($25 per basis point gain) = $500 per contract × 5,000 contracts equal to a $2,500,000 gain (of course this would be a loss if interest rates had gone down 20 basis points instead).

To show that this is correct we calculate the new delivery price for the Eurodollars where Price = Amount $[1 - (d \times n/360]$,

Contract price = $1 million $[1 - (0.0069 \times 90/360)]$ = $998,275

New price = $1 million $[1 - (0.0089 \times 90/360)]$ = $997,775

Futures gain = [$998,275 Sell price – $997,775 Buy price] = $500 per contract.

Since you made a gain, you can take the gain by reversing your trade (no delivery needed).

EXAMPLES OF LONG AND SHORT HEDGES WITH EURODOLLAR FUTURES

Example: Long Hedge with Eurodollar Futures

Suppose in January 2016 a money market portfolio manager will be receiving $10 million cash in March to invest in Treasury bills. The current discount yield in January for a 3-month (91-day) T-bill is 0.23% (i.e., quote price = 100% – 0.23% = 99.77%). So currently, the spot price for 10 million T-bills is:

$P_0 = \$10$ million $[1 - (0.0023)(91/360)] = \$9{,}994{,}186.11$.

The manager is afraid that the discount rate on the money market securities will fall (i.e., money market security prices will rise) in March, so wants to hedge against such a spot opportunity loss. Since the CME Group no longer trades T-bill futures, the manager decides to hedge with a long position with 90-day Eurodollar futures contracts (contracts to buy) that will give him a gain if money market security prices rise (i.e., rates fall) in the future. The manager decides to hedge this risk by taking a long position on the March 2016 Eurodollar futures contracts quoted on the CME Global website on January 16, 2016 with the last price as 99.310%, so [100% – 99.310%] equals a 0.69% discount yield.

To calculate the number of contracts to get, a general formula is:

No. contracts = [Spot position / Futures contract amount] × HR

where HR is the hedge ratio estimate reflecting differences in the movement in spot and future prices. The hedge ratio is generally based on historical data on how spot and future prices move together, similar to a stock market beta, and is often calculated as:

$$HR = \frac{\text{Cov (changes in spot prices and futures price)}}{\text{Variance (change in futures prices)}}$$

Where HR is the hedge ratio, Cov (spot prices and futures price) is the covariance between changes in spot prices and change in future prices, and Variance (changes in future prices) is the variance for changes in future prices. Many other types of hedge ratios, including more sophisticated hedge ratios are also used.

Since each futures contract is for $1 million, the portfolio manager will get 10 long Eurodollar futures contracts to hedge the $10 million, assuming hypothetically a hedge ratio of 1. The portfolio manager is cross-hedging for the hedge, since the spot position to be hedged is T-bills, but money market securities tend to move together as liquid, substitutable securities.

Suppose in March 2016, the price of T-bills goes down by 0.10% (10 basis points) to 0.13%, the new price for the T-bills will be:

$P_0 = \$10$ million $[1 - (0.0013)(91/360)] = \$9{,}996{,}713.89$.

So the spot opportunity loss = higher price – previous price. Or,

Spot loss of $9,996,713.89 – $9,994,186.11 = $2,527.78 *Spot loss*.

Suppose, the Eurodollar futures price also goes down by 0.10% (10 basis points), so you have a futures gain on your long position of 10 basis points × $25 per contract × 10 contracts = *$2,500 Futures gain*. By reversing the trade and selling the futures contract at the new higher price, the money market portfolio manager can take the futures gain and get out of the position. The net hedging result will be:

Net hedging result = Spot loss – Futures gain

which results in:

Spot loss of ($2,527.78) – Futures gain $2,500 = ($527.78).

The portfolio manager is happy, since the spot loss was reduced, with the futures gain reducing the net cost of purchasing the T-bills in March.

Example: Short Hedge with Eurodollar Futures

Suppose in March 2016, the liability manager of a major bank will be issuing $10 million of 90-day negotiable bank certificates of deposit (CDs). Currently, it is January 2016, and the manager is concerned that interest rates will rise, and the liability expense of the CDs will go up. Currently, the rate for the bank's CDs is 0.55%. Negotiable CDs, rather than selling for a discount and paying a higher maturity value, sell at par value and pay interest and principal at maturity. So the interest expense expected for the bank for the $10 million of CDs is:

$$\text{Interest expense} = \text{Amount of CDs} \ [(d \times n)/360]$$
$$= \$10,000,000 \ [(0.0055)(90/360)] = \$13,750.$$

To hedge against a rise in the interest expense if interest rates rise in March, the bank will engage in a short hedge cross-hedge with March Eurodollar futures contracts quoted on the CME Global website on January 16, 2016, with the last price as 99.310% or $100\% - 99.310\% = 0.69\%$ yield. If interest rates rise, there will be a gain on the short futures contract to offset the higher interest cost for the bank.

Suppose in March, interest rates rise, and the market rate for CDs rises by 0.25% (25 basis points) to 0.80%, and the discount yield for March Eurodollar futures rises by 25 basis points to 0.94%.

The new interest expense for the CDs for the bank is now

$$= \$10,000,000 \ [(0.0080)(90/360) = \$20,000$$

so the spot opportunity loss is the difference between the new $20,000 cost and the previous expected interest cost of $13,750:

$20,000 – $13,750, which equals a $6,250 spot opportunity loss.

The gain on the futures contracts is [10 contracts × $25 gain per basis point × 25 basis points rise] = *$6,250 futures gain.*
So the net hedging result is

$6,250 Spot loss – $6,250 Futures gain = $0.

This is a perfect hedge, since the spot loss equals the futures gain. So the bank effectively locked in its desired CD interest expense, with the futures gain offsetting the higher interest expense.

RISKS ASSOCIATED WITH INTEREST RATE FUTURES

In the hedging examples above, perfect or almost perfect hedges are assumed, where the spot and future rates moved the same amount and in the way expected for each respective long and short hedge. However, this doesn't always happen, so there are disadvantages/risk associated with futures:

1   *Opportunity losses:* If rates go the opposite way expected, there will be a loss on your futures position that will offset the spot position opportunity gain, and you'll have to take this futures loss against the spot gain.
2   *Margin calls:* Even if you have a perfect hedge, you may still have daily losses that will have to be covered daily to get back up to margin before the end of the hedge, with daily resettlement. Thus, the hedger needs to hold adequate liquidity to cover any margin calls.
3   *Basis risk:* Hedgers have the risk of the gain or loss on the respective futures and spot positions not being equal if futures and spot prices (rates) don't move together, that is, if the basis, change in price on the spot position less the change in price on the futures positions, doesn't equal zero. Hence, determining the correct number of future contracts to buy or sell (long or short position) based on the historical correlation of futures and spot prices is very important.
4   *Cross-hedging risk:* Since contracts are standardized, there may not be a perfect instrument (delivery date, maturity of underlying instrument, type of security) to hedge with. With cross-hedging with different instruments, the hedge has greater basis risk with greater risk of spot and future prices not moving together. Thus, a future loss could occur that is larger than the offsetting gain in the spot market if rates go the opposite way expected. Cross-hedging is often necessary, since futures contracts are not offered on every type of security.
5   *Analyst, regulatory, and accounting risks:* Other risks include misinterpretation by analysts or investors concerning a hedge and what a financial institution is trying to achieve, which can cause a drop in a firm's stock price. Also, there is regulatory risk of a hedge not being accepted by regulators. Regulators of depository institutions in hedging generally support microhedges, but not always macro hedges.

Similarly, accounting rules support microhedges, but rules, such as FAS 133 in the U.S. "Accounting for Derivative Instruments and Hedging Activities" can be complex and require detailed information on the hedging instrument, the link between the hedging instrument and the hedged item, the type of risk that is being hedged, and documentation required by auditors to record the hedging relationship, objective, and strategy for undertaking the hedge, among other requirements. If a hedge is not considered to be qualified, a firm's financial statements must include the amount that is not perfect for a hedge on the income statement, increasing the financial statement's volatility. Firms must also describe their derivative and hedging activities in the footnotes of their financial statements.

Depository institutions also must meet special guidelines, including having a high-level management committee to establish hedging policy and guidelines for establishing hedges and monitoring results. Regulators assign an overall risk management rating as part of the CAMELS ratings. Examiners must determine whether bank managers understand all the risks entailed with derivatives, and have accurate models to measure and monitor risks. Managers must implement controls to quantify and manage these risks effectively, including setting limits on risks, as well as procedures and internal controls to make sure that policy limits are enforced. Also, internal and external audits must be performed, focusing on how effective internal controls and management information systems are.

STOCK INDEX FUTURES, OPTIONS, SWAPS, AND OTHER DERIVATIVES

Stock Index Futures

In 1982 the first stock index futures contract based on the Value Line Composite Index was traded on the Kansas City Board of Trade. Three months later the S&P 500 Futures Contract was traded on the Chicago Mercantile Exchange, and the NYSE Contract was traded on the New York Futures Exchange. New futures contracts for new indexes are constantly being developed. Special characteristics of stock index futures include:

1   *No delivery* (simply reverse your trade and take the gain or loss).
    If closure doesn't occur before the delivery month, the contract's settlement level is the same as the level on the index on a given date when the contract expires (contracts for March, June, September, December).
2   *Exchanges place overall price limits*, since there is often greater volatility for futures prices for stock index futures than the stock market prices for an underlying stock index.
3   *The value of a stock index futures contract is equal to an index level times an established multiple* (such as $50 for a mini-stock index futures contract) an amount that varies by contract.
4   *Quoted future stock index price.* On some exchanges, you need to know the spot index level to interpret the price, since decimals may not appear.
5   *Settlement price = index at settlement x multiplier.* For instance, for an S&P futures contract offered by the CME Group, the multiplier on a S&P 500 futures contract is $250. So if the futures price index was 1875.50, the settlement price would be:

Settlement price for 1 contract = 1875.50 × $250 = $468,875.

For the E-Mini S&P 500 futures contract, which is a smaller contract, the multiplier is $50, so for the same index, the settlement price for 1 contract = 1875.50 × $50 = $93,775.

CME Group Stock Index Pricing

On the CME Group website for equity index products, the E-mini S&P 500 futures and S&P 500 futures contract prices for March 2016 contracts were listed on January 17, 2016 as follows:

Product	Contract	Last	Change	Open	High	Low
E-mini S&P 500 futures	Mar 2016	1876.50	+ 3.50	1869.75	1879.	1859.75
S&P 500 futures	Mar 2016	1875.50	+ 0.50	1867.90	1875.5	1860

For this date the Globex volume for the E-mini S&P 500 futures contract was 78,242, and for the S&P 500 futures was 55 for the March 2016 contract, indicating greater trading for the E-mini contract that has a smaller multiplier. The electronically traded E-mini S&P 500 contract is one-fifth the size of standard S&P futures. Both contracts are a way to manage exposure to leading large-cap stocks (companies with market capitalization values of more than $5 billion) for the U.S. stock market. The contract's underlying asset is S&P 500 stock index that includes 500 individual stocks that represent the market capitalization of large companies. *The S&P 500 futures contract has a $250 multiplier, and the E-mini S&P 500 futures contract has a $50 multiplier.* Options on futures including the S&P 500 options are also offered (CME, 2016c).

FINDING THE APPROPRIATE NUMBER OF CONTRACTS FOR A FUTURES HEDGE

To find the appropriate number of contracts for a hedge using stock index futures contracts, the value of the stock portfolio is divided by the futures index times the multiplier for the particular contract used times the beta of the portfolio as the hedge ratio as follows:

$$\text{No. contracts} = \frac{\text{Value of stock portfolio}}{\text{Futures index} \times \text{Multiplier}} \times \text{Beta of portfolio}$$

For instance, hedging with the E-mini S&P 500 futures contract for March 2016 with a last index price of 1876.50 and a $50 multiplier, if a portfolio of $750,000 needed to be hedged with a beta of 1.20, then the appropriate number of futures contracts to acquire would be:

$$\text{No. contracts} = \frac{(\$750,000)}{(1876.50 \times \$50)} \times 1.20 = 9.59 \text{ contracts (round up to 10)}$$

Note whole contracts must be taken, so if the number of contracts is uneven, if the decimal is > 0.50 round up or < 0.50 round down. So here 10 contracts would be the appropriate number of contracts.

EXAMPLE OF A HEDGE USING STOCK INDEX FUTURES

Short Hedge to Protect a Portfolio against a Market Downturn

Suppose in January 2016 the investor with the $750,000 portfolio wants to hedge against the stock market falling in March 2016. Based on the calculation above for the number of E-mini S&P 500 futures contracts, the investor will take a short position for 10 contracts. With a short position (contracts to sell the index), if the index goes down, the investor can reverse the trade and get contracts to buy the index, and take a gain equal to the (sell price – buy price) × $50 multiplier. This futures gain if the stock market goes down would offset the expected loss on his portfolio.

If in March, the stock market falls by 10%, the loss on the investor's portfolio is equal to $750,000 (0.10 × 1.20 beta) equal to a $90,000 loss. However, suppose the E-mini index also goes down by 10%, falling to 1876.50 (1 – 0.10) = 1688.85, the gain on the futures contracts will be:

Futures gain = 10 contracts × [1876.50 – 1688.85] × $50 multiplier = $93,825.

Because of rounding for the contracts, the futures gain in this example is a little larger than the spot loss, and the net hedging result will be:

Net hedging result = Futures gain of $93,825 – Spot loss of $90,000 = $3,825.

Of course, if the stock market went up 10% instead, the investor will lose out on the $90,000 spot gain that would occur, and would have a net hedging result instead of

Spot gain of $90,000 – Futures loss of $93,825 = ($3,825).

Long Hedge to Protect Against a Market Rise if Buying Stocks in the Future

Similarly, an investor that plans on buying stocks in the future, such as a portfolio manager for a mutual fund planning to purchase stocks in March with cash inflows coming in, could take on a long stock index futures position (to buy stocks in the future). Suppose the portfolio manager needs a hedge for $10 million, and will use the S&P 500 index futures contract with an index price quoted at this time as 1875.50 with a $250 multiplier. The portfolio of stocks the portfolio manager plans to purchase will mimic the S&P 500 with a beta of 1.

The number of contracts he will purchase will be:

$$\text{No.contracts} = \frac{(\$10,000,000)}{(1875.50 \times \$250)} \times \text{beta of } 1 = 21 \text{ contracts.}$$

The portfolio manager takes a long position (to buy the index futures), so that a gain will be made on the futures contract if the market goes up.

Suppose in March, the market goes up 20%, so the cost of purchasing the $10,000,000 stocks is 20% higher, resulting in a $2,000,000 spot position opportunity loss.

With this rise, the S&P 500 index futures index also goes up by 20% to 1875.50 (1.20) = 2250.60, so the gain on the long futures position when the portfolio manager reverses his trade will be:

Futures gain = (2250.60 – 1875.50) × $250 multiplier × 21 contracts
= $1,969,275

So the net hedging result will be:

$1,969,275 Futures gain – $2,000,000 Spot loss = ($30,725) Net loss

This is not a perfect hedge, but the loss is small relative to the $2 million opportunity loss the portfolio manager would have had without the hedge.

OPTIONS ON FUTURES CONTRACTS

The CME Group and other futures exchanges also offer options on futures contracts, which require a premium to be paid to buy a long (call) option or a short (put) option that gives the right to a futures contract by exercising the option.

The advantage of options on futures contracts is that if rates go the opposite way expected, they do not have to be exercised, so the full spot opportunity gain can be taken. Also, problems of meeting margin calls and daily resettlement do not have to be worried about until the option is exercised. The disadvantages for options over futures are that at times they are more thinly traded, and may have a high premium cost, although the loss on options for futures contracts is limited to the premium cost. An American option can be exercised over a given period, while a European option can only be exercised at expiration.

A *call option*, providing the right to buy a security at the exercise or strike price for a long position is *in the money* when the exercise price is less than the current price of the security, and a *put option*, providing the right to sell a security is considered *in the money* when the exercise or strike price is greater than the current price of the security. As volatility increases for underlying prices for a futures contract, options premiums increase, since there is a greater chance of an option being in the money.

Similarly, the strike price affects the intrinsic value and premium cost for an option. For a call option, the intrinsic value is the futures price less the strike price, and for a put option, the intrinsic value is the strike price less the futures price.

As volatility increases for underlying prices for a futures contract, option premiums rise with a greater chance of the option having value, increasing the premium cost. A commonly used term for options is the delta, which is a measure for the rate of change of the premium for an option relative to a price change in an underlying futures contract, measuring price sensitivity to the movement of an underling futures contract. For instance, if an option moves half as much as futures prices move at a particular moment, its delta would be 50%, with the option only half as sensitive to the price movement of the underlying futures contract. Once an option on a futures contract is exercised, a margin as on a future contract is required (Options Guide, 2015).

On the CME Group website, (www.cmegroup.com) under short-term interest rate futures, options are given for futures contracts, such as the March 2016 Eurodollars futures contract discussed earlier, by clicking on the option link, which provides prices for the option on that contract on January 18, 2016 at 4:45 pm as follows:

Underlying future	Last	Change	High	Low	Volume
Mar 2016	99.335	0.00	99.345	99.325	45,153

Below this, call and put prices are provided for different strike prices. For instance, for a 99.500 strike price (given as 9950.0), the settle for a call option is 0.75 and for a put option 17.25. For a 99.25 strike price (given as 9925.0), the prior settle price for a call option is 10.25

and for a put option 1.75. Note the put option premium is higher for a higher strike price, and the call option premium is higher for a lower strike price.

INTEREST RATE SWAPS AND SWAPTIONS

Beginning in the late 1990s, interest rate swaps became widely used for risk management for financial institutions, accounting for the majority of derivative activity by banks. A *swap* is an exchange of cash flows between two parties (counterparties). An interest rate swap is a transaction where two parties agree to pay the interest obligation on a specified debt obligation of the other party (liability swap) or to exchange the cash flows on assets of the other party (asset swap). A *swaption* is an option giving the right but with no obligation to engage in a swap. A *plain vanilla swap* is when one counterparty exchanges a fixed-rate payment obligation for a floating-rate one, while the other counterparty exchanges a floating for a fixed.

Example of a Plain Vanilla Swap

An example of a swap to reduce interest rate risk is when a savings institution that has variable-rate liabilities and fixed-rate assets desires to lock in its cost of liabilities to reduce the risk of a large negative funding gap. The savings and loans (S&L) institution makes a 10-year annual swap agreement to pay interest on a notational principal of $50 million at a rate of 1.6% and will receive cash flows from a counterparty bank at the 1-year LIBOR rate plus 25 basis points. Suppose the 1-year LIBOR rate is 1.15%, so the exchange currently for the bank counterparty would be 1.15% + 0.25% equals 1.4%.

For the first year, the exchange in payments would be the S&L would pay the higher excess payment to the bank of 1.6% − 1.4% = 0.0020 x $50,000,000 notational principle, equal to a payment to the bank of $100,000.

If the second year of the swap, the LIBOR rates goes up to 1.35%, so LIBOR + 0.25% equals 1.6%, there would be no exchange of payments, since both parties would be paying each other 1.6%.

If the third year, the LIBOR rates goes up to 1.6%, so LIBOR + 0.25% equals 1.85%, the bank would pay the higher excess payment of 1.85% − 1.60% which equals 0.25%. So the bank would pay the S&L 0.0025 × $50,000,000 equal to a payment of $125,000 to the S&L.

The agreement would be more or less favorable to each respective party depending on the fluctuation in the LIBOR rate. However, from an interest rate risk perspective, the S&L has locked in a fixed liability rate to match its fixed-rate loans, reducing its negative funding gap. Also, if the counterparty bank has a positive funding gap, the swap would reduce that positive funding gap by giving the bank a variable-rate liability stream of payments to match its variable-rate loans.

Benefits of swaps include: (1) can hedge for longer periods of time without having to roll over futures or options contracts, and contract can be tailor-made, over-the counter for desired number of years and terms; (2) maturity can vary from a relatively short time to as long as 20 years; (3) shorter swaps are more popular with termination clauses in the agreement in the event of unfavorable rate movements; (4) can arrange swap to lower a firm's cost of funds if one firm has an advantage of financing in one type of the market (such as fixed-rate versus variable-rate borrowing).

Disadvantages of swaps include: (1) legal contractual fees with a broker intermediary to make the swap arrangement; (2) the risk of a spot situation changing and having to go through with the swap for many years; despite this change, however, the swap market for trading swaps has grown; (3) often the fixed rate agreed upon on a swap may be initially less than the floating rate, which reflects a willingness to pay an insurance premium to transfer interest rate risk to the other party; and (4) swaps are generally longer-term arrangements.

Other Features of Swaps

Other features of swaps include: (1) the role of brokers and dealers often with large financial institutions taking that role; (2) institutions need to be concerned about the counterparty risk of the other party not going through with a swap; (3) the interest rate index is negotiated, with LIBOR commonly used; (4) swaptions and futures on swaps are available to provide the buyer with the right to exercise some choice during the life of the option; (5) the market for trading swaps among parties has grown tremendously for standardized swaps; and (6) regulatory and accounting issues: details must be disclosed including unrealized gains and losses from swap agreements and the potential loss if a counterparty fails to perform. Under the Dodd–Frank Act of 2010 regulations for swaps as derivatives have become more stringent, with rules to allow greater transparency and financial guarantees, including higher margin requirements for over-the-counter swap participants.

Swaps Used to Reduce an Institution's Cost of Funds

Swaps can be used to lower a firm's cost of funds through currency swaps, with exchanges of cash flows in different currencies where different parties have different advantages in terms of exchange rates internationally, and interest rate swaps where different parties have different advantages for the cost of funds in fixed- and floating-rate markets.

Interest rate swaps can take advantage of lower interest costs, particularly if one party has an advantage, such as a lower fixed or floating cost of debt.

Interest rate swaps can be of two types:

1   A *liability interest rate swap*, such as a fixed- or floating-rate swap where one party (Party 1) with floating-rate debt agrees to pay another party who has fixed-rate debt a fixed-interest payment based on the notational amount stated in the agreement in exchange for the receipt from the counterparty (Party 2) of a floating-rate payment. In this case the first party may have a low cost of floating-rate debt, but a high cost of fixed-rate debt, but prefers to have fixed-rate debt, so the swap with Party 1 in effect reduces that party's fixed-rate debt cost. Party 2 may have a low cost of fixed-rate debt.

2   An *asset interest rate swap* is when two parties exchange payments based on variable- and fixed-rate assets, such as to reduce interest rate risk. For instance, a finance company might have long-term fixed-rate liabilities, but short-term variable-rate consumer loans as assets and would prefer to receive fixed-rate cash flows to better match the variable-rate liabilities it has to pay.

CALCULATING THE EFFECTIVE RATE FOR EACH PARTY FOR AN INTEREST RATE SWAP

Financing Advantages for Parties in a Liability Interest Rate Swap

The effective rate that each party pays on its debt with a swap is basically the interest rate on the type of debt they issue, debt rate (d_r) plus the payment made to the other party, payment out (p_o) less the payment received from the other party, that is, payment in (p_i) plus any brokerage fee (fee%):

Effective liability swap rate % = d_r% − p_i% + p_o% + fee%.

So, for example, a savings association (Party 1) would prefer to have fixed-rate debt but has a high cost of fixed-rate debt of 4%, while its cost of variable-rate debt of LIBOR + 1% is cheaper. A bank (Party 2) would prefer to have variable-rate debt, but has a cheaper cost of fixed-rate debt of 3% versus a variable-rate cost of LIBOR + 1.80%. The brokerage fee for each party for the swap is 0.10%. Each party will finance at their respective cheaper cost and Party 1 will make a fixed-rate payment of 3% to Party 2, and Party 2 will make a variable-rate payment of LIBOR + 1% to Party 1 with details as follows with the notational amount of the swap for $5 million for 10 years.

Swap details Notational amount of swap is for $5 million.

Party 1: Saving association debt it issues has a rate (d_r) of LIBOR + 1%.

Pays out to Party 2 a fixed-payment of 3% (p_o).

Receives from Party 2 a payment of LIBOR + 1% (p_i).

Swap rate Party 1 = d_r% − p_i% + p_o% + fee%
= [LIBOR + 1%] − [LIBOR + 1%] + 3% + 0.10% = 3.10%.

Party 2: Bank's debt it issues has a rate (d_r) of 3% as a fixed rate.

Pays out to Party 1: LIBOR + 1% (p_o).

Receives from Party 1: 3% (p_i).

Swap rate Party 2 = d_r% − p_i% + p_o% + fee%
= 3% − 3% + [LIBOR + 1%] + 0.10% = LIBOR + 1.10%.

The savings association in effect has gained a fixed-cost of debt of 3.10% and the bank a variable cost of debt of LIBOR + 1.10%.

Since the savings association's cost of fixed-rate financing was 4%, its financing advantage for the swap is: 4% − 3.10%, a financing advantage of 0.90% with the swap.

Since the bank's variable cost of financing was LIBOR + 1.80%, it financing advantage for the swap is [LIBOR + 1.80%] − [LIBOR + 1.10%] = 0.70%.

Asset Rate Swap

An asset interest rate swap is when two parties exchange asset payments, which could be beneficial to reduce interest rate risk. For example, a swap of variable-rate asset payments, for a finance company (Party 1) for fixed-rate asset payments to have a better funding gap match for liabilities that are fixed rate. Such a swap would be with a counterparty, a bank (Party 2) who wants variable-rate asset payments to match with variable-rate liabilities to have a better funding gap, closer to zero.

For an asset swap, the effective interest rate that each part receives is:

$$\text{Effective asset swap rate} = a_r\% + p_{ri}\% - p_{ro}\% - \text{fee}\%$$

where: $a_r\%$ is the rate on the firm's assets on its balance sheet;

$p_{ri}\%$ is the payment coming in from the counterparty;

$p_{ro}\%$ is the payment going out to the counterparty; and

fee% is the brokerage fee.

For instance, suppose an asset swap is made for a notational value of $10 million for a 10-year swap as follows for each party, with a brokerage fee for each party of 0.10%. Party 1 receives on its variable-rate loans a rate of LIBOR + 0.50% ($a_r\%$), and Party 2 receives a 6% rate ($a_r\%$) on its fixed-rate loans.

For the asset swap, Party 1 will receive a fixed-rate of 5.5% ($p_{ri}\%$) from Party 2 and pay a rate of LIBOR + 0.50% to Party 2 ($p_{ro}\%$). So Party 2 receives LIBOR + 0.50% from Party 1 ($p_{ri}\%$) and pays 5.5% ($p_{ro}\%$) to Party 1.

The effective swap rate for each party = $a_r\% + p_{ri}\% - p_{ro}\% - \text{fee}\%$ is:

Party 1 Effective swap rate = [LIBOR + 0.50%] + 5.5% − {LIBOR + 0.50%] − 0.10% = 5.4%.

Party 2 Effective swap rate = 6% + {LIBOR + 0.50%] − 5.5% − 0.10% = LIBOR + 0.90%.

Thus, Party 1 in effect has a net fixed-rate as a cash flow on its loans, and Party 2 has a net variable rate. So each party benefits by having better matched assets and liabilities, reducing their interest rate risk in terms of smaller funding gaps.

Understanding Deliverable Swap Futures (DSFs)

As noted by the CME Group (2013b) under the Dodd–Frank Act of 2010, clearing mandates for greater transparency and financial guarantees in the over-the-counter swap markets. This led over-the-counter swap participants to seek alternatives. Deliverable swap futures (DSFs) were launched by the CME Group on December 3, 2012 to allow interest rate swap exposure, but also to provide efficiency and margin savings as obtained with standardized future contracts. DSFs provide the opportunity for trading actual interest rate swaps on a *forward basis,* with the advantages of standardized future contracts. By being deliverable DSFs the advantages of trading futures and over-the-counter derivatives are consolidated in one package for interest rate risk management. DSFs contracts allow for the delivery of "plain vanilla" fixed-rate interest rate swaps that are carried by the CME clearing house. DSFs similar to futures can be reverse traded versus being delivered. These require less than half of the required margin that would have to be provided over the counter, with benefits of lower margins and standardization. Deliverable swap futures have diverse participants, including banks, hedge funds, asset managers, mortgage servicers, and proprietary trading firms, with futures traded for interest rate swaps (CME Group 2016a,b)

INTEREST RATE CAPS, FLOORS, AND COLLARS

Interest rate caps, floors, and collars are synthetic agreements offered by large financial institutions (banks, investment banks) and other institutions that provide long-term protection against losses with future interest rate changes. Often large financial institutions earn fee income by doing the hedging for other institutions. A *cap* is an arrangement whereby cap protection is purchased, so that the institution owning the cap receives funds if interest rates go over the cap that is set. An institution might purchase a cap to hedge against a loss if interest rates rise on a spot position. A *floor* is an arrangement whereby the institution purchasing the floor receives funds if interest rates go below the floor. An institution could use a floor, for instance, to hedge against a loss if interest rates fall on a spot position. A *collar* is a combination of a cap and floor that in effect guarantees a given rate.

WEATHER DERIVATIVES

Futures exchanges offer weather-based index future products including temperature-based indexes for major cities in the United States and Europe. With estimates that 20–30% of the U.S. economy is affected by weather, futures and options on futures have been developed by futures exchanges over the counter and by the CME Group. The entry of weather derivatives provides a financial tool making weather a commodity that can be traded to provide protection for companies for risks that are weather-related. Examples of industries affected by weather include the ski industry, vacation destinations, utility and energy companies, and even retail stores and restaurants. The first over-the-counter weather derivative came about in 1997. In 1999, the Chicago Mercantile Exchange (now the CME Group) developed exchange traded weather futures and options on futures, as standardized contracts that can be publicly traded. These weather derivatives make use of specific indexes for average monthly and seasonal temperatures for 15 U.S. and 5 different European cities, with index values set by Earth Satellite (EarthSat) Corp., an international firm specializing in geographic information technologies in the United States, and by other European weather firms for European contracts. Data from the National Climate Data Center is also utilized for CME Group indexes and other over-the-counter weather derivatives (Carabello, 2015).

The CME Group developed specific indexes for different types of weather risk, including temperatures, frost, hurricane damage, or snowfall deviations from monthly or seasonal averages in particular cities or regions. Variations are based on specific indexes, and dollar amounts attached to deviations in excess or below an index point. Hurricane products are based on an index measuring how much damage a hurricane is likely to cause. An example is a cooling degree day (CDD) index, with summer weather measured for temperatures greater than a base of 65°F (18°C in Europe). Similarly, a heating degree day (HDD) index measures winter weather based on the degree temperatures fall below 65°F. Frost and snowfall indexes are also used to measure snow below or above a benchmark index. Market participants include markets with a wide range of industries, including the insurance and reinsurance industry, hedge funds, energy companies, pension funds, state government, and utility companies (Weather Futures, 2016).

CREDIT DERIVATIVES

Credit derivatives are risk management tools that transfer credit risk from one party to another. Credit derivatives of different types are similar in terms of retaining assets on the books of originating institutions, while transferring some portion of the credit exposure of these underlying assets to other parties.

By 2003, U.S. banks had a notional amount of $710 billion in credit derivatives, and by the end of 2007, the credit default swaps (CDS) market had a notional value of $62.2 trillion. With huge defaults during the subprime crisis, the notional value declined to $36.6 trillion by the end of 2008. At this time, the majority of swaps were traded over the counter and had no required governmental reporting transactions. This lack of transparency make it difficult for analysts to value CDS, and given the huge size of the market created great risks, particularly with CDS used for speculative bets. Under the Dodd–Frank Act a mandate was given for the regulation and greater transparency for credit default swap markets and trade compliance.

Credit derivatives have the advantage of not requiring the sale of assets, which would weaken relationships with borrowers. Also, credit derivatives allow the reshaping of an institution's credit exposure by improving diversification, such as when an institution has too large a loss exposure in one region.

Total Return Swaps and Credit Default Swaps

Two of the major types of credit derivatives are total return swaps and credit swaps. With a *total return swap*, cash flows are exchanged between a total return payor and a total return receiver. The total return payor pays out a return based on the return from its holdings of a risk debt obligation or portfolio of risk debt obligations, based on an interest income stream. The counterparty, the total return receiver, bases what it pays on a default-free obligation and receives a total return from the income stream from the other party's risky debt. The swap allows participation in the return stream of the underlying debt without having to purchase a risk bond itself.

With a *credit swap*, a fixed payor insures against credit events by periodically paying a fixed percentage of the loan's par value. If a credit event such as a loan default occurs, the contingent payor makes a payment that compensates the insured for part of its loss, but otherwise the contingent payor pays zero. Financial institutions, instead of holding a pool of liquid assets against future loan losses could alternatively engage in a credit swap. Hence a CDS provides a type of insurance to the buyer. However, unlike insurance, a buyer does not have to own an underlying security, loans, or form of credit exposure, so the buyer may not really suffer any loss from a credit event. Also, previously, the seller did not have to be regulated, so did not have to maintain reserves to be able to pay off a buyer in the event of a credit event. If banks are sellers, they do not have capital requirements for swaps. CDS contracts previously were not subject to mark-to-market accounting, so this affects the volatility of their balance sheet and income statements.

Under the Dodd–Frank Act new rules for regulating derivatives include: (1) a new regulatory framework capturing derivatives transactions that were previously exempt; (2) mandatory clearing and trading on regulated exchanges; (3) having swap dealers and major swap participants subject to capital and margin requirements and business conduct rules and other special requirements in dealing with governmental entities; (4) a swaps push-out rule that includes collateral segregation, real-time swap transaction reporting requirements, position limits, large trader reporting, and the application of securities laws to swaps that are security-based; and (5) other significant rule-making efforts.

OTHER TYPES OF CREDIT SWAPS

Credit-linked notes are when a risk-seller bank, for instance, sets up a trust (special purpose vehicle) separate from the bank to issue notes or security certificates. The proceeds from the security issue are invested to build up cash collateral for an amount to protect the buyers. The yields from the loans or other collateral, plus fees paid to the protection buyers, are passed on to investors. In the event of default the cash collateral is liquidated to protect the buyer with any remaining proceeds passed on to investors.

First-to-default swaps are credit swaps developed on a whole basket of assets with the default event triggered by any of the assets in the basket.

An *index swap* combines both a bond and a credit option allowing coupon or principal payments to be recalculated (lowered) in the event of a change in expected credit defaults. For example, a finance company that finances its loans with fixed-rate bonds could have a credit option attached that allows the finance company to reduce the coupon payment by a given number of basis points for every increase in the national rate of past due loans or loan defaults. The finance company is protected since if its loan revenues fall with greater loan defaults, it will still have sufficient revenues to repay its bonds that were issued to finance the loans.

EXAMPLE OF A PLAIN VANILLA CREDIT SWAP

Bank Florida has a $5 million credit exposure with Alligator Swamp Corporation, a large tourist corporation in Florida for 5 years. Bank Florida would like to sell off part of the loan to reduce its risk, but Alligator Swamp Corporation does not want part of its loan sold, since it likes dealing with Bank Florida. Bank New York thinks that the loan to Alligator Swap is a good risk, and agrees to enter into a credit swap arrangement in exchange for a fixed fee each year of 50 basis points, that is, 0.0050 x $5 million = a $25,000 year fee. Bank New York agrees that if Alligator Swamp defaults on its loan, Bank New York will pay Bank Florida a given sum representing the loss for the portion of the loan that Bank New York has taken on. The benefits of the swap are that Bank New York gains fee income and can diversify its risk by geographic diversification to Florida. Bank Florida has reduced its overall risk by passing on part of that risk to Bank New York.

CREDIT SWAPS AND THE SUBPRIME LOAN CRISIS

Although credit default swaps (CDS) were created to reduce risk for financial institutions for hedging credit risk for loans and bonds, speculators also used credit swaps for trading profits. Financial institutions might figure there may be a very small chance of a credit event occurring, but to hedge this risk they may buy a CDS paying a premium for it that provides insurance if the firm given credit goes under. The sellers/issuers of credit default swaps include large financial institutions, such as large investment banks, hedge funds, and insurance firms. These include well-known firms that collapsed during the U.S. subprime loan crisis (AIG, Lehman Brothers, and Bear Stearns), when what is known as black swan, highly improbable events (Taleb, 2008) occurred, with a housing market collapse and what issuers thought were low probability events, triggering large payouts.

Many CDS also were issued; all covered very complex financial instruments, including more complex mortgage-backed securities and collateralized debt obligations whose value collapsed with the subprime loan crisis. Also, a number of large financial institutions, in addition to issuing CDS to investors, bought CDS protection at the same time, so that if an event occurred they would have protection with money coming in as well as having to pay money back. AIG did not do this, selling only CDS, so AIG had to cover more than $440 billion out with no money coming in from CDS purchases, like other large financial institutions. When AIG was not able to make its promises of payment, large financial institutions lost their protection, putting these institutions at risk, and reducing liquidity for the entire banking system, with these banks having to curb their lending, leading to a reduction in global pools of money, and new rounds of CDS payouts with bonds of collapsed banks leading to the failure and collapse of other banks. In addition, there was little transparency in the CDS market with CDS primarily over-the-counter instruments, not traded on exchanges at this time (Davidson, 2008). In addition to the contagion extending to other banks in the United States, the onset of the global financial crisis in 2008 led to even higher CDS spreads for other countries, especially in Europe, with greater reliance on foreign capital flows to roll over debt obligations (North and Sengupta, 2012).

Credit default swaps also may have contributed to the crisis by providing incentives for excessive risk taking, and a lack of monitoring by investors, since banks purchasing CDS had protection against large loan losses. CDS may have contributed to market manipulation, with purchasers of CDS, not having to hold the underlying bonds of a credit default swap. Also, indices are traded on baskets of credit swaps. The size of the CDS market was also huge, rising from $6 trillion in 2004 to $57 trillion by June 2008. Regulators globally also reduced the capital required for institutions with protection through credit default swaps (Stulz, 2010).

Under the Dodd–Frank Act of 2010, a number of different provisions were put in place under Title VII with requirements for swap dealers, regulations on swap clearing and exchange trading, swap margin and collateral regulations, risk capital requirements for derivatives exposure, bank lending limits modifications to include derivative swaps, the application of securities laws to security-based swaps, and swap antifraud rules, among many other swap regulations. Under Section 619 of the Dodd–Frank Act, "the Volcker Rule," banking entities including most commercial banks in the United States and their affiliates are prevented from engaging in proprietary trading (trading for their own account), including proprietary derivative trading. Bank affiliates are also restricted in their investment in hedge funds and private equity funds. Mandatory clearing and exchange trading for certain CDS and interest rate swaps is also included (with some limited exceptions) (Practical Law, 2016).

SUMMARY

Financial institution managers hedge interest rate risk by using derivatives, including forwards, futures, options on futures, and interest rate swaps.

In the aftermath of the U.S. subprime loan crisis, which involved speculative bets on credit derivative contracts, new regulations were imposed on derivative use by financial institutions and over-the-counter derivatives, particularly new regulations for interest rate swaps, leading to greater offerings on future exchanges. Understanding how to hedge and the pros and cons of using different types of derivatives is important for hedging the interest rate risk of a financial institution.

INTERESTING WEBSITES AND VIDEO

CME Group: http://www.cmegroup.com/
Futures Industry Association: https://www.fia.org/
Frontline. The financial crisis, Default swaps: http://www.pbs.org/wgbh/pages/frontline/oral-history/financial-crisis/tags/credit-default-swaps/
This is a PBS video documentary on credit default swaps during the U.S. S Loan Crisis and global financial crisis.

BIBLIOGRAPHY

Acworth, Will (2016). "2015 Annual Survey: Global derivatives volume: Asia takes the lead." *Market Voice: The Magazine of the Global Futures, Options and Cleared Swaps Markets*, March 15, 2016. Accessed on August 28, 2016 at: http://marketvoicemag.org/?q=content/2015-annual-survey-global-derivatives-volume

BCC (2015). "Libor: What is it and why does it matter?" BBC News, August 3, 2015. Accessed on January 17, 2016 at: http://www.bbc.com/news/business-19199683

Blystone, Dan (2014). "Introduction to Trading Eurodollar Futures," *Investopedia*, January 22, 2014. Accessed on January 16, 2016 at: http://www.investopedia.com/articles/active-trading/012214/introduction-trading-eurodollar-futures.asp

Carabello, Feliz (2015). "Market futures: Introduction to weather derivatives." *Investopedia*, December 8, 2015. Accessed on January 19, 2016 at: http://www.investopedia.com/articles/optioninvestor/05/052505.asp

CME (2006). *An Introduction to Futures and Options*. Student Manual. Chicago Mercantile Exchange. Accessed on January 11, 2016 at: http://www.cmegroup.com/files/intro_fut_opt.pdf

CME Group (2007). "CME and CBOT complete merger creating the leading global financial exchange." CME Group website. Accessed January 10, 2016 at: http://investor.cmegroup.com/investor-relations/releasedetail.cfm?ReleaseID=254207

CME Group (2010). "Understanding treasury futures." CME Group website. Accessed on January 11, 2016 at: https://www.cmegroup.com/education/files/understanding-treasury-futures.pdf

CME Group (2013a). "Understanding deliverable swap futures." CME Group website. Accessed on January 17, 2016 at: http://www.cmegroup.com/trading/interest-rates/files/understanding-dsf.pdf

CME Group (2013b). "Understanding deliverable swap futures." *Hedge Week*, May 28, 2015. Accessed on January 17, 2016 at: http://www.hedgeweek.com/2013/05/23/184823/understanding-deliverable-swap-futures

CME Group (2015). "Deliverable interest rate swap futures." CME Group website. Accessed on January 17, 2016 at: http://www.cmegroup.com/trading/interest-rates/files/dsf-overview.pdf

CME Group (2016a). "Short-term interest rate products." CME Group website. Accessed on January 11, 2016 at: http://www.cmegroup.com/trading/interest-rates/stir.html

CME Group (2016b). "Finding opportunities in a new interest rate environment." CME Group website. Accessed on January 11, 2016 at: http://www.cmegroup.com/trading/interest-rates/files/eurodollar-trading-basics.pdf

CME Group (2016c). Price quotations on CME Group website, January 17, 2016. Accessed on January 17, 2016 at: www.cmegroup.com

Davidson, Adam (2008). "How AIG fell apart." *Reuters*, September 18, 2008. Accessed on September 18, 2008 at: http://www.reuters.com/article/us-how-aig-fell-apart-idUSMAR85972720080918

FIA (2015a). "FIA releases SEF tracker for November." FIA SEF Tracker, No. 20, January 2014 – November 2015, Futures Industry Association. Accessed on January 22, 2016 at: https://fia.org/articles/fia-releases-sef-tracker-november

FIA (2015b). "Futures Industry March 2015." *Futures Industry Magazine*, Futures Industry Association (FIA), March 9, 2015. Accessed on August 28, 2016 at: https://fimag.fia.org

FIA (2016). "FIA annual futures and options volume survey: Asia takes the lead," March 15, 2016. Accessed on August 28, 2016 at: https://fia.org/articles/2015-fia-annual-futures-and-options-volume-survey-asia-takes-lead

FRBSF (2006). "What is LIBOR and why do LIBOR interest rates move closely in line with short-term interest rates in the U.S.?" Dr. Econ, Education, Federal Reserve Bank of San Francisco. Accessed on January 17, 2016 at: http://www.frbsf.org/education/publications/doctor-econ/2006/july/libor-interest-rates-london-interbank-offered

FinCad (2015). "Types of credit derivatives." FinCAD Resources. Accessed on January 10, 2016 at: http://www.fincad.com/resources/resource-library/wiki/types-credit-derivatives

Frontline (2015). "The financial crisis: Credit default swaps." Frontline: Money, Power & Wall Street website. Accessed on January 22, 2016 at: http://www.pbs.org/wgbh/pages/frontline/oral-history/financial-crisis/tags/credit-default-swaps/

Kawaller, Ira (2014). "Is it time to hedge interest rate risk? Swaps, caps & swaptions oh my." *AFP Exchange Magazine*, July/August 2015, Association for Financial Professionals. Accessed on January 10, 2016 at: http://www.futuresmag.com/2014/08/26/it-time-hedge-interest-rate-risk

Labuszewski, John W. (2013). "Understanding Eurodollar futures." CME Group website. Accessed on January 16, 2015 at: https://www.cmegroup.com/trading/interest-rates/files/understanding-eurodollar-futures.pdf

Labuszewski, John H. and Richard Co (2004). "Eurodollar futures: Interest rate market building blocks." CME Group website. Accessed on January 16, 2016 at: https://www.cmegroup.com/trading/interest-rates/files/Eurodollar_Futures_Interest_Rate_Building_Blocks.pdf

Maness, Terry S. and John T. Zietlow (2005). *Short-Term Financial Management*, 3rd ed. Mason, OH: Thomson/Southwestern.

North, Bryan and Rajdeep Sengupta (2012). "A look at credit default swaps and their impact on the European debt crisis." St. Louis Federal Reserve website. Accessed on January 22, 2016 at: https://www.stlouisfed.org/~/media/Files/PDFs/publications/pub_assets/pdf/re/2012/b/credit_default.pdf

OCC (2015). "OCC's quarterly report on bank trading and derivatives activities, third quarter 2015." Accessed on January 10, 2016 at: http://www.occ.gov/topics/capital-markets/financial-markets/trading/derivatives/dq315.pdf

Options Guide (2015). "CME group options on futures." CME Group website. Accessed on January 18, 2016 at: http://www.cmegroup.com/education/files/options-on-futures-brochure.pdf

Practical Law (2016). "Summary of the Dodd–Frank Act: Swaps and derivatives." Accessed on January 23, 2016 at: http://us.practicallaw.com/3-502-8950#a1008086

Stulz, Rene M. (2004). "Should we fear derivatives?" National Bureau of Economic Research (NBER) Working Paper 10574, June 2004. Accessed on April 13, 2015 at: http://www.nber.org/papers/w10574.pdf

Stulz, Rene M. (2010). "Credit default swaps and the credit crisis." *Journal of Economic Perspectives*, 24(1) (Winter 2010), 73–92.

Taleb, Nassim Nicholas (2008). *The Black Swan: The Impact of the Highly Improbable*. New York: Random House.

Weather Futures (2016). "Weather futures and options: Financial tools that provide means of transferring risk associated with adverse weather events." CME Group website. Accessed on January 19, 2016 at: https://www.cmegroup.com/trading/weather/files/Weather_fact_card.pdf

QUESTIONS AND PROBLEMS

1   A treasury manager of a corporation wants to protect against a fall in the value of a $150 million portfolio invested in short-term securities against a rise in interest rate (fall in value). Suppose the treasury manager gets Eurodollar futures for the hedge.

   a   Should the treasury manager take a long or short position? Explain why this position in futures should be taken.

   b   How many futures contract should be gotten, if the treasury manager expects the hedge ratio for the contracts to be 0.80?

   c   What is basis risk, and what is cross-hedging risk?

2   A money market portfolio manager needs to hedge against an expected rise in interest rates (fall in the price of securities) that need to be sold for liquidity needs in three months.

   a   What futures position should be taken (long or short)? Explain why.

   b   Suppose the futures contract sells at a quoted price of 98.50%, and at the end of the contract the price falls to 98.00%, what is the gain or loss on one futures contract.

   c   What are the advantages and disadvantages of hedging with futures contracts versus forward contracts?

3   In April, an insurance company portfolio manager has a stock portfolio of $850 million with a portfolio beta of 1.15. He plans on selling the stocks in the portfolio in June to be able to pay out funds to policyholders for annuities, and is worried about a fall in the stock market. At this time the CME S&P 500 index is 2,061.02 and for a June E-mini S&P futures contract is 2,052.25 ($50 multiplier for the contract).

   a   What type of futures position should be taken to hedge against the stock market going down and how many future contracts are needed for this hedge?
       (Hint: No. contracts = [Amount hedged / Futures index price x multiplier] x beta of the portfolio.)

   b   Suppose in June the stock market (S&P500 index) falls by 2% and the S&P500 futures index falls by 2% as well, what is the portfolio manager's opportunity loss (gain) on his portfolio, and his futures gain (loss) and the net hedging result?

4   Suppose a large commercial bank has taken a short futures position in three month Eurodollars to protect against a rise in interest expense in 30 days when it issues $3 million in 90-day commercial paper for short-term financing needs. Given the changes in the discount

interest rates on the contracts, 30 days from now shown below, what will be the net hedging error (excluding any margin or brokerage fees)?

(Hint the change in the spot or futures position = [3 million (change in rate) x (90/360)], and the Eurodollar futures contract amount is 1 million.)

	Today	30 days from now
90-day commercial paper rate	3.75%	4.25%
90-day futures contract	3.60%	4.10%

5. The manager of a large commercial bank forecasts an increase in interest rate over the next two months, and is concerned since the bank will be issuing $20 million in 90-day CDs with a 6% fixed rate in three months to finance a loan. The manager hedges against the expected increase in interest rates by taking a short position in 90-day Eurodollar futures, with a minimum contract of $1 million. The discount yield on the Eurodollar futures is 6.50%.

   Later when the manager wants to unwind his hedge by reversing his position, the 90-day CD rate has gone up to 7.5%, and the discount yield on the futures contract has gone up to 8.02%.

   What is the net gain or loss on respectively the spot and the futures position and the net hedging result?

6. A pension fund and a savings institution want to do an asset swap for a notational value of $50 million. The pension fund holds a variable-rate investment that earns LIBOR + 1%. The savings institution holds a fixed-rate investment that pays a fixed rate of 5%. The swap will be based on partial payments.

   With the swap, the pension fund will receive a fixed rate of 4% from the savings institution and will pay the savings institution LIBOR + 0.50% each year. The brokerage fee is 0.10% for each party. What is the effective asset swap return for each party?

7. A finance company (Party 1) has a favorable fixed debt rate of 8%, but would like to have variable-rate debt, but its cost of variable-rate debt is high at LIBOR + 5%. A bank (Party 2) has a favorable rate for issuing variable-rate debt of LIBOR + 2%, but would like to have fixed-rate debt, but has a high cost of fixed-rate debt of 10%. The two parties agree to go ahead and issue their most favorable debt and then do a swap, where Party 1 pays Party 2 LIBOR + 2%, and Party 2 pays Party 1 a fixed rate of 8%. The brokerage fee for each party is 0.10%.

   What is the net effective rate each party will be paying with the swap, and what is the net advantage in financing for each party with the swap?

Part Four

Asset and Liability Management

Chapter 9

Loan Analysis, Credit Risk Management, and Loan Securitization

Statistical models that predict loan defaults failed to warn lenders about risky borrowers, because these models relied too much on hard information, such as credit scores and loan-to-value ratios, and not enough on soft information from personal contact with borrowers, such as a person's job security, upcoming expenses or other observable behaviors that may help prevent the likelihood of default... A fundamental cause for this failure was that the models ignored changes in the incentives of lenders to collect soft information about borrowers and residential properties,…. When incentives change, the link between the data and predicted outcomes changes in a fundamental manner.

(Uday Rajan, quoted in DeGroat, 2009)

While the banking industry had another positive quarter, there are signs of growing interest rate risk and credit risk that warrant attention.

(Gruenberg, 2015)

THE large number of bankruptcies during the U.S. subprime loan crisis and global financial crisis emphasize the great importance of understanding and analyzing financial statements, with even credit analysts and regulators surprised by large net loan losses during the subprime crisis and great recession, with 432 federally insured banks failing as a result of huge loan losses in the United States, as well as bank failures in other countries. Loan analysis and credit management are important aspects of financial institution management, particularly for depository institutions, as well as financial analysts for all financial institutions. Most banks that failed also had undiversified loan portfolios, with a majority of real estate loans.

As noted in the first quote above, prior to the U.S. subprime loan crisis, banks in the United States, particularly larger banks, relied heavily on statistical models in evaluating loans, with less reliance on traditional loan analysis and greater monetary incentives for loan officers to make large volumes of loans versus a focus on the quality of a loan. In many cases loan officers had no responsibility for monitoring loans that were made in the future, with loans pooled together and securitized as collateralized mortgage securities or more complex collateralized debt obligations (CDOs) sold to investors. In the case of subprime loan securitizations, with guarantees provided and great complexity for these securitizations, credit agencies rated these as investment grade securitizations, which investors purchased, while these securitizations had significant risk. This chapter examines bank lending, credit risk management, and loan securitization.

LENDING TRENDS

In the United States alone, total loans for FDIC-insured banks and savings institutions were greater than $8.6 trillion in 2015, with loans representing about 55% of average total assets (FDIC, 2015a). Of 6,270 FDIC-insured depository institutions (5,410 commercial banks and 860 savings institutions), 62 were diversified lenders with assets greater than $1 billion, 663 diversified lenders with assets less than $1 billion, 337 other specialized lenders with assets of less than $1 billion, 57 consumer lenders, 515 mortgage lenders, 3,124 commercial lenders, 1,494 commercial banks, 4 international banks, and 14 credit card lenders according to FDIC classifications (FDIC, 2015a).

Financial institutions focus on different strategies, including the specific types of loans they make and industry loan/leasing specializations (i.e., consumer banks, small business lender, asset-based lender, aircraft leasing, and other industry-specific types of loans, among others). Depository institutions have strategic goals for the types of loans they wish to make, and how diversified they want their loan portfolios to be. Loan growth generally rises in expansions and falls during recessions. Relationship lending is important, particularly for community banks that lend to medium-size and small firms. Large corporations have come to rely on direct financial markets (bonds / commercial paper for financing), and banks have limits on loan concentration as a percentage of capital to one borrower, so often work in loan syndicates with other financial institutions for large loans.

Banks still have information and monitoring advantages in lending to small and medium-size firms that many times are not publicly traded. With more widely dispersed information in the information age, banks have less of an informational advantage than in the past, since information on publicly traded companies is readily available, and firms have alternative financing sources through issuing commercial paper and bonds. However, for private firms and small to medium-sized firms, banks still have an informational advantage in analyzing and monitoring loans. For consumer lending, economic cycles also tend to follow stock market rises and falls, with consumers feeling wealthier in rising stock markets.

With the U.S. subprime loan crisis and global financial crisis from 2008 to 2010, banks had huge loan losses, and in the United States took much larger provisions for loan losses averaging about 1.80%. Since loan losses are often associated with industry sector difficulties, industry analysis is very important in credit analysis. In 2012, the average net charge-off rate for all FDIC-insured institutions was 1.38% (1.26% for real estate loans, 0.78% for commercial loans, and 1.41% for consumer loans). As of the third quarter of 2015, in the United States the average net charge-off rate for insured depository institutions fell to 0.45%, with an average 0.18% net charge-off for real estate loans, 0.22% for commercial and industrial loans, but rose to 1.83% for consumer loans (FDIC, 2015a).

215

Loan Analysis,
Credit Risk
Management,
and Loan
Securitization

The health of the banking industry improved greatly in the United States over time following large losses during the U.S. subprime loan crisis. The number of failed institutions peaked on an annual basis to 157 institutions in 2010 and fell to 6 as of the third quarter of 2015. Similarly, the number of problem institutions fell from a peak of 864 in 2010 to about 203 in 2015 (FDIC, 2015c). As of the third quarter of 2015, all FDIC-insured institutions as a percentage of total net loans held on average about 50% of their loans secured by real estate, 21% in commercial loans, 17% in loans to individuals, less than 1% in farm loans, and about 11% in other loans and leases. The growth rate for loans was about 4.14% versus the previous year. A favorable trend was a reduction in other real estate owned (OREO) falling by 35.2% from the previous year, noncurrent loans falling by 19.1%, and loans and leases 30 to 89 days past due falling by 7.6% (FDIC, 2015b).

In the United States for the third quarter of 2015, for mortgages, there was about $13.701 trillion in mortgage debt outstanding, with about $2.792 trillion representing about 20.38% held by mortgage pools or trusts, including about $1.609 trillion held by the Government National Mortgage Association representing securitized loans. Overall, federal and related agencies held about $5.032 trillion of all mortgage assets, and depository institutions held about $4.303 trillion of a total of about $4.711 trillion held by both depository institutions and insurance companies (Board of Governors, 2015).

FUNCTIONS OF THE CREDIT PROCESS: THE CREDIT PROCESS AS PROTECTION AGAINST DEFAULT RISK

Financial institutions need to underwrite (structure) loans to reduce the risk to their institutions. Credit policies also need to be uniform and fair to all borrowers, and to follow the strategic policies of the institution, including the types of loans the institution wants to underwrite. Risks of loans include default risk as the result of both firm-specific practices that could lead to a firm's bankruptcy (fraud, mismanagement, poor working capital management practices) and industry risks (such as problems for the telecommunications industry in the early 2000s). Hence, loan officers and credit analysts need to be able to understand different industries and analyze industry trends as well.

The pricing of loans also affects their credit rate risk. With variable-rate loans, borrowers take on more interest rate risk, which in turn increases the credit risk of a loan, with the potential for a borrower's loan payment rising increasing the risk of nonpayment. Given that borrowers are taking on greater interest rates, adjustable mortgage rates typically at the time a loan is made offer lower rates at the time they are issued.

Other factors that affect the risk of a loan are a borrower's debt to income ratio, with a rule of thumb that a home mortgage payment should not be greater than 30% of a borrower's gross monthly income before taxes. Most lenders also look at a borrower's equity (i.e., total assets less total liabilities), credit scores, such as FICO scores, and the amount put down on a loan. Typical rules of thumb for example are requiring a higher required credit score when borrowing more than 80%, and a higher required down payment of 30% and required FICO score for self-employed individuals.

The loan-to-value (LTV) ratio is also important, with high LTV ratios suggesting greater risk. One important form of self-protection for lenders of consumer and mortgage loans is to make sure that the value of the property at the time of a loan application is greater than the loan amount by enough to protect the lender in case of default. This provides an incentive for the borrower not to default. For a mortgage loan, the LTV is the mortgage amount divided by the appraised value of the property. Generally banks like to have a maximum ratio of 75% (but at times previously a 95% maximum ratio has been used). The difference between the outstanding loan balance and the value of the property is the borrower's equity in the home. The rationale is that if the mortgage amount is much greater than the appraised value of a property, a borrower has only a small equity investment, and the borrower will have a greater incentive to walk away from a loan. Research shows a positive relationship between the initial loan-to-value ratio and both delinquency and default. Prior to the U.S. subprime loan crisis, when housing values in particular regions were high, however, LTV ratios were low. When there was a real estate bust, LTV ratios rose significantly, and borrowers in many cases walked away from their loans, contributing to hundreds of bankruptcies. For securitizations, often certain loan-to-value ratios are required, before loans can be securitized, among other stipulations.

Proper appraisal of property values Lenders need to have policies in place for having certified, well-trained real estate appraisers. Prior to the U.S. subprime loan crisis, many financial institutions allowed unqualified appraisers to make appraisals, which resulted in inflated valuations that made lenders more willing to lend to subprime borrowers with low downpayments. Since appraised values are historically based, it's also important for lenders to consider future cash flows expected, especially for commercial real estate loans to determine if cash flows projected will be sufficient for loan repayments.

Hence, the structuring of loans to ensure repayment by the borrower is one of the keys to having an effective bank lending process. The credit evaluation process is also critical. To protect the bank and maximize the profitability of loans that are made, banks must have a credit process in place including a carefully written loan policy, loan request procedures and a process for credit analysis, a process for credit execution and administration, and a credit review process to identify problems early for loans that have been made. The loan process must also conform to a large number of lending regulations, with a number of other specifications and regulations to follow if loans are to be securitized including maximum loan-to-value ratios.

THE ROLE OF THE CREDIT PROCESS IN BUSINESS DEVELOPMENT

In addition to protecting a financial institution, its credit process includes business development for the institution. This includes loan call programs, advertising, marketing, and relationship development. Decisions have to be made including what areas will be targeted for potential business, what the forecast demand for bank services is, and how employees will be trained for cross-selling all bank products. For instance, the recipient of a small business loan may also benefit from a bank's working capital management services. Loan officers have become more market-oriented, gathering business for the bank, including being active in community organizations and calling on desirable firms to get their business. Credit analysts assist the loan officer in obtaining financial statements, credit reports and ratings, and in performing

217

*Loan Analysis,
Credit Risk
Management,
and Loan
Securitization*

financial statement analysis. Bank procedures ensure that credit information is collected and presented in a uniform fashion.

LOAN COMMITTEE REVIEW

Loan officers are given some flexibility depending on their seniority and bank policies in determining whether loans should be granted. Larger loans must be approved by a loan committee consisting of loan officers, the bank's regulatory compliance officer, and for smaller banks, often the chief officers for the bank. A loan officer presents the loan request information and the weaknesses and strengths of the loan. Usually, loan officers have close relationships with loan customers, so they act as the advocate for their customers at the loan committee meetings. In turn, bank officers and other lending officers grill the loan officer presenting the loan in terms of potential weaknesses or problems that the loan might have. Underwriting guidelines have a uniform format for ease of presentation. Considerations also need to be made for local market conditions for general types of loans that will be approved, such as if loans are given for commercial development of apartment complexes, whether there is a saturation of new apartment buildings would be carefully considered, along with projected occupancy rates, which are important factors determining whether a loan will be repaid. For more risky construction development loans, often the bank will only lend for a short period of time, under the condition that the loan will be purchased by an insurance company or other long-term lender. Alternative uses for buildings that are collateral for such types of loans would also be important, in the event the bank had to foreclose on a property and how marketable the building would be including considerations of location, and the future value of the property.

BANKS' WRITTEN LOAN POLICIES

A bank's overall loan policy reflects long-term strategic planning for the overall asset portfolio, including setting general guidelines for the size of the loan portfolio, its composition, and the maximum acceptable level of default risk. For example, in a commercial bank, decisions must be made about the proportion of loan funds to be invested in different types of loans. These decisions influence the way a depository advertises its services, the customers whose loan applications will be given preference, and many other aspects of lending. Specific industries or markets that the bank wishes to target where lending officers have expertise are also included. Goals for loan volume and loan quality balances and loan portfolio diversification goals with a bank's liquidity, capital, and rate of return objectives are also incorporated, along with systems and controls to reduce credit risk. In addition, standards and procedures are included in terms of loan quality and procedures for documenting and reviewing loans and loan pricing.

COMPLIANCE POLICIES

Loan policies and procedures for complying with lending regulations also need to be put in place. Some of the major consumer lending regulations in the United States, for example, are as follows:

- *The Equal Credit Opportunity Act (Reg. B)*, whereby the bank is forbidden to discriminate in lending on the basis of race, color, national origin, sex, age, marital status, and/or receipt of public assistance.
- *The Fair Housing Act*, which forbids discrimination based on any handicap or family status.
- *The Fair Credit Reporting Act of 1970*, which requires consumer credit reporting agencies to stress accuracy, correct errors promptly, and release individual's consumer histories only for legitimate purposes. Customers also must be told why they are not given loans and have the right to know of any discrepancies in their credit reports.
- *Truth in Lending (TIL)*, which requires that a bank must quote its rates as annual percentage rates (APRs).
- *Reg. Z*, which sets standards for disclosing the terms and costs of a consumer credit agreement before the borrower becomes obligated, establishes a period during which a consumer may cancel a transaction, and procedures through which a consumer can challenge billing errors on revolving credit agreements. Institutions must comply with both state and federal legislation; if there are any contradictions between the two, federal statutes prevail.

In the United States, there are many mortgage lending regulations as well, including the following:

- *A Uniform Residential Loan Application (FNMA)* for home purchase or refinancing of home purchase of the applicant's principal dwelling where the dwelling that will be used as collateral also must be provided, along with a notice of the right to receive a copy of the appraisal if applicable.
- *The Real Estate Settlement Procedure Act (RESPA)* which provides servicing transfer disclosure and a good faith estimate (GFE) within three business days of receipt of a completed application, the provision of a settlement cost brochure for home purchases only, and a HUD-1 or HUD-A1A Settlement Statement provided at loan closing that must be prepared and made available prior to loan closing.
- *The Home Mortgage Disclosure Act (HMDA)*, which obligates a bank to obtain HMDA information (race, sex, national origin) for home purchases, home improvement, or refinance applications.
- *The Community Reinvestment Act (CRA)*, which requires that the bank meet the credit needs of its area, especially low and moderate-income areas. Institutions are required to disclose the CRA ratings they receive from examiners that range from outstanding to noncompliance. CRA ratings are posted on the Office of the Comptroller of the Currency's website (at: http://www.occ.gov/topics/compliance-bsa/cra/perfomance-evaluations-by-month/2015/cra-performance-evaluations-jan-2015.html).

Since 1992, lenders are required to analyze their lending on a detailed geographic basis, correlating the loans against demographic data for that location, such as income, percentage of minority, population, and other characteristics. CRA has historically focused on mortgage lending, and commercial lending to small businesses. In 1995, new regulations attempted to

219

*Loan Analysis,
Credit Risk
Management,
and Loan
Securitization*

make CRA assessments more objective and performance-based and less burdensome, allowing investments in investment groups that invest in low-income areas. Institutions that fail to demonstrate community reinvestment can face denial when they seek regulators' permission to branch, merge, or acquire another institution.

- *Loans to Insiders Act (Reg. O)*, which states that banks are not allowed to give preferential loan terms to insiders. Loans given to insiders are limited, must be submitted to regulators, and require prior board approval.
- *Limits on lending to one party as a percentage of total capital*, which means that banks are not allowed to make loans to one individual or firm greater than 15% of capital, 25% if collateralized by safe securities.

There are a number of different types of loans as well. The FDIC website (www.fdic.gov/regulations/laws/rules) provides details for each of these regulations. Similarly, bank regulators in different countries have many different regulations that can be found on their regulatory websites.

In the United States the Dodd–Frank Act also instituted new lending regulations under the new Consumer Financial Protection Bureau (CFPB) including new mortgage rules that can be found at: http://www.consumerfinance.gov/regulatory-implementation/. The rules amend several regulations including Regs. Z, X, and B, under the Dodd–Frank Act, Title XIV Rule. These amendments attempt to remedy abuses for consumers that occurred during the U.S. subprime loan crisis, including making higher priced mortgage loans and other types of consumer credit loans that consumer borrowers could not afford, very high prepayment penalties, errors in mortgage obligations, having loan servicers provide information to borrowers, protections for home ownership and home ownership counseling, the provision of free copies of appraisals and valuations to borrowers, having appraisals by a certified or licensed appraisal for higher-risk mortgage loans, and the imposition of requirements and restrictions on loan originator compensation, qualifications and registration or licensing of loan originators, compliance procedures for depository institutions, mandatory arbitration, and the financing of credit insurance, and new requirements and two disclosure forms that consumers receive in the process of applying for and consummating a mortgage loan, among others (CFPB, 2014). Similarly in other countries, more stringent rules for lending for financial institutions have been adopted following the global financial crisis.

CREDIT EXECUTION POLICIES

Policies also include an overview of credit execution and administration process in terms of loan committee reviews, collateral, and documents required for loans and loan reviews, and the follow-up procedures for loans once they have been made. From these policies specific procedures for the credit analysis, credit execution and administration and credit review process are put in place. Policies also include a code of ethics and conflict of interest policy for boards of directors and senior management, including treatment of confidential information from customers.

LENDER COMPENSATION POLICIES

In addition to policies for the bank's overall lending strategy and regulatory compliance policies, banks also have lender compensation policies that are crucial to the bank's business development process. In the 1990s and later, compensation policies for lenders became more performance-based. Bonuses were given based on how well lenders performed in bringing in new loans. With incentives for the quantity versus the quality of loans, often with fee income to brokers for making loans, this led to poor underwriting and little attention paid to the quality of the loans. Low documentation (low doc) loans encouraged such practices, with borrowers not having to provide documentation of their salaries and other information important to their ability to repay loans. Similarly, loan officers actively solicited customers in a predatory fashion (predatory lending) without regard for whether subprime loan customers would be able to repay the loan.

Loan officer bonus incentives should include the future performance of loans including having low loan losses, careful monitoring of loans that were made, serving current loan customers, and helping customers solve problems, such as offering banks working capital management services. Many U.S. states have passed laws against predatory lending practices, although such practices are often difficult to monitor.

THE 5 C'S OF CREDIT

Basically, the loan procedures focus on the risks inherent in the business of the loan applicant, how risks have been mitigated, the use and amount of the loan, the ability of the borrower to repay the loan in terms of cash flow, and secondary sources of repayment including collateral.

The framework of this presentation includes what bankers call *the 5 C's of credit (Character, Capacity, Capital, Conditions, and Collateral).*

- *Character* (the willingness of a customer to pay). Often loan officers use their experience to evaluate the character of individuals during a loan interview. Other evidence of character includes past credit history, credit ratings of firms and individuals, and for firms, reputation from customers and suppliers.
- *Capacity* (the ability of a customer to pay in terms of cash flow). Capacity is often evaluated by looking at current and projected cash flow statements of corporate customers to determine if cash flow will be adequate to cover loan payments. For consumer loans, annual income from tax returns and an employment contract and paystubs are often used. For mortgage loans, comparing the borrower's gross monthly income with the monthly loan payment is widely used to assess the burden on the borrowers. The payment is sometimes adjusted to include homeowners' insurance and property taxes, although some research suggests that the payment to income ratio is not always a reliable predictor of default.
- *Capital* (the soundness of a borrower's financial position in terms of equity). The net worth or equity position of a corporate borrower relative to assets provides information on the cushion that the borrower has to absorb potential losses. For consumer customers, net worth is estimated as personal assets less personal liabilities.

221

*Loan Analysis,
Credit Risk
Management,
and Loan
Securitization*

- *Conditions* (the industry and economic conditions that may affect a firm's ability to repay a loan). For corporate borrowers, external conditions related to the industry a firm is in and the economic environment of the firm are particularly important for the loan officer to analyze. In certain regions that depend on particular industries, industry performance can also affect the economy in a region, such as the effect of a fall in oil prices, which can affect otherwise healthy companies in the oil industry and other firms related to this industry. Similarly, during recessions, mortgage delinquencies also tend to rise, and real estate booms and busts in particular areas can affect the likelihood of foreclosures, such as occurred during the U.S. subprime loan crisis.
- *Collateral* (secondary sources of repayment) (asset-based lending). Collateral and, at times for private firms personal guarantees based on personal assets, are used as a secondary source of repayment for the bank, particularly for more risky company loans. However, taking possession of the collateral is expensive, so lenders should reply on cash flow for primary payment of a loan, with collateral only as a secondary source of repayment, with the hope of not having to take possession.

EVALUATING AND STRUCTURING BANK LOANS TO MANAGE CREDIT RISK

Loan Request Procedures

Loan request procedures are the implementation of a bank's overall lending policy. By having loan request procedures, loan presentations are uniform and accessible to loan committee members. Loan procedures generally include the following:

1 The *source* of the business (is this a new or existing customer? Information about the customer's past relationships and type of business and industry as background).
2 The *principal contacts* for the loan (the contacts with whom the bank regularly communicates).
3 The *participation structure* (optional: if other banks are participating in the loan). If the credit accommodation is either a bought or sold participation then all the pertinent details of the participation need to be spelled out, including the lead bank and its role in the management of the credit and other participants and each participant's share and effective yield that the bank will receive on the credit accommodation.
4 The *amount and reason* for the loan request (the purpose for the funds to be borrowed and a narrative about the rationale for the transaction and structure).
5 Brief *history and operations* of the firm. Include how and when the company was formed, general background and the firm's products, services, and markets, and how it has evolved over time and details about the firm's operations including the geographical and customer market it serves, products it sells, and the competitive environment in which it operates. The competitive advantages or disadvantages the firm enjoys and how these relate to the overall economic environment in which the firm operates should also be discussed.
6 Optional *industry analysis* if needed for large or unusual borrowing requests, or a credit request in which the bank/division has a large concentration.

7 *Management performance profiles.* Assessment of management including practical resume information on the top management of the company and comments for the account officer's assessment of managers and their professional accomplishments and capabilities.

8 *Financial performance*, including a historical financial performance analysis with headings for subsections for Income statement, Balance sheet, and Uniform cash flow. This should include a narrative for the trends occurring, including insights for why trends are positive or negative and the mix of sales if applicable and complexion for the cost of sales. Any unusual expenses or revenues should be explained clearly. The balance sheet should include explanations for all major accounts, with insights for trends regarding asset turnover and special emphasis on working capital management, including accounts receivable, inventory, accounts payable, and accruals. The rationale for the firm's capital structure should also be explained with a discussion about its appropriateness for the firm's operating strategy. For the cash flow statement, there should be insights on the sources and used of cash and the firm's ability to generate sufficient cash flow to be able to repay debts and sustain its growth.

Also future prospects should be discussed in terms of a firm's markets, products, competition, and management; and general capabilities and financial projections with these reconciled with historical statements for creditability, including discussion of any operating changes that the firm is contemplating and the effect on the firm's future operating results.

9 *Collateral/risk analysis*, summarizing collateral available and risks involved in the loan, such as barriers for entry to a particular industry. Preferably a narrative on the collateral, liquidation analysis, and a general risk analysis should be included.

The risk analysis is a summary of the risks for the loan taking account of barriers to entry for this specific industry, management quality, product and service quality for the firm, and the franchise value of the assets along with other factors that might affect the company's ability to operate in the future.

This section should have a conclusion that clearly demonstrates to the loan committee that the loan is collateralized or if a gap exists and the rationale for the bank taking on the loan including such a gap risk.

10 *Loan review and rating recommendation* by the loan officer, which includes whether the loan would be categorized as A, B, or C (or other types of categories) from excellent to average or below rating, based on the bank's classification of ratings for loans.

11 *Conclusion and opinion* (favorable or unfavorable factors for the loan). The conclusion should summarize all the important items that lead the underwriter to conclude that there is a reasonable risk for the bank to take on the loan, including favorable and unfavorable considerations.

Sample Loan Request for the Big Denver Real Estate & Storage Company

I. BACKGROUND

The Big Denver Real Estate & Storage Company was organized in 2000 for the purpose of acquiring, holding, and operating transportation storage facilities in downtown Denver.

223

*Loan Analysis,
Credit Risk
Management,
and Loan
Securitization*

The firm is a general partnership, and the guarantor, Mike Bronco, owns 60% of the partnership. Three other partners own respectively 20%, 10%, and 10% of shares in the partnership. The partnership also owns 100% of three other transportation storage facilities. The company has had a loan with the bank since 2012. At that time, the company was much larger. Since that time it has scaled down, selling two facilities that it owned.

II. REQUEST

The request is for the renewal of its term debt, which originated in 2012 on its facility in downtown Denver. It should be noted that the mortgage on another facility matures in 2018, which could also be a future business opportunity for the Bank for a second lending opportunity.

III. REPAYMENT ANALYSIS

Primary repayment is from cash flows from property. A summary cash flow of the downtown Denver facility on a standalone basis is as follows:

(In $ thousands)	2012	2013	2014	2015
Revenue	365,298	386,783	414,524	428,161
Operating expense	296,921	289,486	316,959	282,579
Net income	78,377	107,297	97,565	145,582
+ Depreciation and amortization	45,214	44,630	44,871	44,883
+ Interest expense	90,597	89,265	87,231	85,985
Net operating income (NOPAT)	214,188	241,192	229,667	276,450
Less debt service*	101,784	101,784	101,784	101,784
Net cash flow	112,404	139,408	127,883	174,666
Debt coverage ratio	2.10	2.37	2.26	2.72

* Debt service based on proposed loan structure.

Summary Points for Table Showing Debt Service

1   The historic debt service coverage is more than adequate in the years reviewed. The facility's percentage occupancy ranged from a low of 87 to a high of 95% in the summer peak period. Based on 2015 operating expenses, rental income would have to drop by over 40% (or $174,666) to fall below break-even.
2   Revenue growth over the past three years is due to price increases, with occupancy expenses fairly stable. The rise in operating expenses in 2014 is due to paying the wages of a hospitalized manager along with the wage expense of a temporary employee to replace that employee on the job.
3   A first quarter interim income statement ending April 30, 2016 on the downtown Denver facility shows annualized revenue of $408,501, which is on schedule with 2015, taking seasonality into account.

Secondary Source

The secondary source of payment is the collateral for the loan (see collateral section) with the refinance or sale of the subject property.

Overall Financial Analysis for Provided Financial Statements

The financial statements were provided for the company for 2012 to 2015, which were Certified Public Accountant (CPA) reviewed. For each of the years, the accountant's review report notes a GAAP (generally accepted accounting practice) exception in the firm's accounting practices, with the firm amortizing its nonpurchased goodwill based on management's assessment that there has been no reduction of value. GAAP requires the amortization of goodwill over the less of its estimated useful life or 40 years.

Balance Sheet

The firm's balance sheet has improved over the past 5 years, particularly with the sale of assets in 2014 and in early 2015. Total assets dropped to $3.16 million in 2015, while net worth rose to $978 million. The firm's leverage position has gradually improved to a debt to tangible net worth of 4.27 in 2015 with over $1.44 million in cash distributions taken in 2014 and 2015. The firm's cash balances grew to $847 thousand at the end of 2015, resulting in higher current and quick ratios with a current ratio of 3.90 and quick ratio of 3.65 in 2015.

Income Statements

Revenue and operating margins have fluctuated over the past 5 years as the firm grew and sold off assets. Operating profits dropped off in 2015 as the result of extra professional expenses that were incurred with the asset sales and are expected to return to their normal range of 40 to 50%. The partnership has had a healthy operating profit each year for the 5 years reviewed. Net profits were particularly strong in the last two years as a result of the gains realized from the sale of the partnership interests. The 2015 property distribution was recorded with the resulting gain reflected under "Gain on sale of assets."

Collateral

The bank has a first mortgage on the downtown Denver Transportation Storage Center, consisting of a 15,600 square-foot lot with a 62,687 square-foot building with an 8,000 square-foot basement. The moving company originally built this building about 1970. The building is several stories tall, and the original open warehouse space on each floor has been finished with individual storage spaces. The large freight elevators are located in the center of the building, and there is office space on the first floor for the business's operations. An appraisal was prepared in 2015 assigning a fair value of $1.6 million to the property. The valuation was done based on an income approach using a capitalization rate of 12.5%. Using the 2016 net income capitalized at the 12.5% rate as a conservative estimate based on market conditions, the property is valued at $2.21 million. This results in a loan-to-value (LTV) rate of 38%. At a more reasonable capitalization rate of 10%, the valuation is $2.76 million for a LTV of 30%. A Phase I performed by Environmental Property Audits in 2015 gave the property a clean bill of health, with no potential hazards revealed from present and past use of the property.

Risk Analysis and Recommendation

The real estate investment does not show any underlying economic and market risk associated with the investment. Risks are mitigated by a profitable history for the firm, the extensive experience of the partners, and a solid collateral position. The loan is recommended as presented with a Grade of 1-C.

Proposed Loan Structure

Credit request renewal—Real Estate Loan Grade 1-C

Amount $835,314

Rate/index 5-year Treasuries + 2.65%, fixed rate at the current rate of 10%

Loan fees: 0.5%

Collateral: First Deed of Trust on Downtown Denver Facility.

As shown in Table 9.1 for the financial ratios above, the firm's sales growth fell in 2015, with a reduction in assets, but its profit margin improved with a bigger reduction in expenses than sales, and in 2015, although it had a slight decline in asset turnover, this was greatly offset by the huge rise in the profit margin, resulting in the large rise in return on assets (ROA) and huge rise in return on equity (ROE), given the company's high financial leverage. The current ratio and quick ratio also improved dramatically in 2015, as did interest coverage, and the firm's bankruptcy risk zeta score, which will be discussed in the next section. Working capital to assets went up dramatically in 2015, with the sale of fixed assets, so the company's liquidity improved, and its bankruptcy risk went down with positive tangible equity and a higher debt to tangible net worth equity.

Often analysts use a Dupont Analysis approach to examine rises in ROE and ROA. Recall that ROE is equal to NPM x AU x EM, where NPM is the net profit margin, AU is asset utilization, and the equity multiplier is total assets to equity.

Given the company's business, as a storage firm, asset turnover is low and fairly stable, rising a bit in 2015. The firm's equity position improved, lowering the equity multiplier. The primary reason for both the higher ROA and ROE was the much higher net profit margin in 2015.

QUANTITATIVE CREDIT SCORING MODELS

Credit Scoring and Zeta Models for Commercial Loans

Quantitative credit scoring models are widely used by financial institutions to integrate information from a variety of sources. Data for an applicant or company are weighted according

TABLE 9.1 | Financial statements: Big Denver Real Estate & Storage Company

Indirect cash flow statements ($ thousand)

	2012	2013	2014	2015
Cash from operations				
Net income	159	326	1,188	1,234
Adjustments:				
Depreciation and amortization	247	245	179	113
Change in accounts receivable	(41)	12	54	13
Change in prepaids	(33)	6	58	8
Change in accounts payable and accrued expenses	(39)	179	(57)	(275)
Change in other assets and liabilities	(94)	(279)	(300)	(21)
Total adjustments	40	163	(66)	(162)
Net cash operations	199	489	1,122	1,072
Cash from investing				
Capital expenditures (if expense negative)	(38)	(40)	2,309	1,415
Cash from financing				
Change in long-term debt	(97)	(153)	(2,563)	(1,832)
Change in contributed capital	124	41	56	(1)
Dividends or owners' withdrawal	0	0	(838)	(579)
Net cash financing activities	27	(112)	(3,345)	(2,412)
Change in Cash	188	337	86	75
Beginning Cash	233	421	758	844
Ending Cash	421	758	844 919	

Income statements ($ thousand)

	2012	2013	2014	2015
Revenues				
Rent	1,524	1,729	1,349	800
Management consulting fees	196	222	197	106
Late charges and other	246	218	305	114
Total revenues	1,966	2,169	1,851	1,020
Gross expense	0	0	0	0
Gross profit	1,966	2,169	1,851	1,020
Payment to partners	129	135	135	135
Other operating expenses	747	731	667	484
Depreciation and amortization	247	245	179	113

227

*Loan Analysis,
Credit Risk
Management,
and Loan
Securitization*

Total operating expenses	1,123	1,111	981	712
Operating profit	843	1,058	870	308
Gain on sale assets	0	0	1,734	1,133
Operating profit and gain	843	1,058	2,604	1,441
Interest expense	651	656	493	207
Other expense	0	0	36	0
Loss minority interest	33	76	887	0
Total other expenses	684	732	1,416	207
Profit before tax	159	326	1,188	1,234

Balance sheets ($ thousand)

	2012	2013	2014	2015
Assets				
Cash	362	668	774	847
Escrow	59	91	70	72
Net accounts receivable	122	110	56	43
Prepaid expenses	113	107	49	41
Total current assets	656	976	949	1,003
Land	1,937	1,937	1,230	492
Buildings	5,941	5,945	3,600	2,605
Furniture and fixtures	91	95	59	49
Gross fixed assets	7,969	7,977	4,889	3,146
Accumulated depreciation	(2,069)	(2,282)	(1,682)	(1,467)
Net fixed assets	5,900	5,695	3,207	1,679
Other assets	111	85	27	10
Nonpurchased Goodwill	467	467	467	467
Total assets	7,134	7,223	4,650	3,159
Liabilities and equity				
Accounts payable	335	514	457	182
Security deposits	28	28	10	8
Prepaid rental income	123	122	96	67
Total current liabilities	486	664	563	257
Mortgage notes payable	6,472	6,319	3,756	1,924
Due to related parties	619	314	0	0
Minority interest	6	7	7	0
Total liabilities	7,583	7,304	4,326	2,181
Minority interest	(92)	(55)	0	0

(Continued)

TABLE 9.1 | (Continued)

Balance sheets ($ thousand)

	2012	2013	2014	2015
Partners equity	(357)	(27)	324	978
Total net worth	(449)	(82)	324	978
Total liabilities and equity	7,134	7,222	4,650	3,159

Financial ratios

	2012	2013	2014	2015
Sales growth	12.41%	10.33%	(14.66%)	(44.89%)
Gross margin	100%	100%	100%	100%
Profit margin	8.09%	15.03%	64.18%	120.98%
Asset turnover	0.28	0.30	0.40	0.32
ROA	2.23%	4.51%	25.55%	39.06%
ROE	17.36%	59.38%	830.77%	241.49%
Current ratio	1.35	1.47	1.69	3.90
Quick ratio	0.95	1.20	1.56	3.65
Working capital	170	311	386	746
Working capital to assets	2.38%	4.31%	8.30%	23.62%
Days accounts receivable	45.63	52.14	60.83	52.14
Days inventory	0	0	0	0
Days accounts payable	0	0	0	0
Plant turnover	0.33	0.38	0.58	0.61
Working capital turnover	11.56	6.97	4.80	1.37
Interest coverage	1.24	1.50	3.41	6.96
Debt/tangible net worth	(8.28)	(13.30)	(30.25)	4.27
Owner equity to assets	(6.29%)	(1.14%)	6.97%	30.96%
Bankruptcy risk Z-Value	0.58	0.75	1.67	2.36

to predetermined standards, and a score for creditworthiness is calculated. Applicants falling below a predetermined minimum acceptable score are rejected or given more attention in the loan application process before loans can be made. As noted in the introductory quote, critics often note that too much dependence may have been placed on credit scoring models versus more relationship-type indicators, such as character, reputation, and willingness to pay, job security, and other more qualitative factors. Credit scoring models are widely used, and facilitate the quickness in underwriting loans for widespread loan securitizations.

Example of a Zeta Model for Commercial Loan Credit Scoring

One of the most popular classification models for commercial loans is Zeta Analysis, designed by Edward Altman at New York University in 1968, which has endured and been refined over the past decades. The model uses a multiple discriminant analysis technique to identify important ratios used to classify firms likely to fail from those that are not likely to fail. For instance, in an early model for manufacturing firms, significant ratios included:

1 *Working capital to total assets (WC)*, i.e., (current assets − current liabilities) to total assets.
2 *Retained earnings to total assets (RE)*.
3 *Operating return on assets (ROA)*, i.e., earnings before interest and taxes to total assets.
4 *Market value of equity to book value of debt*, i.e., equity.
5 *Asset turnover (AT)*, i.e., revenues to total assets.

Given statistically determined weights for each of the ratios, a zeta or Z-score can be calculated by plugging in a firm's ratios (as decimal ratios) as follows:

$$Z = 1.2 \, WC + 1.4 \, RE + 3.3 \, ROA + 0.6 \, Equity + 0.999 \, AT.$$

As an example, suppose a firm has a WC of 0.41, a RE of 0.355, OROA of 0.154, and equity ratio of 2.48, and an AT of 2.84, its zeta score would be:

$$Z = 1.2 \, (0.41) + 1.4 \, (0.335) + 3.3 \, (0.154) + 0.6 \, (2.48) + 0.999 \, (2.84) = 5.794.$$

If the score is greater or equal to the cutoff score of about 2.675, the firm is more like the nonfailed group, and the loan is less likely to default. So this firm is well above that threshold. The lower bound zeta score of 1.81 (failed) and upper bound of 2.99 (nonfailed) are optimal, with any score in between this zone more in the zone of ignorance. The Z-score model's classification accuracy based on a development sample was 95% a year before bankruptcy and 82% two years before. Type II errors (classifying healthy firms as bankrupt) ranged from 15 to 20% in secondary samples.

Classification models, such as the Zeta model, can be purchased by banks as computer packages or developed in-house. Different models have been developed for different industries and for firms in different countries. Other credit risk classification models include neural networks, expert systems, and credit risk models based on a firm's stock price, such as the KMV model. Consumer credit scoring models have also been designed to allow lenders to classify credit applicants into "good" or "bad" risks based on past credit history, employment history and other variables.

Research shows that the accuracy of classifying loan applicants improves when a combination of statistical credit scoring models and judgmentally determined decision rules are used. Like all models, credit scoring has limitations. The statistical complications of gray ranges are one problem. Also models focus only on default risk and may ignore important information, such as deposit and other service relationships with a customer. They also must be carefully structured to comply with Reg. B: Applicant characteristics included in a model must be demonstrably and statistically sound, as defined by the Fed in the United States. But despite these limitations, banks and retailers regularly used these models, as do depositories offering credit cards.

CREDITMETRICS AND OTHER PORTFOLIO APPROACHES

Other measures of a financial institution's credit risk have been used taking an overall portfolio approach, looking at the diversification of a bank's loan or total asset portfolio. In 1997, J.P. Morgan with several other large banks released to the public a model for quantifying portfolio risk based on a value at risk (VAR) approach. The CreditMetrics approach estimates changes in the market value of a bank's loan portfolio as well as other financial instruments in the event of a credit upgrade or downgrade as well as potential loan defaults. Probabilities based on historical data are calculated for the occurrence of such events. Using these probabilities, the expected change in the value of loans, value at risk, for a given confidence level can be calculated. Correlation between the value at risk for different loans and other financial instruments can be used to derive an aggregate measure of the volatility or value at risk for a bank's entire loan portfolio and other instruments, such as swaps, futures, and forward contracts.

PROPOSED LOAN STRUCTURE AND TERMS AND CONDITIONS

Establishing the loan structure and terms and conditions is also critical to ensuring the repayment of a loan. Since loans dominate depository institution's asset portfolios, keeping loan rates at appropriate levels is a prerequisite to earning a target NIM and target ROE. Loan terms include the lending rate, noninterest terms and fees for the loan, the maturity and timing of payments, the loan amount or other secondary sources of payment, and any restrictive covenants associated with the loan. The base lending rate for the loan plus a premium to cover expected default risk, administrative costs, capital costs for expected losses (as discussed in Chapter 5 on capital management for the risk-adjusted return on capital, RAROC) and the bank's desired spread to achieve its NIM and ROE targets are discussed in the following sections.

BASE LENDING RATES

Base lending rates are established at the institutional level and are used as benchmarks for determining specific loan rates. Higher risk customers are charged a risk premium, so the base rate sets the boundaries within which the loan officer can exercise discretion. For a depository institution, the composition of its assets and their rates of return must be considered in planning the total interest spread, interest revenues (IR) – interest expenses (IE), where the interest spread is the sum of each asset x its rate less the sum of each liability x its rate. So if a bank knows its cost of funds and the interest spread it desires, given the rates on its other assets, it can solve for the base loan rate needed for a new loan to achieve that interest spread.

So, for example, if a bank has a desired interest spread of $3.2 million, and cash of $10 million and $30 million of loans that pay a 10.5% rate, the base rate on a particular loan of $60 million can be solved for as:

Spread of \$3.2 million = (0% x \$10 million) + (r_L x \$60 million)

\$3.2 million = (r_L x \$60 million)

Solving for r_L = (\$3.2 million / \$60 million) = 0.0533 or 5.33% as a minimum base rate for a customer of average cost and risk as a starting points for the loan. Competitor conditions including loan rates offered by other banks also affect base lending rates.

Other base lending rates that are often used are the Treasury bill (T-bill) rate, the Fed Funds rate, the London interbank offered rate (LIBOR), the prime rate, or a bank's weighted average marginal cost of funds used to finance the loan plus a mark-up for administrative costs.

RISK PREMIUMS ON LOANS

Once the base lending rate is set, the loan officer needs to set a risk premium for the loan. As discussed in Chapter 5, pricing can be used to add a premium based on the capital needed to cover a potential loss on the loan based on its risk. Other strategies for risk premiums include loan ratings based on rules of thumb, such as commonly practiced in the industry, such as adding 0.10% for a loan with a very high "A" rating, and then additional premiums for credit, maturity, and collateral risk as well. Loan rates typically are priced as a base rate plus a default risk premium plus a maturity risk premium. Examples of risk premiums for a term loan might be: if a loan has a high rating, a risk premium of 0 to 0.50%; an average rating, a risk premium of 1 to 1.50%; and if a lower than average rating, a risk premium of 2–2.50%, with a floor rate of 5%. Another example would be a risk premium of 0.10% for excellent loans, 0.20% for very good loans, 0.50% for good loans, etc., with risk premiums based on credit, maturity, and collateral risk.

For a hypothetical loan rate using RAROC, with the base rate the weighted average cost of funds for the loans: Loan rate = bank's transfer cost of funds (weighted average cost of funds for the loan), such as 5%, + required loan loss provision, such as 1.25%, + administrative costs, suppose 1.70%, + capital charge (RAROC) for the loan's cost of equity capital needed for the loan's risk, such as 3%, would equal a loan rate of about 10.95%.

Loan pricing is important since often loans and risk premiums can be underpriced. Yet loan rates need to be competitive with rates offered by competitors as well.

NONINTEREST COSTS OF LOANS

Banks often adjust the effective loan rate by using *compensating balances* (about 10% of the remaining balance of the loan) to be held as deposits with the institution, which guarantees the lender access to inexpensive funds and liquidity, increasing the actual cost of the loan to the borrower. *Lines of credit and commitment fees* are also used, which are agreements to extend funds to the borrower over some prearranged time period. While a *line of credit* is informal and can be revoked, a *loan commitment* is a formal, legal guarantee that funds will be available at a given rate, amount, and maturity. Terms of commitment usually require a commitment fee on any amount of unused credit over the life of the arrangement, plus a fee on the amount actually borrowed.

For example, for a hypothetical bank, Bank Royal, suppose a firm is offered a line of credit for $2,000,000 that the firm can draw down on at a stated rate of 11.5% plus a risk premium with a 0.25% commitment fee on the unused portion of the line of credit for the term of 1 year. The loan also has a compensating balance that is equal to 8% of the loan commitment, plus a 4% compensating balance on borrowed funds. The estimated average loan balance is 60% of the commitment, and the maximum line of credit is $2,000,000, so the average loan balance is $2,000,000 x 0.60 = $1,200,000. The calculation for the effective annual rate for the loan is shown in Table 9.2.

Hence, the additional compensating balance and commitment fees for the loan increase the effective annual loan rate.

Discounted Loans

Discounted loans are loans where a percentage of the loan is taken out up front, such as with points for mortgage loans, which also increases the effective annual loan rate, since only the loan amount after the discount percentage is usable, so:

TABLE 9.2 | Example interest and implicit interest terms in pricing

Hypothetical loan terms

Line of credit for $2,000,000 (that the firm can draw down on)

Stated rate: 11.5% (bank's cost of funds (base rate) + risk premium)

Commitment fee: 0.25% on unused portion of the line of credit.

Term: 1 year.

Compensating balance: 8% of the loan commitment + 4% compensating balance on borrowed funds

Estimated average loan balance: 60% of the commitment

Maximum line of credit: $ 2,000,000

Average loan balance = $2,000,000 x 0.60 = $ 1,200,000

Loan interest and noninterest revenues for the bank

Interest of $2 million line x 0.60 used x 0.115 = $138,000

Fees: $2 million x 0.40 unused x 0.0025 = 2,000

Total interest and fee revenues $140,000

Net funds invested

Average loan balance: $1,200,000

Compensating balance less 10% reserve requirements = [$2,000,000 (0.08) + 1,200,000 (0.04)] (1 − 0.10) = $160,000 + $48,000 = $208,000 (0.90) = $187,200

Net invested funds = average loan balance less compensating balance = $1,200,000 − $187,200 = $1,012,800

Implicit return to bank = (interest + noninterest expenses) / investable funds

= [$140,000 / $1,012,800 = 13.82%

233

*Loan Analysis,
Credit Risk
Management,
and Loan
Securitization*

Actual loan rate for discount loan = Interest expense / [Loan Amount (1-discount)].

Example Suppose a borrower borrows $100,000 with a 10% stated annual rate, but with a 10% discount.

Effective annual rate = $10,000 / [($100,000 (0.90)] = 0.111 or 11.11%.

Points for loans have a similar effect in increasing the effective annual rate.

CUSTOMER PRICING USING PROFITABILITY ANALYSIS

With profitability analysis, a spreadsheet is set up listing all the revenues a customer brings in less all the costs the bank spends on the customer. A loan rate is solved for that makes revenues equal to the banks costs plus the profit the bank wants to make.

OTHER NONINTEREST LOAN STRUCTURING DECISIONS

Restrictive Covenants

Banks often protect their interests by establishing restrictive covenants, such as minimum liquidity or debt ratios, or a borrower taking on additional debt, limitations on dividend payments, or minimum current and quick ratios, among others. Covenants may require life insurance on key personnel, that the bank be notified of any change in management, and that the bank should receive quarterly financial statements from the firm. The loan may state that if the covenants are not met, the loan will be called.

TYPE OF LOAN AND PROPER STRUCTURING AND MATURITY

A loan should be structured to ensure that borrowers will be able to make loan payments. Often borrowers also request too much or too little funds, so the amount and structure of the loan are important.

Loans should be structured so projected cash flows of a borrower will be adequate to make loan payments. By forecasting financial statements, including an indirect cash flow statement or source and use statements, the proper amount needed for a loan can be determined, as the missing source that makes sources equal to total uses.

Amortized loans have equal loan payments each year that include interest and principal payments, where interest is paid as a percentage of the remaining unpaid balance and the remaining portion of the loan payment goes to pay back principal. For example, for a $600,000 amortized loan for 5 years with an annual 10% rate, the calculation of the loan payment would be

Annual loan PMT = Loan amount / (Present value interest factor annuity r, n)

For example, a $600,000 loan for 5 years with a 10% rate:

Annual loan PMT = $600,000/3.7908 = $158,278.49

PVIFA = $\{[1 - (1/(1 + r)^n]\} / r = [1 - 1/(1.10)^5] / 0.10 = 3.7908$.

By using the number of months, in this case 5 x 12 = 60 months, and 10%/12 as the monthly rate of 0.833%, monthly payments can also be calculated:

PVIFA = $[1 - (1/(1.00833)^{60})] / 0.00833 = 47.070$.

So the monthly loan PMT = $600,000/47.070 = $12,746.97 a month.

Bond type payments have interest only and the principal (balloon payment) is due at maturity. For this type of loan, sometimes the principal payment is rolled over if the loan is re-approved. Banks often change the maturity of the loan through its life or having a revolving loan where the loan will be reviewed for renewal (shorter-term loan will be reviewed for renewal after a certain number of years).

SPECIAL CONSIDERATIONS FOR DIFFERENT TYPES OF LOANS

Seasonal Working Capital Loans

- Seasonal working capital loans are used to finance seasonal inventory and accounts receivable and are usually paid back within a year.
- Quarterly cash flow statements should be forecast for peak and low seasons to determine the appropriate loan amount.
- Looking at the cash cycle days is very important. A rough estimate of annual working capital needs is the daily cost of goods sold (CGS) x no. cash cycle days.
- Seasonal working capital loans are typically collateralized by inventory and accounts receivables.

Term Loans

- Longer-term loans to purchase depreciable assets with maturity from 1 to 7 years.
- Amount of loan equals purchase price of an asset.
- Loan is typically amortized to generate a gradual repayment of interest and principal over the life of the loan.
- Term loan payments should be structured to match cash flows generated by the firm over the life of the equipment.
- Projected cash statements are important to look at to ensure that payments can be made.

235

*Loan Analysis,
Credit Risk
Management,
and Loan
Securitization*

Commercial Real Estate Loans

- Commercial real estate loans or constructions loans with real property as collateral often involve interim (temporary) financing by a bank with a takeout commitment from a long-term lender, such as a life insurance company or a pension fund, after the completion of a project or a certain number of years.
- Bankers have to be very careful to ensure that the takeout commitment protects the bank from being stuck with a long-term loan.
- Projected vacancy rates are important to reduce risk.
- Fees must be amortized over the life of the loan for accounting purposes.
- Other construction loans have higher rates as well, often 1–1.5% above typical commercial loan rates to compensate for the greater risk of these loans.
- Surety bonds guaranteeing the completion of a project should also be purchased.

OTHER LENDING CONSIDERATIONS

- *Loan participations:* Arrangements by two or more lenders to share a loan in some agreed upon proportion.
- *Loan syndicates:* Several lenders simultaneously lend to a single borrower and all lenders have a direct relationship with the borrower. Loan participations are often necessary in large loans because of regulatory limits placed on the amount that a commercial bank may lend to a single borrower as a percentage of capital, and they allow institutions to share the risk of a large loan.
- *Loan sales:* Banks that would rather not make longer-term loans can engage in selling loans to longer-term lenders, such as insurance companies or pension funds. Banks can maintain the servicing arrangement and receive fee income and gain liquidity and lower interest rate risk through loan sales.
- *Loan securitization:* Because commercial loans are less homogeneous than other loans, being tailored and negotiated in terms of size, rate, and maturity, they are not securitized into pools as often as other types of loans, but the securitization of commercial loans has grown dramatically.

COLLATERAL

With asset-based lending, collateral is often matched with the use for the loan. For example, banks often collateralize the assets that are being financed for a loan, such as using temporary accounts receivables and inventory as collateral for a one-year seasonable working capital loan. In turn, once the company sells and collects on these, the loan is paid back during the year. Hence, collateral is matched with the use and term of the loan. For instance, with a longer-term loan to purchase equipment and machinery, the purchased equipment and machinery would be used as collateral for the loan.

Asset-based lending often incorporates costly monitoring, so loan rates are often higher than unsecured loans for the same degree of safety, often 2–6% above a bank's basic lending rate, depending on the risk of the borrower. Maintaining accurate records (loan documentation) is important when examiners are assessing the quality of outstanding loans. Determining the value of the assets to be pledged as collateral, including how liquid and marketable they are, is important, and for accounts receivables, the quality of the accounts receivables, and if they are concentrated towards a few large customers that could default, and reviewing an aging schedule for accounts receivables. The *security agreement*, the legal agreement assigning the assets as collateral is important, and in the United States the *Uniform Commercial Code*, the body of law adopted individually by states containing many common provisions across states, establishes guidelines under which these agreements are drawn.

Factoring can be used as a way to finance higher risk loans, whereby the financial institution purchases accounts receivables at a discount from the borrower, and assumes the default risk and collection responsibility.

Rules of thumb for the maximum loan amount to value ratio (LTV) are lending 40–60% against raw materials and finished goods inventory, which are easier to collect on, but must be marketable, and perhaps 50–80% against accounts receivables depending on the aging schedule and collection experience. For consumer and mortgage equipment loans that are asset based, a loan-to-value ratio should be low enough to ensure that at the time of the application the market value of the property is greater than the loan amount by enough to protect the lender in case of default and to provide the borrower with an incentive not to default.

For real estate loans, the LTV ratio is equal to the balance of the loan divided by the market value of the property. For example, if a property has a loan balance of $400,000 and the market value of the property is $500,000, the LTV ratio is (400/500) = 0.80 or 80%, implying that the borrower has a 20% equity stake for the property. Lenders often require mortgage insurance on real estate loans with a LTV ratio greater than a given amount, such as 80%, so the borrower has at least a 20% equity stake. Many subprime types of real estate loans were made on the basis of collateral of a home or property alone, without requiring borrowers to put down a sufficient down payment or stake in the loan. When the market value of homes fell with the real estate downturn in 2007 and 2008, many borrowers walked away from expensive homes whose value plunged, since the loan amount was greater than the value of the homes.

Different types of collateral arrangements include a *floating lien* that gives the lender recourse to a borrower's entire inventory, even if portions are acquired after the loan is made. *Warehouse receipts* place specific inventory items assigned as collateral under the control of a third party and the goods may be physically transferred to a bonded warehouse for safekeeping. *Floor planning* is often used by car dealers, which allows the borrower to retain possession of the collateral. For this purpose it is often used to finance expensive retail items that are designated by a serial number or description.

POLICIES USED IN LOAN MONITORING

Monitoring procedures are designed to identify problems early enough to circumvent a need for legal action later. Loan officers may be asked to contact and maintain relationships with customers to be aware of potential problems. A comprehensive loan review system also serves to monitor the effectiveness of an institution's loan officers by providing incentives for them to make good decisions initially and then periodically to assess the borrower's subsequent financial position.

237

*Loan Analysis,
Credit Risk
Management,
and Loan
Securitization*

Workout specialists are often used by larger institutions to work on working out loans in an effort to avoid default. Workout specialists know that most of the financial problems of borrowers are traced to mismanagement by borrowers arising from inadequate training and inexperience or even fraud or poor economic conditions.

CLASSIFICATION OF PROBLEM LOANS

- Past due are loans with payments past due for 30 to 89 days.
- Nonperforming are loans where payments are past due for 90 or more days.
- Nonaccruing are loans where payments are not received.

Examiners periodically review a bank's loans and classify problem loans into categories of standard (20% write-down), doubtful (50% write-down) and loss (100% write-down) against capital.

SPECIAL CONSIDERATIONS FOR DIFFERENT TYPES OF LOANS

Seasonal Working Capital Loans

Seasonal working capital loans are generally repaid within one year once inventory has been sold and accounts receivables have been collected. Often seasonal working capital loans are given out as lines of credit that can be repaid over the year. To determine the approximate loan amount needed for a seasonal working capital loan, quarterly balance sheets need to be projected. Performing a sources and uses statement based on the differences between the balance sheet for the peak and low seasons will determine the total uses and sources needed, with the difference between uses and sources as the approximate amount of the loan needed from the bank or another external source.

A rule of thumb method for determining the amount of a working capital loan needed is often calculated as a firm's cash to cash cycle times its daily average cost of goods sold (CGS/365). A firm's cash to cash cycle is typically calculated as:

Cash to cash cycle = Days inventory + ACP – Days accounts payable and Accruals

where:

Days inventory = 365/(CGS / Inventory);

Average collection period (ACP) = 365/(Sales/Accounts receivables); and

Days accounts payable and Accruals = 365/(CGS / Accounts payable and Accruals).

For example, if a firm had days inventory of 60 days, ACP of 30 days, and days AP and accruals of 20 days, the cash to cash cycle would be 70 days. If the daily average cost of goods sold was $1 million, the approximate working capital loan needed would be 70 days x $1 million = $70 million. If the firm was able to reduce its inventory cycle days to 30 days, then the cash to cash cycle days would be only 40 days, and the working capital loan needed would be only $40 million. Since this is just an approximation, it would be better for a lender to use projected cash flow statements to determine the appropriate amount of the loan that is needed. Quarterly cash flow statements are helpful to determine the financing needed for particular quarters. Seasonal working capital loans are typically collateralized by inventory and accounts receivable.

Commercial Real Estate Loans

Commercial real estate loans or construction loans with real property as collateral often involve interim (temporary) financing by a bank with a *takeout commitment* from a long-term lender, such as a life insurance company or pension fund, after completion of a project or a certain number of years. Bankers have to be very careful to ensure that the takeout commitment protects the bank from being stuck with a long-term loan. Projected vacancy rates are important to reduce the risk of the project failing. Bankers also need to work with reliable developers, have third-party appraisals, and demand upfront fees to reduce their risk. Fees must be amortized over the life of the loan for accounting purposes. Often construction loans have higher rates as well, usually 1–1.5% above typical commercial loan rates to compensate for the greater risk of these loans. Surety bonds are also necessary to ensure completion of a project.

Agricultural Loans

Agricultural loans are also often collateralized by land and equipment and are very cyclical and seasonal, with banks providing seasonal funds for planting that are repaid at harvest time, as well as providing long-term loans for land and equipment. Lenders have learned to lend on cash flows versus the value of real estate. In 1984 to 1986, for instance, about 40% of bank failures for agricultural banks were associated with loans based on the value of collateral. When agricultural real estate values dropped incredibly in value with a large drop in commodity prices at this time, many farms went bankrupt, and banks were left with collateral that had lost its value. In the United States a number of government-sponsored agencies also provide loans to farms, including production credit associations, which are part of the cooperative Farm Credit System. The Farmers Home Administration, a federal government agency, provides guarantees for farm loans made by banks and also provides direct lending. The Commodity Credit Corporation, which is also a government agency, provides price support and crop storage loans. Rural banks make about half of all the farm loans made by commercial banks.

Consumer and Credit Card Loans

Consumer loans are usually short-term, between 1 and 4 years, and often have fixed rates paid in installments. Consumer loans are subject to many different regulations and bankruptcy laws. Credit card loans are a popular type of consumer loans, known as *revolving credit*, whereby the lender designates a prearranged interest rate and maximum line of credit. The cardholder chooses when and whether to borrow, repaying the lender partially or in full on receipt of a monthly statement. An annual card fee that most credit card holders pay is

239

Loan Analysis,
Credit Risk
Management,
and Loan
Securitization

similar to a commitment fee in commercial lending. Depository institutions receive fee income from credit cards and interest on outstanding balances, and institutions that process credit transactions and bill customers for depository institutions are able to earn additional revenues, including fees from merchants accepting cards. In the United States under the Fair Credit and Charge Disclosure Act of 1988, regulations require card issuers to disclose interest rates, grace periods, and other terms and conditions at the time of application.

Consumer Installment Loans

Some types of consumer loans are made on an installment basis. Sometimes these loan rates are deceptive, so have been targeted by Congress, because of confusion in stated rates, with the loan amount not being amortized over time, so consumers are still paying a rate on the original amount borrowed versus the principal remaining on the loan under an add-on interest method. For example, if an individually purchases a used car priced at $12,000 and makes a $2,000 down payment, and makes a $10,000 installment loan with a financial institution with an add-on rate quoted at 9% for 4 years with equal payments each year, the borrower will be repaying $10,000 (0.09) x 4 years + $10,000 principal repayment = $13,600 or on a monthly basis: $13,600 / 48 months = $283.33 per month, i.e. a monthly interest rate of 1.3322 % x 12 = a 16% annual rate (a little less than double the stated 9% annual rate). Regulation Z in the United States requires lenders to disclose the annual percentage rate (APR) to borrowers.

The Rule of 78 is also used by some lenders as a prepayment penalty for installment loans for calculating the remaining principal balance. This approach, also called the sum of digits method, involves adding together the digits for the number of payments to be made. The 78 comes from the sum of digits for a 12-month loans, where $12 + 11 + 10 + 9 + 8 + 7 + 6 + 5 + 4 + 3 + 2 + 1$ equals 78. For example, for a 4-year, 48-month car loan, the sum of digits is 1,176 $[(N/2)$ x $(N+1)]$ where N is the number of payments. If a borrower pays off this loan early, the charge would be 48/1,176 of their total interest payments owed in the first month, 47/1,176 in the second month, etc., as interest. So, for example, if a borrower repaid the loan after 1 year, having paid 12 payments of $283.33, the total paid was $3,399.96. Under the Rule of 78, the borrower would be charged with (510/1,176) or 0.43367 of the total interest payment of $3,600 [$10,000 x 0.09 x 4] x 0.043367 equals $1,561.22 as interest. The $3,999.96 already paid less $1,561.22 charge equals $1,838.74 to be considered as repaid principal, so to repay the loan principal of $10,000 − $1,838.74 equals $8,161.26 that the borrower would have to repay the financial institution. Since the loan is not amortized, this repayment is much higher than that for an amortized loan, amounting to an APR of 16%. A few states have adopted laws specifically prohibiting this type of loan as unfair to borrowers.

Home Equity Loans (HELs)

Home equity loans (HELs) differ from second mortgages, which are additional loans backed by the property on which a first mortgage loan has been issued, with fixed dollar amounts, specified maturity dates, and a higher interest rate than a first mortgage. The amount a homeowner can borrow for a second mortgage loan is limited to the amount of equity they have accumulated in their homes. A home equity loan, however, is a revolving line of credit against which a homeowner can borrow with the loan maximum allowed as 70–85% of the equity the borrower has in the home. Since the lender has the security of a junior lien on the borrower's home in the event of default, HELs are offered at lower interest rates than credit card or unsecured consumer loans. Interest rates are variable (sometimes changing monthly) and are often tied to movements in base rates such as a prime rate or T-bill rate index. Repayment schedules are more flexible than second mortgages, and the borrower may often draw on unused but approved credit limits by writing a check. In the United States, the Competitive Equality Banking Act (CEBA) of 1987 mandates that HELs must have lifetime interest rate caps. The Home Equity Loan Consumer Protection Act of 1988 specifies rigid disclosure rules and restricts the right of creditors to charge loan terms after a home equity loan has been approved.

SPECIAL CONSIDERATIONS OF MORTGAGE LOANS

Adjustable Rate Mortgages (ARMs)

There are many special regulations for mortgage loans including adjustable rate mortgage loans (ARMs), such as the indexes that can be used. The lender must explain to the borrower exactly how the loan interest rate is related to the index and how it will be adjusted as the index changes. A 15-year history of the index must be provided. Banks also have limits called *caps* on the size of the periodic rate adjustment, with an overall cap required by federal law in the United States. Federal regulations prohibit prepayment penalties on ARMs. Convertible ARMs have been developed whereby borrowers can switch ARMs to fixed-rate mortgages (FRMs) during a specified period. Many loan customers prefer ARMs because they offer lower rates than FRMs, since the borrower takes on the interest rate risk. However, ARMs increase the credit risk for a loan, since if rates suddenly rise, such as during the subprime loan crisis, borrowers may not be able to make their loan payments.

Due on Sale Clauses

Mortgage loans often have a due on sale clause, whereby the lender can require the borrower to repay the outstanding loan balance when the mortgage property is sold. Mortgages without due on sale clauses are assumed by the new homeowner. Due on sale clauses protect the lender by allowing the lender to evaluate the financial position of the new owner before deciding to continue the loan, and setting a higher interest rate if necessary than the original loan.

Other Types of More Unusual Mortgages

Other types of mortgages that are less usual include *graduated payment mortgages* (GPMs) where monthly payments are set at a low level in early years, then payments increase according to a known schedule before stabilizing. *Reverse annuity mortgages* (RAMs) allow seniors that face cash shortages to gradually in effect sell their property to a depository institution, whereby the owner of the property receives cash payments. When the borrower with a RAM moves out or dies, the property is sold and the lender receives the repayment with interest from the proceeds. *Growing equity mortgages* (GEMs) have initial payments set at the level that would amortize the mortgage over 30 years, but scheduled increases in payments result in a shorter actual maturity. *Price-level adjusted mortgages* (PLAMs) have an adjustable

241

*Loan Analysis,
Credit Risk
Management,
and Loan
Securitization*

interest rate tied to an inflation index rather than an interest rate index, whereby a borrower pays for actual versus expected inflation and benefits from lower initial interest costs that are not adjusted for expected inflation.

SMALL BUSINESS LOANS

Community banks and many large banks with small business specialty divisions help small businesses with loans, working capital management, and other needs, often associated in the United States with Community Reinvestment Act lending activities. Also, community banks have become specialists in small business lending. Banks often become designated as small business lenders, with the ability to make small business administration (SBA) loans. To be eligible to apply for an SBA loan, a borrower must first be denied a conventional loan. A borrower can then apply for an SBA loan through a designated lender. The SBA guarantees a portion of the loan, so the lender is protected against default risk, which allows the lender the ability to take on a loan to a small business, which can entail considerable risk. The SBA-guaranteed portions of SBA-guaranteed loans, however, are securitized with yields close to those of government-issued securities.

MEZZANINE LENDING

Mezzanine loans are longer-term unsecured loans, unsecured loans in which a firm's cash flow is the major source of repayment. In addition, the financial contract contains an option through which the lender can share in the increased value of the business if the venture is particularly successful. The potentially high return on the option is designed to compensate for the relatively high risk of the loan, allowing a lower interest rate. Loans are for more established firms that have stable cash flow to make loan payments. Mezzanine financing often contains layers of investors with senior and junior debt, including warrants attached that allow future equity stakes in a firm. Bond financing is privately placed. With mezzanine financing, different layers appeal to the risk/return preferences of different groups of investors, with venture capital also often involved. Bonds issued with payment in kind (PIK) are similar to zero coupon bonds with interest accumulating, so the principal payment at maturity gets larger and larger. Mezzanine lending provides an additional financing choice for firms that are not large enough to issue public debt.

LENDING TO HEDGE FUNDS

Large banks may lend funds to hedge funds, with guidelines by regulators for assessing bank lending to hedge funds including self-imposed limits by banks on the amount of their loans to hedge funds and having models for credit risks and monitoring. In 1998, bank loans made by larger major banks to Long-Term Capital Management, L.P., a highly leveraged giant investment fund for wealthy private investors was close to failure, and the Fed had to arrange a $3.625 billion bailout by 14 banks and security firms. Following this bailout, the Federal

Reserve Board and OCC in 1999 requested that banks tighten their standards for lending and limits on lending to hedge funds, avoid focusing too much on easy profits while ignoring credit risks posed by some funds, and provide better monitoring and modeling for credit risk for hedge fund loans.

LENDER LIABILITY INCLUDING ENVIRONMENTAL LIABILITY

Lenders can be subject to the threat of a lawsuit by a borrower if the borrower is in financial difficulty and an institution refuses to advance funds, renew a loan, or attempts to take possession of collateral; defendants have in the past claimed that these actions led to a firm's failure. Lenders are also at times cited in environmental liability suits if collateral used for loans is associated with environmental hazards. Consequently, lenders perform environmental audits on land or buildings used as collateral. Lawsuits are expensive for lenders even if they win cases. Hence, it's important for lenders to follow institutional procedures on monitoring and foreclosure scrupulously to give ample time and notice to borrowers if their credit is not to be extended, and to keep excellent records. For this reason, risk premiums are higher for high-risk borrowers to cover the extra cost involved with the higher costs involved.

LOAN SECURITIZATION AND SALES

Securitizations

Securitization, as an innovation, began in the 1970s and grew dramatically in the 1980s and 1990s and on through the 2000s with technology allowing numerous records and information to be gathered, stored, and transferred easily. At the beginning of 2004, ABS Market Statistics reported an estimated $63.3 trillion in asset-backed securities (ABS) outstanding worldwide. With the U.S. subprime loan crisis and global financial crisis, collateralized debt obligations suffered a serious decline, particularly for collateralized mortgage securitizations, but rebounded in recent years.

With securitizations, loans are packaged into portfolios, sold off-balance sheet to a specialized securitization enterprise, and passed on to a trust organization to be repackaged as participating securities with cash flows received by investors on principal and interest. Meanwhile, the bank that originated the loans often maintains the servicing rights and receives fee income for continuing to collect interest and principal payments from the loan customers, which in turn, are passed through to the trust organization to pass on to investors owing the pass-through mortgage securities.

Participants in Securitizations

Government-sponsored enterprises (GSEs) have been active in securitizations, since the first securitization took place in 1970 when the Government National Mortgage Association (GNMA or Ginnie Mae) developed the first mortgage-backed security that passed through interest and

243

*Loan Analysis,
Credit Risk
Management,
and Loan
Securitization*

principal payments for 1–4 family home mortgage loans, known as mortgage-backed or pass-through securities. GSEs buy mortgage loans from banks and savings institutions and repackage them as securities. The Federal Home Loan Mortgage Corporation (FHLMC or Freddie Mac) developed similar pass-through securities and later the Federal National Mortgage Association (FNMA or Fannie Mae) followed with its own pass-through securities in 1981.

Private-sector securitization began in 1977 when Bank of America began securitizing conventional mortgages, and other innovative private-sector securitizations have followed including: *certificates of automobile receivables* (CARs), *credit card receivables* (certificates of amortizing revolving debts, CARDs), and *home equity and subprime loan securitizations*. For securitizations loans must be homogeneous (similar characteristics in terms of payments, maturity, risk, and other characteristics), so small business loans are more difficult to securitize. Large specialized credit card banks and other large financial services firms have been innovative in designing new types of securitizations for credit cards and other consumer loans.

Credit enhancements: Public securitizations generally have part of their issuance insured or have a standby letter of credit from large creditworthy banks to guarantee part of the issue in the event of default, with the guarantee bank receiving fee income. By having a credit enhancement, this reduces the risk of a securitization often raising an issue's credit rating.

Structure and Mechanics of Securitizations

Loans are removed from the balance sheet and packaged into securities with characteristics that make them attractive to large and small investors. Banks gain liquidity by receiving cash to make new loans. The mechanics of securitizations are subject to a wide variety of tax, securities, regulatory, and accounting laws.

Steps in securitizations include:

1   Banks sell pools of loans on a nonrecourse basis to a limited purpose corporation or special enterprise vehicle.
2   A limited purpose corporation (often an investment bank or special subsidiary) buys the loan pool, and a trust company is set up to purchase loans from the limited purpose company. The trust company packages the loans into certificates that can be sold to investors.
3   An agency rates the issue. Often a reserve for losses as well as credit guarantees from large creditworthy banks are included to gain a favorable rating.
4   The bank gets two forms of noninterest revenues:

   a   the profit made on selling the loans; and
   b   fees for continuing to service the loans over their life.

Example Pricing summary of a hypothetical automobile loan securitization with automobile receivables as collateral:

Details of securitization	
Face amount:	$500 million of automobile receivables
Amortization method: effective interest	

(Continued)

(Continued)

Maturity range: 18–48 months	
Weighted average maturity: 24 months	
Payment frequency: monthly	
Weighted average annual percentage rate (APR):	11%
Servicing fee:	2%
Excess servicing fee:	2%

Asset-backed security

Face amount:	$500 million
Coupon rate:	6% (monthly payments)
Maximum maturity:	4 years
Average life:	2 years

Proceeds

Gross (sold at par):	$500,000,000
Underwriting fee:	(2,500,000)
Issuing expenses:	(1,250,000)
1st year credit enhancement:	
(letter of credit for 10% value of cost of 1%)	(500,000)
Net proceeds:	$495,750,000
Plus present value of excess	
servicing flows	$20,800,000*
Net present value	$516,550,000

*The present value of excess servicing flows can be reported as income at the time of the sale under generally accepted accounting practices after the deduction of an appropriate loan loss and prepayment provisions. The NPV would be slightly less after deductions for the cost of subsequent credit enhancement. The added cost would be a function of the amount of actual loans outstanding in years 2, 3, and 4.

As shown in the example above, the bank originates the loans, sells the loans, and services the loans. A limited purpose company purchases the loans that are then immediately sold to a trust. The loans are enhanced for a fee by a guarantor (a very creditworthy bank), which issues a letter of credit or surety guaranty for a certain percentage of the loans (such as 10%). The trust that purchases the loans issues certificates that are sold to investors who own a portion of the loan pool and accordingly receive their share of interest and principal or prepayments if loans are prepaid by borrowers. Hence, investors take on the prepayment risk (risk of their investment maturing early and not getting the desired interest rate that they wanted).

The cash flows of the hypothetical automobile securitization are 11% loan interest. The interest is distributed as follows: The bank receives a 2% servicing fee and excess servicing fee of 2% (part of the fee is put in a reserve for loan losses); the credit-enhancing bank receives a 1% fee; and investors receive a pass-through rate on their securities of 6%. Investors receive scheduled interest and principal payments or prepayments as cash flows.

245

*Loan Analysis,
Credit Risk
Management,
and Loan
Securitization*

LOAN SALES

Financial institutions are also active in selling loans to other financial institutions, including pension funds, insurance companies, and other depository institutions. Loan sales have economic and risk-reducing advantages as due securitizations including: (1) receiving fee income as a broker; (2) reducing interest rate and credit risk for long-term loans that are sold; (3) gaining liquidity and the ability to make new loans for customers with funds received from selling the loans; (4) by removing loans from the balance sheet, capital requirements or insurance premium costs for deposits to finance the loans are removed from the balance sheet as well; and (5) by selling loans and purchasing other loans or mortgage securities geographical diversification of the loan portfolio can be achieved.

Types of loan sales include:

1 *Participation.* Originating bank continues to hold the formal contract between the bank and the borrower.
2 *Assignment.* The loan is assigned to the buyer, but the originating bank may retain the lien on any collateral backing the loan or some other obligations.
3 *Novation* (least common arrangement). All rights and obligations are transferred to the buyer and the originator is free of any legal obligations to the buyer or the borrower.
4 *Distressed loan sales.* Such as international loans that are sold at large discounts. With the Brady Plan of 1989 countries allowed, for instance, the exchange of loans for long-term bonds with longer maturities and more favorable terms with U.S. government guarantees for interest payments (debt for debt swaps). By the mid-1980s, a strong secondary market for trading less developed country debt emerged with large commercial banks and investment banks serving as brokers and dealers. Debt for equity swaps are also used to clean up distressed loans.
5 *Syndicated loans.* These are loans sold by large banks with prices quoted in the financial news. This market has become very large with prices quoted and data available through groups such as Reuters Loan Pricing Corporation. In this way, banks can abide by capital regulations concerning the amount that can be lent to one lender and reduce risk by having other banks take on portions of large loans.

STRUCTURED FINANCE TRANSACTION

Asset-Backed Commercial Paper (ABCP)

In addition to traditional securitizations, banks use structure securitizations to provide financing to businesses in creative ways that avoid limitations placed on banks in terms of the maximum that can be lent to a borrower or as a percentage of total capital and other regulatory restrictions. An example is asset-backed commercial paper (ABCP) that is used for off-balance sheet lending. With ABCP, accounts receivables of multiple corporate clients of banks are put in a special purpose vehicle (SPV). A trust in turn issues high-quality commercial paper backed by the underlying accounts receivables. Often credit enhancers are used, such as credit and liquidity lines from a bank or group of banks. The ABCP proceeds in turn are passed on to the corporate clients to use for liquidity needs and to pay for the accounts receivables that were sold. The advantage of ABCP is a lower cost of financing and access to markets for commercial paper that generally would require high credit ratings. Banks benefit by receiving fee income and better customer lending relationships.

Structured Project Finance Securitization

Similarly, project financing (for large public or capital-intensive projects) can be facilitated using structured finance. A special purpose vehicle (SPV) is created to issue debt serviced by cash flows from underlying assets held by the SPV. Long-term bank project loans are put in an SPV, which in turn issues senior and subordinated debt that will be serviced by cash flows that come from underlying projects. For instance, a bank may initiate the construction of a plant for a 2-year phase, with an SPV taking on the loan, thereafter removing the loans from the bank's balance sheet. Since banks don't like to take on permanent long-term financing of projects, the project financing securitization lessens the problem and provides cheaper fixed-rate financing than if the bank initiated the loan and later sold it to a long-term lender.

Catastrophe-Linked Securities

Insurance companies at times cannot get reinsurance to handle potential large losses, but can use structured finance arrangements, CAT bonds, as a solution to this problem. With a CAT bond, similar to other structured bonds a remote SPV is set that is backed by collateral provided by an insurance firm.

With a CAT bond the securities are issued by the SPV for the risk of a catastrophic loss in a particular region, such as a hurricane in Florida. The coupon rate on the bond is set to be greater than the return on the collateral for the bond, with the excess premiums from the insurer paying for the excess return. The SPV in effect serves as a reinsurance contract for the insurance firm against the risk of a larger loss than expected. The cash proceeds from the security issuance is usually invested in high-quality fixed-income investments that generate funds to use for payments against claims, with the yield that bondholders receive conditional on whether the insurance firms files claims for excess losses above the expected (attachment) point.

SUMMARY

Loans are the largest category of assets for depository institutions, and although depository institutions specialize in different types of loans, all depositories share important elements of successful lending. Lending policies must incorporate specific objectives for the size, composition, maturity, interest rate characteristics, and default risk of the loan portfolio. Procedures for evaluating and approving loan applications and careful credit analysis are entailed to achieve these objectives. Similarly, the loan structure of a loan should be carefully prepared to help ensure loan prepayment by a borrower. The pricing of the loan should be carefully determined to provide a desired profit for the bank and protect the bank against losses, including a capital charge for expected losses, such as under risk-adjusted return on capital models. Environmental liability and Community Reinvest Act assessments are also very important

247

*Loan Analysis,
Credit Risk
Management,
and Loan
Securitization*

considerations for lenders. With large amounts of loans securitized, a careful securitization process, including having diversified loans for securitization pools, is very important.

BIBLIOGRAPHY

Allen, Linda, Jacob Boudoukh, and Anthony Saunders (2003). *Understanding Market, Credit, and Operational Risks: The Value at Risk Approach*. London: Blackwell Publishing.

Altman, Edward I (1968). "Financial ratios, discriminant analysis and the prediction of corporate bankruptcy." *Journal of Finance*, 23 (September), 589–609.

Altman, Edward I (1983). *Corporate Financial Distress*. New York: John Wiley.

Altman, E. I., R. G. Haldemann, and P. Narayanan (1997). "ZETA Analysis: A new model to identify bankruptcy risk of corporations." *Journal of Banking and Finance*, 1–29.

Board of Governors (2015). "Mortgage debt outstanding." Board of Governors of the Federal Reserve System, December 2015, Accessed on February 21, 2016 at: http://www.federalreserve.gov/econresdata/releases/mortoutstand/current.htm

CFPB (2014). "2014 CFPB Dodd–Frank mortgage rules readiness guide." Consumer Financial Protection Bureau, September 2014. Accessed on February 20, 2016 at: http://files.consumerfinance.gov/f/201409_cfpb_readiness-guide_mortgage-implementation.pdf

DeGroat, Bernie (2009). "Subprime mortgage crisis: Failure to predict failure." News Service University of Michigan, Record Update, September 8, 2009, p. 1. Accessed on March 30, 2015 at: http://www.ur.umich.edu/update/archives/090325/28

FDIC (2015a). "Industry statistics at a glance." Federal Deposit Insurance Corporation. Accessed on February 20, 2016 at: https://www.fdic.gov/bank/statistical/stats/2015sep/industry.pdf

FDIC (2015b). "Quarterly banking profile." Federal Deposit Insurance Corporation. Accessed on February 20, 2016 at: https://www.fdic.gov/bank/analytical/qbp/2015sep/all2a.html

FDIC (2015c). "Statistics at a glance." Federal Deposit Insurance Corporation. Accessed on February 20, 2016 at: https://www.fdic.gov/bank/statistical/stats/2015sep/fdic.pdf

Gruenberg, Martin J., (2015). "FDIC-insured institutions earn $40.4 billion in third quarter 2015," FDIC Press Release, November 24, 2015. Accessed on April 15, 2016 at: www.fdic.gov

QUESTIONS AND PROBLEMS

Questions

1 Why do banks need an overall lending policy? What does a bank's lending policy include? Explain the lender's role in bringing business to the bank. How can this role conflict with the lender's credit analysis role? How have lender compensation policies created moral hazard problems? How can these lender policies be changed to encourage lenders to make "good" loans?

2 What are the 5 C's of credit? How are each of these measured objectively?

3 Why are loan-to-value ratios important in making collateralized loans, such as home mortgages? Explain what a loan-to-value ratio is and the rules of thumb for lending on collateral.

4 Explain what a quantitative scoring model is, such as Zeta Analysis. Why have these models been popular? In the quote by Professor Uday Rajan at the beginning of the chapter, what criticisms are made for lending based on quantitative score models alone. What are the limitations of these models?

5   What are some noninterest terms and conditions for structuring a loan? Include in your discussion compensating balances, loan commitments, loan fees, and discounts (or points). How do these increase the actual annual percentage rate for a loan?

6   How are risk premiums on loans set? Give an example including RAROC? How do restrictive covenants help to protect a lender? Give some examples of restrictive covenants that could protect a depository institution's interests.

7   Briefly define the following types of loans: seasonable working capital loans, term loans, commercial real estate/construction loans, and agricultural loans. What special considerations need to be made for each of these respective loans?

8   Discuss how consumer installment loan rates are set. What is the effect on the actual annual percentage rate for these loans?

9   Explain how home equity loans differ from second mortgage loans. Define and explain special details and risks for ARMs, GPMs, RAMs, GEM, and PLAMs.

10 Discuss how securitizations are created. What are the advantages and disadvantages of securitizations? What moral hazard problem can they create? What solutions can be imposed to reduce the risks of securitizations?

Problems

1   Minicase: The Bronco Badges Company has applied for a loan and has projected the financial statements for next year shown in Table P9.1. Answer the following questions for the bank thinking about lending to the Bronco Badge Company.

    a   Fill in the missing items in the sources and uses statement and indirect cash flow statement. How much does the firm need to borrow next year?

    b   Based on the uses (increases in assets in this case) for funds for next year, how would you structure the loan in terms of short-term notes payable (1 year or less maturity) and long-term debt?

    c   Analyze the projected key ratios compared with last year's ratios and the industry averages. What strengths and weaknesses does Bronco Badges have?

    d   As a lender, what other types of information would you like to know about the company or its managers in determining whether to grant the loan?

    e   How would you price the loan? What kind of loan structure (maturity, terms, loan covenants and collateral) would you suggest?

TABLE P9.1 | Exhibits: Current and financial statements projected for Bronco Badges Company

Income statement projected (in $ million)	
Sales	3,000
CGS	1,000
Gross profit	2,000
Depreciation	500

249

*Loan Analysis,
Credit Risk
Management,
and Loan
Securitization*

Operating costs				500
Operating profit				1,000
Interest expense				200
Earnings before tax				800
Taxes (30%)				240
Net income				560
Dividends				380
Addition to retained earnings				180

Balance sheets ($ millions)

Balance sheets	Projected	Last year	Source	Use
Cash	500	450		50
Accounts receivable	1000	900		100
Inventory	1500	1350		150
Net fixed assets	2000	1800		200
Accounts payable	500	450	50	
Accruals	500	450	50	
Notes payable	?	142	?	
Long-term debt	?	500	?	
Common stock	2000	2000		
Retained earnings	1138	958	180	
Total		500		500

Indirect cash flow statement projects for next year

1. Cash flow from operations ($ million)

Net income	560
+ Depreciation expense	500
− Rise in accounts receivable	(100)
− Rise in inventory	(150)
+ Rise in accounts payable	50
+ Rise in accruals	50
Cash flow from operations	910

2. Cash flow from investing activities ($ million)

Change in gross fixed assets:	
Change in net fixed assets	200

(Continued)

TABLE P9.1 | (Continued)

Income statement projected (in $ million)

+ Depreciation expense	<u>500</u>
Cash used for investing activities 700	

3. *Cash flow from financing activities*

– Dividends paid	(380)
+ Increase in notes payable	?
+ Increase in long-term debt	<u>?</u>
Cash flow from financing	?
Change in cash = CFO – CFI + CFF = 910 – 700 – ? = 50	
Beginning cash balance	450
Ending cash balance	500

Financial ratios and other information for projected and current year

Key information	Projected year	Current year	Projected growth
Sales ($ million)	3,000	2,700	+ 11.11%
Total assets ($ million)	5,000	4,500	+ 11.11%
Financial ratios	*Projected*	*Current year*	*Peer average*
Overall profitability			
Return on equity (ROE)	17.8%	21.3%	25%
Return on assets (ROA)	11.2%	14.0%	15%
Debt to assets	37.2%	34.2%	40%
Equity multiplier	1.59 x	1.52 x	1.67 x
Cost efficiency			
Net profit margin (NPM)	18.67%	23.33%	30%
Operating profit margin (OPM)	33.33%	40.00%	45%
Gross profit margin (GPM)	66.67%	70.00%	80%
Asset utilization			
Total asset turnover	0.6 x	0.6 x	0.5 x
Fixed asset turnover	1.5 x	1.5 x	1.2 x
Inventory turnover	0.67 x	0.6 x	0.7 x
Average collection period	122 days	122 days	120 days
Bankruptcy risk			
Times interest earned	5 x	6 x	5 x
Liquidity risk			
Current ratio	3 x	3 x	3.5 x
Quick ratio	1.5 x	1.5 x	2.0 x

2   The Bank of Mountain View is negotiating with a company Enchanted Forest Delights in Santa Fe, New Mexico. The 1-year agreement requires a 0.20% loan commitment fee for a $4 million line of credit, with a 12% compensating balance on the entire commitment and an additional 1% fee on the amount actually borrowed. The annual percentage stated rate on the loan is 8%. The firm expects to use on average 85% of the line. What is the actual annual effective rate for the loan?

3   What is the annual yield on a 1-year consumer loan if interest is discounted, and the stated rate is 10%?

4   What is the effective annual rate for a home mortgage loan for $100,000 with annual loan payments for 15 years and a stated annual rate of 6%, with two points on the loan?

5   You are planning on purchasing a car for $24,000 and will make a 20% down payment. A finance company will finance the remaining payment at an 11% add on rate for 48 months (4 years). What is the annual percentage rate?

Suggested Loan Analysis Case Studies (Darden School and Harvard Business School Case Catalogs)

Darden School cases: Padgett Blank Book Company on "Structuring a term loan"; Hoosier Hose Company on "Restructuring a troubled seasonal loan"; and Patriots Hall on "Evaluating a proposed commercial bank loan."

Harvard Business School: U.S. Bank of Washington Case by Elizabeth R. Lawrence, Case 9-292-057, "Loan analysis for Redhook Ale Brewery."

Useful links for financial analysis and market information:
www.finance.yahoo.com
www.sec.gov
http://www.sec.gov/edgar.shtml

Chapter 10

Liquidity and Liability Management

Uninsured bank debt is vulnerable to panic … [t]he panic starting in August 2007 involved firms withdrawing from other firms by increasing repo haircuts. [A] banking panic occurs when information-insensitive debt becomes information sensitive due to a shock, in this case, the shock to subprime mortgage values due to house prices falling.

(Gorton, 2010, pp.16–17)

Liquidity is the ability of a bank to fund increases in assets and meet obligations as they come due, without incurring unacceptable losses…. Liquidity risk management is of paramount importance because a liquidity shortfall at a single institution can have system-wide repercussions. Financial market developments in the past decade have increased the complexity of liquidity risk and its management.

(Bank for International Settlements, 2008, p.1).

ALMOST all financial institutions, by their nature, are subject to investment management and liquidity problems related to potential withdrawals by liability holders, including policyholders for insurance companies, uninsured depositors and other liabilities for depository institutions, and for open-ended mutual funds when many investors redeem shares in a market downturn. Securities firms also borrow short-term to finance security inventories, often with very short-term borrowings, such as repurchase agreements for which they need collateral. If the value of the collateral declines in value or funding sources quickly withdraw, this can cause a severe liquidity problem as during the subprime crisis for Lehman Brothers, and many other firms. Given the importance of liquidity for a financial institution's survival, regulators also impose liquidity requirements, which have increased for major financial institutions under new regulations, including the Dodd–Frank Act and under Basel III.

Access to cash is important in the financial management of all businesses, since often providing liquidity for customers is an intermediation function. Depository institutions obtain many deposits with the promise of immediate or almost immediate repayment on demand, so the investment and financing decision for a depository institution are closely intertwined. Liquidity is also important for depository institutions for regulatory purposes to have sufficient liquidity for deposit transactions and for holding required reserves with a central bank, as well as having sufficient liquidity for future borrowing needs by their customers. Pledged deposits from governments held by banks also often are required to be kept in liquid, safe securities. Depository institutions use both liquidity and liability management to assure they have sufficient liquidity for both deposit withdrawals and loan commitments to satisfy important loan customers. As noted in the beginning quote, contagion occurred during the U.S. subprime crisis with large purchased fund withdrawals from major financial institutions, putting them on the brink of bankruptcy, necessitating government rescues. This chapter examines liquidity and liability management for financial institutions, focusing primarily on depository institutions.

IMPORTANCE OF LIQUIDITY MANAGEMENT UNDER BASEL III

As of December 2010, the Basel Committee on Banking Supervision issued Basel III's International Framework for Liquidity Risk Measurement, Standards, and Monitoring. With the global financial crisis, both regulators and financial institutions recognized the importance of liquidity and the need to include liquidity in the risk management framework of financial institutions. As noted in a report by Ernst & Young (2011), a majority of large financial services firms have invested in data and technology to enhance their liquidity risk management frameworks to improve their reporting and stress testing capabilities. This includes the incorporation of liquidity within both enterprise risk and funds transfer pricing as a core part of proactive balance sheet management within a strategic planning framework. The new Basel III rules require the *liquidity coverage ratio* (*LCR*) to be met from January 2015 on for large international financial institutions, following previous observation and adjustment periods. The *net stable funding ratio* (*NSFR*) will also be required and will have a longer observation period with an introduction planned for January 2018 (Ernst & Young, 2011).

The *liquidity coverage ratio* (*LCR*) applies to internationally active banking organizations with $250 billion or more in consolidated assets or $10 billion or more in off-balance sheet foreign exposure. In the United States the Federal Reserve Board separately adopted in 2015 a less stringent, modified LCR requirement for bank holding companies and saving and loan holding companies with $50 billion or more in total consolidated assets that are not internationally active and do not have significant nonbanking types of activities, such as insurance operations. Basically, the LCR ratio is the ratio of an institution's high-quality liquid assets (HQLA) relative to its projected net cash outflows over a 30-day period. At full implementation, a large, international depository institution will be required to maintain an LCR equal or greater than 100% (i.e., hold HQLA that are equal or greater than its projected total net cash outflows over this 30-day period). There are three different levels of HQLA (level 1, level 2A, and level 2B) that are defined, including qualifying criteria and limits for inclusion in HQLA. The transition for LCR is 80% by January 1, 2015, 90% for January 1, 2016, and 100% by January 1, 2017 (BIS, 2013; OCC 2014).

The *net stable funding ratio* is basically the amount of stable funding that is available (based on the reliable portion of capital and liabilities over a given time period) divided by the required amount of stable funding required for a specific institutions. The amount of stable funding required is based on the liquidity characteristics and residual maturities of various assets held by the institution as well as off-balance sheet exposures (BIS, 2014).

In addition, banks are required to observe the Principles for Sound Liquidity Risk Management and Supervision set out in September 2008 and used in the foundation for the U.S. Interagency Policy Statement on Funding and Liquidity Risk Management introduced in 2010. Also, in the United States, the Dodd–Frank Wall Street Reform and Consumer Protection Act calls for the enhancement of prudential requirements for liquidity and capital for financial service institutions (Ernst & Young, 2011).

Under the BIS Principles for Sound Liquidity Risk Management (BIS, 2008), more detailed guidance is provided for large, international banks including:

- Establishing a liquidity risk tolerance
- Maintaining adequate liquidity, including a cushion of liquid assets
- Allocating liquidity costs, benefits, and risks to significant business activities
- Identifying and measuring a full range of liquidity risk, including "contingent liquidity risks"
- Designing and using "severe stress test scenarios"
- Managing intraday liquidity risk and collateral
- Promoting market discipline, public disclosure.

An interesting aspect of the BIS Principles and for U.S. Interagency Policy Statement is the importance of corporate governance in managing liquidity, including articulating a financial institution's risk tolerance in its business strategy. Also senior management is asked to develop strategy, policies, and practices to manage liquidity risk in accordance with this risk tolerance to ensure that a bank has sufficient liquidity. Liquidity costs, benefits, and risk are to be incorporated in the institution's internal pricing and practices, performance measurement, and new product approval process for significant business activities both on and off balance sheet. Other guidance includes putting together a sound process for identifying, monitoring, and controlling liquidity risk, and having active monitoring and control for liquidity risk exposures and funding tends. Firms are also asked to have a diversified funding strategy, including strong relationships with fund providers on the liability side. Other guidance includes active management of intraday liquidity positions and risks to meet payment and settlement obligations in a timely way, and managing and monitoring collateral positions. Banks are asked to have a formal contingency funding plan (CFP), which provides clear sets of strategies to address liquidity shortfalls in emergency situations, and to have a cushion of *unencumbered, high-quality liquid assets* as insurance against different liquidity stress scenarios.

LIQUIDITY: THE RISK/RETURN TRADE-OFF

Liquid assets, such as cash and marketable securities, have low rates, so financial institutions have a return/liquidity trade-off to negotiate between the risk of illiquidity and earning lower returns. There is also the trade-off between depending on short-term borrowing (liability management) for liquidity, which allows a financial institution to hold a lower amount of cash and short-term securities, but has greater risk as a strategy. With greater liability management, the financial institution depends on having sources readily available for borrowing, which could dry up if other financial institutions offer higher returns or there is bad news about the financial institutions. Hence, since these are short-term borrowing, they have the risk for the potential, if rates rise or a risk premium is imposed on a financial institution, of the financial institution having a much higher interest expense, as well as not being able to renew borrowing relationships. This was the case for Lehman Brothers and other large financial institutions depending on liability management for short-term funds during the subprime loan crisis.

Central banks require depository institutions to hold reserves with the central bank for monetary policy purposes. Hence deposits held with the Fed or another central bank cannot be used to meet liquidity needs. Hence, liquidity available for normal and unexpected loan demand and deposit withdrawals must be estimated above amounts of vault cash and deposits held with a central bank, such as a Federal Reserve Bank or, for smaller depository institutions, held with a larger correspondent bank in a pass-through relationship for reserves required to be held as reserves with the Fed. Hence, depository institutions must also engage in reserve management to ensure they are holding adequate reserves and at the same time avoiding opportunity costs of holding too many reserves, as illiquid assets.

EXAMPLE: RESERVE REQUIREMENTS REQUIRED BY THE U.S. FED

Under the Federal Reserve Board's Regulation D, reserves must be held on net transaction accounts. Statutory formulas specified in the Federal Reserve Act require adjustments to be made annually. As shown in Table 10.1, in 2016 the Fed amended Regulation D, Reserve Requirements of Depository Institutions, to reflect the annual indexing for the reserve requirement exemption amount for the low reserve tranche. At the time of this writing in 2016, a *0% reserve requirement* was set for *$15.2 million of net transaction deposits* (rise from $14.5 million in 2015) that in effect is *exempt from holding reserves*. The amendment also set the amount of net transaction accounts at each depository institution *greater than the exemption amount* known as the *low reserve tranche* at *$110.2 million* (from $103.6 million in 2015) to be subject to a *3% reserve requirement*. For deposits over this low reserve tranche, the reserve requirement is *10% of the amount over $110.2 million*. At this time, there was a 0% reserve requirement *for nonpersonal time deposits and euro-currency liabilities* (Board of Governors, 2015, 2016). Annual updates can be found on the Federal Reserve website (www.federalreserve.gov/monetarypolicy/reservereq.htm).

Required reserves must be held as vault cash, and if vault cash is insufficient also in the form of deposits maintained with a Federal Reserve Bank. Reserve requirements are imposed on commercial banks, savings banks, savings and loan associations, credit unions, U.S. branches and agencies of foreign banks, Edge Act corporations, and agreement corporations.

Net transaction accounts are calculated by taking total transaction accounts less any demand balances due, less cash in the process of collection. The total vault cash held over a 2-week lagged computation period is subtracted, since it contributes to the reserve requirement, leaving the total required reserves to be held at the Fed during the maintenance period.

As an example, suppose a bank has net transaction deposits of $600 million, the first $15.25 million will be exempt, so reserve requirements will be required for $600 million less

TABLE 10.1 | Federal Reserve depository institution reserve requirements 2016

Liability type	Requirement	
	% of liabilities	*Effective date*
Net transaction accounts		
$0 – $15.2 million	0	1/21/16
More than $15.2 million – $110.2 million	3	1/21/16
More than $110.2 million	10	1/21/16
Nonpersonal time deposits	0	12/27/90
Eurocurrency liabilities	0	12/27/90

Source: Board of Governors of the Federal Reserve System https://www.federalreserve.gov/monetarypolicy/reservereq.htm

$15.2 million equal to $584.8 million. For the first $110.2 million the reserve requirement is *($110.2 million x 0.03), which for this example equals $3.306 million*. The remaining $584.8 million less $110.2 million is $474.6 million that will have an additional reserve requirement of *(0.10 x $474.6 million), which equals $47.46 million*, so the total reserve requirement will be $3.306 million plus $47.46 million equal to *$50.766 million total reserves* required to be held in vault cash or with a Federal Reserve Bank.

MANAGING THE RESERVE POSITION

As of 2016, the Fed requires depository institutions with net transaction accounts greater than $15.2 million or with total transaction accounts, savings deposits, and small time deposits of $1.901 or greater to file a *Report of Transaction Accounts, Other Deposits and Vault Cash* (*FR 2900 report*) either weekly or quarterly, depending on the size of the bank. Institutions with total deposits greater than the $15.2 million, but with total transaction accounts, savings deposits, and small time deposits less than $1.901 billion only have to file an annual report of deposits and reservable liabilities (FR, 2910a report).

The Federal Reserve Bank now pays interest on required reserve balances and excess reserve balances, under the Financial Services Regulatory Relief Act of 2006, which went into effect advanced to October 1, 2008 by the Emergency Economic Stabilization Act of 2008. The Board of Governors of the Federal Reserve System determines the interest rate on required reserves (IORR rate), which was established to eliminate an implicit tax that was previously imposed on depository institutions by the Fed not paying interest. The interest rate on excess reserves (IOER rate) also provides the Fed with an additional tool that can be used for the conduct of monetary policy. At the March 2015 Federal Open Market Committee (FOMC) meeting, the minutes noted that the FOMC intended to set the IOER rate equal to the top of the target range for the Fed Funds rate, with evaluations for the appropriate settings in the future to be based on evolving market conditions, with adjustments made as needed. As of December 17, 2015, the IORR rate was set at 0.50% and the IOER rate at 0.50%.

Large banks have reserve desks, where Fed Funds are sold daily to keep the reserve position at the optimum level. Branches report their deposits during the day and any large changes in deposits, so the bank can forecast its reserve requirements relative to the reserves it is holding. If an institution's reserves are greater than 4% below the daily average minimum reserve required, it is subject to a penalty imposed by the Federal Reserve. If there is a deficit or excess of 4%, the deficit or excess can be carried over into the next 2-week reserve period. Depositories attempt to estimate their reserve requirements as accurately as possible.

DISCRETIONARY AND NONDISCRETIONARY FACTORS INVOLVED IN LIQUIDITY MANAGEMENT

Financial institution liquidity management includes discretionary items (that can be forecast or acted upon such as repurchase agreements or Fed Funds) and nondiscretionary items, such as unexpected deposit fluctuations, loan demand, and reserve requirements. The better a depository institution can forecast its expected loan demands and deposit withdrawals, the lower excess liquidity it needs to hold. Often depository institutions separate out liquid and illiquid assets and funding sources into volatile and nonvolatile funding source categories. For example, liquid assets include cash and short-term investments and other liquid assets, and core (insured deposits) and less volatile sources of funding versus uninsured deposits and other short-term borrowings. By predicting additional loan demand, net liquid assets equal liquid assets less expected loan demand. For instance, if liquid assets held were $645 million and loan demand expected was $12.1 million, net liquid assets held would be $633 million. Then the banks liquidity deficit would be equal to liquid assets held less volatile funds, for this example equal to $633 million less $679.7 million, which equals $46.7 million. The bank could then line up sources of liquidity to cover this liquidity deficit, such as selling long-term securities, securitizing or selling loans, or issuing additional short-term liabilities, such as Fed Funds purchased, repurchase agreements, short-term borrowings, commercial paper, and/or other short-term liabilities.

BORROWING VERSUS SELLING SECURITIES

Two general liquidity management strategies are available. One strategy is to use stored liquidity by liquidating assets from the securities portfolio, although if market interest rates are high, this approach can be undesirable particularly if securities are being used for other purposes, such as generating income. The second approach is to use liability management by borrowing funds either from regulatory agencies or from nondeposit or uninsured depositors in financial markets. Factors that influence which strategy is used primarily by a depository institution include size and financial stability, with very large financial institutions that are active in financial markets with high credit ratings more able to engage in purchased funds strategies. Smaller financial institutions have to depend more on stored liquidity strategies. Risk/return preferences are also important, since liability management exposes an institution to greater risk when cash is needed, particularly at times when an institution is facing liquidity difficulties.

BORROWING FROM REGULATORY AGENCIES AS A SOURCE OF LIQUIDITY

The Discount Window

Central banks in most countries allow for temporary emergency borrowing for insured depository institutions. In the United States, the Fed administers discount window borrowing under Regulation A, which allows institutions to borrow under three conditions to meet temporary liquidity needs, including: (1) to meet seasonal credit demands, such as for rural banks during planting season; (2) for special "extended credit" purposes, after disasters, such as hurricanes, among others; and (3) when unusually heavy withdrawals occur, such as uninsured deposit runs, as occurred during the U.S. subprime loan crisis. For banks the interest cost and availability of these borrowings and collateral needed to be posted are major factors in the decision to use the discount window. Ordinarily banks have to post risk-free collateral, such as Treasury securities, and borrowings are very short-term and only used to meet genuine liquidity emergencies.

FHLB Advances

The Federal Home Loan Banks (FHLB), as privately owned wholesale banks, raise funds by selling AAA-rated bonds to investors, which allows the FHLB to lend money at low rates (smaller spreads over comparable Treasuries) to member banks than other privately offered debt. In 1999, the Financial Services Modernization Act amended the authority of the FHLB to make advances secured by small enterprise loans of community financial institutions as well. In the event of emergencies, eligible institutions must be solvent and must present substantial evidence that they can repay the debt. The FHLB was originally chartered in the United States by Congress in 1932 to provide member financial institutions with financial products and services to promote housing and community lending. Eleven FHLBs were originally set up as cooperatives owned by member financial institutions and now include all types of depository institutions (savings associations, commercial banks, and credit unions, as well as insurance companies) with over 7,300 regulated financial institutions in 50 states.

Members must purchase stock in the FHLB, which gives them accessibility to low-cost financing and the receipt of dividends based on their percentage of stock ownership. Members get access to liquidity through secured loans as advances that are financed by FHLBs financing in the capital markets, including discount notes and term debt, with each FHLB having a requirement to register at least one type of equity with the SEC. Each FHLB offers different products and services, which can include overnight funding, short-term advances, long-term advances, fixed-rate advances, variable-index advances, and funding for community development (FHLB Boston, 2016).

Sources of Borrowing for Credit Unions

For credit unions, three sources of short-term funds are available, two of the three from regulatory sources. The Central Liquidity Facility (CLF) is an arm of the National Credit Union Administration and functions as a lender of last resort for CUs that voluntarily choose to join it.

In contrast to FHLB advances, CLF loans are made for liquidity purposes only. Borrowing CUs pay in additional to interest a loan commitment fee of 1%. Fed discount window loans are also available to CUs that offer transaction deposits or nonpersonal time deposits. CUs that are members of a corporate credit union (CCU) may also borrow from the CCU.

THE SECURITIES PORTFOLIO AS A SOURCE OF STORED LIQUIDITY

Depository Institutions use their investment portfolios for both income purposes and for liquidity purposes. When loan demand goes down, investment portfolios get bigger as a source of countercyclical income. For liquidity purposes, under a *stored liquidity approach*, institutions keep a pyramid of reserves, with cash above reserve requirements as primary reserves, along with short-term marketable securities that are not pledged for public deposits (government deposits that require funds be put in Treasury or safe agency securities) as *secondary reserves*. Mortgage securities and other longer-term investment grade securities are used as tertiary reserves that can be sold if necessary. Banks are required to classify their securities as *available for sale* that must be reported at fair market value or *held to maturity* securities that can be reported at book value.

Banks have multiple goals for their holdings of investments, including: (1) to provide stored liquidity; (2) to provide income, particularly when loan demand is low to keep funds fully employed; (3) to satisfy pledging requirements (uninsured deposits by governments, such as tax funds often require that these be held in liquid, safe securities, making these deposits unavailable for use in making loans; (4) to reduce taxes by holding municipal securities that are not taxed at a state level or taking a loss on securities to offset other security gains; and (5) to use the portfolio to make adjustments for the bank's asset and liabilities position, including the bank's overall capital and interest rate risk. Banks generally prefer maturities on the security portfolio to have a maximum maturity of 10 years or less. The security portfolio is generally used to reduce (rather than increase) a bank's overall risk.

Alternative strategies that are used for investments to meet liquidity needs include:

1   *Ladder strategy:* where a portfolio is held that is diversified across maturities, so that a certain percentage of the investment portfolio is maturing each year to meet liquidity needs. This strategy is advantageous for small community banks as a passive strategy that takes less investment expertise. However, studies suggest that although the strategy has less risk, the return is lower than the potential return with other strategies.
2   *Barbell (or split maturity) strategy:* where depending on market conditions, investments are held in short-term or long-term maturity ranges. If interest rates are expected to rise, a larger amount of the portfolio would be in short-term securities to avoid capital losses with rising rates; and if interest rates are expected to fall, a larger amount of the portfolio would be in long-term securities to maximize capital gains. The barbell strategy can generate higher potential returns on investments, but carries more risk of losses in the event interest rate guesses are incorrect.
3   *Hybrid barbell strategy:* where part of the portfolio is held as a ladder approach and part using a barbell approach. This strategy is less risky than a complete barbell strategy.

4   *Buffer strategy:* where a larger portion of the portfolio is concentrated in the short-term end of the maturity schedule, which allows the portfolio to serve as a buffer against even the slightest risk of cash shortages. This strategy has lower liquidity risk, but a lower potential return with the average maturity lower than under the ladder or barbell approach.

Depository institutions are limited in the types of securities that they can hold, which must be investment grade securities (triple B or better ratings) and cannot be equity securities. Hence, the majority of depository institution investments are fixed-income securities. Regulators classify securities into three groups.

Tier 1 securities are securities that carry very low or no default risk, such as U.S. Treasuries, federal agency, and general obligation municipal bonds that are backed by the taxing power of the state or municipal government issuing the bonds. These can generally be held in unlimited amounts.

Tier 2 securities include quasi-public, federal and municipal agency securities, and selected state agencies with public projects, such as housing or universities, with restrictions that no more than 15% of a bank's capital and surplus can be invested in any single issuer.

Tier 3 securities encompass investment grade securities (BBB/B as ratings or better), with no more than 10% of capital and surplus in any single issue. Any issues underwritten or dealt in by the bank are disallowed. There are no specific restrictions on maturity, but as a rule of thumb, banks often do not like to hold securities with maturities greater than ten years, since this increases their interest rate risk, and at times securities are held to reduce a bank's overall interest rate risk profile.

Banks cannot hold common stock in another corporation as part of an investment portfolio. Banks must also distinguish between "investment" securities to be held to maturity (held at book value) and securities available for sales (that must be held at market value with gains and losses taken). Trading securities also must be held at market value. Regulators have permitted banks to own mutual funds for security types that they are allowed to hold, up to 10% of a bank's capital and surplus, with shares required to be marked to market, discouraging banks from investing in mutual funds.

TYPICAL TYPES OF SECURITIES HELD BY U.S. DEPOSITORY INSTITUTIONS

As of December 31, 2015, all U.S. FDIC insured banks and savings institutions (as reported at: https://www5.fdic.gov/SDI/SOB/) held about 21% of total assets in securities and 2.28% in Fed Funds and reverse repurchase agreements. The percentage of securities held to total assets was about 20.93%, with the following types and maturities held in 2015 shown in Table 10.2.

Smaller banks hold smaller percentages of long-term securities over 15 years than large banks, given larger banks have more access to different market and choices for liability management. For all FDIC-insured institutions 7.53% of total securities held were pledged securities for government deposits, about 6.97% were mortgage-backed securities as a percentage of total assets, and 20.50% were debt securities relative to total assets. For the about

TABLE 10.2 | Maturity and repricing data for debt securities for FDIC-insured depository institutions in 2015

Percentage held to total average assets

Mortgage pass-through securities backed by closed-end first lien for 1–4 residential mortgages	
3 months or less	0.18%
Over 3 months to 12 months	0.11%
Over 1 year to 3 years	0.12%
Over 3 years to 5 years	0.15%
Over 5 years to 15 years	1.87%
Over 15 years	4.62%
CMOs, REMICs and stripped MBS (excluding mortgage pass-through securities) with an expected average life of:	
3 years or less	1.04%
Over 3 years	3.23%
Other debt securities	
3 months or less	2.05%
Over 3 months to 12 months	0.57%
Over 1 year to 3 years	1.61%
Over 3 years to 5 years	1.94%
Over 5 years to 15 years	2.57%
Over 15 years	0.88%
Fixed and floating rate debt securities (including above)	
With remaining maturity of 1 year or less	0.90%

Notes: CMO, collateralized mortgage obligation; REMICs, real estate mortgage investment conduits; MBS, mortgage-backed securities.

Source: FDIC (2016) at www.fdic.gov

20.50% debt securities to assets for all institutions only 4.43% to total assets were classified as held to maturity securities held at book value and 16.13% to total assets (about 78.68% of total securities held) were available for sale, held at market value.

DIFFERENT TYPES OF AGENCY AND MORTGAGE-BACKED SECURITIES

Agency securities held by depository institutions include those backed by the U.S. government with the primary purpose of reducing the cost of borrowing against these and increasing the accessibility to funds to particular sectors as collateral, such as for repurchase agreements. Agency securities from government-sponsored agencies that have become private, generally still have a lower cost of funds than other private firms, as quasi-public agencies, that investors assume will implicitly be bailed out. The Government National Mortgage Association (GNMA or Ginnie Mae) is a federal government agency owned by the U.S. government, as are the Federal Housing Administration (FHA) and the Export–Import Bank.

Different types of mortgage-backed securities (MBS) include mortgage-backed bonds, certificates of participation in pools of residential mortgages (either issued or guaranteed by the U.S. government or privately issues), and CMOs.

Mortgage-backed bonds are simply bonds collateralized by mortgages on a financial institution's balance sheet and thus are not securitizations. Banks, for example, can offer bonds with a lower coupon rate, for bonds collateralized by specific mortgage assets on the bank's balance sheet that provides investors with lower risk.

Mortgage pass-through securities or certificates of participation in pools of residential mortgages, in contrast, are securitizations whereby shares in the interest and principal payment on a pool of mortgages are passed on to investors who purchase these securities.

Collateralized mortgage obligations (CMOs), like stripped securities are securities that are created from mortgage pass-through securities with more favorable characteristics than plain vanilla pass-throughs. They can also be pass-throughs originally packaged into several classes (tranches) of securities with different characteristics for each tranche appealing to different types of investors. An issuer of CMOs takes a pool of mortgages and converts them into different maturities. When mortgage holders prepay their mortgages in a pool of mortgages, investors holding the first class (or A-class or tranche) of bonds are repaid their principal payments first. B-class investors are paid off next, then C-class, and so on. Thus, A-class investors have mortgage securities with the lowest expected maturity, B-class the next, and later classes, the highest maturities. Consequently, investors have less prepayment uncertainty than they would with ordinary pass-through securities. This also provides investors with better estimates in terms of the likely maturity and yield that should be offered on a particular type of CMO relative to a similar maturity Treasury security with no prepayment risk.

There are many different types of CMOs. A plain vanilla CMO may have four tranches A, B, C, and Z, with class C receiving no periodic interest until the other three tranches are retired, with at that time the *Z tranche investors* receiving cash payments from the remaining underlying collateral (remaining mortgage pool) for principal plus accrued interest (so they are often called accrual bonds). Z-bonds, hence, are similar to zero coupon bonds and have the most interest rate risk. A *planned amortization class (PAC)* bond is a CMO with lower risk by having a fixed amortization schedule, so investors can better predict when a particular tranche of bonds will mature. If actual prepayment rates differ from the expected prepayment rates, principal payments to designated tranches are reduced or increased to ensure that PAC CMOs mature as scheduled. Stripped mortgage-backed securities separate securities into classes of *interest only (IO)* and *principal only (PO)* paying securities. With prepayment risk, POs and IOs are very interest rate sensitive.

If interest rates fall significantly, IOs decline in market value, since the maturity of the security is shortened with prepayments. If rates rise significantly, however, the prepayment risk falls for IOs, increasing their market value, since the expected maturity and number of interest payments expected increases. In contrast, for POs, if interest rates fall, their market values rise since the principal payments are discounted at a lower rate and cash flows are expected to come in sooner with repayments. When interest rates rise, the market value of POs falls, with a higher discount rate for cash flows that are now expected to come later.

Regulators discourage the holdings of IOs and POs by financial institutions, since they entail greater interest rate and prepayment risks.

Hence, for financial institutions that hold mortgage-backed securities, they need to examine their prepayment risk as well as credit and interest rate risk. When interest rates fall approximately 2% below the average mortgage rate on a pool of securities, prepayments rise with the pool of mortgage borrowers more likely to refinance their loans at lower rates. In this sense, a pass-through mortgage security is similar to a callable bond, and pass-through MBS often demonstrate negative convexity with smaller capital gains when interest rates go down than conventional bonds, but smaller capital losses than other conventional bonds when interest rates go down, since prepayment risk falls. Investors demand a higher interest rate for pass-through securities for their prepayment risk.

Securitization of Loans and Loan Sales as Liquidity Sources

Just as financial services firms invest in mortgage-backed securities, they also use securitization as a source of liquidity as discussed in Chapter 9. Depository institutions can also use loan sales and securitizations as a source of liquidity. Very large bank holding companies often have their own securitization operations through special purpose vehicles (SPVs), while smaller community banks and savings institutions often sell loans to other banks and insurance companies and government-sponsored or quasi-government-sponsored agencies.

LIABILITY MANAGEMENT AS A SOURCE OF LIQUIDITY AND DEPOSIT MANAGEMENT

Trends in Deposit Management

The majority of liabilities held by depository institutions are deposits. For instance, for U.S. FDIC-insured commercial banks and savings institutions at the end of 2015, they held 76 deposits as a percentage of total average assets. The type of business a bank is in will also determine what type of deposits it will attract. For instance, consumer banks attract consumer deposits, and business banks attract business demand deposits. Wholesale banks with no branches rely more on nondeposit funds for financing. Thus, in terms of a bank's market segment and the type of loans it makes, asset management is closely related to the type of deposit and liability management a bank has.

Depository institutions attempt to attract core (insured) deposits that tend to be cheaper and more relationship-based and less interest rate sensitive than other types of liabilities. This is in contrasts to large jumbo $100,000 or more insured deposits and uninsured time deposits over insurance limits (of $250,000 for individual depositors in the United States), and other borrowing and types of liabilities that are more volatile and rate sensitive. These are often called purchased funds or volatile liabilities, since they can leave a bank at any time if other depository institutions offer more favorable rates, or there is unfavorable news about the depository institution. Brokered deposits, deposits that are sold to a bank through a broker, access a large pool of potential investment funds for liquidity. Brokered deposits are also volatile deposits, since the type of customer seeking brokered deposits is looking for a higher yield, and can leave a bank at any time. Under FDIC rules, only well capitalized banks can engage in brokered deposits.

Trends for bank liabilities include low rates for deposits during periods of quantitative easing by central banks, greater use of debit cards and alternative payment mechanisms including apps that allow scanning of checks for deposit, the rapid growth of ATMs, widespread use of PayPal and other new forms of payments, online banking, and new payment mechanisms, and the development of blockchain technologies for future use to increase security for payment mechanisms.

The Check Clearing Act for the 21st Century, effective in October 2004 in the United States, made the payment system more efficient by reducing the legal impediments to check truncation, allowing a new negotiable instrument, "a substitute check." This "substitute check," also known as an image replacement document (RD), is a magnetic ink character recognition (MICR) encoded paper reproduction of an original check and, as a legal equivalent of the original check, can be presented in the same manner. The Act also reduced costs for banks, since substitutes can be used for bank statements.

Banks have also become leaders in electronic check presentment, which is a hybrid electronic/paper method of expediting check collections, where check data are exchanged in advance of presenting actual checks, speeding up payment systems and reducing a bank's operational expenses. Regulators have been concerned about significant changes in the infrastructure of the payment mechanisms and the growth in nonbank (third-party) processors, rapid off-site ATM growth, and consolidation of ATM and debit card networks, making regulation more difficult. Other regulatory and safety concerns include the provision of life-time banking accounts for recipients of welfare payments that are transmitted electronically, with basic banking considered to include the right to a checking account with a low minimum balance requirement and a limited number of free checks per month.

Other important regulations related to deposits in the United States include the Bank Secrecy Act (BSA) and other "Know Your Customer" (KYC) regulations. The BSA requires banks to have surveillance duties for large cash deposits greater than $10,000, whereby they must file forms with the U.S. government for these depositors making large deposits (unless an exemption is submitted for frequent cash depositors such as casinos). Suspicious activity forms must also be submitted for questionable activities that could encompass money laundering or illegal activities. The USA Patriot Act also requested that banks be on the alert for activities associated with terrorist activities as well as helping in detecting money trails leading to terrorist activities.

Liability Management by Large Banks

Larger institutions with greater sources of borrowing engage in greater liability management by attracting more nondeposit types of funds.

Smaller institutions are often limited to Fed Funds purchased (short-term loans of excess reserves at the Fed among banks usually overnight and reversed the next day), repurchase agreements, also known as repos (the sale of marketable securities by an institution with agreements to repurchase at a specified higher price at a specified future date), or other types of borrowing from regulators, such as FHLB advances. Correspondence deposits are also often a significant funding source, whereby smaller banks leave compensating balances with their correspondent bank for their services, including check clearance, investment advice, international entry, and loan participations.

There is a risk/return trade-off as financial institutions take on greater liability manage-ment, since with greater dependence of borrowing short-term funds, there is the risk that sources of funds may dry up if there is bad news about a bank, such as in the case of Lehman Brothers during the subprime loan crisis. Similarly, if interest rates rise, borrowing costs on short-term liabilities could rise, increasing a bank's interest expense. However, by engaging in liability management for liquidity, a bank doesn't have to hold as much stored liquidity that may be very low yielding short-term investments. Hence, most large banks engage in a com-bination of some stored liquidity and the use of liability management to both maximize yields and have sufficient liquidity. With new regulations under Basel III, large banks will need to hold additional liquid assets to reduce their overall liquidity risk.

Different types of money market securities used as short-term sources of funding for larger banks include commercial paper, Eurodollar deposits, negotiable CDs, and bankers' acceptances. These are considered in the following section, including a discussion of how their yields are calculated.

Summary of Characteristics of Different Types of Money Market Securities Used for Stored Liquidity Including Some Types Used by Banks for Liability Management

Characteristics of money market securities with 1 year or less include: (1) maturity of 1 year or less; (2) sell at a discount from maturity value rather than paying interest; (3) have low default risk; (4) have strong secondary markets (over the counter, facilitated by brokers and dealers); (5) liquid: can be sold with little or no loss of value; and (6) have large minimum denominations. In addition to Treasury securities and agency securities that are used as short-term investments, large banks issue commercial paper, bankers' acceptances, and negotiable certificates of deposit, among other negotiable securities for liability management as described in Table 10.3 summarizing different types of money market securities.

TABLE 10.3 | Summary characteristics of different types of money market securities

Treasury bills are short-term U.S. Treasury securities with a maturity of 1-year or less, including 3-month (91 day), 6-month (182 days), and 1-year (52 week) T-bills. The amount of 3-month and 6-month T-bills are announced for sale each Thursday by the U.S. Treasury, with bids due by purchasers by the next Monday and awards announced on Tuesday, while 1-year T-bills are sold monthly. Bids are accepted based on the highest price on down until the offering amount is completed for competitive bids, with bids receiving the highest yield given to any accepted bid. Noncompetitive bids are also awarded at the same yield for given amounts that investors want, and all noncompetitive bids are taken, so investors are guaranteed to get the securities they desire. T-bills are discount securities that pay a maturity value.

Commercial paper are short-term corporate borrowings with a maturity of less than 270 days (9 months to avoid requirements in the United States for registration with the SEC), which increases the borrower's cost and time required to raise funds. Commercial banks, savings institutions, mutual funds, and other large financial institutions are the primary buyers of commercial paper. Like T-bills, commercial paper is purchased on a discount basis and redeemed at par on maturity. The minimum denomination ranges from $25,000 on up, depending on whether the purchase is made through a dealer or directly from the borrowing firm. Finance companies are large issuers.

Most commercial paper is held to maturity, and the secondary market is more limited compared with T-bills, but the rapid growth of money market mutual funds enlarged this market.

Bankers' acceptances are short-term negotiable securities that arise out of bankers accepting payment in association with international trade for the finance, import, or export of a domestic shipment of goods. Thus, bankers' acceptances serve not only as short-term assets to money market investors, but also as short-term sources of funds to large banks that finance international transactions. Similar to T-bills, bankers' acceptances are sold to money market investors at a discount from the face value, and yields are quoted on a banker's discount basis.

Negotiable certificates of deposit issued by large banks have face values with a legal minimum of $100,000, but in practice are usually more than $1 million and can be sold in secondary markets. Innovations in the CD market include variable rate CDs on which the maturity is fixed, but the interest rate can vary every 30 days.

Eurodollar CDs are dollar denominated negotiable CDs issued primarily by London-based branches of American, Japanese, British or other foreign banks. They are popular types of negotiable CDs. The secondary market for Eurodollar CDs is smaller than the secondary market for negotiable CDs in the United States, since a portion of a negotiable CD up to an insurance limit is eligible for deposit insurance, so Eurodollar CDs tend to have higher yields than domestic CDs.

Repurchase agreements are money market transactions in which securities (usually Treasury securities) are sold by one party to another, with the agreement that the seller will repurchase the securities at a specified price on a specified date. For the seller the transaction is called a repo and for the buyer the transaction is called a reverse repo. Repurchase agreements are commonly used by security dealers to finance their inventories. The daily volume of repurchases can reach $1 trillion, with many transactions as short as one day. Reverse repos are used by the Fed as part of open market operations to temporarily decrease the amount of reserves available in the banking system by selling Treasury securities with agreements to repurchase them later, or to increase reserves by purchasing Treasury securities from banks under agreements with the banks to repurchase them later. Repos do not have a secondary market.

Fed Funds are excess returns required by the Fed lent by one institution to another that are very short-term typically with many overnight similar to repos. Fed Funds are typically borrowed either through direct negotiation with the lending institution or through New York brokers. The lending institution instructs the Fed or its own bank to transfer the agreed upon balances to the borrower. Since Fed Funds are typically overnight, the transaction is reversed the next day, including one day's interest. The Fed Funds rate is extremely important in monetary policy decisions on a daily basis. To make short-term adjustments in the supply of funds, the New York Fed will be instructed to keep the Fed Funds rate within a desired range by buying or selling funds.

Sources: See Marcia Stigum (1990). *The Money Market*. Homewood, IL; Dow Jones-Irwin; and Marcia Stigum (1981) *Money Market Calculations: Yields, Break-evens, and Arbitrage*. Homewood, IL: Dow Jones-Irwin, for an in-depth discussion of money market securities and yields.

CALCULATING EFFECTIVE YIELDS FOR MONEY MARKET SECURITIES

Discount Yields for T-Bills

Money market securities are unique in that they are short-term securities with less than 1 year in maturity that generally sell as discount securities, requiring a single cash outflow (price) from the investor, followed by a single cash inflow at maturity. Since they are less than 1 year in maturity, their yields have to be annualized for the number of times a year an investor could earn that yield. For instance, if an investor invests in a 3-month T-bill, the investor could earn that yield 365 days /90 days = 4.06 times a year. The tradition of pricing T-bills began in 1929 when T-bills were first sold and traders found it easier to make computations using a year as 360 days and calculating yields as a fraction of 100% of par value versus price. Hence, by convention, T-bills are priced with discount yields (d). For the formula below for a discount yield, par value is the maturity value (minimum denomination $1,000 or larger amounts such as $10,000 or 100% to get the price as a %) for a 360-day year, and n day maturity for the T-bill is:

$$d = \frac{[\text{Par value} - \text{Price}]}{\text{Par value}} \times [360 / n].$$

So, the T-bill price (P_0) = Par value $[1 - [(d \times n/360)]$.

Since annual effective yields are as a percentage of price, the annual bond coupon equivalent yield (y) is:

$$y = \frac{[\text{Par value} - \text{Price}]}{\text{Price}} \times [365 / n].$$

and including the possibility of compounding effects over a full year, the effective annual compound rate y^* is:

$$y^* = [\text{Par}/P_0]^{365/n} - 1.$$

For example, suppose hypothetically a 91-day T-bill is issued with a 0.92% discount yield based on a 360-day year. To solve for the price = Par $[1 - (d \times n/360)]$ using a par value of 100%:

$$P_0 = \text{Par} [1 - [(d \times n/360)] = 100\% [1 - [(0.0092) \times (91/360)] = 99.768\% \text{ of Par}.$$

If the par value was $10,000, P_0 in $ = 0.9976 \times \$10,000 = \$9,977$.
    Solving for y, the coupon equivalent rate:

$$y = \frac{[\text{Par value} - \text{Price}]}{\text{Price}} \times [365 / n] = \frac{[100\% - 99.77\%]}{99.77\%} \times [365 / 91] = 0.925\%$$

and solving for y^*, the annual effective compound rate is:

$$y^* = [\text{Par} / P_0]^{365/n} - 1 = [100\% / 99.77\%]^{(365/91)} - 1 = 0.928\%.$$

Hence y and y^* are always greater than the discount yield, and y^* is slightly higher than the annual bond equivalent yield.

Calculating Yields for Negotiable CDs and Fed Funds

Some money market securities including Fed Funds and negotiable CDs, rather than selling for a discount and paying a higher maturity value, sell at par value and pay interest and principal at maturity. Effective yields are calculated similar to those for T-bills. In this case, the maturity value (P_1) is equal to the amount invested plus the interest paid on that amount, again annualized, using a 360-day year, where d is the quoted interest rate and n is the number of maturity days as follows:

$$P_1 = \text{Amount invested } [1 + (d \times n) / 360]$$

and the annual effective compound yield $(y*)$ is:

$$y* = [P_1 / \text{Amount invested}]^{(365/n)}$$

So for a 180-day negotiable CD with a face value of $1 million invested and an interest rate (d) based on a 360-day year, the amount received at maturity (P_1) is:

$$P_1 = \$1 \text{ million } [1 + (0.035 \times 180)/360] = \$1.0175 \text{ million and the annual effect}$$
compound yield $(y*)$ is:

$$y* = [\$1.0175 \text{ million} / \$1 \text{ million}]^{[365/180]} - 1 = 3.58\%.$$

Calculating the Yield for Commercial Paper

For calculating the yield for commercial paper or other short-term financing that includes fees and other what's often called out-of-pocket expenses, an effective annual rate can be calculated as:

$$\text{Effective rate} = \frac{\text{Out-of-pocket expenses}}{\text{Usable funds}} \times (365 / n)$$

where usable funds are the net proceeds that the issuer receives when issuing the commercial paper that are reduced by the discount interest paid, and out-of-pocket expenses include the interest expense paid and other fees.

Types of out-of-pocket fees include a commitment fee for the back-up line of credit and a dealer's fee, for instance. For an example, suppose a financial institution issues $5 million as the face value for commercial paper, with a discount yield of 5% for 30 days of a 360-day year, the *interest expense* that will be paid will be equal to:

$$\text{Interest expense} = d \times (30/360) \times \text{Face value}$$
$$= 0.05 \times (30/360) \times \$5,000,000 = \$20,833.$$

So the usable amount that the financial institution will receive will be equal to:

$$\text{Usable amount} = \text{Face value} - \text{Interest expense}$$
$$= \$5,000,000 - \$20,833 = \$4,979,167.$$

For the other *out-of-pocket expenses* in addition to interest, suppose there is a dealer and commitment fee that totals to 0.30% of the face value adjusted for the (30/360) maturity time for the commercial paper.

$$\text{Dealer and commitment fee} = \text{Fee fraction} \times \text{Face value} \times (30/360)$$
$$= 0.0030 \times \$5,000,000 \times 30/360 = \$1,249.50.$$

So total fees and interest expense that are out-of-pocket expenses will be:

$20,833 + $1,249.50 = $22,082.50.

$$\text{Effective annual rate} = [\text{Out-of-pocket expenses/Usable funds}] \times (365/n)$$
$$= [\$22,082.50 / \$4,979,167] \times (365/30) = 0.05396 \text{ or about } 5.40\%.$$

Hence, for commercial paper yields, yields are basically calculated as what the firm pays divided by the funds it has available annualized for the number of times this could occur in a year to get an annual rate.

MARGINAL COST OF LIABILITIES FOR DEPOSITORY INSTITUTIONS

Depository institutions in estimating their costs for different types of deposits need to include the marginal administrative costs incurred by the institution for different types of deposits, with higher costs for administrative costs for transaction types of deposit accounts. Different models are used including tools offered by Federal home loan banks that include the cost of repricing deposits and the marginal administrative costs, often with scenario analysis (FHLB Des Moines, 2016). Watson (1978) presents a model widely used that estimates the marginal interest and noninterest costs of an additional deposit dollar (MCD) as:

$$MCD = [I + S + D_I] / (1 - RR)$$

where I is the market interest rate on this type of deposit, S is the servicing cost per each dollar acquired, D_I is the deposit insurance premium required as a percentage of each insured dollar, and RR is the reserve requirement for this type of deposit.

For instance, suppose a NOW (negotiable order of withdrawal) account has a 0.35% and the servicing cost is 2%, and the deposit insurance premium is 0.254%, and the reserve requirement is 10%, then:

$$MCD = [0.35\% + 2\% + 0.254\%] / 0.90 = 2.89\%.$$

A similar analysis can be performed for each fund source that the institution uses and then a weighted average cost of funds (the sum of each marginal cost times the fraction of funds used as a percentage of total financing) can be found. This in turn could be used for determining how to price accounts to attract the quantity of desired deposits from target customer segments, and also as a base cost to be covered in pricing loans based on their type of funding.

LIQUIDITY RISK OF OTHER FINANCIAL INSTITUTIONS

Although depository institutions have the largest liquidity risk of financial institutions, since deposits can be withdrawn at any time, insurance companies and mutual funds and security companies have liquidity risks as well.

Insurance Companies

Insurance companies have long-term contracts, and therefore have much lower liquidity risk than other financial institutions, but still have some liquidity risk, when they have large investment losses, such as First Executive Life in 1990. Policyholders and annuity holders, and investors in guaranteed investment contracts (GICs) have at times engaged in runs to cash in policies and investments to try to obtain what they could before a troubled institution's closure. Similarly, property/casualty insurance companies (P/Cs) must keep sufficient liquidity to make payouts for contingencies for damages to personal property or individuals. Since policies are shorter-term than life insurance companies, P/C s must keep a larger percentage of shorter-term assets. They are also exposed to the liquidity risk of policyholders canceling or not renewing policies, which reduces cash flow from coming in from premiums, and are exposed to potential liquidity problems.

Mutual Funds

Open-end mutual funds are also subject to liquidity risk in the event of large investor withdrawals, such as in market downturns, since they are obligated to buy back their shares in any quantity offered, generally at the net asset value on the day the redemption is requested. During the financial crisis, regulators were also very concerned about money market funds having sufficient liquidity. Following Britain's decision to leave the European Union in July 2016, two large UK property mutual funds suffered hefty investor withdrawals, with investors fearing declines in British real estate prices, creating liquidity problems for these funds.

Securities Firms and Finance Companies

Finance companies, securities firms, and other types of financial institutions that borrow short-term funds have liquidity risk, including those using repurchase agreements for security firms to finance inventories of securities, and finance companies that use commercial paper and other short-term borrowing instruments. Thus, they are subject to liquidity risk, such as if securities for security firms are not sold quickly. Lehman Brothers was caught, for instance, in a severe liquidity crisis, when it was not able to borrow funds quickly when bad news appeared about the firm during the subprime loan crisis. Better-capitalized institutions with greater reputational capital are able to attract larger sources of short-term financing. Having diversified sources of financing are also key to reducing liquidity risk when purchased funds are used for liquidity.

SUMMARY

Managing liquidity for financial institutions includes both asset management, including holding short-term investments that can be liquidated quickly to meet liquidity demands, and liability management, involving having access to diversified borrowing sources for short-term liabilities. It is important for depository institutions in managing their reserve positions for required deposits to be held with their central bank and for them to forecast discretionary cash inflows and outflows as well as nondiscretionary cash inflows and outflows that are more volatile and unexpected. Large depository institutions are more active in liability management while smaller institutions must rely more on stored liquidity sources and different strategies for investing that allow ample liquidity to be available for expected and unexpected cash flow needs.

During the U.S. subprime loan crisis of 2007 to 2008 and the following global financial crisis, large financial institutions faced severe liquidity problems, emphasizing the need for institutions to hold a larger liquidity cushion. Under Basel III, large internationally active banking organizations are required to meet a liquidity coverage ratio based on the ratio of high-quality liquid assets to projected net cash outflows over a 30-day period in response to potential liquidity risk. In addition, a net stable funding ratio must be met as the ratio of the available amount of stable funding, based on a reliable portion of capital and liabilities over a given time, relative to the required amount of stable funding required for a specific institution, based on the liquidity characteristics and residual maturities of various assets held by an institution, as well as off-balance sheet exposures. Evaluation of a financial institution's liquidity position and risk is based not only on its stored liquidity, but also on its liability and off-balance sheet risks.

BIBLIOGRAPHY

BIS (2008). "Principles for sound liquidity risk management and supervision—Final document." Bank of International Settlements, September 2008. Accessed on February 28, 2016 at: http://www.bis.org/publ/bcbs144.htm

BIS (2013). "Basel Committee on Banking Supervision: Basel III: The liquidity coverage ratio and liquidity risk monitoring tools." Bank of International Settlements, January 2013. Accessed on February 28, 2016 at: http://www.bis.org/publ/bcbs238.pdf

BIS (2014). "Basel Committee on Banking Supervision: Consultative document: Basel III: The net stable funding ratio." Bank of International Settlements, January 2014. Accessed on February 28, 2016 at: http://www.bis.org/publ/bcbs271.pdf

Board of Governors (2015). "Reserve requirements for 2016." Board of Governors of the Federal Reserve System. Accessed on February 27, 2017 at: http://www.federalreserve.gov/newsevents/press/bcreg/20151112a.htm

Board of Governors (2016). "Reserve requirements." Board of Governors of the Federal Reserve System. Accessed on February 27, 2016 at: http://www.federalreserve.gov/monetarypolicy/reservereq.htm

Ernst & Young (2011). "Basel III liquidity requirements and implications: Regulatory rules' operational and strategic implications." EY Building a Better World. Accessed on February 28, 2016 at: http://www.ey.com/GL/en/Industries/Financial-Services/Banking—Capital-Markets/Basel-III-liquidity-requirements-and-implications—Regulatory-rules-operational-and-strategic-implications

FDIC (2016). "Statistics on Banking." Federal Deposit Insurance Corporation. Accessed on February 28, 2016 at: https://www5.fdic.gov/SDI/SOB/

FHLB Boston (2016). "Products & services & about us." Federal Home Loan Bank of Boston. Accessed on April 16, 2016 at: http://www.fhlbboston.com/aboutus/thebank/index.jsp

FHLB Des Moines (2016). "Marginal cost of funds." Accessed on April 16, 2016 at: http://members.fhlbdm.com/analytical-tools/marginal-cost-of-funds/

Gorton, Gary B. (2010). *Slapped by the Invisible Hand: The Panic of 2007.* Financial Management Association Survey and Synthesis Series, Oxford: Oxford University Press.

OCC (2010). "Interagency policy statements on funding and liquidity risk management." Office of the Comptroller of the Currency, March 17, 2010. Accessed on February 28, 2016 at: http://www.federalreserve.gov/board-docs/srletters/2010/sr1006a1.pdf

OCC (2014). "Liquidity coverage ratio: Description final rule." Office of the Comptroller of the Currency, OCC Bulletin 2014-51, October 17, 2014. Accessed on February 28, 2016 at: http://www.occ.gov/news-issuances/bulletins/2014/bulletin-2014-51.html

Watson, Ronald D. (1978). "Estimating the cost of your bank's funds." *Business Review, Federal Reserve Bank of Philadelphia*, (May/June), 3–11.

QUESTIONS AND PROBLEMS

1 Robert Cooperman, President of Snow-City Bank plans to invest $4 million in a negotiable CD for 180 days. The bank offers a discount rate of 6.2%. What is the effective annual yield on the CD?

2 Phil and Ros Lerner, respectively CEO and President of Euphoria Bank Holding Company in New York City had a noncompetitive bid for a $10,000 maturity value, 91-day T-bill. The average discount rate for the auction was 3.4%.

   a What price did the T-bill sell for?
   b What was the annual coupon equivalent rate for the T-bill?
   c What was the annual effective compound yield for the T-bill?

3 Jeff and Lori Cooperman, Executives with the Big Apple Financial Company, are going to issue $1 million of commercial paper with a 90-day maturity at a discount rate of 4%. Other fees for a dealer and back-up line of credit are 0.40%. What is the effective annual interest rate for the commercial paper issue?

4 Suppose a large internationally active banking organization has high-quality liquid assets of $5 billion, and projected net cash outflows of $5.5 billion. What is the bank's liquidity coverage ratio? Will the bank meet the full implementation of the LCR ratio under Basel III?

5 What is the net stable funding ratio under Basel III? What type of liquidity risk is this ratio addressing?

6 Under the BIS Principles for Sound Liquidity Risk Management, what topics does it provide detailed guidance for? How is corporate governance related to liquidity management for a bank?

7 Why do central banks impose reserve requirements on banks? How do banks manage their reserve positions?

8 Why is it important for financial institutions to forecast both discretionary and nondiscretionary factors in determining their liquidity positions?

9 The Mountain Dew bank holds liquid assets of $500 million and loan demand is expected to be $250 million. What is the bank's net liquid assets? If the bank has volatile funds of $300 million, what is the bank's liquidity deficit? What are some different ways to cover this deficit?

10 What are the different investment maturity strategies used by community banks to generate liquidity from their investment portfolios? What are the trade-offs for these strategies in terms of risk and return?

11 For large banks that use liability management for liquidity, what are the risk and return trade-offs versus having stored liquidity? Why is diversification of short-term borrowing sources important?

12 What are some of the liquidity risks for insurance companies, mutual funds, securities firms, and finance companies? Globalization and interconnectedness across hundreds of companies increased this liquidity risk. Give an example for an insurance firm, such as AIG, and a securities firm such as Lehman brothers, looking up an article on the web about their liquidity problems.

Part Five

Overview

Nondepository Financial Institutions and New Forms of Financing

Chapter 11

Insurance Companies: Overview, Operations, and Performance Analysis

With core competencies in risk management and finance, the insurance industry is uniquely positioned to further society's understanding of climate change and advance creative solutions to minimize its impacts.

(Mills, 2015)

INSURANCE companies are contractual financial institutions that collect premiums from customers in return for insurance contracts to provide benefits in the future in the event of future contingencies. Insurance companies pool together and invest premiums in bonds, stock, real estate, and other investments to be able to provide for future contingencies that customers face, as well as investment vehicles including annuities and whole life insurance policies that accumulate a cash balance as an investment vehicle. Insurance companies as in the quote above have core competencies in risk management and investment management.

As the Insurance Information Institute (III, 2015) points out, insurance company activities include the life and health insurance (L/H) sector focusing primarily on life and health insurance and retirement annuities, and the property/casualty (P/C) insurance companies including primarily auto, home, and commercial insurance. While health insurance is generally separate, this sector includes private health insurance companies as well as government health insurance programs around the globe. Some P/C and L/H insurance companies also underwrite health insurance as part of their operations.

Insurance company operations are widespread. The III (2016) reported that in the United States alone in 2014, 6,118 insurance companies had net premiums of over $1.1 trillion. Of these insurance companies, the U.S. National Association of Insurance Commissioners (NAIC) reported that 2,583 were P/C, 895 life/annuities, 857 health, 85 fraternal, 252 risk retention groups, and 1,390 other companies. In 2014, both the L/H and P/C sectors were profitable with the L/H sector having net written premiums of $648 billion and the P/C sector $503 billion (U.S. Treasury, 2015).

Overview:
Nondepository
Financial
Institutions and
New Forms of
Financing

Globally the III (2015) reports the top 10 insurance company groups to include: (1) Berkshire Hathaway in the United States; (2) AXA in France; (3) Japan Post Holdings in Japan; (4) Allianz in Germany; (5) UnitedHealth Group in the United States; (6) Assicurazioni Generali in Italy; (7) Munich Re Group in Germany; (8) Prudential in the United Kingdom; (9) China Life Insurance in China; and (10) Zurich Insurance Group in Switzerland.

RISK POOLING IN INSURANCE

Insurance allows the spreading of financial risks across a large pool of individuals or companies, allowing the transfer of risk, so funds are available to meet unplanned financial catastrophe risks. Premiums are set to be able to have sufficient funds to cover risks. Risk pooling is a key concept of insurance. Insurance began more than 5,000 years ago in Babylonia to protect shipping companies against the loss of ships, crews, and cargos at sea. By pooling funds, risks were spread, so each individual shipper only had to pay a small amount, and loans to shippers could include a rider for a fee for removing the loan if ships were lost at sea (McClintock, 2015).

As McClintock (2015) points out, today insurance companies employ actuaries in finance and probability to predict the probability and severity of different risks, taking into consideration expected returns on investments and claim costs and lapse rates, as well as administrative and marketing expenses and a profit markup to determine appropriate premiums. If future claims are higher than expected, insurance companies suffer losses. So setting premiums is very important for the insurance industry. Some risks are uninsurable. If they are too frequent or are huge risks, companies may need to self-insure such a risk, if the risk is cost prohibitive to pass on to an insurance pool.

ADVERSE SELECTION AND MORAL HAZARD IN INSURANCE

Adverse selection occurs when individuals who are more likely to take risks and, hence, to receive insurance benefits are the ones who are most likely to seek out insurance. Since insurance is based on the theory of pooling risks, pools of individuals with varying risks are needed to be able to have funds available for those needing payouts for adverse events. To reduce adverse selection risk, insurance firms often offer better rates for group insurance, such as everyone working in a business, to avoid adverse selection problems. Other ways to reduce this risk include lower premiums for individuals with lower risks to entice them to be in the insurance pool (i.e., such as nonsmokers, individuals with excellent safety records, and reductions for taking precautions).

Moral hazard occurs when an individual who owns an insurance policy fails to take proper precautions to avoid losses, because losses are covered by insurance. Examples include failing to lock car doors to avoid car theft, failing to tie up a boat properly when bad weather such as a hurricane is expected, and generally failing to take safety precautions to avoid losses. To reduce moral hazard, insurance companies require a deductible, whereby the insured has to pay a given amount of any loss before the insurance company will pay anything, thus, giving the insured a stake in the loss as an incentive to be proactive against losses. Also, insurance

279

*Insurance
Companies:
Overview,
Operations, and
Performance
Analysis*

companies often have terms in contracts to reduce risk, such as requirements that a roof is up to a regulatory standard, a sprinkler system to protect against fires, and other precautions in a building, among others.

OVERVIEW OF INSURANCE OPERATIONS

The extent of insurance company operations is quite broad, as discussed by Outreville (1998) in the *Theory and Practice of Insurance*. Operations include:

1   The *design and development of new products* for customer and market needs strategically considering potential competition, expected losses, legal and regulatory and cost factors.
2   *Production, distribution, and advertisement* for new products.
3   *Product management* including setting the price (rate) for a product for its risk and expected losses based on actuarial considerations and statistics, payments of claim, and other costs, plus a product profit markup.
4   *Underwriting* including strategically determining the risks that the company is willing to take on, based on financial capacity, technical skills and abilities, regulatory restrictions, and the availability of reinsurance and implementation.
5   *Claims adjustment and settlement* including having integrity and being able, fair, and prompt for paying for losses of claimants.
6   *Services including legal, loss control, risk management*, policyholder and consumer and employee educational services.
7   *Administration* including strategic planning, personnel management, branch management, accounting, and public relations.
8   *Finance and investment* including management and valuation of the investment portfolio from strategic and regulatory perspectives, since state regulators often limit the percentage of different types of investments that can be held.

The U.S. Bureau of Economic Analysis reported that insurance carriers and related activities contributed $421.4 billion or 2.5% of the U.S. gross domestic product in 2013, and the Department of Labor reported that the U.S. insurance industry employed 2.5 million people in 2014, including 838,200 employees carrying out operations for life, health, and medical insurers, 596,000 employees for P/C insurers, and 25,200 employees for reinsurers, plus 1 million for insurance agencies, brokers and other insurance-related enterprises (III, 2016).

CHANGES IN MARKETING FOR INSURANCE WITH TECHNOLOGY

Insurance companies use a variety of different distribution channels, including traditional captive agents and independent agents working for a number of companies, as well as commercial insurance brokers that are also often underwriters. With technology both access and exchange of information became easier and faster, and that includes sales by internet and telephone. Also banks, workplaces, associations, and car dealers are often used to gain access

Overview:
Nondepository
Financial
Institutions and
New Forms of
Financing

for potential policyholders. For car insurance, internet sales have risen dramatically with the ability to get quotes and rate comparisons online (III, 2015).

INSURANCE COMPANY REVENUES AND EXPENSES

Insurance entails future payouts for losses, since payments by customers of premiums are made before future services, in terms of payment of claims, are made. Gross written *premiums* provided by policyholders are used to cover the costs of commissions and administrative expenses and claims paid, determined in the event of a loss. Since claims are often not made in the same year that premiums are received, *reserves* are put aside as commitments by the insurer for the insured policyholders. Premiums are invested in securities with similar maturities to expected future cash flows for contracts. A portion of premiums received in a given year may be used to cover claims incurred within that year. Insurers receive income each year from premiums and from investment income. Insurers make profits whenever premium and investment income exceeds the amount that is needed to cover all expenses, claims, and proper provision (reserves) for liabilities to policyholders.

Insurance companies are organized as stock or mutual insurance companies. Policyholders (customers) own mutual insurance companies. Dividends paid to mutual insurance company policyholders are tax free, as a policy expense. Stock companies may have incentives to take higher risks to maximize stockholder wealth, while mutual insurance companies have the goal for long-term safety to protect policyholder owners. Hence managers of mutual insurance companies may tend to be more risk averse. However, studies examining differences in investment holdings find mixed results in terms of the riskiness of mutual versus stock insurance company holdings.

There has been a trend for mutual companies to convert to stock companies over time, in order to benefit from greater access to capital, to merge with other companies, and to retain employees through stock options. Mutual insurance companies hold a much smaller percentage of insurance assets compared to stock insurance companies, so many are smaller than stock insurance companies (NAIC, 2015b).

OVERVIEW OF LIFE INSURERS

Life insurance companies tend to be larger than P/C companies, since economies of scale are necessary for profitability, so the life insurance industry tends to be more concentrated. The majority of L/H insurance companies are stock owned, but in the United States over 100 companies are mutual firms owned by policyholders.

There have also been many mergers in the life insurance industry. For example from 1992 to 2002, the number of life insurers fell by 40% with mergers. In 2013 there were 695 global mergers and acquisitions, a decline from 741 in 2012. The III (2015) points out that an analysis by Conning Research suggests that a recent decline in mergers was likely the result of several factors, including a more favorable economy, regulatory initiatives including the Affordable Care Act in the United States, and higher valuations.

In the United States, about 11% of insurers are foreign owned, with Canada, the Netherlands, France, and Switzerland as the largest foreign insurance company owners. The

281

*Insurance
Companies:
Overview,
Operations, and
Performance
Analysis*

top 10 countries with the largest amount of dollars of life and nonlife direct premiums written include the USA, Japan, the United Kingdom, China, France, Germany, Italy, South Korea, Canada, and the Netherlands. Large financial holding companies, including bank investment banking subsidiaries, are also engaged in insurance brokerage activities. For example, by 2010 there were 3,080 banks reporting insurance brokerage income totaling about $2.76 billion. Insurance companies have also purchased savings banks (III, 2015).

The 10 top writers of life insurance/annuities by direct premiums written reported by SNL Financial, in 2014 in the United States include: (1) MetLife Inc. with 16.14% market share; (2) Prudential Financial Inc. with 7.6%; (3) New York Life Insurance Group with 4.81%; (4) Jackson National Life Group with 4.52%; (5) AEGON with 4.29%; (6) Lincoln National Corp. with 4.12%; (7) American International Group (AIG) with 3.94%; (8) Principal Financial Group Inc. with 3.20%; (9) Manulife Financial Corp. with 3.13%; and (10) Massachusetts Mutual Life Insurance Co. with 2.85% (III, 2016; U.S. Treasury, 2015). The top 10 companies held a total share of 54.38%. All of these companies are very large companies and tend to be stock owned. The top combined 25 groups by direct premiums written held a 79.47 percent share, and the combined top 100 held a 98.06% share (U.S. Treasury 2015).

The top U.S. L/H insurance groups in 2014 by accident and health (A&H) lines direct premiums written include: (1) United Health Group Inc. with a 26.19% share; (2) Aetna Inc. with 13.94%; (3) Aflac Inc. with 8.795; (4) Cigna Corp. with 8.07%; (5) Met Life, Inc. with 4.01%; (6) Unum Group with 3.17%; (7) Mutual of Omaha Insurance Co. with 1.96%; (8) Guardian Life Insurance Co. of America with 1.72%; and (10) Genworth Financial Inc. with 1.57%. The combined top 10 companies held a 71.34% share; the top 25, an 85.57% share, and the top 100, a 98.89% share.

LIFE INSURANCE COMPANY INCOME STATEMENTS

Shown below is the average income statement for U.S. Life Insurers in 2010 and 2014. Life insurers tend to have a variety of different types of insurance products producing premium revenue. Expenses for life insurers include benefits, surrenders of policies, increases in reserves, transfers to separate accounts, commissions, general and administrative expenses, insurance taxes, licenses and fees, among others. Life insurance companies receive tax advantages in terms of mutual policy dividend being deductible and capital gains are not taxed on investments held for long-term investments.

As noted on the life insurance industry income statement, total premiums grew by 15.16% from 2010 to 2014, and total revenue grew by 15.24%. However, total expenses grew by 18.23%, resulting in a lower net gain from operations before tax. However, net realized capital losses were lower in 2014 than in 2010, resulting in a higher average net income in 2014. For life/health insurance companies revenues come from a variety of different types of premiums including life insurance, annuities, accident and health, credit life, credit accident, and health premiums.

Many large life insurance companies are diversified and also have P/C subsidiaries. Expenses also include surrenders of policies, where customers cash in their life insurance policies for their cash values, and commissions for sales made by insurance agents and brokers, as well as general and administrative expenses.

Overview:
Nondepository
Financial
Institutions and
New Forms of
Financing

U.S. life/health insurance industry income statement, 2010 and 2014

Revenue ($ billion, end of year)	2010	2014
Premiums, consideration and deposits	562.1	647.3
Net investment income	164.1	171.7
Reinsurance allowance	(29.3)	(15.0)
Separate accounts revenue	23.4	34.3
Other income	53.0	39.5
Total revenue	*773.4*	*877.9*
Total expenses	687.2	812.4
Policyholder dividends	15.0	16.4
Total revenues less expenses and dividends	71.2	49.1
Adjustments	(18.1)	(0.1)
Net gain from operations before taxes after adjustments	*53.1*	*49.0*
Federal income tax	8.6	10.1
Net realized capital gains (losses)	(16.1)	(1.3)
Net income	*28.4*	*37.6*

Source: SNL Financial LC as reported by U.S. Treasury (2015) and III (2016).

In 2010, the return on average asset (ROA) for the life insurance industry was about 0.56%, which rose in 2014 to 0.61%. The return on average equity (ROE) in 2010 was 9.39% rising to 10.96% in 2014. Similar to depository institutions, L/H insurers have high financial leverage, so despite a small average ROA, this results in a higher ROE.

OVERVIEW OF PROPERTY/CASUALTY INSURERS

The P/C insurance industry consists of a number of very large firms, which dominate the industry, and thousands of smaller firms. With greater ease of exit and entry, there are numerous small and medium-size firms. The largest 50 insurers hold about 50% of market share in the United States. Other insurance companies include financial guaranty and also reinsurance companies that insure risk for insurance companies, among others.

Property/casualty insurance companies underwrite policies to protect against adverse events. P/C insurers have less predictability on future payouts than life insurance companies, so when catastrophic events occur, often premiums are not sufficient to cover the expenses incurred in underwriting insurance policies, so insurers depend on investment income to make a profit. According to the Insurance Information Institute (III, 2016), in the United States alone, P/C insurers paid out $15.5 billion in property losses that were related to catastrophes in 2014, a rise from $12.9 billion in 2013, with 31 catastrophes occurring in 2014 versus 28 in 2013.

With competition in the industry, at times there are periods of chronic underpricing in some lines of insurance, such as commercial lines and low investment returns, known as the *P/C underwriting cycle*, as well as low interest rate periods leading to a shake-out in the industry

283

*Insurance
Companies:
Overview,
Operations, and
Performance
Analysis*

of weaker firms. With many companies relying on income from bonds, low bond rates can hurt profitability. Some corporations when premiums are high from P/C companies have moved into self-insurance by creating their own special insurance entity for self-insurance.

Liability insurance lines can be problematic for P/C insurers since they have what's often called a *long tail of liability*, where insurers are forced to pay millions of dollars for claims arising from injuries that occurred decades earlier.

In the P/C insurance industry in the United States the top 10 underwriters, in terms of their share of U.S. combined lines direct premiums written for all lines of business in 2014, were reported by SNL Financial as: (1) State Farm Mutual Automobile Insurance with a 10.34% share; (2) Liberty Mutual with 5.19%; (3) Allstate Corp. with 5.11%; (4) Berkshire Hathaway Inc. with 4.66%; (5) Travelers Companies with 4.03%; (6) Nationwide Mutual Group with 3.35%; (7) Progressive Corp. with 3.34%; (8) American International Group with 3.30%; (9) Farmers Insurance Group of Companies with 3.29%; and (10) USAA Insurance Group with 2.27%. The combined top 10 shares were 45.37%, combined top 25, 63.54%, and combined 100, 85.18%. Hence, the P/C industry is more competitive than the L/H industry. Different P/C insurance groups also have different rankings for more specialized commercial lines for direct premiums written (III, 2016; U.S. Treasury, 2015).

INCOME STATEMENTS FOR P/C INSURANCE COMPANIES

Sources of income for P/C insurers are net premium income and net investment income and realized capital gains. Expenses include losses incurred, other underwriting expenses, and policyholder dividends. As shown below, a typical income analysis as provided by III (2016) is reported in billions for U.S. P/C companies in, respectively, 2010 and 2014.

U.S. property/casualty insurance industry income analysis 2010 versus 2014 ($ billion)

	2010	2014
Net premiums earned	424.7	493.5
Losses and loss adjustment expenses	312.5	340.6
Other underwriting expenses incurred	121.3	139.1
Other underwriting deductions (add)	(0.81)	(0.48)
Net underwriting gain (loss)	(8.3)	14.3
Policyholder dividends (deduct)	2.7	2.9
Net investment income	48.1	54.9
Net realized capital gains	7.8	11.8
Finance service charges received (add)	3.2	3.3
All other income	(2.0)	(6.2)
Federal and foreign income tax	8.8	10.3
Net income after taxes	37.3	64.9

Source: SNL Financial cited in U.S. Treasury, 2015.

Overview:
Nondepository
Financial
Institutions and
New Forms of
Financing

As shown above, in 2014 U.S. insurance companies had an increase of 16.20% in net premiums earned over 2010. Despite rises in loss and other underwriting expenses, the P/C industry had a net underwriting gain in 2014 as the result of net premiums earned covering losses and underwriting expenses. Net investment income and capital gains were also larger in 2014, resulting in a higher net income rising by about 74% compared to 2010. The importance to the P/C industry of net interest income and capital gains is shown in 2010, when the P/C industry had a net underwriting loss, but because of net interest income and net realized gains, net income was positive. The return on assets in 2010 was 2.45% and return on average equity (capital and surplus) was 6.89%. In 2014, the ROA went up to 3.67% and the average ROE went up to 9.58% (U.S. Treasury, 2015).

KEY PROFITABILITY AND EXPENSE RATIOS FOR THE INSURANCE INDUSTRY

As noted above in the income statements for the U.S. insurance industry, revenues for the insurance industry come primarily from (1) premiums from customers and (2) earnings from investments. Expenses come from (1) insurance payouts when events trigger payments to customers and (2) other operating, marketing, and administrative costs. Analysts use special ratios to examine insurance company operations and these focus on premium income relative to total policy expenses.

Key Financial Ratios for Insurance Companies

Special financial ratios are used to evaluate insurance companies including:

(1) *Net underwriting margin (NUM)* = [Premiums earned − Total policy expenses] / Total assets.

A positive NUM indicates that an insurance firm has made an underwriting profit with premiums earned greater than total policy expenses.

(2) *Expense ratio* = [Operating expenses / Net premiums written]

(Note: If net premiums earned or net premiums written are not available use premiums received as a proxy.)

The lower the expense ratio, the better the insurance company is holding down expenses relative to premiums.

(3) *Loss ratio* = [Loss expenses / Premiums earned]

The lower the loss ratio, the better the insurance company is managing losses relative to premiums (if very high the insurance company may need better risk management policies to avoid against high future possible insurance payouts.

(4) *Combined ratio* = [Loss ratio + Expense ratio]

285

*Insurance
Companies:
Overview,
Operations, and
Performance
Analysis*

The lower the figure the better. A ratio below 100% is a measure of profitability and of the insurance company's underwriting efficiency. Ratios above 100% indicate a failure of the insurance company to earn enough premiums to cover expected claims. High combined ratios can be due to unexpected claims and or underpricing premiums.

For the P/C sector, in 2010, the average loss and loss adjustment expense ratio was 73.59%, with this ratio rising to 79.45% in 2011 and then falling to 74.34% in 2012 and to 67.53% in 2013, and then rising to 69.02% in 2014. The expense ratio was 28.26% in 2010, and remained fairly steady for 2011 to 2013, and fell in 2014 to 27.58%. The combined ratio was 102.49% in 2010, rose to 108.35% in 2011, and then fell in 2012 to 103.15%, to 96.34% in 2013, and was 97.20% in 2014, indicating improvement after 2012 (III, 2016; U.S. Treasury, 2015).

(5) *Investment yield* = [Net investment income / Average investment assets]

Investment yield provides the average return on an insurance company's assets, and is often cited as net yield on invested assets. For the L/H sector, net yield on invested assets was 5.24% in 2010 falling to 4.83% by 2014, with a low interest rate environment after 2010.

For the P/C sector in the United States, the net yield on invested assets was 3.73% in 2010, rising to 3.83% in 2011, and falling to 3.65% in 2014, reflecting a low interest rate environment, and the need for P/C companies to invest in intermediate and shorter-term securities for more unexpected cash payouts (U.S. Treasury, 2015).

(6) *Overall profitability* = 100% − Combined ratio% + Investment yield

If the overall profitability ratio is positive, the firm is making an overall profit. Note many times an insurer depends on a high investment yield for profitability, when combined ratios are greater than 100%.

Dupont Analysis

In addition, a traditional Dupont Analysis can be used for return on assets for insurance companies, similar to the analysis discussed earlier in the text for depository institutions (see Chapter 1), where:

$$ROA = AU \times NPM$$

where:

$$AU \text{ (asset utilization)} = Revenues/Assets$$

and

$$NPM \text{ (net profit margin)} = Net income / Revenues$$

and

$$ROE = ROA \times EM$$

where the EM = Total assets / Total equity.

Overview:
Nondepository
Financial
Institutions and
New Forms of
Financing

A Dupont Analysis examines how well a firm is operating in terms of generating revenues from assets, and managing expenses to produce net income from revenues and for ROE its use of financial leverage.

An example of a financial analysis for a fictional insurance firm, Rock Solid Insurance Company, is described below:

The Rock Solid Insurance Company ($ million)

	2014	2015
Total assets	29,134	39,309
Total investments	15,158	22,470
Total equity	2,019	2,087
Income statements		
Premium payments	3,930	5,760
Investment income	1,693	2,924
Total revenue	*5,623*	*8,684*
Loss expenses	3,091	4,666
Operating expenses	1,961	3,552
Total policy expenses	*5,052*	*8,218*
Net operating income	571	466
Net income	445	277

Questions: Analysis of Rock Solid's trend performance

1   Find the NUM, expense ratio, loss, ratio, combined ratio, and overall profitability ratio, operating profit margin, net profit margin, ROA, and asset turnover.
2   Explain using these ratios, why the firm's ROE and ROA went down in 2015.

Answers

	2014	2015
NUM	− 3.85%	− 6.25%
Expense ratio	49.90%	61.67%
Loss ratio	78.65%	81.01%
Combined ratio	128.55%	142.68%
Average investment yield	11.17%	13.01%
Overall profitability	− 17.38%	− 29.67%
Asset turnover	0.1930	0.2209
Operating profit margin	10.16%	5.37%
Net profit margin	7.91%	3.19%
ROA	1.53%	0.71%

287

*Insurance
Companies:
Overview,
Operations, and
Performance
Analysis*

Calculations for financial ratios

NUM = [Premiums earned* − Total policy expenses] / Total assets

(*for this example, premiums received is used for premiums earned).

2014: NUM = [3,930 − 5,052] / 29,134 = − 0.0385 or − 3.85%

2015: NUM = [5,760 − 8,218] / 39,309 = − 0.0625 or − 6.25%

The firm had a negative NUM, underwriting loss each year with premium income lower than total policy expenses that was larger in 2015 with expenses growing at a larger rate than premiums received in this case.

Expense ratio = Operating expenses / Premiums earned

2014: Expense ratio = [1,961 / 3,930] = 0.4990 or 49.9%

2015: Expense ratio [3,552 / 5,760] = 0.6167 or 61.67%

Loss ratio = Loss expenses / Premiums earned

2014: Loss ratio = 3,091 / 3,930 = 0.7865 or 78.65%

2015: Loss ratio = 4,666 / 5,760 = 0.8101 or 81.01%

Investment yield = Investment income / Investments

2014: Investment yield = 1,693 / 15,158 = 0.1117 or 11.17%

2015: Investment yield = 2,924 / 22,470 = 0.1301 or 13.01%

Overall profitability = 100% − Combined ratio + Investment yield

2014: 100% − 128.55% + 11.17% = − 17.38%

2015: 100% −142.68% + 13.01% = − 29.67%

Asset utilization = Revenues / Assets

2014: AU = 5,623 / 29,134 = 0.1930

2015: AU = 8,684 / 39,309 = 0.2209

Operating profit margin = Operating income / Revenues

2014: OPM = 571 / 5,623 = 0.1016 or 10.16%

2015: OPM = 466 / 8,684 = 0.0537 or 5.37%

Net profit margin = Net income /Revenues

2014: NPM = 445 / 5,623 = 0.0791 or 7.91%

2015: NPM = 277 / 8,684 = 0.0319 or 3.19%

ROA = Net income /Assets

288

*Overview:
Nondepository
Financial
Institutions and
New Forms of
Financing*

2014: ROA = 445 / 29,134 = 0.0153 or 1.53%

2015: ROA = 277 / 39,309 = 0.0071 or 0.71%

Summary Analysis for Rock Solid Insurance Company

Rock Solid had a lower ROA as a result of a lower NPM, resulting from a lower OPM, which in turn was the consequence of both a higher loss ratio and a higher expense ratio in 2015, resulting in a higher combined ratio. This contributed to a larger more negative overall profitability ratio in the current year, despite a slightly higher investment yield. The larger NUM in 2015 suggests that the firm is underpricing its premiums, and also having problems managing both loss and operating expenses.

LIFE INSURANCE COMPANY INVESTMENTS AND CONSIDERATIONS

As of the end of 2013, SNL Financial reported that the L/H insurance industry had cash and invested assets of $3.5 trillion in the United States. About 75% of investments were in bonds, about 2% in common stock, about 10% in mortgage loans on real estate, about 3% in cash, cash equivalents, and short-term investments, about 4% in contract loans including premium notes, about 1% in derivatives, and about 5% in other types of invested assets.

Life/health insurance companies tend to invest in longer-term bonds to match expected maturities and payouts for long-term contracts. Since their investment income is not taxed, they also tend to invest in taxable bonds, with 75.8% of bonds on average for LH insurers in the United States in 2013 held in industrial and miscellaneous bonds, 23% in government and revenue bonds, and 1.2% held in parents, subsidiaries, and affiliates. Many state regulators in the United States have limits on stock holdings for insurance companies, resulting in greater holdings of more conservative investments such as government and other investment grade bonds.

Since life insurers invest primarily in stocks and bonds, investment managers have to carefully analyze default and interest rate risks for bond portfolios. For guaranteed investment contracts (GICs) and annuities, where payouts are made to policyholders, there is a need for liquidity, so hedging techniques and understanding interest rate theories is very important to protect returns on fixed assets from interest rate swings. This is particularly important for insurers with substantial separate accounts, where groups of assets are designated for specific obligations. Earnings pressures often raise public concerns with the temptation for investment managers to invest in more risky types of assets. Hence, risk management is very important.

P/C INSURANCE COMPANY INVESTMENTS

While life insurance companies can better predict likely cash flows for their long-term contracts, P/C insurers subject to catastrophe risks need to invest in more intermediate term assets. The III (2015) reports that in 2013 P/C insurers held about 63% in bonds, about 22% in common and preferred stock, about 0.7% in real estate, about 6% in cash and cash

289

*Insurance
Companies:
Overview,
Operations, and
Performance
Analysis*

equivalents, 0.04% in derivatives, and about 8.26% in other invested assets. Hence, P/C insurance companies have a larger percentage of investments in stock than life insurance companies, a smaller percentage in real estate, and a larger percentage in cash and cash equivalents. The common stock portfolio of P/C companies included 5% invested in mutual funds and money market securities, 23.1% invested in parent, subsidiaries, and affiliates, and 71.9% invested in industrial and miscellaneous stocks. For the average P/C bond portfolio at the end of 2013, 40.1% was invested in industrial and miscellaneous bonds, 27% in special revenue bonds, 16.7% in government bonds, 14.6% in state, territories and other bonds, 1.5% in parent, subsidiaries, and affiliates, and 0.2% in hybrid securities (III, 2015). Since P/C investment income is taxed, the percentage invested in state tax-exempt municipal securities is larger than for L/H insurance companies. State regulators for P/C insurance companies over time relaxed restrictions on common stock, but given real estate market collapses, put greater restrictions on real estate investments.

Property/casuality insurers like life insurers use immunization techniques to reduce interest rate and credit risk. Catastrophic futures hedge against large losses. Insurance company managers also must take care in estimating a firm's anticipated cash outflows from policy claims, many which may not occur until years after a policy is written. With estimates, asset portfolios can be selected that have cash inflows to match estimated anticipated outflows. Interest rate and risk management strategies are important for P/C firms.

INSURANCE COMPANY FINANCIAL LEVERAGE

For insurance companies, capital and surplus is equal to an insurer's assets less its reported liabilities, based, in the United States, on valuations that are prescribed by insurance regulators in each state. Since capital and surplus demonstrates the ability of an insurer to meet its future obligations to policyholders, it is also an indicator of the capacity of an insurer to underwrite new policies for consumers. As reported in 2010, for the L/H sector, using general account assets, the average general account assets to surplus ratio was 10.95 and in 2014 10.84. Similar to an equity multiplier, the reciprocal represents a surplus to general account asset ratio of about 9.13% in 2010 and 9.23% in 2014. Hence life insurance companies in the United States have high financial leverage. In 2008 during the subprime loan crisis in the United States, the L/H sector general account assets to surplus ratio was 12.63 (i.e., a capital and surplus to general account assets ratio of 7.92%), which has improved over time (U.S. Treasury, 2015). For the P/C insurance sector, a typical ratio used is net premiums written divided by average policyholders' surplus. In 2010 this ratio was 87.3, and in 2014 79.47, indicating improvement in terms of a larger average policyholder surplus relative to net premiums written.

STATUTORY VERSUS GAAP ACCOUNTING FOR P/C INSURANCE COMPANIES

In the United States, with states regulating insurance companies, individual states often have accounting statements under statutory (regulatory) accounting principles, which are more cash-based than the accrual accounting required by the Generally Accepted Accounting Principles

Overview:
Nondepository
Financial
Institutions and
New Forms of
Financing

(GAAP). Expenses are not recognized until they are earned under statutory accounting, which is generally more conservative than under GAAP. For example, statutory accounting for P/C insurance companies requires that unrealized gains or losses on stock holdings be reflected on the balance sheet; this reduces the value of a firm's equity compared to GAAP accounting, which requires that equity securities be held at the lower of cost or market value. Statutory accounting only allows "admitted assets," which are assets that can be liquidated if an insurance company faces a financial emergency. Hence, under statutory accounting, reported net worth or policy surplus is understated by the amount of un-admitted assets that do not appear on the balance sheet. This makes it difficult at times to compare financial statements of P/C insurers when different state regulators use different statutory accounting rules.

POLICYHOLDERS' SURPLUS

Insurance companies must maintain a sufficient policyholders' surplus to underwrite risk. Policyholder surplus is the excess capital (assets − liabilities) after an insurer theoretically meets all the payable benefits to its policyholders. This surplus is commonly called "capacity." For P/C insurers in the United States, different states use statutory accounting, so the technical definition for policyholders' surplus would be net admitted assets less statutory liabilities.

As reported by the III (2015) with data from SNL Financial at the end of 2013, net admitted assets were $1,682,073 million, statutory liabilities were $1,014,652 million, and policyholders' surplus was $667,420 million, that is, as a percentage of net admitted assets, 39.68%. This ratio is typically higher for P/C insurance companies than L/H companies, since P/C insurance payouts are less predictable. In 2008, policyholder surplus dropped substantially, reflecting the deterioration in global financial markets, dropping to 32.87% of net admitted assets from about 35.95% in 2007.

Typically, P/C insurers have total loss and unearned premium reserves, while life insurers have policy reserves, security loss reserves (asset valuation reserves), and dividend reserves. Life insurers also typically have a lower equity to asset ratio. For life insurers policy reserves are estimated by taking the present value of future financial obligations (benefits required to be paid out to current policyholders), which are actuarially determined considering mortality and morbidity rates. The present value of future premium payments from the currently insured and the expected rate of return on the life insurance company's investments are also estimated. Policyholder reserves are determined by the present value of expected future financial obligations less the present value of estimated receipts of premium and investment income (U.S. Treasury, 2015).

ADDITIONAL FINANCIAL RATIOS USED BY REGULATORS, AMONG OTHERS

1   Premiums to surplus (gross premiums or net premiums used)
2   Change in net underwriting = (Changes in total premiums written / Previous premiums earned)
3   Change in surplus to total surplus
4   Liabilities to liquid assets.

291

*Insurance
Companies:
Overview,
Operations, and
Performance
Analysis*

SOURCES OF FINANCIAL INFORMATION FOR INSURANCE COMPANIES

Sources of financial information for insurance companies include: *Best's Aggregates and Averages*, with separate life/health and property/liability editions, *Moody's Bank and Finance Manual*, *Best's Reviews* (ratings for insurance companies), *SNL Insurance Quarterly* with year-end financial reports on covered insurances companies and other detailed data (www.snl.com).

REINSURANCE, CATASTROPHE BONDS AND OTHER ALTERNATIVE RISK-SPREADING MECHANISMS

Since insurance companies take on risk, multiple insurance companies share risk by purchasing insurance policies from other insurers that limits the total loss of the original insurer in the case of a disaster, known as reinsurance. Since insurers legally have to meet regulatory capital requirements to ensure an insurer is able to pay its potential liabilities, reinsurance also frees up capital to support larger insurance policies. Reinsurance is a way of transferring or ceding risk to the reinsurer, and is a global business that is complex and evolving. Traditional reinsurance involves the primary insurer selling the original insurance policies to the reinsurance company. Primary insurers can also share both premiums and losses, and a reinsurer can just assume the losses of the primary insurer above a certain dollar limit amount for a fee. In the United States professional reinsurance companies were about 7% of U.S. P/C insurance industry premiums as of 2010 (III, 2014a).

As the III (2014a) reports, because of unusual risks, such as natural disasters with climate change, risks are also being packaged as catastrophe bonds by both insurers and reinsurers to be sold to institutional investors. Other different types of alternative risk-spreading mechanisms are also being used that blend reinsurance and investment banking. With the high risk of natural disasters and capacity limited and prices high for reinsurance, insurance companies turned to capital markets for alternative, innovative risk financing tools.

Catastrophe bonds are issued by insurers and reinsurers, with a special purpose reinsurance vehicle (SPRV) created for this purpose. Often these bonds have complex structures and are initiated offshore in locations with favorable regulatory and tax treatment. The SPRV collects premiums from the insurance or reinsurance firm and the principal paid by investors is held in trust in U.S. Treasury securities or other assets that are highly rated. Investment income is used to pay interest on the principal for the bonds. Given their risk, these bonds pay high interest rates. Upon a trigger event occurring, investors can lose interest and at times the principal, based on the bond's structure, with both used to cover the insurance company's losses from a disaster. The maturity of a catastrophe bond ranges from one year to several years, often set at three years (III, 2014a).

Catastrophe bonds are also being used for residual government entities and wind pools backed by states. For instance, the California State Compensation Insurance Fund issued catastrophe bonds to help cover worker compensation losses if a catastrophic earthquake occurs. **Disaster recovery bonds** provide help for government entities in the event of a

Overview:
Nondepository
Financial
Institutions and
New Forms of
Financing

catastrophic event. An example of this type of pre-financing is the Caribbean Catastrophe Risk Insurance Facility (CCRIF) that provides coverage for hurricane and earthquake damage to member nations, allowing countries to quickly have funds available for recovery needs to enable essential services to continue. The CCRIF allows member nations to combine their risks into a diversified portfolio as a type of mutual insurance company and to purchase reinsurance or other risk transfer types of products on international financial markets at up to 50% over what this would cost each country. Another innovation is the **side-car**, which is a more simple agreement allowing a reinsurer or group of investors such as hedge funds to purchase through private placement catastrophic bonds that provide a share in the profit or loss produced along with a reinsurer (III, 2014a).

The 10 top recent catastrophe bond transactions in recent years include catastrophe bonds for hurricane peril in North Carolina, earthquakes in Turkey, windstorms in France, hurricane and earthquakes nationwide in the United States, hurricane, earthquake, windstorms in the United States and Europe, hurricanes in the Northeast United States, earthquakes in Japan, and hurricanes in Florida (III, 2015). The Reinsurance Association of America (RAA) points out that foreign reinsurers accounted for 91.9% of U.S. premiums for reinsurance versus 8.1% to U.S. professional reinsurers in 2013. Countries where U.S. reinsurance premiums were ceded to either unaffiliated or affiliated offshore reinsurers between 2011 and 2013 include: (1) Bermuda; (2) Switzerland; (3) United Kingdom; (4) Germany; (5) Cayman Islands; (6) Turks and Caicos; (7) Channel Islands; (8) Ireland; (9) Barbados; (10) France; (11) British Virgin Islands; (12) Spain; and (13) Canada, with a total for all countries in 2013 of $65,743 million reinsurance premiums ceded. In world insurance markets, the top 10 global P/C reinsurers by net reinsurance premiums written include Munich Reinsurance Co in Germany, Swiss Re Ltd. in Switzerland, Hannover Re S.E in Germany, Berkshire Hathaway Reinsurance Group in the United States, Lloyd's of London in the United Kingdom, Scor S.E. in France, Everest Re Group Ltd. and PartnerRe Ltd. in Bermuda, Korean Reinsurance Co. in South Korea, and Transatlantic Holdings Inc. in the United States (III, 2015).

MICROINSURANCE IN DEVELOPING COUNTRIES AND EMERGING MARKETS

Microinsurance has been provided by insurers in developing countries through microinsurance projects that offer low-cost insurance to individuals not covered by traditional insurance or government insurance programs. The advantages of microinsurance products are generally a lower cost than traditional insurance products with protection provided to a larger market, with high volumes, low cost, and efficient administration. Sometimes policies are offered with a small loan, with premiums set at a small percentage of the loan amount. The approach is associated with microfinancing as developed by Muhammad Yunus that has provided assistance to millions of low-income individuals primarily in Asia and Africa by providing small loans to assist small business startups. Microinsurance products help to protect poorer individuals who are working against the impact of financial losses. A study by Munich Re Foundation and Deutsche Gesellschaft fur International Zusammenarbeit (GIZ) found that by 2012 more than 170 million individuals had benefitted from microinsurance (III, 2015).

293

*Insurance
Companies:
Overview,
Operations, and
Performance
Analysis*

The III (2015) points out that a recent study by Swiss Re shows that premium growth in developing countries has recently outpaced that of industrialized countries, with growth in South and East Asia, Latin America, the Caribbean, central and eastern Europe, Africa, the Middle East, and central Asia and Turkey, with China the largest emerging market country with insurance premiums written, followed by Brazil, and India.

DIFFERENT TYPES OF INSURANCE POLICIES AND PRODUCTS

Types of Life Insurance Policies and the Determination of Premiums

Life insurance companies have developed new products that compete with investment products offered by other financial intermediaries, and four major types of policies are discussed here:

Whole life insurance has a fixed annual premium that is paid every year by a policyholder, with a known death benefit, the face amount of the policy. The beneficiary of the policy receives this face amount regardless of the date of death. Part of the premium is for insurance and part is for investment purposes. Whole life premiums are set based on the average actuarial amount needed to cover claims for a policyholder's entire life, so excess premiums in earlier years above the actuarial need are invested at a fixed annual rate established at the time the policy is written (with state regulators often setting a minimum yield). Policyholders build up cash values based on the earnings for excess premiums that can be cashed in, in lieu of maintaining full death protection, or against which low rate loans can be made.

Term life insurance, in contrast, is only for a short time period, such as a year, with the premium only the actuarial premium determined for that year based on a person's age, with term premiums rising as a person ages, with no excess premium or savings vehicle or accumulated cash value. Alternative policies offer constant premiums but decreasing coverage with age, and other options are also available. Term policies are frequently offered as group plans as part of employee benefit packages.

Premiums for life insurance policies are calculated by using a mortality table, where death rates per 1,000 are calculated conservatively, according to the number of insured men or women actually dying during the historical period examined, with an increase to allow for a margin of error. For instance, if the rate of death for men before age 43 is 2.2 men per 1,000, the insurer multiplies the face value of the policy, such as for example, $100,000, by the average probability of 0.22%. So the expected payout is $0.0022 \times \$100,000 = \$220$. The present value of this expected payout is then determined as a pure premium by dividing by 1 plus the expected rate of return to be earned on premium payments, taking a conservative rate as required by state regulators. If this expected rate of return is 4%, based on expected claims and if claims are paid by the end of the year, then to get the pure premium:

Pure premium = Present value of (Face amount × Probability of a claim)

so for the example, the Pure premium = [$220 / 1.04] = $211.53.

294

*Overview:
Nondepository
Financial
Institutions and
New Forms of
Financing*

For whole life policies, premiums are based on the present value of the insurer's expected cash outflows over an individual's life, adjusting for the probability that premium payments may not be made. For example, an annual whole life premium based on actuarial estimates coming up with an even premium for an individual's entire expected remaining life might be set for a 43-year-old at $1,260.43. For this 43-year-old suppose the pure premium is $211.53 for the year, so the excess premium is equal to $1,048.90, with that excess increasing the cash value of the policy and invested for the policyholder. The cash value increases based on an assumed fixed rate, which the policyholder earns regardless of the insurer's actual investment earnings. Participating policyholders may receive dividends in good years. Hence, actuarial assumptions and investment assumptions often provided by state regulators are very important in setting life insurance premium amounts.

Other insurance products are more investment-oriented and include:

Variable life policies like whole life policies require premiums over a policyholder's lifetime, but excess premiums earn variable rates rather than fixed rates of return based on a policyholder's choice of investments, passing on investment risk and the opportunity for higher returns to the policyholder. A minimum death benefit is specified on the policy, but no maximum. The actual payment to beneficiaries depends on yields earned on excess premiums.

Universal life insurance combines the death protection features of term insurance with the opportunity to earn market rates of return on excess premiums and take advantage of tax-free investment accumulations, with lump sum premiums allowed as well as a series of payments and a minimum guaranteed return. Unlike whole or variable life policies, the face amount of guaranteed death protection in a universal life policy can be changed at the policyholder's option, including adjustments of death benefits, premium payments, and risk and return selection as needs change. Investors also may have the option of investing excess premiums in different types of investments and mutual funds and allowing loans on policies.

ANNUITIES AND GUARANTEED INVESTMENT CONTRACTS (GICS)

Insurance companies are also popular life insurance company products, and along with guaranteed investment contracts (GICs) provide fixed cash flows and fixed investment returns, respectively, which are particularly helpful for individuals that are retired, who often put in lump sums at retirement in return for fixed cash flows each month with insurance annuity contracts. Insurance companies are also active in the financial planning business, requiring agents with financial planning credentials, such as the Certified Financial Planner (CFP) credential and security licenses to assist customers with their investment and financial planning needs, along with insurance needs. As noted by III (2015), measured by premiums written, the largest L/H product line is annuities, followed by life insurance and health insurance (often referred to as accident and health).

295

*Insurance
Companies:
Overview,
Operations, and
Performance
Analysis*

ACCIDENT AND HEALTH INSURANCE AND CREDIT INSURANCE

Medical expense, disability income, and long-term care are included in different types of insurance policies for accident and health insurance. Insurers also offer credit life insurance, which pays off loans in the event of a policyholder's death or disablement.

Health insurers underwrite private health insurance. Life/health and property/casuality insurers also underwrite health insurance coverage, with about 64.2% of U.S. citizens covered by private health insurance in 2013, 53.9% covered by employment-based health insurance, and 34.3% covered by government health insurance. Disability insurance insures individuals in the event they are unable to work because of accident or illness, paying a certain percentage of salary lost. Long-term care (LTC) insurance provides payments for services to assist individuals needing long-term care, with almost 5 million people covered by long-term care insurance in 2013 (III, 2015).

REGULATORS OF INSURANCE COMPANIES

Countries differ in their regulation of insurance companies. In the United States insurance companies are regulated by each state, but the McCarran–Ferguson Act of 1945 establishes the right of the federal government to regulate insurance companies if states fail to do so adequately. The National Association of Insurance Commissioners (NAIC) sets standards and regulatory support for U.S. insurance companies, which is governed by the chief insurance regulators from 50 states, the District of Columbia and five U.S. territories. With NAIC, state insurance regulators establish standards and best practices for insurance companies, conduct peer reviews, and coordinate their regulatory oversight. The mission of NAIC includes: (1) protecting the public interest; (2) promoting competitive markets; (3) facilitating fair and equitable treatment of insurance consumers; (4) promoting fair and equitable treatment of insurance consumers; (5) promoting the reliability, solvency and financial solidity of insurance institutions; and (6) providing support and improving state regulation of insurance (NAIC, 2016b).

Under the U.S. Dodd–Frank Wall Street Reform Act of 2010, the Financial Stability Oversight Council (FSOC) was charged with: (1) identifying risks to U.S. financial stability; (2) promoting market discipline; and (3) responding to emerging risks to the stability of the U.S. financial system, and designating any nonbank financial institution that could pose a threat to U.S. financial stability by means of its nature, size, scope, interconnections, or mix of activities. The Dodd–Frank Act also established a Federal Insurance Office (FIO) as an entity that reports to Congress and the President on the insurance industry (including reinsurers, as well, but not health insurers).

The U.S. FSOC designated several nonbank financial institutions as systematically important financial institutions (Sifi), requiring them to hold additional capital and have additional oversight. At the time of this writing AIG, GECC (General Electric Capital Corporation, which GE sold in parts to various buyers in 2015 to appeal to remove this designation), Prudential, and Met Life, are very large insurance firms designated in this category. The

Overview:
Nondepository
Financial
Institutions and
New Forms of
Financing

FSOC is required to annually re-evaluate each previous determination (U.S. Treasury, 2015). Met Life challenged its identification as a Sifi by the FSOC in court, based on the use of a flawed and inadequate analysis for making this designation. In late March of 2016, the U.S. District Court ruled in favor of Met Life challenging this aspect of the Dodd–Frank Act (Jopson and Gray, 2016).

The Fed was also given expanded responsibility as the consolidated supervisor for a number of insurance holding companies, including those owning an insured bank or thrift, as well as insurers designated by the Council for Federal Reserve supervision, representing, currently, companies that hold about one-third of U.S. insurance industry assets (U.S. Treasury, 2015).

In December 2014, Congress passed the Insurance Capital Standards Clarification Act of 2014 that was signed into law, giving the Federal Reserve flexibility to tailor its capital framework "substantially engaged in insurance underwriting activity," which the Fed is currently constructing. At the state level, since the subprime loan crisis of 2007 to 2008, both domestic and international regulators have made substantial efforts to develop stronger standards for both the quantity and quality of capital that must be held by insurers, building on existing standards to develop a greater risk-sensitive approach for group capital. In the United States regulators include the Federal Insurance Office (FIO), the Fed, state legislatures and insurance regulators, and the NAIC, and they are all working on more risk-sensitive standards for setting minimum insurer capital requirements as of the time of writing (U.S. Treasury, 2015).

The IAIS, the international standard-setting body for supervisors of the insurance sector also implemented reforms in 2014 to improve financial independence, efficiency, and transparency for insurance companies. The IAIS has continued development on a Common Framework for the Supervision of Internationally Active Insurance Groups (ComFrame), including qualitative standards for group-wide supervision, governance, risk management, and recovery and resolution. The IAIS in 2014 adopted a basic capital requirement (BCR), as the first group capital standard for the insurance sector, and in 2015 a higher loss absorbency (HLA), both of which will apply to insurers that are globally systemically important. It is also working on more risk-sensitive insurance capital standards to replace the BCR as a basis, which with HLA will be a capital standard that is quantifiable for globally systematically important insurers (G-SIIs) (U.S. Treasury, 2015).

U.S. RISK-BASED CAPITAL REQUIREMENTS

The National Association of Insurance Commissioners (NAIC) developed a formula for risk-based capital (RBC) requirements for L/H Companies in December 1993. RBC requirements attempt to estimate the capital needed by a firm to safely absorb the losses to which it is subject. For P/C companies, four risk categories are given:

- Investment or asset risk
- Credit risk, such as reinsurance
- Off-balance sheet risk, such as separate accounts
- Underwriting risk, such as the loss ratio and reserve adequacy.

An RBC requirement is calculated for each category based on calculations of risk charges applying to potential risks for that category. These charges are weighted, based on

297

*Insurance
Companies:
Overview,
Operations, and
Performance
Analysis*

the importance of different types of risk, and summed. Adjustments are then made for covariances to account for diversification to achieve the RBC requirement. Life insurance RBC is calculated in a similar fashion but with a heavier weight on asset risk, given the risk of asset values falling. For P/C companies the risks of underestimating reserves and overestimating the probability of income premiums are given heavier weights. Using special formulas with these weightings, a minimum capital or surplus amount that the insurer should maintain is calculated. If an insurer has a surplus below half that amount, state insurance regulators are mandated to take over the company.

REGULATORY MONITORING FOR SOLVENCY

Regulators use early warning systems to monitor insurance companies for solvency risk. Some states have their own systems, but most use the system developed through NAIC, which prioritizes insurers according to their risk for greater analysis and onsite regulatory examinations. Insurers also receive a normal detailed financial examination every three to five years. NAIC's Insurance Regulatory System (IRIS) involves 11 different financial ratios, which are calculated for each insurer with reviews and analysis by an examiner team. NAIC also developed a new solvency screening system for major insurers known as FAST (financial analysis system tracing) that has separate screen models for P/L and L/H insurers, and an expanded set of financial ratios which each insurer is scored on, with scores used to prioritize how much regulatory scrutiny a major insurer needs.

GUARANTY FUNDS FOR INSURANCE COMPANIES

States and countries often have guaranty funds to protect insurance policyholders in the event insurance companies go bankrupt. In the United States insurers in a state are required to participate in the state's guaranty fund, which is administered by state guaranty associations that operate as nonprofit organizations, subject to the oversight of licensed insurers in a state. Generally states have separate guaranty funds for P/C and L/H lines of insurance (U.S. Treasury, 2015).

ISSUES FACING INSURANCE COMPANIES

Currently, insurance companies are facing many different issues associated with climate change, terrorism risk, and cyber security protection, among others.

Climate Change Risks

As the III (2014b) points out, since climate change is associated with losses on an enormous scale, insurers that normally work to mitigate potential losses are increasing their efforts to make the public aware of climate change and potential damage, and of ways to reduce this damage with more prudence in the use of land, better planning, and stronger building codes. Major insurance firms, such as AIG, have been hiring senior climate scientists, specializing

Overview:
Nondepository
Financial
Institutions and
New Forms of
Financing

in atmospheric perils, for catastrophic risk management and analysis to assess underwriting risk and conduct research, including on the impact of long-term climate factors into modeling frameworks. They are also helping to develop underwriting and risk management strategies, models, and risk management tools, among other responsibilities.

There have also been concerns about full disclosure of climate change risks. As noted in a NAIC (2015a) brief on "Climate change risk and disclosure":

> Disclosure of climate change risk is important because of the potential impact climate change can have on insurer solvency and the availability and affordability of insurance across all major categories. … Experts predict climate change will continue to intensify the frequency and severity of these types of weather related events. Given these trends, it is important for insurers to identify climate-related factors and evaluate how they will impact their business and the exposure they indemnify.

Some major insurance companies have also developed projects that are innovative to help developing countries to adapt to climate change and to invest in renewable energy. Insurance companies have also assisted clients in risk management for climate change, which includes protecting against harm to the environment. With global warming, almost all segments of the insurance industry are affected, including a rise in death rates for life insurers and property losses of all types, with a rise in the risk of wildfires in some regions, rainstorms and flooding in other regions, and the severity and greater frequency of hurricanes. Catastrophe risk is expected to increase by as much as 40% over the next two decades associated with mega disasters. In addition, there are higher commercial liability losses accompanying hurricanes for businesses, including loss of income if property damage prevents a business from operating, as well as property damage and relocation costs. Also, corporations have potential liabilities for increased lawsuits by stakeholders over environmental liabilities (III, 2014b).

The Insurance Information Institute (2014c) reported that insured losses from natural disasters in the United States in 2014 reached a total of $15.3 billion, as estimated by Munic Re, excluding flood insurance losses, with insured severe thunderstorm losses greater than $12.3 billion, the fourth highest total amount on record, insured damages from winter storms and snow damage exceeding $2.3 billion, and the Napa, California earthquake resulting in insured losses of $150 million and economic losses of $700 million. During the first half of 2015, insurance losses as the result of natural disasters were a total of $12.6 billion, with 80 natural catastrophes, including 38 severe thunderstorms, creating $7 billion in overall insured and economic losses, and $5.1 billion insured losses; and 11 winter storms and cold waves resulting in $3.8 billion overall losses, including $2.9 billion in insured losses, a record high.

World insurance losses for natural catastrophes and man-made disasters cost $45 billion in insured losses in 2013 and $78 billion in 2012. In 2013 worldwide weather-related natural catastrophes resulted in $37 billion in insured losses, with the most expensive including massive flooding in central and eastern Europe and typhoon Halyan with the strongest winds on historic records, hitting the Philippines and killing over 7,500 and leaving more than 4 million people homeless (III, 2015).

The Geneva Association, with members that represent the largest insurers and reinsurers in the world is involved in a research project on climate change and its economic impact on insurance, including a detailed report on the insurance industry and climate change and the role of insurance companies in adapting to negative effects with change (Geneva Institute, 2009).

299

*Insurance
Companies:
Overview,
Operations, and
Performance
Analysis*

Efforts that insurance companies have made include reducing greenhouse gas emissions through sustainable policies that reduce fossil fuel emissions and encouraging policyholders to do so as well. In addition, major insurers have developed new insurance products, such as microinsurance policies, disaster recovery bonds and multinational government pools, to help underdeveloped countries through new forms of public/private initiatives for better risk management. To minimize the likelihood of lawsuits, insurance companies also provide analysis of policyholders' liability risks and guidance for the best approach, including adaptations to global warming by companies to ensure they do not cause harm, such as emission reduction programs and energy conservation projects. A number of companies provide consulting on carbon project risk management. For auto insurance, examples of incentives to policyholders to reduce their green footprints include: (1) pay-as-you-drive (PAYD) a usage-based insurance that allows drivers to pay lower premium by driving less, which in turn reduces carbon emissions (with motor vehicles responsible for about 25% of all greenhouse gas emissions); (2) special policies to policyholders for "green" building insurance coverage, such as consumers generating their own solar, wind or geothermal power that they sell back to their local power grids, with the insurance policy covering costs for getting back online when income is lost if a power outage from a peril that is covered is incurred that requires a homeowner to buy electricity from an outside source. Some policies also permit policyholders to rebuild under green standards (III, 2014b).

Mills (2015) lists ten opportunities for insurance companies to improve resilience to disasters and to adapt to climate change and reduce climate change risks including:

1 understanding the problem of climate change;
2 promoting loss prevention through energy efficiency and renewable energy technologies and better infrastructure that is less vulnerable to losses;
3 providing incentives to reduce risk-taking behavior, rewarding policyholders through premium discount;
4 developing innovative insurance products;
5 providing carbon risk management and reduction services;
6 financing climate protection improvements;
7 investing in climate change solutions;
8 supporting public policies that mitigate and are proactive for reducing climate change risks;
9 leading by example by being sustainable and reducing CO_2 emissions; and
10 carbon-risk disclosure such as through the CDP (formerly the Carbon Disclosure Project) that allows insurers to evaluate climate change impacts of a business.

Terrorism Risk Insurance Program

With terrorist attacks, insurance companies are exposed to great risks, with catastrophic, unexpected losses, such as 2,976 people perishing with the September 11, 2001 terrorist attacks in New York, Washington DC, and Pennsylvania, with total insured losses estimated to be about $42.7 billion in 2013 dollars. On April 15, 2013, the Boston Marathon bombing, causing the deaths of 4 people and injuring 264, resulted in claim payments totaling about $24.9 million for medical claims and property damage (III, 2015).

300

*Overview:
Nondepository
Financial
Institutions and
New Forms of
Financing*

After the 2001 terrorist attacks, many insurers and reinsurers withdrew from the terrorism risk insurance sector, which had a potential negative effect on construction, projects of businesses, and economic activities. In the United States, in response, the Terrorism Risk Insurance Act (TRIA) was enacted in 2012, creating a Terrorism Risk Insurance Program (TRIP) under the U.S. Treasury to provide incentives to the private market to offer terrorism risk insurance. TRIA generally requires commercial P/C insurers to participate and have insurance coverage available for terrorism risk. TRIP may reimburse an insurer for insured losses resulting from certified acts of terrorism when the insurance industry losses are greater than a specific trigger amount. On January 12, 2015, the Terrorism Risk Insurance Program Reauthorization Act was signed into law, reforming some provisions of TRIA and continuing the program (U.S. Treasury, 2015).

Cyber Security and the Insurance Sector

In the information age, with significant dependence on computer networks for daily business operations and enormous liabilities for breaches in security and greater vulnerability for consumer fraud and identity theft, new types of losses have arisen that need to be insured. The market for cyber liability insurance is relatively new, and is expected to grow rapidly as businesses become more aware of cyber risks and the need for these risks to be covered. The NAIC (2016a) reports cyber risks to include identity theft, business interruption, damage to a firm's reputation, costs associated with damage in data records, theft of digital assets, introduction of malware, worms, and other malicious computer code, human error leading to the disclosure of sensitive business information or personal identifying information, the cost of credit monitoring services for customers or others affected by a security breach, and lawsuits for trademark or copywriter infringement. Liability policies include coverage for different costs associated with expenses for different cyber risks.

SUMMARY

Insurance companies rely on actuarial science; and premiums and reported obligations are based on estimates of the amount and timing of claims a firm will have to pay in the future. Life insurers traditionally enjoy predictable payout events; however, with separate accounts, annuities and other new products, liquidity is important. Hence, investment management strategies to ensure cash flows are available for given investment horizons are important. Property/casualty insurers have cash payments to policyholders for often unpredictable weather events and large catastrophes, so investment and risk management strategies to ensure liquidity will be available, and losses reduced are very important as well. Assessing and reporting climate change risks, incorporating risks in underwriting policies, and developing new products has become increasingly important for insurance companies.

BIBLIOGRAPHY

Geneva Institute (2009). "The insurance industry and climate change—Contribution to the global debate." The Geneva Reports, Risk and Insurance Research. Accessed on January 9, 2016 at: https://www.genevaassociation.org/media/201070/geneva_report%5B2%5D.pdf

III (2014a). "Reinsurance: The topic." Insurance Information Institute, November 2014. Accessed on December 28, 2015 at: http://www.iii.org/issue-update/reinsurance

III (2014b) "Climate change: Insurance issues." Insurance Information Institute, September 2014. Accessed on January 8, 2016 at: http://www.iii.org/issue-update/climate-change-insurance-issues

III (2014c). "Catastrophes." Insurance Information Institute. Accessed on January 9, 2016 at: http://www.iii.org/fact-statistic/catastrophes-us

III (2015). *The Insurance Fact Book 2015*. New York: Insurance Information Institute.

III (2016). "Insurance industry at a glance." Insurance Information Institute Industry Overview. Accessed on January 1, 2016 at: http://www.iii.org/fact-statistic/industry-overview

Jopson, Barney and Alistair Gray (2016). "Financial. Dodd–Frank challenge: MetLife ruling shakes US post-crisis laws." *Financial Times*, April 1, 2016, p. 15.

McClintock, Leslie (2015). "What is risk pooling in insurance." *Zacks Finance*. Accessed on December 31, 2015 at: http://finance.zacks.com/risk-pooling-insurance-1890.html

Mills, Evan (2015). "Responding to climate change—The insurance industry Perspective." Climate Action Programme. Accessed on December 26, 2015 at: vanmills.lbl.gov/pubs/pdf/climate-action-insurance.pdf

NAIC (2015a). "Climate change and risk disclosure." National Association of Insurance Commissioners, Center for Insurance Policy Research. Accessed on April 10, 2016 at: http://www.naic.org/cipr_topics/topic_climate_risk_disclosure.htm

NAIC (2015b). "Capital markets special report: Mutual versus stock insurance companies & investment portfolio comparison." National Association of Insurance Commissioners, Center for Insurance Policy Research. Accessed on December 27, 2015 at: http://www.naic.org/capital_markets_archive/150428.htm

NAIC (2016a.). "Cybersecurity." National Association of Insurance Commissioners, Center for Insurance Policy Research, January 25, 2016. Accessed on July 5, 2016 at http://www.naic.org/cipr_topics/topic_cyber_risk.htm

NAIC (2016b). "About the NAIC." National Association of Insurance Commissioners. Accessed on January 4, 2016 at: http://www.naic.org/index_about.htm

Outreville, J. Francois (1998). *Theory and Practice of Insurance*. Boston: Kluwer Academic Publishers.

U.S. Treasury (2015) "Annual report on the insurance industry." Federal Insurance Office, U.S. Department of the Treasury, September 2015. Accessed on December 29, 2015 at: https://www.treasury.gov/initiatives/fio/reports-and-notices/Documents/2015%20FIO%20Annual%20Report_Final.pdf

QUESTIONS AND PROBLEMS

Questions

1 Explain how the characteristics of, respectively, life and P/C insurers are reflected in the investment assets they hold.

2 Explain what statutory accounting is and how it differs from GAAP accounting.

3 How do the assets and liabilities of both life and P/C insurers differ from depository institutions? How are services offered and fund sources reflected in balance sheet differences?

4 What are policy reserves? How are they calculated for life insurers?

5 Explain how NUM differs from NIM. How similar a role do the two ratios play in financial management decisions?

6 Explain what the loss ratio, expense ratio, combined ratio, and overall profitability ratios indicate in terms of the profitability of P/C insurers. Why are P/C insurers very depend on investment yields? What is the long-tail of liability? How has it affected the financial performance of P/C insurers?

7 Why do P/C insurers have underwriting cycles?

8 Discuss the different operating areas for insurance companies.

*Overview:
Nondepository
Financial
Institutions and
New Forms of
Financing*

9 Explain the differences between whole life, term insurance, variable life, and universal insurance policies. How are premiums determined for whole life versus term insurance?

10 How does climate change risk affect insurance companies? What have insurance companies done to predict and reduce climate change risks?

Problems

1 The Colorado Best Insurance Company has the following financial statements.

   a Calculate and evaluate the following ratios for the company for each year and analyze the trends for the net underwriting margin (NUM); loss ratio expense ratio; combined ratio; and overall profitability ratio, using the information in the income statement above.

   b Calculate the ROE, ROA, NPM, and AU ratios, and do a Dupont Analysis for the trends for the company for the two years using the income statement and balance sheet information provided. Summarize your overall analysis, and any strengths and weaknesses for the firm.

Colorado Best Insurance Company income statement ($ million)

	2016	2017
Premiums written	78,560	67,819
Income statement		
Premiums earned	76,272	65,801
Loss expenses	58,235	55,030
Other expenses	20,653	17,498
Total policy expenses	78,888	72,528
Net underwriting gain	− 2,616	− 6,727
Net investment income	8,670	8,206
Taxes	1,818	263
Net income	4,235	1,217
Average return on investments	7.26%	6.18%

Colorado Best Insurance Company balance sheet ($ millions)

	2016	2017
Assets		
Cash	241	940
Short-term investments	16,948	43,025
Bonds	102,140	88,883
Interest due	1,371	1,395

303

*Insurance
Companies:
Overview,
Operations, and
Performance
Analysis*

Other assets	349	772
Total assets	121,049	135,015
Liabilities		
Accrued losses	28,371	33,003
Loss-adjusted expenses	10,444	10,914
Taxes, licenses, fees	968	1,550
Unearned premiums	28,647	26,715
Other liabilities	12,991	27,547
Total liabilities	81,421	99,729
Equity accounts	39,628	35,286
Total liabilities and equity	121,049	135,015

2   The Premium Mutual Insurance Company has the following financial statements.

a   Calculate and evaluate the following ratios for the company for each year and analyze the trends: net underwriting margin (NUM); loss ratio; expense ratio; combined
ratio; and overall profitability ratio.

b   Calculate the OROE, OROA, OPM, and AU ratios, and do a Dupont Analysis for the
trends in these ratios for the company for the two years.

c.   Summarize your overall analysis, and any strengths and weaknesses for the firm.

Premium Mutual Insurance Company income statement ($ million)

	2016	2017
Total premiums written	8,011	8,975
Less unearned premiums	(375)	(473)
Net earned premiums	7,636	8,502
Net investment income	682	1,022
Total revenues	8,318	9,524
Expenses		
Loss expenses	6,077	7,276
Policyholder dividends	136	4
Operating expenses	1,355	1,511
Total expenses	7,568	8,791
Operating income	750	733
Net underwriting gain*	204	(285)

*Earned premiums – Loss expenses – Operating expenses.

*Overview:
Nondepository
Financial
Institutions and
New Forms of
Financing*

Premium Mutual Insurance Company balance sheet ($ million)

	2017	2017
Assets		
U.S. Treasury bonds	1,169	1,106
Municipal bonds	2,779	3,505
Other bonds	4,161	4,554
Common and preferred stock	3,192	3,260
Mortgages and other loans	2,422	2,501
Other assets	1,652	1,745
Total assets	15,375	16,671
Liabilities and net worth		
Total loss and unearned premium reserves	7,185	7,879
Total surplus (net worth)	8,190	8,792
Total liabilities and net worth	15,375	16,671

3 The Friendly Property & Casualty Insurance Company has the following trends in financial ratios and other data for the past 5 years.

a Evaluate the trends for the past 5 years for the company including the net underwriting margin (NUM); loss ratio; expense ratio; combined ratio; and overall profitability ratio.

b Evaluate the trends in direct premiums written, net premiums written, total admitted assets, and policyholder surplus over the 5 years, including the average annual growth rates in direct premiums written and net premiums written, total admitted assets, and policyholder surplus. Calculate the ROA each year using net income divided by total admitted assets, and average ROE, using net income divided by policyholder surplus, and evaluate these trends.

c Summarize your overall analysis, and any strengths and weaknesses for the firm.

Friendly Property & Casualty Insurance ratio trends

	2013	2014	2015	2016	2017
Loss ratio	70.5	72.5	62.0	72.3	68.2
Expense ratio	32.0	30.9	34.3	36.7	36.9
Combined ratio	102.5	106.4	96.3	109.0	105.1
Investment yield	5.60%	5.00%	4.80%	5.60%	5.20%
Trends in premiums, net income, assets and surplus *($ million)*					
Direct premiums written	8,386	8,675	8,961	12,651	12,218
Net premiums written	8,004	8,370	8,858	12,563	12,119

Net income	260	246	467	(563)	362
Total admitted assets	12,001	13,438	14,757	18,746	18,854
Policyholder surplus	3,359	4,143	4,481	6,546	6,942

4 The Moonlight Corporation (a multiline insurer) has the following income statements, balance sheets, and reported financial ratios for a 2-year period reported below.

a   Calculate and evaluate the following ratios for the company for each year and analyze the trends for the net underwriting margin (NUM); loss ratio expense ratio; combined ratio; and overall profitability ratio, using the information in the income statement above.

b   Calculate the ROE, ROA, NPM, and AU ratios, and do a Dupont Analysis for the trends for the company for the 2 years using the income statement and balance sheet information provided.

c   Summarize your overall analysis, and any strengths and weaknesses for the firm.

Moonlight Corporation income statements current and previous year

	Previous year	Current year
Balance sheet		
Assets ($ thousand)		
Cash and investments	603,857	677,293
Reinsurance assets	211,386	274,707
Deferred policy acquisition costs	21,985	22,510
Other assets	74,516	38,175
Total assets	911,744	1,012,685
Liabilities and equity		
Policy reserves	532,807	557,546
Debt	24,900	39,644
Other liabilities	87,482	121,536
Total liabilities	645,189	718,726
Total common equity	266,555	293,959
Total liabilities and equity	911,744	1,012,685
Income statement		
Revenues		
Policy revenues	141,884	142,324
Net investment income	24,558	23,937

(Continued)

Overview:
Nondepository
Financial
Institutions and
New Forms of
Financing

(Continued)

	Previous year	Current year
Net realized gains	2,982	1,853
Other revenues	951	1,337
Total revenues	$170,375	$169,451
Expenses		
Policy expenses	61,252	64,728
Other expenses	66,053	64,722
Interest expense	1,548	2,280
Total expenses	128,853	131,730
Net income before taxes	41,522	37,721
Provision for taxes	11,351	9,482
Net Income	30,171	28,239
Reported financial ratios (%)		
Return on average assets	3.43	2.93
Return on average equity	12.93	10.08
Investment yield	4.66	4.03
Operating income to revenues	23.95	22.76
Other ratios reported (%)		
Combined ratio	86.80	88.20
Policy reserves to equity	2.00	1.90
Debt to equity	8.54	11.88

Chapter 12

Mutual Funds and Pension Management

A relaxing retirement is supposed to be the reward for a lifetime of work and yet it seems we must pass an entrance exam to reach it.

(Mullainathan, 2015, p. 11)

INVESTING for future goals, such as for a down payment for a house, saving for college expenses, a trip, or for retirement, poses challenges particularly with volatile financial markets, such as expressed in the quote above. Average life expectancies have increased; so individuals need to save more for retirement to ensure sufficient income. Accordingly to the U.S. Social Security website, a man reaching age 65 today can expect to live to age 84.3, and a women turning 65 can expect to live to age 86.6. Hence, individuals can expect to live 20 or more years in retirement, so need to have funds available to have a regular income during their retirement (Social Security, 2015). There has been a shift in many countries including the United States; individuals are now responsible for investing for retirement, with a movement away from defined benefit (DB) plans, where companies provide retirement payments for employees in retirement, to defined contribution (DC) plans where employee and employer contributions are invested in mutual funds that employees choose based on a menu of different funds offered by employers. Hence, employees have to become educated in choosing and monitoring their investment funds and saving for their own retirement, with employees rather than employers taking on the investment risk.

While many countries have government-defined benefit pension plans for citizens or government and state workers, many DB funds are currently having financial problems, and governments have had to lower benefits or delay the minimum retirement age, such as calls for reforming Greece's ailing pension system, by raising the retirement age to 67 years by 2022 and cutting pensions by 10% for early retirees that have taken benefits (Koutantou and Papadimas, 2015).

Elizabeth Brown (2012) notes that 14 countries that provide government pension benefits to citizens raised their minimum retirement ages as they grappled with deficits, including Spain in 2011 raising the minimum age from 65 to 67, Austria from 61.5 to 65 for men, and from 56.5 to 60 for women, the United Kingdom with a gradual rise from 65 to 67 by 2028,

Overview:
Nondepository
Financial
Institutions and
New Forms of
Financing

Germany with a gradual rise from 65 to 67 by 2029, and Italy initiating a rise from 62 to 69 for men and from 60 to 67 for women by 2050. In the United States, similarly, the minimum age for taking full social security benefits has increased to 67 for those born in 1960 or later, with the emphasis that social security is enacted as only a supplement to provide more adequate provision for old-age benefits, versus being a full retirement plan. In the United States the average monthly security retirement benefit as of January 2015 is $1,328 or about $15,936 a year, so it's important for individuals to save for retirement (Social Security FAQs, 2015).

Since 1980, there has also been a large decline in the number of DB plans offered by companies to employees and a large rise in DC plans, particularly in the United States. The Employee Benefit Research Institute (ebr.org, 2015) reports for the United States that, as of 2012, only 3% of private sector workers participated only in DB plans (this represents 7% of private sector employees with retirement plans), 31% participated in defined contribution (DC) plans (representing 69% of private sector employees with retirement plans), and 11% participated in both DB and DC plans (representing 24% of private sector employees in retirement plans). This compares with 28% of private sector employees participating in defined benefit plans in 1980 (62% of private sector employees with retirement plans), and 8% at that time participating in defined contribution plans (17% of employees with retirement plans). To encourage individuals to save for their retirement, governments have initiated programs for tax-free savings vehicles, such as, in the United States, individual retirement accounts (IRAs) in either traditional IRAs, whereby taxes are paid when distributions on IRAs are taken at retirement, or Roth IRAs, where taxes are deducted at the time of the investment, allowing distributions to be tax-free, when taken at retirement.

With the trend away from DB plans to DC plans, individuals need to become better educated on different types of mutual funds and learn how to invest on their own and plan for retirement. With this in mind, along with poor investment decisions made globally by investors concerning investments in risky, subprime collateralized default obligations and subprime home mortgages prior to the subprime loan crisis in 2007 to 2008, there has been much concern about financial literacy. Governments, such as the U.S. government, are attempting to provide resources for individual investors to increase their knowledge of different types of investments, costs, and risks.

GOVERNMENT EFFORTS TO IMPROVE FINANCIAL LITERACY AND SAVING

Following the subprime loan crisis in the United States, the Dodd–Frank Wall Street Reform and Consumer Protection Act of 2010 mandated a study regarding financial literacy among investors by the Securities and Exchange Commission (SEC). The study examined the existing level of financial literacy among retail investors, and methods to improve the content, and format of investment disclosures to investors. The study also examined the most useful, understandable, and relevant information that investors need to make informed financial decisions. A survey of U.S. retail investors found that on average they lacked basic financial literacy, with even less literacy for minority groups and women. The study also found that investors preferred receiving disclosures from financial intermediaries before purchasing an investment product or service that includes details on fees, disciplinary history, investment strategy, and conflicts of interest, as essential in summary documents (SEC, 2012).

Similarly, the Financial Industry Regulatory Authority (FINRA) (2015), a non-governmental agency regulating the securities industry, did a survey of U.S. retail investors in 2012, and found that 33% of respondents had taxable investment accounts, 29% had just retirement accounts, and 38% had no investment accounts. Among groups in the survey, investors in taxable investment accounts were the most astute with 26% participating in financial education, 60% showing high financial literacy, and 55% having sought advice on saving and investing. This investor group had a higher tolerance for risk (a mean rating of 5.8 on a scale of 1 to 10). Those with no accounts had the lowest percentage of high financial literacy, lowest risk tolerance (mean of 4.2) and were less likely to seek advice and participate in financial education. FINRA has developed a website to provide education to investors at its sites (FINRA.org/Investors and RetirementMadeSimpler.org). Similarly, the Securities and Exchange Commission (SEC) has a financial education website on different types of investments (at: http://investor.gov), including information on diversification and types of mutual funds and operating costs for different funds (at: http://investor.gov/investing-basics/investment-products/mutual-funds).

Often workers are trying to just get by and feel that they cannot afford to save. In the United Kingdom, a law was recently passed requiring employers to offer employees a savings plan and this is currently being phased in. If employees opt in, it will allow employees to start putting just 2% of their salary into a retirement account. Employers match a portion of that, with the total the employer matches gradually increasing over time to at least 8%. As behavioral economists note, employees are more willing to save this way, since by having employers take funds out, there is less a feeling that money is being taken out of their pocket. For the United Kingdom savings program, the early results see over 90% of people opting in, since employees see that they'll be losing money provided by employers if they don't, with 5 million people saving as a start for the program. For more than half the workers in the United Kingdom who have been enrolled, their employers have chosen an investment vehicle set up by the government, run by a former bank executive, Tim Jones, who capped fees at 0.5% a year to allow workers to earn a health investment return over time (Arnold, 2015b).

OVERVIEW FOR MUTUAL FUNDS

Mutual funds are a popular, diversified investment. The SEC's Investor.gov (2015) points out advantages of mutual funds including:

- **Professional management:** Providing expertise and research and monitoring the performance of mutual funds.
- **Diversification:** Not putting all your "eggs in one basket," with investments in a range of companies and industries to lower your overall portfolio risk.
- **Affordability:** Being able to invest in a portfolio of stocks for a relatively low dollar amount for an initial investment and subsequent purchases.
- **Liquidity:** For open-end mutual funds, investors can redeem shares at any time for the current net asset value (NAV) in addition to any redemption fees.

(http://investor.gov/investing-basics/investment-products/
mutual-funds)

Overview:
Nondepository
Financial
Institutions and
New Forms of
Financing

While a small investor would have difficulty creating a diversified portfolio with an investment of $500 to $1,000, purchasing shares of a mutual fund allows the small investor to invest in a diversified portfolio, such as Standard & Poor's (S&P) 500 index with 500 stocks in different industry sectors. Mutual funds also provide accounting and reinvesting of dividend services, as well as offering research and advice on websites or convenient locations, and advice on planning for retirement and handling mandated distributions from IRAs in retirement (in the United States, when an investor reaches age 70½). For open-end mutual funds discussed below, shares can be redeemed at any time at the current net asset value and new shares can be purchased, providing liquidity.

GENERAL TYPES OF MUTUAL FUNDS

As Investor.gov (2015) notes, basic types of mutual funds moving from lower risk and higher liquidity to higher risk and less liquidity include:

- **Money market funds** that invest in high-quality money market securities, such as U.S. government Treasury bills, and other short-term securities with a maturity of 1 year or less that are highly marketable.
- **Bond funds** that invest in government and corporate bonds; different types and maturities, and investment quality defining their risks.
- **Stock funds** that invest in corporate stocks including many different types of stock funds, such as: growth funds that focus on potential financial gains versus dividend; income funds that focus on paying dividends; index funds that track a particular market index, such as the S&P 500 index, and sector funds that specialize in a particular industry segment.
- There are also **hybrid or balanced mutual funds** that invest in both stocks and bonds, among many other types of mutual funds.

OVERVIEW AND HISTORY OF MUTUAL FUNDS

Mutual funds differ around the world, but all mutual funds are organized whereby individual (retail) investors as well as institutional investors purchase shares in different portfolio funds of their choice, including those that are all stocks, all bonds, a mix of stocks and bonds (balanced funds), money market funds, or other types of investments (asset allocation funds, index funds, sector funds, international and global funds, real estate funds, commodity funds, market neutral funds, among others). This allows diversification and management expertise and research at a low cost, with a wide selection of both passively managed index funds and actively managed equity funds based on alternative investment manager styles, such as value investing, growth or aggressive investing, blending (a blend of the two), among others.

As noted in the *Investment Company Institute (ICI) 2015 Fact Book*, the concept of an investment company offering a diversified investment opportunity to smaller investors emerged in Europe in the later 1700s when a Dutch merchant established an investment trust for this purpose. Later in London the Foreign and Colonial Trust was set up to allow smaller investors to supply funds for investments abroad, and in 1873, the Scottish and American Trust was created to allow smaller investors to invest in railroad bonds and other investments supporting the emerging U.S. economy at this time. Many trusts for investment emerged in the 1800s, and the first open-end mutual fund by the Massachusetts Investors Trust in the United States in 1924.

The establishment of regulations for investment company structure and operations provided greater confidence in mutual fund operations. This includes the U.S. Investment Company Act of 1940 that regulates investment company structure and operations and requirements for diversification. In the United States mutual funds grew from 68 funds with $0.45 billion total net assets in 1940 to 7,923 funds with total net assets of $15.9 trillion by year-end 2014. In the United States, as of the beginning of 2015, 43% of U.S. households hold mutual fund shares. On a worldwide level, net assets invested in mutual funds and exchange traded funds by year-end 2014 were $33.4 trillion, growing from about $4 trillion in 1993 (*Investment Company Institute Fact Book*, 2015).

As a force in financial markets, investment companies managing mutual funds in the United States hold a 30% share of corporate equities, 26% municipal securities 46% share of commercial paper, and 11% share of government securities (*Investment Company Institute Fact Book*, 2015). As large institutional investors, mutual funds are active participants in corporate governance and trading and investing in financial markets.

ORGANIZATION AND DIFFERING REGULATIONS FOR MUTUAL FUNDS GLOBALLY

Mutual funds differ in their structure in different countries, with various cultural and regulatory environments affecting the construction and organization of mutual funds and restrictions on who can purchase funds and what funds can be purchased, such as capital controls on foreign investors. The stability of a country's financial system and regulatory environment, economic development income and wealth, market efficiency and liquidity affect the development and growth of mutual funds within a country. Other factors affecting differences include tax rules, a strong legal system, and government tax incentives for retirement vehicles; also, investment restrictions, including how open a country is to foreign direct investment and international trade, and cultural factors, such as a propensity for saving affects global differences in the development growth of mutual funds.

For instance, Mary Brown (2012) points out differences in global regulations affecting mutual fund growth. In the United States mutual funds must be registered with the Securities and Exchange Commission (SEC) and operate under the Investment Company Act of 1940 ("40's Act"), including requirements for diversification, and limits on the use of investments in other investment companies. Under Rule 35d-1 ("name test") 80% of a mutual fund's holdings must reflect the name of the fund and its mission provided in its prospectus. In European Union (EU) countries, mutual funds for sale are under regulations enacted under the Undertakings for Collective Investment in Transferable Securities (UCITS), including rules on monitoring the risk of derivative positions under UCITS III. Funds need to be registered in an EU country under the auspices of that country's financial regulator, such as, for Ireland, the Irish Financial Services Regulatory Authority (IFSRA). Regulatory authorities are also part of the Committee of European Securities Regulators, given the task of the coordination of all EU country security regulators.

Overview:
Nondepository
Financial
Institutions and
New Forms of
Financing

There are many other different mutual fund regulations country by country. In some countries, regulators have very specific rules and restrictions to protect investments against speculation, such as in Hong Kong, where the Mandatory Provident Funds Authority (MPFA) has very specific rules and regulations with other broader rules under the Securities and Futures Commission (SFC) as the two major governing bodies (M. Brown, 2012).

There are also regulations concerning cross-listing of funds and selling shares across country borders. In July of 2015, China and Hong Kong started cross-border sales of funds for approximately 100 Hong Kong funds and 850 qualifying counterparts in China, with combined assets of 2.3 trillion yuan, providing a channel for Hong Kong asset-management firms to provide mutual funds to smaller investors with about $8 trillion of household savings in China (Nishizawa, Li, and Chan, 2015). Although some countries allow the purchase of mutual funds by noncitizens directly through fund issuers, others restrict ownership to investors that are citizens in their countries (Hirby, 2015).

DETERMINANTS OF RAPID MUTUAL FUND GROWTH IN DIFFERENT COUNTRIES

ICI Global Research (2014) in a study of global mutual funds found that from 1993 to September 2013, European mutual fund assets grew by 640% to almost $9 trillion, the U.S. fund assets by close to 600% to $14.3 trillion, Asian Pacific fund assets by 450% to $3.3 trillion, and funds in the rest of the world by 2,200% to $2.3 trillion. Studies of factors that have led to the global growth of mutual funds point out important factors including: (1) capital market development; (2) investor confidence in the integrity, liquidity, and efficiency of markets; (3) a financial market orientation; (4) increased globalization of finance; (5) the presence of large multinational financial groups in a large number of countries; (6) transparency in markets to allow market to market valuation for assets; (7) stronger performance for equity and bond markets, stable capital markets with a larger supply of investable securities; (8) effective and robust regulatory frameworks and auditing rules for the disclosure of information to maintain transparency; and (9) the rise of a large middle class in many countries and the movement away from defined benefit to defined contribution plans and other individual retirement vehicles to encourage retirement savings (ICI Global Research Perspective, 2014; Klapper, Sulla, and Vittas, 2003). With a strong regulatory framework, and greater confidence in financial markets after the subprime crisis, by year-end 2014, there were 16,660 investment companies, employing 166,000 (34% in fund management, 30% in investor servicing, 10% in fund administration, and 26% in sales and distribution), operating in the United States, including 9,260 open-end mutual funds, 568 closed-end funds, 1,451 exchange traded funds (ETFs), and 5,381 unit investment trusts (UITs) (Icifactbook.org, 2015a,b).

MUTUAL FUND REGULATIONS

Mutual funds are subject to strict regulations and oversight. As an example, in the United States mutual funds are overseen by the SEC, which requires complete disclosures to investors in a written prospectus, including the fund's goals, fees, expenses, investment strategies, and risk, along with information on purchasing and selling shares. The *Investment Act of 1933* mandates specific disclosures, and the Securities Act of 1935 sets out antifraud rules covering the purchase and sale of fund shares. The *Investment Act of 1940* requires all funds to register with the SEC and to meet certain operating standards. Section 18 of the 1970 Act also limits the financial leverage of mutual funds (with open-end funds not allowed to issue debt securities and only allowed bank loans up to 33% of a fund's total assets, as long as assets are greater than three times outstanding loans). Funds must hold securities (marked to market daily) in segregated accounts that are no less than equal to the values of the liabilities created. The *1940 Act (subchapter M)* requires mutual funds to pass-through distribution of 90% of income and capital gains to shareholders to allow these not to be taxed under the Internal Revenue Code.

U.S. mutual funds also must meet tests including: (1) the *Short 3's Test,* whereby no more than 30% of gross income can come from the sale of securities held for less than three months; and (2) *diversification tests*, whereby no more than 25% of assets can be held in securities of any one issuer for diversified funds, excluding government securities. Also, subject to limitations, at least 50% of assets must be invested in securities and cash equivalents (cash or short-term securities). With a boom in mutual funds in the 1990s, the SEC mandated clearer prospectuses for mutual funds, so average investors could understand the content, including having a statement of a fund's objectives and a brief risk/return summary at the start of each prospectus with a narrative risk summary; a bar chart showing annual return over 1, 5, and 10 years compared to benchmark indexes; the highest and lowest return in any one quarter; a table of performance figures; and a fee table.

Other rules have been passed to encourage greater transparency, ethics, and fiduciary duty for the mutual fund industry, including in the United States the *Mutual Fund Reform Act of 2004* amending the 40's Act to: (1) reduce from 60% to 25% the maximum number of interested directors on boards of registered investment companies; and (2) prohibiting an interested person from serving as chair of the board of directors, with the fiduciary duty of the board of directors to act in the best interests of shareholders, and an investment adviser is required to supply material information needed for the independent directors to review and govern a company.

The SEC was also asked to require a registered investment company and its investment advisers and principal underwriters to adopt a code of ethics. Provisions include the certification by each senior executive officer to certify in periodic reports to shareholders that specified procedures are in place to verify compliance with transparency and specific ethical considerations, along with whistleblower protection for employees of publicly traded companies and registered investment companies. The SEC is also directed to develop standardized disclosures for: (1) expense and transaction cost ratios; (2) cost structures; (3) investment adviser compensation; (4) point of sale; and (5) additional disclosures of broker compensation (Congress.gov, 2015).

Following the subprime loan crisis, in 2010, the SEC enacted amendments mandating liquidity baskets in money market funds, improving underlying credit quality, shortening the maturities of holdings, and introducing stress testing (Prior, 2015). In 2014, the SEC adopted money market reform rules making structural and operational reforms to address risks of investor runs, requiring a floating net asset value for institutional prime money market funds versus special pricing and valuation conventions that permitted a constant share price of $1.00 to be maintained. Money market fund boards also have the right to impose fees and gates during periods of stress. The SEC also imposed enhanced diversification, disclosure and stress

Overview:
Nondepository
Financial
Institutions and
New Forms of
Financing

requirements, and updated reporting by money market funds and private funds acting like money market funds (SEC, 2014).

DIFFERENT TYPES OF MUTUAL FUNDS

Open-End versus Closed-End Mutual Funds

Two kinds of mutual funds are open-end and closed-end mutual funds. The majority of mutual funds are open-end funds (in the United States $15.9 trillion of net assets managed at year-end 2014), where open-end funds are often referred to just as "*mutual funds*" versus other types of funds. *Open-end funds* continuously offer new shares to the public and redeem (buy back) shares at any time upon a shareholder's request (unless a fund becomes too large and is sometimes closed to new investors). By federal law, *mutual funds* in the United States are required to redeem (buy back) outstanding shares upon a shareholder's request at a price based at the current value of the fund's net asset value (NAV), where the calculation for NAV is:

$$NAV = (Market\ value\ securities - Liabilities)/(No.\ shares\ outstanding).$$

NAVs are calculated and posted at the end of each day of trading and reported in the financial news the following day. An example is the *Wall Street Journal* Market Data Center, which posts NAVs for mutual funds alphabetically by fund family listings (at: http://online.wsj.com/mdc/public/page/2_3048-usmfunds_A-usmfunds.html), such as below for the Vanguard S&P 500 index (VFINX) fund on July 15, 2015 as:

Name	Symbol	NAV	Change	% YTD return	3-year % change
500	VFINX	194.57	− 0.14	3.4	18.1

The NAV is given for the end-of-day trading, along with the change from the previous day, the percentage year to date (% YTD) return, and the percentage 3-year change in NAV.

The *Wall Street Journal* and the *New York Times, Forbes, Money Magazine*, and many other news sources have special informational issues on mutual fund rankings for different funds by:

1   *Type*, the investment type of the fund based on the investment style of the fund.
2   *Rating (RAT)*, the performance rating for the past three years, reported by Morningstar, Inc. with ratings from 1 to 5 (5 high) for each fund, with ratings adjusted for risk and sales charges for funds with at least a 3-year history.
3   *NAV*, net asset value of the fund.
4   *Total % return* usually for the total calendar quarter, the past 12 months, and 5-year returns, including invested dividends.
5   *Expense ratio (Exp. Ratio)*, the percentage of fund assets paid for operating expenses and management fees including 12b-1 fees and administrative fees (brokerage costs and sales charges are not included).
6   *Turnover*, the rate at which the fund buys and sells assets (100% is when a fund's trading over a year equals its assets).
7   *Manager years (Mgr. Yrs)*, the average number of years the current manager has managed the fund.

As an example, *The New York Times*, Sunday, July 12, 2015, special section on Mutual Funds and ETFs (on p. 19) reported for American Century Funds for its Equity Income Investment (EqIncInv) as:

Fund name	Type	RAT	NAV	Total % return Qtr.	12-Mo.	5Yrs.	Exp.Ratio	Turn over	Mgr. Yrs.
EqIncInv	LV	3/2	8.52	− 1.6	+ 2.1	+ 12.4	0.93	56	16.3

The type indicated is large value (LV). Large value is an investment style, whereby stocks are selected for a portfolio with an intrinsic value larger than the average stock market value. For this equity income fund the (RAT) rating of 3/2 shows a 3 Morningstar weighted average rating for the last 3, 5, and 10 years (about average; with ratings of 1 to 5) and a 2 rating for the last 3 years compared to other similar funds of this type. The NAV of 8.52 is for the end of the quarter. The fund had a quarterly total percentage return of − 1.6%, a 12-month return of 2.1%, and 12.4% over the past 5 years. The expense ratio is 0.93%, the average turnover ratio 56, and the fund manager has managed the fund for 16.3 years.

Websites for different fund families, such as Fidelity (www.fidelity.com), Vanguard (www.vanguard.com), and T.Rowe Price (www.individual.troweprice.com), among many others, provide research and fund comparisons. Comparisons include ratings developed by Morningstar, a prominent mutual fund information company. Morningstar's ratings are for different types of funds, along with comparisons on fund expenses. For instance if you go to the Fidelity website and click on research, you can select an asset class or a fund type and see a comparison of matching funds. You can also reduce your search by selecting different attributes, such as Morningstar rankings (5 stars highest); type of fund; average returns; and net and gross expense ratio; among other choices. For example, for a moderate allocation fund, the Fidelity Balanced Fund (FBALX), the following information is provided:

Morningstar symbol	YTD (Daily)	1 year	3 year	5 year	10 year	Net Exp.Ratio	Overall
FBALX	4.12%	6.38%	12.76%	12.59%	7.49%	0.56%	*****

For this balanced fund that includes stocks and bonds, the 10-year average return is 7.49%, with other returns listed including the daily year to date mean return (YTD) of 4.12% as of July 16, 2015, and a 5-star overall Morningstar rating reflecting both risk and return. By clicking on other choices, searches can be made on different criteria including volatility measures (the 3-year Sharpe ratio, the standard deviation of returns, the beta of the portfolio, and the R^2 as a diversification measure), among many other search choices.

More detailed information can be found on a particular fund. For instance, on the Vanguard website, by clicking on Vanguard Dividend Growth Fund from the Vanguard Fund family, a Morningstar Snapshot is provided for the fund, with a net expense ratio of 0.32%, a $3,000 minimum investment, 23% turnover rate, a 30-day yield of 1.97%, a 4-star Morningstar rating, and an overview of the fund's objective, strategy, and risk information. For this particular fund, the strategy is provided to invest in stocks with a stream of growing income over time. The fund has a secondary objective of long-term capital appreciation and current income. The top 10 holdings of stocks in the fund are given, along with other more detailed information.

Overview:
Nondepository
Financial
Institutions and
New Forms of
Financing

Closed-End Funds and Unit Investment Trusts

In the United States at year-end 2014, closed-end funds managed $289 billion in net assets. *Closed-end funds* issue a fixed number of shares that trade over the counter or on a stock exchange. Once closed-end funds are issued, they are sold in public markets at their current market value, just like stocks. Thus closed-end funds can trade below their net asset value and have brokerage commissions. They are less popular than open-end funds, since open-end funds are more liquid and redeemable at any time. However, closed-end funds can be traded more frequently. An investment company manages the fund according to the policies and objectives of the fund. Many closed-end funds are bond, convertible bond, or preferred stock funds, that allow trading of a bond portfolio dedicated to a particular type of bond, such as municipal bond funds, high yield bond funds, U.S. government bond funds, or investment grade bond funds, among others.

Closed-end funds price quotes include the NAV, along with the most recent market closing price from the exchange in which the securities are primarily traded. Closed-end funds often sell at a discount from their NAV. Closed-end funds can also include portfolios of global stocks. An example is the Morgan Stanley China A Share Fund, Inc. where on July 17, 2015, the NAV for the fund was reported on the Closed-End fund Center (cefa) (www.cefa. com) as $42.17 (net change from the previous day of $1.19), with a market price of $31.17 (market change of $0.51), and selling at a discount from its NAV of − 6.08%. The inception date, number of managers, portfolio turnover ratio, management fee, and expense ratio are all provided. The 5-year average discount is − 5.30% and year to date discount, −15.72%, with a fund objective of seeking capital growth by investing with normally at least 80% of its assets in A shares of Chinese companies on the Shanghai and Shenzhen Stock Exchanges (http://www.cefa.com/FundSelector/FundDetail.fs?ID=111897).

Unit investment companies often issue investment trusts (UTIs) that offer interests in a fixed portfolio of securities held passively for an agreed-upon period of time, whereby assets are distributed among the shareholders. As of year-end 2014, UITs managed $101 billion in net assets (*Investment Company Institute Fact Book*, 2015). Real estate investment trusts (REITs) offer shares in real estate investments. Unit trusts may redeem shares at net asset value but only in large blocks. Hence, closed-end funds and UITs do not have the liquidity concerns of open-end funds that agree to redeem shares upon request to investors at NAV.

As Morningstar.com points out, a REIT is generally operated by a company that owns and manages real estate that produces income, as established in the United States by an act of Congress in 1960 to allow small as well as large investors to earn rental income from commercial property. REITs must obey many regulations, including the distribution of 90% of their taxable income as dividends to shareholder each year; having 75% of assets in real estate, cash, and government securities; having at least 75% of gross income from rents, mortgage interest, or other investments in real estate; and shares owned by at least 100 shareholders.

Different REITs have different specializations, with a majority investing in malls, shopping centers, offices, and industrial centers, while others invest in many other types, such as movie theatres, golf courses, hotels, self-storage unit facilities, among many others. Investors benefit from higher dividend yields secured by long-term leases and gaining diversification by having real estate as part of a larger investment portfolio (Morningstar.com, 2015a). Although REITs are sometimes used to diversify stock portfolios, care has to be taken in selecting REITs, since some REITs are very specialized, and can actually reduce portfolio diversification.

Exchange Traded Funds (ETFs)

Exchange traded funds (ETFs) have been very popular in recent years with about $2.0 trillion managed by year-end 2014. ETFs trade on the market like closed-end funds do. An investment company with ETFs has shares that are traded during the day on stock exchanges at market prices. ETF shares are purchased just like stocks from brokers or mutual fund families. They are similar to index mutual funds in being passively managed and mimicking an index. ETFs are "securities certificates" that provide a legal right of ownership for a share of the basket of individual securities, and are flexible in being able to be bought and sold throughout a trading day and being bought on margin like a stock, and also offering short positions to be taken. As passively managed funds, they have low annual expenses. ETFs like closed-end funds are like stocks and can potentially trade below net asset value like other closed-end stocks.

ETFs come in different types and often have interesting names, such as the Diamond Trust Series (DIAMONDS), which track the Dow Jones Industrial Average; fixed-income exchange traded securities (FITRs), which track various Treasury securities; holding company depository receipts (HOLDRs) that track narrow industry sector groups; Standard & Poor depository receipts (Spiders or SPDRS), which track a number of different S&P indexes, and Vanguard index participation receipts (VIPERs), that track several Vanguard fund family index funds. There are hundreds of different types of ETFs including those that track different commodity share prices. Many mutual fund family companies also have their own ETFs.

Alternative Strategies Funds

Following the 2008 subprime loan crisis, investment companies created alternative or hedge mutual funds to meet the desires of investors to broaden their portfolio holdings to reduce the correlation of their investments with the market, by including small amounts of leverage and investing in alternative financial securities and instruments, such as derivatives to hedge against declines in different market sectors. An example would be using options and short positions in securities and sectors that seem overvalued to hedge long positions. Both equity and bond alternative strategies can be used (*Investment Company Institute Fact Book*, 2015).

Diedrich (2014) points out that this newer type of "hedged mutual fund" is often offered by large hedge funds that have gained scale and expanded into mutual fund markets. Alternative strategies funds try to have a hedge fund-like exposure within a mutual fund structure by utilizing leverage, derivatives, and short selling. By this means mutual fund investors in alternative funds gain some access to strategies traditionally used by hedge funds, such as merger arbitrage, convertible arbitrage, long/short equity, and macro trading, among others. However, performance manager fees are not allowed for mutual fund managers and, unlike hedge funds, mutual funds are under greater regulations and have a greater need for liquidity. Consequently, fund managers do not have the flexibility of hedge funds, and mutual fund investors primarily use them for diversification purposes (Diedrich, 2014).

A number of different news sources, such as *U.S. News Money* (2015) and Morningstar (2015b) provide ratings on multi-alternative strategy funds that use different alternative strategy tactics, with a gross short exposure greater than 20% as defined by Morningstar. Some alternative funds that are more defensive include market neutral, bear market, managed futures, and commodity funds among others. Some funds invest in EFTs to get this exposure, while other funds use options and other types of hedging instruments.

HEDGE FUNDS (THAT ARE NOT MUTUAL FUNDS)

Hedge funds are another popular type of fund for wealthy, accredited investors, as defined by the U.S. Securities and Exchange Commission (SEC) under Regulation D (adopted by the SEC to assist small businesses in selling unregistered security to accredited investors). Investments are only allowed in hedge funds for financially sophisticated investors that are assumed to need less regulatory protection (investors with net worth over $1 million and income greater than $200,000; $300,000 for couples). Hedge funds are set up as limited partnerships with private, unregulated investment funds. Accredited investors are generally required to have large minimum investments of $1 million and typically pay high fees such as 1 to 2% of assets, as well as about 20% of profits. With the Dodd–Frank Act, the SEC is required to review the definition of an accredited investor every four years. Hedge fund managers look for market inefficiencies to take advantage of.

Typically, hedge funds are not liquid and strategies often go along with hedging against market downturns, and often make use of derivatives, short selling, and high financial leverage, so are more risky than mutual funds, and some have failed, such as Long-Term Capital Management in 1998. As unregulated funds, hedge funds are not subject to SEC monitoring and reporting, so investors have less information on previous performance to consider. As noted by Diedrich (2014), hedge funds experienced great consolidation in recent years, with lower growth in client flows, the top 287 hedge funds managing $1.5 trillion in total assets (about 60% of the total) of 10,000 hedge funds operating. Consequently, some of the largest hedge funds achieved the scale necessary to allow for greater asset growth.

MUTUAL FUND FAMILIES OR COMPLEXES

Mutual fund families (or complexes) offer investment research and advice and are managed by investment company fund families (complexes) that offer different mutual fund choices. As noted by the *Investment Company Institute Fact Book* (2015) fund families provide economies of scale and scope, allowing lower costs for investors in funds. Often within a country, fund families dominate mutual fund markets, but other types of financial institutions also offer mutual funds, including banks and insurance companies. For instance, in the United States, 80% of fund complexes were independent fund advisers, 8% non-U.S. fund advisers, 5% insurance companies, 5% banks or thrifts, and 2% brokerage firms. Overall 867 financial companies from around the world compete in the United States to provide investment management services to fund investors. In the United States the largest five companies have 43% of total net assets for mutual funds, with the largest 10 companies holding a 55% share, and the largest 25 mutual fund families holding a 74% market share. The 10 largest fund complexes also manage the majority of assets for passively managed index mutual funds (*Investment Company Institute Fact Book*, 2015). The largest U.S. mutual fund families include Fidelity Investments, Vanguard, American Fund, Franklin Templeton Investments, and T. Rowe Price, among other large fund families.

THE AFFILIATE MANAGEMENT
STRUCTURE OF MUTUAL FUNDS

Mutual funds make up about 95% of professionally managed assets. The companies that manage the funds are generally privately or publicly owned and may be subsidiaries of large financial services companies or financial holding companies that include banks, securities firms, and insurance companies. Almost all mutual funds are externally managed, with operations conducted by investment companies and other affiliated organizations and independent contractors.

Mutual funds are unique since typically many activities are outsourced to different companies, creating a complex network of companies as principal service providers. Investment adviser affiliates manage funds and receive annual fees based on percentages of average net assets they control. They often provide administrative and accounting services, or an unaffiliated party does this work. Separate organizations designated as principal underwriters usually distribute shares for mutual funds, which are regulated as brokers and dealers to continuously offer new shares to the public. Mutual funds are required by law to protect portfolio securities by placing them with custodians that are usually qualified banks. Transfer agents help mutual funds to conduct record-keeping and related functions and maintain customer service. Independent public accountants are also employed to certify a fund's financial statements. The fund's board of directors oversees the fund's activities including approving contracts with management companies and other service providers. The investment adviser's job includes portfolio management and securities trading. Traders place orders with broker/dealers and try to obtain the most expedient and lowest cost execution of these orders. Affiliates may be part of a single company or a collection of different companies.

Although a mutual fund is owned by its shareholders, the investment firm that runs a mutual fund's operations can be mutually owned by shareholders, privately held, publicly owned, or be subsidiaries of other companies. Many large funds, such as Fidelity Investment Company, which is privately owned by the Johnson family, have their investment operations centered in one area, such as the East Coast, with affiliates in other areas, and may be very diverse with other subsidiaries as well including a life insurance, real estate, or other interests. Mutual funds are "jacks of all trades" offering a wide variety of financial services, including brokerage operations, management and research, wealth management, institutional retirement services, credit and debit cards, securities execution and clearance, corporate systems and services, insurance, automated bill paying, and annuities, among other services. In terms of ownership structure, Vanguard is one of the few U.S. funds that is mutually owned by its fund investors, which allows the company to keep its expenses low.

In the United States funds are organized under state law, often as a Massachusetts business trust, Delaware or other state statutory trust, or as corporations under Maryland law. Each fund has a board of trustees or directors that are elected by shareholders, with 40% required to be independent, with most funds having a majority of independent directors, and typically funds within a complex have a common board or at times two or more boards over all funds. "Interested" directors typically include executives of a sponsor or fund management company.

Hoene and Bressler (2015) point out that mutual fund boards are unique in being charged to serve the interests of shareholders, while fund sponsors or distributors who collect asset-based fees for managing funds may have incentives to increase assets under management and to charge higher fees. This can result in potential conflicts of interest, such as in association with the approval of the investment advisory contract and fee. The U.S. Investment Company Act (ICA) of 1940 requires investment advisers to register with the SEC, to provide disclosure about themselves and their business to clients, and imposes fiduciary duty and anti-fraud standards on investment advisers. Hence, independent directors serve as "watchdogs" for funds and there are tensions between independent directors and fund managers, with two independent director trade associations, the Independent Directors Council and the Mutual Fund Directors Forum, to provide support, education, and policy development for positions on independent directors that are submitted to Congress and regulators.

*Overview:
Nondepository
Financial
Institutions and
New Forms of
Financing*

MARKETING OF MUTUAL FUNDS

Fund families use a combination of direct and indirect marketing. With direct marketing, investors contact a fund directly on their website or use toll-free phone numbers or contact local mutual fund offices. Often funds advertise on television and magazines and other media to increase retail investors' awareness of a fund and its services, including advice for saving for retirement. With indirect marketing funds are sold through brokers or investment advisers with securities firms, banks, insurance companies, and other financial services firms. A retirement channel also is often used where employer-sponsored defined contribution plans give defined contribution pension plan investors a choice of mutual funds to invest in. Other channels are through discount brokers who offer different mutual funds from a large number of sponsors, and institutional channels where endowments, foundations, businesses, financial institutions, and other institutional investors engage in transactions with mutual funds or through third parties to mutual funds.

THE COST OF MUTUAL FUND OWNERSHIP: UNDERSTANDING FEES

Mutual fund shareholder fees must be disclosed in a standardized fee table at the front of a fund's prospectus. This fee table classifies fees and expenses so that shareholders can see what they will be paying for when purchasing fund shares and can use these to compare the investing costs of other funds. Fees include two main categories: shareholder fees and annual fund operating expenses. FINRA has a Mutual Fund Analyzer (at: http://apps.finra.org/fundanalyzer/1/fa.aspx) that allows you to enter ticker symbols for funds and to compare up to three funds to compare costs, with a data bank of 18,000 mutual funds, and exchange traded funds (ETFs) and exchange traded notes (ETNs). Fund websites also often give the operating cost percentage for different funds.

To cover the costs of doing business, mutual funds have fees and expenses that differ for different funds. These include shareholder redemption fees and operating costs, which can reduce net returns. Mutual funds are often classified as *no-load*, *low-load*, and *load funds*. Load funds are generally sold through brokers that have a *front-load* (upfront) sales charge or a *back-end load* charged at the time of the fund's redemption, compensating the broker for this service. At times the back-end load is amortized so that it disappears if the fund is not redeemed for several years. A *redemption fee* is paid to a fund to cover the costs (other than the sales charges) associated with a redemption. An *exchange fee* may also be charged for a transfer of money from one fund to another fund within a family (often after a certain number of free transfers). An *annual account maintenance fee* also is charged by funds to cover costs, such as for providing service to customers with low-balance accounts.

DIFFERENCES IN EXPENSES FOR TYPES OF MUTUAL FUNDS AND SERVICES OFFERED

As pointed out by the *Investment Company Institute Fact Book* (2015) the expenses of individual mutual funds differ considerably, since funds offer an array of different products, so expense ratios of individual funds reflect many factors, including investment objective, fund assets, and payments to intermediaries. Examples of fund expenses varying by objective, for instance, are higher expense ratios for equity funds (mean 1.33%) over bond (mean 0.98%), hybrid funds (mean 1.33%), and money market funds (0.12%), (means for 2014), and expenses tend to be higher for funds specializing in a given sector, such as health care, real estate or in international equities, since these funds are more costly to manage. Index equity funds, which are more passively managed, also have a lower mean expense ratio of 0.70%, as do target date funds (mean 0.99%). Within a given investment objective, fund expense ratios can also vary dramatically. The ICI points out that the expense ratios for 10% of equity funds focusing on growth stocks have expense ratios of 0.74% or less, while 10% of these funds have expense ratios of 2.0% or more, with differentials often explained partially by the higher cost to manage small- and mid-cap stocks than large-cap stocks.

ANNUAL FUND OPERATING EXPENSES

Operating fees are associated with "normal costs" of fund operations and expenses that are deducted from fund assets before earnings distributions to shareholders. These include: (1) a *management fee*, a fee to the fund's investment advisers for managing the fund portfolio and related services; (2) a *distribution (12b-1) fee* that may be deducted from fund assets to compensate sales professionals for providing advice and ongoing services to mutual fund shareholders for fund marketing and advertising expenses; and (3) *other expenses* that include fees paid to a fund's transfer agent for providing fund shareholder services (i.e., toll-free phone numbers, computerized account services, website services, record-keeping, printing, and mailing, among other expenses.

With the U.S. SEC's approval of Rule 12b-1 in 1980 allowing the continuation of annual charges to cover the cost of sales commissions and other marketing expenses, previous no-load funds became, in effect, low-load funds. The SEC limited 12b-1 fees to 1% annually, with a 0.25% maximum allowed for brokers, with the intention that fees be used to fund advertising to increase fund size and lower costs through economies of scale.

It is important for investors to monitor fund expenses, since they can significantly lower net returns and result in negative returns in down markets. An example is if a fund has a 12-month return of 19% and operating expenses of 5.5%, the net return would be 13.5%. In recent years, funds have also increased their minimum investment requirement, often to $1,000, although minimums are often lower for IRAs and reinvestments.

INDEX FUNDS UNDER PASSIVE INVESTMENT STRATEGIES WITH LOW FEES

Under the capital asset pricing model (CAPM) the best strategy for the highest return and the lowest risk is to invest in an entire market, leading to the development of index funds. Index funds are popular in providing wide market diversification. In the United States for households owning mutual funds, as reported by ICI (*Investment Company Institute Fact Book*, 2015), 31% owned at least one equity index future fund in 2014, with 382 index funds managing $2.1 trillion in net assets, with 41% invested in funds tied to domestic stock indexes, 26% in world stock indexes, and 33% in bond or hybrid indexes, used as common benchmarks.

Overview:
Nondepository
Financial
Institutions and
New Forms of
Financing

Jack Bogle, a long-time investment guru, who founded the Vanguard Group about 40 years ago, points out that by investing in the S&P 500 index mutual fund with low fund fees can result in investors earning more money over time. He notes that costs can be everything, such as even a fee of 2% that seems small for managed funds. This contrasts with investing in an index fund that has a fee of just 1/20 of 1%. He notes that index funding currently makes up about 34% of the market for stock mutual funds (Arnold, 2015a). With a more long-term buy and hold strategy, investors may do better versus instincts noted by behavioral financial economists, noting that there is a strong tendency to sell stocks when they go down significantly, which is often the worst reaction, resulting in a *buy high, sell low* result. As Justin Wolfers, a University of Michigan economist notes "…in a financial market, randomness may be the norm, even if in much of the rest of our lives, order and predictability is the norm" (Arnold 2015b).

ASSET MIXES FOR ACTIVELY MANAGED PORTFOLIOS OF MUTUAL FUNDS

Often mutual fund investors hold several different types of mutual funds in one or several different fund families. The type of funds they choose are based on a target level of risk (tolerance for volatility), investment goals, the desired time horizon for investing, and the desire for diversification and liquidity. With diversification, an investor holds a diverse portfolio with shares in numerous stocks and industry sectors, often as a rule holding no more than one stock as 5% of a stock portfolio or holding a passively managed stock index mutual fund, based on the S&P 500 for instance. Diversification can also include being diversified by holding stocks with different market capitalization (small-, mid-, and large-caps), geography, and industry sector and by bonds, stocks, and cash, depending on an investor's need for liquidity.

LARGE-CAP, MID-CAP, AND SMALL-CAP STOCK FUNDS

In terms of diversification by *market cap*, Morningstar Stock Research (2015) points out differences in *large-cap*, *mid-cap*, and *small-cap stocks* and potential benefits by diversifying among these. Large-cap stocks are generally stocks for mature, established companies that have market capitalizations of greater than $5 billion, while mid-cap stocks are companies that have market capitalizations of $1 billion to $5 billion, firms that may be younger but have gotten through their startup years, and small-cap companies, as the youngest and least established of the three categories have market capitalizations of less than $1 billion. Historically, the research points out, based on return and risk over 1976 to 2005, investors might potentially (hypothetically) benefit in terms of a higher return without an increase in risk by adding a mix of mid-cap and small-cap stocks to a large-cap portfolio based on historical risk and return measures.

MANAGED DIVERSIFICATION ALLOCATIONS

Diversification is also often discussed in terms of investing in a combination of domestic and foreign stock, bonds, and short-term investments. Fidelity (2015) proposes different hypothetical holdings based on an investor's risk/return profile that would be have to be monitored and rebalanced over time. A more conservative investor might select fund holdings with 50% bonds, 30% short-term investments, 14% U.S. stock, and 6% foreign stock. This compares with an investor with more balanced holdings of 35% U.S. stock, 40% bonds, 15% foreign stock, and 10% short-term investments. An investor with a more growth focus might choose holdings of 49% U.S. stock, 21% foreign stock, 25% bonds, and 5% short-term investments, or taking a more aggressive growth approach, holdings of 60% U.S. stock, 25% foreign stock, and 15% bonds. Ibbotson Associates, an investment research firm, using a simulation over 1926 to 2014 finds the mean return and mean average return for the five worst years in this period for: (1) the conservative investor, a mean return of 6.01% and worst years mean of -0.37%; (2) for the aggressive growth portfolio, 9.64%, with a worst years mean of -13.78%; for the balanced mix, 7.98% and for the worst years a mean of -6.18%, and for the growth portfolio, 8.97%, and for the worst years a mean of -10.43%. An appropriate asset mix would vary by an investor's risk tolerance, financial situation, liquidity needs, and time horizon with a longer-term horizon more likely to smooth out some of the volatility on average (Fidelity, 2015).

SECTOR INVESTING

Another type of diversification and investment strategy used by investors is sector investing, targeting stocks of companies in different industry sectors of the economy that can be used for diversification, managing risks, and for growth strategies. Sector funds in an industry are offered by fund families as mutual funds and as sector ETFs managed by a fund's asset managers. Different sectors include consumer discretionary, consumer staples, energy, financials, health care, industrials, information technology, materials, real estate, telecommunications, and utilities, among others. Fund families offer many different types of actively managed sector funds. For instance, Fidelity Investments offers 44 different funds, with an overview of sector investing on its website (at: https://www.fidelity.com/sector-investing/overview) where characteristics of different industry sectors are described.

STYLE INVESTING

Mutual funds have different investment styles, including:

1   *Value investing*, a style originally developed by Dodd and Graham, known as the fathers of value investing, whereby securities are analyzed and a fund manager seeks to find securities that are underpriced to purchase and hold until their prices rise to their intrinsic value.
2   *Growth investing*, a style where an investment manager purchases securities in a growth stage of their life cycles, and securities are held to produce a risk-adjusted return.
3   *Blend*, a style combining both value and growth investing strategies.
4   *Aggressive growth*, a style that expands upon a growth strategy by employing alternative methods, such as momentum investing, whereby securities with above average risk may be included and at times debt and derivatives may be used to increase a fund's overall risk and return potential.

(Mutual Fund Styles, 2015)

*Overview:
Nondepository
Financial
Institutions and
New Forms of
Financing*

Styles are often used by both index and actively managed funds and some funds are concentrated, having 30 to 60 different companies. Commodity funds can also be included in index funds, stock funds, or managed future funds.

TRENDS IN U.S. MUTUAL FUNDS

The *Investment Company Institute Fact Book* (2015) notes that for the United States at the end of 2014, equity funds held 52% of total U.S. mutual fund assets, bond funds 22%, money market funds 17%, and hybrid funds 9%. Retail investors held 89% of mutual fund assets, with institutional investors (nonfinancial businesses, financial institutions, and nonprofit organizations) holding about 11%, with 62% held in money market funds to manage cash balances. Equity fund net cash flows are related to market performance and market volatility, often with the Chicago Board Options Exchange *Volatility Index* (*VIX*) tracking the volatility of the S&P 500 index used as a proxy for market risk, with values greater than 30 usually reflecting greater fear in the market and values less than 20 associated with market calm. While equity funds had strong inflows throughout 2013 when the VIX was never above 21, in 2014, the daily VIX averaged 14 but peaked at 26 in October and 24 in December, reducing the number of equity mutual funds receiving lower net inflows in 2014. Bond funds are affected by the performance of bonds driven by interest rates. With a decline in interest rates and more baby boomers planning for retirement, bonds had net inflows in 2014. With a larger percentage of the U.S. population reaching retirement, inflows rose for both bond funds and *target date mutual funds* that gradually reallocate assets away from equities and towards bonds as the fund's target date is reached, often transferring investments from other equity and bond funds. *Hybrid (asset allocation or balanced) funds* that invest in a mix of stocks and bonds also have had net inflows each year since 2008, with their popularity based on their help to investors in achieving a balanced stock and bond portfolio. Often particular funds provide in their prospectus the percentages they use for, respectively, stocks and bonds, such as a 60%/40% approach. *Index funds* are particularly popular, with 31% of households owning at least one index mutual fund in 2014. For 2014, 41% of new inflows to index funds were tied to U.S. stock indexes, 26% to world stock indexes, and 33% to bond or hybrid indexes, such as used for target date funds. Money market funds only had modest inflows with very low interest rates at this time (*Investment Company Institute Fact Book*, 2015).

SOCIALLY RESPONSIBLE INVESTMENT COMPANIES AND INVESTING

Socially responsible investment (SRI) funds offer investors the ability to invest in different types of environmental, social, and governance (ESG) responsible investments. SRI has become mainstream, with a large number of different funds available to investors. These include opportunities to invest in sustainability indexes including the Dow Jones Sustainability Indexes (DJSI), the FTSE4Good Index series, the Goldman Sachs GS SUSTAIN ESG index, the Domini 400 Social Index, MSCI World, and the KLD Broad Market Social Index (BMSI), among many others (Cooperman, 2013). The 2014 Report on U.S. Sustainable, Responsible, and Impact Investing Trends reports $6.57 trillion in professionally managed portfolios that use ESG or other socially responsible investment strategies, a huge rise from about $639 billion in 1995, with almost 18% of $36.8 trillion in total assets professionally managed in the United States involved with SRI (Schueth, 2015). Mahn (2015) points out that the number of funds incorporating ESG factors at the end of 2014 was 925 compared with only 55 in 1995.

As noted by Fung, Law and Yau (2010), major categories of SRI portfolios include environmental, religious or ethical, social and corporate governance, with portfolios also including a combination of these, with different strategies used for the construction of SRI portfolios focusing on both ESG factors and long-term risks associated with these factors, as well as time horizon, and risk considerations. Strategies used include: (1) investment screens (both positive and negative types of screens); (2) a best in class approach comparing and ranking firms by industry sector or benchmark indexes: (3) engagement with companies where a critical, large amount of capital is being invested, such as by institutional investors; (4) shareholder advocacy and activism supporting specific causes; and (5) an integrated approach involving a combination of strategies (see Cooperman, 2013 for more details).

Schueth (2015) points out that the modern roots of SRI can be traced to the concerns for social and environmental issues, from civil rights, equality for women, labor/management, the anti-apartheid movement, corporations with environmental disasters in the 1960s to 1980s, to more concerns about school human rights, respect for indigenous peoples, safe and healthy working conditions today, along with most recently the climate change crisis awakening investors to the opportunities of directly investing in companies that would help to create a sustainable future. An SRI portfolio management approach includes qualitative and quantitative analysis from both a profit potential and the integration of environmental, social, and governance factors into the investment decision-making process, keeping "a keen eye on the impact portfolio companies have on our world." SRI notes that ESG investing considers "a double bottom line approach," attempting to both achieve an investor's financial goals, but also to align these goals with ESG factors based on an investor's priorities.

Different aspects of SRI investing include:

1 integrating ESG factors that can also affect a company's profitability, value and share price and can help to identify better managed companies;
2 shareholder engagement efforts including both dialog with companies and filing proxy resolutions to encourage more responsible citizenship by corporations to have a positive effect on society at large—including pursuing the well-being of "all stakeholders," including customers, employees, suppliers, communities, shareholders, and the natural environment; and
3 community impact investing whereby capital is directed by low-income, at-risk communities that have difficulty financing through conventional channels, with many socially conscious investors allocating a percentage of their funds to community development financial institutions (CDFIs) whose work is to reduce poverty, create jobs, provide affordable housing, and finance small business development in disadvantaged communities (Schueth, 2015).

Schueth (2015) points out several factors fueling the growth of SRI funds, including higher quality information and more well-informed investors; climate change risks that offer opportunities to reduce these risks by investing in solutions; impressive performance shown

*Overview:
Nondepository
Financial
Institutions and
New Forms of
Financing*

in academic studies for SRI funds; accessibility of SRI funds for both small and large investments; corporate scandals driving investors to seek ESG investments; an increase in women investors interested in an ESG approach to investing; and investors from the 85 million in the milliennial generation (born between the early 1980s and the early 2000s) that seek to make a difference in society) (Schueth, 2015).

Social Funds (www.socialfunds.com) has a search function for different SRI funds, including those managed by Calvert, Green Century, Domini, Dreyfus, Legg Mason, TIAA-CREF, PIMCO, Pax World, Parnassus, New Covenant, Neuberger, Vanguard, and Utopia, among others. Some SRI firms, such as First Affirmative Financial Network, a professional investment management firm in Colorado, prepare individually tailored portfolios for individual investors. Screening can be both positive, for firms engaged in responsible actions, or negative, such as screening companies engaged in tobacco, environmental derogation, or other unsocial or nonenvironmental actions.

As pointed out by Cooperman (2013), many SRI mutual funds also act as advocates for social/environmental issues, using manager funds (versus funds being managed) to purchase the minimum share-holding requirement to meet SEC proxy resolution filing conditions for proposals to be voted on at annual meetings. Other social activists include a mixture of SRI mutual funds, private equity investors, state and city and union pension funds, religious groups, private foundations, and social–environmental nonprofit groups. The As You Sow Foundation and Ceres are nonprofit groups that assist social activists with resolutions, with a group of investors often submitting a resolution together. Often a company will agree to negotiate in return for a withdrawal of a resolution, so that it won't have to be voted on at an annual meeting. Often votes at annual meetings, if with a majority vote, are nonbinding.

PENSION FUNDS AND RESPONSIBLE INVESTING

Groups of pension funds in the United Kingdom and Europe, as well as the United States including the California Public Employees' Retirement System (CalPERS), often require ESG screening before they will invest in a company's stock, and often engage in social activism in terms of negotiating with companies to improve upon corporate environmental, social, and governance (ESG) practices, at times filing proxy statements for changes in corporate practices for annual meetings. In 2015, for example a group of 16 UK pension funds, representing more than $300.9 billion of assets joined together to back "A Guide to Responsible Investment Reporting to Public Equity" that was published as part of a wider effort to incorporate responsible investment in the money manager selection and monitoring, and reporting process. The goal is for the guide to be used by all pension funds to assist them in their engaging and monitoring activities (Baker, 2015). The United Nations Environment Programme Finance Initiative (UNEP FI) (2007) points out in a joint report with the United Kingdom Social Investment Forum (UKSIF) and the Sustainable Pensions Project (SPP) how leading public pension funds are meeting the challenge for responsible investment, highlighting responsible investment case studies for different pension funds, including CalPERS, TIAA-CREF, ABP in the Netherlands, the Swedish National Pension Fund AP Funds Family, the Australian Reward Investment Alliance, Caisse de depot et placement du Quebec, the Environment Agency Pension Fund in the United Kingdom, the

Government Pension Fund Global in Norway, the Government Pension Fund in Thailand, PGGM in the Netherlands, among many others.

RISK-ADJUSTED PERFORMANCE MEASURES

There are a number of different risk-adjusted performance measures for mutual fund portfolios. Katerina Simmons (1998) in the *New England Economic Review* at the Federal Reserve Bank of Boston examines several of the most commonly used measures, including (1) the standard deviation of returns; (2) value at risk; (3) the Sharpe ratio; (4) the M-square measure and (5) the Morningstar return and risk measures, betas, and asset class measures.

Standard Deviation of Returns

The monthly standard deviation of returns is calculated as the square-root of the sum of the squared differences between each monthly return from the average monthly return, divided by the number of observations. Mutual fund analysts are usually interested in the standard deviation of excess returns over the risk-free rate or some appropriate benchmark index based on a fund's objective, known as the tracking error, which indicates its volatility over the average volatility of the market.

Value at Risk

Value at risk (VAR) is a risk measure that provides an estimate of how much a firm's portfolio can decline with a given probability over a given time period, indicating the likely range of losses based on historical data. If a 95% probability is used, based on a normal distribution, 95% of all observations will occur within 1.96 standard deviations from the mean, with only 5% deviating from that mean, that is, a 2.5% chance of falling below the mean. For example, if a fund has a mean monthly return of 2% and a standard deviation of 4%, its monthly VAR would be 2% less $[(1.96)(4.00)] = -5.84\%$, or a 2.5% probability of losing no more than $58.40 a month for a $1,000 investment. Although VARs are based on historical volatilities, estimated volatilities and correlations can be used. Risk managers can also find a VAR for underperforming a fund's selected benchmark, known as a "relative" or "tracking" VAR.

Sharpe Ratio

To calculate the Sharpe ratio or index, a fund's average excess return over the risk-free rate or an appropriate benchmark is divided by the standard deviation of the fund's excess return. For instance, if the monthly mean excess return of a fund is 1%, and the monthly standard deviation for the excess return is 4%, the monthly Sharpe ratio is 0.25. To annualize this ratio, the monthly Sharpe ratio can be multiplied by the square root of 12 or 3.46. Multiplying 0.25 by 3.46, the annualized Sharpe ratio is 0.865.

An alternative measure that is often used is the Treynor index, which is a fund's average excess return divided by the beta of the fund portfolio. These ratios are measures of a fund's excess return adjusted for risk, allowing a comparison for funds with different levels of risk.

Overview:
Nondepository
Financial
Institutions and
New Forms of
Financing

The Treynor ratio is based on the capital asset pricing model (CAPM), which assumes that investors can achieve any level of risk by investing in the fund with the highest ratio and reduce that risk by investing part of the portfolio in risk-free securities or leveraging the investment by increasing its risk by borrowing at the risk-free rate to purchase more of the portfolio.

Modigliani or M-Square Measure

Modigliani and Modigliani (1997) proposed a different measure that they believed would be easier for an investor to understand; often known as the M-square measure it measures a fund's performance relative to the market in percentage terms defined as:

$$M\text{-square} = \frac{\text{Fund's average excess return}}{\text{STD of fund's excess return}} \times \text{STD of index excess return}$$

Modigliani and Modigliani proposed using the standard deviation of the S&P 500 or another broad-based market index for the second term. The M-square provides a measure equivalent to the return the fund would earn if its risk was the same as the market index. Similar to the Sharpe ratio, the higher the M-square, the higher is the fund's return for any level of risk. As an example, if the fund's average excess return over the S&P 500 index is 15% and the STD of the fund's excess return is 10%, and the standard deviation of the S&P 500 Index return is 25%, the M-square would be $(15\% / 10\%) \times 25\% = 37.5\%$. Hypothetically, investors could take on greater financial leverage to increase the STD of the fund's excess return to achieve the 37.5% return.

Morningstar Ratings

Morningstar, Inc. publishes its own risk return measures, which are used for its widely used star ratings. Morningstar divides mutual funds into four asset classes: domestic stock funds, international stock funds, taxable bond funds, and municipal bond funds. An excess return is calculated for each fund adjusting for sales loads and subtracting the 90-day Treasury bill rate. This load-adjusted excess return is then divided by the average excess return for the fund's asset class as:

$$\text{Morningstar return} = \frac{\text{Load-adjusted fund excess return}}{\text{Average excess return for asset class}}$$

A measure of downside risk is estimated by counting the number of months that a fund's excess return was negative, summing all negative returns, and dividing this sum by the total number of months over the measurement period. The same measure is calculated for the fund's asset class as a whole. The ratio of the two, Morningstar's risk measure is as follows:

$$\text{Morningstar risk} = \frac{\text{Fund's average underperformance}}{\text{Average underperformance for the asset class}}$$

To rate funds, Morningstar subtracts the risk score from the return score and ranks funds by this raw rating within their asset class. Stars are then assigned, with the top 10% rankings receiving five stars, the next 22.5% four stars, the middle 35% three stars, the next 22.5% two stars, and the lowest 10% one star. Overall rankings are calculated by combining stars that are calculated for 3-, 5-, and 10-year periods. Category ratings for each fund are also calculated for more narrowly defined fund categories; however, these ratings are not adjusted for sales loan and are only calculated for a 3-year period. Morningstar has 16 style-based indexes that are used as benchmarks. Morningstar also has a U.S. Market Index to represent 97% of the U.S. market.

Katerina Simmons performed a detailed examination of these rankings and found them to be highly correlated. Some analysts, such as Bogle (1994) point out that investments in value funds or specialty funds imply taking on extra risk and accepting a lower level of diversification, such that the rewards of investing in such a fund might be near the top 10% of funds for a given period, but might underperform the bottom 10% of funds during different market periods, since performance for value funds has varied; in the 1980s they performed well in the bull market, but not during the bull market of the 1990s.

Morningstar in 2011 launched a new, additional forward-looking rating system for mutual funds, with the intention of better predicting future performance. These new ratings were based on a study that found that fund fees were a better predictor of future performance than star ratings, with combined star ratings and fund fees the best predictor of future performance for a fund within its particular category. The new rating system for 349 funds provides a rating of gold, silver, bronze, neutral, or negative. About 75% of the funds were initially rated gold or silver, funds known as *analyst picks*. The new methodology includes five pillars: (1) *people*—who is running the fund; (2) *process*—how the fund selects its holding; (3) *parent*—evaluation of the parent company as well as its stewardship rating; (4) *performance*—the risk-adjusted performance within a category; and (5) *price*— the expense ratio relative to other funds with similar investment objectives and means of distribution. Funds with positives across all five pillars received a gold rating; while funds with primarily negatives received a negative rating (Roth, 2011). Morningstar also has fund sustainability ratings.

TYPES OF PENSION FUNDS AND OTHER RETIREMENT VEHICLES

Defined Contribution Plans

For retirement, as mentioned earlier, pension funds have moved from defined benefit (DB) plans, where companies managed pension funds on behalf of employees based on employee and employer contributions and where employers take on the investment risk and promise fixed benefits, to defined contribution (DC) plans (in the United States these include primarily 401(k) plans, and also 403(b) plans for educators and certain nonprofits organizations allowing additional deferred tax savings). Defined contribution plans include 457 plans (for employees of state and local governments and certain tax-exempt organizations), the Federal Employees Retirement System (FERS) Thrift Savings Plan (TSP), Keoghs, a type of retirement plan designed for self-employed individuals and their employees and other private sector plans, holding about $6.8 trillion in assets. About $4.6 trillion is held in 401(k) plans. Under 401(k) plans tax-free contributions are put into a set of mutual funds that employees can choose from, and employees need to monitor their mutual funds and

Overview:
Nondepository
Financial
Institutions and
New Forms of
Financing

take on the investment risk of having sufficient funds for retirement. Taxes are deferred on investment earnings until later when individuals take out funds in retirement (*Investment Company Institute Fact Book*, 2015).

Other retirement vehicles that governments set up include individual retirement accounts (IRAs); these are investment vehicles that individuals can invest in to earn tax-free income until retirement. As tax-advantaged retirement savings vehicles these are also often invested in mutual funds. In the United States $7.3 trillion was invested in mutual funds for IRA and DC plans at year-end 2014 (*Investment Company Institute Fact Book*, 2015).

Services and Expenses in 401(k) Defined Contribution (DC) Plans

The ICI observes two competing economic pressures for employers in the design of employee retirement plans: (1) the need to attract and retain quality workers with competitive compensation and retirement packages; and (2) the need to keep these products and services priced competitively. Hence, employers need to access the benefits and costs for DC plans, with costs including employer contributions and the ongoing costs for setting up and administering plans. Employers providing and maintaining 401(k) plans must meet a number of different administrative, employee-focused regulatory and compliance services, so typically hire service providers to operate plans, with providers charging fees for services, and the employer typically deciding the sharing of these costs between the employer and employees. Fees can be paid directly by the employer or directly by the employee, or indirectly by the employee in terms of a reduction in investment returns (with part of the return paid to the investment provider).

Studies suggest that plans with a greater number of participants and larger average account balances tend to have lower fees overall than smaller plans with smaller average account balances (i.e., economies of scale—with fixed costs spread across more participants and/or a larger asset base). Expense ratios also tended to be higher for equity versus fixed-income investments. In the United States at year-end 2014, investors were holding $3.7 trillion or 55% of total DC plan assets in mutual funds. Among DC plans, 401(k) plans held $2.9 trillion in mutual funds, followed by 403(b) plans holding $456 billion, other private sector DC plans $287 billion, and 457 plans $112 billion. In terms of employee options for mutual fund choices, employers often provide choices of domestic and international equity funds, balanced funds, primarily domestic bond funds, and other funds including money funds, guaranteed investment contracts (GICs) and others. GICs are contracts that guarantee the repayment of principal at a fixed or floating interest rate for a given period of time, typically insured by insurance companies, with a favorable tax status for saving for retirement (*Investment Company Institute Fact Book*, 2015).

U.S. PRIVATE SECTOR DB PLANS, ERISA, AND THE PBGC

In the United States following World War II, with firms competing for workers and with support from labor unions, companies developed retirement benefits to attract workers, and in 1949 the Supreme Court ruled that pension benefits could be included in collective bargaining agreements, resulting in plans doubling by 1960. As pension plans grew, so did the possibility of sponsoring firms failing to meet their pension obligations, such as the 1964 failure of Studebaker, which left its employees with few or no pension benefits. In response,

Congress passed the Employee Retirement Income Security Act (ERISA) in 1974 to prevent fund insolvencies, ensuring that employers work towards full funding. A DB pension plan is fully funded if the present value of its assets equals the present value of future contributions, known as its funding target. Since the total amount of the fund's liabilities are not known with certainty, the fund's liabilities are estimated using actuarial methods based on the actuarial assumptions, including the retirement age of covered employees, their expected salaries at retirement, how long they are expected to live after retirement, and the interest rate that will be earned on assets (used as the discount rate to find the present value of pension liabilities). Employer contributions are based on these calculations, with a major question in the management and regulation of DB plans being whether an employer's contribution to the fund is sufficient to meet future pension liabilities.

ERISA established the Pension Benefit Guaranty Corporation (PBGC) to assure within limits the payment of up to 85% of vested benefits if a defined benefit pension fund fails. The PBGC is supported by annual premiums based on the number of participants covered. If a plan is terminated, the PBGC becomes the trustee, taking control of the fund's assets and using them to pay as large a portion of the basic vested benefits as possible. The sponsoring company of a terminated plan may be held liable for unfunded benefits based on a formula established by Congress in the Single Employer Pension Plan Amendment Act of 1986. As noted earlier, many corporate DB plans have switched to DC plans, owing to higher costs and management risks for DB plans, with corporate DB plans in the United States representing only 20% of plans for total private sector employees.

OVERVIEW TRENDS FOR GOVERNMENT DEFINED BENEFIT PENSION FUNDS

Defined benefit (DB) plans pay an annuity for a retiree's lifetime, based often on an employee's number of years of service and final salary. Many governments and states have defined benefit plans, but in the corporate sector the percentage of employers with DB plans has been on the decline. In the United States for instance, over the past 30 years, there has been a steady decline.

From 1980 to 2008, for instance, Butrica, Iams, Smith, and Toder (2009) report the percentage of private wage and salary workers in DB plans fell from 38% to just 20%, while the percentage for DC plans rose from 8% to 31%, and many companies have frozen their DB pension plans to be eventually terminated, whereby current participants receive retirement benefits that are based on the accruals they have up to the freeze date, but do not accumulate additional benefits, and new employees are not covered under the DB plan with employees having the option to enter a new DC plan or increase contributions for existing DC plans. With this change, there have been some concerns from a policy standpoint whether income generated from increased DC plans will compensate for the loss of DB plan benefits.

A similar trend has occurred in the United Kingdom for private sector DB plans. Butrica, et al. (2009) point out that on the public sector side, however, there has been very little shift from DB to DC plans, although in the United States some states have introduced DC plans in different forms. However, these may face rising stress with, from 2006 on, about a third of state and local government pension plans in the United States being less than 80% funded, with underfunding rising to 46% during the subprime crisis. Similarly with the great

Overview:
Nondepository
Financial
Institutions and
New Forms of
Financing

recession, government pension plans have had funding difficulties, leading to a rise in the minimum retirement age for retirees in some countries. There have been pension crises in many countries, such as Brazil in 2015, where the average retirement age is 54, and other factors including greater longevity leading to high spending for pensions, and a large deficit with the president at the time proposing cuts, contributed to political turmoil (Romero, 2015).

RECENT DEFICITS FOR PUBLIC EMPLOYEE PENSION PLANS

Defined benefit pension plans experience difficulties in their management, since future pension liabilities have to be predicted based on current as well as expected retirements in the future, with benefits based on often the highest average salary in the last 3 years of retirement, which depends on an expected growth rate in salaries over an employee's work career, along with other stipulations for benefits, such as annual cost of living adjustments (COLA). Similarly, funds available to pay liabilities also depend on employer and employee contributions, and the interest rate that contributions will earn, among many other formula rules, to determine the percentage of salary provided as benefits during retirement for a particular employee.

Hence, the present value of future liabilities at retirement for an employee using a reasonable discount rate must be compared to the present value (PV) of future investment assets in terms of value of investments funded by employer and employee contributions available to draw upon for future retirement benefits. From a theoretical perspective, if the PV of assets of a plan are less than the PV of future benefits based on the expected life retirees in retirement, then there could be a deficit in the funding of the pension plan.

Since DB plans for government plans (federal, state, municipal) are backed by taxpayer dollars, any large deficit puts a strain on government finances and may require either higher taxes to cover the deficit and/or changes in pension stipulations, such as a higher minimum retirement age, lower COLA, or lower benefit rates, which in turn can lead to political discord, such as observed recently in Brazil and Greece, among other countries.

Private sector DB pension plans have also faced serious pension plan underfunding issues as the result of poor stock returns and very low interest rates, with the 30-year Treasury bond discount rate for finding pension liabilities extremely low. In the United States this led to Congress passing the Pension Funding Equity Act of 2004, providing temporary relief for corporations having to pay deficit reduction contributions and replacing the discount rate used with a longer-term corporate bond rate for a 2-year period. The bill also helped to keep the PBGC solvent and, with the failures of Enron and WorldCom resulting in large pension losses for employees; the new law increased the liability of pension fund managers and officers of companies with DB plans.

ASSET ALLOCATION ISSUE FOR DEFINED BENEFIT PLANS

With many defined benefit plans facing large deficits, there has been a tendency for funds to take on more risky types of investments to achieve higher investment returns. The optimal allocation for pension assets has been an ongoing theoretical issue. Theoretical studies including Sharpe (1976) and Harrison and Sharpe (1983) propose that if pension plans are partially insured by the PBGC, they should invest in more risky assets, with the majority of the investments in stock, which will allow a firm not to have to make as large a contribution. Logue and Rader (1998) point out that asset allocation generally should reflect a firm's financial condition and the characteristics of its DB plan, with surveys showing more profitable plans taking on a greater percentage of equity and more risky firms taking on a greater percentage of debt for plans. With low interest rates on bonds, and bull markets, there are temptations to invest more in equities, with some funds investing with hedge funds or more risky types of real estate assets if allowed by government regulations.

Other considerations involved in active asset management include investment style, management fees, derivatives, rebalancing, evaluation of money managers, and whether tactical asset allocation should be used. Management fees are also a significant consideration, with active management fees for a pension fund averaging about 50 basis points, whereas passive index funds for a broad market often average 2 to 10 basis points. Mutual funds and other funds for managing employee pension plans have higher active equity fund expense ratios, averaging 100 basis points. Pension fund managers need to monitor fees carefully as part of their due diligence.

Some pension fund managers may want to use smoothing techniques to reduce the plan's risk, although at the expense of higher potential returns. One smoothing technique is to reduce the plan's risk, although at the expense of higher potential returns. Another smoothing technique is to use guaranteed investment contracts (GICs), whereby a pension fund contracts with a life insurer to earn a fixed rate of return over a specified period, in which a lump sum is invested in return for a fixed annuity return. GICs are only as sound as the financial condition of the life insurer issuing the GIC. Alternatively, dedicated bond portfolios are designed to be immunized from changes in interest rate risk by matching the duration of the bond portfolio with the time horizon for the pension obligation. Careful monitoring must be done, since if pension liabilities change, a fund could be at risk and have insufficient income to match pension liabilities.

USING A RANVA APPROACH TO COMPARE RETURNS WITH ACTIVE VERSUS PASSIVE MANAGEMENT

Ambachtsheer and Ezra (1998) point out that the choice of an asset mix policy and the way in which such a policy is implemented depends on a number of different considerations, including the nature of the pension liabilities, risk tolerance of managers, the funding status of a pension plan, the prospects for long-term capital markets, and current perceptions for the standard asset mix of pension funds. They suggest using a *risk-adjusted net value added (RANVA)* approach to determine the performance of a fund; this is equal to the gross annual return less the expected annual compound return for a passively managed (index fund) benchmark less the average extra cost of active management less the average risk penalty for active management risks. For instance, they note that in the early 1990s, 98 pension funds in North America had a 10.7% gross return. When a RANVA was calculated (10.7% minus the 10.7% return for a passively managed index fund less a 0.2 active management cost less a 2.3% risk premium), it was − 2.5%, suggesting that passive management using an index fund would have been better.

SUMMARY

According to the Investment Company Institute (ICI) over $33.4 trillion was invested in mutual funds and exchange traded funds by year-end 2014. In the United States alone, total retirement market assets were $24.7 trillion, with $7.3 trillion investments in mutual funds for IRA and defined contribution retirement plans and $18.2 trillion net assets managed by U.S. investment companies, including $15.9 trillion for mutual funds, $2 trillion for exchange traded funds, $289 billion for closed-end funds, and $101 billion for unit investment trusts.

With greater investment risk for companies and greater longevity for workers in retirement increasing defined benefit plan costs, companies have switched to defined contribution plans, often giving employees a choice of mutual funds in which to invest. With the subprime crisis, followed by the great recession, and thousands of investors losing savings on subprime collateralized debt obligations (CDOs) and real estate investments, efforts have been made to improve financial literacy for individuals and to provide better information on mutual funds as investment choices for defined contribution plans. This chapter gives an overview of different types of mutual funds, their organization, and regulation, along with an overview of different types of pension plans, management issues, and information on costs, fees, and performance for mutual funds.

SOURCES OF INFORMATION ON MUTUAL FUNDS AND PENSION FUNDS

Good sources of detailed information on mutual funds include the *Investment Company Fact Book* (at: www.icifactbook.org) which provides up-to-date information on U.S. registered investment companies and details about mutual funds (Icifactbook.org 2015a,b). The U.S. Securities and Exchange Commission provides a free publication to download, *Mutual Funds: A Guide for Investors* (Mutual Funds, 2015a at: www.investor.gov). The Investor.gov website offers information on investment basics and detailed information on mutual funds and other investment vehicles. The U.S. News.com website gives advice on "Best mutual funds" (at: http://www.forbes.com/sites/samdiedrich/2014/02/28/alternative-or-hedged-mutual-funds-what-are-they-how-do-they-work-and-should-you-invest/).

A good source for mutual fund performance for different types of funds is Morningstar, which gives rankings for funds by different categories (at: http://news.morningstar.com/fund-category-returns/). Some information is proprietary, while other information is published on Morningstar's website.

BIBLIOGRAPHY

Ambachtsheer, Keith P. and D. Don Ezra (1998). *Pension Fund Excellence: Creating Value for Stakeholders*. New York: John Wiley & Sons.

Arnold, Chris (2015a). "The George Washington of investing wants you for the revolution." NPR, Colorado Public Radio-News, Special Series: Your money and your life, October 21, 2015. Accessed on October 22, 2015 at: http://www.npr.org/2015/10/21/443192311/the-george-washington-of-investing-wants-you-for-the-revolution

Arnold, Chris (2015b). "Why is it so hard to save? UK shows it doesn't have to be." NPR, Colorado Public Radio-News, Special Series: Your money and your life, October 23, 2015. Accessed on October 23, 2015 at: http://www.npr.org/2015/10/23/445337261/why-is-it-so-hard-to-save-u-k-shows-it-doesnt-have-to-be

Baker, Sophie (2015). "Group of 16 UK pension funds publish responsible investment guide." *Pensions & Investments*, January 26. Accessed on October 20, 2015 at: http://www.pionline.com/article/20150126/ONLINE/150129903/group-of-16-uk-pension-funds-publish-responsible-investment-guide

Bogle, John C. (1994). *Bogle on Mutual Funds.* New York: Irwin Professional Publishing Co.

Brown, Elizabeth Nolan (2012). "The takeaway: 14 countries raising retirement age." *AARP Bulletin Today*, July 12, 2012. Accessed on October 20, 2015 at: http://blog.aarp.org/2012/07/12/europe-pension-reform-retirement-age-increases/

Brown, Mary (2012). "How mutual funds differ around the world." Investopedia, Yahoo Finance, January 12. Accessed on July 14, 2015, at: http://finance.yahoo.com/news/mutual-funds-differ-around-world-180413379.html;_ylt=AoLEVi7ApqVVtMsAlosnnIlQ;_ylu=X3oDMTEzaDk2NWhzBGNvbG8DYmYxBHBvcwMzBHZoaWQDRkZHRTAxXzEEc2VjA3Ny

Butrica, Barbara A., Howard M. Iams, Karen E. Smith, and Eric J. Toder (2009). "The disappearing defined benefit pension and its potential impact on the retirement incomes of baby boomers." *Social Security Bulletin*, 69(3), 1–27. Accessed on October 19, 2015 at: http://www.ssa.gov/policy/docs/ssb/v69n3/v69n3p1.html

Congress.gov (2015). "Summary S. 2059-Mutual Fund Reform Act of 2004." Accessed on October 19, 2015 at: https://www.congress.gov/bill/108th-congress/senate-bill/2059

Cooperman, Elizabeth S. (2013). "The greening of finance: A brief overview." *International Review of Accounting, Banking and Finance*, Spring, 5(1), 42–59.

Diedrich, Sam (2014). "Alternative or hedged mutual funds: What are they, how do they work, and should you invest?" *Forbes*, February 28. 2014. Accessed on July 19, 2015 at: http://www.forbes.com/sites/samdiedrich/2014/02/28/alternative-or-hedged-mutual-funds-what-are-they-how-do-they-work-and-should-you-invest/

Ebr.org (2015) "What are the trends in U.S. retirement plans?" Employee Benefit Research Institute. FAQs about benefits—retirement issues. Accessed on October 16, 2015 at: http://www.ebri.org/publications/benfaq/index.cfm?fa=retfaq14

Fidelity Investments (2015). "The pros' guide to diversification." Fidelity website. Accessed on July 17, 2015, at: https://www.fidelity.com/viewpoints/guide-to-diversification

FINRA (2015). "2015 ICI Retirement Summit—Session 1: What do retirement savers need & what can providers give them? The roles of education, advertising & advice," April 8, 2015 (Washington, DC), Financial Industry Regulatory Authority. Accessed on October 14, 2015 at: https://www.ici.org/pdf/ppt_15_summit_walsh.pdf

Forum for Sustainable and Responsible Investment (2014). "Report on sustainable and responsible investing trends in the United States, 2014." Accessed on October 17, 2015 at: http://www.ussif.org/content.asp?contentid=82

Fung, Hung-Gay, Sheryl A. Law, and Jot Yau (2010). *Socially Responsible Investment in a Global Environment.* Northampton, MA: Edward Elgar.

Harrison, J. Michael and William F. Sharpe (1983). "Optimal funding and asset allocation risks for defined benefit pension plans." In Zvi Bodie and John B. Shoven (Eds.), *Financial Aspects of the United States Pension System* (pp. 91–103). Chicago: University of Chicago Press.

Hirby, James (2015). "Can non-U.S. residents and non-citizens invest in IPOs and mutual funds using an online broker?" *The Law Dictionary.* Accessed on July 25, 2015 at: http://thelawdictionary.org/article/can-non-u-s-residents-and-non-citizens-invest-in-ipos-and-mutual-funds-using-an-online-broker/

Hoene, Mary Joan and Gregory N. Bressler (2015). "Mutual fund governance—independent directors rule." Association of Corporate Counsel, Corporate Governance Seminar, sponsored by Carter Leyard & Milburn, New York, September 17, 2015. Accessed on October 16, 2015 at: https://www.acc.com/chapters/gny/upload/7677924_2-c-2.pdf

Icifactbook.org (2015a). "Table 1: Total net assets, number of funds, and number of share classes of the mutual fund industry, year-end." *Investment Company Institute (ICI) Fact Book.* Accessed on July 12, 2015, at: http://www.icifactbook.org/pdf/2015_factbook_1.pdf

Icifactbook.org (2015b). "Chapter One U.S.-registered investment companies." *Investment Company Institute (ICI) Fact Book.* Accessed on July 12, 2015 at: http://www.icifactbook.org/fb_ch1.html

ICI Global Research Perspective (2014). "Globalisation and the global growth of long-term mutual funds," *ICI Global Research Perspective*, (March), 1(1), 1–43. Accessed on July 14, 2015, at: https://www.ici.org/pdf/icig_per01-01.pdf

*Overview:
Nondepository
Financial
Institutions and
New Forms of
Financing*

ICI Global (2014). "Insights from the 2014 Global Retirement Savings Conference: Common principles for a diverse world." Accessed on July 25, 2015 at: https://www.iciglobal.org/pdf/pub_14_grsc_insights.pdf

Investment Company Institute Fact Book (2015). Investment Company Institute. Accessed on July 12, 2015, at: http://www.icifactbook.org/pdf/2015_factbook.pdf

Investor.gov (2015). "Mutual funds." U.S. Securities and Exchange Commission. Accessed on July 12, 2015, at: http://investor.gov/investing-basics/investment-products/mutual-funds

Klapper, Leora, Victor Sulla, and Dimitri Vittas (2003). "The development of mutual funds around the world." World Bank Working Paper. Accessed on July 14, 2015, at: http://siteresources.worldbank.org/DEC/Resources/MFNov03.pdf

Koutantou, Angeliki and Lefteris Papadimas (2015). "Greek experts call for pension reform amid protests." *Reuters*, October 15. Accessed on October 16, 2015 at: http://www.reuters.com/article/2015/10/15/us-eurozone-greece-protest-idUSKCN0S90J020151015

Logue, Dennis E. and Jack S. Rader (1998). *Managing Pension Plans: A Comprehensive Guide in Improving Plan Performance.* Boston: Harvard Business School Press.

Mahn, Kevin (2015). "Modern sustainable responsible impact investing versus traditional socially responsible investing." *Forbes*, April 16. Accessed on October 20, 2015 at: http://www.forbes.com/sites/advisor/2015/04/16/modern-sustainable-responsible-impact-investing-versus-traditional-socially-responsible-investing/

Market Data Center (2015). *The Wall Street Journal* Market Data Center. Accessed on July 16, 2015 at: http://online.wsj.com/mdc/public/page/2_3048-usmfunds_V-usmfunds.html

Modigliani, Franco and Leah Modigliani (1997). "Risk-adjusted performance." *Journal of Portfolio Management*, 23 (Winter), 45–54.

Morningstar.com (2015a). "Benefits of REITS." Stocks 500, Investing Classroom. Accessed on July 24, 2015 at: http://news.morningstar.com/classroom2/course.asp?docId=145579&page=2&CN=

Morningstar.com (2015b). "Fund category performance: Total returns." Accessed on October 22, 2015, at: news.morningstar.com/fund-category-returns/

Morningstar Stock Research (2015). "The perfect mix of large-, mid-, and small-cap stocks." Accessed on July 25, 2015 at: http://www.morningstar.com/products/pdf/MGI_StockResearch.pdf

Mullainathan, Sendhil (2015). "Investing in the dark: Even an economist is confounded by the complex world of mutual funds." *The New York Times*, Mutual Funds & E.T.F.s, Sunday, July 12, 2015, pp. 11, 14.

Mutual Fund Styles (2015). "Mutual fund styles." Mutual Funds website. Accessed on July 12, 2015 at: http://mutfunds.net/stock-funds/mutual-fund-styles/

Mutual Funds (2015a). *Mutual Funds: A Guide for Investors.* Securities and Exchange Commission, Investors.gov. Accessed on July 12, 2015 at: http://investor.gov/sites/default/files/mutual-funds.pdf

Mutual Funds (2015b). "Types of mutual funds." Fidelity website. Accessed on July 16, 2015 at: https://www.fidelity.com/learning-center/investment-products/mutual-funds/types-of-mutual-funds

Nishizawa, Kana, Fion Li, and Billy Chan (2015). "China opens door to $97 billion of fund sales via Hong Kong." *Bloomberg Business*, May 22. Accessed on July 17, 2015, at: http://www.bloomberg.com/news/articles/2015-05-22/china-hong-kong-to-start-cross-border-mutual-fund-sales-july-1

Prior, Nancy (2015). "The SEC's recent money market mutual fund reform proposal." Fidelity Market Perspectives. Accessed on October 19, 2015 at: https://communications.fidelity.com/wi/2013/moneymarkets/pdfs/Call%20Summary_The_SECs_Recent_Money_Market_Reform_Proposal_Fidelity_FINA.pdf

Romero, Simon (2015). "An exploding pension crisis feeds Brazil's political turmoil." *The New York Times: International*, October 21, 2015, pp. A4–A7.

Roth, Allan (2011). "Morningstar's new forward-looking fund ratings." MoneyWatch, November 28, 2011. Accessed on October 22, 2015, at: http://www.cbsnews.com/news/morningstars-new-forward-looking-fund-ratings/

Schueth, Steven J. (2015) "The history of SRI." SRI Conference on Sustainable, Responsible, Impact Investing. Accessed on October 17, 2015 at: http://www.sriconference.com/about/what-is-sri/history-of-sri.html

SEC (2012). "Study regarding financial literacy among investors: As required by Section 917 of the Dodd–Frank Wall Street Reform and Consumer Protection Act." Staff Study, U.S. Securities and Exchange Commission, August 2012. Accessed on October 14, 2015 at: http://www.sec.gov/news/studies/2012/917-financial-literacy-study-part1.pdf

SEC (2014). "SEC adopts money market reform rules." U.S. Securities and Exchange Commission, July 23, 2014. Accessed on October 19, 2015 at: http://www.sec.gov/News/PressRelease/Detail/PressRelease/1370542347679

Sharpe, William F. (1976). "Corporate pension funding policy." *Journal of Financial Economics*, 4(2), 183–193.

Simmons, Katerina (1998). "Risk-adjusted performance of mutual funds." *New England Economic Review*, Federal Reserve Bank of Boston (September/October), 33–48.

Social Funds (2015). "SRI fund finder." Social Funds website. Accessed on October 17, 2015 at: http://www.socialfunds.com/

Social Security (2015). "Calculators: Life expectancy." Social Security website. Accessed on October 16, 2015 at: http://socialsecurity.gov/planners/lifeexpectancy.html

Social Security FAQs (2015). "Social security frequently asked questions." Social Security website. Accessed on October 17, 2015 at: https://faq.ssa.gov/link/portal/34011/34019/Article/3736/What-is-the-average-monthly-benefit-for-a-retired-worker

UNEP Finance Initiative (2007). "Responsible investment in focus: How leading public pension funds are meeting the challenge." Report jointly prepared by The United Nations Environment Programme Finance Initiative (UNEP FI) Asset Management Working Group (AMWG) and The United Kingdom Social Investment Forum (UKSIF) Sustainable Pensions Project (SPP). Accessed on October 20, 2015 at: http://www.unepfi.org/fileadmin/documents/infocus.pdf

U.S. News Money (2015). "Best fit multialternative." Investing. Accessed on October 22, 2015 at: http://money.usnews.com/funds/mutual-funds/rankings/multialternative

ACTIVITIES AND QUESTIONS

1   Go to www.http://investor.gov/investing-basics/investment-products/mutual-funds. Look on the left-hand side at the list of different investment products and find information on a particular product. What are the different types of mutual funds, and why have they become so popular? Why has financial literacy become an important issue, and what have governments done to improve financial literacy?

2   Go to http://www.ici.org/fb_data.html and download the latest ICI Factbook to see details about investment companies and mutual funds. What is the total investment globally in mutual funds at this time, and what are recent mutual fund trends, and the characteristics of mutual fund owners?

3   What are the advantages of mutual funds for small investors and what are general types of funds? Why are regulations important to provide greater confidence in mutual funds?

4   In the United States there are a number of different mutual fund regulations. Give a brief summary/overview of these. Following the subprime loan crisis, what additional regulations were instituted? Why is it very important to have independent directors on mutual fund boards?

5   What is the difference between a closed-end and an open-end mutual fund? Which type is more popular? Explain why.

6   For open-end mutual funds, what is net asset value (NAV) and how is it calculated? What is a net expense ratio listed for a fund, and why is it important in selecting a particular fund in which to invest?

7   What is a unit investment trust and a real estate investment trust and how do they operate? What is an exchange traded fund, and how is it like a closed-end fund? What are alternative strategies funds? What are hedge funds? How do these differ from open-end mutual funds?

8   What is a mutual fund family? What advantages do mutual fund families have and what services do they provide? Give an example of a mutual fund family and look up the fund

338

*Overview:
Nondepository
Financial
Institutions and
New Forms of
Financing*

on Google to see the services and research that the fund family provides. How are mutual funds marketed?

9   What are typical fees and operating expenses for mutual funds? Why do index funds have lower expenses?

10 Discuss different types of actively managed portfolio mutual funds, including type of capitalization, managed diversification allocations, sector investing, and style investing.

11 What are socially responsible investment funds, and what are their goals versus traditional investment funds?

12 What are the different risk measures for evaluating mutual funds and pension fund performance? What are Morningstar ratings and how are they calculated?

13 What is the difference between a defined contribution (DC) and a defined benefit pension (DB) plan? Why are the majority of private pension plans in the United States DC plans?

14 What trends have occurred for government defined benefit pension funds and what problems do they face? What regulations in the United States were developed to help protect corporate DB pension plans?

15 What are asset allocation choices for managers of DB plans?

16 What is RANVA and how is it used? Suppose an actively managed pension fund has a gross return of 20%, a 0.50% active management cost, and a 2.5% risk premium for active management, and a passively managed pension fund has a gross return of 18%. What is the RANVA? Would the pension fund management do better using an index fund or not

Chapter 13

Investment Banks and Securities Firms and Dark Pools and High-Frequency Trading

> Investment banking is a peculiar business. It takes decades and, in some cases, over a century to build a market-leading operation, only to then watch as it falls in a matter of days. While overleverage is often the predicate, a loss of confidence is the exciting cause. It's like a roaring avalanche triggered by an otherwise benign disruption far down the mountain.
>
> (Maxfield, 2013)

> This new bank holding structure will ensure that Morgan Stanley is in the strongest possible position—with the stability and flexibility to seize opportunities in the rapidly changing marketplace. It also offers the marketplace certainty about the strength of our financial position and our access to funding.
>
> John J. Mack, quoted in De la Merced, Bajaj, and Ross, 2008)

> The dark pool fines in the US … tend to affect the volumes for a period of time. …Bank trading desks are becoming leaner. People are asking "how do you do your job more efficiently, how do you source liquidity more efficiently?" The market is changing and asset managers are getting used to it.
>
> Mark Pumfrey, quoted in Stafford, 2016)

INVESTMENT banks, securities firms, and hedge funds have characteristics in common in that they all deal with investing or facilitating investment in different ways, as financial intermediaries providing research, advice, and expertise to facilitate investing for institutional investors, individual investors, and wealthy accredited investors, or providing funds and advice. Investment firms also facilitated initial public offerings for entrepreneurial firms as well as established firms for secondary offerings, among other roles. With the information age, the nature of these firms has changed dramatically. As early as the 1990s, online trading of securities grew dramatically, with the role of facilitating investors in handling their own

*Overview:
Nondepository
Financial
Institutions and
New Forms of
Financing*

investments and providing lower trading costs. Mutual funds companies also have their own discount brokerages, along with online trading. With the global financial crisis, however, many individuals have returned to seek advice from these intermediaries and also assistance in retirement planning. Today, there is also less differentiation between large commercial banks, investment banks, and securities firms with firms operating under the same bank or financial holding company, with universal banking that had been prominent in Europe, allowed in the United States after the passage of the Gramm–Leach–Bliley Act of 1999 through today.

In addition to online trading, the nature of both investment banking and financing for entrepreneurial firms is changing in the information age. By early February 1999, William Hambrecht, former CEO and founder of Hambrecht & Quist, an innovative investment bank, announced the startup of an innovative Internet investment bank, WR Hambrecht + Co that uses an internet Dutch auction for initial public offers (IPOs) as opposed to setting the price of an IPO, a traditional convention for investment banking firms. High bidders versus preferred investors (as is often practiced) are given shares. This process reduces the cost of underwriting issues for firms going public, including reducing underpricing for issues through the OpenIPOAuction. WR Hambrecht notes on its website that the auction process is set up to "help companies of all sizes efficiently access capital at the lowest possible cost in order to accelerate disruptive growth" and "enable the distribution of issuer disclosure and research to any investor, and the collection of bids in a fair and systematic fashion" (Hambrecht, 2016). FinTech, startups that offer digital financial services, have rapidly grown including crowd-funding as a new source of financing.

Securities firms and investment banks have faced a number of challenges in recent years, including a lack of confidence in the industry following scandals involving conflicts of interest between credit rating agencies and issuers of subprime loan securitizations, among others, and the failure of Lehman Brothers and bankruptcy of Bear Stearns in 2008. Securities firms during the subprime loan crisis often suffered liquidity problems, with contagion effects. Goldman Sachs and Morgan Stanley converted to bank holding company structures to allow for Federal Reserve borrowing privileges.

This chapter examines the securities industry with an overview of securities and investment banking firms and their operations, including new online FinTech securities and investment firms.

INVESTMENT BANKS AND SECURITIES FIRMS

Structure and Types of Firms

Investment banks and securities firms are often part of the same financial holding company. Investment banks finance major capital financing for corporations, launch initial public offerings (IPOs) and secondary offerings, negotiate private placements, and assist in mergers and acquisitions, and other more wholesale level services. Securities firms perform services related to investment management, portfolio management, risk management, brokerage and dealer services, and trading of derivatives. Today securities firms, commercial banks, investment banks, and private banks often operate under one umbrella.

The Securities Industry and Financial Markets Association (SIFMA, 2015) points out a number of different types of securities firms, including:

*Investment Banks
and Securities
Firms and
Dark Pools and
High-Frequency
Trading*

1   *National full-line firms* offer both investment banking and corporate advisory services and trading activities for customers and for the firm itself as principal transactions, along with retail brokerage services and advice; these include Bank of America Merrill Lynch, and UBS, among many others. National full-line firms often receive the largest percentage of their revenues from brokerage commissions on securities firms as well as from the net interest spread (interest revenues from loans to customers less interest cost to borrow). Customers are loaned securities that are in the firm's name for short selling and provided with margin credit. National full-line firms also have a large number of employees with a national branch network, and financial advisers often receive fee income from customers for financial planning advice.

2   *Large often global wholesale investment banks* usually focus on wholesale (corporate) underwriting and advisory services, underwriting and distributing common stock and corporate and municipal debt, arranging private placements, acting as advisers in mergers and acquisitions, and providing other corporate services; these include, for instance, Goldman Sachs in New York and Credit Suisse First Boston in Boston. Note that this category is not mutually exclusive, since many full-service and New York investment banks are also large. Top global investment banks often cited include Bank of America Merrill Lynch, Barclays Capital, Citi, Credit Suisse, Deutsche Bank, Goldman Sachs, J.P. Morgan, Morgan Stanley, and UBS.

3   *Regional securities firms* are based in a particular region, such as Brown Brothers Harriman, that serves the North America region and primarily provide private banking, investment management, and other investor services. Regional firms often are also involved in underwriting the stock or debt of select firms in their region and providing institutional investor and other services depending on the particular nature of the firm. Piper Jaffray, for instance, provides asset management, investment banking, public finance, and institutional brokerage services across the United States, but also has special regional offices, such as its Denver Public Finance office serving public finance issuers in Colorado, Montana, Idaho, and the Rocky Mountain region.

4   *Global regional securities firms* focus on particular regions of the world. Examples include: Piper Jaffray, Raymond James, SunTrust Robinson Humphrey, and Wells Fargo & Co, in the United States; RBC Capital Markets, Scotiabank, and TD Securities in Canada; HSBC Holdings, RBS, Credit Agricole, BNP Paribas, ABN AMRO, and Commerzbank in Europe; Vermillion Partners, Guosen Partners, China International Capital Corporation, and CITIC Securities International in China; Mizuho Financial Group, Nomura Holdings, Sumitomo Mitsui Financial Group, and Mitsubishi UFJ Financial Group in Japan; Macquarie Group and BBY in Australia; SMI Capital Markets (State Bank of India) and Maple Capital Advisory in India; and Daewoo Securities in Korea, among many others (WSP Resources, 2016).

5   *Discount firms* trade for customers and offer online trading with lower fees and commissions for retail customers, such as Charles Schwab, which also offers banking, trading, and financial consultant services. Many discount firms also receive commission fee income from selling mutual funds for mutual fund companies as well. There are also pure online securities firms including E*-Trade, that allow investors to invest and trade, taking control of their own investments, including some online advice, such as a retirement planning calculator and other educational services.

342

*Overview:
Nondepository
Financial
Institutions and
New Forms of
Financing*

6   *Online platform investment banking firms* such as WR Hambrecht + Co, discussed earlier, use a Dutch auction platform. Other FinTech firms have rapidly evolved in recent years for investments and securities trading.

7   *Boutique investment banks* focus on particular industries or types of underwriting. Examples include: Miller, Buckfire & Co that focuses on restructuring; Montgomery & Co. that is media and internet and technology focused; Berkery, Noyes & Co that is financial services focused; Cain Brothers that is health care focused, as well as global boutique investment banks, such as Perella Weinberg Partners and Lazard, Global M&A advisory firms. These categories are not mutually exclusive and are in constant flux. Many mutual fund companies including Fidelity and Vanguard, for example, offer brokerage services for customers.

With the growth of mega bank holding companies and financial holding companies, many of these categories have become blurred, with many investment banks and securities firms operating under the umbrella of larger bank and financial holding companies.

PRESTIGIOUS AND NONPRESTIGIOUS INVESTMENT BANKS

Investment banking firms also are often classified as prestigious or nonprestigious based on their syndicate participation in advertisements, often called tombstone ads, because of their shape. Lead underwriters in charge of an issue are listed first, followed by other underwriters based on their relationships with lead investment banks and their reputation in handling and selling an issue. Firms with continuous top rankings are deemed prestigious underwriters, such as Morgan Stanley and Goldman Sachs, as examples. Prior to the 1970s primarily New York wholesale investment banks were deemed as prestigious, but soon full-service firms entered the ranks, such as Merrill Lynch (now part of Bank of America) which made the industry more competitive.

OVERVIEW OF KEY AREAS OF ACTIVITIES FOR SECURITIES FIRMS

Securities firms are engaged in many different activities, and often benefit from principal trading (transaction) activities and fee income for advisory services in bear markets when underwriting revenues are down. Key areas of activity and revenues for securities firms include the following:

1   *Investment banking underwriting fees and gross spread* (difference between the price paid for securities from a corporation and the offering price securities are sold for to the public) for debt and equity securities, private placements, management fees, mergers and acquisitions (M&A), restructuring, advisory services, among others.

2   *Principal transactions* involving trading and investments; for trading this involves making securities, foreign exchange, or commodity trades that are profitable for the firm. For investing it means managing an investment portfolio to reap returns for the firm itself. Principal transactions also include revenues from mortgage-backed securities, swaps, derivatives, hedging strategies, among others.

343

*Investment Banks
and Securities
Firms and
Dark Pools and
High-Frequency
Trading*

3 *Selling and dealing activities and trading for customers as an agent* involve marketing and distributing securities and receiving commission income, making trades for customers in foreign exchange, commodities, bonds, or other instruments, and margin lending to customers.

4 *Investing activities as an agent* involves managing mutual funds and pension funds or portfolios for wealthy investors, receiving fee income for this activity.

5 *Back office activities* include clearing and escrow services, research services, and advisory services, and M&A advice.

6 *Other types of activities*, such as merchant banking in which the securities firm takes an equity financing position in a merger or leveraged buyout (for instance, venture capital and private equity subsidiary activities) and real estate subsidiary activities, including real estate investment trusts and real estate partnerships, among others.

Investment banks have entered many other new areas as well, including banking type services, such as small business, consumer, and mortgage loans and small business consulting services. Also, many investment banks are part of a financial or bank holding company. During the U.S. subprime crisis, on September 21, 2008 both Goldman Sachs and Morgan Stanley, as the remaining independent, major U.S. investment banks became traditional bank holding companies, which allowed the Fed to provide liquidity through its discount window. The two investment banks' previous nonbank deposit-taking activities were rolled into their new bank subsidiaries. During the crisis, the Fed arranged mergers for some investment firms with bank holding companies to prevent their failures, including Merrill Lynch with Bank of America (De la Merced, et al., 2008).

SOURCES OF REVENUE

As shown in Table 13.1, investment banks and securities firms have a wide range of sources of revenue.

TABLE 13.1 | Sources of revenue for investment banks

Revenue	Typical percentage
Commissions	18.35
Trading gain (loss)	9.34
Investment account gain (loss)	0.40
Underwriting revenue	9.59
Margin interest	1.95
Mutual fund sale revenue	7.38
Fees, asset management	12.80
Research revenue	0.04
Commodities revenue	0.81
Other revenue related to the securities business	22.78
Other revenue	16.54
Total revenue	100

Source: FINRA, 2016b (for 4,679 member firms for the most recent year reported, 2010).

Overview:
Nondepository
Financial
Institutions and
New Forms of
Financing

For revenues, there are a variety of different sources with commissions, trading gains, underwriting revenue, mutual sales revenue, asset management fees, and other revenue sources as key sources, with investment account gains, margin interest, research revenue, and commodities revenue, as other sources of revenue.

As noted in Table 13.2, compensation is the largest expense for the firms reporting, as a little over 46% of total expenses, followed by other expenses as about 25% of total expenses, by floor costs as 10.41% of total expenses, and interest expenses as 10.01% of total expenses. In 2010, 4,679 firms reported to FINRA with a total of 365,524 million personnel, with 188,521 million income producing and 177,003 nonincome producing.

Performing a Dupont Analysis, where ROE is a function of NPM and AU and EM, for securities firms the NPM is 9.74%; the asset utilization (AU) is also low at 0.0549 x, resulting in a small ROA of 0.53%. Since securities firms had a very low equity to assets ratio of just 4.75%, this high leverage results in an equity multiplier (EM) of 21.05 x, so the ROE is 11.16%.

It is worth noting that in 2008 during the U.S. subprime loan crisis, for 4,923 firms reporting, the average NPM was – 8.52% and AU was 0.0657 x. The ROA was – 0.56% with an EM of about 24.07 x. This large EM magnified the negative ROA, resulting in a larger, negative ROE of about – 13.48%.

TABLE 13.2 | Sources of expenses for investment banks and securities firms

Expenses	Typical percentage expenses
Total compensation	46.16
Total floor costs	10.41
Communications expense	2.60
Occupancy and equipment costs	3.14
Promotional costs	0.96
Interest expense	10.01
Losses from error accounts and bad debts	0.13
Data processing costs	1.45
Regulatory fees and expenses	0.03
Nonrecurring charges	0.85
Other expenses	24.26
Total expenses	100
Pre-tax net income % revenues (pre-tax NPM)	13.66
Net income % revenues (NPM)	9.74
Asset utilization (revenues to assets)	0.0549 x
Net income % average total assets (ROA)	0.53
Equity to total average assets	4.75
Equity multiplier	21.05 x
Net income as a % ownership equity (ROE)	11.16

Source: FINRA, 2016b (for 4,679 member firms for the most recent year reported, 2010).

345

*Investment Banks
and Securities
Firms and
Dark Pools and
High-Frequency
Trading*

Over the last few decades, for the securities industry as a whole, revenues have been spread over a larger variety of activities. Other revenue related to the securities business and other revenue for the year examined in Table 13.1 are about 39% of total revenues. Other revenue-generating activities include M&A fees, private placements, market making, asset management, other security related and unrelated (such as back office type) activities, and global investment management, with fee-based businesses increasing in importance. Fees for services to institutional investors are a large source of revenue, with institutional investors holding over 65% of total equities in the United States, with shifts of participants in capital markets towards pooled investment vehicles, including mutual funds and exchange traded funds (ETFs).

As noted by Aguilar (2013) the percentage of U.S. public equities managed by institutional investors grew from about 7 or 8% of market capitalization in 1950 to about 67% by 2010, and institutional investors owned in aggregate about 73% of the outstanding equity of the largest 1,000 U.S. corporations. Institutional investors include mutual funds and ETFs regulated by the SEC, along with pension funds, insurance companies, and diverse types of hedge funds and managed accounts, with many of these unregulated (Aguilar, 2013).

NEW TRADING VENUES INCLUDING DARK POOLS AND HIGH-SPEED TRADING, AND ELECTRONIC TRADING PLATFORMS AND ALGORITHMIC TRADING

Dark Pools and High-Speed Trading

As Aguilar (2013) notes, over the past few decades the growth in assets that are managed by institutional investors had had a significant effect on, and has been also significantly affected by, dramatic changes in market structure and trading technologies that includes new trading venues (including dark pools, electronic trading platforms, and high-speed trading) and the development in the United States of a national market system.

Dark pools opened up in Europe in about 2008, resulting in many European investors trading in dark pools, estimated to be about 8% of total books trades by ITG Europe, an operator of a dark pool, with Bats Chi-X-Europe, a pan-European exchange, increasing its market share to 24% in early 2016 from 21% in 2014, with gains made in Spain and Germany. Advantages for asset managers and pension funds are that venues, such as Liquidnet, match trades in private, whereby prices aren't displayed until after a deal's completion, permitting asset managers to make large block trades off exchange to avoid the risk of prices going against the seller to the buyer, but frustrating regulators and other asset managers, with much publicity making asset managers aware that, through dark pools, trading games are often played at their expense (Stafford, 2016).

Dark pools are used to facilitate block trading by institutional investors who wish to hide their trades to avoid large impacts in financial markets of large orders that could adversely affect their trades. Michael Lewis's *Flash Boys: A Wall Street Revolt* discusses these along with high-frequency trading used to both hide and speed up trades. The net result of this nontransparent trading can be disruption of markets and lower costs for the traders involved at the expense of other traders and small investors (Picardo, 2016).

*Overview:
Nondepository
Financial
Institutions and
New Forms of
Financing*

Regulatory Actions against Dark Pools

Regulators have taken actions against institutional investors for engaging in dark pools that limit market transparency, and in legal actions won $150 million from Credit Suisse and Barclays for oversight failures and/or misleading consumers with respect to their dark pools operations, including Crossfinder, one of two dark pools for Credit Suiise, and Barclay's LX dark pool; there were also fines for ITG and UBS for oversight failures. Despite this, dark pools continue to operate and grow, such as Credit Suisse's Crossfinder, a popular pool, and Liquidnet Europe, a block-trading venue, experiencing a record year in 2015. Dark pool trading in Europe rose by 45% for value traded and by 25% for volume traded in December of 2015 versus 2014. Data from the U.S. Financial Regulatory Authority reveals a similar 22% rise in the number of stocks traded in dark pools for 2015:Q3 versus 2014:Q3. European regulators plan the introduction of caps on the amount of trading that can be done in dark pools in an attempt to return trading to the exchanges. London Stock Exchange's Turquoise, Bats Chi-X Europe, and Deutsche Borse also provide discreet block trading services, with benefits of both exchanges and dark pools (Fahey, 2016; Stafford, 2016).

Electronic Trading Platforms and Algorithmic Trading Apps for Selecting Investments

In recent years computers have been used to not only go through algorithm rules to make trades at opportune times, but also to make decisions how to invest. Millennial investors have increased their use of apps from investment companies (Betterment, Wealthfront, Acorns, among others) that provide access to robo-computers to allocate funds to ETFs, based on an individual's goals and target retirement date, in a similar way to target funds, with computers changing allocations such as a customer's age or their goals change. These companies are now managing several billions of dollars in assets, with Betterment's assets under management growing from $1.1 billion in 2015 to $3.5 billion in 2016. Although, the amount of assets managed is relatively small compared to the total wealth management market, the technology offers a massive disruption potential for wealth management advising. Many millennial investors prefer this type of simple investment advice where investment choices are made for them based on their profiles and goals rather than choosing from a myriad of mutual funds. Apps, like Acorns also round up customer purchases, so an excess amount is invested as savings, such as 75 cents on a $15.25 purchase, with customers averaging about $50 to $60 a month in savings. Since computers are cheaper than hiring expert employees as advisers, fees can also be lower, with portfolios prices at just a fraction of those for more traditional wealth advisers, along with fees charged by the ETFs in which a customer's funds are invested (Sweet, 2016).

Automated Trading Systems

Automated trading systems, often called *algorithmic trading*, permits traders to set up specific rules for trades that then can be automatically executed by a computer, based on either simple rules or complex strategies using programming language on a trader's

347

*Investment Banks
and Securities
Firms and
Dark Pools and
High-Frequency
Trading*

platform and an expert programmer. Once rules are established, the computer monitors markets for buy or sell opportunities based on the specifications of the trading strategy, which allows for instantaneous order entry in fast moving markets. As Folger (2016) points out the advantages of automated trading systems include: avoiding human emotions that can lead to overtrading; the ability to try out algorithms on historical data first; keeping discipline in volatile markets; achieving consistency for a trading plan; improved order entry, since computers immediately respond to changes in market conditions and allowing diversity in trading for multiple accounts and strategies at the same time, with a computer scanning for trading opportunities across markets. Disadvantages include: the potential for mechanical failures; the need for monitoring to avoid potential mechanical failures and identify and resolve problems; and over optimization with some trading systems doing fine on historical data with backtesting, but doing terribly in real markets (Folger, 2016).

Regulators have been concerned about the increasing risk of computerized trading in the U.S. bond market with the potential for creating turmoil, such as the dramatic price swing that occurred on October 15, 2015. While those in favor of automated trading see high-frequency trading using complex models as useful in terms of instantaneous purchases and sales for huge volumes to enhance liquidity and bring down trading costs, critics see automated trading as disruptive and a means to manipulate markets. This in turn leads to greater operational risk and disruptions in markets. The Treasury Markets Practice Group (TMPG) sponsored by the Federal Reserve made a recommendation for a set of industry practices for the automated trading of bonds to avoid short-term disruptions. Potential risks cited by the TMPG report include operational risks, such as program malfunctions to unexpected reactions if algorithms reach "wrong or unexpected data," and the potential for "rogue" traders to use automated systems to manipulate markets. Electronic trading now represents more than half of the overall trading volume for Treasuries, with the remainder performed over the phone between dealers and investors or among dealers (Leong and Reese, 2015).

THE VOLCKER RULE

Under the Volcker Rule initial provisions of the U.S. Dodd–Frank Act of 2010, insured depository institutions, bank holding companies and their affiliates are prohibited from engaging in proprietary trading or acquiring or having an ownership interest in covered funds (hedge funds or private equity funds, among others) with a number of exceptions. A final version was adopted in December 2013 by the CFTC, OCC, Fed, FDIC, and the SEC. The final rule allows a phasing in over time, and requires that such investments need to be fully deducted from Tier 1 capital. "Proprietary trading," which means engaging as principal for the trading account of a banking entity for buying or selling a financial instrument, cannot be larger than 3% of Tier 1 capital. Banking entities that engage in proprietary trading and/or covered fund investments also have to establish a specific compliance program related to the Volcker Rule, with an exception for specific permitted activities, such as underwriting, market-making, hedging, and risk management (Raymond James 2015).

*Overview:
Nondepository
Financial
Institutions and
New Forms of
Financing*

U.S. DEPARTMENT OF LABOR FIDUCIARY RULE FOR INVESTMENT ADVISERS

On April 6, 2016, the U.S. Department of Labor released a final rule for fiduciaries for investment advice provided to retirement savers by investment advisers. Under this rule, anyone that provides investment advice on retirement accounts that is given in exchange for compensation must act as a fiduciary and must put "the investors best interest ahead of his or own interests." Hence, a securities broker for instance would not be allowed to steer investors into house funds, for instance, that have higher fees than other nonhouse funds. Formerly, brokers generally only needed to recommend suitable funds for clients, which provided a lower than fiduciary standard, so the new rule provides a more stringent standard. The standard also applies to advisers that act as fiduciaries, setting a standard above the existing legal standard, where, previously, investment advisers could recommend investment options that gave them a larger commission, as long as they disclosed this conflict of interest. While consumer groups praise the new rule, other are concerned that this will result in fewer choices and higher fees to offset the security industry's costs in complying with the new standard, and that the higher compliance costs including potential costly litigation could put smaller adviser firms out of business, reducing choices of personalized investment advice (Leary, 2016; Savage, 2016).

CAPITAL STANDARDS UNDER BASEL III FOR LARGE INVESTMENT BANKS WITH BANKING OPERATIONS

Under Basel III regulatory capital rules and new capital regulations under the Dodd–Frank Act, large financial services firms with banking operations must make adjustments including holding a capital conservation buffer, along with adjustments for the calculation of risk-weighted assets and new minimum capital ratio requirements beginning January 1, 2015. For large investment banks with banking operations, this increases capital requirements and requires the raising of additional capital for growth.

RISK MANAGEMENT IN SECURITIES FIRMS

Trading Risk

Securities firms have been exposed to huge losses by rogue traders, going back to the late 1980s, when one young trader in Singapore, Nick Lesson, accrued huge losses on Japanese stock index futures, and a trader for Daiwa Bank, a leading Japanese investment bank, lost $1.1 billion through 30,000 unauthorized trades over 11 years as a senior manager in Daiwa's New York branch. Securities firms have attempted to develop better information on the risk exposure of traders, using *daily earnings at risk (DEAR)* and *value at risk (VAR) measures*. They have also attempted to allocate greater capital against potential losses associated with the risk of different activities, using the risk-adjusted return on capital *(RAROC)* approach.

349

*Investment Banks
and Securities
Firms and
Dark Pools and
High-Frequency
Trading*

Position limits for traders have also been devised, based on the market risk of traders' portfolios, and compensation methods also now consider traders' returns, along with the additional risk that riskier trades impose on a firm. Higher market trading risk capital requirements are required for large international banks with subsidiaries engaging in trading activities.

Underwriting Risks

Investment banks have considerable underwriting risk, the risk of adverse price movements immediately after the issue of new securities. Under a negotiated offering, investment bankers purchase securities at a given price and sell securities at a higher offering price to the public (i.e., a gross spread). To reduce selling risk, syndicates of securities firms are often formed to take on a portion of the offering and reduce the underwriting and selling risk of the lead underwriter. To retain the prestige associated with being a leading firm in syndicates, firms must manage a large volume of new offerings, putting them at greater risk.

Underwriters take on greater risks with SEC 415 shelf registration deals; they are often asked to provide bids for an offering, particularly debt offerings that may have to be offered in just a few days. With a shelf registration, the SEC gives prior approval for an issue and may take as little as two days to give final approval based on the final price and contract rate for the offering. Consequently, underwriters do not have time to market the bonds before making a bid. A bought deal is such an accepted bond transaction, often for Eurobonds, whereby an investment bank has not had time to develop a syndicate or access market interest before submitting a bid. A kamikaze offer is an offer by a prospective underwriter for a bought deal at such a low spread that other underwriters may decline to participate in a syndicate for it. Despite lower spreads, underwriters may feel compelled to participate in an offering to retain other types of business from corporations. Technological innovations have also allowed corporations to bypass securities firms. For instance, CapitalLink, a system innovation that was made available in 1990 allows blue chip corporations to issue bonds directly to institutional investors. Rapid technological changes and instantaneous trading can increase the operating risk of securities firms.

HEDGING OF UNDERWRITING

Hedging using futures basically entails taking a position on bonds in the futures market that will provide a gain to offset a loss on a spot position on bonds. Hedges are commonly used by securities firms.

Underwriters are allowed to use stabilization techniques during the first 30 days of a new stock issue, whereby they purchase or sell securities to stabilize the security's price. Often negotiated in an offering are overallotment (greenshoe) options, which allow a maximum of an additional 15% of the number of shares included in the basic offering. This allows the underwriter to sell to the public more shares than it must purchase under the underwriting agreement and to cover its short position to help stabilize the price of an issue. In a falling market, the lead manager may attempt to use overallotments with syndicate participants as a way to encourage sales efforts.

Overview:
Nondepository
Financial
Institutions and
New Forms of
Financing

LIQUIDITY RISK

Investment banks and securities firms are subject to liquidity risks, since they often must borrow to purchase securities that they sell at a later time as security issuers and dealers. Hence, having sufficient liquidity to meet contractual obligations, including cash and available access to credit and capital markets for borrowing, is highly important. The demise of Lehman Brothers and Bear Stearns discussed in a later section clearly emphasizes how not having sufficient access to liquidity can lead to severe risks that can affect a firm's financial condition. Securities and investment firms are also subject to regulatory risks of higher liquidity or capital requirements being imposed. During the global financial crisis, markets for short-term borrowing dried up quickly.

As Gorton (2010) points out, securities firms also depend on short-term borrowing using repurchase agreements in the repo market, which like demand deposits "can be withdrawn at any time." Repos are backed by collateral, and collateral at times of scarcity may take the form of bonds issues by special-purpose vehicles, which as demand grows come to include securitized products. When the housing market collapsed, the value of such collateral fell in value, resulting in repo haircuts and withdrawals for other firms, creating a panic. Money market mutual funds also purchased various structured assets, and had to be bailed out by sponsors when they suffered value losses and rapid withdrawals. Since many securities firms have money market funds, this creates further liquidity risks.

In July 2014, the U.S. SEC adopted amendments to the rules governing money market mutual funds in response to excessive withdrawals over short time frames during the U.S. subprime loan crisis, with structural and operational reforms addressing this risk while attempting to preserve the benefits of these funds. The new SEC rules require that institutional prime money market funds must use a floating net asset value (NAV) based on market-based factors, with shares sold and redeemed based on changes in the market value of fund assets versus a previous convention allowing a constant share price of $1.00 to be maintained. Nongovernment money market fund boards also in the rule are provided new tools to address runs that include the ability to impose liquidity fees and redemption gates during periods of stress. The rules also add enhanced diversification, disclosure and stress testing requirements, and updated reporting for money market funds and private funds that operate similarly to money market funds. Funds have a two-year transition period to allow for full adjustments for their systems, operations, and investing practices (SEC, 2014; Raymond James 2015).

REPUTATIONAL RISK

Reputational risk is very important for securities firms, with administrative proceedings by regulators having a serious effect on reputation risk. Similarly, any violation affecting operations and financial results, liquidity and trading price of a company can cause serious damage to a firm's reputation that is critical for companies in attracting and maintaining their clients, customers, investors, and associates. Such risks can harm a firm's business and prospects. Reputational risks include: dealings that have conflicts of interest; that violate legal and regulatory requirements; ethical issues; money laundering; cybersecurity; privacy; recordkeeping; sales and trading practices; any failure for selling securities underwritten at the price levels

351

*Investment Banks
and Securities
Firms and
Dark Pools and
High-Frequency
Trading*

that are anticipated; and failure of due diligence for firms, as well as credit, liquidity, and market risks that go with the nature of the products of securities firms. Other reputational risks include any failure regarding standards of service and quality, whereby failure to treat customers and clients and employees fairly could lead to customer complaints, lawsuits, and higher regulatory scrutiny, and to lower revenues and higher operating and reputational costs and harm to prospects for future business for a firm. With international operations and globalization, these risks increase (Raymond James, 2015).

THE IMPORTANCE OF LIQUIDITY AND RISK MANAGEMENT FOR SECURITIES FIRMS

As in the quote from John Maxfield at the beginning of this chapter, investment banking is a business that depends on a firm's reputation and it take many decades for a firm to build up to be a leading organization. However, investment banking is also a highly leveraged business, with typically low capital ratios, engaged in activities that can reap great returns, but also involve significant risks. Investment banking average returns on equity and returns on assets are also quite cyclical, with high returns during boom times and lower returns during recessions, when demand for new public issues is low. The size of investment banks in terms of employees also tends to rise during expansions and falls during downtimes.

Bear Stearns is an example of an investment firm that had a change in the "character" and "culture" of its organization over time. As Maxfield (2013) notes on the 5th anniversary of Bear Stearns' collapse, a change in culture came about with a new CEO in 1993 moving from a previous CEO that was a "democratic, humble, hard-charging, risk-obsessed, and penny-pinching leader" to a CEO with less interest in or knowledge of risk management and more interested in lavish spending. Monitoring of Bear Stearns' real estate traders became lax, allowing for the accumulation of almost $50 billion in mortgage-related assets by 2007, the time of the U.S. real estate market collapse. Two Bear Stearns managed hedge funds that specialized in mortgage-backed securities went under, as housing prices declined and delinquencies for mortgages increased, and subprime mortgage security prices plunged. For the fourth quarter of 2007, for the first time in 85 years, Bear Stearns had major losses, and the CEO was ousted. However, just after this replacement in March 10, 2008, a major rating agency downgraded mortgage-backed securities issued by the firm. The Fed in response launched a $50 billion lending facility to support troubled financial institutions. Hedge fund investors began a run on Bear Stearns' brokerage unit, pulling out deposits. This run resulted in the firm having insufficient liquidity for its survival. The Fed provided a bridge loan through JPMorgan and Bear Stearns' board of directors, with the firm agreeing to be sold to JPMorgan for just $2 a share, less than a week from trading at $65 a share, ending the firm's 85-year history. Bear Stearns' failure emphasizes the importance of risk management for securities firms (Maxfield, 2013).

Similarly, other long-standing investment banks failed or had to be merged over the crisis including Lehman Brothers on September 15, 2008, days later the bailout of insurer AIG by the federal government, and a massive stock decline for Merrill Lynch, which Bank of America agreed to buy for $50 billion. Britain's Barclays acquired the core capital-markets business of Lehman Brothers as it came out of bankruptcy (De la Merced, et al., 2008; Salisbury and Lim, 2014).

Overview:
Nondepository
Financial
Institutions and
New Forms of
Financing

On September 8, 2008, Goldman Sachs and Morgan Stanley, who had plunges in their stock prices as well as liquidity difficulties, as the last two independent U.S. investment banks converted to bank holding companies to allow for the Federal Reserve to provide liquidity. This conversion also allowed the two investment banks to combine these operations with larger capital cushions that could be generated with low-cost retail deposit financing. These actions put the two investment banks under more stringent banking regulations, including holding higher equity to asset ratios, and made Goldman Sachs, the fourth largest bank holding company in the United States, with its deposit-taking activities rolled over into GS Bank USA; Morgan Stanley's Utah industrial bank became a national bank, Morgan Stanley Bank (De la Merced, et al., 2008).

CONFLICTS OF INTEREST AND NEW REGULATIONS

In reaction to conflicts of interest associated with the U.S. subprime loan crisis and global financial crisis, new rules were adopted to avoid these. This includes, as of July 1, 2014, mandatory registration of "municipal advisers" as stipulated under the Dodd–Frank Act, requiring a fiduciary duty for municipal advisers when advising municipal entities with an effect on the interaction with municipal issues, with additional regulation and oversight by the SEC that affects the nature of interactions with public finance clients for securities firms involved in public financing transactions.

In April 2016, the U.S. Labor Department also announced a new "fiduciary rule" that adopts a new standard for brokers and advisers that is more stringent than current regulations, which only require that brokers recommend "suitable" products, even if they might not be the best option for investors. Under the new rule, a broader group of investment professionals are included as fiduciaries, with the role of putting investors first, whereby they are not allowed to accept compensation or payments that create a conflict of interest, with the exception if they qualify for an exemption that ensures an investor is protected. As more U.S. savers are being put in charge of their own retirement security with a large movement from defined benefit to defined contribution (401k) plans, the rule was established to provide an additional layer of protection to protect workers from "poor or conflicted investment advice" and to make improvements in disclosures and reduce conflicts of interest. Such conflicts of interest could include a securities firm or mutual fund or other third party receiving compensation for recommending a particular investment. Although this new rule will not ban commissions, brokers may have to provide explanations for why they are recommending particular products, if a less expensive option is available or if they recommend "complicated products" (Marte, 2016).

SUMMARY

Investment banks and securities firms depend on their reputation to allow their businesses to maintain and attract future business. Investment banks do due diligence for businesses and underwrite new issues (initial public offerings) and secondary offerings to attract external equity capital to them. Securities firms distribute offerings and buy and sell securities for customers, as well as many other advisory services. Securities firms take on greater risk than

353

*Investment Banks
and Securities
Firms and
Dark Pools and
High-Frequency
Trading*

other types of financial institutions, and business can be very cyclical with large profits during bull markets and lower profits during bear markets. They face market, liquidity, operating, and reputation risks that have to be carefully managed. Many securities firms are part of larger financial or bank holding companies, so have a diversified mix of assets in different financial service areas. Following the U.S. subprime loan crisis and global financial crisis, technology has been a driver for disruptive new business models and more more stringent regulations and technology have been introduced as forces for changing the nature of the industry.

BIBLIOGRAPHY

Aguilar, Luis A. (2013). "Institutional investors: Power and responsibility." Speech at J. Mack Robinson College of Business, Center for the Economic Analysis of Risk (CEAR), Department of Finance CEAR Workshop-Institutional Investors, Atlanta, Georgia, April 19, 2013, U.S. Securities and Exchange Commission. Accessed on March 4, 2016 at: https://www.sec.gov/News/Speech/Detail/Speech/1365171515808

De la Merced, Michael J., Vikas Bajaj, and Andrew Ross Sorkin (2008). "As Goldman and Morgan shift, a Wall St. era ends." DealBook, *The New York Times*, September 21, 2008. Accessed on March 4, 2016 at: http://dealbook.nytimes.com/2008/09/21/goldman-morgan-to-become-bank-holding-companies/?_r=0

Deloitte (2016). "Forward look: Top regulatory trends for 2016 in securities." Deloitte. Accessed on March 3, 2016 at: http://www2.deloitte.com/us/en/pages/regulatory/securities-regulatory-outlook.html

Fahey, Mark (2016). "Dark pools still popular, despite year of regulatory attention." CNBC, February 1, 2016. Accessed on March 4, 2016 at: http://www.cnbc.com/2016/02/01/regulators-may-dislike-dark-pools-but-investors-love-them.html

FINRA (2016a). "FINRA's 2016 focus: Supervision, liquidity and securities firms' culture." Financial Industry Regulatory Authority (FINRA), January 5, 2016. Accessed on March 3, 2016 at: https://www.finra.org/newsroom/2016/finras-2016-focus-supervision-liquidity-and-securities-firms-culture

FINRA (2016b). "Total FINRA member firms' income statement & selected items." FINRA website. Accessed on March 4, 2016 at: www.finra.org

Folger, Jean (2016). "The pros and cons of automated trading systems." Investopedia. Accessed on March 6, 2016 at: http://www.investopedia.com/articles/trading/11/automated-trading-systems.asp

Gorton, Gary B. (2010). *Slapped by the Invisible Hand: The Panic of 2007.* Oxford: Oxford University Press.

Hambrecht (2016). "About WR Hambrecht + CO." WR Hambrecht + Co. Accessed on March 3, 2016 at: https://www.wrhambrecht.com/about/

Hart, Rupert M. (2012). *Crowdfund Your Startup! Raising Venture Capital Using New Crowdfunding Techniques.* CordaNobleMedia Publications.

III (2016). "Financial Services Fact Book Archive." Insurance Information Institute. Accessed on March 3, 2016 at: http://www.iii.org/financial-services-fact-book/archive

Leary, Elizabeth (2016). "Retirement savers get new legal protections." *The Denver Post*, April 17, 2016, 6K.

Leong, Richard and Chris Reese (2015). "Automatic trading brings growing risks to U.S. bond market: TMPG." *Reuters*, New York. Accessed on March 6, 2016 at: http://www.reuters.com/article/us-usa-bonds-algo-idUSKBN0N01XS20150409

Lewis, Michael (2014). *Flash Boys: A Wall Street Revolt.* NY: W.W. Norton & Co.

Marte, Jonnelle (2016). "New rules set standards for retirement advice." *The Denver Post*, April 7, 2016, 8A–9A.

Maxfield, John (2013). "A timeline of Bear Stearns' downfall." *The Motley Fool*, March 15, 2013. Accessed on March 3, 2016 at: http://www.fool.com/investing/general/2013/03/15/a-timeline-of-bear-stearns-downfall.aspx

Picardo, Elvis (2016). "An introduction to dark pools." Investopedia, February 20, 2016. Accessed on March 4, 2015 at: http://www.investopedia.com/articles/markets/050614/introduction-dark-pools.asp

Raymond James (2015). Annual Report 2015, Form 10-K for Fiscal Year ended September 30, 2015.

Salisbury, Ian and Paul J. Lim (2014). "6 years later, 7 lessons from Lehman's collapse." *Money*, September 15, 2014: Accessed on March 3, 2016 at: http://time.com/money/3330793/lessons-from-lehman-brothers-collapse/

Savage, Terry (2016). "Fiduciary rule meant to protect investors, may cost them dearly." *The Denver Post*, April 17, 2016, 6K.

354

*Overview:
Nondepository
Financial
Institutions and
New Forms of
Financing*

SEC (2014). "SEC adopts money market fund reform rules." U.S. Securities and Exchange Commission, July 23, 2014. Accessed on September 5, 2014 at: https://www.sec.gov/News/PressRelease/Detail/PressRelease/1370542347679

SIFMA (2015). "US Research Quarterly, Fourth Quarter 2015." Securities Industry and Financial Markets Association, February 24, 2016. Accessed on March 3, 2016 at: http://www.sifma.org/research/item.aspx?id=8589959017

Stafford, Philip (2016). "Dark pool operator Liquidnet Europe enjoys record trading year." FT Trading Room, *Financial Times*, January 18, 2016. Accessed on March 5, 2016 at: http://www.ft.com/cms/s/0/b38cb846-bb87-11e5-b151-8e15c9a029fb.html#axzz423qblREm

Sweet, Ken (2016). "Millennials hiring computers to invest their money." *The Denver Post*, March 6, 2014, 9K.

WSP Resources (2016). "List of investment banks." Wall Street Prep website. Accessed on March 3, 2016 at: https://www.wallstreetprep.com/knowledge/investment-banks-list/

QUESTIONS AND PROBLEMS

Minicase for questions 1 to 3: Securities firm analysis for a financial holding company with broker–dealer subsidiaries engaged in various financial services businesses (that include engagements in various financial service businesses, including underwriting; distributing; trading and brokers of equity; debt securities; sales of mutual funds; other investment products; institutional and retail investment management services; corporate and retail banking; and trust services). About 67% of revenues come from the firm's private client group, 18% from capital markets, 7% from asset management, and 8% from the firm's banking operations.

1. Using the data in Table P13.1 do a Dupont Analysis for the firm by calculating the following, and analyzing trends: (1) asset utilization (revenues/assets); (2) net profit margin; (3) equity multiplier; (4) ROA; and (5) ROE.

TABLE P13.1 | Summary key financial data this year and previous year

	This year ($ thousand)	Previous year ($ thousand)
Revenues	5,200,210	4,861,369
Net income	502,140	480,248
Total assets	26,479,684	23,325,652
Total long-term debt	1,495,613	1,712,894
Equity	4,522,031	4,141,236

2. Using the information in Table P13.2, explain why the NIM went up. The company predicts that a 100 basis point rise in short-term interest rates would increase the firm's pre-tax income by about $150 million. What type of funding gap does this suggest?

TABLE P13.2 | Net interest analysis

The firm has certain assets and liabilities held for its Personal Client Group and Bank segments, which are interest rate sensitive, so can have an impact on the firm's overall financial performance with changes in interest rates.

Average yield/cost	Current year	Previous year
Interest-earning assets		

355

*Investment Banks
and Securities
Firms and
Dark Pools and
High-Frequency
Trading*

Margin balances	3.74%	3.88%
Assets segregated	0.55%	0.55%
Bank loans	3.34%	3.39%
Available for sale securities	1.00%	1.01%
Trading instruments	2.71%	2.84%
Stock loan	2.78%	2.06%
Loans to financial advisers	1.54%	1.55%
Corporate cash and all other	0.43%	0.40%
Total average IR%	2.53%	2.39%
Interest-bearing liabilities		
Brokerage client liabilities	0.03%	0.03%
Bank deposits	0.08%	0.09%
Trading instruments sold but not yet purchased	1.53%	1.78%
Stock borrow	3.88%	2.51%
Borrowed funds	0.84%	0.81%
Senior notes	6.62%	6.62%
Loans payable of consolidated variable interest entities	5.66%	5.63%
Other	1.79%	1.50%
Total average IE%	0.62%	0.63%
Net interest income % (NIM)	1.91%	1.76%

3 The firm has the following consolidated income statement in Table P13.3 for the current and previous year (revenues shown first and then expenses):

TABLE P13.3 | Consolidated income statements

	Current year ($ thousand)	Previous year ($ thousand)
Revenues		
Securities commissions and fees	3,443,038	3,241,525
Investment banking	323,660	340,821
Investment advisory fees	385,238	362,362
Interest revenue	543,207	480,886
Account and service fees	457,913	407,707
Net trading profit	58,512	64,643

(Continued)

356

*Overview:
Nondepository
Financial
Institutions and
New Forms of
Financing*

TABLE P13.3 | (Continued)

	Current year ($ thousand)	Previous year ($ thousand)
Other	96,596	67,516
Total revenues	5,308,164	4,965,460
Interest expense	(107,954)	(104,091)
Net revenues	5,200,210	4,861,369
Noninterest expenses		
Compensation, commissions and benefits	3,525,378	3,312,635
Communications and information	266,396	252,694
Occupancy and equipment costs	163,229	161,683
Clearance and floor brokerage	42,748	39,875
Business development	158,966	139,672
Investment sub-advisory fees	59,569	52,412
Bank loan loss provision	23,570	13,565
Other	183,642	172,885
Total noninterest expenses	4,423,498	4,145,421
Income before taxes	776,712	715,948
Taxes	296,034	267,797
Net income (including noncontrolling (NC) interests)	480,678	448,151
Income attributable to NC interests	(21,462)	(32,097)
Net income attributable to firm	502,140	480,248

a   What were the firm's primary five sources of revenues? Explain why net revenues went up from the previous to the current year? Which revenue areas declined?

b   What are the four largest noninterest expenses for the firm? Which expenses went up and which went down comparing the current year to the previous year?

c   What are the strengths and weaknesses revealed from your analysis?

4   What types of risks do investment and securities firms face? Why are their returns on assets and returns on equity more volatile than traditional depository institutions?

5   What are some different types of securities firms? What are prestigious versus nonprestigious investment banks?

6   What are key different areas for securities firms? Give an example of a diversified securities firm. What are the advantages of investment banks becoming bank holding companies?

7   What are dark pools and why are regulators concerned about dark pools and high-speed trading? What regulatory actions have been taken against dark pool operations?

8   How are electronic trading platforms and algorithmic trading used to make trades? What advantages and disadvantages do they have? Why are regulators concerned about automated trading systems?

9   Discuss the Volcker Rule and its restrictions. Why was this rule passed?

10 Discuss the different risks that must be managed by securities firms. How did securities firms contribute to the U.S. subprime loan crisis? Why is liquidity risk management so important for securities firms?

Shadow Banking, Finance Companies and Diversified Financial Firms, Venture Capital, Crowdfunding, and MicroFinance

> For years now, big bank lenders have warned the public about the dangers of dealing with "shadow" (i.e. non-bank) lending institutions. ... However, with the astronomic recent rise of technology based, non-bank, lending alternatives such as peer-to-peer (P2P) lending, it's really the big banks that should be afraid ... very afraid.
>
> (Zeoli, 2015)

> There are close to 7,000 banks in the U.S. The biggest six have $10 trillion in assets, well over twice as much as the next 30 combined. Globally, the six biggest banks have increased their assets more than five-fold since 1997... Global regulators have been working ... to make it possible for even the biggest financial institutions to close their doors without triggering an economic meltdown. There's plenty of skepticism about whether they've succeeded.
>
> (Hopkins, 2015)

WITH the growth of technology, it became easier for larger and larger financial institutions to be managed under one umbrella. Also with deregulation, such as in the United States with the passage of the Gramm–Leach–Bliley Act of 1999 (allowing banks, insurance, investment and security firms to operate under the same umbrella), more than 640 bank holding companies elected to become financial holding companies (FHCs) in order to become diversified financial firms. Many financial services firms started out as finance companies, while others began with the merger of several finance, insurance, and investment companies over a decade. With cultural, regulatory, and other country differences, management complexity increases. Regulators have been concerned about the challenges of corporate control and risk management for diversified financial companies. Since a number of huge financial services firms were having severe liquidity problems and were on the brink of bankruptcy during the subprime crisis and the global financial crisis, these fears appeared to be justified.

Overview:
Nondepository
Financial
Institutions and
New Forms of
Financing

New regulations under the U.S. Dodd–Frank Act of 2010 and under Basel III have been established to reduce the risk of very large nonbank financial institutions, as well as extremely large financial services firms. Under Dodd–Frank, the Financial Stability Oversight Council (FSOC) was established and this is required to supervise and regulate nonbank systematically important financial institutions (SIFIs) that have systemic risk because of their size, interconnectedness, leverage, liquidity, risk and maturity mismatch, as well as lack of a substitute and lack of existing regulation. Evaluation criteria initially include: (1) consolidated assets greater than $50 billion; (2) credit default swaps (CDS) outstanding greater than $30 billion; (3) net derivative liabilities greater than $3.5 billion; (4) total debt outstanding greater than $20 billion; (5) a leverage ratio greater than 15 to 1; and (6) a short-term debt ratio greater than 10%. A company meeting these thresholds is subject to further tests to see if it is systematic. Even if a nonbank is not given a SIFIs designation, it may still be under greater scrutiny by other regulators as it gets larger, including scrutiny by the Consumer Financial Protection Bureau or state financial regulators, and all nonbanks are subject to the Truth in Lending Act (TILA) and other consumer protection acts. There has also been concern over nonbanks with large amounts of short-term wholesale funding, such as tri-party repos, with proposals to limit this type of liquidity risk (Goldman Sachs, 2015b).

While mega financial institutions are under greater regulatory scrutiny, new innovative disruptive types of financing that are not regulated have been growing rapidly, often referred to as "FinTech". Also, portions of the banking system are not regulated, often referred to as the "shadow banking system".

This chapter examines nonbank financial institutions and the shadow banking sector, with disruptive technology and the desire to circumvent more stringent regulations acting as impetus for alternative types of nonbank institutions. The chapter also provides an overview of FinTech and shadow banking, venture capital, microfinance, and crowd financing as alternative means of financing.

FINTECH AND SHADOW BANKING

The term "shadow banking" today encompasses any financial intermediaries that engage in bank-like activities but are not regulated and do not have access to deposit insurance or a central bank for liquidity. The term was coined in 2007 by Paul McCulley, an American economist and former managing director of PIMCO, to describe the structured investment vehicles (SIVs) used by banks to sell loans that were repackaged as bonds and mortgage-backed securities. Nonbank shadow banks include hedge funds, finance companies, asset-backed commercial paper (ABCP) conduits, structured investment vehicles (SIVs), credit hedge funds, money market mutual funds, securities lenders, limited purpose finance companies (LPFCs), government-sponsored enterprises (GSEs), and pawn shops, among many others (Pozsar, Adrian, Ashcraft, and Boesky, 2012).

This term has expanded to include what is often called FinTech firms. With new disruptive technology different players are included, from mobile payment systems to pawnshop to bond-trading platforms, peer-to-peer (P2P) lending websites, and other mortgage loans websites, such as Rocket Mortgages by Quicken Loans. Technology firms have rapidly entered the payments arena as well. As Wolf (2016) points out: "Finance is an information business.

*Shadow Banking,
Finance
Companies,
Diversified
Financial Firms,
Venture Capital,
Crowdfunding,
Microfinance*

Indeed it already spends a higher share of its revenues on information technology than any other. It seems ripe for disruption by information technologies."

Wolf (2016) points out problems with traditional inefficiencies, conflicts of interest, and ethical problems in the finance industry that new technology could help in three ways: (1) by allowing for instantaneous settlement for payments with improvement in the "robustness of record keeping" that could "revolutionize domestic and foreign payments;" (2) by a transformation via peer-to-peer (P2P) lending, a form of disintermediation by matching savers with investments including equity crowdfunding, invoice trading, P2P consumer and business lending, and others; and (3) by serving as a potential source of transformation via "big data." Wolf also points out that as well as opportunities, there are difficulties, including ensuring that benefits accrue to the public versus a small number of parties, which needs careful watching by policymakers. Opportunities for malfeasance could also occur, he notes and could be "inevitable with transactions that rest on promises against an inherently uncertain future."

With rapid growth in global market based financial systems, shadow banks (unregulated nonbanks that provide banking-like activities) have taken on a major role as nonregulated financial intermediaries that are involved in maturity, credit, and liquidity transformations. The size of the shadow banking sector was almost $20 trillion at its peak in 2007, and despite a shake-out during the U.S. subprime loan crisis, today shadow banks have about $15 trillion in assets (as large as the traditional banking system). The Financial Stability Board estimates that the shadow banking sector serviced assets worth $80 trillion globally in 2014 (*The Economist*, 2016: Noeth and Sengupta, 2016; Pozsar, et al., 2012).

As can be seen in the quotes at the beginning of this chapter, there are differing opinions on shadow banking. While regulators, politicians and economists are concerned about the large size and unregulated nature of shadow banks and lack of transparency, others point out that some nonbank lenders are more transparent than traditional banks. Zeoli (2015) observes the level of transparency for many peer-to-peer (P2P) lending platforms. Prosper Marketplace (one of the largest), provides 200 data points for investor consideration, including, among others, FICO scores, employment, income, and any change or updates in information. Advantages for both borrowers and investors with P2P lending and other FinTech platforms include: (1) greater availability of funds, since nonbanks do not have to be concerned with new regulations and capital requirements that have led to traditional banks shying away from lending; (2) better rates, since P2P lending and other FinTech platforms don't have regulatory hurdles and high overheads, allowing savings to be passed on to borrowers; (3) trust, with a loss of faith in traditional banking firms with the global financial crisis, as the result of lost personal relationships and more commoditization of loans, these platforms can engage and update in real-time borrower and investor information, enhancing transparency of deals and avoiding hidden fees (Zeoli, 2015).

A Goldman Sachs (2015a) research report "The future of finance: Part 1: The rise of the new shadow bank" points out that the P2P lending sector is the fastest growing of the nonbank lending industry, expected to capture about 8–10% of the traditional banking market over the next five years. The report observes that new companies in the lending sector, including Lending Club, Quicken Loans, Kabbage, and CommonBond, are taking advantage of twin forces: regulation and technology that opens the door for the expansion of shadow banking, with securitization also beginning for some P2P and other FinTech loans (Goldman Sachs, 2015a; Zeoli, 2015).

Overview:
Nondepository
Financial
Institutions and
New Forms of
Financing

The Goldman Sachs report (2015a) shows a shifting landscape in terms of numbers, including: (1) growth on the two largest peer-to-peer (P2P) lending platforms with Lending Club and Prosper growing more than 65 times from 2008 to 2014; (2) direct lending of over $30 billion by alternative asset managers compromising up to 12% of private equity credit fund assets under management (AUM); (3) alternative lenders approving 62% of small business loan requests in January 2015 versus just 21% by large banks; (4) nonbanks' share of mortgage originations jumping to a record 42% in 2014 from 10% in 2009; (5) banks stepping back from mortgage servicing; (6) total student loans outstanding since 2008 growing 70%, primarily through the government's Direct Loan Program; and (7) a total of $4 trillion in shadow bank loans across six prime lending segments (personal and small business, leveraged lending, commercial real estate, and mortgage and student loans) for a $12 trillion loan market (about 41% of the market for nonbanks).

The report notes emerging disrupters and players include Lending Club and Prosper for personal lending; OnDeck and Kabbage for small business lending; alternative asset managers, such as Wealthfront that focus on underserved HENRY (high earning, not rich yet) Millennials; as well as new and growing players for leveraged lending, including Quicken, Freedom Mortgage, PennyMac, Ocwan, and Nationstar for mortgage banking; Starwood Property, Colony Financial, and Blackstone for commercial real estate lending; and SoFi, CommonBond, and Earnest for student loans.

Henry (2016) points out that in 2014, the global investment in financial technology companies tripled to more than $12 billion and continued in the first three quarters of 2015 with $20.49 billion invested, including investments in payment processors, alternative lending firms, and automated robo-advisory investment services. Lending Club went public in 2014 for a valuation of $8 billion, while other companies, such as Wesabe and Bitinstant failed. Since alternative lending firms collect hundreds of points of data for underwriting clients, there are also security concerns, and new startups may need major investments in working capital that can reduce profitability for the long-term. TransferWise, a London P2P money wire platform has processed as much as $750 million a month in personal global transfers, indicating trust by online customers.

Henry (2016) highlights eight FinTech firms to watch, including: (1) Betterment, a New York City based startup providing automated investment services and personalized advice; (2) WePay, a San Francisco startup processing credit card payments online for platforms such as GoFundMe or CrowdRise; (3) Affirm, which offers installment loans to help users to finance e-commerce purchases; (4) CommonBond, an alternative lending firm based in New York City, which has refinanced over $100 million worth of student loans; (5) Kabbage, a small business lender that uses a number of complex data points to underwrite short-term business loans; (6) Orchard Platform, that connects investor clients to about 130 lenders in the marketplace and sells services to third-party lenders, such as Lending Club, Prosper, and Funding Circle; (7) Transfer Wire based in London that provides a cheaper, efficient platform for foreign exchange; and (8) Meniga based in Iceland that licenses money management software to banks (Henry, 2016).

Lohr (2016) points out a millennial-led shift towards new digital financial services, with preferences for doing financial services electronically on smartphones including money transfers from one person to another, and bill paying and loan refinancing online. Challenges, however, include FinTech firms lacking the legal and regulatory apparatus that traditional financial institutions have. He also points out that wealth management services often skew

361

*Shadow Banking,
Finance
Companies,
Diversified
Financial Firms,
Venture Capital,
Crowdfunding,
Microfinance*

towards older demographics while startups for online investments services such as SigFig, based in San Francisco, have an average age for users of 47. Some online payment services are more personalized such as Venmo, which allows small monetary gifts to be sent to friends and relatives with messages (Lohr, 2016).

However, regulatory scrutiny and competitive actions from traditional banks may increase as nonbanks get larger or move more into traditional bank lending areas. Regulators have increased some regulations on shadow banking. This includes in the United States requirements that banks include structured investment vehicles on their balance sheets.

The Federal Housing Finance Agency also recently proposed new rules whereby nonbanks would have to have minimum net worth of $2.5 million in addition to a 0.25% of the outstanding loan stock being serviced before loans could be sold to quasi-government mortgage security agencies, such as Fannie Mae and Freddie Mac.

OVERVIEW FINANCE COMPANIES AND DIVERSIFIED FINANCIAL SERVICES FIRMS

Many of the largest financial services firms began as nonbank finance or mortgage banking companies and eventually became diversified financial service companies. Finance companies since they engage in banking-like activities, but are less regulated, because they do not have deposits, are included among shadow banks. Finance companies make loans, but unlike banks they finance lending activities by issuing commercial paper or bonds or borrowing from other financial institutions including banks. Finance companies also frequently do what is called subprime lending, granting loans to more risky customers who would not qualify for bank loans. Finance companies generally charge higher rates than banks given a higher risk profile for customers.

TYPES OF FINANCE COMPANIES

There are several types of finance companies, including consumer and captive (sales) finance companies that specialize in making consumer loans for automobiles and consumer retail goods, often as a captive or sales company subsidiary of large manufacturing or retail firms to provide financing for these products. Finance companies in the United States are subject to state and federal laws governing the provision of credit, including usury statutes and truth-in-lending regulations. Captive sales companies remain popular for floor financing of retail dealers for their inventory from manufacturing firms, as well as for consumer financing. Well-known captive financing firms include Toyota Motor Credit and Ford Credit Corporation. Some top finance companies include subsidiaries of large financial services firms. Finance companies make both unsecured and secured personal loans, with secured lending including residential mortgages, second mortgages, home equity loans, and second mortgage loans.

Industrial loan companies (ILCs) (sometimes called industrial banks) are an unusual type of finance company that nonfinancial (commercial) companies took advantage of as a loophole prior to be able to engage in banking activities not allowed under the Glass–Steagall Act. Walmart, for example, in the early 2000s acquired a number of ILCs. ILCs were initially

Overview:
Nondepository
Financial
Institutions and
New Forms of
Financing

chartered in some states to provide credit for blue collar workers by being allowed to engage in making nondepository credit and to offer certificates of deposit (called certificates of investment) accounts and provide consumer cash loans secured by personal property, agricultural lending, and short-term inventory credit. Over time, most states changed their regulations to disallow ILCs. Congress, in response to regulatory concerns about commercial firm purchases of ILCs, as well as the potential for money laundering and other criminal behavior by unregulated ILCs, passed legislation as part of the Financial Services Regulatory Relief Act of 2004 to limit the freedom of ILCs.

Commercial finance companies make loans to businesses to provide equipment leasing, asset-based loans and factoring (purchasing accounts receivables from businesses at a discount). In the past, commercial banks shunned asset-based lending (business loans collateralized by the borrowing firm's inventory or receivables). In the United States after 1954, states' widespread adoption of the Uniform Commercial Credit Code clarified the rights of asset-based lenders and provided strong impetus for the growth of commercial finance companies, which today offer both short-term and long-term asset-based loans and leasing. Commercial finance companies are often captive companies of large manufacturing companies, providing financing and leasing services for customers' purchases of machinery and equipment, such as John Deere Capital Corporation, Caterpillar Financial Services, and McDonnell Douglas Finance Company. Commercial finance companies also often sell participation in an asset-based loan to banks in exchange for cash. Proceeds from the loan are then divided between the finance company and the banks according to their relative shares in the participation. Although some loan participations are actually arranged by banks and then sold to finance companies, most require the finance company to remain active in tracking the performance of the assets pledged as collateral. Commercial finance companies are also often subsidiaries of large financial services firms or "specialty" finance companies that specialize in particular types of lending, such as inventory lending, factoring, leasing of aircraft or financing or leasing particular types of equipment. Diversified finance companies make both consumer and business loans and are often subsidiaries of financial holding companies or insurance companies.

Finance companies have less interest rate and liquidity risk than depository institutions, since their loan maturities on average are short with securitizations to match with liabilities that can be short-term using commercial paper and bank loans or long-term to match longer-term loans by issuing bonds. Since finance companies do not have deposits as liabilities, they have less liquidity risk, although they do have liability management risks for short-term financing.

TYPICAL FINANCIAL STATEMENT FORMAT FOR FINANCE COMPANIES

Large finance companies tend to be diversified finance companies with numerous financial services activities included in their financial statements, ranging from insurance activities, brokerage, and other securities and banking activities for subsidiaries, as well as finance company activities. Finance companies or finance company subsidiaries typically have the balance sheet and income statement formats and special ratios shown in Table 14.1. Usually, loans are listed as receivables under assets on the typical balance sheet for a finance company

363

*Shadow Banking,
Finance
Companies,
Diversified
Financial Firms,
Venture Capital,
Crowdfunding,
Microfinance*

with consumer, business, and real estate receivables. Like banks, finance companies have reserves for loan losses, and also reserves for unearned income. Unlike banks, short-term liabilities include bank loans and commercial paper. Long-term debt includes parent company financing, debentures, and other debt. Finance companies are a major issuer of commercial paper for short-term loans. Because they do not have insured deposits, total equity to total asset ratios are usually higher than banks.

Typically, finance company gross income includes interest and fee income on receivables (loans) and securitizations as well as revenue from credit insurance payments and fees on other services. Operating expenses often range from 40–50% of expenses. Usually, finance companies have a higher rate on loans and a higher interest expense than traditional depository institutions, given higher risk for loans and typically higher bankruptcies and lower returns during recessions and higher profitability during economic expansion periods.

Like other consumer lenders finance companies are affected by state usury laws, which restrict rates that lenders can charge on specific types of loans. Personal bankruptcy laws also have a significant effect on the profitability of consumer finance companies in terms of their ability to collect on loans that default.

TABLE 14.1 | Typical balance sheet items for finance companies

Assets	Liabilities
Receivables (loans)	Bank loans
Consumer	Commercial paper
Business	**Long-term debt**
Real estate	Owed to parent
Less reserves for unearned income	Debentures
Less reserves for losses	Other debt
Net receivables	Total liabilities
Other assets	**Equity**
Total assets	Common stock
	Retained earnings
	Total liabilities and equity
Typical income statement	**Special liquidity ratios**
Interest revenue	Maturing receivables in 1 year / Total receivables
Interest expenses	Unused credit lines / Open market debt
Interest spread	Cash / Short-term debt
Other revenues	**Special efficiency / Productivity ratios**
Other expenses	Operating expenses / Average net receivables
Income before taxes	Average monthly principal collections /
Taxes	Average net monthly receivables
Net income	Annual gross finance revenues /
	Average net receivables

Overview:
Nondepository
Financial
Institutions and
New Forms of
Financing

CREDIT CARD COMPANIES

Credit card companies are finance companies that issue credit cards to consumers and businesses. They make significant fee income from selling and securitizing credit card loans and continue to earn fee income by servicing these loans. Examples of credit card companies include American Express Credit Corporation and Discover Bank, as well as credit card companies that are subsidiaries of financial services firms, such as Capital One. Many of these companies operate internationally and are very profitable, issuing specialty credit cards, purchasing consumer loans from financial institutions, and packaging and securitizing loans. In addition to major credit card companies, many consumer finance companies entered the credit card business to supplement personal cash loans, with most joining the national Visa and MasterCard networks.

GOVERNMENT-SPONSORED ENTERPRISES

Often categorized among the largest finance companies, government-sponsored enterprises (GSEs) and other large mortgage banks originate loans and sell or securitize these loans, receiving a profit. They also often receive fee income for servicing contracts for these loans. In addition to purchasing and securitizing primary loans, secondary mortgages are also purchased. More risky loans can be brought to the market by obtaining sufficient credit enhancement from other institutions involved in the securitization process, giving the securities a higher credit rating.

As noted by Pozsar, et al. (2012) the beginning of the shadow banking system occurred in the United States with the creation of government-sponsored enterprises (GSEs), including the Federal Home Loan Bank (FHLB) system in 1932 and the Federal National Mortgage Corporation (FNMC, known as Fannie Mae) under the National Housing Act as part of Roosevelt's New Deal (originally chartered as the National Mortgage Association) in 1938. While FHLBs provided warehousing for loans, Fannie Mae and Freddie Mac were initiators of the "originate-to-distribute" model for securitized credit intermediation. Freddie Mac, for instance, was chartered by Congress in 1970 and given the mission of stabilizing the residential mortgage markets and expanding homeownership opportunities and affordable rental housing by providing liquidity and affordability to the U.S. housing markets. In 1954, Fannie Mae became a "mixed ownership corporation" with the federal government holding the preferred stock interest, and investors the common stock interests, and in 1966 became a privately held corporation and the previous Fannie Mae was divided into Fannie Mae and the Government National Mortgage Association (GNMA; Ginnie Mae) which became a government organization that is not part of the shadow banking system, since it is backed by the U.S. government. Ginnie Mae supports FHA-insured, VA (Veterans Affairs (VA), and Farmers Home Administration (FmHA) mortgages.

In 1970 Fannie Mae went public and was authorized to purchase conventional mortgages, and in 1981 issued the first mortgage-backed security, followed by Freddie Mac issuing the first mortgage pass-through (participation certificate) with primarily private mortgages included. In 1989, Freddie Mac went public, with its stock converted, so that it could be owned and traded by investors, as voting common stock (Freddie Mac, 2016b).

*Shadow Banking,
Finance
Companies,
Diversified
Financial Firms,
Venture Capital,
Crowdfunding,
Microfinance*

GSEs are funded through capital markets by issuing short- and long-term agency debt securities purchased by money market and mutual funds and other investors. GSEs purchase mortgage loans and mortgage-related securities for investment. Ginnie Mae, the Government National Mortgage Association (GNMA), is a government agency versus a GSE that supports affordable housing for millions of low- and moderate-income households in the United States by guaranteeing loans allowing mortgage lenders to offer lower pricing for GNMA guaranteed mortgage loans. Lenders can then sell the guaranteed mortgage loans in the secondary mortgage market, providing lenders with funds to make new loans. Ginnie Mae does not buy or sell loans or issue mortgage-backed securities (MBS), but does provide a "full faith and credit guaranty of the U.S. government, guaranteeing that investors will receive timely payment of principal and interest on MBS that are backed by federally insured or guaranteed loans. These are primarily loans that are insured by the Federal Housing Administration (FHA) or guaranteed by the Department of Veterans Affairs (VA), as well as other guarantors or issuers of loans with eligible collateral for GNMA MBS, such as the Department of Agriculture's Rural Development and the Department of Housing and Urban Development's Office of Public and Indian Housing (Ginnie Mae, 2016).

Likewise, Fannie Mae provides a critical role in the U.S. housing finance system by acting in a similar way in the secondary mortgage market to provide large-scale access to affordable mortgage credit, so individuals can buy, refinance, or rent homes. As of the fourth quarter of 2015, Fannie Mae was one of the largest single issuers of single-family mortgage-related securities in the secondary market and a source of liquidity in the multi-family market in the United States. For all of 2015, about $516 billion in liquidity was provided to the market, assisting individuals and families to buy, refinance or rent 2.7 million homes. Fannie Mae also assisted families in distress to keep their homes and avoid foreclosure through about 122,000 loan workouts in 2015 that included about 94,000 loan modifications.

Because of their near collapse during the subprime loan crisis with the collapse of the mortgage market together with high leverage and concentration exposure to U.S. residential mortgages, both Fannie Mae and Freddie Mac were rescued and taken over by the U.S. government and operated under a conservatorship that began in September 6, 2008. Congress under the Housing and Economic Recovery Act of July 2008, gave the United States unlimited investment authority for the two firms, with the Federal Housing Finance Agency (FHA) placing the two into conservatorship, which prevented additional contagion, and allowed conservation of the two firms' values, with taxpayers injecting $187.5 billion overall (Frame, Fuster, Tracy, and Vickery, 2015). The bailout for Fannie Mae was about $116 billion of funds from the Treasury department. In May of 2012, the executives of Fannie Mae announced that after three and a half years in conservatorship, the firm was profitable, with profits larger than the bailout amount, and in August of 2012, the Treasury department announced that Fannie Mae's profits would be taken for a general purpose fund to help finance government operations and reduce debt to better protect taxpayers. This led to investor lawsuits for stockholders of Fannie Mae, in terms of changes to the terms of the bailout, with Fannie and Freddie sending the Treasury more than $50 billion over the amount they drew down in the bailout. New capital requirements were also required for Fannie and Freddie Mae to build up their capital to absorb greater losses. These GSEs guarantee about 80% of mortgages nationwide in the United States (Morgenson, 2015, 2016).

Overview:
Nondepository
Financial
Institutions and
New Forms of
Financing

PRIVATE AND PUBLICLY TRADED MORTGAGE BANKS

Unlike banks, mortgage banks originate loans with the intent to sell or securitize them right away, removing them from their balance sheets, reducing liquidity concerns, and funding gap problems. However, mortgage banks still face the risk of interest rates changing between the time they purchase and sell mortgage loans, which can result in having to sell loans at a loss. Their profits are also subject to real estate market cycles.

Although many private and publicly traded mortgage companies are well managed, as subsidiaries of bank holding companies and financial holding companies, just as with other lenders, some finance companies have in the past been involved with predatory lending, that is, targeting disadvantaged borrowers and charging high rates. While subprime lending is not necessarily a bad thing, if borrowers are charged higher rates than they could find elsewhere or given loans that they cannot afford, and are not educated in the loan risks, such as for adjustable rate loans, where loan rates can rise above a borrower's ability to make payments, they are being treated unethically. Some states passed anti-predatory lending laws to discourage subprime and predatory lending.

An example of a mortgage company that was not well managed is the case of Countrywide Financial, co-founded by two New Yorkers in 1968 and which by 1992 had become the largest mortgage loan originator in the country for single-family mortgages, with almost $40 billion in mortgages issues in a single year. As described in *All the Devils Are Here: The Hidden History of the Financial Crisis* by Bethany McLean and Joe Nocera, in an attempt to grow, Countrywide engaged in poor underwriting and risky subprime lending and refinancings, and eventually failed and was merged with Bank of America under a Fed arranged merger, with Bank of America later suffering large loan losses from its acquisition. The former CEO of Countrywide, Angelo Mozilo, was put on trial by the SEC after being accused of failing to tell investors about Countrywide's risky mortgage exposure and agreed to pay a $67.5 million penalty and reparations to investors, and accepted a ban permanently prohibiting him from serving as an officer or director for a public company (McLean and Nocera, 2011; Olsters, 2010). Later, Bank of America's Countrywide mortgage unit appealed the ruling on fraud for one of Countrywide's former executives in not disclosing to Fannie Mae and Freddie Mac that the subprime loans it was selling were not up to contractual requirements. The federal appeals court ruled that this was not technically fraud, upholding this decision on August 22, 2016 (Henning, 2016).

PRIVATE EQUITY, HEDGE FUNDS

Nonventure private equity firms, often *hedge funds*, are firms that invest in private firms with the goal of "buy and build" strategies, turning companies around and increasing their value. Many nonventure private equity firms started out as leveraged buyout firms that provided debt and equity investments to help firms go private through leveraged buyouts (LBOs) or manager buyouts (MBOs). While private nonventure equity firms engaged in highly leveraged corporate breakups in later years, they relied more on equity to make deals. Private equity firms have also been active in global expansion. Strategies by private equity firms to maximize the value of firms that they acquire include strengthening management, adding complementary

Shadow Banking,
Finance
Companies,
Diversified
Financial Firms,
Venture Capital,
Crowdfunding,
Microfinance

companies, or rolling up companies and fragmented sectors. Different private equity capital firms have different strategies and expertise in the type of firms they acquire for classic buy and build deals. Prominent private equity firms include Kohlberg, Kravis Roberts & Co., Warburg Pincus, Apax Partners, Forstmann Little & Co., and Hicks, Muse, Tate & Furst, Inc., among others. Often private equity firms specialize in different industries or regions or private investments in public equity.

VENTURE CAPITAL

Venture capital (VC) firms are organized as limited partnerships with managing partners and limited (passive) investors, with the majority of investors being institutional investors, including insurance companies and pension funds, corporations, endowments, foreign investors, and wealthy individuals, often known as "angel" investors. Venture capital firms are investment firms that provide: (1) seed capital to firms just starting; (2) startup capital to firms beginning to operate or manufacture a product; and (3) later stage capital and temporary (bridge) financing. Many investment banks have VC firms as subsidiaries. The goal of VC firms is to make a large return on a portfolio of companies, averaging about 50% a year, for investors who are willing to take the risk of investing in relatively new companies. Returns are higher depending on the risk and stage of the firm's growth. For instance, for firms just getting started (seed financing), sometimes an 80% return is required, 60% is required for a startup actually beginning operations or manufacturing, 50% for a third stage firm, and 25% for bridge financing. To make an average return VCs invest in a portfolio of firms with high expected growth, with the VC generally taking an equity interest. Some firms will fail, but a few star winners can compensate for this. In order to make a return, they must "harvest" their investments by having an initial public offering (IPO) for the firm, where VC investors can sell their shares, or sell the firm to another company for profit in a relatively short time frame of 5 to 7 years. Normally, VC firms consider investments in excess of $2 million. Firms must give up a portion of control of the business, whereby the VC provides expertise and financial backing. Venture capital firms prefer firms in such high-growth areas as biotech, software, media communications, and information technology.

Different types of venture capital firms include: (1) private VC firms, which are often subsidiaries of investment firms or other corporations, or limited partners, angels, or other wealthy individuals; (2) venture capital networks (VCNs), which provide anonymous matching; (3) small business investment corporations (SBICs), which are funded by $4 of low-cost government debt for every $1 of stockholder equity and which provide capital often in the form of convertible debenture debt for small businesses capable of an annual cash flow that will allow SBICs to cover their commitments; and (4) minority enterprise small business investment companies (MESBICs), which provide debt and equity to small businesses that are at least 51% owned by socially or economically disadvantaged persons. Like SBICs, MESBICs receive low-cost government debt financing.

Capital deals are designed by VC firms with commitment letters, investment agreements, loan covenants, rewards for performance, and penalties for failures. If goals are met, entrepreneurs reap financial rewards when the company goes public, is sold, or is refinanced. Through VC subsidiaries, investment banks can take promising firms public with initial public

Overview:
Nondepository
Financial
Institutions and
New Forms of
Financing

offerings (IPOs). VCs prefer to harvest companies within five years. VC portfolio returns can be volatile, with higher returns in bull markets, and in recent years averaging about 20%.

There have also been disruptions for capital raising for new ventures, such as WR Hambrecht + Co's OpenIPO auction that provides a level playing field for initial public offerings by allowing individuals and investors to be able to bid online for shares of an IPO, with all investors paying the same price and leveraging the internet to allow efficient marketing and allocation for IPOs. Other auction systems include the A+ IPO based on a SEC proposed Regulation Tier 2 change that would allow growth companies a more streamlined access to public capital, allowing an A+ IPO marketplace (WR Hambrecht + Co., 2016).

The Jumpstart Our Business Startups (JOBS) Act directed the SEC to adopt rules allowing the offering of up to $50 million of securities within a 12-month period, which would require audited statements to be filed with the SEC. Under Regulation A+, two tiers of offering would be allowed, with Tier 1 for offerings of securities up to $20 million in a 12-month period, with not more than $6 million in offers by security-holders that are affiliates of an issuer, and Tier 2 for offerings of securities up to $50 million, with not more than $15 million in offers by selling to security-holders that are affiliates of an issuer, along with basic requirements for additional disclosure and reporting requirements (SEC, 2015).

OVERVIEW OF CROWDFUNDING

Goldman Sachs (2015b) in "The future of finance: Part 3: The socialization of finance," points out that the enablers of the socialization of finance, changing the impact of technology and behavior for financial services markets, includes social networks, such as social payments platforms like Venno and social investing communities like OpenFolio,; alumni lending groups on platforms like SoFI, a technology-enabled lender that provides tools to better measure and manage default risk; millennials as agents of change in shifting behavior-reducing frictions in payments, investing, and lending processes, technology, and data; and the emergence of marketplaces and the sharing economy (these include "disruptive" sectors that benefit from the socialization of finance, including crowdfunding, wealth management automated advisers, such as Wealthfront and Betterment, peer-to-peer lending platforms, and socialized payments).

Crowdfunding is the funding of a project or venture by raising small amounts of funds from a large number of people via the internet, commonly used by musicians, filmmakers, and artists who not only raise funds, but also raise awareness of their product/production through crowdfunding. Some crowdfunding platforms were originally focused on artistic endeavors, such as Kickstarter.com. Goldman Sachs (2015b) notes that $1.6 billion was pledged on Kickstarter as of March 2015, with the largest single campaign (Pebble Time) having raised over $18 million. In addition to raising funds and reaching a huge audience through platforms such as Kickstarter and Indiegogo to enable innovators and their products and artists, Goldman Sachs notes that investment platforms, such as AngelList initiated new methods to match companies with accredited angel or venture investors to allow them to source and fund startups. The Goldman Sachs report also notes that enablers of growth for this alternative funding include innovations in crowdfunding, changing demographics and consumer behavior, the potential for viral growth, strong network effects, and regulatory changes (Goldman Sachs, 2015b).

Entrepreneurs raising funds on crowdfunding platforms in the past prior to January 2016 generally were not allowed to raise equity capital from small investors, so instead rewarded backers with gifts, such as T-shirts, coffee mugs, a cameo role in a film, among others. Entrepreneurs with innovative ideas or products also provided a sample of their product. Different models for crowdfunding include: (1) a pre-order model where potential customers pre-order a product or service, such as, for a musician, a CD for a planned album or an invitation to an event; (2) a donation model where small funds are requested as donations from individuals interested in an entrepreneur's products or services; (3) a reward-based model where providers of funds receive a reward. Although this reward could not be shares in a company for small unaccredited investors, recently in the United States the SEC adopted rules allowing small equity investments with crowdfunding.

The new U.S. SEC rules, adopted on October 30, 2016 to take effect in May of 2016, allow small investors to purchase shares of private companies on designated crowdfunding platforms under the JOBS Act. Under the new rules companies can raise up to $1 million for a 12-month period through a crowdfunding campaign, but firms must provide potential investors with financial statements. This rule has exceptions for some first-time issues, and for those that seek less than $500,000, with companies raising between $500,000 and $1 million for the first time allowed to submit "reviewed" financial documents rather than formal and more expensive audited statements. Entrepreneurs that raise less than $500,000 are also allowed to provide specific information from their tax returns that are reviewed by an independent tax accountant. Previously, only accredited investors with annual income greater than $200,000 or net worth of at least $1 million were allowed to invest. Some portals that were set up for accredited investors are planning expansion into the unaccredited market, such as SeedInvest, which has been assisting funding deals from accredited investors (Clifford, 2015; Cowley, 2015).

Companies can advertise their offerings in different ways, such as posting them on a crowdfunding platform, if allowed by that platform. How much an unaccredited investor can invest depends on their income and net worth. Investors with an annual income or net worth less than $100,000 can only provide up to $2,000 a year or 5% of the lesser of their income or net worth. Investors with a net worth greater than $100,000 are allowed to invest up to 10% of the lessor of their income or net worth. Whether an individual is wealthy or not, the maximum investment that can be put into startups through online equity crowdfunding in any given year is $100,000. Shares are not liquid, however, with no marketplace for shares and must be held for at least one year, and not all crowdfunding platforms wish to be part of raising funds for equity (Clifford, 2015; Cowley, 2015).

Popular crowdfunding websites include Kickstarter, Indiegogo, RocketHub, FundRazr, GoGetFunding, Crowdfunder, and Start Some Good, all with different focuses and requirements, some with an all or nothing focus, where all funds are lost unless a financing goal is met. Transaction fees vary as a percentage of total funding. Some platforms are a mixture of donation-based and investment crowdfunding models, which encourage both online and off-line crowdfunding, and many focus on social entrepreneurs and nonprofits. There are also respective debt and equity crowdfunding (peer-to-peer platforms), which have focused on the facilitating of friends and family loans, and accredited investor loans and bank loans for business borrowers looking for funding, with different platforms having different restrictions and focusing on different types of entrepreneurial ventures. Hence, fund-raising is made easier for startups, reducing dependence on financial intermediaries.

Overview:
Nondepository
Financial
Institutions and
New Forms of
Financing

Concerns for crowdfunding and the new SEC rules include how to expand capital markets that have been underutilized, but at the same time to protect investors who are unsophisticated from losing their savings to startup ventures that may be risky or unrealistic and to avoid fraud and scams. There are also concerns that rules have complex provisions and requirements for compliance that may create problems for unwary small business entrepreneurs and may deter them from using crowdfunding as a viable source for raising funds. The rules include a SEC inter-divisional staff working group to monitor fraud for the new category of securities and for the SEC to file a comprehensive report on the functioning of the new marketplace three years after the rules' implementation on the rules' effectiveness. Funding portals also must register with the SEC, as from January 29, 2016 (Clifford, 2015).

Crowdfunding is also used for the greater good, such as a recent Kickstarter campaign with the UN Refugee Agency that raised over $200,000 for refugees fleeing conflict in the Middle East, and crowdfunding campaigns are used increasingly for humanitarian aid and development purposes as well. Other crowdfunding platforms have also harnessed the power of private individuals, using "crowdfunding for the global good," such as Indiegogo Life, Catapult, Kiva, and GlobalGiving, allowing connection to popular causes regardless of distance, and with some campaigns helping specific individuals, such as particular refugees needing help for their families, while others support particular microfinance type projects to help connecting artisans in poor countries to designers and markets for products, for example. Other platform's such as Google's One Today app allows users to donate a dollar a day to organizations and causes highlighted by Google, such as Nepal's earthquake fund and a single campaign to help refugees and migrants crossing the Mediterranean, which raised over $10 million. By partnering with development organizations and charities, Google's One Today has provided confidence for donors that their money will be utilized by these causes (Fredieu, 2015).

MICROFINANCE

Global envision (Mercy Corps' blog) in an article on the history of microfinance points out that microfinance has a long history, with savings and credit groups providing funds for others in their community globally for centuries and the development over the years of formal credit and savings institutions, which became more formal in the 1800s as people's banks, credit unions, and savings and credit cooperatives. In the 1950s and 1970s governments and donors provided agricultural credit to small and marginal farmers to increase productivities and incomes. Later in the 1970s, microenterprise credit began as experimental programs in Bangladesh, Brazil, and several other countries to provide loans to groups of women in poverty to invest in microbusinesses. These were typically organized as solidarity groups where each group member provided guarantees for the repayment of all members. Well-known microfinance organizations include:

1   *ACCION International*, providing a network of lending partners in Latin America, the United States, and Africa and helping to found Banco Sol in 1992, the first commercial bank that is solely dedicated to microfinance, delivering financial services to more than 70,000; along with 15 ACCION-affiliated organizations that became regulated financial institutions;

2   *SEWA Bank* (Self Employed Women's Association), which began as a registered trade union in Gujarat, India and which in 1973, addressing the lack of access to financial services, founded the Mahila SEWA Co-operative Bank;

3   *Grameen Bank* founded in 1983 by Professor Muhammad Yunus in Bangladesh, which stimulated the development for several other large microfinance institutions including BRAC, ASA, and Proshika, among others.

4   *Bank Rakyat Indonesia (BRI)*, a village banking unit system, the largest microfinance institution in developing countries servicing 22 million microsavers with self-run managed microbanks, among many others.

(Global Envision, 2006)

Large financial institutions also engage in microfinance. Deutsche Bank, for instance, has established very innovative microfinance instruments and processes, being the first operating private bank to launch a microcredit fund in 1997, in 2005 a microfinance fund for institutional investors, including advisement on microfinance risks, and in 2008 establishing the Tsunami Loan program for regions affected by the pacific tsunami to receive favorable credit conditions.

In 2008 Deutsche Bank also organized a meeting of leading microfinance organizations to draft a formal code of ethics for the microfinancing sector, and in 2010 launched with FINCA, the FINCA Microfinance Fund as one of the largest microloan networks. In 2012, Deutsche Bank established the Global Commercial Microfinance Consortium II to focus on customer protect, product innovation, and service, and in 2013 the bank secured $75 million from institutional investors for the Microfinance Enhancement Facility (MEF) to provide funding worldwide to microfinance institutions (Deutsche Bank, 2014). Investment firms have also provided funds for microfinance, including ResponsAbility Investments AG, a global leading independent asset manager that specializes in the development of related sectors of emerging economies, and is one of the world's largest microfinance investors, with investments and reinvestments (responsAbility, 2014).

As noted in its annual outlook report for microfinance responsAbility (2014, p. 4) points out that the purpose of microfinance is to facilitate lending to micro and small entrepreneurs, building financial sectors closely interconnected with local economies. This includes the enablement of establishing payment systems and new savings opportunities for households. In this way capital is put in place for production use, contributing to the growth of other sectors of an economy as well, such as small-scale industries for construction and trade. From this perspective, companies providing a full range of financial services are important, with providers active in microfinance designated as microfinance institutions (MFIs), which today includes thousands of providers in different stages of operational development and of different legal status. In turn the report notes that for investors, it is also important that MFIs operate profitably and effectively, with professional structures and processes in accounting and risk management. In 2015, about 500 institutions operated in microfinance worldwide in about 80 countries. ResponsAbility's report on these divides these into two groups: Tier 1 MFIs, including at least 100 firms that have a large and well-diversified client base and an experienced management team in place that have generally realized their potential; and Tier 2 MFIs, with at least 400 firms that are smaller and younger with viable business models that have been implemented to a degree and who would like to be regulated to become recognized officially as financial

Overview:
Nondepository
Financial
Institutions and
New Forms of
Financing

institutions within their countries (responsAbility, 2014). ResponsAbility (2016) in its outlook for microfinance for 2016 notes the global microfinance market is expected to grow by 10–15%, with a solid financial footing keeping this sector resilient, with technology allowing MIFs to access microentrepreneurs in areas that are difficult to reach, and better risk assessment tools, and technology, providing a great opportunity globally for microfinance institutions (ResponsAbility, 2016).

A trend for microfinance institutions is to move from a nonprofit status to a profit status, with some Microfinance firms going public, such as SKS, India's largest microfinance institution. SKS filed a draft prospectus in 2010 for an initial public offering and to sell shares on the India stock exchange for financing, to allow larger scale microfinancing for the poor in India. This evolution occurred as microfinance grew in scale from just reaching tens of thousands to over 150 million of the world's poor, as nonprofits evolved into sustainable microfinance banks with access to capital markets. Large top tier financial institutions entering microfinance allows countries, such as Bolivia, as a "pioneer in building microfinance services," to serve low-income families utilizing top-tier financial institutions competing to serve such families, allowing low microfinance interest rates in this region. Similarly in Peru, rates have declined and product markets have increased, with 44 of 55 regulated banks and lending institutions in Peru contributing to microfinance competition (Schlein and Chu 2010).

MEGA FINANCIAL SERVICES FIRMS AND FINANCIAL CONGLOMERATES

Universal banks where banks and investment banks and insurance companies operate together are prevalent in many countries. In the United States under the Glass–Steagall Act of 1933 passed during the Great Depression, banks and investment banks and insurance companies were not allowed to operate together in the same financial institution. At that time, there was fear that bank funds would be used for speculative purposes for securities and investment banking activities. In 1999, the Gramm–Leach–Bliley Act (GLB) was passed that overturned Glass–Steagall, allowing financial holding companies and bank holding companies to have bank, investment banking, and insurance company subsidiaries under arguments for greater efficiency and competitiveness with other universal banks internationally. As the result of many mergers and acquisition, many large financial and bank holding companies grew to become major firms internationally in both commercial lending and investment banking and securities activities. As Irwin (2015) points out mega bank holding companies today include Citigroup, JPMorgan Chase, and Bank of America and these now have combined assets of about $6.5 trillion or 36% of U.S. gross domestic product (Irwin, 2015).

Although mega banks have been blamed for the global financial crisis, as Irwin (2015) notes, the financial institutions that were involved in the crisis were more traditional investment banks, such as Bear Stearns, Lehman Brothers, and Merrill Lynch, and large mortgage banks that had converted to savings and loan charters, including Washington Mutual and Countrywide that made subprime and other risky mortgage loans, and a large commercial bank, Wachovia, that collapsed as the result of its acquisition of Golden West, a large savings and loan institution that was a major mortgage lender. He points out that two mega banks that

*Shadow Banking,
Finance
Companies,
Diversified
Financial Firms,
Venture Capital,
Crowdfunding,
Microfinance*

had commercial and investment banking divisions received bailouts, but others, JPMorgan Chase and Wells Fargo, accepted bailouts at the urging of the Treasury and Federal Reserve in 2008, but did not really need them, and got through the crisis fairly well (Irwin, 2015).

However, with the huge size of mega banks, there is the fear that their large size in the event of a failure could have a huge effect globally with interconnections with other financial institutions around the world. Hence, there is an argument that, with mega banks having huge deposits invested in global markets, the government will have to step in and bail out mega banks if anything goes wrong. Thus, there is an argument that Glass–Steagall should be reinstated and big banks broken up, involving banks in having to divest their investment banks. However, if Glass–Stegall was enacted, banks would be less diversified, which could impact the wealth management business of banks for high-net-worth clients, retirement services for consumers, and convenience benefits for those who would like to do their financial activities in one place (Bell, 2012).

REASONS FOR THE DEVELOPMENT OF FINANCIAL CONGLOMERATES

The reasons for the emergence of both nonfinancial and financial conglomerates have often been debated throughout the 1990s and 2000s. Reasons include:

1   Firms can smooth their earnings by receiving interest and noninterest income from a variety of sources.
2   Smoother earnings allow firms to have greater debt capacity and a lower overall cost of funds.
3   Firms can achieve operating synergies, including economies of scale and score and more productive resource utilization.
4   Firms in maturing industries, such as the insurance or banking industries, can diversify for long-term survival and greater profitability and growth.
5   Managers can reduce unemployment risk by smoothing earnings or achieving greater ego satisfaction or compensation, if management compensation is related to growth (hubris hypothesis).
6   Through economies of scale and scope and management competencies, firms can improve the efficiency of inefficient firms that they acquire in a related industry.

From a more practical perspective, other considerations for the growth of mega financial services firms include ease of entry, with the cost of entering different aspects of the financial services industry low, since a major investment may not be needed for a firm in the information or retailing business. For instance, telecommunications and high-tech firms, such as Apple, Microsoft, and Samsung, have found it easy to set up joint ventures with banks to offer bill paying, mortgage shopping services, and payment apps, such as Apple Pay, Google Wallet with Android Pay, Samsung Pay, and many others, for ease of payments for consumers. Similarly, large financial services firms in one area can find it easy to expand into other related areas, such as large mutual fund companies offering credit cards, brokerage, and other banking and security-related services.

Overview:
Nondepository
Financial
Institutions and
New Forms of
Financing

With substitutability of products, with many financial products having commodity-like characteristics, all firms also have an equal opportunity to succeed. Other reasons for expansion into new areas include a decline in traditional profits and regulations for traditional businesses, such as lower spreads for traditional banking net interest margins, making noninterest revenue for other nontraditional types of financial services more attractive. Insurance firms, in the last two decades faced slower profit growth in a maturing industry and diversified into areas with more rapid growth, including health insurance, mutual funds, and annuity products.

In addition, high-technology costs and customers demanding new high-tech services increased technological costs for financial institutions. These increased costs needed to be spread over a larger volume of customers to gain economies of scale and score, with spreading the cost of technology across more customers and diverse products reducing the cost of technology per unit. Also, with the information age, there is greater ease in managing mega institutions globally than there was in the past, with technology allowing greater connections internally and internationally for large financial services firms. Technology also results in improvements in efficiency and the ability to enter new markets and geographic regions. A final motivation for diversified financial services firms is a belief that earnings of a diversified firm will exceed two or more firms operating separately and/or reduce the volatility of the earnings of the two individual firms.

Studies examining the success and failure of different financial services firms suggest that important lessons to learn for diversification include:

1   Managing diversification is challenging, especially with differences in business cultures (e.g., an aggressive investment banking culture and a conservative traditional banking culture) and care has to be taken that safeguards are put into place, such as keeping traditional bank underwriting standards in underwriting loans for securitizations, unlike poor underwriting standards for subprime loans and securitizations that contributed to the U.S. subprime loan crisis.
2   The large size of a firm is not always synonymous with efficiency, and larger firms may have more difficulty exerting control over different divisions, resulting in scandals, such as trading scandals that have occurred for many mega banks as the result of poor monitoring.
3   Without adequate risk management, the benefits of diversification in terms of smooth earnings and reducing risk can be lost.
4   Some customers may not prefer diversified financial services and may prefer financial services that are more specialized in different areas as in niche financial institutions.

Thus, enhancing institutional value entails careful identification of market opportunities and analysis of these opportunities, including the use of available risk management tools, with financial deregulation and global markets not changing the determinants of value, but broadening the range of opportunities available.

Diversified financial services firms also need to manage the risk of different product lines, incorporating the risk-adjusted return on capital approach (RAROC) for different businesses, including having sufficient risk capital for credit risk, market risk, operation risk, and insurance risk, and cross-sector diversification assessments for the reduction in risk with diversification.

Shadow Banking,
Finance
Companies,
Diversified
Financial Firms,
Venture Capital,
Crowdfunding,
Microfinance

SHOULD MEGA FINANCIAL FIRMS BE BROKEN UP?

In reaction to damage created during the subprime crisis and great recession as the result of risk-taking activities by mega banks, there has been a popular movement for breaking up banks to end problems of having "too big to fail" financial institutions that could take down an economy. Similar arguments occurred during the banking crisis of the early 1990s, while counter arguments are given that without mega banks, U.S. banks lose economies of scale and their competitiveness with international banks. Under Dodd–Frank, the eight largest U.S. mega banks are required to present "living wills" showing their wind-up provisions in the event of a financial crisis to avoid the chaos and taxpayer bailout that was came about with Lehman Brothers' collapse in 2008.

In April of 2016, five of these banks, including JPMorgan Chase and Bank of America, were told their plans were inadequate and were given warnings that they must seriously revise their plans or face sanctions. These rulings occurred during a U.S. presidential election campaign debate over whether the United States has reached a post-crisis objective to ensure that no bank would be held as "too big to fail" to avoid an economic collapse in the future. The Fed and FDIC directed the five banks to fix their plans by October 2016 or to face more stringent capital, leverage, or liquidity regulations or forced divestment of operations. As Tom Hoenig, vice-chairman of the FDIC reported, each plan had shortcomings and deficiencies, with no firm demonstrating that it would be able to resolve its bankruptcy in an orderly fashion to prevent the government from having to bail it out. For two major U.S. investment banks, the FDIC rejected Goldman Sachs' plan, but accepted Morgan Stanley's, while the Federal Reserve did the opposite. For Citigroup, which had divested $700 billion of its assets previously, the regulators found deficiencies in its plan, but felt that the plan was credible (Jopson, 2015; Popper and Corkery, 2016). In October 2016, plans were resubmitted.

SUMMARY

With technology and dramatic social networking changes, the world of finance is changing. Shadow banking (nonbank) financing has increased dramatically with technology allowing new platforms to bypass traditional financial intermediaries and avoid regulatory costs. Although there are many concerns about a lack of transparency for shadow banking markets, with big data available, peer-to-peer (P2P) lending platforms display large amounts of data to investors for enhanced transparency and are often more transparent in terms of clarity for fees, if any, for transactions. With technology it is also easier for the transfer of information allowing for mega institutions to be managed globally. With the growth of mega banks and other mega financial services firms, this has also increased concerns about the global effects and contagion that could occur with an institution's failure, reminiscent of Lehman Brothers' failure having an effect on institutions worldwide, with interconnectivity across other banks and nonbanks. Technological changes bring about new challenges for managing financial institutions in a FinTech and social media world, but also offer great opportunities and financing models that provide greater access to capital to innovators and entrepreneurs, as well as ways to help the poor through microlending.

Overview:
Nondepository
Financial
Institutions and
New Forms of
Financing

BIBLIOGRAPHY

Agrawal, A.K., C. Catalini, and A. Goldfarb (2013). "Some simple economics of crowdfunding." NBER Working Paper 29133, June 2013. Accessed on September 5, 2016 at: http://www.nber.org/papers/w19133.

Bell, Claes (2012). "Should the big banks be downsized?" *Bankrate*, August 2012. Accessed on March 10, 2016 at: http://www.bankrate.com/finance/banking/big-banks-downsized-1.aspx

Clifford, Catherine (2015). "The SEC just approved rules opening up equity crowdfunding to the general public in a 3-1 vote." Equity Crowdfunding, *Entrepreneur*. Accessed on October 30, 2015 at: http://www.entrepreneur.com/article/252322

Cowley, Stacy (2015). "S.E.C. gives small investors access to equity crowdfunding." *The New York Times*, October 30, 2015. Accessed on March 30, 2015 at: http://www.nytimes.com/2015/10/31/business/dealbook/sec-gives-small-investors-access-to-equity-crowdfunding.html?_r=0

Deutsche Bank (2014). "Infographics microfinance." Deutsche Bank. Accessed on March 11, 2016 at: https://www.db.com/cr/en/datacenter/infographic-microfinance.htm

Fannie Mae (2016). "Fannie Mae progress." Fannie Mae. Accessed on March 10, 2016 at: http://www.fanniemae.com/progress/serving.html

Frame, Scott, Andreas Fuster, Joseph Tracy, and James Vickery (2015). "The rescue of Fannie Mae and Freddie Mac." Federal Reserve Bank of New York Staff Reports, No. 719, March 2015. Accessed on March 11, 2016 at: https://www.newyorkfed.org/medialibrary/media/research/staff_reports/sr719.pdf

Freddie Mac (2016a). "Company profile." Freddie Mac. Accessed on March 10, 2016 at: http://www.freddiemac.com/corporate/company_profile/

Freddie Mac (2016b). "Investor FAQ." Freddie Mac. Accessed on March 10, 2016 at: http://www.freddiemac.com/investors/faq.html

Fredieu, Emma (2015). "Crowdfunding for the greater good." Mobile Technology, Global Envision. Accessed on March 11, 2016 at: http://www.globalenvision.org/mobile-technology

Ginnie Mae (2016). "About us: Funding government lending." Ginnie Mae website. Accessed on September 5, 2016 at: http://www.ginniemae.gov/about_us/who_we_are/Pages/funding_government_lending.aspx

Goldman Sachs (2015a). "The future of finance: Part 1: The rise of the new shadow bank." Goldman Sachs Equity Research, March 3, 2015. Accessed on March 7, 2016 at: http://www.betandbetter.com/photos_forum/1425585417.pdf?PHPSESSID=7406416a94128a8eca87ec315399c75c

Goldman Sachs (2015b). "The future of finance: Part 3: The socialization of finance." Goldman Sachs Equity Research, March 13, 2015, 1–62. Accessed on September 5, 2016 at: www.planet-fintech.com/file/167061/

Global Envision (2006). "The history of microfinance." April 14, 2006. Accessed on March 11, 2016 at: http://www.globalenvision.org/library/4/1051

Harvey, Chris (2015). "What is the future for equity crowdfunding in the USA?" Quora.com. Accessed on March 7, 2016 at: https://www.quora.com/What-is-the-future-for-equity-crowdfunding-in-the-USA

Henning, Peter J. (2016). "Prosecution of financial crisis fraud ends with a whimper." DealBook, *The New York Times*, August 29, 2016. Accessed on September 5, 2016 at: http://www.nytimes.com/2016/08/30/business/dealbook/prosecution-of-financial-crisis-fraud-ends-with-a-whimper.html?rref=collection%2Ftimestopic%2FCountrywide%20Financial%20Corporation&action=click&contentCollection=business&region=stream&module=stream_unit&version=latest&contentPlacement=1&pgtype=collection

Henry, Zoe (2016). "8 emerging Fintech startups to watch in 2016." INC website, Best of Inc., January 15, 2016. Accessed on April 17, 2016 at: http://www.inc.com/zoe-henry/8-emerging-fintech-startups-2016.html

Hopkins, Cheyenne (2015). "Too big to fail." Bloomberg Quick Take, November 9, 2015. Accessed on March 7, 2016 at: http://www.bloombergview.com/quicktake/big-fail

Irwin, Neil (2015). "What is Glass–Steagall? The banking law that stirred the debate." *The New York Times*, October 14, 2015. Accessed on March 10, 2016 at: http://www.nytimes.com/2015/10/15/upshot/what-is-glass-steagall-the-82-year-old-banking-law-that-stirred-the-debate.html?_r=0

Jopson, Barney (2015). "Banks face harsh sanctions as Fed rejects wind-up provisions: Five big names told to fix 'living wills:' bid to end 'too big to fail' on hold until October." *Financial Times*, April 14, 2016, p. 1.

Lohr, Steve (2016). "As more pay by smartphone, banks scramble to keep up." *The New York Times*, January 18, 2016. Accessed on April 17, 2016 at: http://www.nytimes.com/2016/01/19/technology/upstarts-are-leading-the-fintech-movement-and-banks-take-heed.html

377

*Shadow Banking,
Finance
Companies,
Diversified
Financial Firms,
Venture Capital,
Crowdfunding,
Microfinance*

McLean, Bethany and Joe Nocera (2011). *All the Devils Are Here: The Hidden History of the Financial Crisis.* New York: Portfolio Penguin, Penguin Group USA, Inc.

Morgenson, Gretchen (2015). "Fannie and Freddie's government rescue has come with claws." *The New York Times*, December 12, 2015. Accessed on April 17, 2016 at: http://www.nytimes.com/2015/12/13/business/fannie-and-freddies-government-rescue-has-come-with-claws.html

Morgenson, Gretchen (2016). "Documents undercut U.S. case for taking mortgage giant Fannie Mae's profits." *The New York Times*, April 12, 2016, pp. B1, B5. Accessed on April 17, 2016, at: http://www.nytimes.com/2016/04/13/business/fannie-mae-suit-bailout.html?_r=0

Olsters, Scot (Ed.) (2010). "How the roof fell on Countrywide." *Fortune*, December 20, 2010. Accessed on March 10, 2016 at: http://fortune.com/2010/12/23/how-the-roof-fell-in-on-countrywide/

Noeth, Bryan J. and Rajdeep Sengupta (2016). "Is shadow banking really banking?" Federal Reserve Bank of St. Louis. Accessed on March 6, 2016 at: https://www.stlouisfed.org/Publications/Regional-Economist/October-2011/Is-Shadow-Banking-Really-Banking

Popper, Nathaniel and Michael Corkery (2016). "Regulations enforce a diet for Citigroup: A trend of megabanks becoming just big." *The New York Times*, April 16, 2016, pp. A1, B6.

Pozsar, Zoltan, Tobias Adrian, Adam Ashcraft, and Hayley Boesky (2012). "Shadow banking." Federal Reserve Bank of New York Staff Report No. 458, July 2010 (Revised February 2012). Accessed on March 6, 2016 at: https://www.newyorkfed.org/medialibrary/media/research/staff_reports/sr458.pdf

ResponsAbility (2014). "Microfinance market outlook 2015." ResponsAbility, November 2014. Accessed on March 11, 2015 at: http://www.responsability.com/funding/data/docs/es/10427/Microfinance-Market-Outlook-2015-DE.pdf

ResponsAbility (2016). "Microfinance market outlook 2016." ResponsAbility, November 2015. Accessed on March 11, 2015 at: http://www.responsability.com/funding/data/docs/en/17813/Microfinance-Outlook-2016-EN.pdf

Schlein, Michael and Michael Chu (2010). "Microfinance goes public," April 30, 2010. Accessed on March 11, 2015 at: http://www.forbes.com/2010/04/30/india-microfinance-sks-ipo-markets-emerging-markets-accion.html

SEC (2015). "SEC adopts rules to facilitate smaller companies' access to capital." U.S. Securities and Exchange Commission. Accessed on October 15, 2015 at: http://www.sec.gov/news/pressrelease/2015-49.html

The Economist (2016). "How shadow banking works." *The Economist*. Accessed on March 6, 2016 at: http://www.economist.com/blogs/economist-explains/2016/02/economist-explains-0

Wolf, Martin (2016). "Good news—FinTech could disrupt finance." *Financial Times*, March 10, 2016, p. 11.

WR Hambrecht + Co. (2016). "About WR Hambrecht + Co." Accessed on March 3, 2016 at: https://www.wrhambrecht.com/about/

Zeoli, Anthony (2015). "Peer to peer lending: Taking the fear out of 'shadow banking'." Crowdfund Insider, May 27, 2015. Accessed on March 7, 2016 at: http://www.crowdfundinsider.com/2015/05/68355-peer-to-peer-lending-taking-the-fear-out-of-shadow-banking/

QUESTIONS AND PROBLEMS

1   What is shadow banking, and how does it differ from traditional banking institutions? Why are regulators concerned about shadow banking? Give an example of a shadow bank during the U.S. subprime loan crisis or the global financial crisis that posed a risk to the financial system. How big is this sector? Which types of shadow banks are more risky?

2   Why have many financial institutions grown so large? What are the advantages of diversified financial conglomerates? What are the disadvantages? What additional regulations have been imposed on systematically important financial institutions (SIFIs)?

3   What are FinTech firms? Give an example. What advantages do peer-to-peer (P2P) lending firms have, and what disadvantages? Should large banks be afraid of new disruptive technologies? Find an article on a FinTech firm and point out its advantages and disadvantages.

Overview:
Nondepository
Financial
Institutions and
New Forms of
Financing

4   Give an example of a company that you are familiar with that is a FinTech company and the innovations that the company has made.

5   How do finance companies differ from depository institutions? Where do they get their funding? How do their credit, liquidity, and interest rate risks compare to traditional depository institutions?

6   What are the different types of finance companies? Give examples of each.

7   How do credit card companies make money? Why are they so profitable?

8   What are government-sponsored enterprises and how do they make loan markets more efficient? Why did Fannie Mae and Freddie Mac have severe financial problems during the U.S. subprime loan crisis? Should they have been bailed out? Explain why or why not.

9   Give an example of a private or publicly trading mortgage bank. How do mortgage banks operate? Does the nature of their operations increase or decrease their overall risks compared to depository institutions? Why did Countrywide loans have severe problems, necessitating its merger with Bank of America.

10 What are hedge funds? How are they shadow banks? Why aren't hedge funds as regulated as other financial services firms?

11 What do venture capital firms do? Why are high returns and harvesting key for the profitability of these firms?

12 What is crowdfunding, and what are the different crowdfunding models? How have SEC rules changed in the United States allowing greater equity funding on crowdfunding platforms. Give some examples of different crowdfunding platforms and how they differ.

13 What is microlending, and how has it expanded? What are recent trends in microlending?

14 Give some reasons for the development of financial conglomerates. What are special challenges in managing diversified financial services firms? There has been public pressure to break up "too big to fail" financial institutions. What are the pros and cons of these arguments?

Appendices

Overview Liquidity Analysis

HERE is a short tutorial for analyzing the liquidity of a company including how to create a sources and uses statement and indirect cash flow statement and differences between stored and cash flow measures of liquidity.

To evaluate the liquidity of a firm, a credit analyst needs to evaluate both:

1 the *stored liquidity* a firm has on its balance sheet, liquid assets that are marketable that can be sold to meet upcoming liabilities; and

2 *cash flow measures of liquidity* in terms of how efficient a firm is in terms of generating cash flow from its operations. An important part of evaluating a loan includes an evaluation of a firm's liquidity and cash flows. This involves evaluating sources and uses of funds and a firm's indirect cash flow statement.

CREATING AN INDIRECT CASH FLOW STATEMENT

Financial statements can easily be accessed for public firms (U.S. publicly traded financial statements can be downloaded from the U.S. Securities and Exchange Commission's Edgar website at: www.sec.gov/edgar.shtml or search for the company on Yahoo! Finance, www.finance.yahoo.com). For privately held firms, firms provide their financial statements when applying for a loan. Using balance sheets, an indirect cash flow statement is easy to create.

As an example, see the income statement for Susie's Emporium. Susie, the owner has supplied its income statement to you as a credit analyst for the Denver Best Bank. Balance sheets are also supplied for the past two years.

Susie's Emporium, Income Statement, current year ($)

Revenue	7,270,965
Cost of goods sold	5,088,078
Gross profit	2,182,887
Selling and administration costs	1,648,000*
Operating profit	534,887
Interest expense	4,012
Income before taxes	530,875
Taxes	200,484
Net income	330,391
Dividend paid	64,359
Addition to retained earnings	266,052

*Note: The depreciation expense is $83,000, which is included in selling and administrative costs, and dividends paid is $64,359.

Susie's Emporium, Balance Sheets for current and previous years $

	Current	Previous
Assets		
Cash	118,936	221,679
Accounts receivable	66,827	94,585
Inventory	1,527,187	1,390,767
Other current assets	99,740	91,767
Total current assets	1,812,690	1,798,798
Net property, plant and equipment (PP&E)	1,657,919	1,514,138
Other long-term assets	88,727	78,768
Total assets	3,559,336	3,391,704
Liabilities		
Accounts payable	1,006,700	946,037
Accrued liabilities	184,386	172,259
Notes payable	589	537
Total current liabilities	1,191,675	1,118,833
Long-term debt	578,474	440,646
Total liabilities	1,770,149	1,559,479
Equity		
Common stock	51,973	361,043
Retained earnings	1,737,214	1,471,182
Total equity	1,789,187	1,832,225
Total liabilities and equity	3,559,336	3,391,704

CREATING A SOURCE AND USE STATEMENT FOR SUSIE'S EMPORIUM

To evaluate how Susie's Emporium acquired and used funds over the past year, it is useful to do a sources and uses statement first, utilizing the current year and previous year balance sheets Susie provided. To do a sources and uses statement, you just need to take the difference between the current year and previous year for each balance sheet item (omit any total figures). Then you just classify the change in each asset and liability as a use of funds or a source of funds.

For each asset, if the asset goes up, this is a use (*even for cash, which you can think of as cash held in the bank that is held for transactions as a use of funds*). If an asset goes down, this is a source of funds. Any liability or equity item going up is a source of funds, and any decline is a use of funds (i.e., paying back debt or repurchasing equity, etc.). If accumulated depreciation goes up (not shown in this statement), it is a rise in a source of funds, as a noncash payment). The sources and uses for Susie's Emporium are shown below (with total sources equal to total uses).

	Current	Previous	Source	Use
Assets ($)				
Cash	118,936	221,679	102,743	
Accounts receivable	66,827	94,585	27,758	
Inventory	1,527,187	1,390,767		136,420
Other current assets	99,740	91,767		7,973
Total current assets	1,812,690	1,798,798		
Net property, plant, and equipment	1,657,919	1,514,138		143,781
Other long-term assets	88,727	78,768		9,959
Total assets	3,559,336	3,391,704		
Liabilities ($)				
Accounts payable	1,006,700	946,037	60,663	
Accrued liabilities	184,386	172,259	12,127	
Notes payable	589	537	52	
Total current liabilities	1,191,675	1,118,833		
Long-term debt	578,474	440,646	137,828	
Total liabilities	1,770,149	1,559,479		
Equity ($)				
Common stock	51,973	361,043		309,070
Retained earnings	1,737,214	1,471,182	266,032	
Total equity	1,789,187	1,832,225		
Total liabilities and equity	3,559,336	3,391,704		
Total sources and uses			607,203	607,203

The total sources and uses for the current year each equal $607,203. As shown in the sources and uses provided above, cash went down and was used as a funding source, as was the decline in accounts receivables, and rises in accounts payable and accrued liabilities. For external financing items, sources included a rise in long-term debt, along with a rise in internal financing in terms of the rise in retained earnings.

Uses of funds include a large rise in inventory, a small rise in other current assets, a large rise in PP&E (property, plant, and equipment) and a rise in other long-term assets. There was also a large decline in common stock as a use, with a large repurchase of common stock by the firm in the current year.

In summary, the firm appears to have improved on its credit sales collections with a reduction in accounts receivables. However, the firm increased its inventory. Susie's Emporium is also relying more on supplier financing as shown by the large rise in accounts payable. The firm has also purchased plant and equipment, so appears to be expanding its operations in the current year. For external financing, the firm is increasing its financial leverage by taking on more long-term debt and repurchasing common stock.

CREATING AN INDIRECT CASH FLOW STATEMENT FOR SUSIE'S EMPORIUM:

The format for an indirect cash flow statement has three parts:

1   Cash from operations
2   Cash used in investment activities
3   Cash from financing activities.

Cash from operations (CFO) is the cash actually generated by the firm's operations over the year. To get CFO adjustments are made for noncash receipts and noncash payments. So for CFO, net income is adjusted by adding back the depreciation expense that is a noncash accounting expense that was not actually spent. Also, adjustments are made by then adding back operating sources and subtracting operating uses for current operating assets (accounts receivable, inventory, and accrued assets) and for current operating liabilities (accounts payable and accrued liabilities).

Cash used in investment activities (CFI) adjusts for the cash that was actually used to make investments, equal to the change in gross fixed assets. To calculate the change in gross fixed assets, if only net fixed assets are shown on the balance sheet, you can calculate the change in gross fixed assets as the change in net PP&E plus the current year's depreciation expense on its income statement. Changes in other long-term assets or other investments would also be included.

Cash from financing activities (CFF) adjusts for the cash given out for dividends as a deduction, and any change in external financing items (notes payable, bank loans, long-term debt, bonds, common stock, preferred stock, and other externally financed balance sheet items), such as paying back or increasing external debt, stock repurchases or other external financing activities.

A simple format for the indirect cash flow statement is as follows:

1. Cash flow from operations (CFO)

Net income

+ Depreciation

+ Any operating sources (sources that are operating* current assets and operating current liabilities)

– Any operating uses (uses that are operating current assets and operating current liabilities)

= Net cash flow from operations.

*Note: Operating current assets and operating current liabilities exclude any external financing items, such as notes payable or bank loans, only including changes in operating current assets, such as accounts receivable and inventory and accrued operating assets, and changes in operating current liabilities, including accounts payable and accrued liabilities related to operations. Change in cash will be the balancing item, for CFO – CFI + CFF, so should not be included.

2. Cash used in investment activities (CFI)

Change in gross fixed assets (GFA)*

Change in any other long-term assets or investments.

*Note: If net PP&E is given, the change GFA = Net PP&E + Depreciation expense (from the current year's income statement). Note generally CFI will be a use with a rise in gross fixed assets (if there is a decline, the sign will be negative here for that item).

3. Cash from financing activities (CFF):

– Dividends paid

+ Any rise in an external financing item* (source)

– Any decline in an external financing item (use).

*Note: An external financing item includes any externally financed item (that a firm has to go out and get), such as bank loans, notes payable, bonds, short- and long-term loans, etc., common stock, preferred stock, etc. Retained earnings, as internal financing, is not included, since it is already included in net income.

Change in cash for the firm will equal: CFO – CFI + CFF, which should be the same as the change in cash on the balance sheet for the two years as a check.

Creating Susie's Emporium's Indirect Cash Flow Statement

1. Cash flow from operations (CFO) ($)

Net income	330,391
+ Depreciation expense	83,000
+ Decline in accounts receivable	27,758
– Rise in inventory	(136,420)
– Rise in other current assets	(7,973)

+ Rise in accounts payable	60,663
+ Rise in accrued liabilities	12,127
Cash from operations	*369,546*

2. Cash used in investing activities (CFI) ($)

– Dividends paid	(64,359)
+ Rise in notes payable	52
+ Rise in long-term debt	137,828
– Decline common stock	(309,070)
Net cash used in financing activities	*(235,549)*
Change in net PPE + Depreciation expense	143,781 + 83,000 = 226,781
Change in other long-term assets	9,959
Net cash used in investing activities	*236,740*

3. Cash from financing activities (CFF) ($)

Change in cash = CFO − CFI + CFF = 369,546 − 236,740 − 235,549 = $102,743
   Check: Change in cash on balance sheet = $102,743.

ANALYSIS OF THE INDIRECT CASH FLOW STATEMENT FOR SUSIE'S EMPORIUM

Analyzing the indirect cash flow statement for Susie's Emporium, the company has a healthy cash flow from operations of $369,546. The firm used cash for expanding its gross fixed assets of $263,740 and inventory. On the financing side, the firm had a net use of cash to pay dividends and repurchase stock, and also issued additionally a large amount of long-term debt.

On the working capital side, the firm under cash flow from operations had a net rise in working capital (change in current assets less change in current liabilities) of $43,845 (net use). The firm's large rise in inventory and small rise in other current assets as uses were larger than the decline in accounts receivables and rise in accounts payable and accrued liabilities as sources.

With the large depreciation expense adjustment as a noncash flow of $83,000, despite the rise in net working capital as a use, net cash flow from operations was larger than net income by $39,155. The firm had a large rise in accounts payable likely to partially finance the large rise in inventory. The firm appears to be expanding with the large inventory rise and rise in gross fixed assets. In terms of cash flow from financing, the firm appears to be changing its capital structure with the repurchase of equity and rise of long-term debt.

RATIO ANALYSIS TO ANALYZE SUSIE'S EMPORIUM'S LIQUIDITY

Stored Liquidity Ratios

To analyze a firm's liquidity, a credit analyst needs to look at both the firm's stored liquidity and its cash flow available to repay a loan.

Stored liquidity measures include:

Current ratio: Total current assets / Total current liabilities

Quick ratio: (Total current assets − Inventory) / Total current liabilities.

The current ratio indicates the ability to pay upcoming current liabilities in the coming year by liquidating all current assets. The quick ratio indicates the ability to pay upcoming current liabilities using only the most liquid assets that are more marketable, excluding inventory. For both, higher ratios indicate higher stored liquidity. Banks generally have requirements in loan covenants for minimum current and quick ratios to provide greater security for bank loans.

A firm with very high current and quick ratios, however, may be operating inefficiently, in terms of holding excess inventory that is not selling and/or excess accounts receivables if the firm is not effectively collecting on its credit sales or has customers who are unwilling or unable to make credit payments.

Hence, it is also important to examine cash flow measures of liquidity to examine how efficient a firm is in generating cash flow and quickly converting inventory to sales and credit sales to cash payments, as well as examining how efficiently a firm is managing its accounts payable (supplier credit) that reduces the time it takes for a firm to generate cash flow before having to make cash payments.

Other measures for stored liquidity measuring current assets less current liabilities include:

Net working capital = Total current assets − Total current liabilities

Net working capital to sales = Net working capital / Sales

In terms of the ability to have cash to meet upcoming liabilities, the net liquid assets or net liquid balance (NLB) ratio is used as:

Net Liquid Balance (NLB) = [Cash and Equivalents − Notes payable and Current maturities of long-term debt or leases due in the next 365 days].

The Cash Flow Timeline and Cash Flow Liquidity Measures

Given the time it takes from when purchases are made and paid for by a firm and its sales are made and cash is received from accounts receivables, a firm has a cash flow timeline that includes a cash operating cycle, the time it takes for inventory between when inventory is purchased and sold and when accounts receivables are collected. The full cash cycle also deducts the time it takes the firm to pay its suppliers for the inventory purchased.

The quicker a firm's cash cycle, the quicker the firm builds up liquidity and the less financing a firm will need for financing working capital, where a firm's approximate working capital loan is equal to its daily cost of goods sold (CGS) times its days cash cycle.

The formula to calculate a firm's days cash cycle is:

Days cash cycle = Days inventory + Days accounts receivable (AR)

− Days accounts payable*

where:

Days inventory = 365 / (CGS / inventory);

Days AR or average collection period = 365 / (Sales / Accounts receivable);

Days accounts payable (AP) = 365 / (CGS / Accounts payable)

*Note: Often days accrued liabilities is often also used and deducted if the firm has accrued wages or other accrued liabilities, days accrued liabilities would also be deducted, where Days accrued liabilities = 365 / (CGS / Accrued liabilities).

Many firms have adopted a negative days cash cycle, where cash comes in before cash goes out by efficiently managing inventory and collecting on accounts receivables quickly and having a good relationship with suppliers allowing a longer days accounts payable period.

Other cash flow measures to examine are:

Cash flow from operations (CFO) from the firm's cash flow statement

Cash conversion efficiency (CCE) = CFO / Sales, as an indicator of the ability of a firm to generate CFO relative to sales.

Current liquidity index = (Cash assets previous year + CFO)

where a higher ratio indicates greater liquidity with cash and the firm's CFO available to pay off upcoming current liabilities.

Evaluation of liquidity for Susie's Emporium

Given sales in previous year: $6,814,479 and CGS: $4,727,813.

	Current	Previous	Peer average
Stored liquidity ratios			
Current ratio	1.52	1.61	1.60
Quick ratio	0.24	0.37	
Net working capital	$621,015	$679,965	
Net working capital to sales	8.54%	9.98%	
Net liquid balance	$118,347	$221,142	
Cash flow ratios			
CFO	$369,546	Not given	

CFO/Sales	5.80%	Not given	
Current liquidity index	$591,225	Not given	
Days inventory days	109.61	107.35	135.19 days
Days accounts receivables	3.35	5.07	
Days operating cycle	112.96	112.42	
Days accounts payable	72.28	73.15	
Days accrued liabilities	13.23	13.30	
Cash cycle days	27.45	25.97	

From a stored liquidity perspective the firm had a decline in its current ratio. There was also a decline in the quick ratio, which is very low (less than one) reflecting the large amount of inventory held. Net working capital and net working capital to sales declined, despite the rise in inventory in the current year, with a rise in accounts payable and accrued liabilities and a small fall in accounts receivables in the current year.

From a cash flow perspective, Susie's Emporium has a large CFO in the current year and CFO to sales ratio and current liquidity index. The firm's cash cycle days went up slightly in the current year from about 26 days to about 27.5 days. Accounts receivable days fell slightly, and inventory days rose slightly, while days payable and days accrued liabilities remained fairly stable. The firm has a large operating cycle each year of about 3.8 months. However, because of a combined accounts payable and accrued liabilities days of about 85.5 days, its cash cycle days is little less than a month. Although the firm's days inventory seems high, it is below the industry average each year. Hence, from a cash flow perspective the firm appears to be generating liquidity and doing well in contrast to balance sheet liquidity ratios that show a very low quick ratio, but a positive net liquid balance.

Debt Payment Coverage Ratios

Debt coverage ratios also help to evaluate a firm's liquidity in terms of its ability to cover its upcoming payments including interest and lease payments, where:

Times interest earned (TIE) = Earnings before interest and taxes / Interest expense

Fixed charge coverage = (EBIT + Lease payments) / (Interest expense + Lease payments)

Debt coverage ratio = Net operating income* / Debt service

*Where net operating income is defined as net income + depreciation and amortization expense + interest expense.

Often for repayment analysis, the following format is used for analysis:

Revenue

Operating expenses

Net income

+ Depreciation and amortization

+ Interest expense

Net operating income

Less debt service*

Net cash flow

Debt coverage ratio

*The total debt to total assets and total debt to total equity ratios and equity multiplier (assets/equity) are also used to examine a firm's debt capacity.

Debt Coverage Analysis for Susie's Emporium

Debt coverage ratios for Susie's Emporium for the current year are as follows, supposing that with a new loan, the debt annual payment would be $1,589 including the previous notes payable:

Repayment analysis ($)	Current year
Revenue	7,270,965
Operating expenses	6,736,078
Net income	330,391
+ Depreciation and amortization	83,000
+ Interest expense	4,012
Net operating income	417,403
Less debt service*	1,589
Net cash flow	415,814
Debt coverage ratio	262.68

	Current year
Times interest earned	133.32
Fixed charge coverage	133.32
Debt coverage ratio	262.68

	Current	Previous
Total debt to total assets	49.73%	45.98%
Total debt to total equity	0.99	0.85 (Peer average: 2.1)
Long-term debt to total assets	16.25%	12.99%
Equity multiplier	1.99	1.85

Susie's Emporium has high TIE and debt coverage ratios, indicating low liquidity risk from a cash flow perspective, with its net operating income easily covering its expected debt service with a new loan that has an annual payment of $1,000 plus its current notes payable indicating a $1,589 debt service needed to be covered, which would be covered 262.68 x from the firm's net operating income in the current year. The firm increased its financial leverage in the current year, but is still well below the average peer debt to equity ratio.

This analysis shows how important it is to examine cash flow and debt coverage ratios in addition to stored liquidity ratios. With an overview of profitability ratios, the firm appears to be financially healthy in terms of its profitability ratios. While Susie's Emporium had low quick and current ratios, it is generating large cash flows, and has the ability to repay its debt.

Sometimes high current ratios can reflect high inventory and accounts receivable levels that may reflect poor working capital management policies, with a firm holding excessive inventory and uncollected accounts receivables. Thus, it is important to look at cash flow ratios to examine from a flow perspective how much liquidity a firm is generating.

Profitability ratios for Susie's Emporium for the current year

Return on equity (ROE)	18.46%	(Peer average: 15.02%)
Return on assets	9.28%	
Equity multiplier	1.99 x	
Asset utilization	2.04 x	
Net profit margin (NPM)	4.54%	(Peer average: 4.45%)
Gross profit margin	30.02%	
Operating profit margin	7.36%	

From a profitability perspective, Susie's Emporium has a higher ROE in the current year than the peer average and a slightly higher NPM. For this type of business, a high asset utilization is important, and with an equity multiplier of almost 2, the ROE of 18.46% is higher than the peer average of 15.02%. Overall, the firm appears to be generating cash flow well, and the firm is profitable, with a high gross profit margin.

Mini-Loan Analysis Cases

BOOK WORM, INC.

The Book Worm, Inc. is a large bookstore company that sells retail books, textbooks, magazines and newspapers and other related products including eBooks and other digital projects, bargain books, gifts, apparel and gifts, school and dorm supplies, café products and services, educational toys, games, music and movies. These products are sold online on its website and also through its chain of bookstores across the United States, with its headquarters in New York City. The owners of Book Worm have been good customers of the Euphoria Bank in Brooklyn, New York, which has branches across the five boroughs of New York City. Euphoria Bank is a community bank, with Phil Lerner, a well-known financier, the bank's CEO and Ros Lerner, the eminent President of Euphoria Bank, who is well acquainted with the owners of Book Worm, Inc. Eleanor Swanson, the visionary owner of Book Worm, Inc. has submitted a new loan request to Euphoria Bank. You as credit analyst at the bank have been asked to do a liquidity and profitability analysis for the firm.

The financial statements for the firm for the past two years are shown below:

Book Worm, Inc. financial statements ($ thousand)

Income statements

	Previous year	Current year
Total revenue	6,069,497	6,381,357
Cost of revenue	4,196,998	4,523,422
Gross profit	1,872,499	1,857,935
Depreciation expense	194,174	216,807
Selling and administration expenses	1,545,152	1,606,936
Total operating expenses	1,739,326	1,823,743
Operating profit	133,173	34,192
Interest expense	17,890	29,507
Earnings before taxes	115,283	4,685

Income tax expense	78,687	3,198
Net income	36,596	1,487
Dividends	23,105	0

Balance sheets

	Previous year	Current year
Assets		
Cash and equivalents	74,360	340,171
Accounts receivables	241,385	288,711
Inventory	1,348,239	1,284,976
Other current assets	65,331	66,580
Total current assets	1,729,315	1,980,438
Net fixed assets	1,500,190	1,557,011
Total assets	3,229,505	3,537,449
Liabilities		
Accounts payable	1,089,113	1,237,695
Accrued liabilities	358,146	483,950
Total current liabilities	1,447,259	1,721,645
Long-term debt	396,829	578,914
Total liabilities	1,844,088	2,300,559
Equity		
Common stock	1,027,905	892,869
Retained earnings	357,512	344,021
Total stockholder equity	1,385,417	1,236,890
Total liabilities and equity	3,229,505	3,537,449

To analyze the firm, Phil Lerner, the CEO, and Ros Lerner, President of Euphoria Bank ask you to:

1   Prepare a sources and uses statement, categorizing changes for individual balance sheet items as sources and uses and discuss the sources and uses of funds by the firm over the two years.
2   Prepare an indirect statement of cash flows using the format shown below for the current year where for the cash flow from operations (CFO) and cash flow from financing (CFF) for changes in each item, sources are added and uses are subtracted (from your sources and uses statement):

Indirect cash flow statement

Cash flow from operations (CFO)
Net income
Depreciation expense
Change in accounts receivable

(Continued)

Appendix B

(Continued)

Change in inventory	
Change in other current assets	
Change in accounts payable	
Change in accrued liabilities	
	Cash from operations
Cash flow from investing activities (CFI)	
	Change net fixed assets
	+ Depreciation expense
	= *Change in gross FA*
Cash flow from financing (CFF)	
Less dividends paid	
Change in long-term debt	
Change in common stock	
	Cash from financing
Change in cash CFO − CFI + CFF	
Check: Should equal change in cash balance.	

3   Evaluate trends in stored liquidity including balance sheet ratios (current ratio, quick ratio, net working capital, and working capital to sales).

4   Review cash flow liquidity measures including cash flow from operations (CFO), CFO/sales for the current year.

5   Evaluate trends in the cash cycle for each of the two years, calculating the days inventory, days accounts receivables, days accounts payable, and days accrued liabilities. Analyze these trends.

6   Evaluate trends in debt coverage ratios and solvency ratios including total debt to total assets, times interest earned, long-term debt to total assets, and the equity multiplier.

7   Do a Dupont Analysis for the trends for the two years including a review of return on equity (ROE), return on Assets (ROA), net profit margin (NPM), gross profit margin (GPM), operating profit margin (OPM), asset utilization (AU), and fixed asset turnover, along with the trends you evaluated earlier for days inventory, days accounts receivables to explain any change in ROE and ROA for the two years.

8   Do a summary overall evaluation of the firm in terms of your previous analysis. What are the firm's strengths and weaknesses? What suggestions would you give to managers for improvement?

9   Do a loan repayment analysis and calculate the debt coverage ratio based on the current year's income statement. For the debt coverage ratio, assume Euphoria Bank would give the company a loan that had a total annual debt service (including any previous debt service) of $36,000. If the loan is granted, what restrictive covenants would you suggest for the loan to protect the bank's interests?

NAPA VALLEY COMPUTERS

Napa Valley Computers designs, manufactures, and markets specialized smart phones and personal computers, and other technological devices, and sells them through its retail stores in 10 different western states in the United States. David Sussman, the CEO and President of Napa Valley Computers, is thinking of getting additional external equity financing with Strength Capital, a private equity firm in San Francisco. As the credit analyst for Strength Capital, you are asked to analyze the firm's financial statements preparing a sources and uses analysis and indirect cash flow statement for the firm for the current year, and performing a liquidity, solvency and profitability analysis including an analysis of the trends over the two years. Specific aspects that the equity partners of Strength Capital, Herman Asarnow and Susan Baillet, ask you to look for include:

1 A review of the cash flow liquidity measures including cash flow from operations (CFO), CFO/sales for the current year.
2 An evaluation of the trends in the cash cycle for each of the two years, calculating the days inventory, days accounts receivables, days accounts payable, and days accrued liabilities. Analyze these trends.
3 An evaluation of the debt coverage ratios and solvency ratios, including total debt to total assets, times interest earned, long-term debt to total assets, and the equity multiplier.
4 A Dupont Analysis for the trends for the two years including a review of return on equity (ROE), return on assets (ROA), net profit margin (NPM), gross profit margin (GPM), operating profit margin (OPM), asset utilization (AU), and fixed asset turnover, along with the trends you evaluated earlier for days inventory, days accounts receivables to explain any change in ROE and ROA for the two years.
5 An overall evaluation of the firm in terms of your previous analysis. What are the firm's strengths and weaknesses? Give your opinion on whether an equity investment should be made in the firm.
6 Do a cash flow liquidity analysis, calculating the firm's cash cycle days (days inventory, days accounts receivables, days accounts payable, and days accrued liabilities). What do these trends reveal along with the CFO and CFO to sales ratios about the firm's cash flow liquidity and management of working capital?
7 Do a Dupont Analysis for the trends in ROE, ROA, NPM, GPM, OPM, and AU (including an analysis of fixed asset turnover and days inventory and days accounts receivables). Analyze the trends and reason why the ROE changed in the current year, based on $ROE = NPM \times AU \times EM$.
8 What strengths and weaknesses are revealed? Give your advice on whether the firm's financial condition merits taking on additional debt through a bank loan or additional equity through a secondary equity offering.

Napa Valley Computers financial statements ($ million)

Balance sheets

	Previous year	Current year
Assets		
Cash and equivalents	10,746,000	14,259,000
Short-term investments	18,383,000	26,287,000

(Continued)

Appendix B

(Continued)

Balance sheets

	Previous year	Current year
Accounts receivables	21,275,000	24,094,000
Inventory	791,000	1,764,000
Other current assets	6,458,000	6,882,000
Total current assets	*57,653,000*	*73,286,000*
Net property, plant, and equipment	118,411,000	134,137,000
Total assets	*176,064,000*	*207,423,000*

Liabilities and equity

	Previous year	Current year
Accounts payable	32,589,000	36,646,000
Accrued current liabilities	5,953,000	7,435,000
Total Current liabilities	*38,542,000*	*44,081,000*
Long-term debt	0	16,960,000
Other long-term liabilities	19,312,000	22,833,000
Total liabilities	*57,854,000*	*83,874,000*
Common stock	16,921,000	19,293,000
Retained earnings	101,289,000	104,256,000
Total equity	118,210,000	123,549,000
Total liabilities and equity	*176,064,000*	*207,423,000*

Income statements

	Previous year	Current year
Revenues	156,508,000	170,910,000
Cost of revenue	87,846,000	106,606,000
Gross profit	*68,662,000*	*64,304,000*
Depreciation expense	3,277,000	6,757,000
R&D expense	3,381,000	4,475,000
Selling and administration expense	6,763,000	4,073,000
Total operating expense	*13,421,000*	*15,305,000*
Operating profit	55,241,000	48,999,000
Other income	522,000	1,156,000
Earnings before interest and tax	55,763,000	50,155,000
Interest expense	0	0
Earnings before tax	55,763,000	50,155,000
Income tax expense	14,030,000	13,118,000
Net income	41,733,000	37,037,000
Dividends paid	37,977,030	34,070,000
Addition to retained earnings	*3,755,970*	*2,967,000*

PAPER CLIP JUNCTION

Paper Clip Junction, a national office supply store company, sells office supplies and furniture with convenient locations for stores in California, Arizona, Utah, Colorado, and New Mexico. The CEO, Ralph Dangerfield, has asked for your advice as an investment bank adviser for ways to improve the company's performance to make it attractive as an acquisition target, including an analysis of the liquidity, solvency, and profitability of the firm.

1   Do a sources and uses analysis and an indirect cash flow statement for the current year, and evaluate the primary sources and uses of the firm, and other information revealed from these statements. Review cash flow liquidity measures including cash flow from operations (CFO), CFO/sales for the current year.
2   Evaluate trends in stored liquidity including balance sheet ratios (current ratio, quick ratio, net working capital, and working capital to sales).
3   Evaluate trends in the cash cycle for each of the two years, calculating the days inventory, days accounts receivables, days accounts payable, and days accrued liabilities. Analyze these trends.
4   Evaluate trends in debt coverage ratios and solvency ratios, including total debt to total assets, times interest earned, long-term debt to total assets, and the equity multiplier.
5   Do a Dupont Analysis for the trends for the two years including a review of return on equity (ROE), return on assets (ROA), net profit margin (NPM), gross profit margin (GPM), operating profit margin (OPM), asset utilization (AU), and fixed asset turnover, along with the trends you evaluated earlier for days inventory, days accounts receivables to explain any change in ROE and ROA for the two years.
6   Do a summary overall evaluation of the firm in terms of your previous analysis. What are the firm's strengths and weaknesses? What suggestions would you give to managers for improvement?

Paper Clip Junction financial statements ($ thousand)

Income statements

	Previous year	Current year
Revenues	10,696,000	11,242,000
Cost of revenues	8,160,000	8,616,000
Gross profit	2,536,000	2,626,000
Depreciation expense	203,000	209,000
Administration and selling expenses	2,364,000	2,622,000
Total operating expenses	2,567,000	2,831,000
Operating income or loss	(31,000)	(205,000)
Other income	25,000	401,000
Earnings before interest and tax	(6,000)	196,000
Interest expense	69,000	69,000

(Continued)

Appendix B

(Continued)

Income statements

	Previous year	Current year
Earnings before taxes	(75,000)	127,000
Income tax expense	2,000	147,000
Net income	(77,000)	(20,000)
Dividends paid	0	0
Addition to retained earnings	(77,000)	(20,000)

Balance Sheets

	Previous year	Current year
Assets		
Cash and equivalents	671,000	955,000
Accounts receivable	804,000	1,333,000
Inventory	1,051,000	1,812,000
Other current assets	171,000	296,000
Total current assets	2,697,000	4,396,000
Net property, plant, and equipment	1,314,000	3,081,000
Total assets	4,011,000	7,477,000
Liabilities and equity		
Accounts payable	1,872,000	2,893,000
Short-term debt	174,000	29,000
Total current liabilities	2,046,000	2,922,000
Long-term debt	917,000	2,438,000
Total liabilities	2,963,000	5,360,000
Common stock	1,664,000	2,753,000
Retained earnings	-616,000	-636,000
Total equity	1,048,000	2,117,000
Total liabilities and equity	4,011,000	7,477,000

CACTUS RAGS, INC.

Cactus Rags, Inc., with headquarters in Santa Fe, New Mexico operates retail department stores, along with internet sales for designer, southwestern clothes. The stores offer a large range of quality clothes and other merchandise for men, women, and children, with boutique stores in 20 states in the United States. As a financial consultant for small businesses with Sun Best, a major small business lender in the region, the CEO, Skip Wescott, and President, Sharon Curran have asked you to do a liquidity/profitability analysis including preparing an indirect cash flow statement and financial ratios, and to evaluate ratio trends based on year-end figures each year for the company.

Answer the following specific questions for your analysis:

1   Do a sources and uses and indirect cash flow statement for 2015.

 Hint: Be careful for cash flow from investing; you'll note that there is a decline in net property and equipment, so be sure to put that as a negative under cash flow from investing plus your 2015 depreciation expense equals change in gross fixed assets.

2   Discuss the reasons why the CFO on your indirect cash flow statement differs from net income for the current year. Also, discuss the major sources and uses of cash shown by the entire cash flow statement. What does the statement reveal about any changes in the firm's liquidity and solvency risk over the year?

3   Using end of year figures for each year, do a liquidity and bankruptcy trend analysis by calculating and evaluating the trends for the two years for the current ratio, quick ratio, net working capital to sales, days inventory held, days sales outstanding, days payables outstanding, operating cycle, cash conversion period, and net liquidity balance (cash balance less notes payable) for each year. Also evaluate trends in bankruptcy risk by analyzing trends for the two years in total debt to assets, long-term debt to assets, and times interest earned.

4   Do a Dupont Analysis analyzing trends in ROE and ROA and their components (NPM, AU, and EM). Go further to analyze the GPM and OPM to explain any changes in NPM, and then to analyze trends for the days inventory, days AR, and fixed asset turnover to explain any changes in AU.

5   Give a summary of your overall assessment of the firm in terms of its strengths and weaknesses from a liquidity, solvency, and profitability standpoint based on your previous analysis. Also, give any suggestions for improvement.

6   If Cactus Rags requested a seasonal working capital loan from Sun Best Bank, what would be the pros and cons for making the loan? What restrictive covenants should be placed on the loan to protect the bank's interests if the loan is made?

Cactus Rags, Inc. financial statements ($ thousand)

Income statement

	Current year	Previous year
Total revenue	25,003,000	23,489,000
Cost of revenue	14,824,000	13,973,000
Gross profit	10,179,000	9,516,000

(Continued)

Appendix B

(Continued)

Income statement

	Current year	Previous year
Expenses		
Selling, general and administration	7,135,000	6,875,000
Depreciation expense	1,125,000	1,187,000
Non-recurring expenses	25,000	391,000
Total expenses	8,285,000	8,453,000
Operating income	1,894,000	1,063,000
Other income	5,000	6,000
Earnings before interest and tax	1,899,000	1,069,000
Interest expense	579,000	562,000
Earnings before taxes	1,320,000	507,000
Income tax expense	473,000	178,000
Net income	847,000	329,000
Dividend paid	84,000	84,000
Addition to retained earnings	763,000	245,000

Balance sheets ($ thousand)

	Current year	Previous year
Assets		
Cash and equivalents	1,464,000	1,686,000
Accounts receivable	392,000	358,000
Inventory	4,758,000	4,615,000
Other current assets	285,000	223,000
Total current assets	6,899,000	6,882,000
Net property, plant, and equipment	13,732,000	14,418,000
Total assets	20,631,000	21,300,000
Liabilities and equity		
Accounts payable	4,611,000	4,220,000
Notes payable	454,000	242,000
Total current liabilities	5,065,000	4,462,000
Long-term debt	10,036,000	12,185,000
Total debt	15,101,000	16,647,000
Common stock	2,540,000	2,426,000
Retained earnings	2,990,000	2,227,000
Total equity	5,530,000	4,653,000
Total debt and equity	20,631,000	21,300,000

Mini Financial Institution Analysis Cases

INSURED BEST INTERNATIONAL

A major international insurance firm, Insured Best International is having a financial review of its financial statements for the current and previous year, and as a financial analyst for the company, you have been asked to do the review. The financial statements for the company are shown below with all of its global insurance company operations consolidated.

For the review you are asked to:

1   Evaluate the trends in the financial statements, and also calculate and evaluate trends in the (a) net underwriting margin; (b) expense ratio; (c) loss ratio; (d) combined ratio; (e) investment yield; and (f) overall profitability ratio.
2   Calculate the firm's return on equity (ROE), return on assets (ROA), the net profit margin (NPM), the asset utilization (AU), and the equity multiplier (EM), and do a Dupont Analysis of the trends for the two years.
3   Explain why the firm's profitability changed in the current year based on your analysis. Summarize any strengths and weaknesses of the firm based on your evaluation of these trends and give suggestions for improvement.

Insured Best financial statements ($ thousand)

Income statements

	Current year	Previous year
Average investment yield	3.8%	4.5%
Revenues		
Gross written premiums	50,998	54,781
Less premiums ceded reinsurers	(8,078)	(6,101)
Net written premiums	42,920	48,680

(Continued)

Appendix C   (Continued)

Income statements

	Current year	Previous year
Less change in reserves for unearned premiums	(296)	(359)
Net earned premiums	42,624	48,321
Other related revenues	2,786	2,791
Net investment income grp investments	7,462	9,211
Net investment results-unit-linked investments.	6,238	10,784
Net gain/loss on divestments of businesses	10	(259)
Other income	1,448	1,723
Total nonpremium revenue	17,944	24,250
Total revenues	60,568	72,571
Benefits, losses and expenses		
Insurance benefits, losses and expenses		
Gross of reinsurance	36,076	37,452
Less ceded insurance losses	(5,330)	(3,088)
Net insurance losses (net of reinsurance)	30,746	34,364
Policyholder dividends, net of reinsurance	7,863	12,568
Underwriting and policy acquisition costs (net of reinsurance)	9,061	9,835
Administration and other operating expense	8,659	8,858
Total policyholder expenses	25,583	31,261
Total expenses before interest expense	56,329	65,625
Interest expense on debt	431	525
Interest credited to policyholders and other	467	523
Total benefits, losses and expenses	57,227	66,673
Net income before income taxes	3,341	5,898
Income tax expense	(1,294)	(1,670)
Net income after taxes	2,047	4,228

Balance sheets

	Current year	Previous year
Assets		
Investments for group contracts:		
Cash and cash equivalents	8,159	7,600
Equity securities	18,873	16,099
Debt securities	137,730	153,648
Investment property	9,865	8,784
Mortgage loans	7,024	7,826

Other loans	9,569	10,834
Investments in associates and joint ventures	18	70
Investments for unit-linked contracts	126,728	134,416
Total investments	*317,966*	*339,277*
Reinsurers share of reserves for insurance contracts	17,774	16,550
Deposits made under assumed reinsurance contracts	1,708	2,203
Deferred policy acquisition costs	17,677	17,750
Deferred origination costs	506	595
Accrued investment income	1,727	1,912
Receivables and other assets	14,930	16,946
Deferred tax assets	1,455	1,561
Assets held for sale	10	48
Property and equipment	1,140	1,273
Attorney-in-fact contracts	1,025	1,025
Goodwill	1,289	1,661
Other intangible assets	4,765	5,728
Total noninvestment assets	*64,006*	*67,252*
Total assets	*381,972*	*406,529*
Liabilities		
Reserve for premium refunds	537	606
Liabilities for investment contracts	70,627	70,813
Deposits received under ceded reinsurance contracts	903	1,022
Deferred front-end fees	5,299	5,539
Reserves for insurance contracts	237,622	243,719
Obligations to repurchase securities	1,596	1,451
Accrued liabilities	2,849	3,065
Other liabilities	15,051	17,230
Deferred tax liabilities	4,498	5,020
Senior debt	4,471	5,379
Subordinated debt	5,614	5,857
Total liabilities	*349,069*	*369,700*
Equity		
Share capital	3,256	4,854
Net unrealized gain on available for sale investments	2,556	4,068
Cash flow hedges	294	306
Cumulative foreign currency translation adjustment	(9,347)	(6,313)

(Continued)

Appendix C

(Continued)

Balance sheets

	Current year	Previous year
Revaluation reserve	228	218
Retained earnings	34,192	31,602
Noncontrolling interests	1,724	2,094
Total equity	*32,903*	*36,829*
Total liabilities and equity	*381,972*	*406,529*

T. ROWE PRICE GROUP

T. Rowe Price is a global investment management firm with $764.6 billion in assets under management in 2016. In 2016, T. Rowe Price was named one of Fortune Magazine's World's Most Admired Companies, and the founder Thomas Rowe Price Jr. created a firm "with a reputation for the highest character and the soundest investment philosophy" with values of "put clients first, act with integrity, cultivate intellectual curiosity, embrace differences and collaboration, apply disciplined thinking and process," and "pursue excellence with passion and humility" (T. Rowe Price Website, "About." Accessed on June 11, 2016 at: https://www3. troweprice.com/usis/corporate/en/about.html).

    T. Rowe Price provides products for personal investing including mutual funds, brokerage services, advisory planning services, and tax planning, managing workplace retirement plans, institutional investor investing, institutional consultant services, financial adviser/intermediary services, and record-keeping/consultant services, among others.

    As a financial institution investor analyst, you are asked to do a Dupont Analysis using the financial statements provided in the annual report for T. Rowe Price in 2015 (available on its website under TROW Investor Relations at: http://trow.client.shareholder.com/annuals-proxies.cfm). The consolidated income statements are provided below. Do a trend profitability analysis for the two years, calculating return on equity, return on assets, asset utilization, net profit margin, and equity multiplier for each year, and analyzing the trends for 2014 and 2015. Also, do a quick overview liquidity and solvency analysis calculating the current ratio and total debt to total assets ratio.

T. Rowe Price Group financial statements ($ million)

Consolidated statements of income

	2014	2015
Revenues		
Investment advisory fees	3,464.5	3,687.3
Administrative fees	374.0	361.8
Distribution and servicing fees	143.6	151.5
Net revenues	3,982.1	4,200.6
Operating expenses		
Compensation and related costs	1,329.6	1,443.6
Advertising and promotion	76.0	79.7
Distribution and servicing costs	143.6	151.5
Depreciation and amortization of property and equipment	111.7	126.3
Occupancy and facility costs	143.9	159.2
Other operating expenses	286.4	341.4
Total operating expenses	2,091.2	2,301.7
Net operating income	1,890.9	1,898.9

(Continued)

Appendix C   (Continued)

Consolidated statements of income

	2014	2015
Non-operating investment income	112.2	103.5
Income before taxes	2,003.1	2,002.4
Provision for income taxes	773.5	779.4
Net income	1,229.6	1,223.0

Consolidated balance sheets

	2014	2015
Assets		
Cash and cash equivalents	1,506.1	1,172.3
Accounts receivable and accrued revenue	442.8	446.0
Investments in sponsored funds	1,884.0	1,612.3
Other investments	408.3	406.6
Net property and equipment	586.4	607.1
Goodwill	665.7	665.7
Other assets	151.1	196.9
Total assets	5,644.4	5,106.9
Liabilities and stockholders' equity		
Liabilities		
Accounts payable and accrued expenses	143.4	170.6
Accrued compensation and related costs	82.2	153.1
Income taxes payable	23.6	21.2
Total liabilities	249.2	344.9
Equity		
Common stock	808.7	704.7
Retained earnings	4,450.1	3,970.7
Accumulated other comprehensive income	136.4	86.6
Total stockholders' equity	5,395.2	4,762.0
Total liabilities and equity	5,644.4	5,106.9

LEGG MASON, INC.

Legg Mason, Inc. is a prominent global asset management firm, headquartered in Baltimore, Maryland that was founded in 1899, and has been a public company for over 32 years, with 3,000 employees and 31 offices worldwide on six continents. Legg Mason serves both institutional and individual investors with over $671 billion in assets under management. Legg Mason's products include mutual funds, managed accounts, closed-end funds, 529 college savings plans, money market funds, and variable managed investments (including managed portfolios, such as the ClearBridge Variable Aggressive Growth Portfolio seeking long-term, capital appreciation with a "high conviction portfolio of companies offering new or innovative technologies, products and services" with a stock selection process that looks for companies with strong fundamentals, and skilled and committed management teams) (see: https://www.leggmason.com/en-us/products/variable-investments.html). Legg Mason has also been engaged in environmental, social and governance (ESG) strategies since 1987.

As a financial analysis for an investment firm that focuses on financial institutions, you are asked to do an overview of the consolidated balance sheet and income statements for Legg Mason, published in Legg Mason's annual report for 2015 (https://ww2.leggmason.com/annualreport/) with its consolidate balance sheets and income statements, shown in the annual report as of March 21, 2015 and March 21, 2014.

You are requested to do a Dupont Analysis for the firm and review changes in balance sheet composition and income statement changes that occurred for the two years. Using the Dupont Analysis, explain why the return on equity, and return on assets changed in 2015 from 2014. Also, review changes in the firm's net interest margin for the two years (interest income less interest expense) as a percentage of total assets. Also, do a solvency and liquidity trend analysis.

Legg Mason, Inc. financial statements ($ thousand)

Consolidated statements of income for 2015 and 2014

	2015	2014
Operating revenues		
Investment advisory fees:		
Separate accounts	824,211	777,420
Funds	1,544,494	1,501,278
Performance fees	83,519	107,087
Distribution and service fees	361,188	347,598
Other	5,694	8,374
Total operating revenues	2,819,106	2,741,757
Operating expenses		
Compensation and benefits	1,232,770	1,210,387
Distribution and servicing	594,788	619,070
Communications and technology	182,438	157,872
Occupancy	109,708	115,234
Amortization of intangible assets	2,625	12,314

(Continued)

Appendix C   (Continued)

Consolidated statements of income for 2015 and 2014

	2015	2014
Other	198,558	195,987
Total operating expenses	2,320,887	2,310,864
Operating income	498,219	430,893
Other nonoperating income (expense)		
Interest income	7,440	6,367
Interest expense	(58,274)	(52,911)
Other income (expense), net, including debt extinguishment losses	(85,280)	32,818
Other nonoperating income (expense) of consolidated investment vehicles, net	5,888	2,474
Total nonoperating income (expense)	(130,226)	(11,252)
Income (loss) before income tax provision	367,993	419,641
Income tax provision	125,284	137,805
Net income	242,709	281,836
Less net income attributable to controlling interests (plus if negative)	5,629	(2,948)
Net income attributable to Legg Mason	237,080	284,784

Consolidated balance sheets

	2015	2014
Assets		
Current assets		
Cash and equivalents	669,552	858,022
Cash and equivalents of consolidated investment vehicles	2,808	56,372
Restricted cash	32,114	13,455
Receivables		
Investment advisory and related fees	368,399	348,633
Other	118,850	68,186
Investment securities	454,735	467,726
Investment securities of consolidated investment vehicles	48,000	50,463
Deferred income taxes	169,706	186,147
Other	51,750	47,677
Other assets of consolidated investment vehicles	6,121	31,910
Total current assets	1,922,035	2,128,591
Fixed assets, net	179,606	189,241

Intangible assets, net	3,313,334	3,171,773
Goodwill	1,339,510	1,240,523
Investments of consolidated investment vehicles		31,810
Deferred income taxes	161,978	165,705
Other	157,514	183,706
Total assets	7,073,977	7,111,349
Liabilities and stockholder's equity		
Current liabilities		
Accrued compensation	400,245	425,466
Accounts payable and accrued expenses	208,210	214,819
Current portion of long-term debt		438
Contingent consideration	22,276	
Other	177,879	91,586
Debt and other current liabilities of consolidated investment vehicles	6,436	88,936
Total current liabilities	815,046	821,245
Deferred compensation	51,706	49,618
Deferred income taxes	362,209	265,583
Contingent consideration	88,508	29,553
Other	167,998	136,656
Long-term debt	1,058,089	1,038,826
Total long-term liabilities	1,728,510	1,520,236
Total liabilities	2,543,556	2,341,481
Commitments and contingencies		
Redeemable noncontrolling interests		
Consolidated investment vehicles	38,498	43,328
Affiliate management equity plan interest	7,022	1,816
Total redeemable noncontrolling interests	45,520	45,144
Stockholders' equity		
Common stock (par and additional paid in capital)	2,855,588	3,160,113
Employee stock trust	(29,570)	(29,922)
Deferred compensation employee stock trust	29,570	29,922
Retained earnings	1,690,055	1,526,662
Accumulated other comprehensive income, net	(60,742)	37,949
Total stockholders' equity	4,484,901	4,724,725
Total liabilities and stockholders' equity	7,073,977	7,111,349

CALVERT INVESTMENTS

Calvert Investments, a global leader in responsible investing in the United States, with the mission "to deliver superior long-term performance to our clients and enable them to achieve positive impact" (see: http://www.calvert.com/about-us). Calvert as a socially responsible investment firm offers products that include mutual funds, management of separate accounts, separately managed accounts, and variable portfolios, offering socially responsible equity, fixed income, multi-asset, index, and actively managed mutual funds.

Calvert also is active in research and corporate social engagement, including proxy voting, corporate engagement, and shareholder resolutions submitted to companies for, and public policy initiatives to get, corporations to make positive changes related to environmental, social, and governance (ESG) issues, including getting companies to establish certain commitments and make positive progress within each industry. Calvert is also active in public policy initiatives, such as in actively encouraging governments to take on a policy of setting a price on carbon and limits on greenhouse gas emissions to reduce climate change risk and promote innovations to speed up the transition for a low-carbon economy

A defined contribution pension fund is developing mutual fund choices for its employees to invest their employer and employee contributions in. The human resources administrator for the company with the defined contribution plan would like you to research Calvert Investments and the firm's investment philosophy and investment strategies and approach and do a report on the fund's investment strategies and products (that can be accessed at www.calvert.com).

Listed below is a summary of "The Calvert Principles for Responsible Investment" from the Calvert Investment website at: http://www.calvert.com/NRC/literature/documents/TL10194.pdf (accessed on June 12, 2016).

The Calvert Principles for Responsible Investment

Overview statement: "We believe that most corporations deliver a net benefit to society, through their products and services, creation of jobs and the sum of their behaviors. As a responsible investor, Calvert seeks to invest in companies that provide positive leadership in the areas of their business operations and overall activities that are material to improving societal outcomes, including those that will affect future generations."

The principle statement also points out that:

1 Calvert seeks out companies for investment that balance the needs of both financial and nonfinancial stakeholders and that show a commitment to global welfare as well as the rights of individuals and communities.
2 Calvert's principles for responsible investment are used to guide Calvert Investments' selection of companies for both all indexed investment strategies and for its actively managed strategies.
3 Calvert's stewardship on behalf of its clients extends to active engagement with the companies that are held in its portfolios, conforming with Calvert's proxy voting guidelines.

Calvert also has three areas listed in the Calvert Principles for Responsible Investment that include:

1 *Advancing environmental sustainability and resource efficiency* (reducing negative environmental impacts of operations; managing water scarcity and efficient and equitable access to clean sources of water; mitigating the impacts on different types of natural capital; reducing carbon emissions and climate-related risks; innovation in sustainability and resource efficiency with new products and services and operations).
2 *Contributing to equitable societies and respecting human rights* (respectful, ethical marketing of products and services to consumers; integrity in customer relationships; security for sensitive data on consumers; respecting local communities' culture and traditions and economies, and the rights of indigenous peoples).
3 *Accountable governance and building transparency* (acting in shareholders' best interests; accountable governance and effective boards that reflect expertise and diverse perspectives; oversight for sustainability risk and opportunities; integration of environmental and social risks and impacts in financial disclosures; lifting ethical standards in all operations and dealings; transparency and accountability in addressing adverse events; trust building and minimization of risks.

These represent positive screens for investments. Calvert also notes negative screens based on the application of these principles including avoiding investments in corporations that:

1 Demonstrate poor environmental performance or compliance, contribute to local or global environmental problems, or have risks related to the operation of nuclear power facilities.
2 Are subject to critical labor-related actions or regulatory penalties or have a pattern of employing forced, compulsory, or child labor.
3 Show a pattern and practice of human rights violations or are directly involved in human rights violations that are committed by government or security forces, including those under U.S. or international sanction for "grave human rights abuses."
4 Show a pattern and the practice of violation of the protections and rights of indigenous peoples.
5 Show poor corporate governance or engagement of unethical or harmful business practices.
6 Manufacture tobacco products.
7 Have direct and significant involvement in manufacturing alcoholic beverages or gambling operations.
8 Manufacture or sell firearms and/or ammunition.
9 Manufacture, design or sell weapons or their critical components violating international humanitarian law or manufacture, design or sell "inherently offensive weapons" as defined under the Treaty on Conventional Armed Forces in Europe and the U.N. Register on Conventional Arms, "or the munitions designed for use in such inherently offensive weapons."
10 Abuse animals, including causing unnecessary suffering and death, or where a company's operations exploit or mistreat animals.
11 Develop genetically modified organisms (GMOs) for environmental release that do not have countervailing social benefits.

(Source: "The Calvert Principles for Responsible Investment," Calvert Investments. Accessed on June 12, 2016 at: http://www.calvert.com/ approach/how-we-invest/the-calvert-principles).

For your report, be sure to research the www.calvert.com website (accessed September 12, 2016) and review the different areas: Perspectives, Strategies, Our Approach, and Resources. Under strategies look under various categories of funds, and click on different types of mutual funds, such as index strategies listed for different funds.

Using this information, which particular mutual funds would you recommend as being worth investigation to include as a socially responsible mutual fund investment choice, based on performance and expenses, for defined contribution investors. Explain why you would select these funds. You'll notice when you click on a fund, you can also see how a fund compares based on a similar Russell or Lipper fund index. On a 1-year, 3-year, 5-year, and 10-year performance comparison, how do the funds you selected compare to the Russell or Lipper fund index.

Discuss the pros and cons of investing in a SRI fund in your report.

CITI'S GLOBAL CITIZENSHIP REPORT

Incorporating the principles of sustainability into everything we do improves our own operations, enhances our clients' work, and contributes to a better world.

(Corbat, 2015)

Betsy Morris, CEO and President of the Texas Best Bank in Austin, Texas, would like the bank to publish a corporate, social governance or sustainability report. She has asked you to review sustainability reports for different financial institutions to see how the bank can engage in corporate citizenship and sustainability activities. In particular, she has selected the sustainability report that Citigroup Inc. or Citi, a leading global bank issued in 2015 at: http://www.citigroup.com/citi/about/citizenship/download/2015/global/2015-citi-global-citizenship-report-en.pdf (accessed September 12, 2016).

The Citi Global Citizenship Report includes different sections on strategy, conduct, culture and governance, trust, inclusive cities, financing development, human rights, sustainability, diversify, workforce and talent, the Citi Foundation, and the GRI Index and UN Global Compact. Betsy was particularly impressed with the financing development section where partnerships for financing solutions were emphasized, including Citi's 44 microfinance institutions in 25 countries that reached 1.2 million entrepreneurs, for a decade long partnership of Citi with the U.S. government's Overseas Private Investment Corporation. For sustainability, the report points out a 5-year road-map which includes aligning Citi's corporate strategy to create value for the company and for future generations by using a materiality assessment that is focused specifically on sustainability issues, including identifying climate change, sustainable cities, and people and communities as top priority.

Activities that are tackling these issues include three areas:

1 *Environmental finance:* Advising on and financing projects that focus on environmental and climate change solutions.
2 *Environmental and social risk management (ESRM):* Assisting clients in understanding and managing risks of their businesses that impact the environment and communities.
3 *Operations and supply chain:* Citi's management of its operations and supply chain to minimize direct environmental impacts, reduce costs, and exhibit best practices.

The report notes that Citi has an environmental finance goal to lend, invest and facilitate $100 billion over 10 years for environmental solutions and activities to reduce the impact of climate change. In 2015 highlights included participating in $47.6 billion in environmental finance activities towards the $100 billion environmental finance goal, developing a new coal mining standard committed to reducing Citi's credit exposure, achieving a stretch goal of reducing Scope 1 and 2 greenhouse gas (GHG) emissions by 25% without using carbon offsets, and having over 675 suppliers complete Citi's corporate responsibility questionnaire.

Betsy asks you to do a report on other aspects of Citi's sustainability report, including more information on its environmental finance goal and how it defines impact criteria, identifies innovative projects, and measures potential environmental and social impacts. Also, she would like you to give an overview of the report's environmental and social risk management (ESRM), the company's portfolio-level reviews of sectors important to Citi's business that fall into a higher risk category, and their report on their implementation to the Equator

Principles. Also, discuss the operations and supply chain section of the sustainability report and Citi's role in this area. What is meant by Citi's science-based goals for reducing its GHG emissions by 35% by 2020 and 80% by 2050. Discuss Citi's progress on meeting its goals. Briefly give a summary of other areas of the Citi global citizenship report. Also, discuss the benefits for a financial institution in having a sustainability or full global citizenship report from the perspective of customers, reducing costs, and reputation building perspectives.

Find another financial institution's social responsibility or sustainability report, such as that for Wells Fargo in 2015. How do its sustainability goals differ based on the focus of that institution? How have costs been reduced through sustainability and other social responsibility activities and how have employees benefitted?

JPMORGAN CHASE & CO.

JPMorgan Chase is one of the largest global financial services companies and one of the largest asset and wealth managers in the world with assets under management over $1.71 trillion. JPMorgan Chase is a diversified financial firm engaged in multinational banking in consumer and community banking, corporate and investment banking, commercial banking, and asset management and wealth management services and is classified as a money center bank with diversified financial services

As a financial analyst for a major internet financial advice firm, you are asked to do a brief financial analysis overview article for JPMorgan Chase for trends for 2014 to 2015 based on the JPMorgan Chase Annual Report 2015 (accessed on June 12, 2016 at: https://www.jpmorganchase.com/corporate/investor-relations/document/2015-annualreport.pdf).

Do a Dupont Analysis for JPMorgan Chase, analyzing changes in ROE, ROA, asset turnover, net profit margin, net interest margin, and equity multipliers for each year. Also, look at balance sheet changes and analyze how diversified JPMorgan Chase is in its operations. Explain any strengths and weaknesses revealed in your overview analysis. For the article you are writing, the consolidated income statements and balance sheets are shown below from the annual report. Discuss the pros and cons of being a mega-diversified financial services firm. What advantages does JPMorgan Chase have by being a global diversified financial services firm specifically, and what disadvantages?

JPMorgan Chase financial statements ($ million)

Income statements

	2015	2014
Revenues		
Investment banking fees	6,751	6,542
Principal transactions	10,408	10,531
Lending and deposit-related fees	5,694	5,801
Asset management administration and commissions	15,509	15,931
Securities gains	202	77
Mortgage fees and related income	2,513	3,563
Card income	5,924	6,020
Other income	3,032	3,013
Noninterest revenue	50,033	51,478
Net interest revenue (includes net of interest expenses)	43,510	43,634
Total net revenue	93,543	95,112

(Continued)

Appendix C

(Continued)

Income statements

	2015	2014
Expenses		
Provision for credit losses	3,827	3,139
Noninterest expenses		
Compensation expense	29,750	30,160
Occupancy expense	3,768	3,909
Technology, communication and equipment	6,193	5,804
Professional and outside services	7,002	7,705
Marketing	2,708	2,550
Other	9,593	11,146
Total noninterest expense	59,014	61,274
Earnings before income tax expense	30,702	30,699
Income tax expense	6,260	8,954
Net income	24,442	21,745

Consolidated balance sheet ($ million)

	2015	2014
Assets		
Cash and due from banks	20,490	27,831
Deposits with banks	340,015	484,477
Fed Funds sold and securities purchased under resale agreements	215,575	215,803
Securities borrowed	98,721	110,435
Trading assets		
Debt and equity instruments	284,162	320,013
Derivative receivables	59,677	78,975
Securities	290,827	348,004
Gross loans	837,299	757,336
Allowance for loan losses	(13,555)	(14,185)
Net loans after allowance	823,744	743,151
Accrued interest and accounts receivable	46,605	70,079
Premises and equipment	14,362	15,133
Goodwill	47,325	47,647
Mortgage servicing rights 6,608	7,436	
Other intangible assets	1,015	1,192

Other assets	105,572	102,098
Total assets	2,351,698	2,572,274
Liabilities		
Deposits	1,279,715	1,363,427
Fed Funds purchases and securities loans or sold under repurchase agreements	152,678	192,101
Commercial paper	15,562	66,344
Other borrowed funds	21,105	30,222
Trading liabilities		
Debt and equity instruments	74,107	81,699
Derivative payables	52,790	71,116
Accounts payable and other liabilities	177,638	206,939
Beneficial interests issued by consolidated variable interest entities ("VIES")	41,879	52,320
Long-term debt	288,651	276,379
Total liabilities	2,104,125	2,340,547
Stockholders' equity	247,573	231,727
Total liabilities and stockholders' equity	2,351,698	2,572,274

REFERENCE

Corbat, Michael L. (2015). Chief Executive Officer, at Sustainable Progress launch event, February 16. 2015 Citi Global Citizenship Report, Sustainability, 7.1. Accessed on June 12, 2016 at: http://www.citigroup.com/citi/about/citizenship/download/2015/global/2015-citi-global-citizenship-report-en.pdf

Text Chapter Mapping: Harvard Business School Publishing Cases

HARVARD Business School Publishing (HBSP) has interesting cases available on topics related to each module and chapter, including cases and articles by Harvard Business School, Ivey Publishing, Darden Business School, Stanford Business School, and INSEAD, among others. Detailed descriptions can be found on the Harvard Business Publishing Website (https://cb.hbsp.harvard.edu).

PART 1: OVERVIEW FINANCIAL SERVICES INDUSTRY AND ITS ENVIRONMENT

Module I: The Financial Services Industry: Today and the Future

Chapter 1: Financial Institutions as Social Value Creators and Financial Risk Takers

Overview
The Great Recession, 2007–2010: Causes and Consequences
Danielle Cadieux and David W. Conklin
Publication date: Jan. 15, 2010
Ivey Publishing, 910M98-PDF-ENG, 11 pages

Case
Restoring Institutional Trust: A Systemic Approach
Nicole Gillespie, Robert Hurley, Graham Dietz, and Reinhard Bachmann
Publication date: Sep. 01, 2012
Rotman Management Magazine, ROT176-PDF-ENG, 5 pages

Case
Weathering the Financial Crisis in Iceland: Landsbanki Islands
David Beim
Publication date: Jul. 16, 2012
Columbia Business School, CU26-PDF-ENG, 29 pages

Module II: Financial Markets, Interest Rates, and Their Regulatory Environment

Chapter 2: Interest Rates: Theories and Duration as an Overall Risk Measure

Chapter 3: The New Regulatory Environment and the Regulatory Dialectic

Bank planning for new regulations
Deutsche Bank and the Road to Basel III
Yiorgos Allayannis, Gerry Yemen, Andrew C. Wicks, and Matthew Dougherty
Publication/revision date: Oct. 21, 2013
Darden School of Business, UV6662-PDF-ENG, 20 pages

Financial institutions addressing the Dodd–Frank Act
JPMorgan and the Dodd–Frank Act
Yiorgos Allayannis and Adam Risell, Publication/revision date: Mar. 13, 2012
Darden School of Business, UV5660-PDF-ENG, 13 pages

The Dodd–Frank Act and Its Impact
Yiorgos Allayannis and Adam Risell
Publication/revision date: Mar. 05, 2012
Darden School of Business, UV5662-PDF-ENG, 15 pages

PART 2: PERFORMANCE AND RISK ANALYSIS FOR FIS AND ESG CONSIDERATIONS

Module III: Risk and Financial Analysis of Financial Institutions

Chapter 4: Financial Performance and Risk Analysis

Credit Union Acquisition Case
Blue Ocean or Stormy Waters? Buying Nix Check Cashing
Peter Tufano and Andrea Ryan
Publication/revision date: Jul. 31, 2009
Harvard Business School, 210012-PDF-ENG, 28 pages

Savings Association
Canada Wide Savings, Loan and Trust Company
David C. Shaw
Publication/revision date: Jul 09, 2012
Ivey Publishing, W12435-PDF-ENG, 11 pages

Chapter 5: Capital Management

Module IV: Environmental, Social, & Governance (ESG) for FIs

Chapter 6: Social and Environmental Risks and Sustainable Financial Institutions

Social Banking: HBR Article
Collaborating with Congregations: Opportunities for Financial Services in the Inner City
Larry Fondation, Peter Rufano, and Patricia Walker
Publication date: Jul. 01, 1999
Harvard Business Review, 99404-PDF-ENG, 8 pages

Socially Responsible Investing and Shareholder Activism
Doing Right, Investing Right: Socially Responsible Investing and Shareholder Activism in the Financial Sector
Chang Hoon Oh, Jae-Heum Park, and Pervez N. Ghauri
Publication date: Nov.–Dec., 2013
Business Horizons, Article, BH566-PDF-ENG, 12 pages

Financing an Environmental Project:
Windhoek Nature Reserve: Financing a Sustainable Conservation Model in Namibia
Peter Hecht, Brooke Parry Hecht, and Kavita Kapur MacLeod
Publication date: Mar. 04, 2005
Harvard Business School, 205066-PDF-ENG, 11 pages

PART 3: MANAGING FI RISKS

Module V: Managing Interest Rate and Foreign Exchange Risks

Chapter 7: International Markets, Foreign FX Risks, & Hedging FX Risk

Case on Central Bank Policies for a Small Open Economy in a Global World
Dealing with Capital Flows: Thailand in 2006
Wei Li
Publication date: Mar. 13, 2007
Darden School of Business, UVO765-PDF-ENG, 12 pages

Chapter 8: Hedging Interest Rate Risk with Derivatives

Overview Using Derivatives for Asset and Liability Management
Banc One Corp.: Asset and Liability Management
Peter Tufano and Benjamin C. Esty
Publication date: Jul. 01, 2008
Harvard Business School, 294079-PDF-ENG, 29 pages

PART 4: ASSET AND LIABILITY MANAGEMENT

Module VI: Asset and Liability Management and Innovations

Chapter 9: Loan Analysis, Credit Risk Management, and Loan Securitization

Bank Syndicate Lending
Chase's Strategy for Syndicating the Hong Kong Disneyland Loan (A)
Benjamin C. Esty and Michael Kane
Publication date: Jun. 21, 2013
Harvard Business School, 201072-PDF-ENG, 22 pages

Loan Analysis Case
Covalent: Term Loan for Expansion and Modernization
Maram Srikanth and Palanisamy Saravanan
Publication date: Jun. 17, 2015
Ivey Publishing, W15241-PDF-ENG, 10 pages

Loan Analysis Case
Calaveras Vineyards
Robert F. Bruner
Publication/revision date: Apr. 26, 2016
Darden School of Business, UV0255-PDF-ENG, 23 pages

Loan Securitization Option Case
Fremont Financial Corp. (B)
Erik Sirri and Ann Zeitung
Publication date: Mar. 04, 1994
Harvard Business Review, 294099-PDF-ENG, 9 pages

Loan Securitization, Collateralized Debt Obligations (CDO)
Western Asset Arbitrage
Elena Loutskina and Rahul Prahbu
Publication date: Apr. 23, 2009
Darden School of Business, UV2540-PDF-ENG, 19 pages

Project Finance
An Overview of Project Finance and Infrastructure Finance—2014 Update
Benjamin C. Esty, Carla Chavich, and Aldo Sesia
Publication/revision date: Jul. 29, 2014
Harvard Business School, 214083-PDF-ENG, 42 pages

Other Loan Cases can be found at *Harvard Business Review* https://hbr.org/search?N=0+429
4967293&Ntt=Loan+Cases

Chapter 10: Liquidity and Liability Management

Depository Institution Debt Investments
Note: Fair Value Accounting for Investment in Debt Securities
William E. Fruhan
Publication/revision date: Feb. 28, 2011
Harvard Business School, 209134-PDF-ENG, 6 pages

PART 5: OVERVIEW NON-DEPOSITORY FIS AND NEW FORMS OF FINANCING

Module VII: Contractual Financial Institutions and Mutual Funds

Chapter 11: Insurance Companies: Overview, Operations, and Performance Analysis

Investment Strategy for a Life Insurance Company Adjusting to Market Conditions
New York Life Insurance Company: Adjusting the Investment Portfolio to Market
Conditions
Mary Michel and Janet L. Rovenpor
Publication date: Jun. 01, 2013
North American Case Research Association (NACRA), NA0213-PDF-ENG,
38 pages

Troubled Life Insurance Company
First Capital Holdings Corp.
Stuart C. Gilson, Harry Deangelo, and Linda Deangelo
Publication date: May 17, 1996
Harvard Business School, 296032-PDF-ENG, 19 pages

Chapter 12: Mutual Fund and Pension Management

Mutual Funds
Vanguard Group Inc.—1998
Andre F. Perold

Publication date: Sep. 10, 1998
Harvard Business School, 299002-PDF-ENG, 24 pages

ETF Case: Commodities
The market for Gold: SPDR Gold Shares and Beyond
Yiorgos Allayannis and Pedro Matos
Publication/revision date: Jul. 19, 2013
Darden School of Business, UV6706-PDF-ENG, 22 pages

Hedge Fund Manager Selection
Common Fund Hedge Fund Portfolio
Andre F. Perold and William T. Spitz
Publication date: Dec. 30, 1996
Harvard Business School, 297014-PDF-ENG, 15 pages

Pension Case
The Canada Pension Plan Investment Board: October 2012
Josh Lerner, Matthew Rhodes-Kropf, and Nathaniel Burbank
Publication/revision date: Aug. 14, 2014
Harvard Business School, 813103-PDF-ENG, 27 pages

Endowment Fund Investing
The University of Notre Dame Endowment
Andre F. Perold and Paul Buser
Publication/revision date: Jan. 13, 2010
Harvard Business School, 210007-PDF-ENG, 20 pages

Alternative Asset Investing
Vanderbilt University Endowment (2006)
Andre F. Perold and William T. Spitz
Publication/revision date: Dec. 04, 2007
Harvard Business School, 207062-PDF-ENG, 10 pages

Module VIII: Securities Firms and Venture Capital and Crowdfunding

Chapter 13: Investment Banks and Securities Firms and Dark Pools and High-Frequency Trading

Investment Banking
Goldman Sachs History and Its Reputation
David P. Baron
Publication date: Jan. 01, 2011
Stanford Graduate School of Business, P77-PDF-ENG, 13 pages

Goldman Sachs: Anchoring Standards after the Financial Crisis
Rajiv Lai and Lisa Mazzanti
Publication date: May 01, 2014
Harvard Business School, 514020-PDF-ENG, 35 pages

Events Leading to the Collapse of Bear Stearns
Bear Stearns and the Seeds of Its Demise
Susan Chaplinsky
Publication date: Oct. 22, 2008
Darden School of Business, UV1064-PDF-ENG, 27 pages

Predicting Financial Distress for an Investment Firm
Predicting a Firm's Financial Distress: The Merrill Lynch Co. Statement of Cash Flows
Danielle Morin, Julien Lemaux, and Dominque Hamel
Publication date: May 30, 2012
Ivey Publishing, W12114-PDF-ENG, 14 pages

FinTech: Case on HelloWallet, an Online Financial Guidance Service
HelloWallet
Debra Schifrin and John Beshears
Publication date: Feb. 10, 2011
Stanford Graduate School of Business, F275-PDF-ENG, 15 pages

Chapter 14: Shadow Banking, Finance Companies and Diversified Financial Firms, Venture Capital, Crowdfunding, and Microfinance

Shadow Banking in China
Financial Networks and Informal Banking in China: From Pawnshops to Private Equity
Elizabeth Koll
Publication date: Jan. 16, 2009
Industry and Background Note, 80911-PDF-ENG, 18 pages

Banking Conglomerates
Banco Espirito Santo
Walter Ingo, Alvin Chiang, and Pooja Eppanapally
Publication date: Oct. 26, 2015
INSEAD, IN1110-PDF-ENG, 25 pages

Venture Capital
How Venture Capital Works
Bob Zider and Hal R. Varian
Publication date: Nov. 01, 1998
HBR Article, 98611-PDF-ENG, 9 pages

Venture Capital with Cross Border Investments
WI Harper Strategic Crossroads
George Foster and Patrick Arippol
Publication date: Jun. 06, 2007
Harvard Business Review, E257-PDF-ENG, 35 pages

Initial Public Offering
How I Learned to Live on Wall Street
Safi U. Qureshey
Publication date: May–Jun. 1991 (pp. 46–52)
Harvard Business Review (available at: https://hbr.org/1991/05/how-i-learned-to-live-with-wall-street#), 7 pages

Microfinance Models
Contrasting China's Yuan Model with Bangladesh's Yunus Model for Microfinance
Yuping Du, Randall O. Chang, Meng Wu, and Chun Li
Publication date: Jun. 21, 2013
Ivey Publishing, W13266-PDF-ENG, 9 pages

Microfinance with Venture Capital
SKS Microfinance
Shawn Cole and Theresa Chen
Publication date: Mar. 16, 2009
Harvard Business School, 208137-PDF-ENG, 21 pages

New Business Model: Upscaling to Make Microbanks Profitable
Seeing Profitability Through a Banking Lens
Francesc Prior and Javier Santoma
Publication date: Sep. 15, 2011
IESE-Insight Magazine, IIRO57-PDF-ENG, 5 pages

Journey of Microfinancing in India
Krishna Bhima Samruddhi Local Area Bank (KBSLAB): A Decade Review
Puran Singh, Nupur Pavan Bang, Kaushik Bhattacharjee, and Rajesh Chakrabarti
Publication date: Jun. 30, 2013
Indian School of Business, ISB018-PDF-ENG, 24 pages

Glossary

Accredited investors Accredited investors are investors who are sophisticated financially, which includes earning an individual annual income greater than $200,000 per year or $300,000 jointly with a spouse and having a net worth greater than $1 million (excluding the value of one's residence) as defined by the SEC's Regulation D. Banks, insurance companies, employee benefit plans, and trusts are also accredited investors.

Accumulated loan losses A depository institution's accumulated loan loss reserve account is a cumulative account on a depository institution's balance sheet below gross loans. Accumulated loan losses accumulate provisions for loan losses taken each year by the depository institution (taken as an expense on the institution's income statement) less any net loan losses each year (actual loan losses less recoveries). Net loans are equal to gross loans less accumulated loan losses.

Adjustable rate mortgages (ARMs) An adjustable rate mortgage is a mortgage with a rate of interest that is adjusted for given set periods to reflect changes in a specific benchmark rate used for the loan. ARMs have greater credit risk than fixed-rate loans, since with rises in interest rates and loan payments, a borrower may not be able to make higher future loan payments if interest rates rise.

Advance warning systems Advance warning systems are early warning systems that provide a set of processes for identifying risks at an early stage and strengthen the oversight of a bank's assets. Regulators also have advance warning systems as red flags to identify problem banks.

Adverse selection With adverse selection, there is a higher likelihood that potential customers who are less creditworthy or who have a propensity to take on greater risks are more likely to seek out financial products, such as, respectively, loans and insurance.

Agency costs Agency costs entail any reduction in benefits to owners stemming from contracts governing the separation of ownership and control between principals (owners) and agents (managers) that may have different preferences for taking risk or taking perquisites.

Agency securities Agency securities (bills, notes and bonds) are securities issued by government-sponsored or quasi-government sponsored enterprises (GSEs) (such as Fannie Mae, Freddie Mac, and the Federal Home Loan Bank). Thus, they are low risk debt obligations.

Agency theory Agency theory is a theory of managerial decision making, suggesting that if managers are unmonitored they will engage in their own personal preferences as agents versus the interests of principals (owners).

Algorithmic trading Algorithmic trading entails automated trading systems that utilize advanced mathematical models for making transactions in financial markets, whereby the algorithms built into models provide strict rules to find the optimal time for an order to be placed to prevent a significant impact on a stock's price. For institutional investor trades, large blocks of shares are often divided into smaller amounts and complex algorithms determine when the smaller shares should be sold using automated trading systems.

Alternative strategies funds Alternative or "alt" mutual funds are mutual funds that utilize more nontraditional investments (such as global real estate, commodities, investments in startup firms and unlisted securities and derivatives). Alt funds often utilize financial leverage and engage in more complex trading strategies, taking advantage of opportunities as market conditions change. Often alt funds seek higher returns, while some alt funds aim for greater diversification or the reduction of market volatility as strategies.

American Business Act on Climate Pledge Pledge signed by over 154 U.S. companies with over $7 trillion in market capitalization to take aggressive action against climate change including ambitious company-specific goals.

Amortized loans Amortized loans have equal loan payments each year until a loan is paid off after a given number of periods. Amortized loan payments include interest and principal payments, whereby interest is paid as a percentage of the remaining unpaid loan balance. For each loan payment, any amount greater than the interest portion of the payment goes to repaying the principal of the loan over the life of the loan.

Angel investors Angel investors are accredited investors providing financial backing for entrepreneurial businesses, usually providing mentoring and seed money, often preferring to invest in businesses that they have experience and interest in. Angel groups and network platforms assist startups in finding angels or submitting business plans for anonymous review for potential funding (see Angel Capital Association, for example, at: http://www.angelcapitalassociation.org/directory/).

Annual dividends for insurance companies Some life insurance companies may give customers an annual dividend when the firm's investment return, experience (paid claims), and operating expenses for a particular year are better than expected.

Annuity An annuity is a form of insurance or investment that entitles the investor to a series of equal future payments. Investors usually pay a large lump sum, such as at retirement, for the annuity. Annuities can be fixed rate or variable rate, and may have a minimum guaranteed rate.

Aspen Institute The Aspen Institute is an educational and policy studies organization to foster leadership and education based on enduring values and providing a nonpartisan venue for dealing with critical issues including energy and environment issues, such as climate change risks.

Asset-backed commercial paper (ABCP) Asset-backed commercial paper is a short-term investment security (on average 90–180 days) issued by a financial institution with the notes backed by assets, such as trades receivables for short-term financing needs, with the commercial paper backed by expected cash flows from the receivables, which are passed on to the financial institution or another conduit, which in turn passes funds to the note holders.

Asset-backed securities (ABS) ABS are bonds or notes backed by financial assets, such as credit card receivables, auto loans, home equity loans, or manufactured housing contracts, among others. ABS for investors can be an alternative for investing in corporate debt.

As You Sow As You Sow is a nonprofit organization that promotes environmental and social corporate responsibility through shareholder advocacy, coalition building, and innovative legal strategies, assisting shareholders in environmental and social shareholder proxy resolution campaigns (www.asyousow.org).

Asymmetric information The inequality of information between savers and borrowers and financial institutions given the private nature of financial contracts and for, at times, incomplete information about future prospects of borrowers.

Automated clearing house (ACH) network The automated clearing house network is a batch processing system whereby financial institutions accumulate ACH transactions throughout the day for later batch processing. ACH network transactions, including direct deposits and direct payments, are transmitted electronically with faster processing times and cost savings.

Balance of payments (BOP) The balance of payments are bookkeeping accounts for international receipts and payments that directly affect the movement of funds across nations from private and government transactions. The current account reflects international transactions that involve currently produced goods and services, with the trade balance equal to the net receipts from trade (i.e., difference between exports and imports). The capital account is equal to the net receipts from capital transactions, with flows of capital into (out of) a country registered as receipts (payments). A country has a positive capital account when net capital flows into a country. The net change in a government's international reserves is equal to its current account plus its capital account.

Balanced mutual funds Balanced mutual funds (also called hybrid funds) invest in both stocks and bonds, targeted to investors looking for a mixture of safety, income, and more modest capital appreciation, with often set minimums and maximums for each asset class, and at times based on particular investors' risk tolerance.

Bank for International Settlements (BIS) The BIS is an international organization established in 1930 in Basle, Switzerland by major European banks serving as the coordinator of German reparations after World War II. The BIS evolved into a key manager and supervisor for the international financial system, fostering the cooperation of central banks and international policymakers.

Bank holding company A bank holding company owns or has a controlling interest in one or more banks. A one-bank holding company (OBHC) owns or controls one bank and has other types of financial service firms as subsidiaries, such as an insurance company or investment firm or other types of companies as allowed by regulators. A multi-bank holding company (MBHC) owns or controls several different banks as subsidiaries.

Bank living wills Under the Dodd–Frank Act Rule (DFA Rule) applying to large financial institutions operating in the United States and the Insured Depository Institution (IDI Rule) applying to large depository institutions, large financial institutions that may pose systemic risk to the financial stability of financial markets in the United States must have living wills. These living wills are plans on how these institutions would plan to wind down in the event of a crisis, which regulators must approve as a core requirement.

Bank scenario analysis Bank scenario analysis is the process of analyzing the effect of possible future interest rate and economic events to examine their effects on a bank's balance sheet (in terms of both changes in rates and balance sheet mix and volume) to see the effect on a bank's net interest margin and market value of equity. Different scenarios are often used for best, average and worst case scenarios, often using specialized bank analysis software.

Bank Secrecy Act (BSA) The Bank Secrecy Act, also known as the Currency and Foreign Transactions Reporting Act is a U.S. law requiring banks to have surveillance duties for large cash deposits greater than $10,000, whereby banks must file forms with the U.S. government for large deposits (unless an exemption is submitted for frequent cash depositors such as casinos). Banks must also submit Suspicious Activity forms for questionable activities that could encompass money laundering or illegal activities, and cooperate with the U.S. government for cases suspected for money laundering and fraud.

Bank simulation analysis A simulation analysis for a bank's overall interest rate and earnings risks using a Monte Carlo or other type of simulation that considers mix and volume changes in a depository institution's balance sheet, along with valuation changes and changes in a bank's net interest margin and earnings under different economic and interest rate scenarios.

Bankers' acceptance (BA) A BA is a time draft (promised future payment), which is accepted and guaranteed by a bank and drawn on a deposit at the bank. Companies in international transactions use bankers' acceptances to guarantee payments, and facilitate payments among importers and exports for international trade. Bankers' acceptances are marketable and can be traded on secondary markets prior to maturity at a discount.

Barbell (or split maturity) liquidity strategy A liquidity strategy where, depending on market conditions, investments are held in short-term or long-term maturity ranges. If interest rates are expected to rise, a larger amount of the portfolio would be put in short-term securities to avoid capital losses with rising rates, and if interest rates are expected to fall, a larger amount of the portfolio would be in long-term securities to maximize capital gains. The barbell strategy can generate higher potential returns on investments, but carries more risk of losses, in the event interest rate forecasts are incorrect. A hybrid barbell strategy is less risky by having part of the portfolio held as a ladder approach and part using a barbell approach.

Basel III Under the auspices of the Basel Committee on Banking Supervision, Basel III includes a comprehensive set of reforms measures and capital and liquidity requirements for the improvement of the regulation, supervision, and risk management of international banks. Important provisions include improvements in the ability of the banking system to be able to deal with future financial and economic stress with systematic shocks to the financial system by improving capital and liquidity requirements and strengthening the transparency of the banking system.

Basel III additional Tier 1 capital (AT 1 capital) Under Basel III, additional qualifying capital in addition to core equity capital includes qualifying capital instruments that have no obligation for payment in the event of default with no circumstances under which distributions are obligatory and with no credit-sensitive dividend feature (i.e., dividend/coupon reset periodically based in whole or in part on a bank's current credit standing). Hence, AT 1 capital is included as additional core capital that has a greater ability to be loss absorbing, such as noncumulative perpetual preferred stock or other qualifying instruments.

Basel III core equity Tier 1 capital Core equity Tier 1 capital is a new definition known as CET 1 capital that includes predominantly common stock and retained earnings (undivided profits) with some adjustments.

Basel III Tier 2 capital Tier 2 capital under Basel III includes nonequity capital that is allowed as secondary capital, where the investor has no rights to accelerate payment in the future. The instrument also may not have a credit-sensitive dividend/coupon reset periodically based on a bank's current credit standing and must be subordinate to depositors and general creditors of the bank, often including limited allowance for loan and lease losses and preferred stock and subordinated debt instruments.

Basis point (BPS) A basis point is a commonly used measure in finance to describe the percentage change in the value for the rate of financial instrument, with one basis point equal to 0.01 percent, used primarily for examining differences for interest rates.

Basis risk of futures contracts Basis risk for hedging with futures contracts is the risk of prices on the spot position that is being hedged moving differently from prices on the futures contract that is being used to hedge against a loss on the futures position. If a hedge is done with a different instrument than the spot position to be hedged (i.e., cross-hedging), there is greater basis risk of spot and future prices not moving together.

BIS Principles for Sound Liquidity Risk Management These principles include detailed guidance for large, international banks including: (1) establishing a liquidity risk tolerance; (2) maintaining adequate liquidity, including a cushion of liquid assets; (3) allocating liquidity costs, benefits, and risks to significant business activities; (4) identifying and measuring a full range of liquidity risk, including contingent risks; (5) designing and using stress test scenarios for severe liquidity stress; (6) managing intraday liquidity risk and collateral; and (7) promoting market discipline and public disclosure, among other guidance.

Bitcoin Bitcoin is a digital asset and payment system, that was released in 2009 as an open-source software system, providing a virtual crypto-currency not backed by a government, to allow for direct peer-to-peer transactions that are verified by nodes in a network and are recorded in a distributed ledger known as the blockchain, with Bitcoin as the unit of account.

Bond immunization Bond immunization is an investment strategy to minimize the risk of a bond investment by adjusting the bond or bond portfolio duration to match the investor's investment time horizon to offset both reinvestment and price risk with changes in interest rates.

Bought deal A bought deal is an accepted bond transaction, such as for Eurobonds, whereby an investment bank has not yet had time to develop a syndicate or accessed market interest before submitting a bid.

Bretton Woods Agreement The Bretton Woods Agreement was created after the end of World War II in 1945 at Bretton Woods, New Hampshire, where the agreement was negotiated at the United Nations Monetary and Financial Conference. Under this agreement the U.S. dollar was established as a global currency, and at that time the conversion of U.S. dollars into gold was established initially as one U.S. dollar convertible into gold at $35 per ounce, with the fixed rate maintained by central bank intervention (selling and buying of dollar assets) to keep currencies in line. This created a pegged foreign exchange system. Major outcomes also included the formation of the International Monetary Fund and the International Bank for Reconstruction and Development.

Bridge loan A bridge loan is a short-term loan for temporary financing, before a person or company secures permanent financing, to allow the borrower to meet current obligations by providing cash immediately. Usually bridge loans are short-term up to one year with relatively high interest rates and are backed by some form of collateral.

Brokered deposits Brokered deposits are large denomination deposits that are sold through a broker for banks to customers that desire higher yields, including institutional investors. These deposits are interest rate sensitive, so can leave a bank at any time. In the United States under FDIC rules, only well-capitalized banks are allowed to solicit and may accept brokered deposits. Adequately capitalized banks may accept brokered deposits if they are given a waiver, and undercapitalized banks are not allowed to accept brokered deposits.

Burden A financial institution's burden expense is equal to its noninterest expenses less its noninterest revenues. A financial institution's burden or burden ratio as a percentage of total assets is a measure of a firm's operating efficiency, with a higher burden indicating lower operating efficiency.

CAMELS ratings Bank ratings given to depository institutions by U.S. regulators based on capital quality, asset quality, management quality, earnings quality, liquidity, and interest rate sensitivity.

Capital conservation buffer Under Basel III, large international banks are required to hold a capital conservation buffer to ensure that capital is built up during favorable periods, so that it can be drawn upon later in unfavorable periods when losses may occur. The capital conservation buffer requirement is 2.5%, to be phased in by January 1, 2019, comprised of common equity Tier 1 capital. Regulatory restrictions on capital distributions can be imposed if a capital conservation buffer becomes depleted.

Capital Link Capital Link is a system innovation, made available in 1990, that allows blue chip corporations to issue bonds directly to institutional investors.

Capital risk Capital risk is the risk for a financial institution of losses eroding the value of the firm's capital that can result in being below a regulatory minimum, leading to the closure of the institution.

Captive finance companies Captive finance companies are subsidiaries with the purpose of providing financing to customers that are buying the products of a parent company.

Captive insurance agents Captive insurance agents only work for one insurance company and are paid either with a combination of salary and commissions or with just commissions, who can be a full-time employee or an independent contractor.

Carbon asset risk Carbon asset risk or stranded asset risk is the risk of fossil fuel companies losing value with the transition towards a lower fossil fuel economy to avoid catastrophic climate, with future regulatory restrictions likely to be imposed by governments or a low price for fossil fuels making the use of fossil fuel reserves no longer economical to develop.

Carbon Principles (CP) The Carbon Principles are principles to create best practices for the evaluation of options to meet the electric power needs of the United States in an environmentally responsible and cost-effective manner, with undersigned financial institution signatories using an Environmental Diligence Process when evaluating the financing of new fossil fuel generation from a carbon asset risk perspective.

Carbon Tracker Initiative The Carbon Tracker Initiative is a nonprofit initiative focusing on stranded assets for fossil fuel companies, with large carbon asset reserves that are under threat of becoming stranded with a shift to a low-carbon economy and as governments move to control carbon emissions, creating systemic risks for institutional investors.

Cash to cash cycle (C to C cycle) A firm's cash to cash cycle is a measure of the time operating cash is out of reach for use (i.e., the time from when inventory is purchased to the time it is sold and cash is received from accounts receivables less the time it takes to pay suppliers for the inventory and or accrued expenses). The formula for the cash to cash cycle is generally Days inventory plus Days accounts receivables less Days accounts payable and Accruals. The faster a firm's C to C cycle, the more liquidity it generates and the lower its need for a financing of seasonal working capital.

Cash surrender value Cash surrender value is the amount of funds an insurance company pays a policyholder or annuity holder in the event a policy is voluntarily ended before its maturity or an insured event occurs, whereby the cash value represents usually for permanent life insurance policies, such as whole life policies, as the savings component of the policy (also referred to as the surrender value or policyholder's equity for the policy).

Catastrophe bonds Bonds issued by insurers and reinsurers, with a special purpose reinsurance vehicle (SPRV) created for this purpose. Often these bonds have complex structures and are initiated offshore in locations with favorable regulatory and tax treatment. The SPRV collects premiums from the insurance or reinsurance firm and the principal paid by investors is held in trust in U.S. Treasury securities or other assets that are highly rated. Investment income is used to pay interest on the principal for the bonds. Given their risk, these bonds pay high interest rates. When a trigger event occurs, investors can lose interest and at times the principal based on the bond's structure. These funds are used to cover the insurance company's losses from a disaster. The maturity of a catastrophe bond is often set at three years, but can range from one to several years.

Catastrophe-linked (CAT-linked) securities Catastrophe-linked securities are a mechanism to transfer catastrophe risks to capital markets that allow an additional layer of protection to traditional insurance and reinsurance arrangements, covering risks not currently covered by insurance markets. A CAT bond involves the setting up of a remote special purpose vehicle (SPV) that is backed by collateral provided by an insurance firm. The securities issued by the SPV for a CAT-bond focus on the risk of catastrophic loss for a particular region, such as for hurricanes in Florida. The coupon rate on the bond is set to be greater than the return on the collateral for the bond, with the excess premium from the insurer paying for the excess return. The cash proceeds from the security issuance is invested in high-quality fixed-income investments to generate funds used for payment against claims, and bondholders' yields are conditional on whether the insurance firm has to file claims for loss above an expected point (known as an attachment point).

CDP (formerly the Carbon Disclosure Project) The CDP is an international independent nonprofit organization that collects and provides environmental information on issues including climate change and water use for the purpose of promoting transparency and working towards a more sustainable economy. Data is voluntarily reported by companies and cities on their environmental impact to enable companies and municipalities to reduce their carbon emissions and other negative environmental impacts.

Central banks Central banks in different countries are responsible for the oversight of the monetary system for a nation (or group of nations, such as the European Central Bank). Responsibilities include a wide range including the oversight and implementation of monetary policy and currency stability, ensuring low inflation and full employment. Central banks also issue currency, oversee the banking system, manage exchange rates, serve as a lender of last resort, and ensure an efficient payment system.

Central liquidity facility (CLF) For credit unions (CUs) in the United States, the CLF is an arm of the National Credit Union Administration and functions as a lender of last resort for CUs that voluntarily elect to join it. CLF loans are made for liquidity purposes only, with borrowing CUs paying a 1% commitment fee in addition to interest on borrowings. CUs that are members of a corporate credit union (CCU) may also borrow from the CCU, and CUs that offer transaction deposits or nonpersonal time deposits may borrow from the Fed discount window.

Ceres Ceres is a nonprofit organization that advocates for sustainability leadership, mobilizing a network of investors, companies, and public interest groups to both accelerate and expand the adoption of sustainable business practices and solutions for a healthy global economy. Ceres also supports shareholders for environmental and social proxy resolutions to corporations, including climate change resolutions that underscore material financial risk, and urgency for companies to prepare for a low-carbon transition (see www.ceres.org).

Check Clearing Act for the 21st Century U.S. Act passed in 2004 that makes the payment system more efficient by reducing the legal impediments to check truncation by allowing a new negotiable instrument, a substitute check (i.e., an image replacement document (RD)) that is a magnetic ink character recognition (MICR) encoded paper reproduction of an original check as a legal equivalent of the original check that can be presented in the same manner as a check.

Climate Principles The Climate Principles is an organization launched by a group of major international financial institutions with a global climate change framework to guide best practice across the sector to deal with both the risks and opportunities of climate change. The framework enables financial institutions to show the importance they place on the embedment of climate change considerations into core business strategy and activity and to disclose publicly progress against key indicators.

Closed-end mutual funds Mutual funds that are publicly traded, whereby a fixed number of shares for a fund trade over the counter or on a stock exchange. Once closed-end funds are issued, they are sold in public markets at their current market value just like stocks. As publicly traded funds, closed-end funds can trade below their net asset value and have brokerage commissions.

CME Group Inc. The CME Group is a U.S. futures company and globally among the largest options and futures exchanges, with futures exchanges in Chicago and New York City and online trading platforms. The CME group was formed with a 2007 merger of the Chicago Mercantile Exchange (CME) and the Chicago Board of Trade (CBOT), and in 2008 the CME also acquired NYMEX Holdings, the parent company of the NY Mercantile Exchange and Commodity Exchange, Inc. (COMEX). The four exchanges operate now as designated contract markets (DCM) of the CME Group.

Collateral Collateral is used with asset-based lending to secure a loan, where the property or other assets to secure the loan are matched with the use for the loan. If a borrower stops making the promised loan payments, the lender can take the collateral to recoup its losses.

Collateralized debt obligations (CDOs) CDOs are structured financial products that are backed by a pool of loans, such as mortgages, bonds and loans, serving as collateral for the CDO, with different tranches created for different investor profiles.

Collateralized mortgage obligations (CMOs) CMOs are securities created from mortgage pass-through securities with more favorable characteristics than plain vanilla pass-through mortgage securities. CMOs can be packaged into several classes (tranches) of securities with different characteristics for each tranche appealing to different types of investors. When mortgage holders prepay their mortgages in a pool of mortgages, investors holding the first class (A-class or tranche) of bonds are repaid their principal payments first. B-class investors are paid off next, then C-class, etc. with A-class investors having the lowest expected maturity and later classes, higher maturities. CMOs with tranches provide lower prepayment uncertainty and have better estimates for the likely maturity and yield. A plain vanilla CMO may have four tranches A, B, C, and Z with class C receiving no periodic interest until the other tranches are retired, with the Z-tranche investors receiving cash payments from the remaining underlying collateral for principal plus accrued interest.

Combined ratio The combined ratio for an insurance company is equal to the sum of the loss ratio and the expense ratio, sometimes also calculated as the total of both incurred losses and expenses divided by earned premiums. Typically ratios are expressed as percentages, and a combined ratio that is lower than 100% is an indicator that a firm has made an underwriting profit, and a ratio greater than 100%, an underwriting loss (i.e., more funds paid out than premiums received).

Commercial finance companies Commercial finance companies make loans to businesses to provide equipment leasing, asset-based loans and factoring (purchasing accounts receivables from businesses at a discount).

Commercial finance companies use short-term loans, issuing commercial paper and long-term loans and bonds for financing.

Commercial paper Commercial paper are unsecured, short-term debt securities issued by a company, often to finance net working capital, with maturities generally less than 270 days to avoid SEC registration.

Commercial real estate loans or construction loans Loans with real property as collateral often involve interim (temporary) financing by a bank with a takeout commitment from a long-term lender, such as a life insurance company or a pension fund after project completion or a certain number of years. Surety bonds are often used to guarantee the completion of a project.

Community banks Community banks are commercial banks that derive deposits from and make loans to the community where these banks operate. They are typically locally owned and operated. Community banks have assets ranging from $10 million to multi-billion dollar institutions.

Community Reinvestment Act (CRA) CRA was enacted in the United States by Congress in 1997 to encourage depository institutions to assist in meeting the credit needs of communities and to provide financing for moderate to low-income areas. Banks receive CRA examinations and ratings that are published by regulators.

Conflicts of interest When a party in a financial contract has incentives to act in his/her own interests versus the interests of other parties.

Construction and land development loans Real estate loans for construction and land development purposes. A land development loan is secured by a mortgage and is used to finance the costs for converting land into construction-ready building sites for the future construction of homes or commercial buildings. An acquisition and development loan (A&D loan) is a loan with a portion of the proceeds used to purchase the property, part for land development, and part for reserves, such as for a interest expense and sales commissions and a contingency reserve. Construction loans are usually short-term loans (average 3 years) that are secured by the mortgage on the property that is financed for the cost of land development and business construction, with disbursements often made at each stage of completion or when certain conditions are met. Banks and other financial institutions generally have arrangements for these loans to be taken over for permanent financing (20 years or more) by a longer-term lender or investor, such as an insurance company. The long-term lender is repaid from the cash flow generated by the completed building or project.

Consumer finance companies Consumer finance companies specialize in making consumer loans for automobiles and consumer retail goods, often as captive or sales companies of large manufacturing or retail firms to provide financing for these products.

Consumer Financial Protection Bureau (CFPB) The CFPB is a U.S. regulatory agency that was charged under Dodd–Frank Act to oversee financial products and services that are offered to consumers. The CFPB operates as an independent agency of the U.S. government and is responsible for consumer protection in the financial sector with its jurisdiction including depository institutions, securities firms, payday lenders, mortgage-servicing operations, foreclosure relief services, and debt collectors, as well as financial companies operating in the United States.

Consumer installment loans A consumer or sometimes a business loan generally for a vehicle or other goods, where the principal and interest are repaid in equal installments at fixed intervals (often monthly) that are secured by the item purchased.

Contractual financial institutions Financial institutions, such as insurance companies and pension funds that take premiums (or investments) and invest these for customers (employees) for the long-term to be able to meet future contractual obligations, thus providing risk management, maturity, and risk management intermediation services.

Convexity Convexity measures the curvature for the relationship between bond prices and bond yields that is used as an adjustment to duration measures for this curvature, whereby with a change in rates, capital gains with a fall in rates are slightly larger than capital losses with a rise in rates. Convexity is calculated as the second derivative of the price of the bond with respect to interest rates, while duration is the first derivative.

COP21 COP21 refers to the 21st United Nations Climate Change Conference held in Paris in December 2015, where 155 countries submitted intended nationally determined contributions (INDCs) to the UN Framework Convention on Climate Change, as climate action plans for lowering global emissions to avoid catastrophic effects from climate change if temperatures rise by more than 2°C.

Core (insured) deposits Core deposits are stable insured deposits that tend to stay with a bank, so have less liquidity risk and include demand deposits, savings accounts, NOW accounts, Super NOW accounts, money market accounts, and insured time deposits.

Corporate governance Corporate governance refers to the different mechanisms, relationships, and processes that are used to balance diverse interests of a company's stakeholders, including shareholders, managers, customers, suppliers, debt-holders, government, and the community.

Corporate social responsibility (CSR) The responsibility of a corporation to its stakeholders and society at large. CSR as a business approach provides a contribution to sustainable development in terms of providing economic, social, and environmental benefits to all stakeholders and society as a whole.

Country risk exposure Risk for a company operating in a foreign country of a nationwide default by its government on its debt regardless of the condition of a particular borrower; for instance, if a government announces that all dollar debt will not be repaid.

Coupon bond A bond that has both coupon payments paid annually or semi-annually and a maturity payment at maturity.

Credit default swap (CDS) A CDS is a swap that is designed to transfer a credit exposure of a fixed-income product between two or more parties, whereby the buyer of the swap makes payments to the swap's seller until the maturity date of a contract, and the seller takes the risk of having to pay out if a credit event, such as a loan default, occurs.

Credit derivatives Credit derivatives are types of derivatives whereby the risk of a loan not being repaid is sold to another party other than the lender, reducing the default risk for the issuer of the loan.

Credit-linked notes Credit-linked notes are credit derivatives that are structured as a security with a credit default swap embedded allowing for the transfer of specific credit risk to credit investors, transferring the issuer risk to the investors, so in the event of a specified event, the issuer does not have to repay the debt.

CreditMetrics A statistical approach that estimates changes in the market value of a bank's loan portfolio in the event of a credit upgrade or downgrade as well as potential loan defaults. Probabilities based on historical data are calculated for the occurrence of such events to calculate the expected change in the value of loans, value at risk for a given confidence level. The correlation between the value of risk for different loans and other financial instruments can be used to derive an aggregate measure of the volatility or value at risk for a bank's entire loan portfolio and other instruments, such as swaps, futures, and forward contracts.

Credit risk The risk of default on debt, or for a financial institution on loans, that can result in loss of principal and interest payments and loan losses.

Credit union A credit union is a nonprofit, member-owned financial cooperative that provide savings and credit services and other financial services for their members, with membership based on a common bond based on a specific community, organization, religion, or place or type of employment.

Crowdfunding Crowdfunding is the funding of a project or venture by raising funds in small amounts from a large number of people on a web crowdfunding platform. Different countries have different rules on whether or not equity investments can be made and on which platforms they can be made. In the United States the rules allowing small investors to make equity investments with crowdfunding began on May 16, 2016 with detailed regulations imposed.

Currency board foreign exchange rate arrangement Under a currency board arrangement, a country has a currency board as its monetary authority for the valuation of the country's currency, and pegs its currency's exchange rate to that of a larger country, whereby the country has an equal amount of the foreign currency held as reserves.

Currency swap A currency swap is a foreign exchange derivative often between two institutions to exchange the principal and/or interest payments of a security or loan in one currency for equivalent amounts at a future date at a given exchange rate, with periodic interest payments made during the term of the swap. Currency swaps can be tailor-made for longer-term, custom-made arrangements over several years to reduce foreign exchange risk.

Daily earnings at risk (DEAR) Daily earnings at risk are calculated using value at risk models to estimate the amount of potential loss on a daily basis.

Dark pools "Dark pools" is a term for new trading venues that allow nontransparent trading, such as electronic trading platforms and high-speed trading where investors are able to hide their trades to avoid large impacts in financial markets of large orders that could adversely affect their trades and speed up trades. Dark pools by their lack of transparent trading have the potential to disrupt markets and lower trading costs for those engaged in dark pool trading at the expense of other traders and small investors.

Debenture A debenture is a type of debt instrument that is not secured by collateral or other assets and is backed only by the general creditworthiness of the issuer, with corporations and governments frequently issuing bonds of this type.

Defined benefit pension plans Pension plans managed on behalf of companies or governments on the behalf of employees based on employee and employer contributions, where employers take on the investment risk and promise fixed annuity benefits in the future for employees in retirement.

Defined contribution pension plans Pension plans self-managed by employees whereby employer and employee contributions are invested by employees generally in a choice of mutual funds with employees taking on the investment risk.

Depository institutions Depository institutions (commercial banks, savings institutions, and credit unions) take deposits invested by savers and use these deposits to make loans to borrowers, providing liquidity and maturity intermediation services, respectively, to savers and borrowers.

Derivatives Securities that derive value based on the performance of an underlying security or portfolio that are used to hedge risks, such as futures and options and swaps. A derivative contract is a contract between one or more parties, whose value is determined by fluctuations for the underlying asset, such as stocks, bonds, commodities, foreign currencies, and market indexes. Derivatives can be traded over the counter or on an exchange for standardized contracts.

Direct finance Financing that is done directly between borrowers and savers, creating a direct security as a form of IOU for the transaction, such as a company engaging in an initial or secondary stock offering that is sold directly to individuals.

Direct premiums written Direct premiums written are total premiums received before adjusting for account reinsurance ceded for an insurance company, with direct premium written often a proxy for the growth of a company's insurance business over a given period that can include policies written by the company and policies written by its affiliated companies.

Disaster recovery bonds Bonds issued that help government entities if a catastrophic event occurs, such as pre-financing with the Caribbean Catastrophe Risk Insurance Facility (CCRIF) that provides coverage for hurricane and earthquake damage to member nations, allowing countries to quickly have funds available for recovery needs to allow essential services to continue. The CCRIF allows member nations to combine their risks into a diversified portfolio as a type of mutual insurance company, and to purchase reinsurance or other risk transfer types of products on international financial markets at up to 50% over what this would cost for each country.

Discount loans Discount loans are short-term loans whereby the interest amount for the entire loan period (plus any charges) is deducted from the principal of the loan at the time it is provided, and the borrower pays off the loan based on the full principal amount before the deduction.

Discount window borrowing Most central banks globally act as lenders of last resort when a bank has severe liquidity needs. In the United States the Federal Reserve administers discount window borrowing, which allows depository institutions to borrow under three conditions to meet temporary liquidity needs: (1) to meet seasonal credit demands, such as for rural banks during planting seasons; (2) for special "extended credit" purposes after disaster, such as hurricanes, among others; and (3) when unusually heavy withdrawals occur such as in crisis periods with large deposit runs.

Diversification Diversification involves the use of a portfolio of assets for investments that have returns that are not all correlated together to reduce the unsystematic risk (that occurs with specific industries or companies), reducing the volatility of the portfolio, leaving only the systematic risk inherent for the entire market.

Diversification tests Under the US. Investment Company Act of 1940, mutual funds must declare themselves as diversified or nondiversified. A diversified fund is required to invest more than 75% of the value of its total assets in cash and cash items (including receivables), government securities, securities of other registered investment companies, and other securities that are limited in respect to any one issuer to an amount not greater in value than 5% of the value of the total assets of the fund and to not more than 10% of the outstanding voting securities of the issuer. A nondiversified mutual fund is not subject to this requirement, but is subject to a similar diversification rule for 50% of its assets under the qualification requirements of Subchapter M of the Internal Revenue Code.

Divest-Invest Philanthropy Divest-Invest is a nonprofit organization promoting divesting from fossil fuels and investing divested funds in climate solutions.

Dodd–Frank Wall Street Reform and Consumer Protection Act (Dodd–Frank) The Dodd–Frank Act was signed into law on July 21, 2010 as a response to the Great Recession, following the U.S. subprime crisis of 2007 to 2008. Dodd–Frank initiated new regulations affecting all federal financial regulatory agencies and almost all aspects of the U.S. financial services industry. Provisions include the establishment of the Financial Stability Oversight Council; the Orderly Liquidation Authority; Transfer of Powers to the Comptroller, FDIC, and the Fed; Regulation of Advisers to Hedge Funds and Others; the establishment of a Federal Insurance Office and State-Based Insurance Reform; Provisions for the Improvement of Regulation, Wall Street Transparency and Accountability, Payment, Clearing and Settlement Supervision; Investor Protection and Improvements to the Regulation of Securities, the establishment of the Bureau of Consumer Financial Protection; new Federal Reserve System Provisions; the Mortgage Reform and Anti-Predatory Lending Act, among many other provisions. The Dodd–Frank Act also repealed remaining provisions of Regulation Q by allowing banks to offer interest on checking accounts for its business banking customers.

Dollarization Dollarization is when a country aligns its currency with the U.S. dollar either officially or unofficially, whereby the dollar is the legal tender in the country for its transactions.

Due on sales clauses A due on sales clause is often part of a mortgage loan agreement, whereby the lender requires the borrower to repay the outstanding loan balance when the mortgage property is sold. Due on sale clauses protect the lender by allowing the lender to evaluate the financial position of the new owner before deciding to continue the loan and setting a higher interest rate if necessary than that of the original loan.

Dupont Analysis Dupont Analysis is a financial model that was developed by Donaldson Brown at E.I. du Pont de Nemours & Company in 1918 to examine the fundamental drivers of profitability of General Motors when Dupont purchased a large stake in the company. The analysis uses both balance sheet and income statement information to view a firm's financial health and operating efficiency. The first equation is Return on assets (net income/assets) (ROA) = Net profit margin (net income/revenues) (NPM) × Total asset utilization (revenues/assets) (AU). This equation shows ROA to be a function of cost management for generating profit from revenues (NPM) and revenue generation from assets (AU). The second equation is Return on equity (net income/equity) (ROE) = ROA × Equity multiplier (assets/equity) (EM). This equation shows that ROE is a function of both net income produced from assets and a firm's financial leverage, with a higher equity multiplier indicating greater use of debt for levering returns for stockholders. Putting these as one equation ROE = NPM × AU × EM, where return on equity is a function of a firm's cost efficiency generating net income from revenues, its revenue generation from assets, and its financial leverage.

Duration Duration is a measure of interest rate risk that includes both price and reinvestment risk. Duration measures the sensitivity of a bond's price to a change in interest rates, including the effect of coupon payments, maturity, and the yield to maturity rate. Duration is included in the presentation of bond mutual funds and bond information. The calculation for duration is the sum of the weighted present value of cash flows (i.e., the sum of the present value of each cash flow × t, the year the cash flow comes in) divided by the sum of the present value of cash flows (i.e., the bond's price).

Duration gap (DGAP) A financial institution's DGAP is a measure of the institution's overall interest rate risk, calculated as the duration of its assets less [(Total liabilities/Total assets) × (Duration of its liabilities)]. A positive duration gap indicates a longer duration for assets than the duration of liabilities, indicating greater interest rate risk for a fall in the market value of the bank's equity with a rise in interest rates, with the market value of assets falling more than the market value of liabilities with a rise in interest rates. A negative duration gap indicates a longer duration of liabilities than the duration of assets, indicating greater interest rate risk for a fall in the market value of the bank's equity with a fall in interest rates, with the market value of liabilities rising more than the market value of assets with a fall in interest rates.

Economies of scale Economies of scale result in cost advantages that are achieved with greater size or scale, which allows the cost of output to fall with fixed costs spread out over a greater volume of units of output.

Economies of scope Economies of scope arise by producing or having a range of products that result in it being less costly to produce products together versus individually, such as the sharing of centralized functions for the products; for example, financing or marketing or cross-selling advantages.

Effective annual yield (EAY): The effective annual yield is the ex post actual annual compound yield that an investor receives equal to the future cash flows (FV) the investor receives divided by the price paid for the security (PV), annualized by taking the [FV/PV] to the $1/n$ power and then subtracting 1 to get the EAY.

Efficiency ratio A measure for a depository institution's inefficiency with higher ratios indicating higher inefficiency. The efficiency ratio is calculated as noninterest expenses divided by (net interest income plus noninterest revenues).

Environmental liability Environmental liabilities for a financial institution include environmental contamination and related liabilities affecting the value of real estate or other collateral held by a financial institution. A financial institution may be held directly liable for court-ordered cleanups for environmental damages, such as for hazardous substance contamination. Lenders can reduce their environmental risks by requiring environmental assessments as part of a mortgage application process, by lending only for classes of properties that do not have the potential for increased environmental risks, or by purchasing environmental insurance or lender liability insurance, among other protections.

Environmental, social, and governance (ESG) factors ESG factors are three primary criteria for screening investments for socially responsible investment companies, as well as for financial institutions and other companies in making decisions, providing a more complete investment analysis to make better, more informed investment decisions. The CFA (Chartered Financial Analyst) Institute points out that ESG investing ethics are often used to promote a fiduciary culture and a more sustainable form of capitalism to better serve society, in terms of a *more trustworthy, forward-thinking financial industry*. See CFA Institute, "Explore Environmental, Social, and Governance (ESG) Issues in Investing" (at: https://www.cfainstitute.org/learning/future/knowledge/pages/esg.aspx).

Equal Credit Opportunity Act (Reg. B) U.S. law enacted in 1974 whereby banks are forbidden to discriminate in lending on the basis of race, color, national origin, sex, age, marital status, and/or receipt of public assistance.

Equator Principles The Equator Principles is a risk management framework adopted by financial institutions for the determination and assessment and management of environmental and social risks in projects. Under the Equator Principles bank signatories sign on to conduct due diligence supporting responsible risk decision making for financing decisions for making loans.

Equity multiplier The equity multiplier (EM) measures the degree of financial leverage used by a company or financial institution. EM is calculated as total assets divided by total equity, with a higher EM indicating greater financial leverage. EM can also be calculated as 1 divided by (Total equity / Total assets).

Ethics Moral principles guiding an individual's or group's behavior that distinguishes between human actions that are right and wrong and focuses on virtuous conduct, such as the code of conduct for a business.

Eurodollar CDs Eurodollar CDs are certificates of deposits in U.S. dollars issued and held outside the United States with almost all Eurodollar CDs issued by banks in London.

Eurodollar futures contracts Eurodollar futures are one of the most popular short-term interest rate futures contracts for hedging short-term interest rate risk. The CME Eurodollar Time Deposit futures contract reflects the offered interest rate for the 3-month $1 million deposit that is offered on U.S. denominated deposits that banks hold outside the United States.

Exchange traded funds (ETFs) ETFs are similar to index mutual funds in being passively managed and mimicking an index, but they trade on the market like closed-end funds do. ETFs are securities certificates that provide a legal right of ownership for a share of the basket of individual securities or commodities, and are flexible in being able to be bought and sold throughout a trading day and can be bought on margin like a stock, also offering short positions to be taken. Since they are passively managed funds, ETFs have low annual expenses. There are a variety of different types of ETFs, and many mutual fund family companies also offer their own ETFs.

Expectations theory for yield curves The expectations theory is a prominent explanation for the shape of yield curves, whereby long-term rates for a homogeneous group of securities are determined by the current short-term rates for these securities and expected future short-term rates by investors over the life of a bond.

Expense ratio for insurers For the insurance industry, the expense ratio is a ratio equal to the expenses associated with acquiring, underwriting, and servicing premiums divided by the net premiums earned by an insurance firm. Expenses include operating expenses for employee wages and commissions, and advertising, among others. The expense ratio measures a firm's operating efficiency.

Expense ratio for mutual funds The expense ratio for open-end mutual funds is the percentage of fund assets paid for operating expenses and management fees including 12b-1 fees for distribution costs and administrative fees (brokerage costs and sales charges are not included).

Factoring Factoring is a financial transaction whereby a firm sells its accounts receivables to a third party (factor) for a discount. Forfaiting is a factoring agreement used in international finance by exporters who want to receive cash sooner and hence sell their receivables to a forfaiter.

Fair Credit Reporting Act The Fair Credit Reporting Act is a U.S. law requiring consumer credit reporting agencies to stress accuracy, correct errors promptly, and release the consumer histories of individuals only for legitimate purposes. Customers must also be told why they are not given loans and have the right to know of any discrepancies in their credit reports.

Fair Housing Act The Fair Housing Act is a U.S. law forbidding discrimination of home sales, rentals, and financing based on race, color, national origin, religion, sex, family status, or on disabilities.

Fed Funds rate The Fed Funds rate is the interest rate for short-term lending (often overnight) between the most creditworthy depository institutions for excess reserves held at the U.S. Federal Reserve (Fed) generally for overnight borrowing. The Fed Funds rate is used in the Fed's open market operations as a desired target rate. Fed Funds sold are excess reserves lent to another bank (i.e., a short-term asset on bank balance sheets). Fed Funds purchased are excess reserves borrowed from another bank (i.e., a short-term liability on bank balance sheets).

Federal Deposit Insurance Corporation Improvement Act (FDICIA) FDICIA was adopted in 1991 in response to serious difficulties for the thrift and banking industries with a wave of bank and thrift failures. Major provisions include phasing out deposit rate caps under Reg. Q. to allow banks and thrifts to compete with money market funds, recapitalization of the FDIC's Bank Insurance Fund, authorization to the FDIC to increase insurance deposit premium assessments and to borrow from other sources, expansion of regulatory enforcement powers, and establishing five regulatory categories of capitalization for depository institutions, among other regulations. Under the categories of capitalization, if a depository institution falls in the undercapitalized, significantly undercapitalized, or critically undercapitalized categories it becomes subject to special enforcement actions by its primary federal regulator.

Federal Financial Institutions Examination Council (FFIEC) The FFIEC is a U.S. government interagency body that includes the different depository institution regulators in the United States. Established in 1979 it is empowered to prescribe uniform principles, standards and report forms to promote uniformity in the supervision of financial institutions and oversees real estate appraisal in the United States and facilitates public access to data for depository institutions.

Federal Home Loan Mortgage Corporation (FHLMC) The FHLMC, often called Freddie Mac, is a U.S. government-chartered corporation that purchases qualified mortgage loans from originating financial institutions and securitizes these loans and distributes the mortgage securities through a dealer community. Freddie Mac is a stockholder-owned government-sponsored enterprise (GSE) that was chartered to keep money flowing to mortgage lenders in support of homeownership and rental housing for middle income Americans. Freddie Mac was placed into government conservatorship on September 6, 2008 during the U.S. subprime loan crisis, and has been operating under government supervision since that time, as of the time of this writing, June 2016.

Federal Insurance Office (FIO) The U.S. FIO was established under Title V of the Dodd–Frank Act of 2010 and is housed under the Department of the Treasury, with its head a director appointed by the secretary of the Treasury. The FIO's role is to provide expertise and advice on insurance matters to the Treasury department and other federal agencies, but is not a regulatory agency. The NAIC closely coordinates with the FIO as an information resource to allow international discussion in association with U.S. insurance regulators. The FIO is charged with monitoring all aspects for the insurance industry in the United States, which includes the identification of sector activities that have the potential to contribute to a systemic crisis for the financial system, examining whether underserved communities have affordable access to insurance products, and monitoring the sector's regulation.

Federal National Mortgage Association (FNMA) The FNMA, often known as Fannie Mae, is a government-sponsored enterprise that purchases loans from mortgage lenders and packages them and sells these mortgage-backed securities to investors in the open market. FNMA is a publicly traded company, but was placed into government conservatorship on September 6, 2008 during the U.S. subprime loan crisis and continuing as of the time of this writing, June 2016.

FHLB advances Federal Home Loan Bank (FHLB) advances include funding provided to member institutions, which can be overnight funding, short-term advances, or long-term advances. In the United States there are over 7,300 regulated financial institutions in 50 states as members. Members must purchase stock in the FHLB, which gives them accessibility to low-cost financing and receipt of dividends based on their percentage of stock ownership.

Fiat money Fiat money is currency used based on its backing by the government of a country that is accepted as a means of payment. For example, the United States abandoned the gold standard in 1971 moving to a floating rate foreign exchange system and a fiat money system. A fiat monetary system allows more control for the central bank over a country's money supply to stimulate or contract the money supply as needed. This contrasts with a fixed-rate gold standard that leaves expansion and contraction subject to volatile market fluctuations in the supply of gold, leading to both inflation and economic contraction.

FICO score A FICO score is a credit score used by lenders in the United States to assess an applicant's credit risk that goes into the determination for whether a loan is granted. FICO stands for the Fair Isaac Corporation who originated the score. The FICO score ranges between 300 and 850 with a higher score indicating a higher rating, with 650 categorized as very good and 620 often used as a benchmark, below which individuals may have greater difficulties obtaining a favorable rate based on their credit risk.

Financial holding company A financial entity created in the United States by the Gramm–Leach–Bliley Act of 1999 that allows for the engagement in a broad range of financial activities, including insurance underwriting, securities trading and underwriting, investment advisory services, merchant banking, securitizations, and any other nonbanking activities allowed in the United States by the Bank Holding Company Act, with the Federal Reserve Board responsible for supervision. Any nonbank commercial company predominantly engaged in financial activities that earns 85% or more of its gross revenues from financial services can choose to become a financial holding company, but must sell any nonfinancial businesses within 10 years (see Definition of BHCs and Banking Terms, National Information Center (NIC) at: http://www.ffiec.gov/nic).

Financial Industry Regulatory Authority, Inc. (FINRA) FINRA is an independent regulator of securities firms that operate in the United States, whereby securities are any financial instruments including stocks and bonds that are traded freely on the open market. FINRA is a private corporation and acts as a self-regulatory organization (SRO). FINRA succeeds the previous authority of the National Association of Securities Dealers, Inc. (NASD) and the member regulation enforcements and arbitration operations of the NYSE.

Financial intermediaries Financial intermediaries are financial institutions that serve as intermediaries between savers and borrowers, including creating indirect securities that have more desirable characteristics for borrowers and lenders (savers) than direct securities. Financial intermediaries provide economic functions increasing the efficiency of an economy, including liquidity, maturity, denomination, search, monitoring, and information intermediation benefits.

Financial Stability Oversight Council (FSOC). The FSOC is a U.S. federal government organization that was established under Title 1 of Dodd–Frank in 2010. The FSOC has a charge to monitor the financial system, which includes the identification of potential threats to the nation's financial stability. The FSOC is under the U.S. Department of the Treasury. Voting members include major regulatory bodies including the Secretary of the Treasury as Chairperson, the Chairman of the Board of Governors of the Federal Reserve System, the Comptroller of the Currency, the Director of the Bureau of Consumer Financial Protection, the Chair of the SEC, the Chair of the FDIC, the Chair of the Commodity Futures Trading Commission, the Director of the Federal Housing Finance Agency, the Chair of the National Credit Union Administration, and an independent member with insurance expertise appointed by the President of the United States and confirmed by the Senate for a six-year term.

FinTech Financial technology (FinTech) is a financial industry sector that uses technology to make financial services more efficient. Firms in this industry are often startups that use new types of web-based platforms and disruptive technologies to engage in direct peer-to-peer (P2P) or business-to-business (B2B) transactions. FinTech firms provide efficient financing through new business models, applications, or processes. Examples include new payment mechanisms, such as digital wallets or P2P payments, crowdfunding or P2P lending, "Insur" Tech for insurance transactions, and online robot-type (robo) investment advising services, among many others.

First-to-default swaps A first-to-default swap is an instrument that provides a payment of a predetermined amount when (and if) the first instrument for a basket of credit instruments goes into default, after which the transaction terminates. This in turn makes the derivative price cheaper than if individual contracts on the reference credits were purchased.

Fisher effect The Fisher effect (credited to a 20th century economist, Irving Fisher) distinguishes between nominal interest rates (i_n), the stated rate on a bond that includes the real rate, r, and an inflation premium, IP, for any expected loss in purchasing power over the life of a bond. Under the Fisher effect, the real interest rate, r^*, is calculated approximately as the nominal rate, i_n, less the inflation premium, IP, whereby nominal interest rates include the expected inflation rate over a period to compensate investors for loss in purchasing power.

Five C's of credit The five C's of credit is a lending framework that uses five major factors in determining whether or not to underwrite a loan: (1) Character, the willingness of customers to pay back a loan; (2) Capacity, the ability of a customer to pay in terms of cash flow; (3) Capital, the soundness of a borrower's financial position in terms of equity; (4) Conditions, the industry and economic conditions that may affect a firm's ability to repay a loan; and (5) Collateral, secondary asset sources of repayment (i.e., asset-based lending).

Fixed foreign exchange rate regime A fixed foreign exchange rate regime for a country uses a fixed (pegged) exchange rate for the value of its currency, fixed against the value of another single currency or a basket of currencies or another measure of value, such as gold.

Floating foreign exchange rate regime A floating exchange rate regime is when a country's currency is set based on supply and demand factors for its currency versus other countries' currency in the foreign exchange market.

Floating lien A floating lien is a collateral arrangement that gives the lender recourse to a borrower's entire inventory, even if portions are acquired after the loan is made.

Floor plan A floor plan is a collateral arrangement, often used by car dealers that allows the borrower to retain possession of the collateral. Also often used to finance expensive retail items that are designated by a serial number of description.

Forward markets Forward markets are over-the-counter markets with brokers and dealers where arrangements are made between parties to exchange a specific, tailored amount of an asset for delivery in the future for a specified future date and specified rate of exchange.

Funding gap A funding gap for a financial institution is equal to its rate-sensitive assets (RSA) less its rate-sensitive liabilities (RSL). The larger the funding gap the larger the mismatch in maturities for assets and liabilities and the greater a financial institution's interest rate risk. A positive funding gap is when RSA > RSL, increasing a financial institution's risk of lower net interest income if rates fall and interest revenue falls more than interest expense. A negative funding gap is when RSL > RSA, increasing a financial institution's risk of lower net interest income if rates rise and interest expense rises more than interest revenues. Funding gaps are measured for particular periods, such as a 1-year, 3-year, and 5-year funding gap.

Future value annuity factor (FVIFA) The future value of an annuity factor is used to calculate the future value of a series of equal payments (annuity) over a given period of time, n, given a reinvestment rate, r. The FVIFA is calculated as: $\{[(1+r)^n - 1] / r\}$. The future value of an annuity (FVA) is calculated by multiplying the annuity payment amount times the future value annuity factor.

Future value of a single sum factor (FVIF) The future value of a single sum factor (FVIF) is the factor to find the future value of a single cash flow, invested at a given rate, r, for a given number of periods, n. The FVIF is calculated as $[(1 + r)^n]$, and the future value of the single cash flow today (PV) is equal to the present value (amount today) times the future value of a single sum factor.

Futures contracts A futures contract is a contract to buy or sell an asset on an organized exchange in the future. Futures contracts are standardized contracts for a fixed amount, delivery date, and price in the future. While some contracts allow for future physical delivery, most contracts are settled by reversing the trade and taking a gain or loss (i.e., cash settlement). The organized exchange guarantees the trade, and trades can be reversed at any time, so contracts are very liquid. Futures contracts have margin requirements and daily resettlement, so liquidity is needed to replenish margin accounts.

Futures exchange A futures exchange is a formal financial exchange for trading standardized future contracts, with the exchange guaranteeing that a contract will go through reducing counterparty risk, and providing liquidity through trading of contracts, with the buyer/seller of a contract having the ability to reverse a trade and get out prior to the delivery date of a contract.

G7 Agreement The G7 are seven industrialized countries (Canada, France, Germany, Italy, Japan, the United Kingdom, and the United States) that have agreed to coordinate efforts to keep the U.S. dollar within a specified trading range relative to the currencies of the other countries as trading partners.

G20 group The G20 is an international forum for the governments and central banks from 20 major economies, founded in 1999 for the purpose of study, review, and discussion for promoting international financial stability.

Glass–Steagall Act of 1933 The U.S. Glass–Steagall Act (GS), also known as the Banking Act of 1933, prohibited commercial banks from engaging in investment banking and other nonbank activities, in reaction to 5,000 banks failing during the Great Depression at that time. GS also created the Federal Deposit Insurance Corporation (FDIC) and the Federal Open Market Committee. It also created Regulation Q (Reg. Q) at that time that forbid banks from paying interest on demand deposits and capped interest rates on other deposit products. Reg. Q was completely repealed in the early 1980s and for demand deposits in July 2011.

Global Alliance for Banking on Values (GABV) The GABV is an international banking network that has a commitment to the advancement of positive changes in banking values, including the transparency of banking business models, promoting sustainability, and the reporting of the social and ecological impact of banking within a regulatory framework.

Global Reporting Initiative (GRI) The GRI is an independent institution with the mission to develop and disseminate sustainability reporting guidelines that are globally applicable to help organizations and corporations to report their economic, environmental, and social dimensions for their activities, products, and services.

Globally systematically important financial institutions (GSIFIs) Under Basel III requirements, globally systematically important financial institutions (SIFIs) designated by a country's regulators must have greater loss absorbency capital reflecting the greater risks that they present to the financial system. In the United States GSIFIs are subject to the Federal Reserve's risk-based capital surcharge framework determined by their size and total exposure, interconnectedness, substitutability, complexity, and cross-jurisdictional activity.

Go Fossil Free Go Fossil Free is a nonprofit organization that promotes divestment from fossil fuel companies to avoid damage to the environment and avoid carbon emissions that contribute to climate change. The Divest from Fossil Free movement is an international network of campaigns and campaigners seeking to free communities from dependency on fossil fuels (www.gofossilfree.org).

Gold standard A fixed-rate exchange rate system, where a currency is valued in gold. Problems with a gold standard include a loss of control over a country's currency, since any rise or decrease in gold production affects the amount of currency in circulation, such as increased production leading to inflation, and a contraction in gold production, reducing currency in circulation leading to economic contraction. Britain stopped its use of the gold standard in 1931 and the United States in 1971. Most countries abandoned a gold standard, although many countries still hold gold reserves.

Government National Mortgage Association (GNMA) GNMA (often called Ginnie Mae) a U.S. government corporation within the U.S. Department of Housing and Urban Development (HUD) with the purpose of ensuring liquidity for government-insured mortgages, including those insured by the Federal Housing Administration (FHA), the Veterans Administration (VA), and the Rural Housing Administration (RHA). GNMA purchases and packages bundle mortgages for securitizations that are sold to investors. GNMA securities are government guaranteed.

Government-sponsored enterprises (GSEs) GSEs are enterprises set up by governments to provide a more effective home mortgage market. GSEs purchase mortgage loans from financial institutions, often securitizing them by pooling mortgages and packaging them into securities, providing investors with a return based on the mortgage rates of the pool, and providing liquidity for mortgage markets, by allowing financial institutions funds to make new mortgage loans.

Graduated payment mortgage (GPM) A GPM is a mortgage where monthly payments are set at a low level in early years and then payments increase according to a known schedule before stabilizing.

Gramm–Leach–Bliley Act (GLB) GLB (often called the Financial Modernization Act) was passed by Congress in 1999 in the United States to remove provisions of the Glass–Steagall Act of 1933 to allow bank holding companies to engage in investment, securities, and insurance activities through subsidiaries. The GLB Act also established a new entity, financial holding companies.

Great global recession The great global recession is often used to identify the period of general economic decline in global markets that occurred following the U.S. subprime loan crisis of 2007 to 2008.

Green bonds Green bonds, also known as climate bonds are a fairly new asset class that are issued for the financing of climate change solutions, including climate change mitigation or adaptation-related projects or programs. Most green bonds are green in the use of proceeds bonds that are earmarked for particular green projects or are asset-linked bonds.

Growing equity mortgages (GEMs) GEMs are mortgages that have initial payments set at the level that would amortize the mortgage over 30 years, but have later scheduled increases in loan payments that result in a shorter actual maturity.

Guaranteed investment contracts (GICs) A GIC is an investment product that provides fixed cash flows and fixed investment returns, which are helpful for individuals who are retired, who often put in lump sums at retirement in return for fixed cash flows each month with insurance annuity contracts.

Hedge fund Hedge funds are limited partnerships that manage investments for accredited investors, using alternative investment strategies to earn an active return (alpha) for their investors and often include the use of derivatives and leverage in domestic and global markets.

Hedge ratio A ratio used to adjust for differences in historical movements of spot and future prices to adjust for the number of futures contracts to acquire to hedge a spot position, whereby the hedge ratio represents generally the covariance for changes in spot and future prices divided by the variance for the change in futures prices.

Home equity loans A home equity loan is a loan where a borrower uses the equity that an individual has in the home as collateral.

Home Mortgage Disclosure Act (HMDA) The Home Mortgage Disclosure Act is a U.S. law that obligates financial institutions to obtain HMDA data information (race, sex, national origin) for home purchases, home improvement, or refinance applications, which information is required to be available to the public.

Independent insurance agent Independent insurance agents are professionals who sell insurance and financial services products based on a search for the best products for clients versus direct agents who just sell policies for one insurance company.

Index mutual funds Index mutual funds are mutual funds that are constructed to match or track the components of a market index, such as Standard & Poor's 500 index, to provide diversification and broad market exposure, along with low operating exposure and low portfolio turnover, allowing for a passive investment strategy for investors that want diversification.

Indirect financing Financing wherein more desirable characteristics for borrowers and lenders (savers) are created by a financial intermediary, such as a bank taking in deposits that are liquid and have short-term maturities and lending these to longer-term borrowers as loans.

Industrial loan companies (ILCs) Industrial loan companies or industrial banks are an unusual type of finance company chartered in some states to provide credit for blue collar workers. The growth of ILCs resulted from the recognition by companies of a loophole to the U.S. Glass–Steagall Act that allowed nonfinancial companies to engage in banking activities through ILCs. Industrial loan companies could offer certificates of deposit (called certificates of investment) accounts and provide consumer cash loans secured by personal property, agricultural lending, and short-term inventory credit. Over time, most states changed their regulations to disallow ILCs, and the freedom of ILCs was limited by Congress as part of the Financial Services Regulatory Relief Act of 2004.

Information symmetries Information asymmetry is a special type of agency problem where one party in a contract has more information than another. Financial institutions by their nature have private information on borrowers for lending contracts and other financial contracts whereby there are differences in information between owners and principals, such as managers and stockholders, creating greater agency costs and making it difficult for stockholders to monitor managers.

Initial public offering (IPO) An IPO is the initial sale of stock by a private company that is going public, whereby the issuer gets the assistance of an investment banking (underwriting) firm to do due diligence and meet SEC rules for the registration, and provide advice for the best offering price and timing for the issue to go to market, and marketing and selling of the issue.

Institutional investors Large organizations including many large financial institutions, such as banks, pension funds, insurance companies and other large investors such as labor unions, that have substantial investments in the stock of large corporations.

Insurance premiums An insurance premium is the amount paid by customers for an insurance policy, with premiums depending on the type of coverage, the probability that a claim will be made, the region where a policyholder lives or has a business, the behavior and risks that a person or business takes, and the insurance company's competition and competitor rates.

Interest only (IO) collateralized mortgage obligations (CMOs) Stripped mortgage-backed securities separate securities into classes of interest only (IO) and principal only (PO) paying securities. With prepayment risk, POs and IOs are very interest rate sensitive, with IOs declining in value if interest rates fall significantly, since the maturity of the security is shortened with prepayments.

Interest rate caps, collars, and floors Interest rate caps, floors, and collars are synthetic agreements offered by large financial institutions and other institutions that provide long-term protection against losses. A "cap" is an arrangement whereby cap protection is purchased, so that the institution owning the cap receives funds if interest rates go over the cap that is set. A "floor" is an arrangement whereby the institution purchasing the floor receives funds if interest rates go below the floor. A "collar" is a combination of a cap and floor that in effect guarantees a given rate.

Interest rate parity and FX rates Under purchasing power parity, the expected returns in a country including FX appreciation or depreciation should be equal across countries, where returns on domestic deposits adjusted for FX changes should equal the return on foreign deposits adjusted for FX changes.

Interest rate risk Interest rate risk is the risk that an investment's value will fall due to changes in interest rates for a bond or for a financial institution that its net interest spread between interest revenues and interest expenses will fall. Interest rate risk sensitivity depends on maturity and coupon rate, reflected by a bond's duration.

Interest rate swap An interest rate swap is an exchange of cash flows between two parties (counterparties). An interest rate swap is a transaction where two parties agree to pay the interest obligation on a specified debt obligation of the other party (liability swap) or to exchange cash flows on assets of the other party (asset swap). A plain vanilla swap is a swap where one counterparty exchanges a fixed rate payment obligation for a floating rate one, while the other counterparty exchanges a floating for a fixed.

International Association of Insurance Supervisors (IAIS) The IAIS was formed in 1994, representing insurance regulators and supervisors for over 200 jurisdictions in over 140 countries that constitute 97% of the world's insurance premiums. As the primary international organization of insurance supervisors, the IAIS is engaged in creating international standards and guidelines on insurance supervision, implementing the standards in member jurisdictions, and promoting effective and globally consistent supervision of the insurance industry in order to contribute to global financial stability.

International Monetary Fund (IMF) The IMF is an international organization headquartered in Washington DC with 189 countries as members. The IMF fosters global monetary cooperation for the purpose of financial stability and facilitates international trade to promote high employment and sustainable economic growth and to reduce poverty globally. Key activities of the IMF include: (1) to provide policy advice and analysis to governments and central banks on economic trends and cross-country experience; (2) to provide research, statistics, forecasts and analysis for global, regional, and individual economies and markets; (3) to provide loans to help countries to overcome economic difficulties; (4) to provide concessional loans to help fight poverty in developing countries; and (5) to provide technical assistance and training to assist countries to improve upon the management of their economies.

International Monetary Market (IMM) index The International Monetary Market index is the index used for price quotations on Eurodollar futures, whereby the IMM index = 100% − Discount yield % as percentage price for a Eurodollar futures contract, whereby a one basis point (0.01%) change in the IMM index is worth a $25 change in the contract value.

Investment Company Act of 1940 The U.S. Investment Company Act was created in 1940 by Congress defining the responsibility, fiduciary duty, and limitations placed on open-end funds, unit investment trusts, and closed-end funds that offer investment products to the public, with the act enforced and regulated by the Securities and Exchange Commission (SEC).

Investment yield The investment yield for an insurance company is the ratio of its net investment income from investment activities divided by its earned premiums.

Kamikaze offer A kamikaze offer is a bond offer by a prospective underwriter for a bought deal at such a low spread that other underwriters may decline to participate in a syndicate for it.

Kane's regulatory dialectic Edward Kane, a prominent professor of finance, introduced the concept of a regulatory dialectic to capture the impact of regulations on financial institution managerial decisions. Under the dialectic changes occur by means of a process of action and reaction of opposing forces as described by the philosopher Hegel as: (1) thesis, an initial set of arguments or rules; (2) antithesis, a conflicting set of arguments or responses; and (3) synthesis, a change or modification as the result of an exchange or interaction among opposing forces. For financial institutions, an example of such a thesis is regulations passed following a crisis; followed by attempts by financial institutions to bypass regulations, with regulations becoming out-of-date or reducing efficiency in financial markets; followed by a response from regulators in patching up regulations with amendments, with an eventual synthesis occurring with deregulation.

Ladder liquidity strategy A ladder strategy is a passive investment strategy often used by small community banks where a certain percentage of the investment portfolio is maturing each year to meet liquidity needs.

Letter of credit A commercial letter of credit is created when an issuing bank issues a letter of credit to another bank (advising bank) (often for international trade in another country) agreeing to serve as a guarantee for payments made to a specified person under specified conditions. A letter of credit provides a reassurance that a payment will be made. Standby letters of credit are also used to provide an additional guaranty for securitizations or other purposes to provide an assurance for the performance of the terms of a contract, which is rarely ever drawn upon, strengthening the creditworthiness of the contract.

Leverage ratio A depository institution's leverage ratio is generally defined as its total equity capital to total assets (with some regulatory adjustments made), as a measure of its capital risk and a regulatory capital ratio that must meet regulatory standards.

Leveraged buyouts (LBOs) A leveraged buyout involves the acquisition of another company that uses large amounts of borrowed money (bonds or loans) to pay for the acquisition cost, with the assets or cash flows of the company being acquired often used as collateral for the loan in addition to assets of the acquiring company. LBOs occur primarily for private corporations, but are also employed for taking a company from a public to a private company.

Liability management The use of short-term liabilities for liquidity management often used by large depository institutions, where purchased funds, such as commercial paper, negotiable CDs, and other short-term liabilities, are used to generate liquidity, in contrast to holding large amounts of stored liquidity.

LIBOR LIBOR is the London Interbank Offered Rate that is the rate that major international banks offer for term Eurodollar borrowings to each other, with an active secondary market for the sale of Eurodollar CDs by investors before these deposits mature. The LIBOR rate is a key global benchmark rate used for setting adjustable rates for loan and swaps issued by financial institutions.

Line of credit (LOC) A line of credit is an arrangement between a financial institution and a customer providing a maximum loan balance that a bank allows a borrower to maintain and that the borrower can draw down on at any time, as long as the maximum set in the agreement is not exceeded. A line of credit is informal and can be revoked, versus a loan commitment that is a formal, legal guarantee for a given rate, amount and maturity.

Liquidity coverage ratio (LCR) Under Basel III, LCR is the new liquidity coverage ratio required for large international banking organizations with $250 billion or more in consolidated assets or $10 billion or more in off-balance sheet foreign exposure to allow them to have sufficient high-quality liquid assets (HQLA) to withstand a 30-day period of stressed funding. At full implementation, large international banks will have to hold an LCR equal or greater than 100%.

Liquidity premium theory for yield curves The liquidity premium for yield curves is a prominent explanation for the shape of yield curves, whereby long-term rates are determined by current and expected short-term rates for a homogeneous group of securities plus a liquidity premium added for longer-term maturities to compensate investors for greater liquidity risk. The liquidity premium theory helps to explain why yield curves are more typically upward sloping.

Liquidity risk Liquidity risk is the risk of not being able to meet short-term financial demands for a company or the risk from lack of marketability for a security with a minimal capital loss. For a financial institution, liquidity risk reflects the risk of not being able to cover deposit withdrawals or meet other liquidity needs.

Liquidity risk premium Liquidity risk premiums are additional yields required for longer-term bonds and securities that are not very marketable for their liquidity risk. In contrast, short-term, more liquid money market securities (with less than one year to maturity) that are marketable (with a large secondary market and dealers/brokers facilitating sales) with more liquidity (greater ease of being sold with little or no loss of value) have low liquidity risk.

Load mutual fund A load fund is a mutual fund that has a sales charge or commission, whereby the investor pays the load to compensate the broker for the time and expertise in selecting appropriate funds for the investor. Loads can be front-load (deducted upfront) or back-end load (deducted when sold) or low-load.

Loan commitments Loan commitments are a binding promise that a lender gives that a line of credit or specified amount of loan will be made available in the future to a named borrower at a certain interest rate for a given purpose over a given period. Terms of commitment generally have a commitment fee on any amount of unused credit over the life of the arrangement, plus a fee on the amount actually borrowed.

Loan participation Loan participations are arrangements by two or more lenders to share participation in a loan to a single borrower based on an agreed upon proportion used particularly for very large loans, with one or more banks taking on the role of lead bank that recruits other banks to participate.

Loan sales Banks that would prefer not to make longer-term loans often engage in loan sales, where loans are sold to longer-term lenders, such as insurance companies or pension funds. Banks can maintain the servicing arrangement and receive fee income, and gain liquidity and lower interest rate risk through loan sales.

Loan securitization Loan securitization is the process of pooling loans so that they can be repackaged into interest-bearing securities, with the interest and principal payments from the loans pooled passed on through to the purchasers of the securities.

Loan-to-value (LTV) ratio The LTV ratio for a mortgage loan is the loan amount divided by the appraised value of a property. High LTV ratios suggest credit risk for a loan, since this implies that a borrower has a smaller equity investment, and will have a greater incentive to walk away from a loan. Generally banks often use a maximum LTV ratio for mortgage loans of 75% to reduce the risk of the loan not being repaid.

Loanable Funds Theory of Interest Rates The Loanable Funds Theory of Interest Rates is a widely used theory of interest rates based on the real equilibrium interest rate in an economy being determined by the intersection of the supply and demand curves for loanable funds. The supply curve for loanable funds provided by net savers and changes in the money supply is upward sloping with more funds provided at higher rates, while the demand curve for loanable funds of net borrowers (governments and businesses) is downward sloping with more funds demanded when rates are lower. The intersection of the two curves determines the equilibrium real interest rates with different events and economic factors affecting shifts in each respective curve.

Loans to Insiders Act (Reg. O) U.S. Regulation O is a regulation for Federal Reserve system depository institution members concerning extensions of credit to insiders and transactions with affiliates. Reg. O covers different types of insider loans, extensions of credit by a member bank to an executive officer, director, or principal shareholder of the member bank, a bank holding company of which the member bank is a subsidiary, and any other subsidiary of that bank holding company. Reg. O limits loans to insiders, with depository institutions required to submit information on insider loans to regulators, and requires prior board approval. Banks are not allowed to give preferential loan terms to insiders.

Long hedge A long hedge entails taking a futures position to buy a security or other asset in the future, so a gain on the futures contract is made if prices rise and the price of the asset rises above the buy price locked in with the hedge. The futures gain is used to offset a spot loss that would occur on a spot position if the price of the asset rises. Examples are taking a long futures hedge to protect against a spot loss that occurs with a foreign exchange rate rise for a currency, or for a rise in the price of a security (i.e., hedging against a fall in interest rates).

Long tail of liability The long tail of liability refers to the long period whereby an insurance company may still have claims made on policies, since insurance claims for some types of policies have a protracted payout period, such as for liability insurance that can take many years to settle.

Long-term care (LTC) insurance LTC insurance is insurance coverage for long-term nursing care, home health care or adult day care for senior citizens that need intense supervision for chronic or disabling conditions that can be expensive and above government program amounts.

Loss ratio The loss ratio for an insurance company is the total losses paid by an insurance company for claims divided by total premiums earned. The loss ratio is an indicator of how well the insurance company is managing losses relative to premiums it receives.

Loss reserves Loss reserves for an insurance company are estimates for its liability for future claims. Loss reserves are typically invested in liquid assets and are estimated based on the type of insurance offered, the duration of the insurance contract, and the probability for a claim and the speed of its resolution.

McCarran–Ferguson Act of 1945 The McCarran–Ferguson Act establishes the right for the U.S. government to intervene in insurance activities if needed, but is not exercised if individual states adequately establish and enforce standards for insurance firms in their state..

McFadden Act of 1927 The McFadden Act was passed in Congress in the United States in 1927, and gave individual states the authority for governing branching restrictions within their respective state. The McFadden Act was modified in 1994 with the passage of the Riegle–Neale Interstate Banking and Branching Efficiency Act which allows banks to merge with other banks across state lines.

Managed float regime or dirty float A managed float regime is when a country's exchange rate is allowed to float on a day-to-day basis based on supply and demand factors, but when FX rates get too much out of line, central banks intervene to influence their country's exchange rate by buying and selling currencies.

Management buyouts (MBOs) A management buyout is an acquisition by a company or part of a company by its existing managers either from the parent company or from its private owners.

Managerial expense preference behavior Managerial expense preference behavior refers to the potential for managers to take excessive perquisites or other forms of behavior that maximize their own interests versus the owners of a firm. Managerial expense preference behavior is a form of agency cost in terms of managers engaging in behavior that does not maximize shareholders wealth, such as by increasing a firm's costs, including hiring larger staffs than necessary, lavishly furnishing offices, or enjoying large travel and expense accounts.

Market discipline Market discipline is Pillar 3 under the Basel Committee on Banking Supervision's Basel Capital Accord introduced under Basel II with the recognition that the stock market provides discipline for financial institutions to maintain adequate capital to cover potential losses, and that by having greater market transparency and disclosure, market discipline enhances capital regulation and other supervisory efforts to promote safety and soundness in banks and the financial system, with strong incentives for banks to maintain a strong capital base as a cushion against potential future losses from a bank's risk exposures.

Market segmentation theory for yield curves Under the market segmentation theory for the term structure of interest rates, investors have preferences for different security maturities, such as pension funds or life insurance companies preferring longer-term securities to fund longer-term commitments, and depository institutions preferring shorter-term investments for liquidity purposes. Under the market segmentation theory, interest rates will be determined separately in short-term and long-term markets by supply and demand factors in those respective markets, with little substitution across maturities.

Maturity risk premium A maturity risk premium is a risk premium for longer-term bonds, with investors demanding a higher yield for greater risk for longer-term bonds for capital losses with rises in interest rates and greater liquidity risk (risk of not being sold easily with little or no loss of value).

Mezzanine loans Mezzanine loans are longer-term, unsecured loans in which a firm's cash flow is the major source of repayment. Mezzanine financing often contains layers of investors with senior and junior debt, including warrants attached that allow investors a future equity stake in a firm, which creates different layers for the risk/return preferences of different groups of investors. Privately placed bond financing and venture capital are often involved with mezzanine financing. Payment in kind (PIK) bonds are at times issued similar to zero coupon bonds with interest accumulating, so the principal payment at maturity gets larger over time.

Microfinance Microfinance refers to financial products provided to the working poor, such as small loans, micro-loans, or microsavings products, or microinsurance products by microfinance financial institutions or other nonprofit organizations. While previously microfinance was done primarily by nonprofit firms, large financial institutions also make microfinance loans, and institutional investors also may engage in microfinance-related investments.

Microinsurance Microinsurance has been provided by insurers in developing countries through projects that offer low-cost insurance to individuals not covered by traditional insurance or government insurance programs, with the advantage that policies are generally for a lower cost than traditional insurance products. At times policies are offered with a small loan, with premiums set at a small percentage of the loan amount.

Minority enterprises small business investment companies (MESBICs) MESBICs in the United States provide debt and equity financing at lower costs to small businesses that are at least 51% owned by socially or economically disadvantaged persons.

Modern asset theory of FX rates Modern FX rate models are based on supply and demand factors that affect FX rates between countries based on capital mobility across countries. Different factors that affect FX rates include: (1) the relative supply and demand for goods and services in different countries: (2) the relative inflation rates across countries; and (3) the relative real interest rates in different countries, among other factors.

Modified duration (MD) MD is the price sensitivity of a security as the percentage change in price for a unit change in yield, and is calculated as its duration divided by $(1 + y*)$ where $y*$ is the current yield to maturity for a similar security. Modified duration is the approximate percentage change in a bond's price for a 100 basis point change in yield, under the assumption that a bond's expected cash flow does not change when the yield changes.

Money market funds Money market mutual funds are open-ended mutual funds that invest in short-term debt securities, such as U.S. Treasury bills and commercial paper, or other liquid, marketable short-term securities with maturities of 1 year or less that are generally high-quality and liquid.

Moral hazard Moral hazard is the risk or hazard that a transaction in a party is not acting in good faith or gets involved in risky behavior knowing that the other party will entail the cost of these actions. Examples include a borrower, once having received a loan, of walking away and not repaying a loan; the value of the loan becoming greater than the value of the collateral for the loan; or an individual with an insurance policy engaging in greater risk-taking activities. To reduce moral hazard, insurance companies require a deductible, whereby the insured has to pay a given amount of any loss before the insurance company will pay anything. Similarly depository institutions may require that borrowers have made a significant down payment in a home or a higher loan-to-value ratio to reduce the moral hazard risk of a borrower walking away from a loan.

Morningstar mutual fund ratings Morningstar fund ratings are rates published by Morningstar, a prominent mutual fund rating company. Ratings range from one to five stars (best) for different types of mutual funds. Ratings reflect measures based on a fund's risk-adjusted return relative to similar funds.

Mortgage banks A mortgage bank is a financial institution that originates mortgages utilizing funds borrowed from a warehouse lender or the firm's own funds to fund mortgages. Mortgage banks often sell their loans, and keep servicing rights or sell these to another financial institution. Mortgage funds, by warehousing and selling loans, reduce their risks of holding mortgages, with a business model to earn fees with loan originations and servicing rights versus keeping loans as assets.

Mortgage pass-through securities Mortgage pass-through securities are certificates of participation in pools of residential mortgages as securitizations, whereby shares in the interest and principal payment on a pool of mortgages are passed on to the investors that purchase these securities.

Mortgage-backed bonds Mortgage-backed bonds are bonds collateralized by mortgages on a financial institution's balance sheet. Mortgage bonds typically have a lower coupon rate than traditional debentures, since specific mortgage assets on a bank's balance sheet providing collateral offer bond investors lower risk.

Mutual fund families Mutual fund families are groups of mutual funds offered by a fund company, often called a family of funds, with many different funds over a large range of categories and investment objectives to choose from.

National Association of Insurance Commissioners (NAIC) The NAIC was created in 1871 in the United States and is an organization whose primary responsibility is to protect the interests of insurance consumers nationally. Some of the primary objectives of the NAIC are for the provision of support to insurance regulators nationwide with the promotion of competitive markets, improving insurance regulations, and the fair treatment of insurance consumers.

National Capital Declaration (NCD) The NCD is a finance sector initiative with endorsements at the CEO-level for the purpose of integrating natural capital considerations into loans, equity, fixed-income and insurance products, along with frameworks for accounting and disclosure. Signatory financial institutions provide support for the development of metrics and tools to assist in the incorporation of natural capital factors across their businesses.

National Credit Union Administration (NCUA) The NCUA charters, regulates and examines federally chartered credit unions and administers the National Credit Union Share Insurance Fund (NCUIF) that provides deposit insurance to protect deposits of credit union (CU) members at insured CUs.

National Information Center (NIC) The NIC is a central repository for data about banks and other depository institutions in the United States that includes both domestic and foreign banks operating in the United States, including holding companies with assets greater than $10 billion.

Negotiable certificate of deposit (NCD) Negotiable certificates of deposit are short-term, liquidity securities issued by large banks. An NCD can be bought and sold (traded) in the secondary market prior to maturity with a large denomination of $100,000 or larger. An NCD is generally short-term for 2 to 52 weeks.

Net asset value (NAV) The net asset value for an open-end mutual fund is calculated as the market value of securities less liabilities divided by the number of shares outstanding for the mutual fund. The NAV is the price per share for the mutual fund or for exchange traded funds, the price-share value. NAV is calculated daily based on closing market prices for the securities in a fund's portfolio.

Net interest margin (NIM) The NIM is a profitability measure for a depository institution equal to its net interest spread divided by its total earning assets (or as a proxy if earnings assets are not available divided by its total assets).

Net interest spread The net interest spread is the profit made for a depository institution for its traditional lending activities, calculated as an institution's interest revenues less its interest expenses.

Net loan charge-off A net loan charge-off measures net loans that have been written off by a depository institution. A net loan charge-off is equal to its loan charge-offs less any recoveries. The percentage of net loan charge-offs (net loan charge-offs to gross or net loans) for a depository institution is a measure of an institution's credit risk.

Net stable funding ratio (NSFR) NSFR is a required ratio under Basel III to address liquidity mismatches that can occur long-term encompassing the entire balance sheet. This requirement acts as an incentive for banks to utilize stable sources of funding and as a means for regulatory supervisory monitoring of banks for sound liquidity principles. The NSFR is basically the amount of stable funding that is available (based on the reliable portion of capital and liabilities over a given time period) divided by the required amount of stable funding required for a specific institution. The amount of stable funding required is based on the liquidity characteristics and residual maturities of various assets held by the institution as well as off-balance sheet exposures.

Net underwriting margin (NUM) The net underwriting margin for an insurance company is the difference between premiums earned and total policy expenses divided by total assets. A positive NUM indicates that an insurance firm has made an underwriting profit with premiums earned greater than total policy expenses. A negative NUM indicates an underwriting loss, with total policy expenses greater than premiums earned.

Nonaccruing loans Nonaccruing loans are loans where payments are not being received on the loan by a financial institution. Hence nonaccruing loans are nonperforming and are often related to financial difficulties on the part of the borrower, with these loans likely to default. Under standard banking regulations, nonperforming loans are required to be classified as nonaccrual when principal and interest have to be paid for 90 days or more, with an exception when the lender has collateral that is adequate to cover the loan.

Noncurrent loans For a depository institution, noncurrent loans are financial assets that are not current (up to date) on their loan payments. The percentage of noncurrent assets is used as a measure of an institution's credit risk, as an indicator of the amount of risky loans on the portfolio.

Nonperforming loans or assets Nonperforming loans are assets consisting of nonaccrual loans, accruing loans 90 days past due, repossessed assets, and other real estate owned.

Office of the Comptroller of the Currency (OCC) The OCC was established to create a uniform national currency under the National Currency Act during the U.S. Civil War. The OCC charters and examines federally insured commercial banks, that were authorized for the OCC to charter in 1864 under the National Banking Act, that originated the dual system of federal and state chartered banks.

Open-end mutual funds Open-end mutual funds are mutual funds that continuously offer new shares to the public that can be redeemed (and bought back) at any time upon a shareholder's request unless a fund becomes too large and is sometimes closed to new investors. In the United States mutual funds by federal law are required to redeem outstanding shares upon a shareholder's request at a price based at the current value of the fund's net asset value (NAV).

Open market operations Open market operations are undertaken by central banks to expand or contract the money supply. To expand the money supply and stimulate the economy, the central bank purchases bonds from the nonbank public, in exchange for deposits placed in nonbank public accounts that in turn can be used by banks to make loans. With a greater supply of loanable funds, this in turn reduces the real interest rate (targeted as the Fed Funds rate in the United States) stimulating the economy. To reduce the money supply and contract the economy, the central bank sells bonds to the nonbank public reducing deposits in nonbank public accounts and in turn reducing deposits that banks can use, reducing bank loans. This in turn reduces loanable funds available, resulting in a higher equilibrium interest rate, contracting the economy.

Operation Twist Operation Twist is the name given to the Federal Reserve's policy of selling short-term government bonds and purchasing long-term bonds for the purpose of pushing down long-term rates, encouraging corporations to issue bonds and take on new capital projects that would increase hiring and reduce unemployment following the U.S. subprime loan crisis. The name comes from the effort to twist the yield curve, so long-term rates would fall.

Options on futures contracts Options on futures contracts can be purchased on an exchange for a premium that allows the hedger the right, but not the obligation, to exercise the option. Call options on futures contracts are options to purchase futures contracts in the future. Put options are options on futures contracts to sell in the future. The advantage of options on futures contracts is that they do not have to be exercised if futures prices go the opposite way expected, so a futures loss does not have to be taken. Since they do not have to be exercised, the maximum loss with an options contract is the premium price.

OREO For a depository institution, OREO stands for other real estate owned which includes property taken (as previous collateral) for unpaid loans, listed at market value. Problem banks often have large OREO accounts, with the percentage of OREO and noncurrent assets varying across different regions as a reflection of different regional conditions.

Other borrowed funds Other borrowed funds (short-term commercial paper, Eurodollar CDs, bankers' acceptances) are short-term securities that can be traded prior to maturity. Other types of borrowed money including FHLB advances (short-term borrowings from the Federal Home Loan Bank System), are also often used, along with other short-term liabilities.

Overall operating ratio for insurance companies An insurance company's overall operating ratio is equal to the combined ratio less the investment income ratio. A ratio below 100% indicates the insurer is making a profit from its operations, while a ratio above 100% indicates a loss with costs higher than investment income.

Overall profitability ratio for insurance companies The overall profitability ratio for an insurance company is calculated as 100% less the combined ratio (often after dividends) plus the investment yield. Since property/liability companies have had underwriting losses as indicated by their combined ratios, which have been greater than 100%, their profitability has often depended on generating revenue from their investment yield; hence the overall profitability ratio provides a measure of a property/liability insurance company's overall profitability.

Overallotment or greenshoe option An overallotment option for an investment bank for an offering it underwrites, often called "a greenshoe option," is an overallotment of shares, which the investment bank can choose to exercise to stabilize an issue or make a profit on the spread between the allotment price and the selling price of the securities over a particular period of time. By using a greenshoe option giving the right to sell investors more shares than planned if the demand for a security is higher than expected, the underwriter gets the ability to increase the supply of the issue, and reduces price fluctuations if there is a surge in demand for the issue. Typically, greenshoe options permit underwriters to sell up to 15% more shares than the original number set by the issue.

Past due loans Past due loans are loans with payments that have not been made as of a due date. A borrower may be subject to late fees, unless the borrower is within a grace period, with past due loans generally loans that are past due for 30 to 89 days.

Pay as you drive auto insurance Pay as you drive auto insurance is an individualized insurance policy whereby drivers are charged based on the amount they drive. Pay for drive policies are offered in the United States in over 25 states through several different insurance companies. These policies may entail using a proprietary onboard device measuring mileage or OnStar. For premiums, other factors are also considered, including an individual's accident history, type of car, state, age, gender, and marital status, among others.

Peer-to-peer (P2P) lending Peer-to-peer lending entails debt financing outside of a financial intermediary through P2P online platforms, with popular platforms including Upstart, Funding Circle, Prosper Marketplace, CircleBack Lending, Peerform, SoFi, Lending Club, and The Bottom Line, among others. Many times loans are made for relatively small amounts.

Pension Benefit Guaranty Corporation (PBGC) The PBGC was established under the Employee Retirement Income Security Act (ERISA) of 1974 to guarantee the benefits of defined benefit pension funds for public corporations in the United States regulated by ERISA.

Planned amortization class (PAC) bond A PAC bond is a special type of collateralized mortgage obligation (CMO) with lower risk by having a fixed amortization schedule, so investors can better predict when a particular tranche of bonds will mature. If actual prepayment rates differ from the expected prepayment rates, principal payments to designated tranches are reduced or increased to ensure that PAC CMOs mature as scheduled.

Pledged deposits In the United States for uninsured public deposits (Treasury tax and loan accounts and local and state government accounts), banks are required to hold these or a portion of these in safe, qualified securities (generally U.S. Treasury securities), as a pledging requirement.

Policyholder surplus Policyholder surplus is equal to total assets of a mutual insurance company less its total liabilities. Policyholder surplus is used as an indicator of an insurance company's ability to withstand losses and have additional funds available to be able to pay unexpected amounts of claims.

Preferred habitat theory The preferred habitat theory is a modification of the market segmentation theory for the term structure of interest rates, whereby different investors have preferences for different types of maturities for securities, but substitutions are allowed among security maturity segments, if a premium exists to induce them to switch to a different maturity than their preferred maturity choice.

Premium to surplus ratio The premium to surplus ratio used by insurance companies is equal to net premiums written (or at times gross premiums) divided by an insurance company's policyholder surplus. This ratio is used to measure the capacity an insurance company has to underwrite new policies.

Premiums earned Premiums earned are the total premiums an insurance company collects over a given period based on the ratio of the time passed on the policies to their effective life, as a measure of the pro-rated paid in advance premiums that have been earned that belong to the insurer.

Present value interest factor of annuity (PVIFA) The present value of an annuity factor is used to calculate the present value of a series of equal payments over a given period of time, n, given a discount rate, r. The PVIFA is calculated as $\{[1 - (1 / (1 + r)^n] / r\}$ where r is the market interest rate and n is the number of periods. The present value of the annuity (PVA) is equal to the annuity payment (PMT) times the PVIFA factor, given r and n.

Present value of a single sum factor (PVIF) The present value of a single sum factor (PVIF) is the factor to find the present value of future cash flows, discounting them back to the present. The PVIF is calculated as $\{1 / (1 + r)^n\}$ where r is the discount rate (opportunity cost rate) and n is the number of periods. The present value of a single sum (PV) is equal to the future cash flow (FV) times the PVIF factor, given r and n.

Price-level adjusted mortgages (PLAMs) PLAMs are mortgages that have an adjustable interest rate tied to an inflation rate index versus an interest rate index, so a borrower pays for actual versus expected inflation and benefits from lower initial interest rates that are not adjusted for expected inflation.

Price risk The risk for a bond having to be sold at a capital loss if interest rates rise and the bond has to be sold prior to maturity for a given investment horizon.

Price/yield relationship The inverse relationship between prices and yields for securities, whereby a lower price implies a higher yield, and a higher price, a lower yield.

Principal only (PO) collateralized mortgage obligations (CMOs) Stripped mortgage-backed securities separate securities into classes of interest only (IO) and principal only (PO) paying securities. With prepayment risk, the value of POs declines in value if interest rates rise, since prepayments are not likely to occur, increasing the expected maturity of the PO, and reducing the POs value with principal payments discounted at a higher rate.

Principal transactions Trading activities done for the firm itself to generate income, such as trading, buying or selling for a firm's own account, entailing trades at its own risk.

Private placements Private placements are nonpublic offerings whereby securities are sold through a private offering, generally to institutional investors or other chosen investors, with private investment in public equity (PIPE) deals a special type of private placement.

Project financing Project financing is a loan structure relying on a specific project cash flows for repayment, with the project's assets, rights, and interests used as secondary collateral.

Provision for loan losses (PLL) A financial institution's loan loss provision is an expense set aside for expected future loan losses on its income statement. Managers have some discretion in determining the provision for loan losses taken in a given year.

Purchased funds Purchased funds (often called volatile deposits) are large time deposits including Jumbo CDs and brokered deposits and other uninsured funds. Since these types of deposits are less stable and interest rate sensitive, purchased funds can leave the bank at any time if there is bad news about the bank or more competitive rates elsewhere. Hence, a bank's percentage of purchased fund financing is used as a measure of a bank's liquidity risk on the liability side. Purchased funds are also more interest rate sensitive than core deposits.

Purchasing power parity (PPP) Purchasing power parity is a theory of how foreign exchange rates should act in the long-run, based on the law of one price, that if two countries are producing identical goods, the price of a good should be the same globally regardless of the country producing it. If costs differ, the foreign exchange (FX) rate for two countries' currencies should adjust to make the price identical. Hence, FX rates should adjust to reflect changes in the price levels of the two countries, such as high inflation in a country resulting in a depreciation of that country's FX rate in the long-term.

Pure premium A pure premium is the expected present value of the payout for an insurer based on probabilities of a claim occurring. To calculate a pure premium, generally a conservative discount rate is used as required by state regulators.

Quantitative easing (QE) QE is a nonconventional monetary policy whereby a central bank purchases huge amounts of government securities or other securities in return for money paid back to the nonbank public to increase the money supply, targeting lower interest rates to stimulate the economy, such as the quantitative easing policies that the U.S. Federal Reserve engaged in following the U.S. subprime loan crisis.

RAROC (risk-adjusted return on capital) RAROC is a technique for including the cost of equity capital used in making a loan in pricing the interest rate on the loan and is used by large money center banks, whereby a loan or other particular asset is given a capital charge based on the amount of capital that needs to be held on the asset according to its risk, with a larger amount of capital needed to be held for more risk assets.

Rate-sensitive assets A financial institution's assets that are maturing are variable and hence sensitive to interest rate changes for a given funding gap period.

Rate-sensitive liabilities A financial institution's liabilities that are maturing or that have variable rates and hence are sensitive to interest rate changes for a given funding gap period.

Real estate investment trusts (REITs) REITs are unit trusts with real estate investments that are held passively for an agreed-upon period of time, whereupon assets are distributed among the shareholders.

Real Estate Settlement Procedure Act (RESPA) RESPA is a U.S. law requiring that lenders provide servicing transfer disclosure and a good faith estimate (GFE) within three business days of receipt of a completed application, the provision of a settlement cost brochure for home purchases only, and a HUD-1 or HUD-A1A Settlement Statement that must be prepared and made available prior to loan closing.

Regulation A Regulation A is an exemption from registration requirements that are mandated by the U.S. Securities Act for small public offerings not greater than $5 million in any 12-month period, with a requirement that an offering statement must be filed with the SEC.

Regulation A+ Under Title IV of the U.S. JOBS Act, the SEC was directed to adopt rules allowing offerings of up to $50 million of securities within a 12-month period that would require audited statements to be filed with the SEC. Under Regulation A+ that was approved in 2015, two tiers of offerings would be allowed to be sold to unaccredited investors for startup, including Tier 1 for offerings of securities up to $20 million, with not more than $6 million in offers by security-holders that are affiliated within a 12-month period; and Tier 2 for offerings of securities up to $50 million, with not more than $15 million in offers by security-holders that are affiliates of an issuer, along with basic requirements for additional disclosure and reporting requirements.

Regulation Q (Reg. Q) Regulation Q was part of the U.S. Banking Act of 1933 which prohibited banks from banking interest on demand deposits and putting other restrictions on rates for other types of deposits. Reg. Q interest rate caps were phased out under the Federal Deposit Insurance Corporation Improvement Act (FDICIA) of 1991 and for demand deposits in 2011.

Regulation Z (Reg. Z) U.S. law that sets standards for disclosing the terms and costs of a consumer credit agreement before the borrower becomes obligated, establishing a period during which a consumer may cancel a transaction and procedures through which a consumer can challenge billing errors on revolving credit agreements. Institutions must comply with both state and federal legislation; if there are any contradictions between the two, federal statutes prevail.

Regulatory classifications for securities U.S. bank regulators classify securities into three groups: (1) Tier 1 securities that carry very low or no default risk (i.e., U.S. Treasuries, federal agency securities, and general obligation municipal bonds that are backed by the taxing power of the state or municipal government issuing the bonds) that depository institutions can hold in unlimited amounts; (2) Tier 2 securities that include quasi-public, federal and municipal agency securities and selected state agencies with public projects, with restrictions that more than 15% of a bank's capital and surplus be invested in any single issuer; (3) Tier 3 securities that include investment grade (BBB ratings or better), with no more than 10% of capital and surplus in any single issue.

Reinsurance Reinsurance for insurance companies is a transfer of a portion of risk portfolios to a reinsurer or other institutions through an agreement to reduce the risk to the insurer by spreading the risk across alternative institutions.

Reinvestment risk The risk for coupon bonds of lower coupon income if interest rates fall resulting in lower reinvestment income.

Repurchase agreements (repos) Repos represent the short-term sale of Treasury bills or other liquid securities by a bank to another bank that are agreed to be repurchased at a higher price by the borrowing bank (i.e., an exceptionally short-term, collateralized loan). To the lending bank, this repurchase agreement is a short-term asset called a reverse repurchase agreement, while to the borrowing bank, the agreement is a repurchase agreement as a short-term liability.

Reputational risk Reputational risk is the risk of a financial institution losing its reputation through any dealings that have conflicts of interest, are unethical, or through failure of due diligence or other breaches including failure for standards of service and quality, that harm a firm's future business prospects.

Reserve requirements Reserve requirements (or cash reserve ratios) is a regulation by central banks, and employed by most central banks globally, setting a minimum fraction of a depository institution's deposits that must be held as cash or cash-equivalent reserves with the central bank or in a bank's vaults. Reserve requirements serve as a safeguard against sudden deposit withdrawals, such as a bank run, and are used as a tool by the central bank to inject liquidity into or contract liquidity in an economy.

Restrictive covenants Restrictive covenants are binding legal obligations for a bond or loan agreement requiring borrowers to maintain, for instance, minimum liquidity or debt ratios; restricting borrowers from taking on additional debt or limitations on dividend payments or minimum current and quick ratios, among others, such as requiring life insurance on key personnel, required notification on key personnel changes, and receiving quarterly financial statements from the borrowing firm. The loan may state that if covenants are not met, a loan may be called.

Reverse annuity mortgage (RAM) A RAM is a reverse mortgage that allows seniors facing cash shortages to gradually, in effect, sell their property to a depository institution, whereby the owner of the property receives regular cash annuity payments. When the borrower with the RAM moves out or passes away, the property is sold, and the lender receives the repayment with interest from the proceeds of the sale.

Revolving credit Credit that is automatically renewed as debts are paid off, where generally a customer pays a commitment fee and then is allowed to utilize funds as needed, such as for operating purposes, with amounts varying depending on a customer's cash flow needs.

Riegle–Neal Interstate Banking and Branching Efficiency Act (IBBEA) IBBEA was passed in 1994, which removed most restrictions on interstate bank acquisition and interstate branching allowing banks to engage in interstate banking and branching across state lines, which previously had been restricted and subject to state branching laws under the McFadden Act of 1927. The goal of the act was to restore competitiveness to the banking system in response to relaxed branching regulations for state chartered banks. The act also included a provision that a federally chartered bank that wished to expand needed to undergo a review for Community Reinvestment Act compliance.

Risk-adjusted performance measures for mutual funds There are a number of different risk-adjusted performance measures for mutual fund portfolios including: (1) the standard deviation of returns; (2) value at risk; (3) the Sharpe ratio; (4) the M-square measure; and (5) the Morningstar return and risk measures, betas, and asset class measures.

Risk-based capital (RBC) Risk-based capital is a method used by regulators to recognize the minimum amount of capital needed by an insurance company to support its operations considering both its size and risk profile. In the United States the National Association of Insurance Commissioners developed a RBC system for minimum risk-based capital ratios for insurance firms.

Risk pooling Risk pooling is a key concept of insurance, whereby insurance allows the spreading of financial risks across a large pool of individuals or companies, allowing the transfer of risk, so funds are available to meet unplanned financial catastrophe risks. Premiums are set across policyholders to have sufficient funds to cover risks.

Risk spread A measure of the default risk premium on a bond, taking the rate for a risk bond for a given maturity less the risk-free rate for the same maturity for government bonds guaranteed by the government, such as the U.S. Treasury bond rate with the same maturity. Generally during economic recessions risk spreads tend to get larger and during economic expansions they often get smaller. Risk spreads can be calculated for different bonds based on their credit rating by Moody's or Standard and Poor's (i.e., Aaa or AAA; Aa or AA, Baa or BBB, Ba or BB, Caa or CA or CCC, CC, and D grades). Bonds with greater credit risk tend to have larger risk premiums.

Robo investment firms Online automated investment service firms, often called robo advisers, that allocate funds for investors based on their goals, risk preferences, and profiles, with different robo advisers offering different services and educational and investment tools, including stock/bond allocations, portfolio rebalancing, dividend reinvestment, and other services. ETF and asset allocations are determined by the robo adviser, increasing the ease of investing, but at times limiting flexibility and choices.

Roth IRA A Roth IRA in the United States is an individual retirement account in which an individual sets aside after-tax income up to a specified amount each year to save for retirement. Both earnings and withdrawals after age 59½ are tax free, encouraging savings for retirement.

Savings institutions Financial institutions that accept deposits from predominantly individuals that are used to finance primarily residential mortgage loans. These include both savings banks and savings and loans associations and are also often called thrift institutions since they encouraging savings.

SBA loans SBA loans are loans for small businesses that are generally collateralized with a portion of the loan guaranteed by the U.S. Small Business Administration, so the lender is protected against default risk.

Seasonal working capital loans Seasonal working capital loans are loans financing seasonable inventory and accounts receivable that are usually paid back within a year after sales are made and that are typically collateralized by inventory and accounts receivable.

Secondary offerings A secondary offering is when new stock is issued for public sale for a company that has already gone public, through the assistance of an investment bank that underwrites the offering.

Sector mutual funds Sector mutual funds (specialty funds) focus equity investments on a single sector of the economy (i.e., energy, health care, real estate, technology, consumer staples, precious metals) and often use ETFs for sector investing.

Securities and Exchange Commission (SEC) The SEC was established in 1934 in the United States under the Securities Exchange Act. The SEC regulates organized exchanges and financial markets, including requirements for disclosure and restricting insider trading. The SEC is also responsible for regulating investment companies and investment advisers and mutual funds.

Securitization Securitizations are created when pools of loans are packaged into portfolios and sold off-balance sheet to a specialized securitization enterprise and passed on to a trust organization to be repackaged as participating securities with cash flows received by investors on principal and interest. Meanwhile the bank originating the loans often maintains the servicing rights and receives fee income for doing so.

Self-insurance Self-insurance is when companies or individuals set aside their own money to be able to pay for a potential loss versus purchasing insurance, where funds are paid out of pocket if an incident occurs, often for risks of a smaller nature versus expensive risks.

Shadow banking system A shadow banking system is the system of financial intermediaries who facilitate and create financial transactions, including expansion of credit across the global financial system, but who are not technically banks, so are not subject to regulatory oversight. Shadow banking also often includes unregulated activities that regulated financial institutions engage in.

Short hedge A short hedge is a hedge that takes a futures position to sell an asset in the future to make a futures gain to offset a spot loss if prices fall (i.e., interest rates rise).

Side-car A side-car, an innovative type of catastrophe risk bond with a simple agreement, allows a reinsurer or group of investors, such as hedge funds, to purchase through private placement catastrophic bonds that provide a share in the profit or loss produced along with an reinsurer.

Small business investment corporations (SBICs) SBICs in the United States offer small business funding with $4 of low-cost government debt for every $1 of stockholder equity, providing capital often in the form of convertible debenture debt for small businesses capable of an annual cash flow that will allow firms to repay their commitments.

Social and environmental banks Banks formed with environmental and social goals in addition to economic goals with the aim to have a positive impact through banking on people, the environment, and culture.

Social Capital Protocol The Social Capital Protocol is a challenge by the World Business Council for Sustainable Development (WBCSD), a CEO-led organization of companies that are forward thinking, to create a sustainable future for business, society, and the environment. The Protocol is for the creation of a world where profit and loss, performance, and value creation are redefined to integrate longer-term environmental and social impacts and dependencies (www.wbcsd.org).

Social finance Social finance applies finance for a social objective, which in addition to being the focus of governments and charities has also become a specialized finance area for for-profit companies, including banks, consumer finance companies, and telecom companies, and social entrepreneurs, among others.

Social impact bonds Social impact bonds, also called "pay for success" bonds or social benefit bonds, are contracts made with the public sector that make a commitment to pay for improved social outcomes that contribute to public sector savings.

Social security Social security generally is any government system that provides assistance benefits to its public. In the U.S. Social Security is a federal government insurance program that provides public benefits including retirement income, disability income, Medicare and Medicaid, and deaths and survivorship benefits.

Socially responsible investment (SRI) funds Mutual funds that use positive or negative screens for environmental, social, and governance (ESG) factors in making portfolio decisions. SRI funds also engage in impact investing to generate competitive financial returns and have a positive societal impact. Different funds emphasize different approaches and interests, including community investing, ethical investing, green investing, impact investing, mission-related investing, responsible investing, socially responsible investing, sustainable investing, and value-based investing, among other approaches (see USSIF, The Forum for Sustainable and Responsible Investment, at: www.ussif.org/sribasics)

Special purpose vehicle (SPV) A SPV or special purpose entity (SPE) is created to carry out a specific business purpose as a separate entity used for a structured finance transaction, such as a securitization that allows the isolation of specific company assets or operations.

Stabilization techniques Underwriters of new stock issues are allowed to use stabilization techniques during the first 30 days of a new stock issue, whereby they purchase or sell securities to stabilize the security's price. By making stabilizing bids, underwriters attempt to keep a stock's price from falling if there is selling pressure by investors, such as flipping their shares to make a short-term profit.

Stakeholders Stakeholders are those that can affect or are affected by an organization's or corporation's actions that include in addition to stockholders, creditors, directors, employees, regulators, consumers, suppliers, unions, and community members where a business operates.

Statutory Accounting Principles (SAP) The Statutory Accounting Principles are a set of regulations submitted by state regulatory bodies for insurance companies that are generally more conservative than generally accepted accounting principles (GAAP) for preparing insurance company financing statements.

Sterilized FX intervention A sterilized foreign exchange intervention by a country's central bank takes an offsetting action for the purchase or sale of foreign reserves that has an offsetting effect of reducing or increasing the country's currency in circulation. To offset these respective effects the central bank engages in a respective counteraction by engaging in open market operations to respectively increase or reduce the country's currency in circulation to its previous level before the unsterilized FX intervention.

Stock index futures Stock index futures are futures contracts with an underlying stock index as the asset behind the contract. Stock index futures are used to hedge stock portfolios and have special characteristics including no delivery, overall price limits set by the exchange, and prices set equal to an index level times an established multiple, whereby the settlement price equals the index at settlement times the multiplier.

Stored liquidity approach A stored liquidity approach to managing liquidity involves holding securities to be available for sale for expected and unexpected liquidity needs. Under this strategy a depository institution may keep a pyramid of reserves as primary reserves including cash and short-term marketable securities, along with secondary reserves that are more intermediate term investments that can be sold for secondary reserves as securities that are available for sale.

Stress test Stress tests for banks include an analysis of unfavorable economic scenarios, designed to determine if a bank has sufficient capital to withstand the impact of adverse conditions, in order to evaluate the strength of the institution.

Structured investment vehicles (SIV) A SIV is used by banks to sell loans that are repackaged as bonds and mortgage-backed securities. A SIV contains a pool of investment assets that profits from credit spreads between short-term debt and long-term structured finance products such as asset-backed securities, with funding coming from issuing commercial paper that is constantly rolled over or renewed to invest in longer maturity assets. SIVs also use financial leverage to earn higher returns. SIVs are also often referred to as conduits.

Style investing Style investing refers to the investment style for mutual fund investments that reflect the style of different investment managers of funds. Styles for stock mutual funds include value stocks, value/growth stocks, and growth stocks and style choices of investing in large-cap, mid-cap, and small-cap stocks. For bond mutual funds styles include short-term, intermediate term, and long-term stocks, and different credit qualities from high-credit grade, to mid-credit to low-credit quality.

Subchapter M Subchapter M of the U.S. Investment Act of 1940 requires mutual funds to pass-through distribution of 90% of income and capital gains to shareholders to allow these not to be taxed under the Internal Revenue Code.

Sustainability Sustainability is a method of using resources frugally, so that these resources are not depleted or damaged permanently. From an environmental perspective, sustainability involves not harming the environment, reducing carbon emissions, operating more efficiently and using less energy and reducing costs, as well as not depleting natural resources, and supporting a long-term ecological balance and an economically sustainable business.

Sustainability Accounting Standards Board (SASB) SASB is an independent nonprofit organization, accredited to set standards by the American National Standards Institute (ANSI) to provide sustainability accounting standards for use by publicly listed corporations in their financial statements, which includes disclosing material sustainability issues. SASB has developed standards for 80 industries including for the commercial banking, investment banking, insurance, brokerage and asset management sectors, among many others.

Syndicate A syndicate is a group of financial institutions formed for the purpose of handling large transactions that would be risky or hard for a single financial institution to handle and allowing a pooling of resources and shared risks. For an underwriting syndicate of investment banks, the group is formed to work together to bring out a new initial public offering and sell the issue, with the leading institution, the syndicate manager.

Synthetic CDOs A synthetic CDO is a variation for a CDO that usually entails the use of credit default swaps and other derivatives to meet particular investment goals.

Target date funds (TDF) A target date fund (also called a lifecycle, dynamic-risk or age-based fund) is a hybrid mutual fund that is designed to have a portfolio asset allocation mix that becomes more conservative the closer an individual is to retirement. Target date funds invest in an asset mix of stocks, bonds, and cash equivalents in a portfolio according to a selected time frame that is appropriate for a particular investor. Fund managers rebalance the portfolio each year to keep investments to meet different investors picking different target date fund goals. A deficiency of target date funds is that they don't consider the risk tolerance for different investors within a single target fund, and different target date funds have different risk and investment expenses to consider.

Tax equivalent yield To compare bond rates that are tax-deductible on a before tax basis, the tax equivalent (TE) yield is often calculated to treat municipal bonds as if they would be taxed on a before tax basis by dividing the yield by $(1 - t)$ where t is the marginal tax rate of the investor.

Term life insurance Insurance for a shorter period of time, such as a year, that pays a benefit in the event of the death of the insured during a specified term, with the premium the actuarial premium determined for that year based on a person's age, with term premiums rising as a person ages, with no excess premium or savings vehicle or accumulated cash value. Alternative policies offer constant premiums but decreasing coverage with age, and other options are also available. Term policies are frequently offered at lower rates as group plans as part of employee benefit packages.

Term loans Term loans are longer-term loans used to purchase depreciable assets with maturities from 1 to 7 years generally for the amount for the purchase price of an asset that are typically amortized for a gradual repayment of interest and principal over the life of the loan and structured to match cash flows generated by the firm over the life of the equipment purchased.

Term structure of interest rates The term structure of interest rates is the relationship between yield to maturity (y^*) and time to maturity for a homogeneous group of bonds, with the same characteristics otherwise including default risk and marketability.

Too big to fail (TBTF) TBTF are financial organizations or other businesses that are so important to an economy that a government or central bank feels obliged to keep these from going bankrupt to avoid systemic effects across an economy and contagion effects.

Trading account assets Trading account assets are securities, primarily Treasury or municipal securities traded by large banks (with > $1 billion in assets) to make a short-term profit from trades.

Traditional IRA A traditional IRA is an individual retirement account in the United States that permits individuals to invest pre-tax income up to specific annual limits towards investments that can grow tax-deferred (no capital gain or dividend income is taxed) until later when withdrawals are taken.

Transaction FX risk exposure Risk of a loss if foreign exchange rates change when one party is paid in one currency and must pay for the transaction in another currency. An example is when an exporter is being repaid in a foreign currency and has the risk of the value of the foreign currency falling in value in the future when the exporter is repaid.

Translation FX risk exposure Risk of the market value of a bank's equity falling in value when assets and liabilities for a financial institution are in different currencies, whereby the market value of a firm's equity is the value of assets less the value of liabilities, denominated in the bank's domestic currency.

Treasury bills A Treasury bill is a short-term (less than 1 year) U.S. government security that is sold at a discount with a single maturity value, guaranteed by the U.S. government.

Troubled Assets Relief Program (TARP) During the U.S. subprime loan crisis in 2008, Congress approved a U.S. government program to purchase assets and take a preferred stock equity stake in financial institutions to restore liquidity to the money markets and financial system and reduce the fallout from the subprime loan crisis. TARP provided the Treasury with purchasing power of $700 billion for these purchases.

Truth in Lending (TIL) Truth in Lending is a U.S. law that promotes the transparency of consumer credit and requires disclosures for the terms and costs of loans in a standardized format, and rates quotes as annual percentage rates (APRs).

UN Principles for Responsible Investment (PRI) United Nations Principles for Responsible Investment incorporate environmental, social and governance (ESG) factors into investment decisions for better management of risk and the generation of sustainable long-term returns (see PRI, at: https://www.unpri.org/about/what-is-responsible-investment).

UN Principles for Responsible Management Education (PRME) The Principles for Responsible Management Education initiative was launched in 2007 at the UN Global Compact Leaders Summit in Geneva as the first organized relationship between the United Nations and business schools with the mission of a transformation of management education, research, and thought leadership globally based on six principles including: (1) *Purpose:* Development of capabilities of students as future generators of sustainable value for business and society to build an inclusive and sustainable global economy; (2) *Values:* Incorporating values of global social responsibility; (3) *Method:* Creating educational frameworks, materials, processes and environments to enable effective learning experiences for responsible leadership; (4) *Research:* Engaging in conceptual and empirical research to advance the role, dynamics and impact of corporations in creating sustainable social, environmental and economic value; (5) *Partnership:* Interacting with managers of business corporations to expand knowledge of their challenges in meeting social and environmental responsibilities and exploring effective approaches for meeting these challenges; and (6) *Dialogue:* Facilitating and supporting debate between educators, students, business, government, consumers, the media and interested groups and stakeholders on critical issues associated with global social responsibility and sustainability (see UNPRME at: http://www.unprme.org/about-prme/the-six-principles.php).

Underwriting gross spread An underwriter's gross spread is the difference between the underwriting price received by the company issuing securities and the price that is offered to the public for a security, with the gross spread what compensates underwriters for an initial public offering (IPO) to cover the investment banker's expenses including management fees, commissions, and risk.

Uniform Commercial Code (UCC) In the United States, the UCC is the body of law adopted by states containing established guidelines under which commercial transaction agreements are drawn.

Uniform residential loan application A uniform residential loan application as used by Fannie Mae and Freddie Mac for single-family residential mortgage loans in the United States provides a uniform application for home purchase or refinancing of a home purchase of the applicant's principal dwelling where the dwelling used as collateral must also be provided, along with a notice of the right to receive a copy of the appraisal if applicable.

Unit investment trusts (UTIs) UTIs are interests in a fixed portfolio of securities that are held passively for an agreed upon period of time, whereby assets are distributed among the shareholders.

Universal life insurance Insurance that includes the death benefit protection features of term insurance with the opportunity to earn market rates of return on excess premiums and take advantage of tax-free investment accumulations, with lump sum premiums allowed as well as a series of payments and a minimum guaranteed return. Unlike whole or variable life policies, the face amount of guaranteed death protection in a universal life policy can be changed at the policyholder's option, including adjustments of death benefits, premium payments, and risk and return selection as needs change. Investors also may have the option of investing excess premiums in different types of investments and mutual funds.

Unsterilized FX intervention A unsterilized foreign exchange intervention by a country involves buying or selling international reserves, such as in the case of an unvalued currency, an intervention by selling international reserves of assets denominated in a foreign currency in return for the country's currency. This action has the unintended effect of reducing the country's currency in circulation, which can have a contraction effect on that country. To counter this effect a sterilized intervention is used where the central bank engages in an offset purchase of government securities, putting the currency back in circulation.

U.S. Department of Labor Fiduciary Rule for Investment Advisers A rule released by the U.S. Department of Labor in April 2016 for fiduciaries for investment advice provided to retirement savers by investment advisers, whereby anyone providing investment advice on retirement accounts must act as a fiduciary and put investors interests first, before the adviser's own interests and not steer investors into in-house funds over other nonhouse funds, particularly if given compensation for transactions in house funds.

U.S. subprime loan crisis The financial crisis that occurred in the United States during 2007 to 2008, when a real estate downturn spiral resulted in large subprime loan bankruptcies and collateralized debt obligations tied to these loans becoming worthless, leading to large financial institution failures and contagion.

Value at risk (VAR) Value at risk is a statistical method used to quantify the level of financial risk for an investment portfolio for a given time period, measuring the amount of potential loss based on the probability historically for a loss based on its volatility.

Valuation using discounted future cash flows The present valuation of a security that is calculated as the present value of its future cash flows.

Variable life insurance Variable life insurance policies like whole life policies have premiums over a policyholder's lifetime, but excess premiums over pure premium amounts built up each year earn variable rates rather than fixed-rates of return based on a policyholder's choice of investments, passing on investment risk and the opportunity for higher returns by the policyholder, with a minimum death benefit specified on the policy, with the actual payment to beneficiaries depending on yields earned on excess premiums.

Venture capital (VC) funds VC funds are investment funds that are organized as limited partnerships with managing partners and limited (passive) investors, with the majority of investors institutional investors, including insurance companies, pension funds, corporations, endowments, foreign investors, and angel investors. VC funds provide capital for firms just starting, startup capital for firms beginning to operate or manufacture a product, and later stage capital and temporary (bridge) financing. VC firms look for firms that will make large returns and have high expected growth to be able to harvest investments through initial public offerings or selling the firm in a relatively short time frame of five to seven years.

Volatility Index (VIX) VIX is a popular measure for the implied volatility of the S&P 500 index options, calculated by the Chicago Board Options Exchange (CBOE) which gives the market's expectation for 30-day volatility, as a forward looking measure of market risk.

Volcker Rule Under the Volcker Rule provisions of the U.S. Dodd–Frank Act of 2010, insured depository institutions, bank holding companies, and their affiliates are prohibited from engaging in proprietary trading or acquiring or having an ownership interest in covered funds (hedge funds or private equity funds, among others), with the final version of the rule adopted in December 2013. Proprietary trading whereby a bank is engaging as a principal for the trading account for the buying and selling of a financial instrument cannot be larger than 3% of Tier 1 capital.

Warehouse receipts A collateral arrangement where specific inventory items assigned as collateral under the control of a third party are used, whereby the goods may be physically transferred to a bonded warehouse for safekeeping.

Weather derivatives Future exchanges offer weather-based index future products, including temperature-based indexes for major cities in the United States and Europe offered by the CME Group, providing a financial tool making weather a commodity that can be traded to provide protection for companies for risks that are weather related.

Whole life insurance Whole life insurance is a type of permanent life insurance, with guaranteed equal premiums, that pays a benefit on the death of the insured and also serves partially as an investment vehicle by accumulating a cash value and often allowing for policy loans based on the cash value.

Wolfsberg's Anti-Money Laundering (AML) Principles The Wolfsberg Group of International Financial Institutions are a group of 13 global banks aiming to develop frameworks and guidance for the management of financial crime risks and greater transparency.

World Bank The World Bank is an international organization that provides financing, advice, and research for developing and poorer nations with the purpose of aiding their economic development. The World Bank aims to help to eliminate poverty by means of helping people to help themselves.

Yield to maturity (YTM) The expected annual yield on a bond based on current market rates for similar bonds assuming that this YTM rate continues for the life of the bond and all coupons are reinvested at this rate and the bond is held to maturity.

Yield to maturity (YTM) curves Yield curves are constructed for different types of bonds that are homogeneous, such as U.S. Treasury securities that have the same default risk with yield on the *y*-axis and term to maturity on the *x*-axis for a yield curve graph. Yield curves are reported daily in the financial press as economic indicators. Shapes of yield curves are typically upward sloping (typical during an expansion), but at times are flat (often in an economic transition period) and downward sloping (more typical during a recession) or humped shape with higher yields for very low maturity securities (in times of a liquidity crunch where demand for short-term liquidity securities goes up).

Zero coupon bond A bond that only has a single maturity value and no coupon payments, so its value is equal to the present value of the single maturity payment.

Zeta scores Zeta scores are scores from Zeta Bankruptcy Risk Models, a widely used credit scoring model for commercial loans developed by Edward Altman, that uses a multiple discriminant analysis technique to identify important ratios used to classify firms that are more likely to go bankrupt versus firms that have low bankruptcy risk.

Index

Note: Page numbers in **bold** indicate figures or tables